Memoirs

———

MEMOIRS

A Twentieth-Century Journey in Science and Politics

———

Edward Teller

———

with Judith L. Shoolery

PERSEUS PUBLISHING
Cambridge, Massachusetts

Cataloging-in-Publication Data is available from the Library of Congress
ISBN 0-7382-0532-X

Perseus Publishing is a member of the Perseus Books Group.
Find us on the World Wide Web at http://www.perseuspublishing.com
Perseus Publishing books are available at special discounts for bulk purchases in the U.S. by corporations, institutions, and other organizations. For more information, please contact the Special Markets Department at the Perseus Books Group, 11 Cambridge Center, Cambridge, MA 02142, or call (617)252-5298.

Text design by Trish Wilkinson
Set in 11-point Garamond3 by Perseus Publishing Services

First printing, October 2001

1 2 3 4 5 6 7 8 9 10—03 02 01

This book is dedicated to four of my Hungarian-American friends, all of whom have passed away: Theodore von Kármán, Leo Szilárd, Eugene Wigner, and John von Neumann.

All of them, like myself, came to the United States during the period that Fascism was gaining power in Europe.

All of them played a role in the technical developments of the twentieth century.

In jest, they were called the Martians.

No accolade gives me so great a pleasure as that I was counted one of them.

CONTENTS

ACKNOWLEDGMENTS

MANY PEOPLE ENCOURAGED me to write this book, but four deserve special recognition: Judy Shoolery who, having heard many of these accounts as a friend, persistently pleaded that she not be the only person to know them; Linda G. Regan who as an editor convinced me to commit to the project and then offered suggestions and encouragement for almost a decade; and my son Paul and daughter Wendy, whose interest in and support of this autobiography has been unwavering.

Special thanks are due Hoover Institution for its support during this effort, particularly for making it possible for my collaborator to conduct interviews at Los Alamos and Livermore. I am also most grateful for the advice and counsel that the Hoover directors, W. Glenn Campbell and John Raisian, have offered throughout this period at Hoover. And I thank Directors Roger Batzel, John Nuckolls, and Bruce Tarter of the Lawrence Livermore National Laboratory for their considerable support.

Many friends and acquaintances have consented to be interviewed by Ms. Shoolery or have reminisced with me on one or more occasions. I am grateful to Harold Agnew, Harold and Jean (Anderson) Argo, the late Roger Batzel, John Boyd, Norris and Lois Bradbury, Robert Budwine, W. Glenn Campbell, Gregory Canavan, Karl Cohen, Stirling and Rosie Colgate, the late Charles Critchfield and Jean Critchfield, the late G. Foster Evans and Alice Evans, Leona Fernbach, Edward H. Fleming, John Foster, the late Carl Haussmann, John T. Hayward, Roland Herbst, Gerald W. Johnson, Arthur Kantrowicz, Rolf Landshoff, Cecil E. Leith, the late Carson Mark and Kay Mark, Hans Mark, William G. and Nancy McMillan, the late Nicholas Metropolis, Milo Nordyke, John Nuckolls, Jack and Beverly Peterson, Louis and Mary Rosen, Duane Sewell, Johndale Solem, Wilson Talley, Theodore Taylor, Richard and Mary Taschek, Richard Van Konynenburg, John Wheeler, and Lowell Wood.

I am grateful to the many people who have helped me locate my papers or historical information, in particular, archivist James Carothers and reference librarian Fred Frost (both now retired) and current archivists Beverly Bull and Steve Wofford, and Rich Hunt and the other current reference librarians at Livermore, archivist Roger Meade at Los Alamos, reference librarian Linda Wheeler at Hoover, and my assistant Genevieve Phillips and senior executive secretary Joanne Smith at Livermore. I also thank the University of California, San Diego, Mandeville Special Collection Library, for their courtesy in allowing me to publish portions of the Maria G. Mayer archive.

Thanks are also due to my friends, too numerous to list, who have read portions of this book and offered comments. I also thank Amanda Cook, my editor at Perseus, whose comments and questions have improved the final manuscript. But, of course, the responsibility for the contents of this book is mine alone. It is, as Szilárd would have put it, my version of the facts.

INTRODUCTION

DESCRIBING WHAT I have been up to since January 15, 1908, or rather, describing the fraction I can remember, is neither simple nor straightforward. Our memories are selective; they delete some events and magnify others. Just the simple act of recalling the past affects the recollection of what happened. That some of my remembrances are not the commonly accepted version of events should not be surprising.

Describing those events—and the people who had a hand in making me the person I turned out to be—is even more difficult. We do not easily recognize what shapes us most deeply, and the results of introspection are even less reliable than memory. Anyone optimistic enough to try to understand people— the most complicated entities in the known universe—is entering a morass.

Writing the first five chapters of this book was especially hard. It was like remembering someone I once knew, a person who no longer exists. I felt as I did in 1933, when I wrote a poem called "Air Mail":

> If I tied a letter to a balloon, it would say:
> I must find someone human—
> Male or female, young or old, does not matter.
> But I must find a human.
> Why send such a letter? If even one soul
> finds my letter, it may be read.
> And the finder may consider it fitting
> to write a response
> And tie it to a balloon.[1]

---

[1] I was then living in Germany, but I wrote the poem "Légiposta" in Hungarian:

How should the twentieth century, during which I lived more than nine decades, be described? Its culture was science and technology; its course was unpredictable change; its fate was to suffer two major wars and a confrontation between two visions of mankind that threatened to lead to a third. My own life has been shaped by each of these forces, and I have been a bystander and also a participant in many of the events connected with these major upheavals.

My dreams were of other stuff, but some of my directions were present from the time of my earliest youth. Science was my earliest passion. I cannot divorce any of the major events in my life from the way of thinking that the study of science imposes. Such thought is not necessarily straightforward logic, but it never permits one to ignore facts or to substitute authority for self-conviction.

This book describes events I perceive as unique in the century I have experienced. Yet each observer has not only a time and a place from which he views events but also an inner perspective built from past understanding that cannot be dismissed but only acknowledged. My life has included many experiences alien to the majority of Americans. Some of them, shared by hundreds of thousands of people, are worth remembering in the hope that the condemnation of repeating history does not come to pass. Others may only help to explain the values and visions that color this book. If they add to the reader's objectivity in assessing the validity of my statements, then they have served their purpose.

Edward Teller
Hoover Institution
October 2000

Ha levelet kötnék egy luftbalónra
Ëmbert keresek
Mindegy, hogy férfi vagy nö
Fratal vagy ö reg
De embert keresek
Ès a luftbalónnak a megtalálója
Olvassa a levelet
Ès mivel hogy ö is ember volna
Ir egy feleletet
Is ráköti egy lufbalónra.

1

How Many
Seconds in a Year?

———

1908–1913

WHAT ARE MY earliest memories of childhood? I remember the bridges, the beautiful bridges. My hometown, Budapest, is built around a river. I have lived near the Tiber, the Thames, the Hudson, and the Rio Grande; but no river warms my memory as the Danube does: the river and its beautiful bridges.

The oldest bridge is the Chain Bridge, a nineteenth-century miracle with two stone lions guarding each end. Eighty years ago, my father told me that when the statues were installed, the city praised their sculptor for creating such beauty. Then a small boy had come along and asked about their funny mouths. In shame, the sculptor committed suicide; he had forgotten to give his yawning lions tongues.

The inconspicuous, modern Margaret Bridge has a branch leading to an island in the Danube. I played there in the ruins of the cloister where a king's daughter had lived and died. A great Hungarian poet, Endre Ady, wrote a poem about St. Margaret the year before I was born. He describes the young Princess Margaret (who was later canonized) fearfully fleeing her father's coarse and boisterous friends, but dreaming of a kindly troubadour from the West. The last lines of his poem, even in my poor translation, are poignant:

> She waited long, in vain. Her knight she never met,
> Whose kiss was gentle, gentle as his smile.
> So to Lord Jesus they gave Margaret,
> Who lived and died a nun on Danube's Isle.[1]

———

[1] *Ö nem járt a Duna táján, soha*
Egy halk dalú és halk scókú legény.

3

The Danube, flowing to the south, separates the flat modern city of Pest from the ancient city of Buda, where the conquering Magyars built their forts a thousand years ago. Almost every Sunday when we were small, my father took my big sister, Emmi, and me for a walk in the forests in the Buda Mountains. My mother had the beginnings of arthritis, which later crippled her hands and feet, and she did not walk for pleasure.

The Temes, a little river, is also bright in my memory; my mother grew up in Lugos, which (far to the southeast of Budapest) lies on the banks of the Temes. My grandparents' home, on the north side of the river in Romanian Lugos, faced the Greek Orthodox church across the town square. I remember that house well; it had a fountain in the yard where we drew our cooking and drinking water. But my favorite memory of that place is of the second-floor balcony; it provided me with a wonderful view of the weekly comings-and-goings at the market held below in the square.

Each year, my family, accompanied by a nursemaid or governess, left Budapest during July and August. My oldest memory is our vacation to Lake Balaton in 1910. I hear myself repeating two words: *igazán, igazán* (really, really), and *igen, igen* (yes, yes). Although two words are a tiny vocabulary for a two-and-a-half-year-old, I remember my feeling of pride and the approval of my parents. Emmi, two years older than I and now the family chronicler, says my parents were worried by my silence. She also says that I mispronounced *igazán* by accenting the syllables as if it were a German word. My mother spoke German at home, and I suspect that learning to talk in a bilingual home posed real difficulties for me.

Our family spent the next summers in the mountains; in 1913, we went to Toblach, near Innsbruck in the Austrian Dolomites.[2] While we were there, my parents decided we would take a carriage trip to Drei Zinnen. The trip took a few hours, and several times we had to get out and walk because the horses could not pull the loaded carriage uphill.

During that same vacation, I had an amazing first experience. My mother's parents came for a visit and hired an automobile. We drove the same road to

---

És Jézusnak áldozák Margitot,
Kí ott halt meg a nyulak szigetén.

[2]In 1981, when I was traveling by train through northern Italy, I passed Dobbiaco, a town ceded to Italy after World War I. Dobbiaco was my old vacation spot, Toblach, and for a few seconds I saw the old hotel, with its steep-walled play yard, still standing but deserted.

Drei Zinnen, but this time we covered the distance in thirty minutes, and no one had to get out and walk. That, I suspect, was the beginning of my respect for technology.

The vacation is also memorable because we had left from one flat but returned to another. My father was a lawyer. Because his office was in our home, we lived near the government buildings, all of which were in the center of town on the east side of the Danube. The apartment waiting for us on returning from our vacation in 1913 was in a brand-new, six-story building that had colored panels on the outside and several grand entryways. The name of the building, the Palatinus, brought visions of palaces to my mind. The eyes of childhood are magnifying lenses.

Although the building was not quite two blocks from our old home, the views from the windows were better than those from our previous home. From one I could make out a little piece of the Buda Mountains across the Danube, including the highest mountain, the Jánoshegy. And from my father's inner office—which was the most splendid room in our home—I could see into the backyard of the fire department across Szalay Street; here, firemen raised and lowered the automatic ladders of a beautiful bright red horseless carriage.

Our new home, in which I spent most of my youth, looked directly at the back of the Supreme Court building. Next to the Supreme Court stood the Parliament building; a large, lovely park, Parliament Park, where my sister and I were often taken to play, separated the two buildings. The motto carved into the lintel of the main entry to the court proclaimed: *Justicia Regnorum Fundamentum* (justice is the foundation of government).

Today, I realize that justice was not a common experience for most Hungarians in those days. Hungary was an agricultural nation, just beginning to industrialize. Between 1873—when the twin cities of Buda and Pest were unified—and 1913, the population of Budapest tripled to one million. My parents were among the hundreds of thousands who moved to the first city of the nation during those years. As part of a small middle class of professional people, they enjoyed a comfortable life. Most Hungarians were agricultural workers, employed only part of the year and living in harsh poverty.

My father was a liberal who believed in democracy and in the need to improve the well-being of all the people, but he was not politically active. By disposition, he was moderate, reserved, and quiet. Instead of talking about a specific political party's program, he tried to explain the principles of good government; sometimes he used a few dozen Hungarian words, occasionally just a few words in Latin.[3]

The Austro-Hungarian empire was part of a political world teetering between the old and the new, and wars were common. The first conflict I remember, albeit vaguely, took place in the Balkans in 1912, when Greece, Bulgaria, Serbia, and Montenegro rose against Turkey.[4] I plainly remember our family's concern. In those days, Hungarian men were eligible for conscription until they were forty-two years old. If Hungary had entered the war, my father would have been drafted in his last year of eligibility; but Hungary stayed out, and my father stayed at home.

One of my most distinct memories of my first five years is of an event that occurred not long before we moved into our new home. One morning, my father gave me a little mirror and showed me how to reflect a sunbeam onto the ceiling. I was fascinated; I played with the mirror and sunbeams for hours. At dinner, the doorbell rang, and my father left the table. When he returned, he took the mirror away from me: It seems that I had happened more than once to direct a sunbeam onto the bald head of a Supreme Court justice.

Both my parents were kind, but even though they laughed about my "crime," I was almost overwhelmed by my guilt. As a small child, I had an almost chronic bad conscience. I do not believe it was justified, but I worried most of the time that some absurdity or another was an offense.

My mother was a worrier, and I may have worried in imitation of her. But some fears were uniquely my own. I had such a terrible fear of the dark as a child that I am sometimes amazed, even today, that I no longer have it. Until I was at least seven, my parents always left a light on for me at night.

My early memories of my mother are intertwined with Beethoven's sonatas. She was a small woman, barely five feet tall, but she was a fine pianist. I believe she had hoped to play professionally before she met my father, but she lacked the self-assurance that performing for large audiences requires. She was reserved about playing for anyone other than family members.

---

[3]My father also was the associate editor of *Jogtudományi Közlöny,* the law journal of Hungary. The editor was Rustem Vámbéry. Rustem is an unusual name in Hungary, but fairly common in southwestern Asia. Rustem's father, Armin, had been an explorer, the first westerner to cross the Gobi Desert; he was even received by British royalty. My father, who was impressed with his somewhat exotic colleague, did all the routine work on the journal. Vámbéry added the flair.

[4]Turkey, formerly a great power, was practically squeezed out of Europe.

My love of music grew from listening to my mother play. My love of the mountains may have been inspired by my father's enjoyment of them. My interest in mathematics was self generated. From earliest childhood, in a barely remembered way, I have had an unrelenting desire to understand. Soon after our summer vacation in 1912, when I was about four and a half years old, I began consistently spending time thinking about numbers.

When I was put to bed, I entertained myself with a secret game. I knew that a minute had sixty seconds, and I charged myself to discover how many seconds there were in an hour, a day, or a year. The fact that my answers were different each time I tried only added to the excitement.

Why would a child enjoy such a peculiar pastime? No one suggested the game to me, and I didn't talk about my activity until I was middle-aged. I might have begun it as a rebellion against bedtime or to help myself cope with my fear of the dark. Or it may be that numbers were attractive to me because they were one area where mistakes could be corrected. Or I may have chosen to think about numbers because words had been confusing when I began to talk. Perhaps I liked numbers because, after all, an hour really does have 3,600 seconds. But no matter what the cause, my first desire, as far back as I can remember, was to find patterns and regularities in the world. As a consequence, I learned to calculate in my head at an improbably early age.

A child cannot know how his days and nights will determine his years— how they may make him fit or not fit into his world. Perhaps intellectual independence is a hereditary trait; perhaps it is a universal characteristic of the young that only a few carry intact into adulthood. Whether intellectual independence leads to success, to misfortune, or to both is unclear; but finding the consistency of numbers is the first memory I have of feeling secure.

2

Learning About War, Revolution, and Peace

1914–1919

IN JUNE 1914, news from Sarajevo produced a tension that I have never forgotten: The crown prince and his wife had been murdered. My family was in the dining room of our apartment, the grown-ups with their newspapers, and someone read aloud: "In spite of the tragedy, there will be no war." I was properly worried about war and the likelihood of father's being drafted.

"Why will there be no war?" I asked. "Because there is no reason that there should be war." "But if there is no reason, why does the newspaper say that there will be no war?" I remember my confusion to this day. Until then, my questions had always earned me my mother's immediate attention and an explanation. On this occasion, not only did my questions go unanswered, I was even told to be quiet!

Today, I believe I know the answer. In 1914, Franz Joseph was eighty-four. He had begun his rule in 1848, as part of the resolution of the Hungarian revolt, at the age of eighteen. About two decades later, in the hope of increasing popular support, Emperor Franz Joseph granted considerable autonomy to Hungary and added the title "King of Hungary" to his name. During the following years, Austro-Hungary expanded south into Bosnia-Herzegovina, which then, as now, was a region of intense ethnic pride and nationalistic conflict.

Toward the end of the nineteenth century, the menace of terrorism spread through the western world; the terrorists of the nineteenth century—called anarchists—wanted to bring an end to all government. Like their twentieth-century counterparts, they committed acts of violence to provoke counter-measures that would, in turn, bring down the existing order. Anarchists murdered presidents, prime ministers, and members of royal families. (Today, terrorists are more democratic.)

During my childhood walks, I noticed a statue of Queen Elizabeth, Franz Joseph's wife, beside the Danube. Queen Elizabeth was a beautiful lady. I was curious about her and was told that the Hungarian people loved her and that she had had died at the hands of an assassin. While she was on a holiday in Geneva, she had wanted to take a public boat ride on the lake, accompanied only by a lady-in-waiting. Heavily veiled, she had just boarded the boat when an anarchist approached her, lifted her veil to be sure of her identity, and stabbed her to death with an awl.

Franz Joseph was sixty-eight years old and had ruled for fifty years when he lost his wife to a senseless assassination. Now, at eighty-four, he lost his nephew, the successor to the throne, to similar political violence in Sarajevo. Franz Joseph asked that the investigation of the archduke's death be conducted by the Austrian police rather than the regional police of Bosnia-Herzegovina. The Serbs, who were involved in the assassination plot, protested Austrian intervention in their local affairs; they claimed that it was an Austrian plot to gain a more comprehensive annexation. A stalemate was quickly reached. France and Russia backed Serbia. The Germans backed Austro-Hungary.

A few weeks later, the fate of Austro-Hungary was sealed: Franz Joseph signed the documents that started World War I. He reportedly said at the time, "I have considered everything; I have weighed everything."[1] He responded, as the anarchists had hoped he would, like an emotional old man. The assassin was eventually caught and sent to prison, where he died; but the deep disturbances that would plague the twentieth century had been set in motion.

During the first days of July 1914, we set out for our customary family vacation, this time to Velden, which was beside a pretty lake, but with a promise that we would go Toblach a month later. However, Emmi and I came down with measles at the end of July. We were still miserably sick when the declaration of war came. At the time, measles felt worse than war, but the declaration made our parents decide to return home as soon as could be managed. By then, trains full of soldiers were rolling.

In the days that followed, the soldiers, followed by their cannons, marched down Vaci Street, a few blocks from our home. By that time, I was not asking why. I was caught up by the war fever; I was certain that we would win. My

---

[1] "Ich habe alles bedacht; ich habe erwogen."

father hung a map on his office wall and stuck flags on it to show the location of the battle lines on the eastern front. The dynamic geography of those mobile frontiers marked the beginning of my interest in the larger world.

I remember that early in the war, those fabulous German warriors von Hindenburg and Ludendorff wiped out the Russian troops in East Prussia.[2] But the Russians soon recovered and deployed their forces against a weaker opponent—the Austro-Hungarian army. I remember the gloomy news in the fall of 1914. Lemberg (now Lvov), a city a hundred miles from the border of Hungary, had fallen. I had no doubt that we would take it back; Hungarians were, to my mind, brave and successful warriors. But we did not defeat the Russians. The Germans did.

The next spring, my father took Emmi and me on a long walk in the mountains of Buda. On the slopes of the triple-peaked Hármashatárhegy, we came upon some trenches. My father explained that they had been dug as a defense against the Russians. Suddenly, the war looked very different. On the map in my father's office, I had seen the Russians crossing the Carpathian mountains in the east. The trenches we saw in the mountains that day were west of the Danube. If our soldiers had had to fight there, our house and the homes of all my friends would already have been captured.

My desire to know more about war grew. At home, we had an illustrated history of Napoleon's campaigns. I remember learning that the huge army that had marched into Russia had left in a terrible retreat. The soldiers bled, they froze, they starved. Only a few returned. On Sundays in winter, my father took Emmi and me to the main park in Budapest, which had a zoo and an art gallery. I remember seeing paintings of battles: wounded men and horses intermingled in agony. They held me in horrified fascination.

My father had clerks working in his office in our home, young men fulfilling a four-year-long internship before opening their own practices. One of them, Joseph Bard (who knew and later married the American reporter Dorothy Thompson), came back from the war with terrible stories. I was bothered by his seeming lack of patriotism and by the doubts he cast on the effectiveness of our armies.

A special teacher, a British subject, whom my mother hired for a short time to give Emmi and me English lessons, challenged my patriotism even further. The tutor was furious about the war and blamed Kaiser Wilhelm for

---

[2]That battle, by drawing troops from the western front, ended the possibility of Germany's ending the war quickly. It also laid the foundation for von Hindenburg's fame and his political role in the 1930s.

starting it. His comments about the kaiser, who I knew had often rescued Hungary, upset me. So when the tutor used a somewhat objectionable word for fool in connection with the kaiser, I returned the favor by using the same word in connection with the British. Much to my amazement, my parents were not at all upset by his behavior—only about mine.

However, about the middle of the war, I realized that the Austro-Hungarian armies always seemed to lose. First, we invaded Serbia, but had to retreat. We fought the Romanians when they invaded Transylvania, but the Germans had to come to our rescue. We fought the Italians, and we were beaten again. When the Germans defeated the Russians in 1914, I had thought that the war was as good as won; I was surprised, then, to realize a few years later that we were going to lose.

By the summer of 1918, everyone was desperately eager to have an end to the war. I remember two riddles popular during the final months of the war. The first described countries:

> What is the difference between England, Prussia, and Austro-Hungary? In England, everything is permitted except for a few things that are forbidden. In Prussia, everything is forbidden except for a few things that are permitted. In Austro-Hungary, everything that is forbidden is permitted.[3]

The second riddle circulated about two weeks before the surrender.

> How is the war going? In Berlin, the situation is serious but not desperate. In Vienna, it is desperate but not serious. [That was the atmosphere in Budapest as well.]

Just before war ended in 1918, an independent republican government was formed under Mihály Károlyi, who, I believe, was a Social Democrat, politically to the left. People walked the streets wearing tiny chrysanthemums in their buttonholes, and soldiers marched with flowers in their gun barrels. The blossoms were the symbol of a largely peaceful revolution, the Revolution of Autumn Roses.[4] Franz Joseph's successor, Emperor Charles, finally acceded to popular demands for a new cabinet. The event marked the beginning of an independent Hungarian republic.

---

[3] After I learned group theory, I added a fourth statement for the sake of symmetry: In Russia, everything that is not forbidden is obligatory.

[4] The Hungarian premier, István Tisza, was killed.

During the fall of 1918, I began my second year of gymnasium studies.[5] The only good thing about school, as far as I was concerned, was the mathematics class. A few years earlier, I learned that what I had been doing in my nighttime game should be done on paper and should be correct. I practiced both on paper and at night, so I had become a good and fast calculator, a type of childhood distinction that has completely disappeared with the advent of hand calculators.

I had learned the rule of nines: If I added the numerals in numbers evenly divisible by 9 (18, 27, 36), the result would be 9. (If the result has more than one digit, the process must be repeated.) For numbers not evenly divisible by 9, the total of the numerals will be the remainder. To my delight, our mathematics teacher, Ireneus Juvancz, explained the reason behind that surprise.[6]

Understanding war and politics was impossible. Numbers were much more reasonable. I always understood and enjoyed what Juvancz had to say about mathematics. But Juvancz was also a dedicated communist, and his comments on that topic were confusing.

The communist movement in Hungary, led by Béla Kun, started shortly after the end of the war. Kun, a former army officer and a Jew, was captured early in the war and held in Russia. He and a few hundred other Hungarian prisoners of war became thoroughly indoctrinated as communists. They were promptly repatriated when the war ended in 1918. The postwar period in any nation, and especially in a defeated nation, is a difficult period; for an inexperienced democratic government, it proved overwhelming.

Early in 1919, four Budapest policemen were killed by a few unidentified communists. The memorial service for the policemen was held in Parliament Square. A friend of my father's had an apartment with a balcony overlooking the square, and my father, his friend (and his dog) and I watched the ceremony from there. The crowd was the largest I had ever seen: Close to a hundred thousand people had gathered. The funeral march from Beethoven's Third Symphony, which I had never heard before, was played.

Prime Minister Károlyi arrested the leaders of the communist party for the murders, even though they had not been directly involved. The arrests met with little public support. Then, a little later, the terms ending the war were

---

[5]Elementary schools in Hungary served children six to ten years of age. Children then attended either regular school or gymnasium. The gymnasium had somewhat higher requirements.

[6]The differences of $10 - 1$ (9), $100 - 1$ (99), and $1,000 - 1$ (999) are all divisible by 9. To find the remainder of $751,000$ divided by 9, one may, therefore, substitute the numeral 1 for 1,000, 5 for 50,000, and 7 for 700,000, a total of 13, which, added, gives the remainder, 4.

presented to the Hungarian government. That settlement not only dismantled the Austro-Hungarian empire but tore the thousand-year-old nation of
Hungary apart and distributed it to other nations. Under the Treaty of Tri
anon, Hungary was reduced from a nation of 18 million people of various na-
tionalities to one of barely 8 million. Almost half of those who were ethnic
Hungarians were to live under foreign rule.

The new democracy could not survive the loss of more than half its territory
and almost half its people. In mid-spring of 1919, when I was eleven years
old, the communists took over. The hope held by some people that the Soviet
Red Army, stationed about two hundred miles away, might help restore
the old boundaries if Hungary became a communist country, contributed
to the acceptance of the communist takeover.[7]

The Communist Party included perhaps one-tenth of one percent of the
Hungarian people; only the communists' discipline, organization, and disregard for law enabled them to gain control. The Social Democrats, who vastly
outnumbered the communists, had only a program of slow reform within the
law.[8] They were coaxed into supporting the government formed under Béla
Kun, but even though the Social Democrats represented many more people
than the communists, they had no influence on Kun's policies.

The communists overturned every aspect of society and the economy. My father could no longer practice law. In fact we became social outcasts. A lawyer
was clearly a capitalist; and, unlike a doctor, who provided a service, a lawyer
was a thoroughly worthless person in a "good" society. Two soldiers moved
into our "extra space," the rooms that had been my father's office in our home.

The old blue money, unlike the communists' white money, still had some
value, but the communists demanded that it all be turned in. Magda Hesz,
who worked for our family as a sort of au pair, resourcefully used her skill in
binding books to hide our family cash in the backs of the books in my father's office. Having soldiers billeted in our "bank" was a grave concern for
my parents, but the soldiers never found our money. In retrospect I remember only that they were self-conscious about being in our home and tried
hard to stay out of the way.

Of this time, I remember more clearly the multitude of posters that appeared in the streets and subways. On one of them, a stern man with his arm

---

[7]That was a most unrealistic hope. The Soviet Army was mobilized there because Soviets
were still engaged in securing their power within their own territory.

[8]Because both Károlyi and Kun came to power without benefit of an election, their popular
support can only be estimated.

extended and his fingertip as large as if it were half an inch from my nose, said: "You, hiding in the shadows, spreading horror stories, you counterrevolutionary, TREMBLE." The finger seemed to follow me wherever I went. From the beginning, the new government was afraid of a counterrevolution. Their concern was justified, for the communists had almost no popular support. The régime lasted four months and ten days.

As students, we learned the "Internationale," which we sang to the tune of the "Marseilles"; I even remember all the words.[9] The Hungarian version (in translation) was:

> Capital will not be our master.
> Who lives for the past will perish.
> We are heading into the home of freedom.
> The truth is the goal for us.
> The truth is the goal for us.
> If anyone rises against us,
> Let the people's anger sweep him away.
> Let him be slaughtered for a cowardly slave.
> We are waving goodbye to the night.
> Our hearts burn with fire:
> Charge! And charge again!
> If they step on the necks of their oppressors,
> The people will be free.

I have looked at the words of the "Internationale" as it was sung in Russia, in France, and by the Wobblies in the United States. None of those versions

---

[9]*Nem lesz a töke úr mirajtunk.*
Elvész aki a múltnak él.
A szabadság honába tartunk.
Az igazság nekünk a cél.
Az igazság nekünk a cél.
'S ha ellenünk bárki is lázad.
Söpörje el a népharag.
Pusztuljon mind a gyáva rab.
Búcsút intünk az éjszakának.
A szívünk tüzben ég.
Csak rajta, rajta még.
Ha elnyomónak nyakára lép.
Szabad lesz majd a nép.

approaches the viciousness of the Hungarian version. But I was less upset by the anthem's peculiar message that being free requires stepping on someone's neck than by its grammar. Proper Hungarian uses a suffix on the word *goal* to denote "for us." I could not understand how our brand new national anthem could contain a grammatical error sufficient to earn me a failing grade.

But my biggest problem was that I was hungry. There was no food (or any other kind of goods) for sale in the stores now owned by the communists, because their money was worthless. Each weekend, my father would take some illegal blue money from the bindings of the law books and, accompanied by Emmi and me, walk to the farms near Budapest and buy whatever was available. But there was not much to buy. As I recall, cabbage was often all we could find. I still dislike cabbage.

One day during those months, Juvancz mentioned that we might have heard complaints about the policies of the new government. I perked up. I had a few complaints myself, my hunger among them. Juvancz continued, "Houses must be torn down before new houses can be built. That causes a lot of noise and dirt. Then, when you are building a new house, there are bound to be some kinds of difficulties before it can be finished." I liked Juvancz better when he explained the rule of nines.

In the midst of that time of hunger, my father told me that the communists would soon fall and that anti-Semitism would follow. He explained: "Too many of the communist leaders are Jews, and all the Jews will be blamed for their excesses." I was astonished that, after so many inconsistent events, my father still dared to make a prediction. I was even more amazed when his prediction proved correct: The comment, "The Jews! They cannot even write decent Hungarian," was commonplace even before the communists fell.

In early summer, all the Social Democrats in the government resigned in protest. Their resignations prompted an ill-planned attempt to overthrow the communists by force. Suddenly, we could see the distant terrors of war from the windows of our home. The janitor of our building had a son who had joined the communists and was killed in the fighting. I remember the mother's cries and weeping when she learned that her son was dead.

The counterrevolution against the communists was short lived; after twenty-four hours of fighting, the communists had regained control. The communist dead were buried with great ceremony after a procession that began at Parliament Square. But this time, the huge crowd was whispering that the end of the régime was near. They were right: The communist government collapsed that summer.

In early August 1919, Admiral Miklós Horthy, a purported war hero, led an army gathered in Romania into Budapest and set up a government. For several months, the new government pursued a terrible policy of retribution. Within the first few years after the demise of the Hungarian Soviet, 5,000 people, most of them Jews, were executed, and many tens of thousands more fled to other lands.

These memories are more vivid for my wife because her father, Ede Harkányi, who had died a few years before the war, and her godfather, Péter Ágoston, had been dedicated and influential Social Democrats. Ágoston had been foreign minister under Károlyi and stayed on in that capacity in Kun's government. The new government sentenced all members of the communist government to death. After some time, however, Ágoston was allowed to leave and lived out his days in Paris.

Admiral Horthy, a reactionary conservative, eventually restored peace. The constitution of the old kingdom of Hungary was put back into effect, with one significant difference: Horthy prevented the king from returning.[10]

During my first eleven years, I had known war, patriotism, communism, revolution, anti-Semitism, fascism, and peace. I wish the peace had been more complete.

---

[10]The internal contradictions in post–World War I Hungary were brought out by a joke told in 1941: When Cordell Hull reported to President Roosevelt that Hungary had declared war on the United States, Roosevelt asked, "Hungary? What is Hungary?" "A kingdom, Mr. President," Hull replied. "Who is the king?" asked Roosevelt. "The king is in exile, sir. The nation is governed by an admiral." "What is their navy like?" asked F.D.R. "There is no navy, sir. They lost their seacoast with the Treaty of Trianon. They have only an army." "Where is the army?" "Fighting in Russia." "Do they want territory from the Russians?" "No, from the Romanians." "Why don't they fight the Romanians?" "Because they are their allies." Roosevelt gave up.

3

THE OTHER SIDE
OF THE WAR YEARS

1914–1919

BECAUSE RIDING IN trains was my favorite occupation, I was disappointed that our vacation in 1915 included no travel. After a year full of the uncertainties of war, my parents took us to the mountains across the river; we were so close to home that we could look back and make out our apartment building. The only memorable aspect of that holiday was that Magda Hesz was with us.

Magda was a Hungarian girl who was born in a German region of southern Hungary (now Croatia) and raised in Chicago. Her parents died when she was in her teens, and she was sent back to Hungary to live with relatives. Shortly after the war began, my mother hired her to supervise Emmi and me and teach us English. She lived with us much as an au pair for seven years.

Magda, little more than ten years older than I, seemed more of a friend than a part of the management. She was a big strong girl, with long, thick blond hair, but she was in no way formidable. Missy, as we called her, never was angry, nor disliked anyone. She did the mending for the family; at her instigation, another wonderful device, a treadle sewing machine, came into our house. She had many other talents: She knew all the omens of good and bad luck and could tell the past and future by looking at the palm of your hand. And she told wonderful stories, most of them about Chicago.

My mother was very fond of Magda, in part because of her aptitude and willingness to work, but also because of her disposition. Magda's room could hardly have been ten feet square; its only window overlooked the back area of the building. Yet Magda lacked neither space to set up an easel nor light to copy Raphael's *Madonna and Child.* It was not that she had exceptional talents, but she always had an interest and could find the means to satisfy it.

Magda spoke Hungarian adequately, but because she had had never attended school in Hungary, her spelling was abominable. English was her best language, although what she actually spoke was American. Magda was homesick for the United States and nostalgic about her life there. She introduced us not to the culture of the founders of the United States but to the immigrant culture of Chicago. Before I was ten, I understood that in the United States foreigners are not foreign.

So while Emmi and I read Dickens with Magda, we gained a much clearer picture of Chicago than of London. Chicago, with its traffic and its El, was a very noisy place. But that was all right, for it was a vigorous noise; it was a noise of machines, and of people going places and making things happen. By the time I was ten, I suspected that Chicago was the center of the universe. And at twenty-seven, when I first saw that city, I recognized it.

I was a serious seven-year-old. I still worried about unintentionally doing something wrong, and my fear of the dark had increased when, not long after Magda arrived, I was moved from the room I had shared with Emmi into a room of my own. Magda brought reassurance, humor, and fortitude with her. She put me to bed each night with the ditty:

> *Good night. Sleep tight.*
> *Don't fight with yourself.*

Not only was my English influenced by Magda's Chicago origins but also—between my seventh and fourteenth year—my point of view was slowly, very slowly, colored by her optimism.

During the summer of 1916, our family resumed its treks. All of us, including Magda, went to Lake Csorba in the Tátra Mountains, a few hundred miles north of Budapest.[1] The lake reflects the mountains surrounding it, and I soon knew the name of every peak. Twenty-one years later, looking past Jackson Lake to the Tetons, I remembered the High Tátras; the only difference was that the mountains were slightly out of place.

Many families from Budapest spent their vacations at Lake Csorba. Two childhood friends, Paul Vírágh and Klári Freyberger, also vacationed there

---

[1]Lake Csorba is the largest of the glacier lakes found in the Tátras; their depth gives them their Hungarian name—the eyes of the ocean.

that year. Paul and I had running arguments that summer about whether free will existed, and whether the mountains were getting smaller because of erosion, or were growing higher. I finally resorted to the argument that I was right because my father had told me so. I hope my debating technique has since improved.

Klári, Emmi, and I spent less time talking than playing tiddlywinks. In Hungary, a playing piece is called a flea. We children collected them. One evening, the girls were called away before we had finished our game, but I carefully put away all our disks. When I entered the dining room of our hotel, I spotted Klári with her family at their table, and I hurried over. "Klári," I boomed happily, "your fleas are with my fleas." Klári was reassured. I, to my puzzlement, was shushed by both sets of parents.

My favorite playmate during this time was Lizi Grátz, whom I knew because our fathers were friends. Lizi had many virtues, but the greatest one I recognized then was that she was a very good listener. I was not. I remember in particular retelling her the story of Nils Holgersson, the boy who traveled on the back of a goose.[2] Her attention made me feel certain that I was a great storyteller.

The Gratz family moved to Vienna in 1917, when Gustáv Grátz was made director of the Economic Sector of the Austro-Hungarian Ministry of Foreign Affairs. I missed my visits with Lizi, but our families remained friends. In 1956, when Emmi's son, János Kirz, escaped from Hungary, Lizi took him into her relatively small apartment in Vienna—together with a few dozen other refugees. And in 1959, when my mother and Emmi were finally allowed to leave Hungary, Lizi also took care of them when they arrived in Vienna.

I saw Lizi again in the mid–1970s. Although so much had changed that we could hardly recognize each other, she had retained one quality intact: She was still a good listener. On that occasion, I was talking about the world's need for energy from every source: energy provided by petroleum and coal; nuclear, hydroelectric, solar, and geothermal energy. Lizi then reminded me that as a child I had talked to her about geothermal energy.

She recalled a day when the two of us, then about nine years old, were playing in Parliament Park. I had recently learned that the center of the earth was hot and had decided to verify the fact. I set to work digging a hole;

---

[2] I continue to enjoy one point in the story. Nils is traveling on the back of the tame goose, who is unused to the rigors of migration and to Nils' extra weight. She begs the leader, Akka von Kebnekaise (whose name I recalled on seeing the mountain in Sweden sixty years later), to fly slower, but Akka replies: "It is easier to fly fast than to fly slowly."

but in spite of my industrious efforts, we noticed no temperature change before Magda Hesz arrived to take me home. Lizi recalled my unhappiness at having to leave before I had found the answer.

The most important figures in my childhood world were my parents. My father was a pleasant but reserved man.[3] I was never able to talk to him easily, nor he to me. I doubt that we had more than a dozen good talks together. To all appearances my mother made the decisions in our family, but I do not believe that was the case. When I was a little older, my father, not my mother, made the decisions about my life.

My father's parents had died before I was born, and I knew only his youngest sister, Elizabeth, of whom both he and I were very fond.[4] She and her husband, Géza Kelemen, lived on one of the main thoroughfares of Budapest, and we visited her often. I remember one occasion in particular. In 1917, when Franz Joseph died, his nephew Charles became the kaiser of Austria and the king of Hungary. My family watched the coronation parade from Aunt Elizabeth's balcony. I was especially interested in the small boy riding with his father, King Charles, in an open touring car.[5]

My father was my first chess partner. He taught me the moves in chess when I was about six, and for the next few years, he beat me consistently. I finally asked him how he did it. He told me that I had to think ahead not one move but two or three. So I began to do so. When I was nine or ten years old, I beat him in chess. With thoughtless honesty, I told him that one of his moves was stupid. His reaction shocked me: He was hurt. And I was ashamed. I do not believe we ever played chess together again.

I think my father preferred Emmi to me, but he was circumspect about his favoritism. My mother doted on me, and made no effort to hide her feelings. Fortunately Emmi was unconcerned. When I was five or six years old I asked Emmi what the word *descendant* meant. Emmi told me, "Mother is Grandmother's descendant, I am Mother's descendant, and you are my descendant. However, by the time I was six or seven years old, I was uncomfortable with my mother's preferential treatment of me.

---

[3]He was the oldest of four children and the only son. He grew up in the small town of Érsekujvár (which became Nove Zamky, Czechoslovakia, after the Treaty of Trianon, and is now in Slovakia). Both of his parents died at the time he began his law studies in Budapest. He was a conscientious man, and the family legend holds that he postponed his own thoughts of marriage for almost a decade until he saw each of his sisters safely settled in her own home. His oldest sister, Irma, lived far from Budapest, and I do not remember meeting her. Mariska, the middle sister, lived in Budapest; but about all I remember about her was that she owned a parrot. I remember Elizabeth well.

My mother was also extremely protective of her children. During our summer visit to Lugos in 1916, Emmi and I learned to swim in the Temes River. People could watch the bathers from a pavilion built over the water, but my mother was too worried about the dangers of the river and the inexperience of her children to be satisfied with just watching: Throughout our swimming excursions, she sat rigidly as she gripped the ends of the cords she had tied around the waist of each of us. In Lugos, we were never much embarrassed by her solicitude. The people in my mother's hometown were well acquainted with her tremendous capacity for worry.

Until I was almost nine years old, my mother almost exclusively supervised my time. My parents had enrolled me in Mellinger School shortly before my sixth birthday. I don't know why, but I attended classes there far less than half the time. All I remember about Mellinger School is that I played pleasant games and memorized a few simple Hungarian poems.

Quite a few parents in Hungary during the first decades of the century began their children's education at home. My mother and Magda Hesz taught Emmi and me to read and write at home. The only unusual aspect of my gentle and indulgent early education was how long it was continued. My entry into the larger world came when, a little younger than my classmates and considerably younger in experience, I entered gymnasium in 1917.

My new school, the Minta (Model) School, had been founded before the turn of the century to carry out educational reforms initiated by a friend of my father's, Maurice von Kármán, who was then Minister of Education and Professor of Education at the University of Budapest.[6] Classes met from 8:00 A.M. to 1:00 P.M. six days a week (although we were dismissed at 12 noon on Saturday. For eight years we were required to study mathematics, history,

---

[4]Elizabeth, my last tie to Budapest, died there at the age of ninety-nine in the mid–1970s.

[5]In 1976, I met the boy I had watched that day, Otto von Hapsburg, who, like me, was then close to seventy years old. He had renounced his hereditary rights and become a simple politician. The former crown prince was then a member of the European Parliament and a proponent of more thorough cooperation among the members of the Common Market. When we met more recently, he gave me a copy of his book, *The Idea of an Empire: The Past and Future of a Supranational Order* (Otto Hapsburg, *Die Reichsidee: Geschichte und Zukunft einer Übernationalen Ordnung* [Wien: Amalthea, 1986]). One of his telling points is that nationalism, fostered by President Wilson's Fourteen Points, has served the world poorly. The old empire with its commonality and unrestricted exchange had much to recommend it; breaking up the Austro-Hungarian empire in 1919 did nothing to improve the lives of its people. Nationalism has little to contribute today except further suffering.

[6]Theodore von Kármán, an outstanding expert in the science of aerodynamics and who will figure in the later chapters of my story, was Maurice von Kármán's son and a Minta graduate.

Hungarian grammar and literature, German language and literature, physical exercise, and Latin.[7] That was *not* the program I would have chosen; and the school itself was not academically stimulating. Students were required to participate, but there was little enthusiasm for learning. The teachers were unenthusiastic; most classrooms were in semirevolt. There was no real interest or exchange of ideas.

I had more difficulties. Instruction at home has the advantage of being tailored to the child's interests; but the environment is so unrealistically approving that entering public school is apt to be a shock. A further problem is that being taught at home does little for one's social skills. My first year in gymnasium, the equivalent of fifth grade, was the beginning of a miserable time. I had no friends among my classmates. In fact, during my first few years at the Minta, I was practically a social outcast.

I was happy when school ended for the day so that I could come home and read for fun. I had discovered Jules Verne and I read everything he wrote. I particularly loved *Around the World in Eighty Days* with its surprise of the missing day discovered just in time. I also read many of H. G. Wells's tales with delight.[8] But I probably gave almost as much of my attention to a set of reference books called *Universum*, a sort of abbreviated encyclopedia.

My favorite pursuit was thinking about numbers, and my avocation was enriched because of an incident that occurred in early 1918. Emmi, now attending gymnasium, was at the age when students were introduced to algebra. One evening she asked my father, "Why is $(10 + 1)^2$ not equal to $10^2 + 1^2$?" Mathematics was not one of my father's interests, so I had little trouble including myself in the conversation. I knew by then that to find the answer, one must add 2 ab to a^2 and b^2. My father was impressed and promptly took me to visit his friend, Professor Leopold Klug, a retired professor of mathematics.

---

[7] We had six hours of Latin classes a week for eight years, a total of 1,800 hours. I remember Karl Oberle explaining why so much Latin was required. "The purpose of an education is to develop intelligence. Intelligence requires logic. Latin teaches logic." Even now, I cannot appreciate the relationship between Latin and logic.

[8] To this day, I find one of his less famous tales, *The Man Who Could Work Miracles,* a particular pleasure. In it, a skeptic discovers that he can work miracles. In the process of exploring his new talent, he commands the earth to stand still. That produces a true catastrophe, because he forgets to command the atmosphere to stand still, too, and everything is blown away in the resulting storm. The man wishes he had never been given his power to work miracles, and the story ends happily with the skeptic back in the setting where the story began; here, he performs the greatest of miracles: He undoes his recent past and loses forever the talent to perform miracles.

Klug had befriended my father during his bachelor days and had included him in his hiking circle. Klug seemed to know so many interesting things that I was fascinated. On our first visit, he asked my father to buy me a copy of Euler's *Algebra*, written more than two hundred years earlier.[9] I read the book, not without difficulty but with pleasure.

During the year, I had perhaps six or seven sessions with Klug. His specialty was projective geometry, which involves working out the rules of what happens to a two-dimensional figure when its shadow falls on another flat surface lying at a different angle.[10] Searching for what was preserved in a projection was a wonderful new game. Klug never asked me to memorize anything, but he presented me with problems far beyond my ability to solve. In attempting what was unreachable, I received my first painless lessons in the activity that I liked best. I fell in love with the underlying simplicity of what seems at first complex.

Klug could do mathematics all day long; indeed, he had done so all his life. He was the only adult (other than Magda Hesz, who hardly seemed an adult) I did not feel sorry for. Almost all the others had complaints about their jobs. I became determined to have a job that allowed me do something that I wanted to do for its own sake.

---

[9] *Algebra* starts with a discussion of why −1 times −1 equals +1 and ends with solutions of algebraic equations of the fourth degree.

[10] Projecting a circle will produce a circle, parabola, ellipse, or hyperbola, which are the four conic sections. Projecting any of the conic sections on a further plane results only in another conic section.

4

ROMANIAN INTERLUDE

1919–1920

I WAS THOROUGHLY RELIEVED when my second year in the Minta ended. In the summer of 1919, my father took us all to Lugos, where, because it was a country town, we could again have the pleasure of eating three meals a day. My father stayed in Lugos only briefly; he was anxious to return to Budapest to reestablish his law practice. My sister, my mother, Magda, and I stayed behind to be fattened up. About the time we had planned to return for the beginning of the school year, Emmi and I came down with chicken pox. By the time we had recovered, the Treaty of Trianon had gone into effect: It decreed that Lugos, Hungary was now Lugoj, Romania.

In Lugoj, we got a little taste of the treatment of Hungarians under a victorious and vindictive government: We were not allowed to return to Budapest. My mother, born in Lugos and living there when the treaty went into effect, was considered a Romanian citizen. My sister and I were also classified as Romanians because we were the children of a "Romanian." As Romanians, we had lost our right to emigrate without special permission. We would spend the next eight months in Lugoj, trying to obtain that special permission.

An apocryphal story that I heard during our exile provides a glimpse, from the Hungarian side, of the ingenuity of the Romanian adminstrators:

The Romanian warden of the prison in Lugos was a most humane individual. The inmates of the prison were guilty of petty deviations from standard good behavior, so he let his wards go home for truly justified reasons, such as any wedding, baptism, or funeral. The inmates dutifully returned to prison, expressing their thanks in the form of a chicken or a small sack of potatoes. The system worked beautifully, except for the circumstance that the prison was practically empty all the time.

24

However, the warden was ingenious as well as humane. Lugos had an important weekly market and fair, and the peasants came in from the country on the day before. When the weather was rainy, the warden rented the empty prison rooms for the night to the peasants. Thus, Romanian common sense was served: The people who wanted to be outside were outside, the people who wanted to be inside were inside, and the warden had a prosperous livelihood.

In reality, the attitude of the German-speaking Hungarian community of Lugos toward their Romanian neighbors was not lighthearted. There was an unbridgeable chasm between the two groups. My father, who had grown up in the multicultural northwestern part of Hungary, spoke German as the language of convenience; but he preferred Hungarian. That was not the case in Lugos. Most books my relatives owned, right down to their translations of Shakespeare, were in German. Even my grandfather's love letters were written in German. My mother learned to speak German before she learned Hungarian, a language she never spoke well. For the Hungarians of Lugos, Hungarian culture was second rate, and Romanian culture was an oxymoron.

The transfer of political power in Lugos, from Hungarian leadership to Romanian, created a great deal of unhappiness for the Hungarian community. But my grandmother's miseries had begun years before. Until the middle of the twentieth century, Hungarians reminded each other several times a day of their position within the social hierarchy. In Hungary at that time, speaking to someone involved using (or not using) an honorific, a form of address that reflected class distinctions. Many educated and successful people—including the teachers in the gymnasiums, merchants, bankers, and factory owners—were excluded from "polite" society; they were not worthy of notice.[1]

My grandfather, Ignác Deutsch, was a banker; he also owned a brewery, a mill, and a textile factory, and was one of the richest men in town. The house he and my grandmother Frieda owned was the most imposing in Lugos and had the best location, right on the central square.[2] My grandmother dressed

---

[1]There were six levels of distinction: *tekintetes*—*noteworthy* (used for engineers and lawyers), *nagyságos*—*great* (used for doctors, judges, university professors, and by all servants when addressing their employers of either sex), *máltóságos*—*honorable* (for large landowners, minor noblemen, and high government officials), *kegyelmes*—*your mercy* (for members of the high nobility, such as counts), *fenséges*—*your highness* (for a prince or princess), and the capstone *Felséges*—*your majesty* (for a king or queen).

[2]My grandfather's initials were proudly displayed on the face of the balcony.

well and was extremely decorous, but their social status was practically non-existent. Perhaps as a consequence, my grandmother had strict rules in her home about what constituted respectful conduct toward her. That rigidity distanced her from her daughters (as well as her grandchildren). My mother and aunt were always dutiful, but I never saw an exchange between them and their mother that suggested warmth.

My grandfather was different. He was a self-made man, but this did not bother him; he lived his life by trying to accomplish whatever needed doing. His daughters adored him. When my mother married, she brought life-sized portraits of her mother and father with her from Lugos. She hung her father's portrait facing the piano so that she could see it while she played; her mother's portrait hung on an adjoining wall, where my mother could barely see it from the piano. (I noticed this because I spent many of my childhood hours on the piano stool practicing my piano lesson.)

My grandfather was a nice man, reliable and even-tempered, easy to talk to. He loved his children and adored his grandchildren. He called us by ridiculous love names; but coming from him, they never felt ridiculous. Of all those in my family, I liked him the best. He had many friendly acquaintances, but, as far as I could see, he was close to no one outside his family. Within the family, everyone (except his wife) liked him a lot. My grandfather was hard of hearing and used an old-fashioned ear trumpet; my grandmother claimed that his deafness had ruined her social life. During the last five or six years of my grandfather's life, his wife hardly spoke to him. Although he was always pleasant and kind, I cannot remember hearing him laugh; I suspect he was deeply sad.

My mother was so fond of her father that to say she loved him profoundly is an understatement. I suspect her extreme devotion to me was partly a transfer of her love for him. She and her family used to say that I looked very much like my grandfather and would grow up to be like him. The claim may have some small basis in fact, but it was carried to ridiculous extremes. When he was about sixty, my grandfather was trampled by some horses and afterwards walked with a slight limp. After I lost my foot in 1927, I was even supposed to limp in the same way he did.

Whenever we were in Lugos, my grandfather would take Emmi and me to the weaving factory. He was especially proud of the patterns that could be programmed into his machines. We traveled to the mill, which was on the banks of the Temes, in a comfortable carriage drawn by two horses. Next to trains, I liked my grandfather's carriage best. Until at least 1925, when I made my last visit to Lugos, there were no automobiles in town.

During our lengthy summer visits, we stayed not in my grandparents' house but with my Aunt Margaret and her husband, Eugene Dobó; they lived on the south side of the river, in German Lugos. My uncle, like my father, was a successful lawyer. My aunt Margaret had absolutely nothing saintly about her and was occasionally compared to the wife of Socrates. My mother and her sister Margaret were opposites: My mother was thin, my aunt, plump, my mother was sad, my aunt, laughing, my mother absurd in her devotion to her children, my aunt perfect in her selfishness. Two of my Dobó cousins were as close to me as brothers. George, a year younger than I, and Stephen, two years younger. Their sister, Ily, born when I was six, was named for my mother.

Our eight months of exile in Romania were a time of great upset for my parents, and I expect that with four extra people in the house, for the Dobó family as well. Emmi and I could not attend school with our cousins because the lessons were taught only in Romanian, now the official language. A tutor (who was boring) was hired to teach us at home. My cousins also suffered: They found having to learn their school lessons in Romanian an unpleasant change.

But my cousins had a further problem; one of them, Stephen, was Aunt Margaret's favorite child. Perhaps one of the reasons that I felt so close to my cousins was that I had a similar discomfort. But the dynamics of the Dobó family were more difficult. My mother may have treated Emmi as if she were less important than I, but both our parents gave Emmi love and approval. Aunt Margaret idolized sweet-tempered Stephen, and in her eyes he could do no wrong. George could do no right. As a result, George became more and more prickly and sour and failed to get along comfortably with anyone except Ily, who got along with everyone.[3]

I could not help feeling sorry for George, even though he spread his misery widely. I felt equally sorry for Stephen, who was as unhappy with his lion's share of praise and attention as George was with the absence of approval. Five years later, those tensions led to tragedy. When an itinerant peddler of handguns came through Lugos, Stephen surreptitiously purchased one. He committed suicide with it at the age of fourteen. I was saddened by his death, and neither anticipated nor understood it, but I was not surprised by it.

---

[3]A few years later, my grandfather began proposing that Ily and I should marry; but marriage to anyone remained an outlandish idea until my future wife, Mici, was firmly entrenched.

Although I have seen my two surviving cousins many times since 1919, I will finish their stories here, during the time we were closest. As a young man, George emigrated to Paris, studied anthropology, changed his last name to Devereux, and eventually achieved considerable success as a professor at the Sorbonne.[4] He also distinguished himself by marrying (successively) six women, including a Hungarian countess.

Shortly before World War II, George came to the United States and began studies of the Mojave Indians.[5] Later, I visited him in Hawaii. He was then married to a psychoanalyst who was also an excellent cook, a combination that I would have thought very close to ideal. But that marriage, like each before and after it, ended in divorce. George died in the mid-1980s without ever finding contentment.

Good-natured Ily married shortly before World War II, moved to Budapest, and gave birth to a son. Her husband was sent to a Nazi concentration camp during the war and died not long after his release. Ily returned to Lugos, where a few years later she married a Romanian lawyer and moved to Bucharest. In the early 1960s, the family—which by then included widowed Aunt Margaret—emigrated to Israel, where we have met again on several occasions. Today, Ily lives in Tel Aviv, where she is a moderately popular Israeli painter. Her son teaches applied mathematics at a university in Southern California. Her story—by comparison, the happiest—closes the history of my extended family.

Given all the strains and unhappiness of the period, our stay in Lugos might well have been bleak. Oddly enough, it was almost exactly the opposite. Postwar life in Lugos had a new and different intensity. I can best explain what I mean by mentioning two people who were an important part of my life during those eight months. The first is Burschi Neumann, another eleven-year-old, the son of my mother's dearest friend. Burschi was considerably more sociable and outgoing than I. He also enjoyed talking, and for once I listened carefully.

Burschi had two favorite topics: ideas about moral superiority he had garnered from reading Nietzsche's philosophy; and concepts about the birth and decay of cultures, obtained from another of his favorite books, *Untergang des Abendlandes (The Decline of the West)* by Oswald Spengler. In retrospect, I have to wonder at an eleven-year-old studying and talking about those books. But

---

[4]His theory of the psychology of cultures continues to be of interest today.
[5]After his death, he was buried on the Mojave reservation.

although I never buried myself in either Nietzsche or Spengler, I served as an attentive audience. Having seen the end of Hungary as I had known it, I could imagine the end of Western civilization (whatever those words might mean).

During this period, my mother dedicated herself to seeing that her children's lives proceeded as they would have in Budapest. My mother looked delicate; she was slender and small, and I suspect that many people believed she had a gentle disposition; but she was a strong-willed and determined person where her children were concerned. Emmi and I had begun piano lessons three years earlier, and I remember them a little dubiously. Emmi was allowed to stop her lessons when my mother decided that I was the potential virtuoso. My studies could not be interrupted.

Joseph Willer, my piano teacher in Lugos, was a notary public, not a professional pianist. His house, where I had my lessons, was very fine, and I never saw any other students. I now wonder whether he took me as a student only as a favor to my mother. Willer loved music as Klug loved mathematics; he was not only an excellent amateur but an outstanding teacher. He wanted me to understand and love music, and he succeeded.

When I started my lessons with him, I had already learned the scales and chords of the various keys by rote. I could hear harmonies, but I was not sure why a particular set of notes was harmonic. Willer explained the principles that Pythagoras had recognized a few millennia earlier. Willer explained music to me in a way that made its resemblance to mathematics clear. It is easy to explain mathematics to a mathematician; it is not as easy to explain music, even to a musician. But my teacher explained music to a young boy who never became a musician. Willer described the rules, which are laws neither of nature nor of psychology; they are simply rules of convention. I began to understand what deserved my attention. The rules do not explain the beauty of music, but they do explain the feeling that everything is in its proper place.

Eight months after our vacation began, late in February 1920, we were allowed to return to Budapest. I was glad to be home again, but I missed my lessons with Willer. He had particularly impressed me once when he played a few chords of one of Beethoven's sonatas. I recognized the sonata as one my mother had played in the past, but I didn't then know that the work was Sonata Opus 13 (*Pathetique*). When I described it to my mother, she thought that I meant the *Appassionata;* she was disappointed when I did not recognize it.

I realized as she played that day that my mother paid a little too much attention to whether she played well. Not long after that, she stopped playing altogether. She was losing her old skill because arthritis was beginning to cripple her and she was no longer able to devote enough time to practice; I suspect that she was too proud to play anything less than her best, even if that meant giving up music.

Willer had suggested that I continue my lessons in Budapest with his sister, Otilia. Unfortunately, Otilia was a very different kind of teacher. She emphasized technique and drilled me mercilessly. She paid attention only to details of execution, and she did not allow pleasure or understanding to slip in. Years later, I realized (because of my earlier lessons with the right Willer) that the evenness of touch and timing that Otilia demanded are necessary to bring out the nuances of the melody, that the accompaniment must be uniform so that the smallest variation in the melodic line can be appreciated.

In her enthusiasm to make a musician out of me, Otilia insisted after a few years of study (at my mother's instigation) that I take the examinations at the Academy of Music. I managed to pass the first one, but barely. The next year, for the first and only time in my life, I failed an exam. Although I always wanted my teachers' approval, my distress over that failure was shortlived. I was not meant to be a musician. My mother's dream of having a concert pianist son ended at least partly because the wrong Willer was my teacher.

I was grateful to be able to stop my piano lessons when I went to study in Germany. I came to love playing again only later. I have always had access to a piano, even during my student years when I made it a condition of renting a room. Yet that is not the whole story, either. My enjoyment of music was induced by my mother. My interest in numbers was spontaneous.

5

MY NAME IS KOKÓ

1920–1925

EXTRA HUNGARIAM, NON est vita; si est vita, non est ita: Outside Hungary, there's no life; if there is any, it's nothing like it. For centuries, Hungarians have repeated that remarkable rhyme, a melange of patriotism, exaggeration, and whimsy. I came home full of the strange experience of being *extra Hungariam*, and expected an interested audience for my account. But in the new Hungary, no one was lighthearted. Extreme agitation was compulsory.

At school, I learned a new pledge:

> *I believe in one God;*
> *I believe in one country;*
> *I believe in God's eternal justice;*
> *I believe in the resurrection of Hungary.*

Those lines, which we chanted in assembly, began my school day for the next five years. Statues of four tattered, grieving women were installed in Freedom Square, a few blocks southeast of Parliament Square, to symbolize the lost lands now annexed to Romania, Yugoslavia, Austria, and Czechoslovakia.

My father's prediction that anti-Semitism would greatly increase was fulfilled. The emigration of Hungarian Jews began. Those who remained suffered from lack of professional opportunity and sometimes from real harassment. Yet anti-Semitism in Hungary was very different from that of the Nazis—it was based on religion, not race. Among the 8 million inhabitants that remained in Hungary, slightly less than 1 million were Jews by descent. Far fewer were Jews by religion. Although almost half the students in my class at school were Jews, I can think of only a handful (besides myself) who were not converted Christians. Converted Jews did not actively discriminate against the unconverted, but they felt (and were) socially superior.

Religion was not an issue in my family; indeed, it was never discussed. My only religious training came because the Minta required that all students take classes in their respective religions. My family celebrated one holiday, the Day of Atonement, when we all fasted. Yet my father said prayers for his parents on Saturdays and on all the Jewish holidays. The idea of God that I absorbed was that it would be wonderful if He existed: We needed Him desperately but had not seen Him in many thousands of years.

And there were other troubles. Our savings became meaningless as prices doubled, tripled, and finally reached a thousandfold. Not until 1923 was inflation brought under control. Our vacations became more modest, and my father always left early to return to work. But the financial pressures my family suffered were similar to those of their friends. My problems had no such commonality. The next years taught me a great deal, and the lessons were painful.

Most children enter a broader, more demanding society when they enter school at six. I was overprotected. I reached adolescence still a serious child with no sense of humor. My classmates laughed about our teachers: That was wrong. They also laughed at me: That was intolerable.

When I returned to the Minta from Lugos, I had passed my twelfth birthday, but my growing older had no effect on the intensity of my mother's care. The Minta was located in the center of the city on Trefort Street, right behind the university. The school was a walk of about thirty minutes from my home. My mother found it unthinkable that I should make that trip alone. Magda Hesz was assigned to walk me to school each day—from my first day at school until she left for the United States when I was almost fifteen.

And that unique situation was not my only unwelcome distinction: I also occasionally had to carry Emmi's old lunch box, which had her name on it. Every new student acquired a nickname; the practice was harmless. At first I was called Emma, which I vigorously protested. But the nickname that stuck was Coco (pronounced *TsoTsoh*), a common name for simpleminded clowns. I was not off to an auspicious start.

My early years at the Minta were miserable. The only idea I had about how to remedy the situation was to change schools. My friend Paul Virágh went to the Piarist gymnasium, which was run by the Catholic Church. He did not hate his school, and he belonged to a boy scout troop!

The Piarist gymnasium was well thought of, and I finally convinced my parents that I should transfer there. I was among the best students in my class, and it seemed likely that I would be accepted. I was even allowed to join the boy scout troop for several hikes (with no teasing added). But, unlike Paul, I was not Catholic. I was turned down.

I began to wonder whether being a Jew really was synonymous with being an undesirably different kind of person. The following summer when we visited Lugos, I asked my grandfather whether Christian ideas of mercy were not really superior to Jewish ideas of justice. Was it right, I asked, to encourage taking an eye for an eye, a tooth for a tooth?

I remember his answer. He said: "Laws must be obeyed without exception. The law cannot make everyone a saint. Only a very few people are saints, and obeying the law must be possible for all people. If someone knocks your tooth out, you have a strong urge to hit back. The meaning of the law is that you must never take more than one tooth for a tooth. To forgive is much better. But the law cannot forbid the desire for revenge. It can only limit it by justice."

That fall when I went into ninth grade, Karl Oberle, the headmaster, taught mathematics. On one occasion during the first weeks of class when Oberle called on me, I gave an answer based on material not yet discussed in class. That seemed to involve no risk on my part; Minta teachers universally encouraged students to bring outside information to the discussion. Oberle, however, frowned. He said to me, "What are you? A repeater?" meaning, had I taken the class before and failed?

The practice in the Minta (and in most other schools) was to promote children with their classes, regardless of performance. Certainly, as headmaster, Oberle would have known if I had had so unusual a record. His question was intended, and received, as an insult. Even worse, the incident marked the beginning of a long period during which Oberle never called on me, even when I was the only student to raise a hand. Everyone noticed, but for once it was not the sort of thing that my classmates teased me about.

Both Oberle and Juvancz provided good explanations of mathematics, but they were opposites in their approach to their students. Oberle was a rigid disciplinarian; he directed a major portion of his effort toward making sure his students closed their brackets correctly and turned in impeccably neat papers. Neither was my forte, much less my pleasure. Although I paid attention in class, I lost my taste for mathematics at home. Mathematical skills seem to develop best in childhood. Oberle's teaching method set me back several years.

I wanted very much to be a good student. I was terrified that Oberle would make me a repeater or, hardly better, give me a low grade. But about a week before the end of the term, he began calling on me, four or five times during each class. I always had the right answer. He passed me with an A. On the written record, he not was unfair. But the new semester brought my return to invisibility in his classroom. When he became ill and died early in the term, I felt greatly relieved and only a little guilty.

Not much later, Magda Hesz left for the United States, and a few weeks after that I had my own first brush with a serious illness. I got scarlet fever and then developed a kidney infection. Before antibiotics, recovery took several (dull) weeks in bed, but eventually I was free of the main symptoms. As the doctor continued to give me checkups, I became familiar with the first chemical experiment I had ever seen. The fascinating test showed that I had albumin in my urine. The diagnosis of orthostatic albuminuria (and a heart murmur) kept me in bed for more weeks. Even when I was finally allowed to go outdoors, my regimen almost completely eliminated sports.

When I returned to school the next fall, an eternity of bleak days stretched out before me. Our Latin teacher, Mr. Gröger, who assigned our seats for every class, had assigned me to share a desk with an unfortunate new student, Forgács; my new desk mate was mentally retarded perhaps because of an iodine deficiency. I didn't mind the arrangement. At least he wouldn't tease me.

As it turned out, Forgács's life at school was living proof that mine could be worse. He tried to learn, and I tried to help him, but neither of us was very successful. That in itself was a sufficient misery for him. But the teasing he endured was far worse than any I had encountered. His tormentors would dance around him in a circle, making faces and taunting noises, wiggling their hands in their ears. Forgács would become upset, then frantic, and finally furious. That only delighted his tormentors and attracted more students to the circle. I couldn't help him. The best I could do was sit by and not participate. But that full view of how teasing worked hinted at what had been happening to me.

A few years earlier I had, unconsciously and mostly out of boredom, done the right thing in response to teasing. Once while Magda Hesz and I were on the way home from school, Nándor Keszthelyi, who lived near me, ran by and grabbed my cap off my head. I proceeded calmly on my way, not even bothering to look at him. About a half hour after I arrived home, the doorbell rang. It was Nándor returning my hat. I had failed to make the connection then, but now the principle was clear: Ignore teasing.

Even after I became less entertaining, I still had little in common with most of my classmates. Many enjoyed appearing arrogant, coarse, and gratuitously cruel. My persistence in tutoring Forgács encouraged two students, both of them Gentiles and socially popular, to seek similar help from me. My father was generous in allowing me the use of his office in the evening, provided that we didn't spoil anything. I learned a good deal about teaching and even about my classmates. They did better in mathematics, and my outcast status was modified.

In the meantime, I acquired a new nickname. Our Latin teacher, Mr. Gröger, ranked high among the students as a subject of ridicule. We were studying Caesar's Gallic campaigns, and he mentioned that the *C* (which in Hungarian is pronounced *ts*) may have been pronounced as a *K* in Latin, thus making the connection between *Kaiser* and *Caesar* more obvious. During a parody of the class afterwards, some wag decided that my nickname, Tsot-soh, should be pronounced correctly Kokó.

I had learned my lesson: I did not react. But the name stuck. And I didn't mind it. My new nickname had a small element of acceptance and friendliness in it. Kokó came to seem, by the end of that year, a sort of badge I had earned through a long, unconscious struggle.

Nándor, who a few years before had stolen my hat, enjoyed a dignified Nándi for his nickname, a symbol of his popularity. He was very lively, but he was also a capable student. During the spring of that year, I saw progress: As we walked home, Nándi found occasions to talk pleasantly with me.

Nándi was very close to two of his classmates, with whom he had shared the same tutor during the primary grades. One was a somewhat quieter boy, Ede (nicknamed Suki) Harkányi-Schütz, whose father, like Nándi's own, was dead; the other was a musically and scholastically talented student too dignified to have a nickname, Tibor László. Although Tibor was the most reserved, his company was much in demand—possibly because of his reserve. Suki was particularly kind and good-natured; everyone liked him. He was observant of other people's feelings and had no trace of meanness in him. I was always impressed by his seemingly effortless way of organizing everything, from his tasks to his possessions. I was not surprised when he later decided to become an engineer.

By the beginning of the next school year, when I was almost sixteen, I had become part of their circle. They included me in their sports club of about ten boys, even though I was markedly inferior at everything except the standing jump. By then, we were all taking physics, which I found as fascinating as mathematics.

A cosine occurs in the formula for calculating work. Whenever I was about to jump, they would cheer, "Go cosine energy!" That kind of teasing I liked. The other sport in which I had a little ability was Ping-Pong. But I took sports as seriously as the rest of life; for me, they were not a joke. I played, but I seldom laughed.

During that year, I got to know Suki's family: his mother, who was a warm and charming woman; his stepfather, Aladar Schütz, a pediatrician who was particularly stern and authoritarian; his two considerably younger half-brothers, Steven and Gábor, and his sister, Augusta, who was called Mici.

Mici, like my sister Emmi, attended Maria Terezia gymnasium, and although they were three years apart in age, they knew and liked each other. Yet Mici and Emmi differed in ways other than age. Emmi was a Jew; Mici, a Calvinist. Emmi was obedient; Mici, iconoclastic. Emmi was old-fashioned in dress and manners; Mici objected to stockings and found decorum dull. Emmi was organized and careful (a trait we did not share); Mici was a free spirit. Yet they liked each other, and more surprising yet, Mici seemed to find me quite acceptable.

When I visited Suki, Mici would ask for my help with her mathematics lesson (which I now realize was simply an excuse to talk to me without upsetting her stepfather, who closely supervised her activities). She was very pleasant to me and called me by my reformulated nickname, Kokó. (For almost eighty years, she continued to do so, thus providing one of the few bridges I had with my childhood.)

At that time, though, I thought of Mici only as Suki's little sister. My first romantic imaginings began on less dangerous ground, with a girl whose family lived in another section of the Palatinus. Magda Radó was a cellist and, like me, loved music.[1] I could figure out which operas Magda was likely to attend, go myself, and talk to her during the intermissions. But I never got beyond such small chats about our shared interest. The wonderful benefit of all that effort was that I, like my father, became an opera addict. During those years, I must have seen every opera that was staged in Budapest (mostly Verdi and Wagner), all from the uppermost, cheapest gallery seats. I especially loved the Wagner operas—for instance, *Die Meistersinger* and *The Flying Dutchman*. I played transcriptions of them at home on the piano. In one case, the dramatic first act of *Die Walküre*, I learned the libretto by heart.

During our last two years at the Minta, Suki, Nándi, Tibor, and I were rarely separated. We all liked the teacher who taught Hungarian literature,

---

[1]Magda had a friend who was an almost passable violinist. I managed on one occasion to arrange for the three of us to play a Beethoven trio; but the sounds we made fell far short of music. I tried throughout my gymnasium years to organize a chamber music group. Tibor was a fine cellist, and I asked to play with him, but he was a much better musician than I and could not find time for me. My first success in playing chamber music came many years later.

Zsolt Alszeghy. Alszeghy treated us fairly and even seemed to like us. For the first time, a class did not put me in the no-man's-land of a battlefield between my teacher and my classmates.

Alszeghy made us memorize poems and recite them with feeling. At one point, I was assigned a translation of "The Raven" by Edgar Allan Poe. I had read it earlier in English and liked it. But the word the translator chose for *nevermore*, which has no equivalent in Hungarian, made the translation all but senseless.[2]

The day my assignment was due was also the day the class made an excursion up the Danube. When we had settled down at the picnic spot, Mr. Alszeghy called on me to recite. So there I stood in the fine sunshine and diligently emoted nonsense, my hands crossed behind me. When one of my friends sneaked up and put a pencil into my fingers, I burst out laughing. Perhaps even Mr. Alszeghy had to laugh. He finally gave up on hearing "The Raven." That day was a milestone for me: I discovered that laughter in the classroom is not necessarily wrong.

In Hungary, every gymnasium student takes a comprehensive examination, the Matura, at the end of the senior year. That year, Mr. Alszeghy assigned essays on the topics that would be covered in the examination and announced that five students, the four of us and another classmate, Andor Hlavács, would critique the essays. That was a considerable honor as well as excellent preparation. For the rest of the year, we met in my father's office for evenings of work and discussion. We called ourselves a committee, played at taking ourselves seriously, and discovered the pleasures of teamwork.

But the happiness I enjoyed from friendship and from family life were of minor importance in comparison to another activity. During those growing-up years, the most exciting thing in the world for me was science. During my last two years in gymnasium, I became acquainted with three young men from the Jewish community in Budapest who were studying and working in Germany as scientists. Probably my father mentioned to their fathers, whom he knew, that I was also interested in science and would benefit from meeting them. Two were in their early twenties: Eugene Wigner, who became a great theoretical physicist, and Johnny von Neumann, whose brilliance as a mathematician is internationally acknowledged. The third was almost elderly—in his late twenties: Leo Szilárd, of lesser fame but great ability.

---

[2]For Hungarian readers, I will mention that the words supplied were *soha már*, a choice clearly based on sound.

I looked forward to spending a few hours with them when they were home during academic breaks. The only topic we discussed in those days was physics. Szilárd narrowed the field even further. He said that only two topics in physics were of interest: the theory of atoms and the theory of gravitation, a statement that many physicists could repeat today with slight modification. Most of the time, I simply listened to them, but they were willing to explain if I asked, a privilege I used sparingly.

Throughout my high school years, I dreamed about the best of all vocations—being a professor. Yet that prospect looked hopeless. Not only had anti-Semitism closed many doors to me, but I felt I was far from brilliant; and my teachers offered me little encouragement. I can still remember my frustration and despair when I first tried to understand relativity. I worked for a considerable time during my junior year before I approached my physics teacher, Mr. Szijártó, with my problem. But instead of trying to help clear up my confusion, he asked me where I had come across the problem. When I told him, he asked to borrow the book. He returned it to me the following year after the Matura, saying, "Now you may work on it." Challenging students to explore ideas was not a common aim at the Minta.

The Matura was the apex of gymnasium studies. Seniors were excused from classes for the two weeks before the examination to study. But when the time came, I was full of panic and despair about every subject other than mathematics and physics. If I did not do well on the Matura, I would not be admitted to any university.

Those were two peculiar weeks. I was too terrified even to begin to review. Most of the time, I walked along the Danube. The weather was beautiful. I loved the sunshine. I looked at the bridges, the trees, the flowing river. I liked them the more for knowing that in a few days, the Matura would bring on the end of the world for me. I was wrong; I passed the examination with ease. But having avoided the worst disaster, I was still facing a calamity: I would have to leave Hungary. Anti-Semitism had, if anything, grown worse. My father had said, "Hungary has no place for you." I knew he was right, but I was afraid to go.

The only person to whom I complained was my grandfather. I still remember parts of a crazy conversation that I had with him one day during what proved to be my last visit to him in the summer of 1925.[3] I was mourning: "I have to leave, and I don't know what will become of me." His

[3]My grandfather died soon after I began my studies in Germany, and my grandmother died two years later.

reply was simple. "You have a head, and you have a heart." I knew I had a heart because it felt heavy. My possession of an equally active head was not as clear to me.

My father wanted me to study in Germany. Hungary practiced anti-Semitism; Germany appeared free of it. The war had left few effects on the German universities. In fact, postwar Germany had emphasized science, and the golden age of physics was largely centered there. I wanted to study mathematics, but my father insisted on a more practical course. Aside from teaching, mathematics offered no job opportunities. We compromised: I would study chemistry. But a further compromise was required. My mother insisted that, at seventeen, I was too young to leave home. Her worries won the day, and during the fall I studied at the Institute of Technology in Budapest.

Much that I remember about that period centers around the Eötvös competition, a prestigious contest open to students when they graduate from the gymnasium. I entered in physics and mathematics. On my way to the examination, I stopped by Suki's house; when Mici sent me off to do battle, I understood for the first time that she had a real interest in me.

During the physics exam, I had a strange experience. One question asked: How much would the water level in a glass of water change when the ice cubes floating in it melted? Before I had time to think about the answer (which is: no change at all), the tune of a ditty about the Archimedes principle popped into my mind.[4] In 1987, I mentioned that experience to some Hungarian visitors I met in Phoenix, Arizona. They immediately began singing the song. Both the Eötvös competition and the tune have survived in my hometown.

After the examination, my professor of mathematics at the Institute of Technology had me repeat the questions and my answers. He said I had done well. A few days later, he was proved to be right. I had won the prize in physics individually, and three of us shared the prize in mathematics. One of

---

[4]The lyric, loosely translated, goes:

> If you a body in water submerge, dear pet
> It loses as much of its weight, dear pet,
> As weighs the water by it, dear pet,
> That is thereby forced to emerge, dear pet.

In Hungarian the rhyme goes:

> Minden vizbe másttat test, Kis Angyam,
> A súlyäbid annyit verzt, Kis Angyam,
> Amennyi az általa no-de, bíszan batt vizsulya, Kis Angyam.

the other winners, László (Laci, pronounced *Lotzi*) Tisza, had attended another gymnasium, and we had not met before the awards ceremony. But I took an instant liking to him, and because he was also studying in Budapest that fall, we became good friends.

On January 2, 1926, two weeks before my eighteenth birthday but six weeks after classes had begun in Germany, I was allowed to set out for foreign lands—accompanied by my mother and father. My mother might well have remained in Germany with me to oversee my welfare, but my father claimed his priority as her husband and she returned to Budapest with him.

The night before I left, Suki, Tibor, Nándi, and I spent almost the entire night talking in my father's office. I knew that I was fortunate to be going, but the price of my good fortune felt high. I knew in my heart that my new life away from Budapest would be not only a beginning but an ending.

But our happy times together were not yet over. During my summer vacation in 1927, Suki, Nándi, Tibor, and I went on a hiking excursion to Dobogókö; afterwards we met several times in my father's office to write a lengthy poem describing our adventure, which we called *Epos*.

Climbing the Dobogókö requires the skills not of a mountain goat but of a cow. Nonetheless, the four of us did have some difficulties. The crisis came when the brook we had been following turned into a small pond almost ten feet wide surrounded by slippery banks. I still remember the pleasure of getting wet in excellent company. To prevent my friends from teasing me about my abilities as a guide and rock climber, I described them myself by modifying a few stanzas of a famous heroic poem in which the hero flings a millstone and accidentally kills a knight. By changing only a few words, our bodies were turned into the millstones, and the drama into silly comedy.

Nándi insisted on using the occasion for some friendly criticism of his charming younger sister, whom he described as tame as a snake and clever as a dove. And that led to our describing Suki, on those rare occasions when he could be provoked, as being possessed not by the devil but by his stepfather (whom we all considered an ogre). To round out the story, we introduced three geese named after three pretty girls we knew: "Each was like beauty itself with intelligence radiating from her beak." I was enormously proud of our literary accomplishment, but I was slightly deflated when I brought it to our friend and former teacher, Mr. Alszeghy: He responded with moderate enthusiasm.

As I became more involved with science, I spent less and less time with my friends. They helped me celebrate my marriage to Mici in 1934, and I saw them for the last time in 1936, on what proved to be my last visit to Budapest for more than half a century.

Suki and Tibor both died in Nazi concentration camps; Nándi survived to welcome the Russians in 1945. He saw Emmi occasionally while she was still in Budapest, but he and I exchanged only a few extremely short sentences on the telephone in 1975.[5] He died four years before I returned to Budapest.

Throughout my early childhood I was terrified by the dark and the nightmares that I believed were waiting for me. No nightmare I imagined could have been as awful as the reality these dear friends of my youth lived out.

[5]See chapter 42.

6

How to Become a
Physicist the Hard Way

1926–1928

I WAS ENROLLED IN the Karlsruhe Technical Institute. My parents left me safely settled in a modest room in a modest home near the school; I had the use of an even more modest piano in the family's parlor. Karlsruhe was (and is) a sleepy little town in southwest Germany. Its most noteworthy feature was that the headquarters of I.G. Farben, then the leading chemical company in the world, were located nearby.

Today, nothing is unusual about a scientific discovery's being followed soon after by a technical application: The discovery of electrons led to electronics; fission led to nuclear energy. But before the 1880s, science played almost no role in the advances of technology. For example, James Watt developed the first efficient steam engine long before science established the equivalence between mechanical energy and heat.

Chemistry was the first science to undergo a merger with technology, and the first technology affected was dyemaking. I.G. Farben was among the first companies to sponsor scientific development at an educational institute. I had landed at one of the major crossroads between science and industry. My father had acted on competent advice when he selected Karlsruhe.

Except for the test for albuminuria, I had never seen a test tube, so laboratory work was my first challenge. The chemistry lab was a large room with twenty or thirty stone-topped benches, equipped with balance scales, Bunsen burners, and glass flasks. I still carry the scars that testify to my first discovery—that test tubes are fragile. My shoes were soon spotted by acid, and my lab coat became battle worn as I struggled with the practical realities of performing qualitative analysis.

A few days after I began my classes, I had an experience that shocked me. I went to the chemistry lab assistant with a question about a laboratory procedure I didn't understand. He sent me away with a rude remark and no answer. My fellow students told me not to be upset and explained that the laboratory assistant had lost a leg in the World War and was, therefore, an anti-Semite. Although anti-Semitism was not new to me, the *therefore* was at that time a real puzzle.

But I had few such unpleasant encounters, and learning the elements of chemistry kept me occupied; I had little time to brood. I enjoyed learning the underlying regularities of chemical reactions: that a salt precipitates from solution only when the concentration of its positive ions multiplied by the concentration of its negative ions reaches a particular value;[1] and the law of multiple proportion—only certain amounts of elements or multiples of those amounts combine with one another.[2] Such numerical rules played a basic role in the development of chemistry and led chemists to think in terms of discrete atoms.

Once during my first year, I acted like a physicist. I had to determine the composition of a salt that behaved like NaCl (sodium chloride); but when I tested it on a Bunsen burner, the flame turned deep red rather than the characteristic yellow of table salt. A spectroscope stood in a forlorn corner of the laboratory and readily gave the precise wavelength of that red flame, which corresponded to lithium—a much easier way to determine my compound than by playing chemist with a solution.

The following year, I went on to quantitative analysis. Although I had enjoyed learning the theories of chemistry, the laboratory work of quantitative analysis—weighing and reweighing samples on glass-encased balance scales—was not as much fun. I soon discovered that measurements became unreliable if I touched the sample with my fingers. Until then, I had not suspected dirt had a measurable weight.

Chemistry was not my only occupation. During the 1920s in Germany, a college education could be pursued with freedom of choice, unburdened by a required curriculum. From the beginning, therefore, I studied not only chemistry but also mathematics, the equivalent of today's double major.

---

[1]For example, silver chloride will form if there is one silver ion per 6,000 water molecules and one chlorine ion per billion water molecules. If there were ten times as much silver, one-tenth the amount of chlorine would suffice.

[2]For example, one amount of hydrogen combines with a certain amount of oxygen to form water (H_2O); the same amount of hydrogen may also combine with twice as much oxygen to form hydrogen peroxide (H_2O_2).

The first mathematics lecture I attended was given by an elderly professor who died a few days later. The lecture was confusing; indeed, I couldn't understand any of it. I went with some apprehension to the second lecture, this one given by Professor Karl Böhm. He began by eulogizing his recently deceased colleague and then went on to praise the lecture I had heard, calling it truly great. Then he began to review it. I followed what he was saying very well.

The class period ended before Böhm had covered more than a tiny fraction of the first lecture. When he began the next lecture, he continued the review; several weeks later, he had covered every topic his former colleague had discussed—and I understood them all. Böhm taught by beginning a problem and then calling on a student to develop the steps of its solution, and he often called on me. I thoroughly enjoyed all my classes with him, but I especially liked those on the theory of functions, which includes working with imaginary and irrational numbers,[3] and non-Euclidean geometry, which makes it possible to understand why three dimensions in space, together with time, can be considered four-dimensional geometry. Those topics are two of the most important tools of quantum mechanics. I had great difficulty with my earlier study of Einstein's last great accomplishment, which concerns gravitation, until I became familiar with non-Euclidian geometry.

Not long after my arrival in Karlsruhe, a chemistry student two years ahead of me, Feri (Ferenc) von Körösy, took me under his wing. His sister was part of the party-going circle in which I had been included in Budapest. Feri was a veritable fountain of wisdom; he advised me on everything from lodgings to professors.[4] I soon moved into a much larger room in the home of a widow—about a forty-minute fast walk from the Institute. My new room was the largest in the flat, had a good view of trees from its window, and, most important, contained a grand piano. Now that I no longer had to endure piano lessons and hours of practicing, playing Mozart and Beethoven had become a real pleasure.

I spent what little free time I had playing the piano, reading more widely—for instance, Dostoyevsky—and (in secret) writing a little poetry in Hungarian and German. I enjoyed everything I was doing in Karlsruhe, but I was lonely and terribly homesick for my friends in Budapest.

---

[3] When I asked Professor Böhm whether imaginary numbers really exist, he quoted a well-known statement: "God made the integers; everything else is human creation."

[4] Feri survived World War II in Europe; after the war, he emigrated to Israel, where he practiced chemistry until his death in the late 1990s.

Budapest was only twenty hours away by express train. I still remember the pleasure I felt when the Jánoshegy, with its lookout tower on top, welcomed me home through the window of the train a half hour before I arrived. I spent more than a quarter of my time at home. The Karlsruhe Technical Institute provided four weeks of vacation at Easter, eight weeks during August and September, and two weeks at Christmas.

But even when I was at home, my attention was often engaged by the new ideas I was encountering. I particularly remember the Christmas holidays during my second year. Just before I left for home, a fellow student introduced me to the first step in a new (for me) kind of mathematics: set theory.[5] Two weeks later, I had reinvented the solution to a crucial problem in set theory. But mathematics had absorbed almost all my waking hours during the vacation. My family was not pleased, and my friends thought I was crazy. But I remember the exploration with happiness.

During my second year at Karlsruhe, I was introduced to a spectacular new adventure. Herman Mark, employed as a chemist by I. G. Farben, was a guest lecturer in Karlsruhe. His class in quantum mechanics was the basis not only of my future studies but of a long-lasting friendship.[6]

Quantum mechanics was a new science. In 1926, some of my textbooks still considered the existence of atoms a hypothesis, not a reality. The size of atoms had been measured in the early 1900s; this should have put their existence beyond doubt. The atomic theory remained suspect because, as Wilhelm Ostwald and Ernst Mach pointed out, the theory was in conflict with the established laws of physics. The problem had not been resolved until Werner Heisenberg put the capstone on quantum mechanics—just two years before my arrival in Karlsruhe.

On one occasion in Herman Mark's seminar, I reported on a paper about molecular spectroscopy by Reinhard Mecke. Chemical reactions provide information about the configuration of atoms in a molecule. By contrast, the

---

[5] The question my friend posed was this: Are there greater infinities than those defined by counting? One larger infinity is easy to recognize. Consider all positive integers replaced by women and all negative integers replaced by men. The set of all possible marriages represents a greater infinity than the infinities of mere counting. I set about thinking and found that the kinds of infinities that are essentially different from each other are unlimited. During the following two weeks, I worked out the precise conditions under which two infinite sets can be considered equal and when they cannot be. Neither of the two theorems I worked out were novel, but they were correct.

[6] The friendship included not just Hermann Mark but also his son Hans, who at that time had not yet been born. Many years later, I taught Hans (who will figure in subsequent chapters) quantum mechanics.

spectra of molecules include information on the manner in which the molecules rotate and vibrate. Study of the rotation and vibration makes it possible to infer the distances between atoms and the forces that hold them in position within the molecule.

Professor Tausz, a Hungarian who taught engineering at Karlsruhe, attended that meeting. Although I had not taken any classes with him, he had gone out of his way to befriend me. As an insecure young student, I had confided in him about my feelings of making no progress. After my report he said, "You are stumbling on pebbles. You will do fine."

Another member of the visiting faculty was a very wonderful crystallographer, Peter Paul Ewald. Ewald taught me a great deal about electromagnetism; but his special field was crystallography, so I read a huge tome by Paul Niggli on the subject. Ewald invited me to visit him at home; there I met his family, including his daughter Rose, who would figure in my life in the United States.

During my time as a student at Karlsruhe, I talked with my father about how much more I enjoyed physics and mathematics than chemistry. But he remained convinced that I would make a better living as a chemist. During one of my vacations from Karlsruhe, I worked at Izzó, the Budapest equivalent of General Electric. My boss, a Mr. Selényi, was a very nice man, and I told him about my father's concerns. He promptly sought out my father and told him that I could have a job as a physicist with him anytime.

My father was a conscientious man as well as a practical one, and he wanted me both to be happy and to succeed. Because he didn't understand what I was doing in chemistry, mathematics, or physics, he visited Karlsruhe to ask for advice from my professors. They all recommended my pursuing whatever I wanted. But even that was not quite enough.

My father had a very distant relative in Vienna, Felix Ehrenhaft, a famous-infamous professor of physics.[7] In early 1928, my father decided to get Ehrenhaft's opinion of my prospects as a physicist, so we traveled to Vienna. Ehrenhaft asked me only one question: "Do you know what *curl* is?"

Maxwell's theory of electromagnetism, which I had finished reading shortly before I graduated from the Minta, introduces curl as the connecting link between electric and magnetic fields.[8] I had also taken a course on electromagnetism with Ewald. I replied, "Yes." Ehrenhaft needed no more

---

[7]Ehrenhaft claimed he had observed particles that carried smaller charges than those of an electron. Today, fractional charges exist in theory, but they still have not been observed.

[8]The night is equally memorable because I first heard Beethoven's Ninth Symphony played that evening.

than my monosyllable. Said he, turning to my father, "When I came to Vienna, I knew what curl was. Today I am a professor. Your son should go into physics." And that was enough for my father.

I was relieved. Ehrenhaft's judgment didn't strike me as particularly well-founded, but I was tired of chemistry experiments. Even more important, I was intoxicated by the new and amazing set of ideas known as quantum mechanics. With my father's permission to "do what you like," I left Karlsruhe and chemistry for good at the end of the semester, in April 1928.

A few weeks later, I enrolled at the University of Munich to study under Arnold Sommerfeld, then reputed to be the greatest teacher of theoretical physics. What should have been a dream come true proved to be much less than that. Sommerfeld was very correct, very systematic, and very competent. I disliked him.

The story that John J. van Vleck, who also studied with Sommerfeld, told me a few years later in Leipzig may explain my feelings. Van Vleck, newly arrived from the United States, was struggling to learn German. The first time he saw Sommerfeld in the library, he greeted him with a heavily accented: "Guten Morgen, Herr Sommerfeld." Sommerfeld barely murmured his reply. The next time Van Vleck greeted him, he said, "Guten Morgen, Herr Doktor," and Sommerfeld responded a little more audibly. The next time, when van Vleck said, "Guten Morgen, Herr Professor," Sommerfeld clearly replied and nodded. Then a few days later, van Vleck opened up: "Guten Morgen, Herr Geheimrat." (Geheimrat means *secret councilor* and is far above the American title of *Honorable*). Sommerfeld finally looked van Vleck in the eye and replied with a smile: "Aber Ihr Deutsch wird jeden Tag besser (But your German is improving every day)."

I studied mathematics and physics, but I was on my way to becoming dedicated to quantum mechanics. In spite of my concerns about my abilities, I found the subject irresistible. I was not completely immersed in my studies; on my visits home during the past two years, I had been seeing more and more of Mici, Suki's little sister, now a charming and beautiful young woman. We would meet, unchaperoned, in Freedom Park under the clock, a favorite place for young people's assignations.

Mici had now completed two years in mathematics at the University of Budapest, and she and one of her friends got jobs teaching summer school at the Odenwald Schule in Germany. She invited me to visit her at the school. I promptly did so, a few weeks before the end of the second term.

There she was: Mici, teaching mathematics in a most progressive German school and proud of her independence. Her German sounded a little unusual, but she told me that her pupils understood it very well—except in the evenings, when she mixed a few Hungarian words into it. Then the girls would ask her to give up her *Abenddeutsch* (evening-German). During my visit, I took Mici walking in the forest, and appropriately (and innocently) we got lost. We arrived back at the school late at night, but no one was too upset. I was twenty years old and very happy.

Although Munich was a disappointment because of Sommerfeld, I loved the nearby Bavarian Alps. I often hiked in them with friends from the university and, while walking, even managed to learn to play chess without a board. On Saturday July 14, the weekend after I returned from visiting Mici, on the way to meet my friends for a hike, I absentmindedly rode the trolley past the stop for the railway station. With my knapsack on, full of cheer and invulnerability, I jumped off the front platform of the moving trolley, lost my balance, and fell. The three following cars of the trolley rattled by rapidly. But my Friday-the-thirteenth luck had arrived a day late.

I felt nothing, but as I turned over, I saw my boot at a distance. My first thought was: How can I go hiking if my boot is spoiled? But when the pain began, I realized what had happened. It seemed a long time before the ambulance arrived; but as I lay waiting, my right foot almost severed, I knew that I was far more fortunate than the innumerable soldiers who had lain wounded on battlefields, unattended for hours.

As a university student, I received excellent care. The man who operated on me, a Dr. von Lossow, was an exceptionally kind man as well as an excellent surgeon. Before the surgery, while I was preoccupied with pain, he patiently explained the various procedures in simple and clear terms; he then asked which operation I would prefer and accepted my decision.

One procedure, developed by a Russian surgeon, Nikolay Ivanovich Pirogov, during the Crimean War, would fuse the remaining part of my heel with the two bones of my lower leg. Although that makes for a bulkier prosthesis and one that requires great skill in construction, it has an advantage: That type of amputation allows one to bear weight on the end of the stump and to get around reasonably well without having to hop. Besides, if I did not like the result, I could always have the more radical operation later. I suspect I may be one of the few living examples of this mid-nineteenth-century surgical procedure.

My mother, father, and Emmi arrived within hours of my accident, and my mother stayed with me until I was released from the hospital. For my mother, the accident was a deeply tragic event. Perhaps it is strange, but losing my foot never seemed so terrible to me. I wished very much the accident had not happened, but the important things in my life were untouched by it. I could not even approach being grief-stricken, I could not agree with my mother's perspective, and that hurt her feelings.

My convalescence was necessarily long because the procedure had required saving as much of the damaged portion of my leg as possible. I shared a hospital room with a young boy whose father was an official in the Kuomingtang in China. My roommate told me about Chiang Kai-shek, about the revolution in 1911, about Sun Yat-sen, about the high hopes for a unified China.

I also had a pair of very welcome visitors. Magda Hesz and her American husband were visiting Europe and came to Munich especially to see me. Magda, as was her nature, was full of cheer and brought me a beautiful fountain pen as a get-well gift. They regaled me with stories of their life in America, but the most amazing thing they told me was that they owned a car.

Owning a car was unheard of! Neither my father nor my grandfather— who was more prosperous—could ever have hoped for his own automobile. Cars in Germany were an almost equal rarity. Yet Magda owned a car. That evidence of the American high standard of living was considerably clearer than any other description I had heard. I believe it was my first whiff of the changes that technical development brought.

Still another visit stands out. A student two years my senior, and thus a much more professorial person, was kind enough to come by the hospital. Hans Bethe was then studying under Sommerfeld and preparing for his Ph.D. examination. He had the finest memory and the most comprehensive knowledge of theoretical physics that I had ever encountered. I was touched and honored that he would take the time to visit me; but once in my room, Hans didn't know what to say or do. He was stiff and uncomfortable in the presence of my injury, and he made his escape as soon as he felt it polite to do so.

During my hospitalization, my mainstay was Dr. von Lossow. In talking with me before the surgery, he asked me about my other ailments. I mentioned my orthostatic albuminuria. He was impressed that I knew the term and jokingly called me Herr Professor. He quickly realized he had found my fondest dream. From then on, he always addressed me as "Herr Professor."

After taking painkillers for a few days, I decided that I disliked their effects, even though I suffered from phantom pain. Dr. von Lossow told me that people used to believe that phantom pain was the result of the missing part's having arrived prematurely in hell. He told me, "If you continue to misbehave and go to hell, that's what you will feel like all over." I decided not to take any more painkillers. When I woke up at night, I would swallow water as if I were taking a pill, and then I would stop thinking about the pain. The result was fully satisfactory.[9]

One day in August, without a word, my friend Dr. von Lossow disappeared. I learned from others that he had gone to South America. He had not even said goodbye, and I was bewildered and hurt.

Many years later, I realized what might have happened. When I arrived in Germany as an eighteen-year-old in 1926, I thought of Hitler's 1923 Beer Hall Putsch in Munich as ancient and irrelevant history. But it ws not.

General Otto von Lossow had commanded the German troops in Munich at the time of the putsch. When he was captured by Hitler's forces in the first minutes of the putsch, General von Lossow feigned sympathy and convinced the Nazis to release him. He then gathered and led the forces that captured Hitler and his followers. No single person could be held more responsible for thwarting Hitler's first takeover attempt. I believe now that my surgeon was related to General von Lossow.

While I was recuperating during the summer of 1928, the resurgence of the Nazi party was in full swing. Although the Nazis held fewer than twelve seats in the Reichstag at that time, in the next election, in 1930, they won more than a hundred and comprised a quarter of the membership. Dr. von Lossow probably understood that, with Hitler in power, he should not remain in Germany. Today I consider Dr. von Lossow's departure an example of the tragic means by which a dreadful movement comes to power. Most people don't know what is coming, and those who do dare not resist.

How does one notice that something is wrong? Germany was prosperous. At least it seemed so compared to Hungary. Anti-Semitism, to me as an outsider, didn't seem to amount to much. Even in retrospect, I think the resistance to anti-Semitism in Germany was greater than in Hungary. Anti-Semitism was

---

[9]Physical pain is a most peculiar thing. I could do without painkillers when I was awake, but for the next five years, the pain I would feel if I dreamed about my foot would be acute enough to wake me. I believe that part of the experience of pain is connected with alarm, with a sense that something is wrong and needs fixing. Once I realized in a truly deep way that the fixing not only wasn't necessary but couldn't be accomplished, the nature of the pain changed.

The human nervous system is remarkable. A few years ago when I had spinal anesthesia, I was amazed to discover that I lost all feeling below my waist—except for my nonexistent foot. My sensations told me that my foot was still there, but attached to what? Until the rest of my body regained sensation, I continued to feel the presence of my missing toes; but I no longer experienced it as pain.

largely imported by Hitler from Austria. The proportion of reasonable people in Germany was larger than that in the former Austro-Hungarian empire.

My first hint of the coming trouble came when Dr. von Lossow, a highly respected member of a big hospital and a thoroughly nice, reasonable person, suddenly took off. I could not believe that he would do so on a whim. Something obviously was wrong in Germany.

During my years in Karlsruhe, I had started to realize that the Germans had made enormous sacrifices in their attempt to win World War I. The bloody months of spring 1918 were still fresh in every German's mind. A superior German army, triumphantly returning from defeated Russia, had attempted to break through the well-built trenches in France. Millions of the best of Germany's young men bled to death that horrible spring, in bravery both useless and senseless.

In October 1918, when the German army was in full retreat, the German General Staff, knew that the war must be ended; but they did not want the defeat to reflect on German honor or that of Generals Hindenburg and Ludendorff, who were popular heroes. Instead, the defeat was blamed on "ein Dolchstoss"—a stab in the back by the "communists and Jews," who were seen as the cause of the antiwar strikes and domestic unrest. Because France allowed the German army to march home with their weapons, an acknowledgment of the German army's valor, an illusion arose: Betrayal, not defeat, had ended the war and produced the nation's woes.

Millions of young men had been sacrificed; tens of thousands of German children were physically and mentally damaged by the starvation that resulted from the Allied shipping blockade during the war (and for almost a year afterward). The punitive provisions of the Treaty of Versailles seemed unbearable. The reaction against the Jews was delayed for many years, but by the time I arrived in Germany, the reservoir of hopelessness and hate—the tinder of World War II—was already there, even though I rarely encountered it.

With Dr. von Lossow gone, I had no reason to stay in Munich. At the end of August, I returned to Budapest to complete my recuperation. Because of the nature of the surgical procedure, the wound still had not healed. The doctors in Budapest performed another surgery because they believed that my x-rays showed a bone fragment. They found no fragment, but a few days later the wound finally closed.

My Budapest recuperation was not unpleasant. My family took good care of me. The summer was over, and Mici came to visit me for three hours or so almost every day. I liked her cheerful company much more than my mother's sadness about my misfortune (which, at the age of twenty, I could not understand). I learned to get around again by using an artificial foot.[10] I was grateful for that minor miracle of technology, eventually so successful that I could even go for long hikes in the mountains.

At the end of October, I could walk again. I was eager to return to my studies, but Sommerfeld had gone abroad for a year. I decided to change universities and study with Werner Heisenberg, who had taken Bohr's initial ideas from the realm of magical hypotheses into that of coherent mathematics and science.

I went off to Leipzig and became acquainted with knowledge in a way that I had dreamed of as a child. Heisenberg was only six years older than I, an enormous difference in scientific development, but not so great a hurdle in human relations. He would never play the role of a Geheimrat. When I was studying with him, he was the last hero of the renaissance of physics. His success could not last forever. My respect and admiration for him did.

---

[10]The first, made in Budapest, was barely adequate. Three German prosthesis experts provided me with simple but sturdy, carefully adjusted devices. Today, more than half a century later, they have proved their permanence better than most of my body.

7

BRAVE NEW WORLD

1928–1929

IN MY OFFICE at Livermore, I have a small statue of a bearded Democritos. In ancient Greece, the word *bearded* signified barbaric, an un-Greek appearance; and, indeed, Democritos came from Thessaly, the primitive north. My statue comes from Athens, a gift from an atomic energy laboratory named for Democritos.

Plato's seminar stood open even to the wild man from the north, but what Democritos said was too much for Plato. Democritos, it is believed, asserted that all matter consists of indivisible atoms and that many observed changes in materials, such as water turning to ice, are caused simply by a rearrangement of atoms.[1] Plato shipped Democritos off to Hippocrates, the greatest contemporary physician. After the Greek equivalent of a psychiatric evaluation, Hippocrates and Democritos appeared arm in arm, and the analyst announced, "If this man is crazy, then so am I."[2]

Even that diagnosis could not lend acceptability to the atomic theory. At the beginning of the twentieth century, the existence of atoms was still occasionally questioned. In chemistry, the theory of atoms worked well; but in physics, the theory was in conflict with well-established laws: Atoms crash into one another at tremendous speeds, but their structure and properties remain unchanged; some parts of atoms and molecules do not obey the laws of statistical mechanics; and according to the laws of electromagnetism, the electrons, assumed to orbit the charged nucleus, should quickly fall into the

---

[1] Today, the tiny particles that Democritos was discussing are called molecules, which in turn are composed of atoms.

[2] The story comes from the partisans at Democritos Laboratory, like the statue, and may not be historically accurate.

nucleus.[3] A clash of opinions is commonplace; a clash of facts is alarming; a clash of two sciences, physics and chemistry, is a catastrophe.

There were further oddities. In 1900, Max Planck suggested a wholly unexpected proportionality between frequency and energy, $E = h\nu$. In 1905, Einstein found conclusive evidence that light (known to be a vibration of magnetic and electric fields) consisted of particles, called quanta, whose energy is $h\nu$, where ν is the frequency of the light and h is Planck's constant. My first reaction to that statement was to ask: What does the length of a ship have to do with the age of its captain?

The answer was the beginning of the new science of quanta, the work of an impressive intellectual community. The two greatest contributors were Niels Bohr and Werner Heisenberg. Bohr pronounced Planck's statement so simple that it could not possibly be explained but only applied and its consequences explored. Bohr introduced a trinity of ideas: The first was that, even though atoms consisted of smaller components, they were found in stable and unchanging states called quantum states; the second, that paradoxes are essential to the development of science; the third, that contradictory ideas, when founded in common experience and common sense, cannot be changed but must be reconciled.[4]

In a way, Bohr stood the reasoning process on its head. Instead of deriving quanta from our everyday experience, he accepted the quanta and tried (successfully) to find the laws in the quantum world that fit smoothly into the world of our experience. What Bohr suggested in 1913 was that atoms, defying all plausibility, possess a stability that prevents them from changing through collisions; and that they have a lowest stable energy state as well as higher states (excited states) with sharply defined energies. He further assumed that atoms can jump (in a manner indescribable in terms of classical physics) from one state to another, emitting or absorbing light as they do so.

---

[3]The atom was found to be composed of negatively charged electrons loosely arranged around a much smaller positively charged heavy nucleus. Because the electrons are not pulled into the nucleus, one would assume they move around it the way the planets move around the sun. According to the theory of electromagnetism, however, charged particles moving and changing velocity should radiate energy, like an alternating-current antenna. In fact, according to classical physics, one could calculate that the electrons should radiate away their energy and be captured by the nucleus in less than a millionth of a second.

[4]For this last and most essential part of his philosophy Bohr used the term *complementarity*. The idea is as old as the duality of body and soul. Its new application is illustrated by the duality of waves and particles. Both concepts are necessary to describe the entities in atomic science. The two concepts complement each other in describing reality.

The sharply defined energies give rise to the spectral lines of sharp frequencies observed in atomic spectra (such as the one I used to identify lithium when I was in Karlsruhe).

When atoms pass from a highly excited state to a slightly less excited state, the quantitative change in energy matters as little as spending pennies does to a millionaire because both states contain a great many quanta. In that specific case, the laws according to which atoms jump from state to state correspond to the laws of common physics, where the various characteristics of objects change in a continuous manner. That is the correspondence principle that Bohr established, emphasized, and used as a tool to guess the laws according to which atoms behave in their low-energy states when they are poor in quanta.

Pythagoras was familiar with vibrating strings, whose frequency of vibration (and the note produced) is the same regardless of whether the vibration is strong or weak, loud or soft.[5] Molecular spectroscopists had started to work out the vibrations of atoms within a molecule. Molecular vibrations (but not the electrons within atoms), are also examples of harmonic oscillation. The quantum problem connected with harmonic oscillators is easy compared to quantization of arbitrary motion, because an essential quantity—the frequency of vibration—remains the same in strongly or slightly excited states.

Heisenberg made his first great contribution in 1925, when he gave a quantitative formulation of the quantum laws in the case of such a harmonic oscillator.[6] Not much later, having perfected the mathematical tools of a new science, Heisenberg did what Einstein had done in another field: Together with Bohr, he clarified the philosophical content of the new theory. In those discussions, he formulated the uncertainty principle with which his name will forever be associated.

The idea that quantum jumps occur according to statistical probability and are unpredictable is in direct contradiction to a causal, machine-like

---

[5]Galileo is said to have been attracted to physics when he noticed the chandeliers in the church took the same time to reach the perpendicular regardless of whether their motion was strong or gentle.

[6]On a vacation during his student years at Göttingen, Heisenberg worked out the mathematics of a harmonic oscillator. On his return, he learned from his professor, the much more mathematically minded Max Born, that what he had invented was an offshoot of matrix algebra. Heisenberg's work became a powerful tool in describing the concepts of quantum mechanics. What he found, in fact, was the means to correlate the transition probabilities of quantum mechanics with the Fourier coefficients of classical mechanics.

description of reality. One consequence of quantum mechanics is that the future becomes truly uncertain. Determinism is a myth. Causality is replaced by a much more unusual idea. A single atomic occurrence cannot be predicted, because in the ambiguous world of waves and particles, it cannot be completely described.

The central idea is that the past is a different reality from the future. The events of the past are always compatible with causality. But the present cannot be known sufficiently for an unambiguous prediction to be made about the future. A wag once said that Heisenberg had solved God's unemployment problem: Creating the world was much easier than operating it. The new picture of the universe is that creation of the future is an ever-continuing process.

Such an idea is even more revolutionary than those associated with relativity. Einstein could never accept the idea that science, necessarily based on human perception, can be compatible with any laws of nature that do not operate strictly as cause and effect. Einstein said that he could believe that God governs the world by any set of rules, but he could not believe that God does so by playing dice.

When I arrived in Leipzig, a few weeks after classes began in the fall of 1928, I was eager to start working under Heisenberg. I believed I was on the right track at last. But I was also worried. Two years of studies in chemistry and mathematics were far from adequate preparation. My knowledge of physics had huge gaps. Would I be able to learn the missing pieces and the new ideas without appearing to be an idiot? Would my fellow students accept me socially, or would I find myself on the outside looking in?

Today, I marvel at the youthfulness of Heisenberg's group. At twenty, I was among the youngest, and only one or two people were as old as thirty. But the most consistent characteristic of that community was its determination to understand. The twenty or so of us studying under Heisenberg represented an international mix: some Germans, including Heisenberg's second-in-command Friedrich Hund, Carl Friedrich von Weizsäcker, and Rudolph Peierls; a few Americans, among them von Vleck, Robert S. Mulliken, and Boris Podolsky; two Japanese, Yoshio Fujioka and Seishi Kikuchi; an Italian, whose name was Gentile; Heisenberg's Austrian assistant, Guido Beck; a Swiss, Felix Bloch; a Russian, Lev Landau, and one Hungarian, me.

Those of us studying with Heisenberg met once a week for an evening of Ping-Pong, chess, and tea in the two common rooms of the Institute building, which held Heisenberg's apartment as well as his and Hund's offices. I suspect that some people felt sorry for me because of my accident and treated me better than might otherwise have been the case. But I also believe that my painful and slow education at the Minta served me well in my new setting.

I did my best to make myself useful. On one occasion early in the term, I volunteered to brew the tea for our gathering; and partly by default, partly because it was widely appreciated, I brewed tea (the apex of my culinary achievements) for the social evenings throughout my two-year stay. I also did well at Ping-Pong which, with the exception of swimming, was the sport least affected by the loss of my foot. During my first term, I beat Heisenberg at Ping-Pong.

The next semester, however, he went to Japan by ship and played Ping-Pong during the voyage with a young man who was an expert. After he returned, I never again could beat him. Heisenberg was a young athlete, and being as sympathetic as he was, I think he had imagined my missing foot was a greater loss than it actually was. But after his voyage, when it was obvious that I was getting around in adequate style, he thoroughly enjoyed beating me each time we played.

Heisenberg was competitive in a manner that appeared half serious, half joking. Science was the center of our universe, but it was by no means dissociated from humor. One of my most vivid memories of those years is of Heisenberg as he inquired, when someone tried to relate a new fact or theory in physics, "Wo ist der Witz?" A stodgy translation of the question would be, "What is the point?" But the question is more accurately translated, "What is the joke?" After all, the essence of a joke is the unexpected something that goes to the heart of the matter.

I quickly discovered that there was no trace of intolerance or snobbery in our university group, only openness and sharing. Nationality, religion, and political opinion had no effect on one's welcome. Hund, as well as Heisenberg, was kind to everyone. Gentile had a hard time speaking German.[7] Podolsky, whose ideas included trying to fit electrons into the atomic nucleus, was disappointed when Heisenberg explained the absurdity of the attempt. But when I arrived, I probably knew less than anyone in the group. I spent most of my time just catching up.

A great deal of what I learned about the nature of matter came through the osmosis of knowledge—the diffusion of facts that spreads among a group of friends. In Leipzig, I found something I had never seen before: people

---

[7] Whenever he did not know how to say something in German, he prefaced his remarks with *Wie man sagt*, an improper translation of *come si dice* (as they say).

more interested in science than I was. I also found something I had never possessed before: a home for my spirit.

The first people with whom I became acquainted at Leipzig were Carl Friedrich von Weizsäcker and Lev Landau. Carl Friedrich was the youngest of the group. His father, formerly an admiral in the German navy and currently a diplomat, was a friend of Heisenberg's; Carl Friedrich had known Heisenberg as a family friend long before he became his student. In fact, Heisenberg had explained the uncertainty principle to him when Carl Friedrich was fifteen. About two years later, Carl Friedrich came to Leipzig and spent the same years there that I did.[8] He was close to Heisenberg, extremely quiet, and, in many ways, by far the best of the students. Carl Friedrich enjoyed, then as now, walking in the mountains and discussing everything from philosophy to physics; he mixed the most serious questions with games or gentle jokes.

During that time, I tried out one of my ideas on him. I was attempting to work out a theory of art—what is involved in the transfer of thoughts and emotions, how human experience can be communicated through a medium. Although art takes innumerable forms, I said, only when art is divorced from everything that is practical does it reach its purest form. Music is such a case. Beauty represents an excellence of artistic communication, but beauty in music is pure convention, I went on, convention with a structure. Music must be complicated, but it must also contain hidden streaks of simplicity. Its beauty really consists of the interaction of what is complex and surprising with what is simple and satisfying.

Weizsäcker listened with faint disapproval, but he did not object. He was something of a philosopher. I suspect that he considered my approach much too logical, a fault that, more than sixty years later, I acknowledge.

Lev Landau and I were almost exactly the same age. (He was born in Russia one week after I was born in Hungary.) He had spent the previous year with Niels Bohr in Copenhagen and was already a superb physicist. He was a kind and honorable man, and a dedicated communist. Landau never missed an opportunity to point out the social failures he observed in the capitalist world. He thought that voting was foolish and a source of many problems, yet he was not a demagogue on the topic. He believed in communism in the same way that he believed in the laws of physics: If you wanted a decent social order, you supported communism.

---

[8] I was with Carl Friedrich longer than with any of my other friends from my student days. We left for Göttingen at the same time, and later we moved to Copenhagen at the same time.

In spite of the disaster that communism had brought to Hungary in 1919, I was not an anticommunist. In Central Europe at that time, the choice seemed to be between the communist and Nazi parties. Although my father was a supporter of the democratic process, until I lived in England some years later I did not believe that democracies could be stable. Landau was so much more knowledgeable a physicist than I that I accepted what he said without much question.

Among the most senior of my friends was an American, Robert Mulliken, whose beautiful wife, Mary Helen, had accompanied him to Leipzig. They visited me and my family in Budapest; many years later, I worked with him again in Chicago. Van Vleck had also transferred from Munich to Leipzig when Sommerfeld left; in Leipzig, no one was scornful of his efforts to speak German.[9]

One of the most unassuming and industrious of my friends, Yoshiyo Fujioka, was from Japan. He also visited me and my family in Hungary on a vacation from Leipzig. In 1959, Fujioka was Japan's representative at the International Atomic Energy Agency in Vienna. When, after many frustrating years, my mother and my sister Emmi were allowed to leave Hungary, it was Fujioka who greeted them in Vienna. Thirty years and a world war had not changed our friendship.

Felix Bloch joined the group about a year after I did. When Beck left, Bloch took over his job. After I had completed my Ph.D., we spent many evenings together correcting the exercises of the beginning students. We worked closely again during the first year of the Los Alamos laboratory. Lev Landau and Carl Friedrich were also in Copenhagen while I was there. Actually, there was hardly anyone studying with Heisenberg during those years whose life would not be intertwined with mine in the future.

Heisenberg was an excellent teacher. As soon as I arrived, he gave me a paper by Eugene Wigner on group theory to report on to our seminar. Although I was well grounded in group theory, I could barely understand Wigner's paper, which discussed the application of group theory to quantum mechanics. That it was written by one of my friends from Budapest helped not at all.

That report marked my first experience with Heisenberg's ability to instruct people in the peculiar art of learning while talking. Each of his questions was a

---

[9] We did chuckle a little, though. For instance, Van Vleck had correctly mastered the German pronunciation of *v* in mathematical formulas (*fow*), but he then began pronouncing the German *w* as *wow*.

lesson in itself. As I talked, I discovered that the kernel of Wigner's paper was simple: If a system—regardless of its other complexities—has symmetry, one can derive simple and exact laws applying to the system. Proving these laws is not so simple. The paper I reported on marked the beginning of Eugene's life's work.

A few weeks later, Heisenberg made me a participant in the developing world of physics. Molecules were not yet much understood, and there was even a little confusion about the simplest molecule—the hydrogen molecular ion, which consists of two hydrogen nuclei and a single electron. A Danish physicist, Carl Jensen Burrau, had calculated the lowest energy state in which these three particles could be found. An American physicist, Bright Wilson, found a different answer. Heisenberg called me in and asked me to decide who was right. As it turned out, the answer to the problem turned on function theory; in fact, I already knew the technical expression for the answer. All I needed was a little time. The American author had made a rather obvious mistake.[10]

A few days later, I happily reported that a purely mathematical assumption, which had nothing to do with reality but only with the theory of functions, was the source of the disagreement. But then Heisenberg assigned me the further task of identifying some of the higher energy states (infinite in number) of the hydrogen molecular ion in which the electron possessed more energy. After that, he promptly left for a sabbatical leave.

The assignment became my doctoral project.[11] The problem involved lots of busy work, a little diligence, and no originality. I needed only to imitate Burrau and do what he had done—again, and again, and again, and again. . . . There was no end to the work.

My task was also accompanied by lots of noise. The work would have been impossible without the help of an old calculating machine, a neat little monster that sat on a table in the downstairs common room of the Institute.

---

[10] Wilson had ignored the circumstance that as the electron was moved away from the nuclei to infinity, the function describing it need not be simple but could have (in mathematical language) an essential singularity.

[11] Only the ground state of the ion had been calculated. The higher energy states are difficult to observe and are of little practical importance, but they are similar to electronic states in molecules consisting of two similar atoms. In 1970, Henry Eyring asked me to write an introductory chapter for a book (*Physical Chemistry: An Advanced Treatise*) on calculations as applied to chemistry. In fact, Eyring wanted a repetition of my Ph.D. thesis. Harry Sahlin and I repeated my work, using the Livermore laboratory computer. The results are now much more complete and accurate, but the topic is still unexciting.

When I turned its handle after setting some figures, it creaked in a most unmusical manner and ground out the next step of an endless calculation. Each step took a few seconds, but I spent more than a year arriving at a series of reasonably accurate numerical answers. Every night, I stayed late in the common room and worked on my calculations with the help of the calculator. Heisenberg, passing through to go to his bachelor's quarters on the third floor, would sometimes stop to talk. I particularly remember one such conversation: He complained that physics had ceased to develop; there was hardly anything interesting left to do.

The year was 1929! I felt more than a little indignant. I thought to myself, "You were there when the really great events occurred. You turned physics upside down. What more do you want?" I don't recall my response, but it was considerably more polite. I remember his answer more precisely: "Except for the chance to do that, I never would have become a physicist." I was shocked. I could not imagine Heisenberg as anything but a physicist. Yet his comment told me that he would have found other pursuits rewarding.

I continue to wonder whether, during each age, a major challenge attracts the brightest. In the Renaissance, it may have been painting; in the Baroque period, music; in the eighteenth and nineteenth centuries, literature. In the early part of the twentieth century, the possibilities of science may have been the major challenge. Today, it may be the technologies that are based on that science. During the same period, while the area of challenge is producing giants, other areas of culture languish. What might Heisenberg have done in another age?

One night in the late fall of 1929, I was making the appropriate noises on my antediluvian computing machine in the wee hours of the morning. On that occasion, Heisenberg made a point of coming downstairs to talk: When did I think my project would be finished? I said that I expected I would be through within the next two years. Didn't I think I had already done enough? Why didn't I write up my results? I did so in the next month and handed in my thesis. I have always had the sneaking suspicion that Heisenberg, with his bed above my cacophonous calculator, had a hard time sleeping while a new Ph.D. was being born.

But I had to confront one more hurdle, the oral examinations. My major subject was physics, and by now I was confident that I was adequately prepared; but I had totally neglected my minors, chemistry and mathematics, since I had come to Leipzig. I did not expect difficulties in chemistry, because my examiner, Professor Le Blanc, was reputed to be harmless and benevolent; but the examiner in mathematics, Professor Paul Köbe, was said to be dangerously difficult. One story told about him was that when all the guests at a party he was attending were asked to write down the name of the person present who had the highest opinion of himself, everyone wrote "Köbe." Professor Köbe wrote the only variation: "Köbe, and rightly so."

A few weeks before the exam, I made my required visit. Köbe greeted me with, "I have never seen you in any of my lectures." I explained that mathematics was my minor. "Ah," he replied ominously, "the so-called minor." The customary examination in a minor subject did not require a demonstration of knowledge in the entire field but only in a couple of specialties. Köbe mentioned a few topics and asked me what I knew about them. Trying to be modest and not catching his point, I kept responding, "A little." Finally, Köbe exploded, "Here you come, never attending my lectures, knowing little of anything, and yet you want to pass. You probably even want a good grade."

At that point, I recognized my error and realized that I had made an especially bad impression. So I interrupted, "Yes, Herr Professor. I certainly would like to get a good grade." Köbe stopped in mid-sentence, breathed deeply a few times, and finally said, "Since the subject does not seem to make any difference to you, I shall examine you on the theory of complex functions and on non-Euclidean geometry."

Perhaps because God watches over children and fools, Köbe chose my two favorite topics. I had taken a wonderful course on complex functions with Professor Böhm at Karlsruhe. Furthermore, I had begun studying non-Euclidean geometry with Klug, and I had also had Böhm's excellent course in that subject. But at the same time, I knew the interview had gone very poorly.

At the next Ping-Pong evening, I reported my blundering to Heisenberg. He laughed so long and hard that I started to worry. Finally, wiping his eyes, he reported, "You'll have to look out for yourself. If I were to say anything to Köbe on your behalf, he would certainly fail you." Heisenberg's finding my situation so hysterically funny was clearly a challenge.

Studying math was, as always, a pleasure, but I also took out an insurance policy. I obtained notes of Köbe's lectures from as many of his students as I could locate and talked with as many candidates he had examined as I could find.

At last, judgment day arrived. I could see that Köbe remembered me from the interview as the student who knew little. He asked me first to write down the Cauchy-Riemann relations. In the theory of complex functions, this task is about as difficult as naming the world's largest ocean. Then Köbe said, "Talk about anything you like."

That was not as much a piece of hopeless resignation as it may sound. Because I had discovered through talking to his examinees that Köbe asked that question of about one in three people, I had prepared for it I began discussing the proof that, with the help of a complex function, any simply connected area in a complex plane can be mapped on the unit circle. I talked and talked with considerable enthusiasm, and Köbe listened attentively until the hour was over and the chance for another question was gone.

Finally, he asked, "Where did you get that proof?" I mentioned the author of the standard textbook, "Bieberbach." "I suppose you know," Köbe said, "that I was the first to prove this theorem?" I respectfully replied, "Jawohl, Herr Professor." I did not add, "That is why I chose to discuss it." I got an A. It was a real pleasure to make tea for the Ping-Pong group the next time and tell my tale. (But even on that evening, I could not beat Heisenberg at Ping-Pong.)

That is how in January 1930, almost as a twenty-second birthday present, I earned my doctor's degree. I must sadly confess that I never looked at that proof again, nor could I reproduce it today. Science is unforgettable—but only if you work on it out of interest and not for some other purpose, such as getting a degree.

8

Journeyman
Year in Physics

1929–1930

Just after graduation, Heisenberg offered me a postdoctoral research position as one of his assistants. Although that was unexpected and made me very happy, I was not without concerns. During the next few years, I worked among accomplished scientists who set an incredibly high standard. I worried whether my dream of becoming a professor was realistic.

At the beginning of the second semester, Heisenberg, who wanted his students to know the great scientists, encouraged us to make an excursion to Berlin to hear Einstein lecture. Einstein had set off his first revolution two and a half years before I was born; he initiated a second in the later part of the next decade. When I heard him speak, he was attempting a third. By exaggerating only slightly, one can say that having given a new description to time, and then having explained that God needed gravitation to create a closed world of three dimensions and time, Einstein next wanted to show that God had no choice but to create electricity and magnetism as well.

Sitting for the first and only time in a lecture room at the Kaiser Wilhelm Institute, I heard that the universe would be described in a general manner by assigning four quantities to each point in space and time. Einstein called the quantities four legs and explained that because the earlier theories of relativity and gravitation were overly simple, electromagnetism had been shortchanged. From that point on, his lecture passed over my head.[1]

---

[1]Twenty years later, when Einstein published his results on that topic, a reporter asked him whether his work was correct. His wise reply was: "Ask me again in another twenty years." When the twenty years had passed, the attempt at unifying all theories required more than four legs. Even today, unification remains out of reach.

After the lecture that day, I walked in the lovely spring sunshine with pleasant friends and viewed the residents of the famous Berlin Zoo, but I was without a doubt the most downhearted animal in the park. My friend from Budapest, Eugene Wigner, who was then teaching in Berlin, had been at the lecture and had come along on the outing afterwards. Noticing my state, he asked me what was wrong. I answered without embellishment: "I am so stupid." "Yes, yes," Eugene said. "Stupidity is a general human property."

Stupidity is unavoidable, but at least in that instance its pangs were not incurable. Wigner's revelation of the "general human property" was more to the point than ambitions of finding the ultimate truth. The example convinced me that more limited achievements were my best hope and could well amount to more than what is usually understood as success.

Not long after the trip to Berlin, another group of us, including Carl Friedrich, traveled to Copenhagen to see Niels Bohr. The collaboration between Heisenberg and Bohr had been central to progress in atomic physics. Bohr struggled for words to express the strange ideas that replaced the simple determinism of nineteenth-century science. Heisenberg had the eagerness to listen long enough to get to the essence of the new theory as well as the precision and flexibility to provide the formulation of the new concepts in a mathematical form. They were dissimilar equals—Bohr the oracle, Heisenberg the discoverer.

Shortly after my arrival in Copenhagen, I attended the weekly tea that Bohr held for his collaborators. Because it was my first visit to Bohr's Institute of Theoretical Physics, I was seated at Bohr's side. When Bohr turned his attention to me, I began by saying that the view of the world provided by classical physics was flawed. I went on to ask, "Wouldn't it be better to teach only the correct quantum mechanical version of physics to high school students? Not only could the required mathematics be introduced at an earlier age, but students would not have to unlearn mistakes."

As I spoke, Bohr slowly closed his eyes. I ended as rapidly as possible. A long silence ensued and seemed to engulf the room. At last, after perhaps thirty seconds, and without opening his eyes, Bohr murmured, "You might as well say that we are not sitting here drinking tea at all but only dreaming it."

Almost eighty years later, I still feel the discouragement of that moment. There was no ambiguity about the thoroughness with which Bohr had destroyed the simple ideas I had built up around atomic theory. The embarrassment of being considered a fool didn't worry me, but the feeling of being completely at sea did. To abandon old ideas was one thing, but to abandon them while retaining them and accepting a contradiction was unimaginable. I did not even dare to say, "I do not understand."

I now know where the understanding started; I hardly know when or whether it was completed. Weizsäcker was among the group on that painfully educational occasion. He helped me accept the result, but he could not provide a complete insight into Bohr's insistent claim: There is no short-cut to the new atomic world. The only path is through the old classical ideas.

The dilemma posed by quantum mechanics is that atoms elude the iron necessity of causality, but we never can catch them doing it. In the atomic realm, uncertainties must be admitted. Every experiment performed to learn about atoms must be done with instruments that themselves consist of atoms. Even the experimenter is composed of atoms. How can one ever hope to reach a concrete, certain scientific result? The answer provided by the Copenhagen school, as I understand it today, is that a boundary must be drawn between the world of the observed and the world of the observer. When crossing that boundary, the laws of physics do not, in general, permit categorical statements but only statements of probability.[2]

Even though I was still terribly uncomfortable about the new ideas of quantum mechanics, I enjoyed a little more success with a stimulating controversy between Heisenberg and Lev Landau. At the time, scientists generally believed that the movement of free electrons (whose properties are closely related to those of conduction electrons in metals) should have no magnetic effects: At each point in space, an electron should be as likely to move in one direction as in the opposite one and their action on the magnetic field would cancel.

Landau disagreed. He had extracted evidence about the role of magnetism from a general formulation in statistical mechanics: The motion of free electrons tended to diminish the strength of a magnetic field (diamagnetism). Heisenberg wouldn't believe it. He used an old ingenious argument to show that the action of electrons that tended to avoid the magnetic field would be compensated by the influence of a few electrons on the border of the region that would be reflected again and again by the barrier confining the free electrons.

I had an idea about how the contradiction might be resolved. Beginning the work was easy. Finishing the job took more time. My results, when I had them,

---

[2]Einstein, as well as many of his great contemporaries, rejected the theory; but some of us believe not only that Bohr's view describes what was found but that a similar approach will stimulate understanding in other areas. One may object that we are playing fast and loose with the concept of reality. I believe that we are taking a necessary, careful look into what reality is.

put me firmly on Lev Landau's side of the argument. In the meantime, my work had taken me to Göttingen. I took my report back to Heisenberg in Leipzig.

I was rewarded in three ways. First, as a result of my efforts, Heisenberg understood and agreed. His argument, correct in principle, was quantitatively in error. Free electrons near the border of the confined electrons, because of Heisenberg's own uncertainty principle, sense the proximity of the region they are not allowed to enter. As a result, those electrons contribute less than their full share in influencing the magnetic field. That correction was just sufficient to resolve the difference between Heisenberg and Landau.

My second reward was that Heisenberg invited me to dinner in his bachelor apartment on my first return to Leipzig. I was confused enough to mistake the dessert for cheese and smeared it on a piece of bread. Heisenberg took his revenge by not enlightening me until it was too late.

Heisenberg had an excellent grand piano in his apartment. Until I arrived in Leipzig, I had been playing compositions by Beethoven and Mozart exclusively; but Bloch had advised me to try the preludes and fugues of Bach's *Well-Tempered Clavichord*, which are beautiful and also short. Even I could come close to playing them decently. I mentioned to Heisenberg that I particularly enjoyed the Prelude in E-flat minor (No. 8). My third reward was that Heisenberg played it for me with some small but effective changes, substituting a two-handed *mezzo forte* for a one-handed *forte*. It sounded even better.

During the final month of my position of Heisenberg's assistant, I had chosen—half through conscious effort, half guided by what appeared to be a random opportunity—a different direction for my work. The excellent people around me, who knew relatively little about chemistry, had made huge strides in explaining the structure of matter: Sommerfeld and Bloch made the decisive contribution on the mobility of electrons in metals; Heisenberg explained ferromagnetism; Hund gave beautiful lectures on the details of the spectra of diatomic molecules. Developments involving polyatomic molecules were in their first phases. The field of chemistry, in principle explained by quantum mechanics, called for detailed explanation of innumerable phenomena, old and new. Pauling and Slater had produced a pretty explanation of why the double bonds common in organic chemistry are more rigid than single bonds. They had also explained why some chemical bonds, such as the two between the oxygen atom of water and the two hydrogen atoms, take on an angle differing from 180 degrees.

Explaining the details of the structures represented by the spectra of polyatomic molecules was still almost a virgin field. I had been introduced to that topic during my first encounter with quantum mechanics back in Karlsruhe.

Although this subject was much less important than those in the forefront of physics, I hoped I could make a substantial contribution to it.

In the mid-1920s, Max Born and J. Robert Oppenheimer had clarified the starting point for looking at molecules. Because nuclei are many thousands of times heavier than electrons and move much more slowly, one begins by considering the nuclei as if they were not moving. Then one investigates the behavior of the electrons under the influence of all the nuclei in various arrangements and calculates the energy of the system for each configuration. Finally, the nuclei can be allowed to move very slowly, driven by the average energies already calculated for each configuration.

That is the procedure I had used in my dissertation on the simplest of cases, the hydrogen molecular ion. Born and Oppenheimer's program is so complicated that calculating it accurately is tedious. The chemically uninteresting case of the hydrogen molecular ion represents our limit of effectively complete computation.

Figuring out the mechanics of larger atoms with several electrons, or of molecules made up of three or more atoms, is far too involved; so one makes do with approximations, the results of experiments, and their systematic interconnections. One essential step is to determine the set of relative positions among all the possible nuclear configurations that leads to the lowest energy. Then finally, the manner in which the nuclei vibrate and the molecule rotates can be examined.

In working on my seminar report back in Karlsruhe, I had found a puzzling detail in Reinhard Mecke's paper. Methyl halides consist of a carbon atom, three hydrogen atoms, and an atom of a halogen (iodine, bromine, chlorine, or fluorine). In classical theory, any speed and frequency of rotation is permitted, but according to quantum theory, only certain frequencies occur. From those frequencies, one can deduce the shape of the molecule. The shape changes if the electrons are excited because, after all, they are responsible for holding the molecule together. But according to the Born-Oppenheimer work—and to the established principles of chemistry—the vibrations influence the size by only 1 or 2 percent. Spectral observation of the frequency of rotation indicated that the size of the methyl halide molecule changed by a factor as large as two in different vibrations. Here was a paradox. This much I had learned from Bohr: Where we find a paradox, we find something of real interest.

When my friend from the Eötvós competition, Laci Tisza, had finished his studies at the University of Budapest—about the same time as I had finished mine—I arranged for him to spend several weeks in Leipzig. Laci was as curious about the problem as I, but we started our work in abysmal ignorance.

Because the vibrational forces (proportional to an original small displacement) vary for each particle and direction, the vibrations of the five atoms of a methyl halide appeared to be an impossible jumble. After a few days in hopelessly confused discussions, Laci and I made an amazing discovery, which, unfortunately (and of course), had been known to scientists for a long time: Among all the possible vibrations, there exists a set of very simple vibrations (called normal vibrations) from which all the rest of the vibrations can be composed.[3] I remember telling Hund that we were working on the problem. He was noticeably taken aback and gently inquired, "Do you know what a normal vibration of a molecule is?" By then we had been working for some days, so I was able, by that slim margin, to tell him that I did.

Quantum mechanics and classical mechanics come close to each other in the instance of the vibration of a polyatomic molecule; this aptly illustrates why my remark to Niels Bohr was particularly wrong. A student of quantum mechanics needs all his lessons in classical physics if he wants to understand what he is talking about.

Now that we had discovered normal vibrations, our fun started. In spectroscopy, one does not really see the rotation of a molecule, but only that of an unbalanced charge. Our methyl halide molecule was symmetric when rotating around its main axis (an imaginary line through the carbon and iodine atoms). The vibration produces an imbalance of charge. One sees not a simple rotation but a rotation coupled with a vibration; this brings about the unbalanced charge.

---

[3] The trick is to find a special set of displacements that will cause the molecule to vibrate in such a way that all the particles move with the same frequency in the same phase on straight lines. In that way, they reach their extreme locations and pass through their positions of equilibrium simultaneously. (They overshoot those and thus continue to vibrate.)

A beautiful mathematical theorem proves that one can construct from normal vibrations all possible low-amplitude motions of a complex vibrating system. The effect holds for molecules, airplanes, bridges, and any other thing that can vibrate and move elastically in such a way that the forces are proportional to the displacement.

I enjoy remembering that my most famous graduate student, Chen Ning (Frank) Yang, when still an undergraduate in China, produced a lengthy and detailed paper explaining normal vibrations with great clarity and offered it to me when he asked me to become his advisor. His choice of topic as well as the quality of his work made a good impression on me. That both Yang and I were interested in normal vibrations was not just happenstance. They help to build a bridge between classical and quantum mechanics and they provide a clear illustration of Bohr's correspondence principle.

What Mecke saw and reported was not the frequency of rotation but the progress of the electrical imbalance as its angle changes under the influence of rotation and vibration; once that became clear, we solved the riddle with two pages of algebra.

I have explained this simple work in such detail because I love it. It was my first discovery, the first time I posed and answered a brand new question where the answer was undisputedly correct. The reader will forgive me if my pleasure in this accomplishment is a thousand times greater than any conceivable justification.

When the problem was finished, Laci returned to Budapest. But similar examples of the problem remained. For instance, methane (CH_4) is both simpler and more complex. Because it is more symmetric, it has three symmetrical rotational axes rather than just one. Even though Laci and I were separated, we decided to continue our collaboration on various ramifications of the problem.

Laci, like many of us, was interested in politics. With the Nazi revolution approaching, many of our discussions turned on the controversy between communism and fascism. I was confused and undecided; but Laci was on the communist side, although not a party member. Hungary, under the Horthy régime, had banned the Communist Party. Not long after he went back to Budapest from Leipzig, Laci was caught carrying a message for some communists. He was arrested, beaten, and jailed.

Thereafter, when I went to Budapest, we continued our work in his prison cell. I was deeply distressed by Laci's imprisonment. If, as my father believed, the basis of all good government was *audiatur et altera pars* (letting the other side also be heard), Hungary was badly governed. Laci, unfairly, was paying the price; serving even a short prison term in Hungary meant that his career was ruined. At the time, I could think of nothing I could do to help him.

One aspect of my summer visit to Hungary was much more pleasant. Mici's strict stepfather had given her permission to accompany her friend Klári Rappai to Mátrafüred, a small resort about a hundred miles northeast of Budapest, for a week's vacation. She invited me to join them. Under the guise of taking a solitary hiking trip in the Tátras (which I did for a few days following), I spent the same week at the resort.

By that time, I had no doubt whatsoever that Mici and I would spend our lives together. But I still had said nothing formally to Mici or to my family. I was far from being able to support a wife—I still could not support myself. My postdoctoral salary was only sixty marks a month, equivalent to about two hundred dollars today. Although I lived frugally in a modest lodging, my family still had to provide about half my support.[4] Nonetheless, to my mind and in the eyes of all of our friends, Mici and I were a well-established couple.

After that wonderful interlude with Mici, I returned to Leipzig and resumed my diligent ways; I studied, I worked on my molecules, and I corrected the papers of Heisenberg's students. One night a week, Felix Bloch and I pored over the students' elaborations of Heisenberg's lectures; we found the papers included a multitude of mistakes.

In retrospect, I suspect that those nights spent correcting papers contributed to my expertise fully as much as anything I did during my self-directed days. Bohr defined an expert as someone who, through personal and painful experience, has found all the possible mistakes that can be committed within a very narrow field. The students' errors were painless instruction, but they were not completely painless because each mistake had to be understood and explained.

That autumn, after a little more than two years in Leipzig, I received an offer from a physical chemist, Arnold Thomas Eucken, to serve as his assistant at Göttingen, the historic center of German mathematics and physical science.[5] I would not give lectures, but I would have my own doctoral students and I would be free to conduct research. The bonus was that I would receive a salary equivalent to that of an assistant professor; this meant that for the first time, I would be an independent practicing scientist. I was sad to leave Leipzig, but it seemed the right thing to do. My friend Carl Friedrich had decided independently to go to Göttingen, so my break with friends, my work, and familiar surroundings would be less complete. But my days as a student were truly at an end.

---

[4]In the late spring, my initial slight successes had sufficed to prompt Leonard Jones, a spectroscopist in Britain, to offer me a modest position, but it would have taken me out of the real center of developing physics. Not foreseeing the catastrophe of Nazism, I declined.

[5]Home of the mathematician Gauss (who was as incomparable as Archimedes himself), Göttingen was also Heisenberg's alma mater.

9

THE PLEASURES
OF SMALL SUCCESSES

————

1930–1933

PROFESSOR ARNOLD EUCKEN, the agent of my arrival at Göttingen, was deeply interested in low-temperature physical chemistry, the natural bridge between chemistry and the science of atoms.[1] Eucken had studied under Walter Nernst, the dominant figure in physical chemistry at that time.[2] Nernst had become a sort of father figure to Eucken: the epitome of all Eucken hoped to become and a rival whom Eucken wouldn't mind contradicting.

I never met Nernst, but his personality can be surmised from a story that circulated about his origin:

> God decided to make an exceptional man. He first created an intellect, and that carried the mark of God's own hand. But unfortunately, God was called to the telephone, and Nernst remained unfinished. The archangel Gabriel came by and thought he would provide a body for the brain. He did a creditable job, but Gabriel felt his work was not quite what the plan called for, so he, in turn, left. Then the last participant saw his chance and finished off the creation: The Devil gave Nernst his character.

---

[1] At absolute zero, materials are in their lowest quantum state. In the 1930s, the words *near absolute zero* meant temperatures where the energy available to atoms was perhaps one-hundredth that of room temperature. Today, such studies are conducted at temperatures one-millionth that of room temperature.

[2] Nernst's theorem (which is also called the third law of thermodynamics) states that at absolute zero, order is perfect. Nernst was also an almost successful competitor of Thomas Edison, having invented a high-intensity electric glow lamp.

To compete with Nernst, Eucken had to understand the theory of atoms. I was to be the latest instrument of that long-sustained adventure. My usefulness would depend on my ability to steer him away from errors when he interpreted his findings in the new terms of quantum mechanics.

That role was full of challenge. Years later in London, I saw a fellow Hungarian, Nicholas Kürti, who had been a year behind me at the Minta. He knew of Eucken's reputation and was astounded to learn that I had lasted in my position for three years. His theory about what must have happened went this way: The man who had held the job two years before me did not have his contract renewed because he contradicted Eucken. My immediate predecessor was let go because when Eucken was wrong, he said, "You are right, but . . ." I managed the final improvement: When Eucken was wrong, I replied, "You are right, because . . ." and then added all the information that was necessary.

Eucken was the only professor I recall who had dueling scars on his face. But his physical appearance and his ambivalent idolization of Nernst belied his disposition: He was a kindly man who took great interest in the professional lives of his collaborators, assistants, and students. At least once a week, Eucken made a lengthy round in his laboratory to discuss each person's work, all his assistants, including me, bringing up the rear. And each week he would discuss that work in greater detail with any of us interested enough to accompany him on his walk on Walkemühlenweg or Stegemühlenweg in the outskirts of Göttingen.

I was most anxious to succeed, both in doing science and in my job as an assistant. I often joined the company, which was particularly easy because I lived in a pension on Stegemühlenweg. Not only did I work on parts of the book Eucken was writing but I was also involved in the work of his students. Working with him taught me a great deal about physical chemistry.

Shortly after I arrived, I was surprised to receive a phone call from James Franck. All I knew about him at the time was that, together with his collaborator Gustav Hertz, he had won the Nobel Prize for finding the first experimental support of Bohr's idea that the excited states of atoms possessed considerable stability.[3] Franck invited me to go for a ride, so that, he said, he could show off his car and acquaint me with the environs of Göttingen.

In 1930, Franck was an exception among the professors of Germany in that he owned an automobile, but the conversation that day was far more interesting

---

[3]Franck was one of the very few who tried to believe Bohr when he said that the state of an atom is stable not only when the atom has the lowest energy but also when the atom is in excited states of higher energy.

than the car or the sightseeing. I particularly remember his remarks about his work on Bohr's theory. "Bohr's ideas did seem absurd," he said, "but Bohr was such a nice fellow that I felt he should at least be given a try."[4]

Franck, as it became clear during the ride, now had quite different interests: He wanted to understand the spectra of polyatomic molecules—which coincided perfectly with my fantasies. Not much later, he took me over to meet the members of his spectroscopy group, and, in the end, he negotiated an appointment for me in which I was equally responsible to him and to Eucken.

Both men were interested in the application of quantum mechanics to the borderline of chemistry and physics, but both demanded an explanation in accordance with the terms of classical physics. Bohr at his tea party had rigidly rejected any other approach, but classical ideas obviously had limited validity. The road to understanding was full of signs saying, "Watch out—dangerous curve ahead."

From our very first meeting, Franck exerted a profound influence on me. Our friendship lasted until his death. Before I met him, I was fully aware that questions of physics raised in nonmathematical form could make a lot of sense. But most theorists did not admit that the answers to those questions could be really far-reaching without mathematics. Franck's position was: "Here is the answer. You serve up the integral salad." I spent many happy hours in Göttingen providing the salad of pertinent mathematics for Franck's experimental entrees.

Franck was gregarious, unpretentious, and good-humored. The group he had gathered shared many of the same characteristics. The outstanding theoretical physicist in Göttingen at that time was Max Born. He was too formal a man for me and, I suspect, much too formal (and mathematically oriented) for Franck and his crew. Because my interests were different from those of Eucken, and I did not fit in well with Born, Franck's adopting me to help part-time in his spectroscopy work was a great boon. I became his consultant and the theorist for his group; he became my mentor.

---

[4]In their experiment, Franck and Hertz bombarded a series of atoms with electrons of various energies. Only when the amount of energy that the electrons carried reached a particular resonant level did the atoms begin absorbing energy. If the electron carried a little more energy, the emission was the same resonant amount, and the electron carried away the excess energy. The atom was unwilling to accept either more or less energy. That was explicit proof that the excited state of an atom as well as the ground state has fixed amounts of energy that it will accept and emit. The remarkable point is that the Franck-Hertz work, the first proof of Bohr's ideas, was not performed until 1919, a full five years after Bohr had published his theory. Bohr received the Nobel Prize for his work in 1922. Franck and Hertz jointly received the Nobel Prize for their work in 1925.

About once a week, Franck's assistant, Herta Sponer (whom he married many years later after his wife died), would arrive with a question. Herta, an exceedingly orderly German, would also stand guard over me and make sure that when I delivered a paper to Franck, the pages were numbered. Although I have made few other concessions toward becoming orderly, I still number my pages.

Everyone I met during my years at Göttingen was intensely dedicated to his or her studies, but most of us were not exclusively serious. Herta wrote an alphabet ditty for one of our parties in which various physicists were described. She flattered me so much that I still can quote the rhyme for T. A very bad (but therefore perhaps appropriate) translation of it might be:

> *Theory's light is less than stellar,*
> *Give us, O Lord, our daily Teller.*[5]

In Leipzig, my being accepted by the group of scientists and students working with Heisenberg had amazed me and given me intense pleasure. But I had made a very conscious effort to be pleasant and to fit in Leipzig. In Göttingen, a circle of new friends developed even before I had time to wonder how I would find new friends.

A group of us met at my pension every day to eat lunch. The regulars included Carl Friedrich and me, Lothar Nordheim (who also lived in the pension), Traute Pöschl (who later became Lothar's wife), Walter Heitler, occasionally Gerhard Herzberg, and a variety of physicists from outside Germany. For Born's birthday, we wrote and put on a review of poems and songs, some flattering, some not. I got into a little trouble during that exercise; because not being Hungarian, my friends failed to appreciate my sloppy rhymes. I did manage to contribute the verses we sang to the tune of Kurt Weill's song "Mac the Knife" from Bertolt Brecht's *The Threepenny Opera*:

> *All the books that Maxie's written*
> *Contain equations thick and dense,*
> *For the books with no equations*
> *Never make a lot of sense.*
> *For the vector and the matrix,*
> *Special symbols have to stand*
> *Of each shape and each variety*

---

[5] *Von Theorie wird man nicht heller.*
Gott geb' täglich unsern Teller.

And alphabets of every land.
And the tensor has a subscript,
And the subscript has a prime.
You're confused when first you read it
And go mad the second time.[6]

At one of our noontime gatherings, I proposed that we modify the game of Twenty Questions by keeping the subject to be guessed unchosen. Everyone, except the guesser, of course, was aware of that fact. We tried to keep our answers more or less consistent so that the guesser, at least temporarily, would believe that we really had a particular subject in mind. But, naturally, some of us took a perverse pleasure in giving seemingly contradictory answers.

On the first occasion we played, the questions and answers went like this: Is it an object? Yes. Is it a solid? No. A liquid? No. A gas? No. The victim started to protest. I suggested taking another approach. It soon developed that the answer was a commonplace, familiar object, found primarily in bathrooms.

At that point, I felt I had to make a little speech: "Now it really should be obvious to you. There can't be many objects that are neither solid, liquid, or gas that are found primarily in bathrooms." With my convincing delivery, I managed to persuade the guesser of the existence of that object, and he soon came up with an answer: a soap bubble.

For me, the game's attraction resided in its similarity to the physical theories of the times, which held that everything could be modified except for the demand for consistency. Sometimes I have a horrid suspicion that God plays a similar game with scientists.

We amused ourselves with the game for some weeks before we played it on a newcomer who was a philosopher. The game, of course, was steered by the interests of the victim, and the object in this case turned out to be a relationship. Then there was a seemingly endless succession of questions about who and what

---

[6]*Und der Maxl der schreibt Bücher*
Und es stehen Formeln drinn.
Denn die Bücher ohne formeln
Machen meistens keinen Sinn.
Für den Vectors und die Matrix
Stäts ein and'res Zeichen steht.
Jeder Form und jeder Grösse
Und aus jedem Alphabet.
Und der Tensor hat 'nen Index,
Und der Index hat 'nen Strich,
Und man liesst's und liesst es wieder
Doch kapieren tut man's nich'.

could have that relationship. The philosopher began by asking, "Do you have it to a newborn baby?" "Yes," someone replied, "if you are its father." Someone else asserted that an object could not have this relationship to a person, but a Japanese student volunteered that he had this relationship to the Eiffel Tower. Finally, the philosopher asked us, pair by pair, if we had the relationship to one another. Most of the responses were "yes," with a "no" here and there.

Because we were playing during the lunch hour, the philosopher finally had to quit, but he would continue later, he said. The rest of us stayed behind a few minutes, unsuccessfully trying to come up with some answer. We decided that the next noon we would simply have to confess our teasing, apologize, and hope he would not be offended.

That evening, the philosopher came to my room. "I want to talk to you about the game this noon," he said. I cleared my throat slowly and in embarrassment over having to explain what now seemed like rude behavior. But before I could begin, he went on. "I have at last thought of the answer. The relationship is that of 'being interested in.'" He was right. Our answers, though not by conscious design, did fit that pattern. I congratulated him on his ingenuity in guessing the correct answer. Never again did we dare to play that game.

When I went home for the spring break, as usual, my hair was too long, and I had to go to the barber shop. This time, I had my head shaved. On a few earlier occasions, I had had my head shaved, a process that spared me having to waste time in the barber shop for a while. Each time I did this, my family denounced my baldness as pure and simple craziness, and Mici complained that I looked horrible. On this occasion, which was the last time I was bald, I gained an unexpected advantage. When I returned to Göttingen, several of my casual acquaintances did not recognize me. I had the opportunity in several instances to find out what people thought of me. That was most interesting but sometimes painful.

My years as a young scientist in Germany were the most satisfying years of my life. Central Europe during the period between the World Wars appeared to be in a state of universal decline; yet I was part of a great enterprise, a very small part, but connected with it nonetheless. The work on polyatomic molecules that I had begun in Leipzig intensified with Franck, who took as his starting point the Franck-Condon principle.[7] As I knew from Hund's lectures,

---

[7] The Franck-Condon principle describes the behavior of the atomic nuclei while the electrons make a transition to another state. According to Heisenberg, one can't know both the position and the momentum of any particle at the same time with complete accuracy, but to the extent that it can be known, the Franck-Condon principle describes the behavior of nuclei during transitions: As the electrons in a molecule absorb light, the nuclei don't change their state: neither their position nor their momentum.

Condon had completely described the principle mathematically for diatomic molecules. But the application of the principle to polyatomic molecules was novel and promised to be most interesting.

At the same time I worked with Franck on his spectra, I collaborated with Gerhard Herzberg on applying the Franck-Condon principle to polyatomic molecules; this work was one of the projects that I most enjoyed during this time. One can appreciate a simple point: When a diatomic molecule vibrates, it doesn't change its symmetry. A polyatomic molecule does. My friend from Budapest, Laci Tisza, and I had already worked on molecules whose triangular symmetry had an effect on the interaction of the vibrations and rotations. Herzberg and I considered molecules with an emphasis on their symmetrical properties and found ways to obtain information about the molecule in its various electronic states.[8] There are plenty of applications for those ideas, and much of Herzberg's later work used our early, simple results.

When I returned to Budapest for the summer at the end of my first year, I received quite a shock: Mici announced that she was going to study overseas for a few years and that she was leaving in the early fall. But far worse than that, she broke off our relationship. The summer before, I had truly believed that Mici was as fond of me as I was of her. But now, it seemed, our romance was over. I had no idea why. I was depressed and hurt.

Fortunately, science seemed not so completely incomprehensible as love or war, and there at least I was enjoying some success. Returning to the university that fall, I set about my research with renewed diligence. I had met another young physicist, George Placzek. Czechoslovakian by birth, Placzek had moved to Vienna before coming to Göttingen. He was only a few years older than I, but he had a much greater knowledge of physics. He reminded me of my friend Landau in two other ways: He was also a communist, and he was wickedly sarcastic about the stupidities of the social system in Central Europe.

When I told Carl Friedrich that I found the two men similar, he disagreed. Landau, he pointed out, was much nicer to children. My youthful assessment of Placzek's abilities in physics was also flawed: Landau was incomparably more original. Most of all, George Placzek reminded me of my cousin

---

[8]Polyatomic molecules that are symmetrical, for example, where the atoms form a tetrahedron have peculiarities; these are visible in their spectra. If the electrons move in a similarly symmetrical manner, radiation cannot be emitted or absorbed, because such transitions are associated with the molecule's having an electric dipole that points in a specific direction; great symmetry may interfere with the singling out of one specific direction. In such cases, a vibration that changes the symmetry can break the deadlock. The result is that some symmetrical molecules can radiate only to the extent that they change their state of vibration.

George, who, bitter and unpleasant as he was, had a fine mind.

Placzek showed me a nice paper by Jean Cabannes and Yves Rocard that explained the Raman effect (a peculiarity associated with the scattering of light) in the simple terms of classical physics. Cabannes and Rocard's paper explaining the role of vibration in the Raman effect simplified many rules about it, particularly those involving quantum changes in symmetrical molecules.[9] Placzek proposed that we should do for the rotation of molecules what Cabannes and Rocard had done for vibration. Our joint effort turned into a long, complicated paper.[10]

I began my collaboration with Placzek with enthusiasm, but, as it turned out, our joint effort was one of the few times I did not enjoy a friendship with a collaborator. Placzek treated me to a large dose of derision, most of it trivial; for instance, he called me "Herr Molekular-Inspektor." The inference was that such a pursuit was a lower-class activity. As far as I was concerned, what happened in physics between 1920 and 1933 was so magnificent that it was a privilege to work even on minor details, and I thought it perfectly grand to be recognized even in an unglamorous field. I had made that decision in all consciousness, and I was content to remain Herr Molekular-Inspektor. Placzek's other colleagues did not appear to share my discomfort, but he treated them differently.

We wanted to finish the work, but Placzek was going to spend the spring vacation of 1932 in Rome with Enrico Fermi. Accumulating extra money as an assistant professor then was certainly no easier than it is today. I had enough money to get to Rome, but I didn't know how to finance living there for several weeks.

Placzek reminded me that a Hungarian college in Rome—the Collegium Hungaricum—was run by the government of Hungary and provided free room and board for Hungarian scholars. But as a Jew, Hungarian or not, I

---

[9] The Raman effect occurs when a molecule absorbs and promptly re-emits a light quantum. Usually, in scattering, the light quantum is re-emitted without a change in its frequency. However, if the electrical properties of a molecule change in an appropriate way during vibration, the vibrational frequency will be added to or subtracted from the original frequency. Then the final scattered light shows up with a different frequency, a situation called the Raman effect.

[10] Our work on the role of rotation in the Raman effect can be visualized by considering the nitrogen molecule, which is composed of two atoms. The change in the frequency of the light quantum emitted is not found by adding the rotational frequency to the original frequency but by adding two times the rotational frequency. That is true because the nitrogen molecule, in interacting with the electromagnetic vibration, will return to its original properties after one-half a rotation. If the molecule rotates 10 trillion times per second, it has the same interaction with scattered light 20 trillion times. Analogous statements hold for all rotations.

was not in a good position to ask for that help. Still, the relations between Hungary and Italy were very good at that time (both had fascist governments); there was always a possibility that if a famous Italian were to write asking that I be given accommodations there, it might help.

Placzek, with a really generous gesture, talked with Fermi, whom I had never met, and in the holidays between semesters, I heard from Fermi. He had written an official letter to the Hungarian government. It called me a great physicist (which I certainly was not), asked for the privilege of collaborating with me (which could hardly have been a privilege for him considering my ignorance of his area of study), and expressed the hope that some means could be found through the Hungarian government to make my stay possible. A handwritten note accompanied a copy of the official letter.

> Dear Teller,
>   Please excuse the formal tone of my enclosed letter. You would be very welcome with us.
>
> Enrico Fermi

I do not believe that as a total stranger I have ever been more warmly welcomed.

So for three weeks in the late spring of 1932, I enjoyed free room and board in the Collegium Hungaricum on the Tiber River, in an old palace, the Palazzo Falconieri. My small and somewhat bare room in the attic was furnished with a table, a water pitcher, a single chair, a bed, and a small window looking out on the Tiber. My room was also supplied with a peculiar alarm clock. As was usual, I worked late into the night and slept late in the morning. On more than one occasion, a cannon, which was located directly across on the river from my room and was fired daily at noon, awakened me most effectively.

Fermi turned out to be just as wonderful a person as his letter had suggested; during my stay, I became very fond of him and his wife, Laura. Fermi also enjoyed playing Ping-Pong, although he took the game much less seriously than Heisenberg. Nonetheless, he was enthusiastic about the game, and we often played. Fermi won only once. At that game's end, when he began to crow, I raised my left arm, paddle in hand, thus pointing out that I had played left-handed.

During my stay in Rome, Fermi and his group of young physicists were just starting to bombard every element in the periodic table with neutrons, which had been discovered a year earlier by James Chadwick. Fermi and his group observed as neutrons were attached to the atomic nuclei of various elements and examined the new kinds of nuclei that were created. They observed the resulting beta radioactivity (in which an electron is emitted by the nucleus and the nucleus itself is changed). The work was uncovering new information almost every day.

After my visit, Fermi arrived in that systematic study at the heaviest element, uranium. When he bombarded that nucleus with neutrons, he observed scores of radioactive substances instead of one or two. Naturally enough, since in all previous cases heavier elements had been produced, Fermi suspected that these new substances were heavier than uranium, that he had opened the door to the transuranic elements.

The story of Fermi's discovery is peculiar and in many ways ironic. Soon after Fermi published his findings, he received a letter from a German chemist, Ida Tache Noddack. Together with her late husband Walter, she had discovered two new elements they called masurium and rhenium (only rhenium really exists). Dr. Noddack suggested to Fermi that the effect he had observed from bombarding the uranium nucleus was a split of the uranium nucleus into two portions.

Fermi refused to accept that idea. For fission to occur, a certain amount of energy must be added to the nucleus. Only after the nucleus has become quite deformed does repulsion (based on like electrical charges) take over as a predominant force. The probability of that happening could be calculated according to quantum mechanics, but the probability depends on how much energy is needed.

Basing his calculations on some erroneous data that were accepted at that time, Fermi concluded that the probability of breaking the nucleus apart was astronomically low. He discarded Dr. Noddack's suggestion. He had the right theory but the wrong experimental information. Had he guessed the right result, the hunt for chain reactions would have started sooner. Who knows what the outcome might have been had that been the case?

But when I heard the cannon on the far side of the Tiber, all that was still in the future. Fermi had merely taken hold of Pandora's box and begun peering into it with his ingenious eyes. I enjoyed my stay in Rome and was delighted to finish my paper with Placzek. I returned happily to Göttingen to look at more molecules and to compare quantum mechanics with classical comprehensible pictures. But I did not look for a girlfriend; I had already had one, and she had gone off to America.

10

THE FUTURE
BECOMES OBVIOUS

1933

Russian and Japanese physicists regularly joined our luncheon table at the Stegemühlenweg pension, but we rarely talked about politics; we were much too interested in our own narrow topic, the structure of matter, to discuss the structure of the international community. Yet some of the most disastrous political developments of the century took shape during the years we met for lunch—from 1930 to 1933.

I remember one Russian for a charming error he made. Waxing enthusiastic about our pension, he praised its *flüssiges wasser* (liquid water). He meant *fliessendes wasser* (running water). At that time, I had heard much about a communist paradise and a little about its problems.[1] That physicist provided me with a startling picture of Stalin's régime: when Leon Trotsky, one of the founders of the Russian Revolution, was mentioned at the table one day, the Russian was obviously disturbed and maintained a silence that was more expressive than a fifty-minute lecture.[2] A situation where a political difference

---

[1]However, the following story made the rounds: Two friends disagreed about the glories of the Soviet Union. They decided that the true believer should go to Russia, find out what was happening, and report by letter. To avoid the possibility of censorship, they decided that if the letter was written in black ink, what it said was true; if it was written in red ink, the opposite would be the case. The enthusiast left and was not heard from for several years. Finally, a letter written in black ink arrived: "Everything in the Soviet Union is wonderful. Goods are available in great abundance. There is, however, one peculiar though insignificant exception. Although I have looked diligently for years, I have not been able to find any red ink."

[2]In 1928, the conflict between Trotsky and Stalin had resulted in Trotsky's expulsion from the Soviet Union. That persecution of a political rival was the first suggestion that the communist movement under Stalin was undergoing a Robespierrean change into a reign of terror. By

had to be passed over in silence and fear was more serious than a shortage of indoor plumbing.

In 1931, I was ignorant of most of the facts about political affairs. Certainly I was unaware that World War II was beginning on the other side of the world with the Japanese takeover of Manchuria. But when the invasion occurred, I remembered my nice Chinese roommate in the hospital in Munich whose father had been part of Chiang Kai-shek's government.

So I asked my new Japanese friend, Horiuchi (whose first name I believe was Seishi), about the conflict, and he explained co-prosperity to us. Japan, Horiuchi said, needed a sphere of order and influence, just as the nations of western Europe needed their governments and those of their neighbors to be stable. The Japanese were merely providing order among the "practically barbaric" Chinese. I was confused over the conflicting claims of the warlords, the central government, and Japan. Horiuchi's explanation left me unconvinced, but he was a good scientist as well as a nice person, so I did not pursue the question further.[3]

Those are the only two discussions that I remember before 1933 that concerned international affairs. Today, it seems incredible that we never even mentioned the terrible cloud that was hovering over our heads. All of us could see that things were not right in Germany: Our haven of physics was surrounded by what I see in retrospect as a sea of frustration and despair.

Because of the war reparations payments, Germany had had a postwar inflation rate that was even worse than Hungary's (where it was more than a thousandfold). I still remember a German advertisement, which I heard about in the early 1920s, for a *nullensicherer Buchführer*, an accountant who

---

the time Trotsky was murdered in Mexico in 1940, the pattern was visible to all who chose to recognize it; not until 1989 was it possible for Russians to say aloud that Stalin's murderous brutality was almost as great as Hitler's.

[3] Horiuchi was older than most of us, a bit more formal and dignified. On one of our modest excursions, he appeared with his umbrella, which was quite unnecessary for the weather. We had some reasonably harmless punch at our destination, and although Horiuchi liked it very much, he did not seem accustomed to it. On the way back, his stride was somewhat unsteady, so he opened his umbrella and used it as a primitive parachute for the purpose of balance. It was an incredibly funny performance.

Almost forty years later, having been on opposite sides in a war of terrible violence, I visited Horiuchi in Japan. Our friendship was unchanged, and we had a good conversation about our common interests in science and our disturbing experiences during the years of the student revolt around 1970. Horiuchi had been held captive by Japanese students, who demanded an outlandish confession, but he could not confess to any sin greater than having been dean of a university.

could keep track of his zeros. Thirteen or more zeros appeared in the price of most items, so the possibility of error was appreciable. Yet when I arrived in Germany in 1926, even in the wake of that terrible inflation, the nation appeared more prosperous than Hungary.

The German people felt not prosperous but defeated and hopeless. I vividly remember a remark made by a German student in Leipzig. He said that the Industrial Revolution was over; no more technical improvements could be expected. Since the Treaty of Versailles had taken away Germany's colonies, people's only chance for improvement was the redistribution of wealth (an idea that the communists helped to popularize).[4]

Like most of my friends, I knew how badly Germany had suffered during World War I, and I believed that the treaties at the end of that war were unjust. But Erich Kästner, my favorite contemporary German poet, wrote: "Wenn wir den Krieg gewonnen hätten, dann wär' die Welt ein Irrenhaus." (Had we been victors in the war, the world would be a loony bin.) Safe in the ivory tower of academia and saturated with the delight of having understood atoms, none of us realized how great and imminent our current danger was. We managed, with some determination, to ignore the contradictions in German politics, the turmoil of world finances, the festering aftermath of World War I, and the prophets of racial superiority.

I think, too, that many of us were misled about the state of affairs in Germany, because the community we were a part of was close to an ideal in social relations. Not age, nationality, or religion were obstacles to warm relationships. The physics professors had good friendships, both professional and personal, with each other and with their students. I was blinded by that happy situation.

I also did not foresee the terrible type of anti-Semitism that developed in Germany. Even today, I do not think that anti-Semitism was a major factor in bringing Hitler to power.[5] I believe that Hitler's attractiveness was based

---

[4]Today, early in the twenty-first century, we can see how enormously wrong that pessimistic prediction was. Preoccupied with social justice, the student, like many Germans, remained completely unsuspecting of the enormous developments in productivity that lay immediately ahead. Commonly held misconceptions such as that were a powerful factor in creating a hopelessness that led to Nazism. Those beliefs in turn brought on the horrors of World War II and delayed the fruition of the positive aspects of technology in Europe.

[5]I remember a contemporary German joke. A Nazi and a Jew are traveling on a train. The Nazi puts down his newspaper and declares, "The Jews are at fault." The Jew replies, "Yes, yes. The Jews and the cyclists (Radfahrer)." The Nazi asks: "Why the cyclists?" The Jew: "Why the Jews?"

on a simple need: The German people were famished for hope. Hitler was saturated with certainty: His answers were indubitably correct. He also had many distinguished supporters, among them General Erich Ludendorff.[6] The failure of the Nazi's 1923 takeover attempt in Munich led to Hitler's spending nine months in prison, and in the years following, the Nazi party had few successes.

In 1925, General Paul Hindenburg, the other World War I hero, was called out of retirement, this time to save his nation from its economic woes and political instability. He was elected president of the Weimar Republic, but he was not a universally popular choice. He had already been accused of senility when he came out of retirement in 1914 to lead the German forces.[7] But inflation slowed and a slight recovery brought new jobs, prosperity, and hopes for the future during his first term of office. He might have managed to keep the republic functioning except for the economic problems that followed the collapse of the New York stock market (an event I noticed long after it occurred).

In 1929 in Leipzig, I had rented two small rooms in the home of a widow, who also prepared my evening meals. I was her only roomer. She seemed a decent sort of person, and the piano and good books in my rooms suggested that she was proud of her cultural background. The terrible inflation of the 1920s had robbed her of her savings. Even taking in a roomer gave her little economic security. She was an example of the part of the German middle class that, ten years later, was still suffering financially.

The depression that followed the stock market crash reached Germany about the middle of 1930. As unemployment spread, more and more members of the German bourgeoisie faced the prospect of joining the ranks of the

---

[6]Ludendorff, one of the two great German heroes of World War I, was a particularly early Nazi supporter and had marched side by side with Hitler in the Putsch attempt of 1923. When the first shots were fired, Hitler dropped to the ground while Ludendorff marched on. That, I remember, led to claims that Hitler was a coward. But Hitler's response was perfectly natural for a World War I corporal who had served in the most dangerous role of courier (and who had been repeatedly decorated for bravery). Ludendorff knew that he would never be shot by German troops because they idolized him.

[7]The people whom I talked with during those times were all academics and almost all liberals. Today, I have no idea whether they were correct in calling Hindenburg senile. It is an easy aspersion to cast.

despised proletariat. With no changes in sight, Hitler's promises to remove the shame and correct economic woes had a powerful effect.[8]

In 1930, the resurgence of the Nazi party was under way. In the elections that year, the Nazis captured about a fifth of the Reichstag seats. Two years later, while I was visiting Fermi in Rome, von Hindenburg narrowly defeated Hitler for the presidency. We heaved a sigh of relief. But in the same election, the Nazi party more than doubled the seats they held. Yet we still did not believe our danger was rapidly increasing. We did not want to.

On the evening of January 30, 1933, I attended a party at James Franck's house. When I arrived, Professor Franck asked me, "Do you know who your new chancellor is?" I did not. It was Adolph Hitler. Hindenburg, in the hope of providing a workable coalition by gaining the support of the Nazis, had made Hitler chancellor.[9]

As chancellor, Hitler set the new elections in a completely normal manner. But within a week, I caught a glimpse of the future. Throughout the city, people pasted their advertisements onto innumerable bulletin board posts (*Litfassäulen*). Under Hitler's chancellorship, all the posts were stripped bare: Everything was scratched off them. From then on, nothing could be advertised without government permission. From my worm's eye view, that was the first sign of what was to come.

The election campaign lasted for the month of February. Almost at its end came the thunderclap: The Reichstag burned down. On the evening after that fire, I had dinner with Walter Heitler at his apartment. Wolfgang Pauli, who had just returned from a visit to the Soviet Union, was the other

---

[8]Because of the financial wizardry of Hjalmar Schacht, the first years under Hitler did turn out to be a great economic success. A story has it that Schacht even tried to convince Hitler that the Jews could be useful by taking Hitler on a shopping expedition. In the first store, Schacht asked for a dozen left-handed coffee cups. He said that the führer was going to give an afternoon party for veterans of the war who had lost their right arms. The shopkeeper said that not only had he no left-handed cups but he had never heard of that variety. Further inquiries turned out to be no more successful until they came to a Jewish shop. There, the owner answered with a bright smile, "This is a most lucky coincidence. I am almost out of them, and as you know, import of them has been banned. I have just a dozen left, but I can let the Führer have them for only twice the regular price." As they left the store, Schacht said, "Mein Führer, do you see why we need the Jews?" Hitler replied, "Ach was? (What of it?) They were his last ones."

[9]Hitler's ascension to power had the immediate effect of making the German communists, who had become the third largest political party in the nation in 1932, extremely bitter that Stalin had not done more to prevent Hitler's rise. That was the first occasion I recall communist supporters talking about Stalin's selling them out.

guest. Heitler had been in the Soviet Union earlier, and neither he nor Pauli had anything good to say about the communist dictatorship.

They were in absolute accord on the further question: "There never could be a dictatorship in Germany. How could such a thing even be imagined? Hitler was an irresponsible madman. He probably put the torch to the Reichstag, which he hated. But a dictatorship in Germany? That just couldn't happen." After the thirteenth denial of that possibility, I was less convinced than after the first.

The Nazis claimed that the communists were the real instigators of the Reichstag fire and arrested all the communist deputies (who committed the incredible folly of not going into hiding). In the last free elections held a week later, the Nazis received 44 percent of the votes, more than any other party but not enough to give them a majority in the legislature. But with the communists locked up, the absolute majority was theirs.

After that, the German people didn't have another real chance. During March, the rapid dismantling of the Weimar Republic was unmistakable. The word for what was happening was *Gleichschaltung*.[10] Hitler destroyed all local autonomy and authority while preaching a unified Germany that would allow the same wonderful reforms to be realized everywhere. Hitler's henchmen took over every level of state and local government. Constitutional guarantees were disregarded. By April 1933, there could be no doubt about what was happening.

About that time, Placzek made me buy *Public Faces* by Harold Nicholson, a novel published in 1932 about a new, terribly destructive weapon made from a raw material found in Iran and called an atomic bomb.[11] The book was and

---

[10]The literal meaning is equality in practice. It turned out to mean equality in obeying Hitler.

[11](London: Constable & Co., 1932). The author held an office in the British State Department, and his descriptions of bureaucratic function and malfunction are most entertaining. What is most striking today is his prescience. Writing seven years before the discovery of fission, Mr. Nicholson has this to say about his fictional new weapon: "[The committee's report claims] that [a] deposit might produce in large quantities an element so unstable that beside it radium would be as dull as lead; an element, some physicists began to speculate, that as soon as it was reduced to its pure state must transmute itself, as radium transmutes itself into lead, but with infinitely more violence; in fact with an explosion that would destroy all matter within a considerable range and send out waves that would exterminate all life over an indefinite area . . . the experts had begun to whisper the words "atomic bomb" . . . a single bomb, no longer than this inkstand, [that] could by the discharge of its electrons destroy New York." Mr. Nicholson errs only in that an inkstand is an underestimate of the weapon's size and that electrons have little to do with the process.

is enjoyable reading, but Placzek wanted me to have a copy because he intended to base a code on it. He was certain that we would need to communicate secretly before we would be able to leave Germany. Although many of us thought the future ominous, Placzek's response was the most extreme.

I knew that my job with the university was likely to end at any moment.[12] I could not return to Hungary. Although the problems there now looked mild by comparison, they were bad enough. Both the countries with which I had ties were closed to me. I applied for a Rockefeller Foundation research fellowship with Niels Bohr in Copenhagen. The foundation turned me down because, they explained, Rockefeller fellowships were given only to scientists who had assured jobs.

When I saw my parents during the usual spring vacation, my mother opposed my ever returning to Göttingen, to that terrible world of Nazism. I had a sense that the danger in Hungary would not be much less than that in Germany and that being at home had nothing to do with security. I told my mother that by going back, I would stay in touch with the world of science, the world I wanted to live in. It turned out to be the only world I could live in.

I was surprised by how seriously the scientific community of Great Britain took the threat of Nazism and how quickly they responded. By April 1933, the British had begun a rescue operation on behalf of the scientists in Germany whose ethnicity or politics placed them at risk. Called the Academic Assistance Council, it was financed by the Imperial Chemical Industries (I.C.I.), the British analog of I. G. Farben. Every scientist at risk who had ability, whether the British needed him or not, was being welcomed in Britain. Indeed, the British went further and sought out the people who were likely to be forced to leave. The purpose was to get us out.

In Göttingen, James Franck's house was the hub of that activity. Franck had already accepted an offer to go to the United States and was doing everything he could to help the rest of us get out of Germany. I was invited for interviews with two well-known British scientists, Frederick A. Lindemann and George Frederick Donnan, who were practically on recruiting missions. It soon became evident that an element of competition was at work between the two in their recruitment efforts.

Lindemann was a great physical chemist who played an important role in world events as Winston Churchill's science advisor. I was very interested in physical chemistry, but when I met with Lindemann in Göttingen, we did

---

[12] The dismissal of Jews from the university faculties did not begin for another year or two.

not discuss common interests. Instead, he lectured me on the ineffectuality of the scientists who were trying to explain numbers such as 1,840, the ratio of the masses of the smallest negative and positive particles. Nonetheless, probably because of Franck's recommendation, Lindemann invited me to Oxford.

Donnan wore a black eye patch to cover his missing eye. Although his field of interest, biochemistry, was rather remote from my own,[13] his manner was most engagingly direct. He emphatically and at once made me a different offer: Come to London and get acquainted. I promptly did so.

That trip was my first real exposure to the West. I had not realized how many people lived in their own houses rather than in apartments. I spent the day with Donnan and he put me through my paces—table manners, science, politics—everything. Donnan learned a lot about my personal life, in part by telling me quite a bit about his own, including his closeness to his two sisters, which had probably come about because he was not married. He took me through his laboratory and was obviously pleased to find that I was not bored by listening for several hours to descriptions of individual research projects. (After Eucken's training, his test was easy for me.)

During that visit, Donnan asked me, "What should we British do? Should we invade Germany and expel Hitler?" I said, "The Germans elected Hitler. If he is disgraced by a foreign power, the protest will come back in a worse form. You had better do nothing."[14] I still believe that invasion would have been wrong, but I now believe that the free nations should have resisted Hitler's expansion by all other means possible.

I explained to Donnan that I had tried to obtain a Rockefeller Foundation fellowship to work in Niels Bohr's laboratory in Copenhagen, and that I could go providing I had a position waiting for me. Donnan told me that I would be welcome to come, collaborate, and leave whenever I liked. That kind of generosity went far beyond what was required to help people in trouble. Such acts are the basis of the spirit of community.

---

[13] His name is famous for the Donnan equilibrium, which discusses the ratio of concentrations on the two sides of a biological membrane, such as the lining of the digestive tract. It is really not an equilibrium at all because it is an active process that selectively brings the food into our bloodstream.

[14] My opinion in 1933 was only a more moderate form of a resolution that the Oxford Union Society passed at that time: "Under no circumstances will this house fight for King and Country." If one believes what Mussolini's and Hitler's confidants wrote after the war, that statement by the intellectual elite of England affected the dictators' planning in a most unfortunate manner.

I must have passed most of Donnan's tests, because he offered me a very good job (which actually paid considerably more than my salary in Göttingen) at University College in London. But the offer, he explained, was contingent on my completing some reading before I returned. He thereupon gave me a volume of Lewis Carroll's *Alice in Wonderland* and *Through the Looking Glass*: He did not want to import a barbarian into England.

Before making final plans to go to London, I felt that I needed the consent of my original boss. In sharp contrast to most other professors, Eucken was very much a political conservative. Although he rarely mentioned his personal life, when his son passed an examination for a position of high status in the German armed forces, he had told me about it with great pride. But as the changes under Hitler began, Eucken was embarrassed and unhappy. His sense of decency was offended by the predicament of his Jewish colleagues. When I mentioned my job prospects in England, Eucken encouraged me to take whatever was offered; he explained that I would soon be unemployable and that he could not help me.

I had promised to write summary articles for an important yearbook on many aspects of my work on the spectra of molecules.[15] The time pressures were great, and Eucken offered his help. As a going-away present, he offered me the services of an excellent young woman, a graduate student who not only had some understanding of what I was doing but also had splendid secretarial skills. Her name was Miss Behrmann. She was nice looking, but she was very large (although smaller than a bear).

I remember her particularly from one of our exchanges. She asked me whether I could explain Professor Franck's behavior to her, and added, "We all know he is a patriotic German, and yet he is planning to leave Germany. Why in the world would he do such a thing?" Her lack of understanding was so incomprehensible to me that I could not think of an answer. Yet that conversation should stand for many others that made it clear how poorly many German people were prepared for what would befall them.

What I did not tell her, I confided to my diary. I wrote several poems in Hungarian and German. A period of beauty and excitement was ending, a refuge for mind and spirit was being destroyed. I was full of anger and

---

[15] R. Mecke, O. Reinkober, and E. Teller, *Molekül - und Kristallgittspektren, Bd. IX, Abschnitt 2 of Hand - und Jahrbuch der chemischen Physik* (W. W. Finkelnburg); E. Teller, "Theorie der langwelligen Molekülespektren"; E. Teller, "Theorie der Kristallgittspektren" (Leipzig: Akad. Verlagsges, 1934).

anguish. The translation fails to convey what I felt. The original did not do it justice, either.

> *October, 1933*
> *These times are for passion, not for doubt.*
> *The people awake to the dawn of greatness.*
> *(You don't think so? Still shout it out.*
> *The demand is for an unconditional great Yes!)*
> *The idea's victorious. The people learn.*
> *They do their duty, and they enjoy it.*
> *(Magnificent Mr. Heroes have no concern*
> *For what is lost: they just destroy it.)*
> *Take the plane; with fervor, smooth the plank.*
> *Small loss if most planks break in two.*
> *(Small loss, if war—barbarity most rank—*
> *Should come with miseries old and new.)*
> *The times are great. No one can change the fact.*
> *The God of Nations has a plan.*
> *(Perhaps worlds with a lesser lack*
> *Of modesty have gods for a mere man.)*[16]

Another poem reflected the nightmarish quality of the times. The fears of my childhood—war, destruction, and death—were being made reality, but the German people around me were unprotesting.

---

[16]*Es schäumen der Begeistrung wilde Wogen,*
Das Volk erwacht, die grosse Zeit ist da
Von jedem fordert sie das unbedingte Ja!
Laut muss man's rufen, und sei es auch gelogen.
Es schreitet die Idee zu neuen Siegen
Mit Freude und mit Lärm erfüllt man seine Pflicht
Was tritt man in den Staub, was bleibt zerbrochen liegen
Die Herrn Heroen denken daran nicht.
Es wird gehobelt, Späne müssen fallen
Man hobelt frisch d'rauf los und geht das Brett entzwei
Und gibts auch Krieg und geht es mit uns allen
Zurück ins Elend, in die Barbarei.
Die Zeit is gross, daran ist nichts zu ändern
Der Gott der Nationen will das so
Oder leben vielleicht irgendwo
Noch andere Götter in bescheiderenen Ländern?

He was upright and modest, accustomed to toil,
A proper man of the native soil.
Each day at dawn, he promptly arose.
He finished his work at the hour to close.
When his work was done, his time was his own.
But no adventurer, he promptly went home.
For a proper man of the native soil
Is upright and modest and accustomed to toil.
While not a learned or clever guy,
In his everyday life, he'd not harm a fly.
Off to the war, one must shoot, one must kill,
Which has nothing to do with any ill will.
One day at the front, a bullet found him,
And lodged in his head, not in a limb.
What bothered him then was an odd sort of pain:
Facing death now, he'd ne'er do so again.
His head was bloody and ablaze. To die!
There must be much better ways.
Not only agony that made him cry
But failure to know the right way to die.
The chaplain is nearing, dignified, fast.
It's almost too late. He arrives at last.
The dying man sees him. His doubts are now mended.
Hands folded, his life is peacefully ended.[17]

My efforts at writing poetry slackened after I left Göttingen and vanished within the decade. Hungarian and German are the languages I learned before

---

[17]*Es war einmal ein braver Mann*
Bescheiden und stolz und arbeitsam
Am Morgen stand er stets früh auf
Dann nahm der Tag seinen täglichen Lauf
Und Abends ging er aus.
Doch er kam zur Zeit nach haus
Denn er war, wie gesagt ein braver Mann
Bescheiden und stolz und arbeitsam.
Er war nicht klügner als undere Lent'
Und tat niemanden 'was zu Leid
Im Kriege schoss er auf den Feind
Aber das war nicht persönlich gemeint.

the beginning of time; English I acquired when I was a grown-up eight-year-old. I suspect that the intimacy with words needed to write poetry has deep roots. My second emigration took me to a new world where I had to work and live with a different language. I also became involved more and more with realities outside science.

Today, English feels like my language, even if it doesn't sound quite that way to my listeners. I left behind a piece of my connection to literature when I left Germany. But, greater loss by far, the unique and wonderful community that was German physics in its golden years was destroyed.

Doch eines Tags da traf ihn das Blei
Und da wusste er es: jetzt ist's vorbei
Und da fühlte er eine seltsame Qual
Denn sterben, dass kann man ja nur einmal
Und es fiel ihm ein, dass er nicht wusste.
Wie man das Sterben anfangen musste.
Seine Haare sind vom Blute feucht
Das Sterben, das Sterben, ist garnicht leicht
Es naht der Feldpfarrer, würdig doch schnell
Im letzten Moment, da ist er zur Stell'
Der Sterbende sieht ihr, er faltet die Hände
Dies war sein seliges Ende.

11

COPENHAGEN

1933–1934

A S A TEENAGER, I had known that Budapest could not be my home. Now, at twenty-five years old, I painfully discovered that the community of German physicists was also closed to me. And for the two long years that Mici—the one person who still tied me to the many things that were dear to me from my youth—had been in America, we had neither spoken nor written to each other. As I was finishing in Germany, I learned that she was coming home; so before I left for London, I went to Budapest.

I went to see Mici almost immediately. As I climbed the stairs in her apartment building, a completely inappropriate quote from Goethe popped into my head. Mephistopheles says to Faust: "Ihr sollt in eures Liebchens Kammer, nicht etwa in den Tod." (You go to the chamber of your sweetheart, not to your death.)[1] I suspected that if I were ever to marry, I would marry Mici. I also knew that if I were to marry her, I should marry her now.

Seeing Mici again swept away all my sorrows and questions. She was enchanted with America and enthusiastic about her switch from mathematics to personnel work. She was now studying sociology and psychology and had learned of a wonderful scientific discovery that made the precise measurement of intelligence possible! I protested: "IQ tests have nothing to do with science, and they certainly cannot measure a person's intelligence, whatever that is." Mici began a spirited defense of her new studies.[2] We managed to avoid irrational debate on an irrational subject only because we were so pleased to see each other again. We made a date to go walking the next day.

---

[1] *Goethe's Faust* (Hamburg: Christian Wegner Verlag, 1949), p. 107.
[2] Forty years later, after many decades of experience in personnel work, Mici was noticeably less enthusiastic about IQ tests.

In the hills of Buda a little less than twenty-four hours later, we stopped for lunch on a meadow. About a dozen geese gathered to greet us, and there to the loud approval of those birds, I proposed [3]

Mici is and always has been decisive. Her answer was yes. The wedding was set for Christmas, 1933. Mici's stepfather gave his consent, grudgingly. Her warm-hearted mother, Ella, insisted that no self-respecting gentleman should wed without owning a hat. (After my friend Nándi had run away with my cap, I had gradually given up the habit of wearing one.) I quickly acquired the necessary status symbol and, with our plans complete, set out for London and my new job.

On the way, I stopped in Copenhagen, the first assembly point of the Diaspora of the German physicists. Many of my friends and acquaintances were spending time there: Bethe, who would later make his way to Manchester; Placzek, who was trying to make up his mind about where to go; and Landau, who was on his way back to Russia.

But for me, the most important man there in early fall was James Franck, who was on his way to Johns Hopkins University in the United States. He was the one person who seemed interested in my big piece of news; Franck thought that my decision to marry was a wonderful idea.

Once in London, I hardly had time to catch my breath before I was confronted with the agreeable news that, as an employed physicist, my application to the Rockefeller Foundation would now be welcome. But the application form asked: "married or single." The correct answer, of course, was single at present, married before the start of the fellowship.

I had inadequate knowledge of verb tenses and of protocol, so I took the application form to Donnan. After listening to my dilemma, he pronounced the form grossly incomplete. "Far more alternatives are needed. The form should read single, married, divorced, widower, intending to marry, intending to divorce, and intending to become a widower." But then Donnan told me to take the next train to Rockefeller headquarters in Paris and explain my situation to them.

I did so and as a consequence had my first encounter with an American bureaucrat. He began in a mild, slightly embarrassed way: "Dr. Teller, the last thing I want is to give you the impression that we, at the Rockefeller Foundation, are opposed to the institution of marriage. But . . ." He then

---

[3] According to Konrad Lorenz, those long-lived bipeds mate for life and are monogamous, so their presence may have been auspicious.

explained that being a newlywed was not apt to lead to proper concentration on scientific work. If I really wanted the fellowship, it would be wise to postpone my marriage. Indeed, he was quite sure the New York office would make that decision, so I should let him know promptly what I was to do. (I later heard that a Hungarian recipient had used his Rockefeller fellowship for an extended honeymoon.)

I was, of course, very upset. I decided to call Mici, but long distance calls in those days were unusual and expensive. So I sent her a telegram telling her when I would call. The time in Paris and Budapest differs by one hour. But in my worry and confusion, I failed to find the correct answer to the profound question: Does the sun rise sooner in Budapest or in Paris? Mici received the phone call two hours later than my telegram had specified. Her younger brothers had spent that interval jumping around and teasing her about the intelligence and/or reliability of her fiancé.

Once connected, I simply asked her to decide whether I should forget about the fellowship or postpone our marriage. As usual, she took less than five seconds to come up with her answer: "You need the fellowship. If we have to wait a little longer, we shall wait."

So that is how, a month or so later, I happened to land in Copenhagen and into another boarding house, this one run by a Frøken Thalbitzer. She had only one other customer, Carl Friedrich. Until the following March, when he returned to Germany, we saw a great deal of each other: on the tram ride to and from the Institute (Frøken Thalbitzer's house in Hellerup was one-half mile beyond the longest tram line in Copenhagen), at the Institute, and in each other's rooms in the evening.

At that time, I did not realize how influential the Weizsäcker family was. Their family history was long and distinguished, and the government post that Carl Friedrich's father, Ernst von Weizsäcker, held was that of undersecretary of state for the Weimar Republic.[4] Carl Friedrich, although he was

---

[4] Ernst von Weizsäcker stayed on in that job under Hitler. Because of that, after World War II he spent, unjustly I believe, two years in prison. During those years he wrote, "He, who fails, within these walls or outside them, to help the next generation avoid what we have had to experience, is a war criminal." (Wer—intra muros von Landsberg et extra wärend den nächsten Jahren nicht seinen Anteil beiträgt, den Kommenden zu ersparen, was wir Abtretenden erlebten, der is ein Kriegsverbrecher." Quoted in Martin Wein, *Die Weizsäckers: Geschicte einer deutschen Familie* (Stuttgart: Deutsche Verlags-Anstalt, 1989), p. 340.

The family tradition of service to the nation has been continued by Carl Friedrich's younger brother, Richard, who in 1989 was the popular president of West Germany.

four years my junior, was more experienced than I in several respects. He made a great difference to my way of looking at the world.[5]

In our after-hour sessions, we spent a time on games that could hardly be called elaborate. On one occasion, we decided to write our own sets of ten commandments. One of Carl Friedrich's was "Do not believe that you have understood something unless you can explain it in the simplest terms." One of mine was stranger: "Live in such a way that at sometime you shall be able to think of your life as finished."

On another evening, he surprised me during a discussion of the types of dispositions identified by Aristotle (melancholic, phlegmatic, choleric, sanguine) by correctly identifying my disposition. I doubt that anyone else among my friends or family members could have done so at that time.[6]

Carl Friedrich talked to me about the literature he loved. I had been exposed to the German classics as part of my education at the Minta, but much more so by my mother, who was an ardent admirer of Schiller and Goethe, in that order. But when I met Carl Friedrich, my appreciation of them changed. His enthusiasm convinced me that I should tackle Goethe again. (On that occasion, I read the second part of *Faust* and found it wonderful.) I disagreed with Carl Friedrich's low opinion of Heine, but I fully shared his appreciation of Christian Morgenstern, a unique master of language.

Morgenstern was whimsical and satiric. In one of his poems, he has an architect removing the spaces in a picket fence and building a house with them. In another, a discarded paper sandwich wrapping, blowing about on a cold winter day, comes to life, "short-circuiting the wearisome ways of evolution"; but the new and irreplaceable life form is soon swallowed by a big greedy black bird.

Carl Friedrich and I spent one evening translating Morgenstern's nonsense poem, "Das Grosse Lalu La" ("The Great Lalu La") into German. The only analogy in English that comes to mind is "Jabberwocky" by Lewis Carroll, but in many ways, "The Great Lalu La" is even more unique.[7] The sound of the title told us that we were dealing with wailing, and, having "discovered" that *Kwasti* meant to destroy, and that *Basti* was the accusative form of the word for life, we determined that the lament was over the death of the hero

---

[5] In midcareer, Carl Friedrich changed from physics to philosophy and became deeply interested in religion.

[6] Carl Friedrich correctly named me, not as sanguine as some of my critics have claimed, nor as melancholic, as I sometimes feel, but as choleric, a flaw I struggled against in my youth.

[7] See footnote 37, Chapter 21, for the complete text of the poem.

"Siri Suri Sei." (We had to work out the grammar of the language before we could properly translate it.)

Carl Friedrich and I also conducted formal debates in the Socratic style. During one of them, Carl Friedrich defended the absurd thesis: Standing at attention is ecstasy.[8] He won the debate because his arguments were much too amusing to contradict.

Our main occupation was interpreting modern quantum mechanics and the cryptic statements of Niels Bohr. Indeed, Bohr's great contribution was not in finding the truth earlier than anyone else but in calling attention to ideas that without him might have remained buried under layers of complex mathematics. I had started to learn that new view of the world from Heisenberg, but I came to understand it fully with Carl Friedrich.

Understanding began with rejecting two generally held conclusions: determinism and the nature of a scientific explanation. The idea of determinism is beautifully summarized in Edward Fitzgerald's translation of the *Rubaiyat of Omar Khayyam*:

> *With Earth's first Clay They did the Last Man's knead,*
> *And then of the Last Harvest sow'd the Seed:*
> *Yea, the first Morning of Creation wrote*
> *What the Last Dawn of Reckoning shall read.*[9]

The depiction of a machine-like universe is rather dismal, but quantum mechanics invalidates that view. The past remains unalterably determined. To quote Fitzgerald again,

> *The Moving Finger writes; and, having writ,*
> *Moves on: nor all thy Piety nor Wit*

---

[8] When I saw Carl Friedrich in 1984 on the Starnbergersee, he and I gave a public exhibition of the formal Socratic debate. It still was fun. Five years later, in September 1989, the University of Gratz in Austria arranged a television debate between his son Ernst and me. Ernst has his father's voice and mannerisms; he also has a beard. Ernst argued for the conservation of natural resources; I tried to defend progress. I found that in the progressive state of Austria, as in the United States, conservation is much more popular. Yet the debate—which extended my good feelings from the father (who began the debating) to his son (who kept alive our old habit of friendly controversies)—was a great pleasure.

[9] *Rubaiyat of Omar Khayyam: Rendered into English Verse by Edward Fitzgerald.* (New York: Grosset & Dunlap, 1947), stanza 73, p. 91.

Shall lure it back to cancel half a Line
Nor all thy Tears wash out a Word of it.[10]

Although we cannot change the past, we can know it. But according to the new theory of atoms, the future is undetermined and therefore truly unknowable. We can change it, but we cannot know it, at least not completely.

For example, during the course of a year, 1 out every 4 billion uranium atoms will emit a fast particle and turn into thorium. But there is no prior difference among the uranium atoms, nor can there ever be.[11] Similarly, if sodium atoms are heated, they emit a characteristic yellow light in about one hundred-millionth of a second on the average. The sodium atoms are identical; it is impossible to say which atoms will emit in the first half of the period, and which ones later. Whether we talk about a process of radioactive decay that takes billions of years or the emission of light that requires less than a microsecond, the future behavior of individual entities cannot be predicted, not now, not ever. The job of creating the future remains incomplete forever.

Newton's laws about the mechanics of the universe worked so well that they seemed to apply forward and in reverse. In that sense, the future and the past were treated as equivalent. True enough, there appeared to be exceptions. If the cook oversalts the soup, she can't unsalt it. But salting soup is merely a question of mixing molecules. If the atomic level were understood (so the scientists hoped), everything could be determined, including the future. Heisenberg, in carrying out Bohr's program in consistent detail, found it necessary to deny that point.

Quantum mechanics demonstrates that the behavior of the individual entity cannot be predicted. Every atom, every star, and every living thing participates each microsecond in creating its part of the future. That is a different view of the universe; under it, God may be employed as the conductor of the universal orchestra. In that scenario, the scientist may be said to be reading the score, an exciting task that is not entirely hopeless; although the future is undetermined, it is not without laws and order.

The other commonly held belief that had to be discarded is the essence of the story of atoms. Immanuel Kant pointed out that the thing itself (das Ding

---

[10] Ibid., stanza 71, p. 89.

[11] This statement is not limited to asserting that no one has yet found a difference between uranium atoms, but rather that a difference between uranium atoms is inconsistent with the known mathematical rules of quantum mechanics.

an sich) is different from our concept—the model in our minds—that represents the thing. But traditionally, science had tried to present a single well-determined picture of the object. With the revolution of atomic theory, science was forced to use two mutually exclusive models consistently: the particle picture and the wave picture. That is the real cornerstone of the new discoveries.

So there was science, confronted with one fact and two explanations. One was based on continuum physics, or waves; the other on discrete quantum states, or particles. That problem had another side: When does causality apply, and when must statements of probability replace it? A general answer can be given. As long as we stay in the realm of particles or in the realm of waves, we have causality. But when we try to move from one description to another, we must introduce probability.

Uncertainty and dualism are connected. Understanding in science requires acts called measurements. To make measurements that would clarify the nature of light or the position and speed of an electron, instruments are needed. But every instrument (being made up of atoms) has the identical problematic nature. The point is that if the uncertainty principle were violated in any one case, it would hold nowhere.[12]

There is a link between the world of atoms and the world of classical, continuum physics. For example, radio waves, which are miles long, consist of particles, quanta of $h\nu$; but because their frequency and energy are exceedingly small, the quanta are incredibly hard to find. They illustrate Bohr's *correspondence principle*, that the laws of quantum mechanics and the more familiar laws of classical physics fade into one another when the quanta are numerous.[13]

My life in Copenhagen was stimulating and challenging. I missed Mici a great deal, but I was far too busy to brood over our change of plans. Still, I felt that I should write James Franck (who by then was in the United States) because of his interest in my wedding. I reported on my activities at the Institute and then explained why my marriage had been postponed. It was a short comment and not a complaint.

---

[12] That idea was not readily obvious. I argued the uncertainty principle with Franck in Göttingen. When Chadwick found the neutron in 1932, Franck said, "Now we have a new particle. We can make new measurements where we can find both its position and its velocity." I replied, "If that were possible, we could use the neutron as a measuring instrument and measure everything."

[13] My job with Franck and Eucken in Göttingen had been to point out the behavior in continuum physics to which the quantum laws corresponded.

But the answer, which arrived by return mail, went something like this: "I was shocked and scandalized to hear that the Rockefeller Foundation forced you to postpone your wedding, I immediately went to their office in New York. They agree that you should marry without delay. But you should try not to embarrass the people in the Paris office. So simply write them about how intolerable life is without your fiancée and beg for a change in their decision. Not only will your request be granted without delay, but it will allow them to save face."

The letter I promptly wrote may have been in imperfect English, but I still imagine that it had great style: The subject of missing Mici was a natural stimulant to eloquence. If I had possessed common sense, I would have simply sent the letter on its way. Unfortunately, I had the feeling that because I worked for Bohr, I ought to tell him about the situation. So I showed him the letter; he took it and said he would think about it.

For days, which stretched into weeks, I could not approach him. If I spotted him at the end of a corridor, he would turn and flee. But at last he appeared voluntarily and invited me to a nearby cafe, nicknamed Quaterne, that served chocolate and cookies. Taking an extremely serious tone, he began, "I have always found that the best policy is complete openness. The Rockefeller Foundation has been extraordinarily good to us here and is helping people escape the Nazis. You should not tell them that you can hardly work without your beloved by your side. Your work is satisfactory. You should write them the full facts. You should tell them that you are writing on Franck's suggestion and will they please permit you to marry."

I told him that Franck had explicitly asked me not to do that. "But," said Bohr, "Franck is our friend." I expressed my dissatisfaction with that argument. Bohr replied, "Perhaps we should write to Franck and ask what to do." I protested: "That would take weeks, and besides Franck already said what should be done." Finally, Bohr took my letter back and said, "I shall ask Harald (his older brother, a great mathematician) what to do." The next day, Bohr handed me the letter and said, "Harald says send it."

Placzek was in the room when Bohr capitulated, and, since our community did not practice secrecy, Placzek was fully aware of the situation. When Bohr left, he said with a laugh, "Quick, go post it before he changes his mind." I rushed to the mailbox in front of the Quaterne. As the letter slid down the chute, I remembered that it was dated three weeks earlier. I consoled myself that the Rockefellers would think that I was wrestling with indecision, not quite daring to send my plea. They would never guess that I was wrestling with the conscience of a great physicist.

When the reply arrived, it turned out to be difficult to decipher. The first sentence said, "We were happy to receive your letter and request." The second sentence, "The Foundation's decisions are always correct and unalterable." The third, "But, in your case . . ." The fourth, "On the other hand, . . . " Up to the very last sentence of the letter, I was in doubt about what the letter was saying. But the last sentence said, "Please inform us of the date of your marriage." I decided that I could not do so without marrying.

I went back to Budapest and on February 24, 1934, I married Mici. Because I am Jewish and Mici Calvinist, we were married in a civil ceremony. It was held in the same city office building whose courtyard hosted the Fire Department's exercises, directly across the street from my home in the Palatinusz. The official who married us weighed well over two hundred pounds. He wore a wide sash of red, white, and green that practically encased his body, and he fulfilled his duties with few words. Only our closest family members and friends were present, but Nándi said that the ceremony was touching.

Mici and I promptly left Budapest by train, but we stopped for a day in Leipzig, where I visited Hund. Even then, a year after the Nazi takeover, Hund did not believe that Hitler would last. The most memorable event of our brief stay was that I lost my second (and last) hat, which I had bought to wear at the wedding. I had it when we arrived at the Leipzig station, but I did not have it when we boarded the train to leave. I didn't lose it on purpose; I was just unaccustomed to remembering extraneous gear. I never bought another hat.

We finished our honeymoon by traveling to Copenhagen, and I was back at work at the Institute within three days of my marriage.[14] The enlarged sample of Hungarian newlyweds might have led the Rockefeller Foundation to conclude that, although Hungarian behavior was not consistent, Hungarians were always extreme.

Mici and I moved into Frøken Thalbitzer's house; almost at the same time, Carl Friedrich returned to Germany. Mici was unhappy with the food (which included cold sweet soups), so not long after moving in, we moved again, this time into our own apartment. A few days later, Heisenberg came to visit us. Mici says that he taught her to make coffee on that visit, out of necessity. Seeing him was a real pleasure for both of us.

---

[14] Just before I left for Budapest, the proofs of the articles I had contributed to Eucken's *Hand- und Jahrbuch* totaling more than 140 pages—had arrived, together with the plea that they must be completed immediately.

I was much happier with Mici by my side, and I was more eager than ever to accomplish something in physics.[15] For the first time in my life, I had no obligation to satisfy anyone else's requirements. There was Niels Bohr, but satisfying him was beyond my imagination. I could observe a star of his magnitude only from afar.

My relationship with Bohr, whether because of age or temperament or some other factor, was much more distant than the one I enjoyed with Heisenberg. Heisenberg was warm and direct and loved jokes. Bohr loved paradoxes and was at his brilliant best when he explained them, carefully emphasizing the contradictions. He also liked to talk about subjects that he did not understand, although he always made sense in an inspirational and ambiguous way. His sentences were long and convoluted. I remember his friend Paul Dirac once asking him, "Were you never taught in school that before you begin a sentence you should have some plan as to how you are going to finish it?" Bohr turned to the rest of us and commented: "Dirac may also think that one should not start life until one has a plan about how to end it."

Bohr's concept of politeness was truly amusing. A young Danish physicist, Fritz Kalckar, and I had developed a theory about the conversion of two forms of hydrogen (para- and orthohydrogen).[16] The two forms retain their identity for long periods, but they can also change into each other under the influence of magnetic forces. Our work was just a small and happy adventure for a couple of young physicists, but is memorable to me for the peculiarities connected with reporting our results to Bohr. The seminar in which that was to occur did not meet regularly. A time was set for our report, and we appeared. Bohr did not. Therefore, there was no seminar.

---

[15] Not only was Mici an extremely patient wife but she was helpful as well. We worked together on proofreading my articles for Eucken, and when they were finally finished (which was after we had moved to our own apartment), Mici, with considerable pleasure, saw them off at the post office.

[16] The difference between them is that in one (orthohydrogen), the spins and magnets of the nuclei are parallel; in the other, they are opposed. A further difference is that in the one, the angular momentum of molecular rotation is an odd multiple of Planck's constant h divided by 2π, and in the other, an even multiple. Those two facts were well-known and well-understood. They also were of peculiar, practical interest.

Liquid hydrogen is necessary for work in low-temperature physics and can be stored in a well-insulated bottle; but containment can be tricky and dangerous because the heat liberated in the transition from ortho- to parahydrogen can evaporate the liquid. Observations showed that inhomogeneous magnetic fields are the reason for the ortho-para transformation. We worked out in detail how the transformation occurs: It is due to the close interaction of molecules that carry strongly inhomogeneous magnetic fields.

The same pattern occurred on other occasions. Because of my marital bliss, my mornings started even later than formerly. One day, arriving at about 1:00 P.M., I found an unannounced seminar in session, with Kalckar reporting our work to Bohr and everyone else. As I entered, Bohr exclaimed, "But here is Teller, and he speaks English. It would be better to have the report in English."

Bohr performed that peculiar machination because out of politeness he felt that he should allow me to give the talk. But he also wanted to be polite to Kalckar. Bohr said that to be properly understood, one should not lecture in his native tongue. He knew that Kalckar did not speak English and that I did; so he provided that spurious reason to allow me to give the talk. No one's feeling were hurt, and no one smiled. At the Institute, Bohr determined the proper style. That was the first lecture I ever delivered in English, but (memories of Magda Hesz!) I managed.

Only once did I directly contradict Bohr, and, of course, I lost. During an informal discussion one day, Bohr described the electronic structure of an oxygen molecule starting from the most elementary principles, but[17] he happened to come out with the wrong answer. The topic was a favorite of Hund's and one I was familiar with, so I attempted to make the appropriate corrections. The physics of the discussion was hardly of great difficulty.

When I finished my statement, Bohr started in: "Teller knows a hundred times more about molecules than do I." Here I interrupted with inexcusable directness: "That is an exaggeration." Bohr assumed an air of indignation: "Teller says I exaggerate. Teller does not want me to exaggerate. If I can't exaggerate, I can't talk. But you are right, Teller, you know only ninety-nine times as much as I do." I never again interrupted Bohr. But I have quoted him in many discussions in defending my own right to exaggerate.

During the time I was at the Institute, Bohr had a conference with several famous positivist philosophers. Positivism holds that no reality exists other than what the senses report, and that truth is the sum total of impressions that the world makes on you. By means of that extreme simplification, positivists manage to sidestep all the difficult problems of philosophy.

Bohr used observations to overcome the prejudice against the reality of the dual nature of waves and particles. To those unfamiliar with his intensive considerations about the nature of observations, his approach might appear to be a straight application of positivism. But in contrast, Bohr could hardly utter a

---

[17]Oxygen carries a magnetic moment, and the question, as I recall, arose in connection with our work on paramagnetic hydrogen.

sentence without criticizing it in his next remark and then criticizing the criticism in his following murmured words. There may have been a superficial similarity between the substance of Bohr's new physics and positivist philosophy, but there was a fundamental antithesis in style and approach.

During the meeting, the positivists agreed with Bohr in much too simple a manner and created the impression that they accepted the role of observation in quantum mechanics as a simple affirmation of their point of view. Bohr pointed out in lengthy and painstaking detail the divergence inherent in the application of their views.

I expected Bohr would be satisfied with the result, but when he appeared the next day, he seemed discouraged. Asked why, he muttered, "If someone talks about Planck's constant and does not feel a little dizzy, clearly he does not know what he is talking about." From my first acquaintance with Bohr, I had recognized that there was something unique about him. He described at least part of his unique nature as being "dizzy," but his associates agreed that he was "dizzy" in a particularly ingenious manner.

The point of view that has guided my thoughts and actions throughout my mature years was formed during my young adulthood in Europe, particularly during my year in Copenhagen. The most important perspectives were connected with science. Other influences were connected with the political changes that were occurring. Although the changes in Germany profoundly affected my life and perspectives, the changes occurring in Russia during this time also made a deep impression on me.

My memories of the four months of communist rule in Hungary during my childhood are the first source of my dislike of communism. The hunger of that period and the longer-lasting consequence of increased anti-Semitism bring memories only of misery and unhappiness. But if my understanding of communism had begun and ended with the clumsy experiment in Hungary, I doubt that I would have been much concerned about it. Much more important to me was what I learned about communism from people I knew well who had direct experiences and whose words I could evaluate.

One such person was my collaborator George Placzek. When he visited Russia, he was an admirer of the communist system and a thin man. When he came back, he weighed even less and appreciated food much more. He gained back his lost weight and then overshot the mark to become overly well-rounded. Placzek never regained his confidence in the communist system. During World War II, he opposed extending the lend-lease program to Stalin. Placzek had strong opinions about what was evil, but he judged Hitler a lesser evil than Stalin. At that time, his opinion greatly surprised me.

When Placzek returned from the Soviet Union, he amused us all by announcing that the Pauli principle applied not only to electrons but also to catastrophes. The original Pauli principle explains why atoms do not collapse.[18] The Pauli principle, Placzek claimed, also applied to catastrophes and in this way saved the Soviet Union from collapse. The example he offered was that in the Soviet Union, you may get a room with running water if you are lucky. If it then turns out that the drain is stopped up, that is a catastrophe. If you turn on the faucet and you get no water, that is another catastrophe. But if both catastrophes occur together, the situation is no worse than it was with either catastrophe alone. That, said Placzek, is the basis of the stability of the Soviet Union. Two electrons or two catastrophes never occur precisely in the same place and manner.

My friend Landau took a different approach to politics. He was concerned only with principles, and, even before Hitler's rise to power in Germany, he pronounced the democratic West ridiculous. In his lively, sardonic manner, he demonstrated his convictions by always wearing a bright red jacket. I remember Niels Bohr's wife, Margarete, with a kind smile on her face, praising Landau on more than one occasion for the remarkable similarity his costume had to that of the Danish letter carriers. Landau was a wonderful and entertaining companion. He and Mici often played tennis together, a game they both loved; but I could not compete with them after my accident.

Above everything else, Landau was a dedicated physicist. During our stay in Copenhagen, we had some interesting discussions about how collisions between molecules transfer energy to molecular vibrations.[19] Shortly after I left Copenhagen, Landau published a paper on the subject. Although my

---

[18]Wolfgang Pauli, a most ingenious Austrian physicist who spent much of his life in Switzerland, formulated the law that no two electrons can be in precisely the same state. Some electrons in strongly charged atoms, such as gold or uranium, are strongly bound and lie very close to the nucleus. But not all the electrons can crowd into this small orbit. Instead, they spread themselves over a variety of energy positions farther from the nuclei. Less strongly charged atoms, such as hydrogen, carbon, and oxygen, have a less extended electronic structure. The size of the heavy atoms is directly related to the Pauli principle.

[19]As it turned out, the energy exchange is quite small, and the chance that some molecular vibration will change by one quantum is often as low as one in a million. Landau's contribution to the topic was to recognize that as the temperature rose and collisions became more energetic and penetrating, the probability that such an energy transfer will occur should increase rapidly.

contribution was modest, he made a joint publication of it. Thus I gained my only publication in a physics journal of the Soviet Union.[20]

My year in Copenhagen was the last time I saw Landau, but it was not the end of our interaction. After Landau had returned to the Soviet Union, I wrote and asked him to help find employment for my Budapest friend Laci Tisza, whose prison record—for delivering messages for the communist party—had made him unemployable in Hungary. Lev promptly gave it, and Laci accepted the offer of a position in the Soviet Union.

I did not see Laci again until four or five years later, after we both had come to the United States. Laci was most enthusiastic about Landau as a person and about Landau's work on superfluidity.[21] But terrible changes were taking place in the Soviet Union during the mid- and late 1930s, and Laci had been delighted to leave Russia and communism behind forever.

I do not believe that anyone I knew in Copenhagen in 1934 had any idea of the problems on the horizon. But in the terrible years that followed, Hitler was not the only terror that overtook us. During one of Stalin's paranoiac searches for dissenters in 1939, Landau—whose equal for sincere devotion to communist ideals I have never met—was charged with disloyalty and sent to jail. I learned with relief that the politically influential physicist Piotr Kapitsa managed to rescue Landau, but only after a year had passed; during that time, Landau's health had suffered.

In the 1970s, while visiting in Israel, I met Alexander Voronel, a low-temperature physicist who had recently emigrated from the Soviet Union. I asked about Landau, calling him "a physicist I knew." Voronel promptly contradicted me. "No. You didn't know him," he announced.

This is absurd, I thought. Voronel's English must be the problem; but then I realized what he was trying to tell me: The Landau who returned from prison was a different man from the idealist I had known and enjoyed.

---

[20] L. Landau and E. Teller, "Zur Theorie der Schalldispersion" (Theory of Sound Dispersion), *Phys. Zeits. d. Sowjetunion* 10, 1 (1936): 34–43.

[21] Helium becomes superfluid at very low temperatures; that is, it flows without friction, much as electrons flow in superconductivity. The factor that produces superfluidity is inherent in quantum mechanics. According to Heisenberg's uncertainty principle, a small amount of velocity is always present in particles; this, according to Landau, causes superfluidity. In 1962, Landau earned his Nobel Prize for that work. Unfortunately, he was badly injured in an automobile accident shortly before he was awarded the prize. He died in 1968 without recovering from his injuries, which included brain damage.

Voronel went on to explain that Landau, long before his death, had lost his faith in communism.[22] That indirect, painful message was the last I heard of a great and exceptional friend, Lev Landau.

My year in Copenhagen was marked by change. When I arrived in Copenhagen, I was single; when I left, I was married to the only woman I have ever known well. When I arrived, I was supposed to be an expert in quantum mechanics; when I left, I was not sure that I would ever become one.

Even before I arrived in Copenhagen, I was a sponge for information about the Soviet Union and the United States, the two countries that would determine the future. Strangely enough, nothing I heard about the United States proved to be as simple and as relevant as what I had learned a dozen years earlier from Magda Hesz.

In one important way, Copenhagen was a disappointment. Niels Bohr had turned out to be an embodiment of the paradoxes of science.

Physics so far has taken three great steps, and each one originally appeared absurd. The first introduced the Copernican system, which showed that our world was a small part of an incomparably bigger system and expanded our idea of space in a way that we don't find uncomfortable only because we are rarely forced to think about it. The second was Einstein's relativity, accepted by scientists for its mathematical brilliance and simplicity; for that very reason, it is still not understood by the general public. The third brought an understanding of atoms; this changed our outlook on causality, a change that even contemporary physicists try to forget. Replacing the theory with its mathematical consequences seems, in comparison, less disturbing than accepting Bohr's challenge to older, more primitive ways of thinking.

Bohr invented paradoxes because he loved them. I imagine that I understand those paradoxes, but I failed to understand Bohr. In human terms, understanding means being able to put yourself in the place of a fellow being. In those terms, I can understand Heisenberg; if my abilities were much greater than they are, I could imagine myself in his position. In no way can I imagine myself in Bohr's place. Even though I spent a year working under him, Bohr remains an unknown and inexplicable person to me. I became acquainted with the amazing nature of his brilliance as a physicist, but we never met as human beings.

---

[22]By the 1970s, my role in the development of nuclear weapons was widely known. Voronel, a recent emigrant, also provided an insight into the political division in his country: "Landau and others of us in the Soviet Union agreed with what you were doing."

12

THE JOY OF
BEING A FOREIGNER

1934–1935

IN SEPTEMBER 1934, I took the train from Copenhagen to London; Mici, who had been my girlfriend for a decade and was now my bride of six months, accompanied me. We spent most of our time on a ferry and suffered through the roughest ride I've ever had on air, land, or sea. (I avoided sea-sickness, but barely.) We brought with us everything we owned, which didn't amount to much but somehow filled seventeen pieces of luggage.

Almost as soon as we arrived, I went off to a physics conference sponsored by the British Association of Science (The British Ass, as it was fondly called). I wanted to hear Lord Ernest Rutherford, one of the earliest contributors to atomic theory, who was to speak at the conference.[1] His demonstration that most of the atom's volume is empty space had provided the initial impetus for Niels Bohr to work on atomic theory.

Early in his career, Rutherford had advocated the impossible—that elements mutated when they emitted an alpha particle. He had also found that a great amount of energy was released in such emissions. The Rutherford I heard was a very different man. On the day of the meeting, Rutherford spent his time railing indignantly against the "idiotic" proposition that the great

---

[1]Rutherford, who was born in New Zealand, began his career teaching physics at McGill University in Canada. He studied the alpha particles released by some elements and decided that such emissions transmuted the element. His Canadian colleagues denounced him as a fool for ignoring the basic fact that elements are immutable. Rutherford proved more immutable than the elements. He went to Manchester, England, and then to Cambridge, where he established the Cavendish Laboratory as a leading center for the experimental study of the atom.

amounts of energy stored in the nuclei of atoms could be put to practical use. The people who imagined that nuclear energy would ever be anything but a part of pure science were crazy. To think otherwise was simple lunacy.

A few weeks later, I discovered the cause of that diatribe. I saw Leo Szilárd. I had met Szilárd in Budapest, and I had seen him on a few occasions when we were both in Germany. But at the time we landed safely in England, I did not know him well. Szilárd, like me, was a refugee, but his was an unusual case. He was influential, I have been told, in setting up the British Academic Assistance Committee, the organization that had helped me and so many others escape the Nazi threat. I find that easy to believe; for Szilárd, a versatile and brilliant scientist, also possessed a talent for anticipating the future.

At Lindemann's invitation, Szilárd had gone to Oxford; there he was conducting his first experiments with neutrons, the particles discovered by James Chadwick, Rutherford's protégé, a few years earlier. Szilárd had the idea that neutron bombardment of nuclei might release additional neutrons. If 1 neutron could produce 2, after ten generations of release, 1,000 neutrons would be released and, after twenty steps, 1 million. Assuming that not many neutrons escaped from the material, more and more neutrons and energy would be released, resulting in a powerful explosion. Szilárd made an appointment to discuss his work with Rutherford, but he had hardly begun when Rutherford denounced Szilárd's ideas as crazy. What I heard Rutherford say at the conference that day was a result of his interview with Szilárd—Rutherford was still angry.

Szilárd just became more determined to prove that nuclear energy could be used in some way. Having heard that I was in London, Szilárd came looking for me, knowing that I would provide him with an appreciative audience. He was not disappointed. The idea he suggested—that a critical mass of material would retain a sufficient fraction of the neutrons and produce an extremely powerful explosion—was interesting, frightening, and logical.

On that occasion in London, Szilárd mentioned that he planned to take out a patent on his idea.[2] After the war, the United States paid him some

---

[2]Szilárd accomplished unprecedented things but often didn't receive credit for them. For example, Szilárd's doctoral thesis consisted of an ingenious solution to a problem posed by Clerk Maxwell. Gases in two adjoining regions spontaneously equalize their temperatures. The opposite process does not occur: Starting from one temperature, they do not spontaneously develop two different temperatures. Maxwell had invented a demon that seemed to make that happen, thus contradicting the laws of heat (thermodynamics).

thousands of dollars for it. I suspect that he took out the patent because he was angry with Rutherford.

In the patent, Szilárd listed the three possible elements by which nuclear energy might be released: thorium, uranium, and beryllium. Uranium was first used, and thorium is the fuel of the future. Only in the case of beryllium was Szilárd wrong; there his error was due to a commonly accepted but incorrect measurement of atomic weight. The same measurement had led to Fermi's error in failing to accept Ida Tasche Noddack's suggestion about fission in uranium.

Throughout his life, Szilárd made great efforts to find reason in his fellow humans, and he never stopped giving advice. His clash with Rutherford was neither the first nor the last time that his surprising and absolute pronouncements provoked a strong negative reaction. He even acquired a nickname, The General, among his friends.[3] (Somewhat irreverently, I think that even he, the Apostle of Reason, was not wholly reasonable). But he was never boring, and he always remained a friend.

My life in London was very satisfactory. Mici found a house for us to rent on Gower Street, a less than lovely section in the heart of the city, close to Soho and the University College of London. We liked our landlady, who was very proud of her "rose garden," a plot of land about three feet square, full of roses. Under Mici's tutelage, the flowers behaved in a gorgeous fashion, and our landlady became very fond of Mici. We rented the lower two of the three floors in the house, and, aside from the garden, our arrangements were notable in only one regard: The toilet was located between the two floors, and everything in it was green. Thus, "the green room" entered Tellerese. Thereafter, Mici and I automatically called its kin by that name, but we failed to find one that matches the original color.

In Maxwell's design, the demon opens a gate between the chambers for fast molecules coming from the left and for slow molecules coming from the right, so that starting from an equal temperature, the left chamber will get cold while the one on the right will grow hot.

Szilárd proposed that the rules of thermodynamics remain valid if one includes the demon in the system rather than talking exclusively about the state of disorder (entropy) in the separate chambers. He assigned a value of entropy (or of order) to the pieces of information received by the demon. Szilárd's work gave rise to a practical and famous branch of science called information theory, important today in transmitting information at minimum cost. Yet his name is hardly ever mentioned in that connection. Szilárd never mentioned that portion of his work to me.

[3] After fission was discovered, Szilárd wrote an article on the topic with Bernie Feld and John Marshall, signed according to convention Feld, Marshall, Szilárd. That listing inspired the comment that Szilárd had grown more ambitious: He had decided that the few stars of a general were insufficient and had promoted himself to field marshal.

At University College, Donnan gave me the task of lecturing regularly on the principles of quantum mechanics, a job I had not undertaken in my earlier positions. Donnan had correctly guessed that I enjoyed lecturing. On the basis of my single lecture in Copenhagen, I felt that I had little difficulty with English; and, on the whole, my audiences seemed to get along very well. On some occasions, they even corrected my pronunciation, but I fear they did so less frequently than was justified.

My first impression of Donnan as an unpretentious, exceptionally kindly person had proved valid. He went out of his way to make his refugees feel at home. I suspect that Donnan had some cause to regret his bachelorhood: He treated us like the children he had never had. Concentrated tea was served at the College on Gower Street each afternoon at a less concentrated social hour. One day each week, German was the language spoken during tea time "for the instruction of the staff," but in reality for the purpose of making the refugees feel at home. Donnan also saw to it that I paid a courtesy call on the people from Imperial Chemical Industries who were funding me (and hundreds of others) though the Academic Assistance Committee.

Professor Donnan was an excellent public speaker. In almost every one of his lectures, he exhibited his modesty with appropriate moderation. One quote I particularly remember is, "I know I am a fool, but you should not believe that I am a bloody fool." I have wanted to plagiarize that line so many times.

Donnan asked me to review the latest book of the great astronomer Sir Arthur Eddington. With advancing age, Eddington developed more and more ambitious yet nonsensical theories. In that volume, for example, Eddington developed an unconvincing theory about a famous pure number (the light velocity c, times Planck's constant h, divided by the square of the charge of the electron e; that is, hc/e^2). After reading the book, I could not think of an appropriate and polite way to review it, but how could I tell Donnan without seeming harsh in judging so notable a British scientist?

When I next saw Donnan, I began by asking whether it would be all right to begin the review with a quotation from *Alice in Wonderland*. Donnan seemed pleasantly surprised and immediately agreed. He then asked me which passage I would use. I promptly exhibited my recently acquired knowledge of English literature:

> *"You are old, Father William," the young man said,*
> *"And your hair has become very white;*
> *And yet you incessantly stand on your head—*
> *Do you think, at your age, it is right?"*

"In my youth," Father William replied to his son,
"I feared it might injure the brain;
But, now that I'm perfectly sure I have none,
Why, I do it again and again."

The idea of my reviewing Eddington's book was dropped.

My scientific work went on along its previous lines, with more work on molecular structure, and along a new line with the beginnings of my interest in the theory of atomic nuclei. Hans Bethe was also in London, another recipient of the kindness of the British rescue service. I had met him in Munich, seen him several times during my stay in Rome, where he was working with Fermi's group, and had become better acquainted with him in Copenhagen. We were together on so many occasions because of the political pressures faced by scientists exposed to Hitler's anti-Semitism and also because the community of physicists interested in quantum mechanics was small.

Bethe had a physicist friend from Germany, Rudolf Peierls, who had ended up in Manchester, and the three of us almost published a joint paper on the proton-neutron interaction while we were in England; but Fermi published a paper on the same subject before we submitted ours. The small remainder of our paper that Fermi had not covered seemed too minor to be worth publishing. I vetoed the submission; Bethe and Peierls agreed. Hans was not happy about it, but the future stretched before us, bright with unlimited possibilities.

I have always enjoyed working with friends. Sharing and exchanging ideas is far more pleasurable than contemplating them in solitude. Although I felt like a stranger, I developed pleasant working relationships with several of my new British colleagues. Bryan Topley was a chemist who came to my lectures on quantum mechanics; he was so enthusiastic about them that he convinced me that we should try to put them together in book form. But although I spent many happy hours working on that project in Topley's very pretty Georgian home, the only result of our efforts was that my future lectures were more complete.

I also collaborated with another chemist, Christopher Ingold, who was later knighted. In Copenhagen, I had done a little work on the shift of vibrational frequencies that occurs when an isotope of the element is substituted. One can calculate the shape of the vibration from the shifts. Ingold, who was working on the benzene ring, wrote a paper applying my work on isotopes to benzene.

One collaborative effort with a new British friend earned some fame. In Copenhagen, I had told Landau about the dissertation work of one of my

Göttingen students, Rudolf Renner.[4] I had suggested that he look at the excited states of the linear (and therefore symmetrical) carbon dioxide molecule, in which the electrons rotate around the axis of the molecule. I suspected that in that case, the Born-Oppenheimer approximation separating the motion of nuclei and electrons did not hold. Renner found that the two kinds of motion were mixed in a more thorough manner, and that, in this case, one cannot describe the motion of the electrons by starting from an approximation in which the nuclei are at rest.

"Wait a minute," said Landau. "You are talking about a symmetrical molecule, and if the electrons are degenerate [the technical expression for different electron orbits having the same energy], then the symmetry will be destroyed. Degenerate electronic states are not compatible with the stability of the molecule."

We argued the case in detail, and eventually Landau gave in. That was quite unusual. Landau was an excellent physicist and was almost never wrong. When all the atoms in a molecule lie on a straight line (as is true in carbon dioxide), it makes no difference in energy whether an electron rotates clockwise or counterclockwise around the line. That sort of degeneracy, or equality of energy, is compatible with a situation where moving a nucleus away from the straight line always increases the energy, which results in the stability of the straight line.

I began wondering how many other exceptions to Landau's postulate there really were. I mentioned the question to various people without creating much excitement. When I mentioned it to my new friend Hermann Jahn, I suggested that it would be interesting to find out whether there were other cases in which Landau's proposed statement didn't hold. He was fascinated, and we began a thorough search of all the possible kinds of symmetry. No other exception turned up. We wrote a paper stating that in a stable polyatomic molecule, two or more electron configurations cannot have the same energy state unless all the atoms lie along a straight line. The phenomenon is known as the Jahn-Teller effect. It should be called the Landau-Jahn-Teller effect.

The subject has turned out to have significant applications; but in some respects, it has remained both incomplete and interesting. One unresolved

---

[4]Renner was an exceptionally bright student. During World War II, he worked in the German meteorological service. He was married, and during the hard postwar period, he had to take over his father-in-law's store to make a living. He was never able to return to physics and died at a relatively young age.

point that I find interesting is that when we consider solid metals rather than molecules, we find that many, highly symmetrical electron configurations possess nearly the same energy. Does anything like the Jahn Teller effect apply to them?

Many metals have a strange property known as superconductivity. At a sharply defined point at very low temperatures, the conductivity of some metals becomes infinite. Currents, once started flowing along a ring, never cease flowing. I began wondering whether something similar to the Jahn-Teller effect occurred in superconducting metals.

One of my famous fellow refugees, Fritz London, was then working on superconductivity and he discussed his ideas with me in detail. The Meissner effect had just been discovered: A superconductor does not tolerate magnetic fields. (A metal, when cooled to its point of superconduction, expels the magnetic field present earlier.) London wanted to talk to me because of the paper I had written three years earlier that clarified the debate between Landau and Heisenberg about the behavior of free electrons in a magnetic field.

London had a beautiful theory that showed the magnetic field did in fact penetrate into superconductors to a very shallow depth, usually the thickness of a few thousand atomic layers. That magnetic interaction did not lead directly to the explanation of superconductivity. After thirty years and one world war, superconductivity was explained by a most ingenious theory.[5] Under it, superconductivity is a result of an interaction between electrons and lattice distortions. The interaction is made possible because electrons in a metal are capable of exchanging very small amounts of energy with vibrations of a crystal lattice, a point that was somewhat distantly yet obviously related to the Jahn-Teller effect.

Science is a pyramid of puzzles. More than once, I have been aware that I did not yet understand everything about a single pyramid that I have tackled, such as the puzzle of superconductivity. The great pleasure afforded in sharing an expedition up such a pyramid with friends was a sustaining force during my year in unfamiliar England. Common interests are a strong basis for good human relations. Those relations may be good or they may be excellent, but they are longer lasting and more pervasive than differences of personalities.

Scientists, of course, disagree and harbor jealousies among themselves. The Germans had a sardonic explanation for this: When God created the scientist (one of the later acts of creation that occurred around 1600), He gave

---

[5]The theory, developed by Bardeen, Cooper, and Schrieffer, is known as the BCS theory.

him everything: comfort, security, and an appetite for knowledge that was always satisfied to an extent that left more appetite. The Devil was therefore most upset. So he created a colleague for the scientist.

I find Oppenheimer's comment, made quite independently a few decades later, much more to the point. He suggested that the reason scientists put up with each other is that even though others make discoveries, they provide you more opportunities to make one yourself.

Although I think of myself during this period as having shown some interest in political affairs, I paid far more attention to science than I did to political questions, even those that were connected to my survival. Of the two invitations I received to work in England, I accepted Donnan's. As it turned out, Lindemann, who had invited me to Oxford, was the science advisor to Winston Churchill and was to play a part in Churchill's heroic career in World War II. Had I worked with Lindemann instead of Donnan, I would have been involved in the war effort, and I probably would not have left England.

Donnan and Lindemann were not particularly close, but Donnan told me an interesting and appreciative story. One of the flaws of the early airplane was that it went out of control easily. If the angle of ascent was too steep, the airplane would develop a spin, lose altitude, and crash. According to Donnan, Lindemann figured out how to correct the problem and, being unwilling to risk anyone else's life to prove his theory, he demonstrated the means himself.

First, he put the plane into a spin; then he turned the nose down and applied full throttle. Instead of sliding slowly around in a conical pattern—which prevented the pilot from regaining control—the plane accumulated enough speed to be brought out of the dive. The technique, I realized not much later, was also the beginning of the dive bomber. Lindemann's proposal was meant to save pilots' lives. Its application eventually had a different and terrifying effect.

A few months before Mici and I arrived in England, the Royal Air Force had conducted maneuvers connected with defense against bombing. When they did not succeed, an angry public debate ensued: Should an attempt be made to improve that situation or was appeasement preferable? Lindemann took a strong stand in his letter to the editor of the *London Times*, which appeared August 8, 1934. I discovered it many years later, but it is worth repeating:

> That there is at present no means of preventing hostile bombers from depositing their loads of explosives, incendiary materials, gases, or bacteria upon their objectives I believe to be true; that no method can be devised to safe-

guard great centres of population from such a fate appears to me to be profoundly improbable.

If no protective contrivance can be found and we are reduced to a policy of reprisals, the temptation to be "quickest on the draw" will be tremendous. It seems not too much to say that bombing aeroplanes in the hands of gangster Governments might jeopardise the whole future of our Western civilization.

To adopt a defeatist attitude in the face of such a threat is inexcusable until it has definitely been shown that all the resources of science and invention have been exhausted.

Scientists are only human beings with specialized knowledge. They are subject to the same moods, discouragement, and frailties as other people. Fortunately, a few scientists and a few political leaders in Britain managed to keep their heads during those difficult times. They developed radar and other defenses against aerial bombing; as a consequence, many lives were saved, and the course of history was directed toward a future that did not include Nazism.

At Christmas, Mici and I went home to Budapest. Before we left, Mici found a pleasant and more permanent home for us, and we signed a six-year lease. When we returned to London, two invitations for teaching positions in the United States awaited us, one from Princeton, where my friend Eugene Wigner had found a position, the other from the George Washington University in Washington, D.C. The second offer was for a full professorship, and it came from George Gamow.

When Landau and I were visiting Copenhagen in 1930, I met his good friend George Gamow, also from the Soviet Union, who was working in Copenhagen that year. Gamow was extremely fond of Landau, but the two could hardly have been more different. Where Landau was of medium height, Gamow was of towering stature. Where Landau was satiric and reserved, Gamow was jovial and impetuous. Where Landau often expressed deep concern about a just political organization, Gamow never uttered a word on the topic.

Gamow found life a great adventure. He overflowed with new ideas, and his physical stamina was equally abundant. My friendship with him had grown during the spring break in 1931, when I went to Copenhagen alone. Gamow, four years older than I, had already made a considerable name for himself as a young physicist by the time we met. But he had also established his reputation as a wild man. Motorized vehicles were far from commonplace in Europe, even in 1931. But Gamow, a mostly penniless Russian, had managed to acquire a motorcycle; and that wonderful instrument of the Devil had a passenger seat behind the driver's.

The year before, he and Landau had made a grand tour of England, where Gamow had been working with Rutherford. But in 1931, Landau was back in Russia, so Gamow adopted me. He invited me to join him for a vacation trip over the Easter holiday in 1931. Thus it was that I traversed the main island of Denmark and traveled north to the tip of the middle island, all the while clinging to the back of George Gamow. But if Gamow was unrestrained in theoretical physics, he had good driving habits. The most exciting occurrence we had on the road was seeing a total eclipse of the moon. When we had viewed the Danish countryside, we spent several days on the beach at Fynf Hoved and talked about physics in a light-hearted way.

At the end of the holiday, I went back to Göttingen, and Gamow returned to the Soviet Union, where he married a very beautiful Russian girl. I met his wife, whom he called Rho, for the first time when I was in Paris trying to arrange my own marriage.[6] But both Mici and I got to know Rho a bit better when the four of us were together in Copenhagen in the spring of 1934.

Mici, who had enjoyed her student years in Pittsburgh, wanted to go back to the United States. I asked Donnan's advice. The job offers were excellent, I said, but I would be happy to stay in England. Donnan replied that I must do whatever seemed best to me. I was welcome to stay as long as I liked; but, he added, I should feel no obligation to stay. Britain had wanted to come to the rescue of science and had done so. That was all the British had hoped to accomplish. Then he added that he believed it was probably best for me to accept.

During the early weeks of 1935, neither Mici nor I considered the possible advantage of putting an ocean between ourselves and the Nazi menace. We had not yet grasped the immediacy and the extent of the danger, nor had we an inkling that our kindly hosts would in so few years become the heroes of one of the great tragedies of our century. But finally we made a decision. The offer at Princeton paid less and did not have tenure. Being with Gamow as a full tenured professor was our best choice. Besides, it would be a lot of fun.

After we had decided to go to the United States, Mici's brother Suki visited us in London, and we all decided to make a trip to Copenhagen. While I was there, I met another visitor, an official of the Rockefeller Foundation. He was quite fatherly and told me about Washington, D.C. "It is very hot

---

[6]I believe Rho's given name was Lyubov (in Russian, Love); but Gamow nicknamed her Roxanne after the legendary sixteenth-century woman who, after becoming the captive of Mohammed the Magnificent, conqueror of Hungary, became his wife.

there," he said, "and the best way to cool off is to take lots of cold showers. Stay in until the low temperature penetrates your fat layer and you get a second set of shivers. Get out then, but don't dry yourself with a towel. Just let the water evaporate. That will keep you cool for the next six hours." I have used the technique many times during our years in hot places without air conditioning; it works.

He continued: "You are Jewish. One terrible thing about Jews is that they have only Jewish friends. Don't do that." As it turned out, many of my future friends in the United States—George Gamow, Merle Tuve, Cloyd Marvin, Charles Critchfield, the Brickweddes—were not Jewish. It was not so much that I took his advice as that I had neither the opportunity nor the incentive to make Jewish friends, except for a few other refugee scientists, among them Bethe, Bloch, and Weisskopf. Maria Mayer, who was to become a favorite collaborator, had a Jewish grandfather, but her husband, Joe Mayer, was not Jewish; nor were Montgomery Johnson, Bill McMillan, or Luis Alvarez, my later friends and collaborators. All my Hungarian friends were Jewish, but when we got together, we were conspicuous not as Jews but as Hungarians.

Because Mici was much more eager than I to accept the invitation, she immediately went to the American embassy to arrange for nonquota visas for us. Because I had a specific offer for employment, we thought we did not have to worry about obtaining quota visas (which were allotted by nationality). We arranged to sail in late summer.

After a few months we still had no visas, so Mici returned to the embassy to ask about them. She was told that we were not eligible for nonquota visas. When she asked why, she was given no answer. I was quite willing to stay in London. I was happy with my friends and with my work, and Donnan assured me again that he would welcome my staying indefinitely. But Mici was determined to go to the United States.

We had a mutual Hungarian friend who had become a well-known economist in London, Thomas Balogh. Years before, when we were high school students together in Budapest, Tommy had been nicknamed Sir Thomas. He later became the economic advisor of the Labor government and was knighted. But as children, we underestimated him; he was Sir Thomas for only a few years before becoming Lord Balogh. Making predictions about Hungarians, even for Hungarians, is a difficult proposition.[7] Balogh was the

---

[7]Nicholas Kaldor was another great economist from Budapest who settled in England and became a lord. He was very overweight. British wags had names for the pair from Budapest: Kaldor they called Buddha; and Balogh, Pest.

gregarious sort of person who seems to know everyone; Mici was certain he would be able to do something at the American embassy.

She was right. The answer came back—fast, unexpected, and satisfactory. The embassy people promptly disclosed to Balogh what they had failed to tell Mici: One requirement of a nonquota visa was that the immigrant had practiced the profession he was to fill in the United States for the previous two years. The year that I had taught at London University College was acceptable, but the previous year as a Rockefeller fellow at Niels Bohr's Institute was not. Even though such a position was a higher honor in my profession than a professorship of the somewhat modest and temporary grade I had in London made no difference.

But Balogh had discovered a further important fact that resolved all the trouble. The Hungarian immigration quota was not filled. All we had to do was apply for a regular visa.

Before leaving, I had a brief encounter with British bureaucracy. I had reported my financial status, and I was notified that I had to pay what seemed to me a remarkably high income tax before leaving England. Unlike the official at the American embassy, the Britisher in charge was willing to explain that the high tax was due on the money I had saved from the Rockefeller fellowship of the previous year.

That was money that I had brought into the country, I protested. Taxing it seemed unfair. The bureaucrat scratched his head and departed for a protracted period. Finally, he returned and inquired when I would leave the country. On hearing my reply, he asked whether I was sure of that date, and then declared: "Your stay in England will be two weeks short of a year. You owe no tax!" I have never decided whether British bureaucracy is superior, or if it is simply that all British bureaucrats prefer to see foreigners outside their country.

London in 1934 made the lot of the refugee tolerable. The foreigner remained a foreigner, but he was not made to feel inferior, only different. In London, I had been a guest, and I was extremely fortunate to have been there. But it was only later that I realized how truly magnificent the work of the rescue committee was. They accepted many more scientists than Britain could possibly use, and all of us were welcomed as permanent residents.

My appreciation of the British was helped along when, not long before Mici and I left, I read a newly published book: *Foreigners, or The World in a Nutshell*.[8] It begins:

---

[8]Theodora Benson and Betty Askwith, *Foreigners, or The World in a Nutshell* (London: Victor Gollancz, Ltd., 1935).

There is an old saying, "Tout comprendre est tout pardonner" (French). For the benefit of those Englishmen who have abstained, and rightly, from learning any language but their own we will translate this: "To understand all is to forgive all. Looking around the world today we see that the need (the need rather than the demand) for forgiveness far outruns all available supply. The Englishman sees that most foreigners are in a mess and is apt to reach the conclusion that almost every foreigner is a mess.

The authors explain that their book should strengthen the reader in the task of dealing patiently with foreigners and adds, "As many of them have had the elementary decency to learn English, it will teach them to understand each other."

A few pages follow about each of forty or so countries, appropriate to the times.[9] The book closes with sections on what the Continent, the Americans, and the English know about the English. They report the Continental view that the British are "mad and hypocritical" and the American view that the British "live on boiled beef, boiled cabbages, and boiled potatoes, and give themselves the most awful airs." About themselves, they say that they have "a passion for fresh air and have guts and grit and all that sort of thing," but regret they are without "temperament, a sense of logic, and a sense of humor."

I thoroughly enjoyed this irreverent little book, but the authors fail to mention one of my own findings: The English are truly among the most hospitable and ethical people in the world.

---

[9] For example, the description of Germans closes: "So far we have not mentioned three recent phenomena: Göring's lion cub, Göbbels's Jewish grandmother, and Hitler's face. A nation that can put up with such a face has no sense of humor." Hungarians, they claim, do better at unloving their neighbors than any others, except possibly their neighbors.

13

FIRST YEARS IN
THE UNITED STATES

1935–1941

T HE GEORGE WASHINGTON University, today as then, is a city university without a large campus, similar in setting to University College, London. In September 1935, it consisted of a few buildings that occupied not much more than a square block, a short distance west of the White House.

We had sailed from England to New York, and one of our fellow passengers was Hans Bethe. Soon after our arrival, I saw Geo Gamow. The New World was not a completely foreign place; physics, a large part of my existence, had come with me, and so had Mici. But I knew I was going to miss my second set of friends even more than I had missed my friends when I left Budapest.

On our arrival, we moved into a small hotel on Franklin Square between Thirteenth and Fourteenth streets. The hotel was less admirable than the square, which was full of squirrels. Half a century of time has not been kind to the area. My salary was more than twice as much as I had earned in England, and because that munificent sum was paid for nine months' work (leaving me the summer for my own pursuits), I had a comfortable situation.[1] Mici and I felt that we were well on our way to becoming a prosperous, established married couple.

Within a few weeks of our arrival, Mici found a furnished house on Garfield Street, near Connecticut Avenue, at a bargain price. Part of the reason for the

---

[1] I made $5,000 per year as opposed to about $2,000 in England and $1,000 per year in Göttingen. In those days, a very nice lunch in a restaurant cost about fifty cents, so my salary was indeed generous.

reduced rate was that it was available only for nine months of the year. The owner wanted to spend her summers in Washington, D.C., but most of the year she lived in Oklahoma because Washington was too cold. Only the summers, according to our landlady, were warm enough to live in Washington. Like most people, Mici and I found the summers too hot, so the arrangement worked very well for all of us. We stayed in the Garfield Street house for five years. My only complaint with those lodgings was that the piano, an old upright, was no good. However, I used it.[2] Even with my greatly increased prosperity, owning a piano would have to wait.

Not only were our living arrangements pleasant but my teaching responsibilities were light. In 1935, quantum mechanics was still news in the United States. My main duty was to give lectures on that topic similar to those I had offered at University College; I used as little mathematics as could be managed. About a dozen students attended my class, almost all of them older than I. We met three times a week in the late afternoon so that my students could leave their laboratories and offices and get to class. The hours suited my preference for working at night and sleeping in the morning, and I thoroughly enjoyed my students.

My only other daily routine was to receive my morning wake-up call. At about 11:00 A.M., Geo Gamow would phone our house on Garfield Street with his latest theory for me to disprove. Gamow chose me to fill the second slot at George Washington because I was a good second fiddle: I listened carefully to his craziest ideas. Bethe was disdainful; Placzek would interrupt and tell him to shut up; I was a more flexible foil.

I appreciated Gamow. He generated one new theory every day, which made him a sort of force of nature. But if the theory turned out to be nonsense, as most of them did, one could tell Gamow this in a straightforward way, with no need to say, "You are right because . . ." Unlike many geniuses, Geo discarded his theories with the same ease as he created them. On the rare occasions when I couldn't fault his notion, we wrote a joint paper. It was usually a good one, because Gamow had excellent taste in selecting questions. In addition, neither of us was a highbrow; indeed, we may even have revolted against formality, so we got along very well.

During the Christmas holiday that first year, Geo and Rho invited Mici and me to drive to Florida with them. On the day we arrived in Miami, the weather

---

[2] At that time, the nicest piano I had played was in my second lodgings in Karlsruhe; it had been a good grand piano.

was windy and the water beautiful. I was excited about swimming in the ocean, but I couldn't keep my balance and quickly escaped from what seemed to be ten-foot waves. On the beach, Geo and Rho were having a tense discussion, and Geo was in a bad temper, a rare occurrence. At dinner that night, Rho, whom I liked very much, blurted out, "Geo is really anti-Semitic, and he can't stand all the Jews in Miami." Geo was embarrassed. In spite of Rho's assertion, I couldn't take Geo's anti-Semitism seriously. Lev Landau, his dearest friend, was very much a Jew, and Geo had adopted me, another Jew. So what kind of an anti-Semite was he? Thus began the first and last political discussion I had with Geo. He turned out to be more anticommunist than anti-Semitic.

Geo hated pretense, dogma, and constraints. He scornfully described the self-criticism/self-improvement sessions in the Soviet Union, which were required of all workers involved in "building socialism." I knew that Geo could not possibly fit into such a straitjacket; it was not surprising that he had a history of trouble with the communists.

In one instance, he had drawn a cartoon showing a cat dragging in ether, a material that nineteenth-century scientists imagined filled space and propagated light waves. Although Einstein's Relativity had disproved the idea, Frederick Engels had mentioned it; in the Soviet Union, therefore, the existence of ether was a sanctified, immutable fact. Gamow's cartoon led to his chastisement, and some of his friends lost their academic positions. Having to reject the theory of relativity because it contradicted some of Engels's rambling was, for Geo, sufficient cause to reject communism and all communists with the exception of Landau.

When Geo returned home in 1931, Stalin's régime had become even more oppressive; he discovered that he could no longer get permission to travel outside the country. Geo and Rho tried to row across the Black Sea to freedom, but exhaustion forced them to turn back. In the fall of 1933, through an amazing stroke of luck combined with Gamow's persistence, they were allowed to attend the Solvay Conference in Belgium. They never returned to the Soviet Union.

Like many others, Geo blamed the Jews for establishing the Soviet system of government, and he was disturbed by the many Jews in Miami. I hadn't even noticed them. There could be no doubt that Geo needed a change. We took the Tamiami Trail west and spent the rest of our time near the shallow, placid water of the Gulf; we were bothered only by some sharks circling in the deeper water.

I was twenty-seven when I began teaching at George Washington, and I was the second youngest person in my classroom. Several of my students were established scientists who wanted to learn more about the new theories that had stood physics on its head. Many of them became personal friends. Sterling D. Hendricks was probably the most able of my students. He was also a wonderful man and a passionate mountaineer.[3] Our tastes in music were similar; he gave me a recording of what has become one of my favorite pieces of music, Mozart's Piano Concerto in E-flat Major. Sterling, his pleasant wife, and I often engaged in a highly intellectual game—hearts. Mici chose not to play.

Toward the end of my stay in Washington, Sterling and I collaborated on a complicated paper on crystal structure, but his interests were broad. In his later position with the Department of Agriculture, he made some great contributions to understanding the mechanism by which plants recognize the approach of spring. His comparatively early death was a great loss.

Another of my students, Ferdinand Brickwedde, and his wife Lange, a real Southern belle, became our close friends. Although we have seldom lived in the same section of the country, with rare exceptions, we enjoyed each other's company at least once a year until the late 1970s. Ferdinand had worked on the discovery of heavy hydrogen with Harold Urey; I met Harold through Ferdinand.[4]

My first group of students included a Hungarian, Stephen Brunauer, with whom I developed another lifelong friendship. We also published a paper together. Adsorption—the deposition of foreign molecules on the surface of a solid—had been well explained by Langmuir, but only for the first layer.

---

[3] A few years later, his partner was hurt on a very difficult climb in the Canadian Rockies. Despite tremendous obstacles, Sterling carried his friend all the way down the mountain.

[4] I enjoyed the story they told about the history of their discovery of deuterium. In about 1913, two chemists at the Carnegie Geophysical Institute wanted to measure the precise density of water. To obtain a pure sample, they distilled their water sample, again and again and again. Each time, the residual water grew in density. Finally, they published a paper saying they couldn't determine the density of water. The explanation is, of course, that the distillate tended to leave behind water containing the heavy isotope of hydrogen. The existence of isotopes had just been proved, but the people with the right data did not recognize that they were dealing with the isotope of hydrogen and stopped inches away from the discovery.

A dozen years later, Harold Urey noticed that the atomic weight of hydrogen seemed to be off. He explained the difference by assuming that two isotopes were involved, with the heavy isotope constituting one part in a few hundred. To separate isotopes most effectively, Urey wanted to distill liquid hydrogen; and in low-temperature work, Brickwedde was the expert. They succeeded but found that heavy hydrogen made up only one part in a few thousand. The mistake in atomic weight, mentioned earlier, had again led to an error. But here, the right atomic weight would not have provided a sufficient difference to awaken Urey's interest. The lesson is that the correct theory applied to the wrong data is better than no theory applied to correct measurements.

Brunauer tried to explain adsorption of further layers by postulating an attractive force that extended from the solid beyond the first layer. Such a force, I told him, was much too weak. Brunauer was by no means a submissive student. "Either offer me a better explanation than the one I gave you," he said, "or I won't believe you're right."

Extending the theory of monolayer adsorption in a natural way, I cooked up a formula in a few days whereby the first layer adsorbed holds the second, the second holds the third, and so on, in a manner that explained the experimental observations. Even after I offered the outline to Brunauer, he wasn't convinced. "I want to show this to Emmett," he said. "Emmett knows everything." That turned out to be true: Paul Emmett, a physical chemist at the Fixed Nitrogen Laboratory in the Department of Agriculture was an expert on catalysis.[5] The joint paper we eventually turned out (nicknamed B.E.T. for Brunauer, Emmett, Teller) became widely known because of its applications to catalysis and measurements of surface areas. Until 1980, the three of us gathered to reminisce at least once a year. But with our increasing years, the discomforts of travel multiplied. Today, I am the only surviving member of the trio.

In addition to my daily activities with Geo and my students, I also developed ties to the larger community of physicists in the area. I took part in the weekly seminar the Bureau of Standards held in their old building on Connecticut Avenue; I made what contributions I could to the discussions, and occasionally suggested speakers. Twice a month, I traveled to Baltimore for a seminar.

Papa Franck, as he was known to the large group of young scientists whom he had befriended, had organized the twice-monthly seminars. Because the ranks of émigré scientists in the United States were continuing to grow, the seminars developed the flavor of reunions. James Franck, my old sponsor from Göttingen days (who had resigned his position there in 1933 in protest against Hitler's policies), had accepted a position at Johns Hopkins University. Herta Sponer, my formidable friend from Göttingen, had found a position at Duke, as had Lothar and Traute Nordheim, my friends from the pension on Stegemühlenweg.[6]

---

[5] Catalysts are chemical matchmakers that allow various reactions to occur without participating in the reaction. In some cases, they are simply surface areas that act as a meeting place.

[6] I received the offer of a professorship at Duke in 1938, I suspect because of some prompting from my friends there. I eventually declined, but not without lots of deliberation.

At the seminar, I was reintroduced to Maria Göppert Mayer. Maria, the daughter of a medical school professor at Göttingen, had studied under Max Born and had made some important contributions during that period. I briefly met her there when she and her new American husband, chemist Joe Mayer, were visiting. In addition to being an extremely able physicist, Maria was also very beautiful. Slender and blond, she had a natural delicacy and grace as well as considerable strength of mind. She had married soon after earning her Ph.D. and, in the following years, had been occupied with her two small children. Joe, a pleasant man, was now teaching at Johns Hopkins; but Maria had not yet returned to physics because the body of knowledge had grown considerably since her student days. I gave her some brief tutorials and encouragement, and we soon became good friends.

The seminar also included two of my friends from Washington, Francis Owen Rice, a chemist with whom I later published a book, and Karl Herzfeld; both were at the Catholic University. Herzfeld enjoyed fencing and because of him, I tried that sport. I made another lifelong friend within the seminar group: Alfred (Freddie) Sklar, a student at Johns Hopkins who had worked with Maria Mayer in Germany.

Except for my forays into nuclear physics at Geo's prompting, I remained, as Placzek had called me, a molecule inspector. I collaborated with several members of the seminar during this time; but a joint paper by Herta, Traute, Freddie, and me illustrates the continuity of the work I began in Göttingen with Gerhard Herzberg on the interaction between vibrations and the electronic motion within a polyatomic molecule. It also illustrates the kind of small success in which I had a passionate interest.

(As an ex-chemist, I particularly enjoyed this paper, a summary of which follows in the text. The reader not interested in the details should skip ahead a few pages.)

We applied quantum mechanical methods to an old chemical problem connected with bonds and double bonds. The double bond, where two pairs of electrons are shared between two atoms, provides a firmer bond between the atoms than do single bonds. Chains of alternating bonds and double bonds give the molecule an even greater stability, and the benzene molecule (six carbon atoms arranged in a hexagon with six hydrogen atoms arranged in a larger hexagon around them) is the best example of that stability. Either of two conjugated double-bond structures can represent benzene. (See fig. 13.1 on the following page.)

In 1865, Kekulé suggested that benzene needs both formulas to describe it. That sounds like an absurdity, but Linus Pauling provided the explanation.

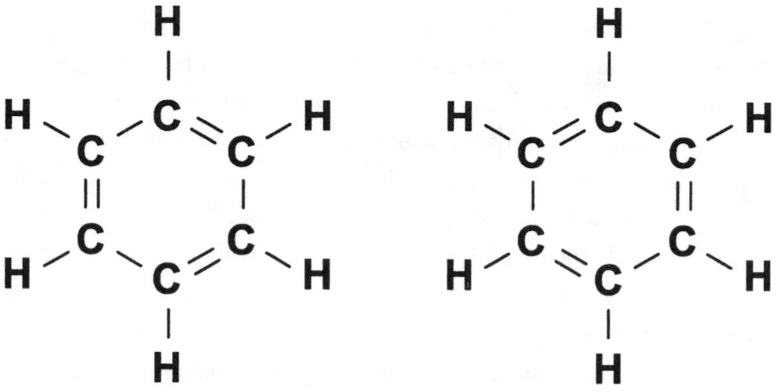

FIGURE 13.1   The configurations assigned to benzene by Kekulé

Quantum mechanics describes each electron as waves of an amplitude that depends on its position in space (the wave function). The greater the amplitude, the higher the probability of finding the electron at that place. The probability of finding electrons is greater around the locations of double bonds. The peculiarity of quantum mechanics (the logical jump that Bohr described as causing dizziness) is that such amplitudes can be added. Pauling suggested that describing benzene in quantum mechanics required the addition of the two wave functions that correspond to the two Kekulé formulas. That addition produces a smoother dependence of the amplitudes on position—which means that the electron has less momentum, velocity, and kinetic energy—and explains the lower energy and exceptional stability of benzene.

Two formulas for one molecule was one too many for the Soviet authorities in those days: They restricted the circulation of Pauling's paper.[7] Still, the Soviet objection had some logical validity. If two wave functions representing two chemical formulas can be added, what corresponds to the wave function that is the difference of the two amplitudes? In that wave function, the dependence of amplitude on position becomes more abrupt and the electrons have more momentum, velocity, and kinetic energy. Thus, this wave function

---

[7]It is ironic that Pauling was politically far more sympathetic to Moscow than most of his contemporaries, yet, until Stalin's death, his work was proscribed in the Soviet Union.

represents a higher energy (excited) state of the benzene molecule. All that was accepted before we began our paper.

My collaborators—Herta Sponer, Alfred Sklar, Traute Nordheim and I were interested in identifying the least amount of electronic energy the benzene molecule could accept and in seeing whether, after accepting that amount, the benzene molecule could be identified with the state where the amplitudes are subtracted. The correspondence principle, which links the world of quanta and common observations, says that the transition between the sum and the difference of the amplitudes has properties similar to the transition from one Kekulé structure to the other. The change between structures does not affect the average position of the electrons, which remains in the center of the hexagon, so the transition is not connected with an oscillation in the position of the electrons. Therefore, there should be no absorption or emission of light (the transition should be forbidden).

Spectroscopy showed that this particular transition in benzene, instead of being absent, was very weak. It had one further property that was a giveaway: The electronic transition never occurred without a change by at least one quantum in a vibration that affected the hexagonal symmetry (e.g., it changed from a roughly circular configuration to an almost circular ellipse). In the original hexagonal symmetry, the electronic transition changed the electronic orbits in a symmetric manner so that the averaged charge would remain centered in the middle of the hexagon.

If the hexagon is distorted, the electronic motion may be connected with a small displacement of the average position of the electrons. More precisely, the intensity is proportional to the square of the displacement. Thus, the motion of the electrons can give rise to an oscillation and radiation of the electronic charge.[8] Our paper provided no novelties, but it increased the common ground between chemistry and physics by showing that describing chemical formulas by amplitude functions leads to verifiable consequences in spectroscopy.[9]

My job involved one other major activity: helping Gamow plan and run the annual George Washington University conferences on theoretical physics. That was at least part of the reason that Geo had invited me to join him.

---

[8] Here is the connection with the work that Herzberg and I did.

[9] Three years later, having arrived belatedly at the Metallurgical Lab in Chicago, I wrote a paper on the behavior of methyl iodide at high energies with my old friend from Leipzig, Robert Mulliken. I believe that was the end of my work as a molecule inspector.

When Cloyd Hecht Marvin, the president of the university, had begun thinking about how to strengthen the physics program of his school, he had first considered placing greater emphasis on the experimental program and adding new equipment. When he mentioned his ideas to Merle Tuve, a physicist at the Carnegie Institute of Terrestrial Magnetism who was about ten years older than Geo and I, Tuve pointed out that there were no theorists in Washington, and that theorists needed only pencils, not a lot of expensive equipment.

When Geo was offered the position, he accepted on the condition that another theorist be added and that there would be a well-funded yearly conference. Tuve persuaded the Carnegie Institute to sponsor the conference jointly, but planning and managing that event belonged to Geo. My duties in that regard were undefined in detail but well defined in purpose. Geo was primarily interested in selecting the topic of the conference; his delightful book *Matter, Earth and Sky* was just one of many of the pleasant results of those gatherings.[10]

The first conference was held before I arrived, but I remember three of the topics of following conferences. One was on geophysics. At that gathering, which included many distinguished physicists, I learned a lot about the composition of the earth and its various layers, and about its magnetism. The topic in 1938 was astrophysics and the nuclear reactions in the sun, one of Gamow's special interests. Atkinson and Houtermans had suggested the thermonuclear process in the stars in the 1920s. The conference was intended to extend the initial efforts Geo and I had made to understand the relevant reaction of atomic nuclei in a quantitative way.

Both of us agreed that Hans Bethe could make a real contribution, but Bethe didn't think he wanted to get involved. Gamow's whimsical approach to the topic was far removed from Bethe's, and I had to work very hard to persuade him to attend. But once he was there, he, too, got interested in Geo's game.

We had acquired a few graduate students in theoretical physics by then; two of them, Charles Critchfield and Harold Argo, became lifelong friends.[11] As a result of the conference, Critchfield correctly proposed the reaction between protons as the source of the sun's energy; he, Geo, and Hans published a joint paper on the topic. Hans proved himself the real master of Gamow's

---

[10] George Gamow, *Matter, Earth and Sky* (London: MacMillan, 1958.)
[11] Charles Critchfield died in 1994.

game, however: Soon after the conference, he published a comprehensive paper on the subjects discussed, which also delineated the role that carbon
plays in the cycle of thermonuclear stellar reactions. That work figured quite
substantially in Hans's Nobel Prize.[12]

Over the years, the attendees varied depending on the topic. Each year,
about two dozen people participated in discussions during the day. Mici
found herself in charge of a day program for wives, and the two of us provided
hospitality during the evenings; this meant that about fifty people gathered
to socialize in our home. Our house was often full of friends in those days, but
throughout our six years at George Washington, the conference was always
our most hectic time.

When the first summer rolled around in 1936, Mici and I were, by agreement, homeless. We sailed back to Europe on the *Báthory*, a Polish ship
named after a famous king of Poland.[13] Placzek, who had at last found a position he was satisfied with at Cornell, was among our fellow passengers. As
with us, his first stop was a conference in Copenhagen.

After the meeting, Mici and I went on by train to Budapest; travel
through Nazi Germany was still safe enough for this. My memories of that
time have dimmed not only because so many years have passed but because
our vacation there was filled only with the comfortable joys of familiar and
happy surroundings. The year 1936 seemed little different from 1926.
Nothing particularly memorable happened, and none of us dreamed that
1936 would be our last visit to Hungary for more than half a century. But it
was. We never again saw Mici's parents, her brother Suki, my father, or most
of our childhood friends. A period was coming to an end, and we didn't notice. It was not a shining period, except in comparison with the darkness
that followed.

On the way back, we made a side trip to Switzerland to see Carl Friedrich
von Weizsächer. We met in Switzerland because having a Jew as a friend
wasn't a good idea in those days in Germany, and Weizsäcker was particularly constrained by his father's political position. As I recall, his mother
had driven him to Switzerland, and I met her there for the first time. We
went rowing on a lake and talked about our friends and the old days. When
the subject of war came up, Carl Friedrich said, "Hitler's planes and tanks

---

[12] The 1939 conference dealt with the topic of low-temperature physics—which includes
the phenomenon of superconductivity—and is discussed in Chapter 14.

[13] King Báthory's nephew became prince of Transulvania, a part of Hungary.

don't work. None of the military equipment is any good. There is no possibility of war."

He was partly right. German armaments in the mid-1930s were poor. When Hitler occupied Austria two years later, his unopposed tanks broke down before they could reach Vienna; however, Nazi armaments improved at an incredible rate. In comparison, the armaments in France and England were obsolete. Carl Friedrich's conclusion was tragically wrong.

Earlier that spring, under pressure from Mici, I had taken an important step toward becoming Americanized: She insisted that we buy a car. I was firmly opposed to such extravagant nonsense, but Mici had the full weight of American society behind her. In particular, Larry Hafstad, Merle Tuve's senior associate, aided and abetted the plan. He selected the used Ford we bought and taught Mici how to drive. There was nothing I could do but learn to drive myself.

Shortly after I had succeeded (beyond my expectations) in passing my driver's test, we accepted Bethe's long-standing invitation to visit him in Ithaca. And so Mici and I, two novice drivers, slowly wended our way through the snow over unfamiliar roads to Ithaca.

Once there, we heard news of Peter Paul Ewald, one of my favorite Karlsruhe professors. I do not remember which member of his family had Jewish ancestry, but Ewald had decided to come to the United States about the same time Hans and I had. I had last seen his daughter, Rose, during my Karlsruhe days when she was a lovely fourteen-year-old in pigtails. Ten years later, she had become the focus of Bethe's romantic interests.

Hans and I wanted to attend a physics conference at Stanford during the summer of 1937. As it turned out, Rose Ewald and Hans invited Mici and me to accompany them as chaperones; and so we all piled into Hans's car and drove across the nation. Bethe and I loved the mountains. Our first extended stop was Estes Park, Colorado. Hans offered beginning lessons in mountain climbing, but we three were good only for extended hikes.[14] We then went on to the Tetons, where my student Charles Critchfield and his charming wife, Jean, joined us for a few days.

---

[14] Our cabin was not far from Bear Lake. That was the first of perhaps a hundred times that I walked from Bear Lake to Nymph Lake, which was a few hundred feet above. In 1937, I didn't meet anyone that I knew on that little hike. When years later I took the trail with my teenage children, I seemed to meet someone I knew every hundred feet. My son, Paul, enjoyed teasing me about my inability to remember the names of some of the people I chatted with.

Our next stop was Mount Rainier. On the day we attempted our climb, a thunderstorm burst on us when we were halfway up the mountain. We fled with the help of gravity, sliding down the gently sloping snowfield on our bottoms. Next, we admired Crater Lake—from the car, having run out of time—and then drove directly on to Stanford. Although I was looking forward to the conference, I was sad to see our small and wonderful company dissolve into the beehive of physicists.

Just before the conference at Stanford, Hans published an article in *The Review of Modern Physics*. He had written down everything he knew about nuclei (which meant everything that was known) so, of course, it was a massive piece. On our arrival, Fermi, who was there for a visit, greeted Hans with congratulations on his "mattoncino," literally, his little brick.

After the conference, Mici and I stayed on for awhile in Palo Alto. One afternoon, Fermi, Mici, and I decided to swim in the Pacific Ocean, a first for all of us, and we drove over to Half Moon Bay. The water was a bit cool, but this time, there were no big waves. Fermi and I busily paddled about while Mici watched from the beach. When Fermi headed for shore, I was ready to enjoy some sunshine, too. But after some minutes, I was more than a little surprised to discover that, hard as I worked, I was making no progress toward the shore. When I hollered, Fermi turned back, and with his moral support I managed, not without effort, to make it into shore. Our introduction to the Pacific had included meeting a riptide, although a gentle one.

Fermi had another first experience during our stay, when Mici and he went horseback riding. (I had begged off.) According to Mici, Enrico, once mounted, began in a most natural manner. He told the horse in a firm voice: "I am the boss." It worked.

I also met two Californians during that time. After the conference, Robert Oppenheimer invited me to give a talk at his seminar in Berkeley. I found talking with him very interesting, but dining with him was daunting. Before the seminar, he took me to an excellent Mexican restaurant with food so hot that I could swallow only a few bites. I also had a small difficulty during my first encounter with Ernest Lawrence. He took me out in his motorboat to look at the Golden Gate Bridge. I withstood the choppy waters with a little less than complete equanimity. Californians seemed to be more than I could handle comfortably.

When the Stanford conference was over, Rose and Hans had to return to the East Coast promptly, and Mici and I were elected to drive Hans's car back. Fermi also was in no hurry to get back, so Bethe invited him to ride back with us. A most welcome passenger, he also chose the route we were going to take.

First of all, Fermi wanted to see Los Angeles and Hollywood. When he found out that we knew a famous Hungarian living in that neighborhood, he was particularly pleased. Theodore von Kármán had come to the United States in 1930 when Guggenheim established an aeronautical institute in Pasadena. Both Mici's and my parents knew von Kármán well; but Mici, who had seen a great deal of him during her childhood, was much closer to him. Von Kármán had a well-deserved reputation as a free spirit, and innumerable stories attest to that characteristic. He had two postulates about *true* stories: One should not be unduly limited by the facts; one should never repeat a true story without improving it.[15]

Von Kármán was twenty-seven years my senior, but he was never so old that he failed to notice feminine charms, and he obviously found Mici attractive. He was quite displeased to learn that Mici remembered his name as "Uncle Theodore." (She enjoyed "accidentally" using it.)

While we were there, von Kármán talked about the great advances made recently in understanding aerodynamics, about the necessity of clean lines, and how even a single thin wire could severely disturb the air flow. He mentioned his visit to Chiang Kai-shek in Szechwan to offer advice on Chiang's air force. Chiang's residence was on the top of a mountain beyond the Yangtse gorges, and Fermi asked von Kármán whether he'd been afraid of flying in a Chinese plane. Von Kármán replied, "Not at all. I designed them. But," he went on, "I rode in a palanquin, carried on two long poles by four men. Going around the bends, I would be hanging over a chasm. Then I was terrified."

We were only a few miles away from Hollywood. Because Uncle Theodore knew everybody, a visit to watch a movie being filmed was easy to arrange. Fermi loved it. I was shocked by how the actors had to repeat over and over a scene lasting less than three minutes. To me, it seems amazing that any movie even vaguely resembles art.

---

[15] His explanation of why he transferred from Göttingen is one of my favorites. The Göttingen faculty wives, an esteemed group of ladies, met regularly for lectures. Von Kármán happened to attend when an Honorable Frau Professor reported on a trip to the Middle East and warned at some length of the perils of the white-slave trade. During the question and answer period, von Kármán raised his hand and asked, "Who buys Göttingen girls?" That, he explained, led to his move to Aachen.

Actually, von Kármán left Göttingen to join Prantl's fine aeronautical institute in Aachen. In the late 1930s, Göring invited von Kármán to return to Germany to help develop the Luftwaffe. Von Kármán took the letter around Pasadena, asking, "What shall I do? Send him a picture of my profile?"

Fermi knew that Oppenheimer was fond of the Southwest; so before we left, he had asked him about the route we should take from Los Angeles. Oppenheimer sent us through the Arizona desert, where we got lost, much to Fermi's alarm. When we finally met an old man who gave us directions, Fermi, an agnostic, called him "an angel sent by God."

We went on to explore Canyon de Chelly and Canyon del Muerto in the middle of Navaho country. I believe that the visit was prompted because Fermi's collaborator, Franco Rasetti, in spite of great interest, had not managed to get there during his trip. Near Canyon de Chelly, we camped in the yard of a building that resembled a cross between a school and a factory.[16] We all tried to guess what the structure might be. Fermi suggested that it was a special armed forces project. Six years later, of course, his joke had an eerie feeling of prescience. On Oppenheimer's advice (he owned a ranch nearby), we also visited Santa Fe and had lunch at La Fonda.[17]

Fermi had a few other worries during the trip. In the Midwest, he found a bedbug in his motel; that made it necessary to make a thorough search of both our rooms each night. As I was still a novice driver, Fermi was anxious to help with the driving. When he was not behind the wheel, however, he constantly admonished me. I can still hear him saying, "Zllllooooh!"

I do not consider myself a speed demon, but I have it from such varying authorities as my wife, my children, and my friends that my speed and attention to the road varies with my interest in the conversation inside the car: Increased interest yields increased speed and decreased attention. Fortunately, I caused no mishaps by my unintentional demonstrations of how much I enjoyed Fermi's company.[18]

The summer of 1937 was perhaps the best of a wonderful quiet period in my life. We had planned to return to Budapest the next summer, but in 1938 Hitler took over Czechoslovakia. Suddenly the world seemed ominous, and we dared not return to Hungary. Instead, Mici and I went first to Chicago, where I taught a term of summer school at the University of Chicago; then we went to Wyoming to join Hans and Rose in the Tetons. Our long hikes up to the saddle of the main ridge of the Tetons reminded me of my favorite mountains, the

---

[16] We discovered later that it was an Indian school.

[17] During the wartime years, lunch at La Fonda was a great treat for the workers confined to Los Alamos.

[18] I never have had a serious accident and have received only about five tickets in fifty years of driving. I got my last ticket in the 1980s as a result of taking Eugene Wigner to the airport: Our conversation overwhelmed my ability to determine where left turns were legal.

Tátras. In both those wonderful places, the peaks rise many thousands of feet straight up from the plains. Jenny Lake reminded me of Lake Csorba, a place that had captured my heart when I was twelve. In the Tetons, I missed only the many "eyes of the ocean" in the side valleys.

The crisis of Czechoslovakia was resolved that fall when Neville Chamberlain arrived home with his famous umbrella from the negotiations with Hitler. I remember reading a highly laudatory editorial in the British scientific journal, *Nature*.[19] It expressed delight at the "beginning of a new era in the history of the world" in which there would be "peaceful methods of settling disputes between nations." The paragraph at the bottom of the page, however, read:

> We hope and believe that the resolution now made between the German Führer and Chancellor and the British Prime Minister will have more lasting influence than that reached by Disraeli, of whose treaty it was said soon afterwards:

> *Once "peace with honour" home was brought;*
> *And there the glory ceases.*
> *For peace a dozen wars has fought,*
> *And honour's all in pieces.*

I turned the page, expecting to read on, but, as often happens in England, the reader was left to draw his own conclusions.

Papa Franck, about that time, would say: "It is unimaginable to have a war. Bombing from airplanes would end civilization." His outlook was bleak, and his comment, when one considers London, Hamburg, and Dresden, was not so far wrong. Although I was detached from public life, this did not prevent me from worrying about what would happen nor from wondering why the Americans didn't do something. Our worst nightmares would soon turn into reality.

During those years in Washington, I wrote prodigiously but I do not believe I published a paper by myself; indeed, I enjoyed the best of all pleasures, collaborating on scientific work with friends.

I remember in particular a letter that unfortunately has been lost. After I taught summer school in Chicago, an inquiry came to Merle Tuve asking if

---

[19]"The Promotion of Peace," *Nature* 142, 3597 (October 8, 1938).

I should be invited to be a professor of physics at the University of Chicago. Tuve showed me his reply:

> If you want a genius for your staff, don't take Teller, get Gamow. But geniuses are a dime a dozen. Teller is something much better. He helps everybody. He works on everybody's problem. He never gets into controversies or has trouble with anyone. He is by far your best choice.

I wish I had Tuve's letter framed on my wall today. I do believe it described me as I was during those happy years in Washington. I didn't receive an invitation from Chicago, but that didn't bother me. I had no further ambitions and no interest in changes.

14

FISSION

1939–1941

THE CHAIRMAN OF the physics department at The George Washington University, Dr. T. B. Brown, at first viewed Gamow and me, members of his department selected by President Marvin, with a dubious eye. After a few years, he relented a little as far as I was concerned, and our relationship became comparatively friendly. At the start of my fourth year, Dr. Brown showed his approval by asking me to give a talk about atomic theory to the faculty of the university; nonetheless, his confidence in me was less than absolute. Once I had agreed to speak, he set about examining my adequacy. Not before or since have I been so thoroughly drilled for a lecture. He even put me through a dress rehearsal.[1]

During the question period following my lecture, someone asked, "How long before a practical use of nuclear energy might be worked out?" I predicted, "It may take a year, a hundred years, or it may never happen." I was wrong. As I was speaking, two chemists at the Kaiser Wilhelm Institute in Berlin were beginning to examine the first key to unlocking nuclear energy. That key had been lying around unused for half a dozen years.

I have already mentioned that in 1932, Fermi had begun to bombard, systematically, all the elements with neutrons, a process that produces radioactive substances. He found that if a lightweight element captures a neutron, it produces a single radioactive element with a specific half-life. Heavier elements that have three or more naturally occurring isotopes may

---

[1] That led to a valuable lesson. When I continued talking as I was writing a formula on the blackboard, Brown interrupted me: "When your back is turned, shut up. Maintain eye contact with the audience when you are talking." Since then, I have.

produce several radioactive isotopes.[2] If a heavier element has fewer than three isotopes, neutron capture usually leads to one radioactive isotope, which then decays and may produce another radioactive substance.

During my visit to Copenhagen in 1935, I happened to hear a talk at Bohr's Institute given by Lise Meitner, an excellent physicist who was then working at the Kaiser Wilhelm Institute in Berlin. She was bothered by an inconsistency in Fermi's results. "Something odd," she said, "is going on with uranium. Why does uranium simultaneously produce dozens of radioactive substances when it should produce only one?" Fermi's interpretation of the multiple radioactivities was that new elements (called transuranics because they are heavier than uranium) had been produced. Meitner noted the oddity, but she did not challenge Fermi's interpretation.

In 1938, Fermi won the Nobel Prize for his work. He had become more and more uneasy about remaining in Mussolini's Italy. His father-in-law was a Jew who had retired from the Italian navy as an admiral. That a Jew held so high a rank accurately suggests that historically anti-Semitism was not endemic in Italy. But the Berlin-Rome axis had introduced the Nazi form of anti-Semitism. That completed Fermi's list of reasons why he had to take his family out of Italy. Leaving everything behind, the Fermis went to Stockholm to accept the Nobel Prize; they used the prize money to travel on to New York, where Enrico settled in as a professor at Columbia.

As 1939 began, I was looking forward to seeing Fermi at the fifth theoretical conference at George Washington University, scheduled for January 19–20. Much to Geo's and my pleasure, Niels Bohr, who had just arrived from Copenhagen to work for a few weeks at Princeton, was also going to participate in the program.

Bohr arrived at Gamow's home late in the afternoon the day before the conference began. An hour or so later, Geo called me in great agitation: "Bohr has gone crazy. He says uranium splits." That was all of Geo's message. Within half an hour, I realized what Bohr was talking about. If the uranium nucleus (the heaviest of the naturally occurring elements) were to split, it could split in a variety of ways. That would account for the many simultaneously produced radioactivities.

Meitner's question had been answered, the tool Szilárd had wished for was now available, and Nazi Germany might well develop a devastating new weapon. My sleep that night was uneasy.

---

[2] Radioactive isotopes are easily identifiable because they decay at different rates.

The subject of the conference was low-temperature physics and superconductivity, at that time an unexplained phenomenon. But Bohr was Bohr, and news is news. So Geo opened the conference by announcing (this time politely) that Bohr had something to say. Bohr then described the work in Nazi Germany, the conclusion that fission had occurred, and the decisive confirmation of fission in Copenhagen.

Two German chemists, Otto Hahn and Fritz Strassmann, had decided to investigate the properties of two products that resulted from uranium bombardment. One, called eka-iodine because of its resemblance to iodine, was a halogen; the other was eka-barium, its properties similar to those of barium, an alkali-earth metal.[3] But eka-iodine behaved so exactly like iodine that after a while, they began to suspect, correctly, that they were not dealing with a new element at all but with an isotope of iodine. The same was true of eka-barium; it was just a heavy form of barium. In December 1938, my friend Carl Friedrich von Weizsäcker, then working at the Kaiser Wilhelm Institute, had helped Hahn and Strassman decide that fission must have occurred.

Fission was an amazing discovery. Hahn had promptly written to his friend Lise Meitner, an Austrian Jew who had been forced to leave her position at the Kaiser Wilhelm Institute only a few months before. Meitner, together with her nephew-collaborator Otto Frisch, who was in Copenhagen, immediately designed an experiment to verify the news. If uranium split in two, the fragments would move apart at high speed and lose many electrons. The highly charged fragments would deposit an unusual amount of energy in a Geiger counter (charged-particle detector). Meitner and Frisch discussed their plan with Bohr before he left Copenhagen and wired the successful result of their experiment to him on board ship. Thus he arrived in New York full of the news. Shortly afterward, he came to Washington.

Yet for all that the news was amazing, the discussion that followed Bohr's announcement was remarkably subdued. After a few minutes of general comments, my neighbor said to me: "Perhaps we should not discuss this. Clearly something obvious has been said, and it is equally clear that the consequences will be far from obvious." That seemed to be the tacit consensus, for we promptly returned to low-temperature physics.[4]

---

[3] Elements, ordered according to their weight, show recurrent (periodically occurring) properties. The halogens (fluorine, chlorine, bromine, iodine) and the alkali-earth metals (beryllium, magnesium, calcium, strontium, and barium) are two of those families.

[4] I had glanced at Fermi during Bohr's announcement. Fermi appeared to be experiencing mixed feelings: pleasure at the explanation together with regret and frustration at having been so close to the discovery and yet missing it.

That evening, Merle Tuve invited the conference participants to visit the Department of Terrestrial Magnetism. There we watched him and his collaborators demonstrate the fission of uranium in a Geiger counter. Tuve, after Bohr's announcement, had rushed back to his laboratory and reproduced the Meitner-Frisch experiment in a few hours.

That the secret of fission had eluded everybody for all those years amazed me far more than the demonstration. In one of his experiments, Fermi had bombarded uranium with neutrons to observe the alpha particles that picked up extra energy from the neutrons. Because he carried out the experiment in a Geiger counter, the highly energetic fission fragments would have been unmistakable. But Fermi was a very careful experimenter. He covered his uranium with a thin sheet of inert material to stop the normal alpha particles (without the extra energy) in which he was not interested. That sheet also stopped the fission products, which had a short range but extremely high energy-density. Had Fermi forgotten to cover his sample even once, fission would have been discovered years earlier.

Physicist Paul Scherrer in Zurich had an even closer encounter with the discovery.[5] He bombarded thorium (another of Szilárd's favorite substances) with neutrons and saw the fission fragments that Meitner and Frisch had identified. But Scherrer wouldn't believe his eyes. He thought his Geiger counter was malfunctioning. What wasn't expected wasn't seen!

In 1939, I did not realize how fortunate it was that those slight changes in an experiment in Rome or Zurich did not occur. If fission had been discovered in 1933, work on the topic in Germany and the Soviet Union—two nations that took the military applications of science seriously—would have been well advanced by 1939. Under different conditions, the United States probably would not have been the first nation to possess nuclear explosives. Fermi, Scherrer, and Szilárd, in their different ways, had a profound and beneficent influence on history.

When our conference was over and Mici and I had collapsed agreeably into a well-deserved rest, the telephone rang: "This is Szilárd. I am at the Union Station. Please pick me up." Mici revived and came along, after making me promise not to invite Szilárd to stay with us. (Szilárd was a demanding houseguest, and Mici had worked hard during the conference.) But when we met him in front of the station, her first words to him were: "Would you like to stay with us?" Szilárd accepted with pleasure.

---

[5] Scherrer together with Peter Debye developed the best method for x-ray analysis of crystals.

When we got home, Mici took Szilárd to our small guest room. He sat on the bed, bounced a few times, and said in an unusually cautious voice: "I have tried to sleep on this bed before. The mattress is quite hard. Is there a hotel nearby?" Mici, with a bright smile, pointed out the window. "There is the Wardman Park Hotel (now the Sheraton Park) in our backyard." Half a century later, Mici was still boasting about her tact on that occasion.

Szilárd had found a position at Columbia but had not been invited to the conference (because low-temperature physics was not one of his interests). Nonetheless, he had heard the news about fission; it had spread through the world of physicists like wildfire. He was not surprised to hear that, apart from confirming fission, none of us at the conference had proceeded further. But Szilárd started where the conference had left off. "Now," he reiterated, "nuclear energy and nuclear explosions are feasible, provided only that, on the average, more than one neutron is emitted in the fission process."

Szilárd began designing an experiment to find out whether fission does produce additional neutrons. About a month later, I was playing a Mozart sonata on our landlady's substandard piano with an acquaintance who was a good violinist.[6] In the middle of the piece, Szilárd called from New York. In those days, long distance calls were unusual events at our house, but the message was more so: "I found the neutrons." When I returned to the piano, I knew that the world might change in a radical manner. The prospect of harnessing nuclear energy seemed chillingly real.[7]

Bohr had stayed in the United States to work at Princeton on the consequences of fission. His conclusion, however, was the opposite of Szilárd's: It would be practically impossible to use nuclear energy. By then, most theoretical physicists knew what was at stake. It is hard to separate wishes from conclusions, and Bohr had good reasons to hope that the nuclear age was not a possibility.

In his earlier work, Fermi had found that as a general rule, nuclei more readily capture slow-moving neutrons (because they spend more time nearby). But the neutrons produced by fission are fast-moving.[8] The loop

---

[6] I believe his name was ~~Burke. Mici liked his wife very much, and he and I shared a com~~mon taste in music. In politics, we disagreed. He favored the Soviet system, and not even the Hitler-Stalin pact opened his eyes completely.

[7] Of course, complete confidence and complete incredulity are both mistakes. But for me, and perhaps for many others, a definite way of imagining the future is natural.

[8] Neutrons ejected during a nuclear reaction move with approximately one-tenth the velocity of light and carry 2-MeV of energy. If those fast neutrons collide with nuclei repeatedly and are not captured, they slow until their velocity is only about ten times greater than that of sound. They maintain that velocity on the average because of the agitation produced by temperature.

needed for a chain reaction is this: Fissions produce neutrons, and neutrons produce fissions. Bohr observed, as expected, that slow neutrons increased the rate of fission. But because the rate of fission he saw was a hundred times lower than expected, Bohr guessed that only the rare isotope U-235 was involved. He concluded that the chain reaction would work in U-235 but would not work in natural uranium (which is almost pure U-238). Separating out the tiny fraction of U-235 would be incredibly difficult because isotopes have similar properties. Therefore, a chain reaction in uranium did not seem practical.

Bohr's basic ideas proved correct, but two possibilities still remained: Either separate the isotopes and use only U-235, or systematically slow down the neutrons. If a fast neutron strikes a uranium atom, the neutron usually exits without causing fission (albeit with less energy). When fast neutrons are slowed by a large factor, for example, by many collisions, they cause fission so effectively that the fission occurring in the tiny amount of U-235 present provides a sufficient release of neutrons to continue the chain reaction. That slow release does not lead to an explosion but to a nuclear reactor that is apt to produce both energy and a new element with important properties.

At the end of March, some of us met in Bohr's office in Princeton. In addition to Szilárd and me, the group included Eugene Wigner, our mutual friend from Budapest who was now a professor at Princeton; Victor Weisskopf, a refugee from Vienna now (I believe) working at the University of Rochester; and Johnny Wheeler, a young, modest, and very capable physicist, whom I had come to know in Copenhagen, where he and I were both newly married Rockefeller fellows. (Johnny was now working with Bohr on the paper that would eventually describe the fission process in considerable detail.)

The four of us who had worked in Germany knew well the excellence of the physicists who were likely to be considering similar questions about fission. We argued that, from now on, we should not publish the results of fission research lest the Nazis learn from them and apply them to making a nuclear explosive. Bohr, however, took the opposite view with deep conviction. "Openness," he said, "is the basic condition necessary for science. It should not be tampered with." He thought we were unduly alarmed: Separating the two forms of uranium and accumulating a sufficient quantity of U-235 would require efforts so huge as to be impractical. "You would need to turn the entire country into a factory," he declared.

He threw in another reason to oppose such secrecy: We were not the only people aware of the extra neutrons: Frederick Joliot had found them, too. "Joliot will not like the idea of secrecy at all. He has been hard at work on fission, and he was already disappointed over credit for the discovery of the neutron."[9] Eventually, Bohr gave in (a most unusual occurrence) to Szilárd's arguments. His one proviso was that Enrico Fermi also agree.

As Fermi's former traveling companion, I was delegated to talk to him. I drove to New York late that night. The next morning, Fermi listened patiently to my arguments. I did not expect that he would want to change the practice of complete openness. Fermi's natural inclination was to abide by conventions and not challenge generally held opinions, but I also knew that he had a truly open mind.

After I had introduced my case, I smiled at him and said, "The next time you find me in a riptide, you may give me a shove toward Japan." But after a little more gentle arguing, Fermi agreed to secrecy, again with one condition: He would not publish if everyone else agreed not to.

I was not a witness to the next part of the story. It seems Joliot got a telegram suggesting he not publish his results on fission; however, as the story (which may be apocryphal) goes, the wire arrived on April 1, and Joliot chose to consider it an April Fool's Day joke. He continued to publish with no compunctions. The verifiable facts are that Joliot was asked to hold up publication, but he published his findings.

Still, during the next few months, the idea that the results of fission research should not be published in the open literature spread. Secrecy was not forced upon us; it was established by tacit consent as the importance of the issue became obvious. In this instance, the scientific community was ahead of the government in realizing the danger of the discovery.

A few scientists tried to bring the possibilities connected with fission to the government's attention and to obtain government support to speed the research. Among the branches of the armed forces, the navy had the reputation of being most interested in technical matters. Merle Tuve, who knew his way around Washington, and Enrico Fermi, the foremost scientist working in the field, took the initiative of going to the navy. They got nowhere.

During the summer of 1939, I taught summer school at Columbia. I lectured graduate students, but I was invited primarily as a consultant-peacemaker on the Fermi-Szilárd chain reaction project. Fermi and Szilárd both had asked me to work with them. They were barely speaking to each other.

---

[9] Joliot, an extremely active physicist in the forefront of nuclear discoveries, had been the first person to produce artificial radioactivity. Joliot's work raised a question about priority in the discovery of the neutron, for which James Chadwick of Rutherford's laboratory is commonly given credit. Joliot was clearly interested in the practical possibilities connected with fission. Married to Irene Curie, Madame Curie's daughter, he worked at the Curie Institute in Paris.

Temperamentally, the two men were almost opposites. Fermi was an exceptionally conservative man; scientifically he was careful, methodical, and responsible. Szilárd was imaginative and flamboyant and lacked even an approximation of the qualities Fermi possessed and valued highly. Fermi seldom said anything that he couldn't demonstrate. Szilárd seldom said anything that was not startling and new. Fermi was humble and self-effacing. Szilárd could not talk without giving orders. Only if they had an intermediary could they be in contact with each other for any length of time. So Mici and I spent the summer in New York City as the missing link in the Fermi-Szilárd communication chain.[10] Because I admired and enjoyed working with both men and they were comfortable with me, I became a conduit of information, able to solve problems between them unobtrusively, sometimes even before they occurred.

Heisenberg visited us during that summer. My respect for him usually kept me from inquiring about personal matters. But this time, with the hope for appeasement in shambles and war around the corner, I asked Heisenberg why he didn't stay in the United States. His answer was simple and straightforward: "Even if my brother steals a silver spoon, he is still my brother." I would have liked to change his mind, but I could not find a way to present my arguments that would have fit our relationship.

In retrospect, it is clear that he, not yet forty years old, made a decision that marked a turning point in his life, before he realized how much more than a silver spoon was involved. Heisenberg had confirmed my belief that understanding was the most important function and the highest pleasure that life offered. During the years that followed, he endured profound and painful difficulties.

My other memorable guest that summer, Leo Szilárd, visited often. One day he asked, "Could you drive me to the end of Long Island to see Einstein tomorrow?" Szilárd accomplished the extraordinary, but he had not learned to drive. I told him I could. I knew the general purpose of the visit. Szilárd was determined to alert the government to the possibility of a fission weapon. He had decided to write President Roosevelt a letter, and he expected it to be read because he had convinced his more famous friend, Albert Einstein, to sign it.[11]

---

[10] Our apartment on 120th Street, close to the university, had two very large windows on the same wall. I observed, with proper amazement at the hydrodynamics of the phenomenon, that the air on hot days had the habit of blowing in one window and out the other.

[11] Szilárd and Einstein were well acquainted from their years together in Berlin. They even held a joint patent for a type of refrigerator, which, I am sure, was the least important of their accomplishments.

So one day early in August, we set out for Long Island. Unfortunately, Szilárd knew only Einstein's general whereabouts, not his address. Once we were in the right neighborhood, we began inquiring about the famous professor, with no result. Finally, we asked a little girl with long braids, about eight years old. She had never heard of Professor Einstein, but she knew a nice old man with long white hair. We were, she told us, almost in front of his house.

Einstein invited us in for tea, and afterwards, Szilárd produced a typewritten letter from his pocket.

Old Grove Road
Nassau Point
Peconic, Long Island
August 2, 1939
F. D. Roosevelt
President of the United States
White House
Washington, D.C.
Sir:

Some recent work by E. Fermi and L. Szilárd, which has been communicated to me in manuscript, leads me to expect that the element uranium may be turned into a new and important source of energy in the immediate future. Certain aspects of the situation which has arisen seem to call for watchfulness and, if necessary, quick action on the part of the Administration. I believe, therefore that it is my duty to bring to your attention the following facts and recommendations.

In the course of the last four months it has been made probable—through the work of Joliot in France as well as Fermi and Szilárd in America—that it may become possible to set up a nuclear chain reaction in a large mass of uranium, by which vast amounts of power and large quantities of new radium-like elements would be generated. Now it appears almost certain that this could be achieved in the immediate future.

This new phenomenon would also lead to the construction of bombs, and it is conceivable—though much less certain—that extremely powerful bombs of a new type, carried by boat and exploded in a port, might very well destroy the whole port together with some of the surrounding territory. However, such bombs might very well prove to be too heavy for transportation by air.

The United States has only very poor ores of uranium in moderate quantities. There is some good ore in Canada and the former Czechoslovakia, while the most important source of uranium is the Belgian Congo

In view of this situation you may think it desirable to have some permanent contact maintained between the Administration and the group of physicists working on chain reaction in America. One possible way of achieving this might be for you to entrust with this task a person who has your confidence and who could perhaps serve in an unofficial capacity. His task might comprise the following:

a) to approach Government departments, keep them informed of the further development, and put forward recommendations for Government action, giving particular attention to the problem of securing a supply of uranium ore for the United States.

b) to speed up the experimental work which is at present being carried on within the limits of the budgets of university laboratories, by providing funds if such be required, through his contacts with private persons who are willing to make contributions for this cause, and perhaps also by obtaining the cooperation of industrial laboratories which have the necessary equipment.

I understand that Germany has actually stopped the sale of uranium from the Czechoslovakian mines which she has taken over. That she should have taken such early action might perhaps be understood on the ground that the son of the German Under-Secretary of State, von Weizsäcker, is attached to the Kaiser-Wilhelm-Institute in Berlin where some of the American work on uranium is now being repeated.

Yours very truly,

Albert Einstein

Einstein read the letter with great care. He made only one comment: "This would be the first time that nuclear energy would be used directly instead of indirectly through the processes in the sun." That comment struck me, even before I had read the actual letter some years later, as a peculiar comment for the letter's author to make upon rereading it. The letter, no doubt, had resulted from conversations between Szilárd and Einstein, and probably between Szilárd and Wigner. But of the three, I suspect only Szilárd would have felt so free as to instruct the president of the United States in detail about what to do. Einstein signed the letter, and we left.

I heard that Szilárd gave the letter to Alexander Sachs, a banker and an acquaintance of Roosevelt's, who promised to have it delivered to the president.

That method of postal service proved slow but effective. Almost ten weeks later, a psychologically ideal moment occurred (after Hitler and Stalin had conquered and divided Poland), and the letter arrived. Roosevelt acted at once. The president set up an Advisory Committee on Uranium, and appointed D. Lyman Briggs, the head of the Bureau of Standards, its chairman.

Briggs called a meeting for October 21, and Sachs saw to it that Szilárd, Wigner, Fermi, and I were among those invited. But Fermi didn't want to attend, so I was again delegated to change his mind. On this occasion, however, Fermi could not be moved. His experience with asking for support from the navy had convinced him that he wanted nothing more to do with governmental meetings. "But," he told me, "I will tell you what I'd say if I were to go. You can deliver the message," Thus, I was promoted from chauffeur to messenger boy.

The army was represented at that meeting by a Colonel Keith F. Adamson from the Aberdeen Weapons Proving Grounds. After the initial presentation, Adamson began by voicing his doubts about novel scientific projects: "At Aberdeen, we're offering a $10,000 reward to anyone who can use a death ray to kill the goat we have tethered to a post.[12] That goat is still perfectly healthy. Furthermore, weapons have far less to do with winning wars than does moral superiority." His comment might have been inspiring except that the recent victory in Poland belonged to Hitler and Stalin; I could not associate moral superiority with either of them.

Szilárd and Wigner continued to press the case for supporting research on fission, and after some time, I was called upon. After stating that I was merely transmitting Fermi's message, I explained that the first necessary project was to construct a chain reactor. The researchers at Columbia would volunteer their labor, I noted (on Fermi's instruction); but slowing neutrons without absorbing them requires a great amount of exceptionally pure graphite, and that would be expensive.[13] "In fact," I added, "a sufficient amount of graphite would cost about $6,000." The committee promptly granted us $6,000.[14]

---

[12] Today, of course, the death ray is called a laser, but it was then only a theoretical concept.

[13] In a similar project in Germany, Walther Bothe, a highly reputable experimentalist, measured the absorption of a supposedly pure sample of graphite and found it too great. The Germans, blaming the absorption on carbon rather than on any impurity, changed to a reactor design that relied on heavy water, which was much more difficult to obtain under wartime conditions. The change was made without a careful reexamination of the graphite, a mistake uncharacteristic of Heisenberg, the director of the project.

[14] Considering that the eventual cost of the atomic bomb project (which was code-named the Manhattan Project) was $2,000,000,000, our funding was a modest beginning.

Emmi, fifteen years old, Madga Hesz, in her early twenties, and me at thirteen. 1921.

Graduating from the Minta, 1925.

Me, Emmi, my mother, Yoshio Fujioka, who was visiting on spring break, and my father, Max Teller, spring 1928.

Me, Professor Pogany of Budapest, and Mary Helen and Robert S. Mulliken visiting me in Budapest, about 1928.

On a hike, about 1928.

An unidentified student, me, and Felix Bloch in Leipzig, 1930.

Niels Bohr, probably about 1925.

In Budapest, early summer 1928. Laslo Tiza, Kató Keszthelyi (Nandi's sister), and me, bald, in one of my attempts to delay the bother of wasting time in a barber shop.

My friend Lev Landau, about 1929.

(Photo courtesy AIP Emilo Segre Archive, *Physics Today* Collection, reprinted with permission)

John Wheeler, looking as he did when we met in 1933.

(Photo courtesy of the AIP Emilo Segre Archive, Wheeler Collection, reprinted with permission)

My wife, Mici, and
me, newly and happily
married, in London, 1934.

Leo Szilárd and
Ernest Lawrence
in 1935.

(Photo courtesy of the
AIP Niels Bohr Library,
reprinted with permission)

James (Papa) Franck, about 1930.

Karl Herzfeld,
Maria Goeppert
Mayer, Joe Mayer,
about 1933.

(Photo courtesy of the
AIP Emilo Segre Archive,
Goudsmit Collection,
reprinted with
permission)

Me and Enrico
Fermi, with
Theodore von
Kármán at Cal
Tech during our
1937 trip.

(Photo courtesy of the
California Institute of
Technology Archive,
reprinted with
permission)

Robert Oppeheimer,
Enrico Fermi, and Ernest
Lawrence at the Berkeley
Radiation Laboratory,
about 1940.

(Photo courtesy of the
E. O. Lawrence Archive, reprinted
with permission)

Mici and me on the boardwalk of the Norfolk Ferry in 1940 in a picture taken by my student Harold Argo, who happened to be on that ship.

Some of the
housing barracks
in wartime
Los Alamos.

(Photo courtesy of the
Los Alamos National
Laboratory, reprinted
with permission)

Our son, Paul, in the yard
behind our apartment in
wartime Los Alamos.

In Fuller Lodge at Los Alamos about 1947, Norris Bradbury and me, talking at a party.

(Photo courtesy of the Los Alamos National Laboratory, reprinted with permission)

John von Neumann with his daughter, Marina, in Santa Fe in 1946.

(Photo courtesy of Marina Whitman, reprinted with permission)

In Fuller Lodge at Los Alamos about 1947, talking with Julian Schwinger (at the left) and Dave Ingles while my son, Paul, enjoys his favorite perch.

(Photo courtesy of the Los Alamos National Laboratory, reprinted with permission)

Mary Langs Argo in 1944 exploring the ancient Pueblo dwellings at Bandelier (now a national monument) near Los Alamos.

(Photo courtesy of Harold Argo, reprinted with permission)

Stan Ulam in a photo he gave me, about 1946. On the other side, Stan had printed, "to my enemy."

Emil (Kayski) Konopinski and Chen Ning (Frank) Yang in Kayski's laboratory in the late 1940s or early 1950s, listening to Lawrence Langer.

Harold Urey, in his laboratory in La Jolla, California, in 1958.

(Photo courtesy of the Argonne National Laboratory, reprinted with permission)

Mici and me in front of the "Teller Hotel" in March 1947.

John and Klári von Neumann at home in Princeton around 1954.

Mici and me at KQED, before the filming of the atom series, 1957.

After the meeting, Szilárd nearly murdered me for the modesty of my request; and Wigner, in his gentler way, seemed ready to assist him. My plea that I was merely quoting Fermi's figures did not moderate their attack. (In later years, my budget estimates were attacked for erring on the opposite side.)

The Bureau of Standards did its best to make sure that the graphite was pure; however, when Fermi and Szilárd began experiments using the graphite, they discovered that a reactor based on uranium and graphite would not work. Szilárd didn't like that conclusion and looked into the origin of the graphite. It turned out that between the time the Bureau of Standards ran its tests on a sample and the time the graphite was shipped to us, the plant had changed its method of fabrication. Szilárd, being Szilárd, insisted that a fresh supply of graphite be made under the previous conditions.[15] The trial of the uranium-graphite lattice-work reactor then began to look more encouraging.

During that academic year, the fission research at Columbia developed slowly. I was uncertain whether I wanted to remain a bystander or become a participant. I was content and pleased with the way my small world was running. I was a professor, as I had dreamed of being. Yet, although I was happy in academia, the possibility of the new weapon made me worry.

In early May 1940, together with a few thousand other scientists, I was invited to attend a Pan American Congress at which President Roosevelt was to speak. I did not plan to attend. In my five years in Washington, I had never visited the Capitol or seen an important political figure. Then, two days before the meeting, the phony war turned into a fast-moving conquest.[16] Using modern tanks and dive bombers to prepare the way, the Nazi armies swept triumphantly through Holland, Belgium, and Luxembourg. The Nazi Blitzkreig, the lightning-strike war, was terrifyingly effective. I decided to accept the invitation and hear the president.

President Roosevelt talked that day about inherent human rights and the blessings of democracy, and about the progress made through science and technology in conquering disease and poverty. Then he became more specific about the war:

> In modern terms, it is a shorter distance from Europe to San Francisco, California, than it was for the ships and the legions of Julius Caesar to move from Rome to Spain. . . .

---

[15] In Hungarian, the word *szilárd* can be translated as doggedly determined, or to put it less politely, rather stubborn.

[16] France and England had declared war on Germany a year earlier, but there had been no fighting in the interim; this led historians to use the term "the phony war" to describe the period.

You who are scientists may have been told that you are in part responsible for the debacle of today because of the processes of invention for the annihilation of time and space, but I assure you it is not the scientists of the world who are responsible, because the objectives which you held have looked toward closer and more peaceful relations between all nations through the spirit of cooperation and the interchange of knowledge. . . .

The great achievements of science and even of art can be used in one way or another, to destroy as well as create. They are only instruments by which men try to do the things they most want to do. . . .

Can we continue our peaceful construction if all other continents embrace by preference or by compulsion a wholly different principle of life? No, I think not.

Surely it is time . . . to use every knowledge, every science we possess, to apply common sense and above all to act with unanimity and singleness of purpose.

I am a pacifist. You, my fellow citizens of twenty-one American republics, are pacifists too.

But I believe that . . . you and I, if in the long run it be necessary, will act together to protect and defend by every means at our command, our science, our culture, our American freedom and our civilization.[17]

Seated in the crowd of thousands that day, I had the peculiar feeling that the president was speaking directly to me. Perhaps that is what is meant by charisma. But I also suspected that, out of all those present, the president and I were probably the only people who associated "using every knowledge, every science we possess" with the race for the atomic bomb.

I remember that at the end of his speech, I looked at my watch. Roosevelt's speech had taken twenty minutes, and in that time, he had resolved my dilemma. I was one of the fortunate helped to escape from the Nazi threat. I was now enjoying the comforts and many benefits of living in a democracy. I had the obligation to do whatever I could to protect freedom.

Not long after Roosevelt's address, I went off to give a Sigma Pi Sigma lecture series. The tour, planned weeks earlier, took me to various universities all over the Midwest, where I lectured about nuclear physics and its applications

---

[17] *The Public Papers and Addresses of Franklin D. Roosevelt with a Special Introduction and Explanatory Notes by President Roosevelt, 1940 Volume: War—And Aid to Democracies* (New York: MacMillan Co., 1941), pp. 184–187.

to astrophysics.[18] While I was traveling from campus to campus, the Nazi armies were sweeping through France. Every day, the situation looked more terrible. The brave resistance at Dunkirk provided the only little spark of hope, but in the midst of the Nazi victory, I hardly noticed it.

Throughout the tour, my feelings of deep concern and sorrow were echoed by the people with whom I talked, with only one exception. In Illinois, I was warmly received by Bob Serber, one of Oppenheimer's outstanding students. With well-founded enthusiasm, he showed me their betatron, a machine designed to accelerate electrons. But later, when I asked him about the most recent war news, he shrugged his shoulders. "The war," he said, "is a clash between capitalist interests." That was the first time I had met that attitude in an American.[19]

During the fall of 1940, the uranium project was given more emphasis, but Briggs's committee had a problem: Fermi, Wigner, Szilárd, and I were not citizens of the United States. Because the committee was considering top secret matters, none of us could attend its meetings. Yet, the Uranium Committee was discussing the results of Fermi and Szilárd's work, and our comments were often necessary. The problem was solved when we were made advisors. Official secrecy was already beginning to complicate scientific work.

Meanwhile, on the opposite side of the country, Ed McMillan and Glenn Seaborg had discovered two transuranic elements, neptunium and plutonium;[20] they had determined, as predicted, that plutonium undergoes fission as easily as U-235.

Back home in Washington, Mici and I, having fulfilled the residency requirement and sponsored by Merle Tuve and Ferdinand Brickwedde, were sworn in as citizens of the United States on March 6, 1941. Mici, I suspect, took this new permanency to heart, for within a month she had found a house for us to buy in the Maryland suburbs. Earlier that year, our landlady had told us that we had to move: She had decided to move back to Washington, D.C., permanently.

---

[18] I remember my stop at the University of Iowa, where I was thoroughly upstaged. The audience politely applauded when I went to the podium. During my talk, a dog wandered across the stage. He stopped, faced the audience, and wagged his tail. The audience then clapped and shouted with far greater enthusiasm than they had shown for me.

[19] Later, Serber worked diligently and efficiently at Los Alamos.

[20] After U-238 captures a neutron, the nucleus undergoes beta decay—the loss of an electron—and a neutron is converted into a proton. That results in the formation of an element with ninety-three protons, which was named neptunium. Seaborg determined that neptunium undergoes a second beta decay creating another element with ninety-four protons, plutonium.

Cloyd Marvin, the president of George Washington University, went to see the house; I suspect he wanted to make sure that no one was taking advantage of his immigrant employee. He reported that the house was a good investment. And so we bought our first house. We had saved a down payment of $1,000, but the total price was $9,000, a staggering debt in those days.

We had hardly moved into our new home when I was invited to Columbia for the following year.[21] On the surface, it seemed that I would be filling a teaching role similar to the one at George Washington; but I realized that the post was offered primarily because I was needed on the reactor project. The relationship between Szilárd and Fermi had not improved, and Hans Bethe, who had been helping for a few months, was going back to Cornell.

After I received the invitation, I went to see Harold Urey, who was already working on the Manhattan Project at Columbia. I wanted a clearer picture of what was going on and whether there really was a way for me to make a contribution there. Harold was simple and clear: "By all means, come," he told me.

Without further concerns, I made up my mind to join the work on nuclear energy and nuclear weapons. Did I know what I was getting into? Of course not. Do I regret my decision? No.

---

[21] We rented out our house throughout the war and for some months afterwards. I held my George Washington post by leave of absence, although I was transferred to Columbia, to University of Chicago, to Los Alamos. But at the end of 1945, I accepted an invitation to join the faculty at the University of Chicago, and we sold our house for $15,000, a considerable profit on our investment in little more than five years. Marvin had given us good advice. The house was a good purchase even though we were never able to live in it.

15

ACADEMICIANS
GO TO WORK

1941–1943

ARLY IN THE summer of 1941, Mici rented out our first house, moved
us to New York, and reestablished us in an apartment on Morningside
Drive. For about three months after the move, I dedicated every Sunday to
looking for a piano. In many respects, I am a terrible husband. I have no
ideas about decorating, clothes, or food, I have never entered a store or tailor
shop willingly, I cannot drive a nail into a wall (straight or crooked), and I
am baffled when the plumbing (or any other system or gadget) does not
work. In short, I am worthless both as a fixer and as a purchaser—except in
regard to a piano. There I am enthusiastically my own favorite expert.

During that summer, I played on hundreds of second-hand grand pianos
and fell in love with several that were too expensive. Eventually, I found just
what I wanted: a small concert grand (little more than seven feet long) with
a sweet voice and excellent key action. It was at least seventy years old, and
its original pillar-like round legs, which Mici would not have tolerated in
her home, had been replaced with more graceful angular ones. Because it had
a cracked sounding board, it was priced within our budget—$400. It re-
mains the only possession that I truly appreciate.[1]

---

[1]That Steinway has now been with us for more than fifty years. The Monster, as Mici called
it, has traveled from New York to Chicago, to Los Alamos, back to Chicago, back to Los
Alamos, back to Chicago, to Berkeley, and now resides in Stanford. The sounding board problem grew quite severe in the midst of those moves; as it cracked more completely, parts of it
rubbed on each other, so during our second stay in Chicago, I had it overhauled and repaired.
When the sounding board was screwed down solidly, no more rubbing occurred, and the
sound was lovelier than ever.

The move to Columbia brought a wonderful benefit—working with many excellent scientists. I especially enjoyed working closely with Fermi. The reactor group, which included my old friends Eugene Wigner and Leo Szilárd as well as Fermi, was considering how a reactor should be constructed. The reactor needed to be completed as soon as possible, but deciding its design was a challenge.

Several problems must be solved in achieving a chain reaction. As I mentioned earlier, the speed of a neutron determines whether it has a better chance of being captured in U-238 or of causing fission in the small fraction of U-235 present.[2] When a fast neutron is emitted in a fission process, the most likely result is that the neutron will collide with a U-238 nucleus and be absorbed. That stops the chain reaction (although the resulting heavier nucleus in the end turns into plutonium, a substance of great interest). Because slow neutrons are more likely to cause fission, the uranium should be surrounded by a moderator, a substance that slows the neutrons without absorbing them.

A neutron loses half its energy when it collides with a hydrogen nucleus (which is a proton and almost identical in weight). After twenty-five collisions, a fast neutron would be slowed sufficiently that if it then diffused back to uranium, it would be more likely to cause fission in U-235 than to be captured in U-238. Water, then, would seem to be an ideal candidate for a moderator.

Two difficulties exist with using water: The neutron may get back to the uranium before twenty-five collisions have occurred and be absorbed by U-238. The further difficulty is that hydrogen is a significant absorber of slow neutrons; thus, the neutron would again be lost to the chain reaction.

Either difficulty can be avoided, but not both. Using too little water, the neutrons arrive back at the uranium too soon. Using too much water, they are absorbed. Unfortunately, the compromise zone is too small to be practical. As contemporary reactors prove, if the uranium can be enriched with U-235, ordinary water can be used as a moderator.[3] But in 1941, we had to make do with natural uranium for fuel.

---

[2] Attaching a neutron to the U-235 nucleus produces sufficiently violent motion and vibration to break the nucleus apart. By contrast, a neutron attached to U-238 releases less energy and causes less motion.

[3] A couple of billion years ago, when U-235 (which decays faster than U-238) was more abundant, an appropriate mixture of uranium ore and water occurred naturally in West Africa and produced a reactor of this type by happenstance. That event is evidenced by an ore deposit in which the U-235 is depleted and fission products are present.

The solution was to use another moderator. The moderator chosen for the first reactor was carbon in the form of pure graphite. Because the carbon nucleus is much heavier than the hydrogen nucleus, a neutron loses less energy when it collides with carbon than it does with water, but 150 collisions will do the job. In sufficiently pure graphite, the neutrons can be appropriately slowed without being absorbed to a significant extent.

While the reactor work was going on, methods to separate the uranium isotopes were being sought, and I was a consultant on that project, too. Harold Urey was in charge of the separation project at Columbia, and some of my friends from the Baltimore seminar, including Joe and Maria Mayer, were part of his group. I met Bill Libby at that time, who was also part of the Urey project. Bill was about my age, and we began a series of useful and animated discussions that we continued until Bill's death forty years later.

Urey and his collaborators were designing a series of porous membranes through which to pass uranium hexafluoride. Because uranium hexaflouride is a gas at room temperature, the process involved circulating uranium fluoride gas through an immense number of membranes. The first batch of molecules to get through each membrane, being slightly richer in the lighter isotope, proceeded on to the next membrane; the bulk of the material was sent back to try again. The process can be compared to a school with an enormous number of repeaters; when they fail, they are demoted. Most of the molecules don't make the grade (almost pure U-238); the few molecules (geniuses) succeeding to the end are enriched U-235.

When the diffusion plant at Oak Ridge, Tennessee, began operation, the workers, uninformed about its purpose, shook their heads: "Funny machine. A lot goes in the front and comes back to the same place, but almost nothing comes out the other end." An enormous number of membranes were needed before that "nothing" could be accumulated in a sufficiently pure form.

While Urey's group was working in Chicago, Ernest Lawrence—the master of handling charged particles—was trying to separate the isotopes by electromagnetic means in Berkeley. Around 1940, he had acquired a new 184-inch magnet that he planned to use later in a new and more powerful cyclotron. After the war began, he put that magnet into service in a device he called the alpha-calutron. (Because U-238 has a slightly greater mass than U-235, it moves on a somewhat larger radius when deflected by a magnetic field.) A simple two-step process, in which the output from the alpha calutron separation was fed into a second (beta) calutron designed specifically for this final process would produce sufficiently purified U-235.

The first prototype calutron built on a hill above the Berkeley campus was replicated hundreds of times in the production facility at Oak Ridge (at Y-12), as was the second-stage (beta) calutron. When Urey's diffusion plants (the K-25 project) started to work, the alpha calutrons became obsolete, and the output of the diffusion process was fed directly to the beta calutrons. That was the process that produced the uranium for the gun-assembly atomic bomb.

At Columbia, I spent my time consulting with Fermi's and Urey's groups on various problems that arose, so while I was busy, I was not very deeply involved in any aspect of the program. The advantage was that I had a chance to work with all my old friends and get to know almost everyone working in the Manhattan Project at Columbia.

Formally, my job at Columbia was to lecture, which was a pleasure, and to work with graduate students, an even greater pleasure. The most outstanding of my graduate students at that time, Arthur Kantrowicz, became a lifelong friend. In 1941, Arthur was working as an applied scientist at Langley Air Force Base. He came to my office and showed me a pretty piece of work he had done on some processes in gases where the rapidity of the flow did not quite permit the molecular vibrations to come into equilibrium. He asked whether it would do as a doctoral dissertation. I said yes. He then inquired, "Would you sponsor it?"

I felt uncomfortable. Arthur knew much more about the subject than I did. But when I started to demur on that basis, he explained that he had gone to Fermi, who claimed to know nothing about the subject. Arthur pointed out that my work with Landau, and a recent note that Bethe and I had published, made it impossible for me to deny all knowledge of the subject. Thus, with a little reluctance, I agreed to be his faculty advisor.

Arthur later became an outstanding contributor in the practical use of hydrodynamics. Among his accomplishments are the design that allows a satellite or missile to reenter the atmosphere without burning up, the design of a carbon dioxide laser, and an understanding of the hydrodynamics of inserting a pump into the human aorta to assist the heart during a heart attack. This last invention has probably saved a million lives.

Another ingenious student from that period was Julius Ashkin. I remember our joint paper because it was mathematically the most complicated I have ever participated in. We proved a not very interesting theorem in physical chemistry by assuming that a famous unproved theorem (the four-color theorem) was true.[4] Thus my work at Columbia covered the futuristic, the practical, and the useless but delightful.

Almost every day, I had lunch at the faculty club with a group of coworkers. We usually spent that time talking about politics. Those of us in the immigrant community shared a particularly deep abhorrence of what Hitler and Mussolini were doing. Enrico and his wife, Laura, were saving a special bottle of wine to drink the day that Mussolini fell. Although our American friends were concerned, by and large they did not have the same depth of anxiety.

When I arrived at Columbia, Hitler was fighting deep in the Soviet Union. That attack had surprised all of us. We spent one noon hour speculating about where in the world a person might go to be safe from the ravages of the war. Fermi, who may have appeared prescient about secret government projects in New Mexico, suggested that a particular island group in the Pacific would be a good haven. Ironically, that region included Iwo Jima.

One day during that fall, while a group of us working on the reactor project were walking back to Pupin Hall (the physics laboratory), Fermi asked me whether I thought that an atomic explosion might be used to produce a thermonuclear reaction. Gamow and I had often discussed the thermonuclear process occurring in stars; however, such reactions are made possible not by the momentary heat caused by a neutron chain reaction but by consistently great heat and density near the center of a star. Fermi suggested that if deuterium (which reacts more readily than hydrogen) were used as the fuel, there might be enough heat near a fission explosion—for a very short time—to produce fusion.

I thought about that question for a week or so; and then, during one beautiful autumn Sunday afternoon walk with Fermi, I explained why the reaction wouldn't work: At the very high temperatures we expected, most of the energy would not be present as light but as x-rays. X-rays would be radiated away without bringing the nuclei and particles closer together; they were useless for carrying on the reaction. Fermi accepted my explanation.

Our closest friends that year, the Fermis, the Mayers, and the Ureys, all lived outside New York City, in Leonia; therefore, although we lived near the university, Mici and I did a considerable amount of commuting. One Sunday in December, Mici and I stopped to buy gas on our way to the Fermis. The gas station attendant was listening to a radio inside, and when he finally came

---

[4] The four-color theorem is easily understood: Four colors are sufficient to differentiate between the countries on any map without duplicating the color on any countries with a common border. Years later, the complicated proof of the four-color theorem was provided by an excellent group of collaborators, who found the help of modern computers decisive.

out to the car, he told us that Pearl Harbor had been bombed. "Where is Pearl Harbor?" I asked. So it was that we learned that the United States was at war.

On Monday, the laboratory was a changed place. Overnight, every trace of opposition to the war had disappeared. Everyone's commitment was now whole-hearted, open, and complete. The day before, I had inhabited a nightmare world of colossal dangers and uncertainties; now the world was full of problems that might have solutions.[5]

About a month later, the work on the reactor was transferred to a new location at the University of Chicago. The new undertaking had the cover name of the Metallurgical Lab. Most of the people I had been working with had been asked to move to the new site. My friend from Leipzig, Robert Mulliken, was in Chicago, and I began looking forward to joining the group there.

But I was not invited. Arthur Compton, who headed the theoretical division of the Manhattan Project, explained tactfully that I was not needed because all the theoretical problems connected with nuclear reactors had been solved. The real problem was that I could not be cleared for classified work. Although Mici and I were both citizens, our families were behind the enemy lines.

Then, late in the spring of 1942, I was asked to transfer to Chicago. I accepted right away. I learned later that Robert Oppenheimer had been responsible for the change in my status. After Oppenheimer had been asked to take charge of the theoretical studies for the design of the weapon, he was faced with a limited number of theoreticians with experience relevant to the task. Oppie then managed to obtain clearance for me and several other "unclearables."

When I arrived in Chicago, I was given the first security badge I had ever had in my life.[6] Because I was a late arrival to the work in Chicago, no one seemed able to figure out a role for me in the project, which by then was progressing nicely. Thus, I was told to do whatever I liked. Then I learned that Emil Konopinski (Kayski), who had just arrived after finishing his year of teaching at the University of Indiana, would help me in that onerous task.

I told Emil about Fermi's suggestion—that a fission weapon might produce enough heat to create fusion—and took out a handful of blank paper and said, "Here is the work that has been done on fusion." I then had a hard

---

[5] I have come to realize the great wisdom Roosevelt showed in his earlier restraint. In the history of the United States, World War II was the only conflict our nation has fought in a unified, single-minded manner.

[6] I got it from a smiling and beautiful Beverly Agnew, who, together with her husband Harold, were among the first settlers at Los Alamos. Harold became the director of Los Alamos in 1970 and filled that role in most able fashion for almost a decade.

time explaining that nothing was written on any of the paper. He finally understood that I was merely proposing the two of us prove conclusively that fusion wouldn't work so that no one else would ever need to repeat the effort.

This time, however, we found an objection to my earlier objection. The x-rays that I had assumed would siphon off the energy are not emitted at once. Perhaps the fusion reaction could proceed before too much of the energy was lost to x-rays.

Oppie convened a study group in Berkeley that summer to consider the relevant problems, and Kayski and I were invited to attend. As the study group was to begin in late June, Mici and I, having arrived late in Chicago, decided to stay in a hotel until we left for the conference. Hans Bethe was also going to Berkeley, and Hans and Rose stopped in Chicago so that the four of us could take the train to California together. By the time we reached Berkeley, Hans was equally fascinated with the possibility of a thermonuclear reaction. We decided to rent a house together in Berkeley for the duration of the conference, and soon found a beautiful place to share; it was so luxurious that I described it in my letter to Fermi a few weeks later as a "palace."

Nine of us attended the meetings held in a small room in LeConte Hall—Oppie, Bethe, Kayski, John van Vleck, Felix Bloch, Stanley Frankel, Eldred Nelson, Robert Serber, and me. After a day or so of discussing the fission bomb in a superficial way, everyone decided that the problems looked straightforward. We proceeded with some excitement to find out whether we could make a thermonuclear reaction proceed. During the next few weeks, we convinced ourselves that it could be done.

During the conference, Oppenheimer left Berkeley to meet with Arthur Compton. I discovered in the mid-1980s the reason behind that meeting had two versions. The widely disseminated version seems to have its source, at least in part, in Arthur Compton's memoir:[7]

> One July week-end my wife and son and I broke away from the pressure of the Met Lab for a quick refresher at our summer cottage in northern Michigan. As our car pulled into the local store where the keys were kept, the phone was ringing. It was a call to me from Berkeley. Oppenheimer and his group had found something very disturbing. How soon could he see me? I gave him the directions and told him I would meet him at the train the following morning.

---

[7] Arthur Holly Compton, *Atomic Quest: A Personal Narrative* (New York: Oxford University Press, 1956), p. 127.

I'll never forget that morning. I drove Oppenheimer from the railroad station down to the beach looking out over the peaceful lake. There I listened to
his story. What his team had found was the possibility of nuclear fusion—the
principle of the hydrogen bomb. This held what was at the time a tremendous
unknown danger. Hydrogen nuclei, protons, are unstable, for they could combine into helium nuclei with a large release of energy. To set off such a reaction
would require a very high temperature. But might not the enormously high
temperature of an atomic bomb be just what was needed to explode hydrogen? And if hydrogen, what about the hydrogen of sea water? Might the explosion of an atomic bomb set off an explosion of the ocean itself?

Nor was this all. The nitrogen of the air is also unstable, though in less degree. Might it not be set off by an atomic explosion in the atmosphere?

These questions could not be passed over lightly. Was there really any
chance that an atomic bomb would trigger the explosion of the nitrogen in
the atmosphere or of the hydrogen in the ocean? This would be the ultimate
catastrophe. . . .

We agreed there could be only one answer. Oppenheimer's team must go
ahead with their calculations. . . .

In due time, the calculations gave the firm result that while the nuclei of
hydrogen and nitrogen are indeed unstable, the conditions under which they
can explode are far removed from anything that can be brought about by
atomic explosions.

We were not told that Oppenheimer's trip to see Compton was related to
the possible ignition of the atmosphere or the sea. The question of igniting
the atmosphere, if it was mentioned at all, was not discussed in any detail at
the summer conference. It was not an issue.[8]

Oppenheimer did indeed go back to Michigan to talk with Arthur Compton during the conference. But Oppenheimer led us to believe that the meeting had been planned in advance of the conference, and that he would also
report our exciting results. When he returned, Oppenheimer told me that he
had given the hydrogen bomb as an example to show Compton that the
developing novel possibilities were further reasons for establishing a laboratory to work on weapons design.

Many American physicists at that time, Arthur Compton among them,
had little familiarity with quantum mechanics; their ability to assess the

---

[8] The question was discussed in detail in 1945 in connection with the atomic bomb test.
(See Chapter 18, p. 210.)

possibilities and probabilities of nuclear reactions, therefore, was limited. It is possible that Compton was simply confused about what Oppenheimer had said. No one will ever know for sure.

It is certain, however, that Oppenheimer discussed a thermonuclear explosive with Compton, and that the topic did illustrate the extended scope of possibilities that could best be explored in a new, separate laboratory. It was after Oppenheimer's meeting with Compton that I first heard that such a lab might be established, with Oppenheimer as its director.

The summer conference was the first time I had really worked with Oppie. He was an excellent theoretical physicist, and I enjoyed his company professionally and socially. I was pleased when, during the conference, Oppie and his wife, Kitty, invited us for dinner at their home. I brought along a recording of my favorite Mozart concerto as a hospitality gift; however, Oppenheimer found the recording uninteresting.

The dinner gathering included another couple from Berkeley who were close friends of Oppenheimer's. My only certain recollection is that they were pleasant company, they were not scientists, and they were considerably left of center. I believe that they were Haakon Chevalier and his wife.[9]

Oppenheimer, like most of us, was fascinated with the idea of harnessing atomic energy, and during dinner we all discussed the idea. I was not at all surprised or alarmed by the dinnertime exchange; it considered in layman's generalities the possibility that such a weapon could be developed. I remember specifically Oppenheimer's prediction that only an atomic bomb could dislodge Hitler from Europe. He made the statement in much the same manner as one would state a scientific absolute. I did not disagree. It just surprised me that his belief was so complete.

At the end of the conference, Mici and I returned to Chicago. We couldn't find a furnished apartment, so we ended up taking an unfurnished place. But the only furniture we owned was the Monster. Resourceful Mici discovered that the Congress Hotel of Chicago, which had been taken over by the army, was selling all its solid oak furnishings. Mici was not only the sole amateur at the sale (all the other buyers were jobbers) but also the only woman.

A few of the jobbers helped her buy beds, several easy chairs, a sofa, a dining room table and chairs, a buffet, and several smaller tables, all for a reasonable price. She was appropriately pleased with her purchases; they have served us for more than half a century. Not much later, she made one

---

[9] An incident involving Haakon Chevalier proved to be crucial to Oppenheimer's being denied clearance in 1954. See Chapters 30 and 31.

purchase that seemed a bit extravagant to me—an automatic clothes washer and drier. But Mici claimed a point of privilege: She was expecting our first child.

Pearl Harbor had marked a turning point in our lives. The storm cloud that had driven us from Europe had created a seemingly impenetrable darkness. The Nazis had captured Poland, Belgium, Holland, Denmark, Norway, France, and now were at the gates of Moscow. With his willing allies in Austria, Hungary, and Italy, Hitler and Nazism dominated Europe; there seemed little possibility of stopping the spread of that horror. Mici had been convinced that it was wrong to bring a child into such a world, but when the United States entered the fight, she changed her mind: She was immediately convinced that Hitler would be defeated. A few months later, she was pregnant and buying furniture.

Back in Chicago after the conference, everyone was talking about the laboratory that was to be established at Los Alamos. Because I was very interested in the problems connected with the fission and fusion bombs, I was considering transferring to the new facility. When I mentioned this to Eugene Wigner, he argued against it: The only real problem was obtaining the material for the fission bomb—the rest would be easy and obvious. There was no need for a separate laboratory to develop the new weapon. Once reactors were producing appropriate amounts of plutonium, the problem would be solved.

Eugene was not the only person with that opinion; many other distinguished scientists were of the same mind. I disagreed. Constructing a nuclear weapon didn't look simple to me, and producing plutonium didn't look difficult. But because so many people thought Eugene was right, Oppie had to do some recruiting during the early fall of 1942, and he stopped in Chicago.

In a conversation with several of us working on the project in Chicago, Oppenheimer made a point about the position of the physicist in society. He recalled the painful experiences that physicists had encountered during the depression years—that physicists had even been forced to perform unskilled labor. He reminded us that, in general, physicists were not considered important contributors. "But, if the work on the atomic bomb succeeds," he asserted, "physicists will never again be held in such low regard."

Such a motive for working on a bomb would never have occurred to me. The remark disturbed me (which explains why I have remembered it all these years). Because the issue of Germany's acquiring an atomic bomb was so grave, the statement seemed inappropriate. Such a motive disregarded international affairs and emphasized only personal interest. Should we work on such a bomb simply to be taken seriously as physicists if the weapon was not in the national interest?

During Oppenheimer's visit, Mici and I invited him to have dinner with us, and afterwards he and I went walking along Lake Michigan. We had been chatting about other topics, when suddenly Oppie said, "You know, I am having trouble with my security clearance. Kitty has relatives who are high-ranking Nazis."

The clearance I needed to move from Columbia to the project in Chicago (the Metallurgical Lab, as it was called), had, as I mentioned earlier, been denied for several months. The reason, Urey told me after my arrival, was because Mici's and my family lived in an enemy country. That made it easy for me to believe that Oppenheimer's spousal ties could create a problem. But the comment bothered me a little. I had not thought of Kitty as having German roots. The comment was most memorable, however, because of its completely out-of-the-blue nature. There was nothing in our discussion that had suggested it.[10]

A little later in the fall of 1942, Oppie and I traveled together to Washington. I have forgotten what the purpose of that trip was, but we shared the same first-class train compartment. As we traveled, we talked about the prospects of the Manhattan Project, about the unnecessary obstacles presented by some aspects of secrecy, and about the new laboratory, which was in the planning stage.

The army had taken over the Manhattan Project, and General Leslie Groves of the Army Corps of Engineers, the officer who had been in charge of constructing the Pentagon, was made its commander. Oppie complained about having to work with Groves, whom he considered awful.

I remember clearly one detail of those discussions. I was trying to put a bandage on one of my fingers where a hangnail had become infected, and Oppie had come over to lend me a hand. Continuing the conversation, he said, "We have a real job ahead. No matter what Groves demands now, we have to cooperate. But the time is coming when we will have to do things differently and resist the military."

I was shocked. The idea of resisting our military authorities sounded wrong to me. "I don't think I would want to do that," I said. Oppie changed the subject immediately. I believe that the relationship between us changed at that

---

[10] I never again heard that Kitty had Nazi relatives. It is not impossible that Oppenheimer meant to say communist relatives and misspoke.

instant. Oppie continued to be friendly, and he continued to encourage me to come to Los Alamos, but the warmth of our conversations vanished and never returned.

Perhaps I overreacted. Perhaps, if I had continued the conversation and probed for the point behind his remark, I might have obtained a better understanding. But Oppenheimer did not invite further questions or offer clarification. Probing would have been discourteous, so I did not ask. The incident merely contributed to my impression of the complexity of Oppenheimer's personality.

During the fall of 1942, the fighting continued in Africa and Russia without much change. Although Eugene Wigner and I did not work together, we still saw each other about once a week. Eugene was deeply pessimistic. When the Nazi offensive was halted at Stalingrad, he continued his lament: "The news is terrible, terrible. The Nazis have lost a fortified position here or there, but that will make no difference."[11]

When I next saw Eugene, the Nazi armies, surrounded at Stalingrad, were about to surrender. His mood, however, had not changed: "The news is terrible, terrible. What kind of a peace shall we make?" Most people, including me, were cheered by the Nazi defeat but were far from seeing the distant prospect of victory and peace as more than a dream of paradise. Sometimes, even Hungarians find Hungarians hard to understand.

A few days before the first anniversary of Pearl Harbor, on December 7, 1942, Fermi succeeded in producing the first controlled chain reaction. The first reactor was an uranium-graphite lattice, although there was not enough metallic uranium to make it a simple metal-graphite lattice. The central region was metal and graphite, but some of the regions toward the outside consisted of uranium oxide and graphite.[12]

Many safety precautions were taken. The neutron-absorbing rods were withdrawn very, very slowly. The number of neutrons emitted was measured with great care. The neutron-absorbing rods were set to be put back instantly, should anything go wrong. And on top of the pile of uranium and graphite stood a slightly jittery individual, holding a vessel containing cadmium solution (a very strong neutron absorber that would destroy the effectiveness of

---

[11] The comment is free translation of what I remember him saying in Hungarian.

[12] Uranium metallurgy was in its infancy, and therefore, because the process of turning uranium oxide into metal was so painstaking and slow, oxide had to be used to complete the fuel supply.

the graphite if used), which he was prepared to pour over the reactor should things get out of hand.

But not a drop was needed. All went according to plans and theory. Fermi could play with the new toy at will, and the famous cryptic message flew from Chicago to Washington: "The Italian navigator has landed. The natives are friendly."

Within two months of Fermi's news of "landing," Mici and I had some exciting news: On February 10, 1943, our first child, Paul, was born. Our Chicago friends were pleased for us and did their best to share our happiness. We only wished that we had a way to tell the grandparents about their new status.[13] In comparison to the tragedies of political oppression and war, such a detail can hardly be considered important. Paul's birth was really sufficient joy in itself.

Toward the end of March, construction on the laboratory at Los Alamos, now called Project Y, had advanced far enough that the scientific staff could assemble. Kayski, Nick Metropolis, a student of Mulliken's who had transferred from Urey's project, and I were all planning to go out. Kayski and I decided to drive our cars out, and Nick could not leave until he finished a last piece of work a few days later.

I loaded a few belongings into my black Plymouth, said my goodbyes to Mici and baby Paul (they would follow by train in a few weeks), and set out for the Southwest. A few days later, I crossed the Rio Grande on the small rickety Otowi bridge and approached a place, both peculiar and outlandish, that became dear to many who lived there. But I was moving to Los Alamos willingly, and the change seemed less dramatic than had some of my other migrations.

---

[13] My mother was the only grandparent who saw either of our children. That happy event occurred seventeen years later.

16

Settling In
at Los Alamos

March 1943–November 1943

I WAS A seventeen-year-old student at the Los Alamos Ranch School in 1942. I remember when the bulldozers came through to remake the school. About December that year, two men showed up at school, and we were required to say our yes sirs to a Mr. Jones, who was wearing a fedora, and to a Mr. Smith, who was wearing a porkpie hat. The names were obviously pseudonyms. Not only was everybody showing them great deference, but Mr. Jones seemed most uncomfortable every time someone referred to him by that name.

The four of us who were seniors had studied physics. The pictures in our physics textbook made it easy for us to recognize Mr. Jones as Ernest Lawrence and Mr. Smith as Robert Oppenheimer. Furthermore, the discovery of fission had been big news. In fact, we were even aware of the idea of a chain reaction.

Clearly, the school was about to be converted to a laboratory to work on a very secret physics project. Why else would top physicists be visiting a place out at the end of nowhere with no water, no roads, no facilities? What was really going on was obvious! We were secretly amused by the pretense.

Mr. Smith gave the commencement speech for my class late that winter. It was extremely gracious, but somehow I didn't believe a word of it. By then the school had told us that the government was taking over the school for the war effort and that we shouldn't discuss it after we left. We were sad to have to leave, but we didn't talk.[1]

---

[1] In a free society, individual common sense is far more effective in preserving security than any number of rules.

Thus my friend Stirling Colgate recounted his memories of the founding of the laboratory in an interview. The two physicists from the University of California, Berkeley, were both involved in selecting Los Alamos, but the person who was instrumental to its beginnings, who inspired every aspect of its development, and whose leadership was indispensable to its success was Robert Oppenheimer.

A few months after Oppenheimer had replaced Gregory Breit as leader of the weapon design group, General Leslie Groves was appointed head of the Manhattan Project. From the beginning, Groves liked and appreciated Oppenheimer, and plans for a separate laboratory to design weapons got underway within a matter of weeks.

Oppenheimer had spent time in New Mexico for many years and even owned a ranch east of Santa Fe. He had discovered the Ranch School, a small, exclusive boys' preparatory school, some years earlier while on a horseback pack trip. It appeared to meet all the requirements for the secret lab: It was in a largely uninhabited area and had housing for the thirty or forty scientists who would be needed; in addition, there were several small outbuildings for laboratories, a large building for a dormitory, and Fuller Lodge, an imposing two-story log hall that could house visitors and serve as a dining hall and a setting for social events. Most important, the school was located on top of a mesa, which meant that access to the site could be easily controlled.

The army acquired the school and the few other privately owned ranches in the region in December. But within weeks, the original estimate that 30 people would be needed for the project had been increased to 1,500 people. By the end of the war, Los Alamos held 10,000 people, most of them active workers! I believe that not even Oppenheimer dreamed we would reach that size.

During the winter, Oppie had asked me to help him with recruitment. As part of that task, I wrote a description for a prospectus without having seen the laboratory grounds; I mentioned among other things that the school was built around "a small lake." When I arrived, I came face to face with that body of water: It was and is, in the best of times, a pond.[2] Fortunately, those whom I unintentionally led astray preferred teasing me to being angry.

The first thing I noticed on arriving was that we were all going to be locked up together for better or for worse: The one road up the mesa was barely passable; once we were on top we were confined to the immediate

---

[2] The little pool is named after Ashley Pond, the founder of the Los Alamos Ranch School, which makes it Ashley Pond Pond. However, it is called Ashley Pond.

grounds by barbed wire. Our badges were checked by guards when we entered; our mail was censored; our privacy became a distant memory. Los Alamos, I soon realized, gave one a new appreciation of grass and strangers.

Few of the buildings were completed yet, so together with some of the other early arrivals I was put up temporarily in the Big House, an impressive barn-like building to the east of Fuller Lodge.[3] The beautiful grove of poplar trees, for which Los Alamos was named, stood nearby.[4]

One of the other residents of the Big House was a young, extremely able physicist, Richard Feynman. I can hardly think of that earliest period without recalling the sound of bongo drums: Feynman, just out of graduate school, played them for hours each night. At that time, his fiancée was suffering from tuberculosis and was in a sanitarium in Albuquerque; she died before the war ended. So for him, the security rules that kept us from leaving the laboratory grounds were a particular trial, and the censorship of the mail almost the last straw.

Feynman seemed to be composed in equal parts of physicist and humorist.[5] Laundry and dry cleaning facilities, like most other services, weren't available at Los Alamos until the war was almost over. Feynman's fiancée made arrangements for his laundry to be done in Albuquerque, and at one point he sent her his laundry list. However, the censors decided that the list was some sort of code and called Feynman in for questioning. After that, he devoted considerable effort to bedeviling the security people with everything from working out codes to communicate with his fiancée about various mundane matters to demonstrating that he could get into every locked vault in the laboratory.

Some of the four-unit apartment buildings for families were completed by mid-April when Mici arrived with our prize possessions—six-week-old Paul, the piano, and the washing machine—and our less remarkable goods, including our magnificent furniture with fake worm holes from the Congress Hotel. We immediately moved into an apartment in a fourplex situated near the edge of the mesa.

---

[3] My two bachelor friends from Chicago, Nick and Kayski, had to live at a neighboring ranch and commute up the mountainside on an only slightly modified goat trail until the first dormitory was finished some weeks later.

[4] Unfortunately, after the war, the trees (and the Big House) were leveled to make way for a shopping center.

[5] See Richard Phillips Feynman, *Surely You're Joking, Mr. Feynman* (New York: W. W. Norton, 1985).

The apartments had two bedrooms, but all the rooms were rather small. The nicest thing about them was that, at Oppie's insistence, they had very large closets, a special blessing for families like us, whose gear far exceeded the space in the rooms. Mici's feeling of claustrophobia had a further cause than the apartment size: Although we could not see it from our apartment windows, a barbed wire fence stood within a hundred yards of our back door; it was intended primarily to keep unwanted visitors out but it also served to keep us in. (Given the declivity of the canyon wall, only a young mountain goat would have found the transit easy.)

Mici had not wanted to come to Los Alamos. She was not fond of Oppenheimer, and the idea of living in a closed facility in an isolated desert region did not appeal to her. "What a place for our baby to grow up," she exclaimed somewhat indignantly, "surrounded by a barbed wire fence." But eventually Mici had a different insight on the subject. One night after the war had ended, I came home to find her most upset. Because strict security measures were no longer necessary, the fences had been torn down that day. With Paul now a three-year-old toddler, her lament was: "What shall we do? Without the fence, Paul will fall off the cliff."

By the end of the war, our Spartan apartment looked lavish in comparison to the small Quonset huts and trailers that had been called into service as housing. However, not only were the former faculty homes assigned to the higher ranking administrators and scientists more prestigious but they possessed the ultimate luxury, reflected in the nickname for that housing area: Bathtub Row.

A further source of unhappiness was the limited availability of domestic help. Mici, like most of the wives, eventually went to work at the laboratory (in the computations division) because of the terrible shortage of personnel. With Paul a baby, she had to have help to do so. At that time, household helpers were in such short supply that they were rationed. Their assignments, determined on the basis of need, were made in part by Kitty Oppenheimer (who had a full-time maid). Yet, in spite of the inconveniences and petty frictions, many of the men and women (including Mici and me) who worked and lived in wartime Los Alamos have a deep fondness for that spot.

The majority of people were under the age of thirty, perhaps even under twenty-five, and the intensity with which we were pursuing our goal combined with the isolation and primitive living conditions led to great informality, both in manners and in dress. I remember that the first party at Fuller Lodge, held in May or June, came to be known as the Necktie Party, because the invitations read, "Wear a necktie if you have one."

Our apartment was on the ground floor, and Cyril Smith, a metallurgist, and his wife, Alice, were our upstairs neighbors. Alice, who had a fine sense of humor, was very sweet and often helped Mici with Paul. I also liked Cyril, whom I had met when I briefed him about the work at Los Alamos.

The Smiths approved of their neighbors in a more limited way. One morning, Cyril told me that if Paul screamed one more night the way he had screamed the previous one, he would be happy to strangle him for us. And although he never complained to me directly about my habit of relaxing at night by playing my piano, I later heard that Cyril, an early-to-bed-and-to-rise sort of person, would have found less of my music more enjoyable.

Felix Bloch, the friend from Leipzig with whom I had corrected papers, his wife, Lore, and their three sons moved into the apartment next door to ours. Felix had emigrated to the United States, rather than returning to Switzerland, when Hitler's policies had made him unwelcome in Germany. But almost from the beginning, the Blochs had difficulties at Los Alamos.

Not long after they moved in, I heard that General Groves objected to having Hungarian spoken in Fuller Lodge. Mici and I were the only people living in Los Alamos who spoke Hungarian, and we spoke it only in our apartment, so I couldn't understand the reason for the complaint. The explanation was that the Blochs's twin sons had been speaking a Swiss-German dialect at the lodge, and Groves had confused that strange language with one even more peculiar.

My feelings about Groves, by comparison to those held by many others, were neutral. The first time Oppie brought Groves in to speak to an assembly of about forty scientists, I happened to be sitting next to David Inglis, whom I had recruited. At the end of Groves' talk, Inglis commented about how out of place Groves seemed. I didn't disagree, but I wondered what Inglis had expected him to say. To me, Groves's speech seemed about what would be expected from a person who knew nothing about the project he was supervising.

In time, I have come to appreciate many things about Groves, particularly his common sense in handling his bunch of eggheads and their wives. The army routinely leveled every bush and tree within two hundred feet of a building site before beginning construction, thereby destroying whatever attractiveness the immediate surroundings had. Yet, throughout the war, our apartment building had a pretty stand of pines growing between us and the canyon. I learned how that small blessing came about in 1989, through an interview that Lois Bradbury, the wife of Norris Bradbury, who served as director of Los Alamos from 1946 to 1980, graciously gave my collaborator.

On the morning that bulldozers had appeared to level the area near our apartment as part of the next construction project, Mici had spread a blanket under the trees and settled herself, Paul, his diapers and bottles, and a picnic lunch on it. The young soldier responsible for the bulldozers asked her politely to move; Mici, just as politely, refused. He leveled the rest of the surroundings and returned to ask again—to no avail. Finally the soldier went to General Groves for advice. "Leave the trees," Groves grumbled on learning about the situation. I know of no other case where our general deferred to a civilian, but Groves's engineering expertise seems to have included a little knowledge about human engineering.[6]

Not long after Groves's first speech, Oppie called a meeting for the forty or so physicists working on Project Y. He announced that too many of us, being foreign-born, couldn't be cleared, so he had worked out a compromise procedure with Groves: We would clear each other by writing down what we knew about each other. "Write down why each of you in the group is reputable," Oppie instructed us, "whatever reputable may mean." Oppie had earlier reported General Groves's instructions to him: "You will be collecting the world's prize crackpots here. Take good care of them." Groves may have considered us crackpots; it was clear that Oppie considered Groves something slightly less desirable.

The newly established laboratory procedures were as strange as our setting. Almost all of us were accustomed to an academic atmosphere, to having time to sit and think quietly by ourselves, to nurturing a novel idea slowly, and to casual chats with colleagues. But at Los Alamos, almost constant collaboration was necessary, all the work was done at a feverish pace, and one's new good idea, once hatched, could be taken away and given to others to develop (which, for many scientists, felt a little like giving one's child to someone else to raise).

In addition, theoretical physicists, unused to considering the practical, had to involve themselves in engineering problems. Everything about the project was novel. While one group of scientists worked to develop a supporting theory, other scientists struggled with the practical details for the execution on the basis of the current best guess in the hope of completing the project at the earliest possible time.

One of the first jobs Oppie assigned me, a job that continued throughout the war, was to brief incoming scientists on the nature of our work. Because

---

[6]When I asked Mici why she had not told me about the incident at the time, she said, "I didn't think it was that important." Mici, as I have mentioned before, has always been an independent spirit.

of the secrecy of the project, many of the scientists—for example, the metal-lurgists who would be working on uranium and plutonium—had only general suspicions about the purpose of the project when they arrived.

But one change that would have been a most damaging departure from our customary academic habits did not come to pass. The security officers tried to forbid discussion of problems among the scientists working on different aspects of Project Y. Oppie fought hard for an open exchange so that everyone could contribute, and he won. With that concession, Oppie gave me a second assignment: to organize a weekly colloquium to share progress and problems. I was in charge of those meetings, held Tuesday nights in the multipurpose hall (which was at other times our movie theater, playhouse, and church), until a few months before the end of the war.

From the beginning of our discussions about the work at Los Alamos, Oppenheimer had stressed the idea that the hydrogen bomb was an important part of the work; indeed, the facility that made it possible to measure the pertinent nuclear cross sections of hydrogen was one of the first research tools to be completed. As it turned out, a suggestion that Konopinski had made at the Berkeley summer conference—that we look into tritium, the hydrogen isotope that contains two neutrons, to see how readily it might fuse—proved to be inspired. But at the moment, other problems demanded our attention.

One of them had occupied me in Chicago after I returned from the Berkeley conference. Szilárd's original idea for a fission weapon was simple enough: Start from one neutron and let it multiply. After sufficient neutron multiplication occurs, a few pounds of fissionable material will liberate energy equivalent to thousands of tons of high explosives.[7] There is just one small hitch: that multiplication must occur in less than one one-millionth of a second. Otherwise, the material will predetonate—fly apart with moderate energy before a full chain reaction can occur.[8]

The trick was to assemble the critical mass of fissionable material in the absence of neutrons. However, neutrons are ubiquitous. First, cosmic rays, which produce neutrons, penetrate practically everything above ground.

---

[7] That multiplication occurs after about fifty generations, at which point almost a billion times a billion times a billion neutrons are involved.

[8] Although it takes fifty generations to produce a full-scale reaction, the critical mass begins to come apart a mere one generation after enough heat is available to vaporize the material. If too many neutrons are available, fissionable material brought together with the velocity of a bullet will come apart with a velocity fifty times greater and produce an explosion equivalent to a few tons of TNT.

Second, and more serious, uranium and plutonium emit alpha particles, which can release neutrons from common nitrogen and from isotopes of oxygen and carbon.[9] The project went ahead with the obvious program: Eliminate as much of the nitrogen, oxygen, and carbon as possible, and perform the assembly as fast as possible, so that the probability of neutrons' being present during the assembly process will be as small as possible. Then provide the neutrons at the right moment.

The most obvious way to assemble the critical mass was to use a high-velocity gun to propel one-half of the nuclear material into the properly positioned second half. But this solution created new problems. First, building a device that could be transported by plane was a challenge, and separating the fissionable material into two portions meant that the device had to be large. Second, shooting half of the material with sufficient accuracy, velocity, and reliability was difficult, and there was also a danger that the rebound from the impact of the projected material would break the system apart before the initiating neutrons could be injected and could multiply.

Those problems proved only moderately difficult. Solutions to the mechanics of size and of combining the material were worked out, and the problem of rebound was overcome by activating a neutron source just as the halves were in proper position. But after we had been working for a few months, a real difficulty showed up. We had assumed that a uranium or plutonium nucleus would not split unless it was struck by a neutron. In the summer of 1943, Emilio Segré discovered that uranium-238, plutonium-239, and plutonium-240 all undergo fission spontaneously.[10]

---

[9] When an alpha particle of some 4-MeV strikes a light nucleus (such as carbon, oxygen, or nitrogen), a neutron may be released. The alpha particle has plenty of energy to penetrate the carbon or oxygen nucleus, and isotopes (oxygen-17 and carbon-13) possess a weakly bound extra neutron that is ejected if an alpha particle is added to the nucleus. The neutrons in nitrogen are bound more firmly, but even nitrogen will emit a neutron. (The alpha particle has 4 MeV of kinetic energy, but the binding energy of the alpha particle to the nucleus brings the available total energy to 10 MeV, an amount that suffices to set a neutron free from nitrogen.) Complete elimination of carbon, oxygen, and nitrogen is very difficult, but even if this could be accomplished, the possible presence of neutrons due to cosmic rays would still be a problem.

[10] For fission to occur, a more or less spherical nucleus must be elongated into an ellipsoid. The ellipsoid will be necked down (or develop a waistline), and the neck will eventually break, which leads to the formation of two more or less equal parts. Electric repulsion propels them apart with high kinetic energy. In the initial phases of that process, almost up to the formation of the two halves, the potential energy is higher than it is in the original nucleus. According to

That was a serious problem, because spontaneous fission would produce considerable numbers of neutrons that could start a chain reaction before full assembly was attained. In the case of uranium, the number was small enough that predetonation could be neglected if the amount of U-238 in the U-235 was small. But both isotopes of plutonium release neutrons by spontaneous fission.[11] Using plutonium in the comparatively slow-gun assembly suddenly seemed questionable. That was a real problem, because by then, we knew there would soon be more plutonium available than uranium-235.

One ingenious man, Seth Neddermeyer, thought the problem might be solved by rapid assembly of a fissionable shell. He began working on a scheme that would bring the critical mass together in a three-dimensional rather than in a one-dimensional manner. Instead of simply propelling one piece of fissionable material into another, he suggested using a shell of high explosives to surround and drive an inner shell of plutonium into a small sphere of plutonium at the center of the device.

Seth's effort received limited attention until Johnny von Neumann showed up in Los Alamos that fall. Johnny von Neumann was so valuable, not only as a mathematician but in virtually every field, that he was welcome to work with us even for very short periods. He was allowed to come and go freely. Johnny gave a talk in which he proposed a method of assembly that involved shaped charges.[12] He then came home to see Mici, meet Paul, and have dinner. Afterwards, as we sat in the living room, I told him about Seth Neddermeyer's

---

classical mechanics, the nucleus will never be found in such states of higher potential energy: Those states constitute a *potential barrier*. In quantum mechanics, there is a small probability of penetrating the potential barrier, because in quantum mechanics one can never know precisely where a particle is unless one allows it to have, with some probability, an extraordinarily high momentum and energy.

That problem in connection with nuclei was first tackled by Geo Gamow, and the probability of penetration is called the Gamow factor. The Gamow factor explains why a nucleus of uranium takes billions of years to disintegrate rather than a tiny fraction of a second. In the case of spontaneous fission, the mass that has to be moved is greater, and the Gamow factor is very much smaller and more effective. But, when 10^{25} fissionable nuclei are assembled, the possibility of a single spontaneous fission emitting a neutron becomes decisive.

[11] The probability that plutonium-240 would undergo spontaneous fission is 40,000 times greater than the probability of spontaneous fission in plutonium-239. Separation of plutonium-239 and plutonium-240 is difficult, and plutonium-240 produces so many neutrons spontaneously that preignition seemed an enormous problem.

[12] A shaped charge was a recently discovered device that allows a rapid assembly of material in two chunks, the larger one moving slowly and a very small one moving at high speed.

approach. Johnny immediately got interested in a quantitative manner. Assuming, as was natural, that the fissionable material was incompressible, Johnny could easily calculate the spherical flow of material toward the center.[13]

In the midst of this discussion, our furnace began a booming serenade so impressive that Johnny stopped talking and looked about with some alarm. When I told him that it was only the steam in the system, he responded, "I would never live it down if I were killed by a mere subcritical explosion at this particular project."

After a few more minutes work, Johnny found that, under Seth's proposal, pressures of hundreds of millions of atmospheres would develop. At that point, I was reminded of a fact I had learned at the George Washington University theoretical physics conference on geophysics: Iron in the core of the earth, under an estimated pressure of 5 million atmospheres, is compressed by about 30 percent. I pointed out that at the high pressures Johnny was talking about, the fissionable materials would be compressed. In that case, the critical mass would become much smaller.[14] Needing less fissionable material for an explosion, particularly at the time when such materials were in short supply, seemed to us a splendid idea. At the same time, we could achieve a speed of assembly great enough that premature neutrons would not cause predetonation in plutonium—at least if the percentage of plutonium-240 was not too high.

The next morning, Johnny and I presented our findings to Oppenheimer. He immediately grasped their implications. Within a week, magnificent administrator that he was, he had turned the direction of the research around. From then on, our main efforts were no longer devoted to a gun-assembled weapon but rather to the implosion assembly.

Our next problem was how to produce a sufficiently spherical implosion. Johnny knew enough about explosives to propose the use of explosive lenses. Just as a beam of light changes its direction when it passes through water and can be focused by passing it through a glass lens, the direction of a shock

---

[13] If one assumes that the same amount of material must pass through each sphere, the velocity must increase with a $1/r^2$ dependence, a relationship that allows the accelerations and pressures involved to be derived in a straightforward manner.

[14] The radius of the critical mass must be a fixed multiple of the mean free path of neutrons, and the mean free path is inversely proportional to the density. Therefore, a twofold decrease in radius (which is a eightfold increase in density) will decrease the critical radius to one-eighth and will decrease the critical mass to one sixty-fourth. The actual compression that can be achieved is less, but still important.

wave produced by an explosive can be focused and redirected by passing it through different explosive materials. Explosive lenses consist of various pieces of explosive that are fitted together so that the detonation wave moves at different speeds as it passes through different portions in the explosive. Such a composite of explosives can thoroughly reshape the shock wave and, at least in theory, can produce the desired shock wave along the surface of convergent spheres.

I believe Johnny began what proved to be his third extremely important contribution to the work on the atomic bomb during that same visit: He began persuading us to use computers, pointing out the usefulness that computers would have in our calculations.[15]

Before Johnny left Los Alamos, he had altered the perspective on our work, but he had also gained a new perspective about us. Shortly after his arrival, Johnny had attended a meeting of perhaps thirty senior scientists, at which Oppenheimer reported on a high-level conference between Roosevelt and Churchill. The issues were serious because they involved the future British-American collaboration on the atomic bomb and the current status of the war. When Oppenheimer stopped speaking, he asked for questions. There was a long silence. Then a deep voice (that remains unidentified to this day) boomed from the last row: "Could you tell us, please, when there will be a shoe repair man in Los Alamos?"[16] That first day of his visit, as Johnny and I walked away, he remarked, "Now I understand what Los Alamos is all about." And to a considerable extent, he did.

By the time the work on implosion began in earnest, my friend Hans Bethe had been heading the theoretical division for about four months. I enjoyed Bethe's company and conversation on any number of topics, and most certainly on physics. But as physicists, we approach problems differently. Bethe enjoys turning out what Fermi called "little bricks," work that is methodical, meticulous, thorough, and detailed. He is, as one of my friends characterized

---

[15] Alan Turing of England had done the original work on complex calculating machines in the late 1930s. After the war, we learned that the first primitive computer in England played a role in breaking the German military code during the Battle of Britain.

[16] The answer to that question turned out to be: Not for more than a year. By mid-1945, in addition to the cobbler, our secret mesa had a small grocery store (the commissary), a trading post for sundries, one small laundry and dry cleaner, and two self-service launderettes equipped with about a dozen washing machines—and almost 10,000 people who needed to use them. Mici reminded me once a week of my error in considering her extremely helpful washer-drier extravagant. She was, of course, right.

him, the dean of German physics, almost a Geheimrat.[17] Although I have made a few tiny little bricks, I much prefer (and am much better at) exploring the various structures that can be made from brick, and seeing how the bricks stack up. Oppenheimer, in my view, also approached physics in a manner more like a bricklayer than a brick maker.

When he told Bethe and me that he had named Hans to head the division, I was a little hurt. I had worked on the atom bomb project longer than Bethe. I had worked hard and fairly effectively on recruiting, and on helping Oppie organize the lab during the first chaotic weeks.

Although I appreciated and enjoyed the differences between Hans and me, sometimes I suspected that Hans thought I spent too much time in impractical pursuits, a failing that I could correct if someone disciplined me. I was not happy about having him as my boss. However, the first months passed in a way that made my concerns seem baseless. I was busy with introducing newcomers to the ongoing work and with choosing the problems to present for general consideration. But I did not lose sight of the more distant future or of the alternate ways in which the atomic bomb could be made to work.

A few days after Johnny had left, Hans called me into his office. "Well," he said, "you proposed the idea of implosion. Now I think that you should work on it. I want you to take charge of solving the equations that will be needed to calculate implosion."

The task Bethe was discussing seemed far too difficult. Not only were other people more capable than I of providing such work, but I also suspected that a job that formidable might not be completed in time to have any influence on a bomb that could be used during this war.[18] Although I began explaining all those reasons to Bethe, he was convinced that I needed to tackle the job; I was just as convinced that if I did, I would make no contribution to the war effort. We talked for almost an hour without coming to an agreement. At that point Bethe excused himself to keep another appointment, and I went back to my office.

Fortunately for me, we never had to resume that conversation. Although Hans did not criticize me directly, I knew he was angry. Although I hoped

---

[17] Geheimrat, as I explained earlier, literally means a secret councilor, a privileged, high-ranking member of the government, able to give advice from his elevated position. Among students in German universities, the term was often associated with pomposity.

[18] I was partly wrong and partly right. The mathematics was completed in time, but everyone was too uncertain of its accuracy to want to base the design on it.

that he would come to understand my position, he never did, and the incident marked the beginning of the end of our friendship. Oppenheimer got wind of our disagreement (whether because Hans told him or someone else did, I do not know). He was much more sympathetic to what I was saying and apparently agreed that productive work requires a person to follow his strengths and inclinations. He told me to continue the variety of programs I was working on and encouraged me to look for new approaches and alternative ideas. He also assumed direct responsibility for determining the assignments for me and my group.

A few weeks later, Oppie gave me an assignment I welcomed because it involved a unique privilege: travel. We could discuss our work openly within the confines of Los Alamos, but security measures prevented an exchange of information among the laboratories working on various aspects of the program. Because an exchange of information was badly needed by the laboratories at Hanford, Oak Ridge, Chicago, and Columbia, Oppie delegated four of us to be spokespeople; I was to be largely responsible for communication with Columbia.

Part of the reason for my selection, I suspect, was that I had repeatedly raised a question about the transport of energy within the bomb.[19] I knew from my work with Gamow that *opacities*—the ease or difficulty with which electromagnetic radiation can be transferred through a material—play an important role in determining the time needed for the energy released in the center of the sun to move to a point at the surface of the sun.[20]

Given the temperatures in the bomb, I believed that radiation transfer—in this case, by means of x-rays—might play an important role in determining the effectiveness of the bomb. When opacity is low, radiation escapes rapidly. That means the bomb would develop less energy because the pressure building up during an explosion would be lower. A bomb with more time to develop energy would be more efficient; therefore, easy escape of radiation, or to use the technical term, *low opacity,* might have important effects on the atomic bomb.[21] Superficial estimates suggested that loss of energy through radiation

---

[19] I had begun considering that question on the evening in 1942 that Mici and I had dinner with the Oppenheimers and their friends.

[20] The time needed for that transport in the case of our sun is a little less than 1 million years.

[21] I had brought up the problem of opacity during the Berkeley summer conference, and my work at Los Alamos on the transport of radiation had increased my interest. Radiation is absorbed somewhat differently at different frequencies. At higher frequencies, all frequencies are absorbed. At lower frequencies, absorption occurs preferentially at specific absorption lines,

would not play a great role. Although Oppie agreed that precise statements would be much better, no one at Los Alamos had time to do the calculations needed to prove or disprove the question.

Joe Mayer had entered the armed forces, but Maria was still in New York, teaching at Sarah Lawrence and Columbia and not involved in a wartime project. Even though Maria had not left Germany because she was in danger (only her grandmother or great-grandmother was a Jew), she hated Nazism. I believed that she would be delighted if she could contribute to the war effort and told Oppie so. In November 1943, Oppie made me the intermediary to propose the task to her and, if she accepted, to supervise that effort.

Oppie had also asked me to evaluate the safety of Urey's equipment for isotope separation that was being constructed at Oak Ridge. I had done my best to read the blueprints given me for that purpose, but I still had several unanswered questions and needed to talk with the designer. The engineer who had drawn up the plans for the plant, Manson Benedict, was also at Columbia; by traveling there, I could help to solve two sets of problems. And so I began working on two projects that separated me from the mainstream effort at Los Alamos.

Within a few months after the lab opened, it had become clear that we would have to be allowed off the project lands to purchase supplies and services. About once a month we would be allowed to go shopping in Santa Fe. We made the most of our outings and managed to have lunch at La Fonda, where Mici and I had stopped on our earlier trip with Fermi. We were supposed to look and behave like tourists on those shopping trips, but we made a poor job of it. Quite often after we had made our purchases, the clerk would ask, "Shall we send this to the Los Alamos office here in Santa Fe?"

We were also allowed to explore our immediate surroundings. In retrospect, it is hard to imagine where we found the energy to go hiking and horseback

---

and that is not a great impediment to energy transfer. The absorption lines act like a venetian blind of thin slats that are turned parallel to the impinging sunlight. The result is that most of the sunlight will come through.

As it stands, that picture is incomplete. For a variety of reasons, the lines are not sharp. Even more important, in the relevant portion of the absorbing activities of uranium, there is an incredible multiplicity of lines. If each of the lines is even a little bit broader, they could cover practically all frequencies and make the escape of the radiation much more difficult. The extent to which that broadening occurs at various temperatures was an important problem.

As it turned out, opacity proved unimportant in the case of fission bombs but was very important in connection with the hydrogen bomb, where transferring energy from the primary fission device to the secondary fusion mechanism proved crucial.

riding, visit the nearby Indian pueblos for festivals, explore the ancient Indian ruins a few miles away at Bandelier, give and attend parties, and manage routine chores while working long hours on the atomic bomb as well. But we did.

Los Alamos is sandwiched between the Jemez and the Sangre de Cristo Mountains, and many of us took advantage of this. Dave and Betty Inglis made so many trips to their favorite peak that Los Alamos people still call it Mount Inglis. On one occasion, they dragged me up one of the Truchas Peaks, which are the highest in the Sangre de Cristo range.[22] Many activities took place on the mesa itself. I helped at the radio station, played chamber music, and had my only experience as a thespian when I played the part of a corpse in a production of *Arsenic and Old Lace.*

With my new assignments, I felt useful and productive. But my friend and neighbor Felix Bloch was not so fortunate. He decided to leave. He felt strongly that because of the way the laboratory was organized, he was wasting his time; and to his mind, his differences with Oppenheimer were insurmountable.

Felix was not the first physicist to depart. Several months earlier, Ed Condon, the physicist who had translated Franck's ideas about the effects of molecular vibration into mathematics, had left Los Alamos. He was to have been Oppenheimer's second-in-command; but after a few weeks he departed because he became convinced that he could never be comfortable with Oppenheimer's way of managing a laboratory.

The Blochs were the couple that we socialized with most comfortably, so we were particularly sorry to see them leave. Felix gave me a farewell present: a small carved wooden plaque of the sort found in tourist shops that illustrated his view of Los Alamos: It showed a car driving straight into a tree.[23] Not long afterward, Oppie stopped by to visit us and noticed the little plaque over our fireplace. He immediately asked, "Did Felix give that to you?" Felix had not hidden his opinions.

Many of the physicists at Los Alamos liked to play poker, and during the war Oppie held fairly regular poker evenings. The only time I was invited to join the group was the night that Felix was leaving. I had promised to

---

[22] Lest the reader get the wrong impression, the slopes of that peak are so gentle that a cow could negotiate them with little difficulty.

[23] The plaque went with us to the Ellis Street house in Chicago but then, sadly, got left behind in our next move.

drive the Blochs to Lamy, near Santa Fe, to catch the train. I settled on a compromise: I drove the Blochs to their train and arrived at the Oppenheimers' after the poker game was well underway.

My friendships are deeply important to me. Being part of the most prestigious group matters less. I was unhappy about my disagreement with Bethe about whether I should do the implosion calculations, and I hoped that it might be resolved in time. When I came to Los Alamos, I did not expect that Oppenheimer and I would become good friends. Months before I had become aware that Oppenheimer and I had values that were too different to allow us to be close.

One significant event during my first months at Los Alamos deserves mention. During the summer of 1943, I read Arthur Koestler's novel *Darkness at Noon*, which proved a major milestone in my thinking.[24]

I had been interested in communism since my original negative experience with it as an eleven-year-old in Hungary, but my childhood opinion had been considerably modified during the seven years I spent in Germany between 1925 and 1933. Several close associates presented me with the ideas and ideals of communism. Eric Landauer, a dear friend of my Karlsruhe mentor Feri von Körösy, was the first dedicated communist I knew; and two of my later colleagues, Lev Landau and George Placzek, were also convinced exponents of communism.

Many considered the depression that followed the stock market crash of 1929 the final failure of the capitalist system. (Similarly, some see the collapse of the Soviet economy sixty years later as the final disproof of the communist system.) I had ambivalent feelings about the experiment going on in Russia. I knew that the social and economic conditions in Russia were even worse than those in Hungary, and I appreciated the difficulties of reform. But I was also impressed by Geo Gamow's deep resentment of communism.

My first indication that something about the communist world was peculiar had come in 1931, when a Russian scientist refused to discuss Trotsky at the lunch table in Göttingen. My misgivings were so slight that later that year I was glad to help my friend Tisza move to the Soviet Union.

I delved a little further into communist methods during my last months in Germany in 1933. In the period just before Hitler's accession to power, German communists joined the Nazis in a general strike that brought down the

---

[24] Arthur Koestler, *Darkness at Noon* (New York: Macmillan, 1941).

government. Two German communists complained to me that Stalin betrayed the communist cause in Germany to promote the interests of the Soviet Union. According to them, Stalin's only concern was not with the well-being of the communist movement but the well-being of Moscow.[25]

The show trials in Moscow, which I began to hear about when I arrived in the United States, had a cumulative effect. Famous heroes of the movement—Bukharin, Rykov, and Zinoviev—confessed to being traitors and were shot. Others, with much less publicity, were just shot.

But I still had not made up my mind. Charles Critchfield, one of our graduate students at George Washington, remembers that as late as 1937 I believed that the experiment in Russia might be the answer to that nation's political and economic problems. He recalls my being shocked when he said that he saw no difference between Hitler and Stalin.

For me, as for many other people, Stalin's pact with Hitler in 1939 marked the beginning of the real revision of my feelings. And I was further educated by Laci Tisza, who had left Russia because he was disillusioned with communism. He was staying with us in Washington about the time the pact was signed, and he probably carried with him the news of Landau's arrest. By the time I arrived in Los Alamos, I had no doubt that the defeat of Hitler was of overriding importance. My thoughts about communism were confused and generally unsympathetic. The opinion in the scientific community continued to be divided.

I don't believe I have ever been more fascinated with a book than I was with *Darkness at Noon*. The novel, which takes place during the 1930s, describes what goes on in the mind of a communist accused of treason, and the exchanges between him and his interrogator. Koestler develops the arguments for communism as effectively as those against it. For a considerable part of the book, I was not sure whether the accused or the interrogator was the traitor to the cause. All that was clear was that no compromise could exist.

For most of the book, Koestler presents both sides with equal force; but, by the end of the book, no ambiguity remains. The accused's self-accusations are a lie, a sacrifice to the cause of communism. *Darkness at Noon* brought together and crystallized the objections to the methods of control used by Russian communism, which had been forming and accumulating in my mind for fifteen years.

---

[25] The first thing that Hitler did after he assumed power was order the wholesale arrest of the communists. Stalin issued no complaint even though the German nation was comparatively weak during the reorganization.

At the time I read the book, I knew nothing about the author.[26] Many years later, I read Koestler's autobiographical book covering the years from 1928, when he became a communist agent, to 1938, when, with the publication of *Darkness at Noon*, he became a leading anticommunist. His work as a communist organizer-agitator took him to many countries, including Germany, the Soviet Union, France, Spain, and England. He was exposed to the horrors of Stalin's rule, but he could not abandon the cause during the fight against Franco. Even after he lost his convictions, he retained his loyalty to his community.

Changing one's mind about a deeply held belief is a difficult process. (I like to say that the substance with the greatest inertia known to man is the human brain, and that the only substance more inert is the collection of human brains found in a large organization such as a military service or the faculty of a university.) Change can happen, but it requires an immense amount of energy and no small cost. Koestler changed his convictions. His friends did not. He suffered deeply from that break. Eleven years after I read the book, I began to understand that loss better, because, in a minor way, I went through a similar transformation.

The scientific community at Los Alamos was powerfully drawn together in several ways. Security sharply limited contact with the outside world—not only was there no travel but even correspondence was restricted. The scientists and their wives and families had little contact with the military personnel on the mesa. The scientific community was remarkably homogeneous in its addiction to science and in its liberal political judgments, which were those commonly held on American university campuses.

I slowly came to realize that in two important respects, my views differed from those held by the majority. Perhaps because I had spent the previous four years working for and on weapons research, I saw it as continuing to have great importance for the future. Unlike many in the scientific community at Los Alamos, I had become convinced that the problems connected with Communist Russia were very great. My friend Lev Landau, a deeply committed communist, had been imprisoned for being a capitalist spy! That, together with pieces of information I had gathered over the last decade, led me to conclude that Stalin, who could never catch up with Hitler, was still a close runner-up.

---

[26] Although Koestler was a native of Budapest, and close to a contemporary, I had no contact with him until a decade later, when John von Neumann, who was a friend of Koestler's, introduced me to him. By then, I had read almost all Koestler's books, including those he wrote about the history of science. Koestler, to my mind, was a remarkably thoughtful and honest person with an exceptional talent for writing.

17

ON AND
OFF THE MESA

November 1943–January 1945

L OS ALAMOS, IN some ways, resembled an enormous international reunion of the atomic physics community. The science of quantum mechanics was only fourteen years old when the war began. There were so few
of us working in the field that for the most part we knew one another, and a
sizable portion of our group worked at Los Alamos. In the late fall of 1943,
the British contingent, headed by James Chadwick, the man who discovered
the neutron, arrived to a warm welcome at Los Alamos.

Even so, Project Y, as Los Alamos was code-named, was perennially short-
handed. By the time Los Alamos was organized, most American scientists
were already involved in war work. The several talented British physicists,
among them James Tuck and Rudolph Peierls, were particularly appreciated
because no one needed to orient these newcomers to the work. The British
were firmly convinced, then and afterwards, that they had started the atomic
bomb project with their Tube Alloy program.[1] The following summer, another member of the British contingent, Klaus Fuchs, arrived after having
spent some months working at Columbia.

The newcomers and their families were soon indistinguishable from the
original Los Alamos contingent. James Tuck was self-assured, outgoing and

---

[1] The British began investigating the possibility of an atomic bomb early and had made
slow progress. Given the hardships, dangers, and shortages of wartime, part of their work was
transferred to Canada, and at the invitation of the U.S. government, a group of British theoreticians joined the Manhattan Project.

friendly.[2] Both Fuchs and Peierls were Germans who had been rescued by the Academic Assistance Committee.

Fuchs, a polite and gracious bachelor, was generous with his time. He was willing to help with any project, whether it was to discuss a colleague's problem and suggest possible new approaches or to act as a chauffeur for wives whose husbands had no time for that. His services earned him a fond spot in many hearts.

But he was so consistently quiet in social situations that Peierls's outspoken Russian-born wife, Genia, nicknamed him Penny-in-the-Slot Fuchs. Talking with Fuchs, she said, was like dropping a coin into a vending machine: You got one word back for each question you asked.[3] Usually, he responded with a yes or a no; but if the question interested him, he might even say a whole sentence. Yet I had the impression that he had a lot to say and did not say it.

Maria Mayer, when she met him the following year, independently observed, "In talking, Fuchs's spontaneous emission is very low, but his induced emission is quite satisfactory." In this respect, he was outdone by Chadwick, who had developed his British reserve to perfection.

I had first met another member of the British delegation, Rudolph Peierls, in Leipzig in 1929. A capable and thorough physicist, Peierls was then working with Heisenberg. Bethe had worked closely with Peierls during the period when we were all beneficiaries of British hospitality. Bethe saw Peierls as ready-made for the task he had had in mind for me: Peierls could tackle the calculations of implosion. So Peierls, with the help of a small group, diligently began that Herculean labor.

A few weeks after the British group arrived, two men from Denmark made the reunion as complete as it could be in our divided world. The Bohr family had been rescued from Nazi-occupied Denmark, and Niels Bohr and his son Aage showed up for a visit at Project Y.[4]

One of the more futile security measures was to change distinctive famous names into common ones. Those of us who were not so famous suffered only a minor deprivation of identity. Our driver's licenses were made out with a

---

[2] Tuck was universally popular at Los Alamos. He enjoyed these years so much that after the war he returned to the lab to work on controlled fusion, in which he had an early and continuing interest. Tuck lived in Los Alamos until his death in the mid–1970s.

[3] Genia Peierls was so upset when she learned in 1950 that Fuchs had been spying for the Soviets during and after the war that she visited him in prison to bawl him out.

[4] Details of the escape are provided in Chapter 20.

number instead of a name, and "Post Office Box 1663, Santa Fe, New Mexico" instead of an address.[5] But Niels Bohr was famous, so he was transformed into Nicholas Baker. The group of us who had known him at his Institute in Copenhagen soon modified that alias to Uncle Nick.

When I heard that Bohr was coming, I began looking forward to reminding him that he had said it was impossible to build a fission weapon.[6] But our meeting turned out to be typical. Bohr spotted me at the end of a long corridor, came running, and immediately squelched my chance of having been right. "Teller," he said, "didn't I tell you that you could not make a nuclear explosive without turning the whole country into a huge factory? Now you have gone ahead and done it."

Bohr never wasted another word in arguing about the difficulties of building the bomb; from that day on, he participated diligently in the effort to solve the problems. In one essential respect, though, he did not change. Although he never voiced a word of criticism at Los Alamos, he remained convinced that secrecy didn't help at all.

The new huge factories that Bohr mentioned included one that I subsequently came to know a little about: the gaseous diffusion plant in Oak Ridge. That project, as I have mentioned, contained hundreds and hundreds of cascades to allow the fastest moving gas molecules to collect at the end of a long and repetitive journey. Concerns arose that U-235 might accumulate at an unexpected place in the system, form a critical mass, and explode. When I finally got to New York, I talked with the man who had designed the apparatus, Manson Benedict.

Our discussion proved a little awkward. I could ask Manson questions about his apparatus and how it would function, but I was not allowed to tell him why I wanted to know; this second point, of course, soon became obvious. Courteous and discreet, Manson never appeared to resent my odd procedure, even though my inquiries were directed at finding fault with his work. (I found no flaws during those meetings.)

On that same trip, I saw Maria Mayer for the first time since I had left Columbia. Mici and I had visited Joe and Maria at their home in Leonia regularly during our stay in New York. The war had disrupted the Mayers' lives

---

[5] Post Office Box 1663 actually appears as the official birthplace of my daughter, Wendy, who was born at Los Alamos in 1946.

[6] He had made that claim in 1939 after he had determined that the bomb would require U-235 and before the possibility of using plutonium had become obvious.

even more profoundly than Mici's and mine. Joe, who was a native-born American, was in the South Pacific, eventually in Kwajalin; so Maria, with her partly Jewish family still in Nazi Germany, had several reasons to hope for a speedy conclusion to the war.

Maria immediately agreed to participate in the opacity study, and we spent most of one day discussing what the project would involve. Although Oppie had arranged for her clearance, she needed permission before she could discuss the project with the graduate students who would be doing the calculations. For that, we had to go to Washington, D.C. There, in a building not far from the railroad terminal, we met with Dr. Richard Tolman, a truly outstanding physicist from Cal Tech who was one of the scientists supervising the Manhattan Project, and with an army colonel who was one of the chief security officers.

The meeting turned out to be a further instruction in the idiosyncrasies of wartime secrecy. The colonel understood that Dr. Mayer might have to be told that the study was about uranium, but he saw no reason for her students to know this. "Wouldn't it suffice to tell them it was element 92?" At that point Tolman interrupted, "Every physics student knows that element 92 is uranium." The colonel gave in on that point, but needed to justify his position.

He said, "I know that the word *uranium* isn't classified, but giving away unclassified information sometimes has as bad a result as a real leak. For example, there was the recent case of a newspaper reporter who was aware that we were looking for a place to build large nuclear reactors. He also heard that there was a huge construction project on the Columbia River near Hanford, Washington. Neither piece of information was really classified. But the reporter put two and two together and guessed that the reactors were being constructed at Hanford. We had a very difficult time keeping him from publishing that information."

After the meeting, as Maria and I were walking back to the railroad station, she said, with a twinkle in her eye, "The colonel's comments about Hanford were really quite interesting." The only security breach at the meeting had come from a security officer.[7]

Maria could tell her students that they were working on uranium, but I was not permitted to tell Maria why we were interested in opacity. After the

---

[7] Of course, the story went no further during the war, except that Oppie found the report of my trip entertaining.

meeting, I mentioned the temperatures at which we wanted the calculations made. Maria caught her breath. She quite obviously understood what the study was about. I think we both enjoyed knowing that our knowledge of the real secret remained unspoken.[8]

The work on implosion was continuing at a feverish pace. On paper, implosion looks simple enough. In practice, the solution spawned many new problems. It is easy to assume a spherical implosion. It is much more difficult to produce one. (And even more difficult to determine that a sufficiently perfect implosion was produced.) The problem is that even a small deviation from the initial symmetry of the shock wave may grow exponentially, in which case it quickly produces a dramatic distortion. Many of us were soon learning tricks of hydrodynamics more familiar to engineers than to theoreticians.

Johnny von Neumann brought the first computers to Los Alamos in the spring of 1944. The equipment, provided by International Business Machines, now known as IBM, was advanced only in the sense that it provided electrical connections to drive mechanical motions.[9] But even those machines were a great help. They were promptly put to work for the numerical integration of the hydrodynamics of implosion. But new problems kept arising, such as our ignorance of how much pressure was needed to produce a particular density in the fissionable material.

In spite of a surprising amount of progress, it was hard not to feel that we were far from our goal. Earlier, Bohr had told us that Heisenberg was working on the German atomic bomb and had implied that Heisenberg was doing so in a most patriotic and diligent manner. (That characterization did not ring true for me even then, but, of course, I did not contest it.) For those of us who knew Heisenberg and the many other talented German physicists, the idea of their working on the project in any frame of mind was deeply disturbing. The thought of how far the Germans might have come in the years since the discovery of fission was enough to give us all nightmares.

Throughout the war, I continued my recruiting efforts. On my first trip to the East Coast, I had telephoned Cloyd Heck Marvin, the president of

---

[8] After Hiroshima, Maria commented in a letter: "Well, the cat is out of the bag. Quite a funny cat!"

[9] I like to call that first device a *monoflop*, because, assisted by a (binary) *flip-flop* device, it produces one decision each second. A few years later, Johnny introduced electronics that made *megaflop* machines possible. Today, advanced computers work with *gigaflop* equipment; it is predicted that in the twenty-first century, the equipment will improve a further millionfold, giving us *petaflop* computers capable of making 10^{15} decisions per second.

George Washington University, to ask about prospective workers. The first recruit from that call was his eighteen-year-old son, Cloyd, Jr. But I also learned that Harold Argo, who had completed his master's degree with Gamow and me, had a wartime position at the Naval Ordnance Lab, and furthermore, that Harold had married one of my particularly able young students, Mary Langs. Mary was then teaching physics at George Washington University.

During the war, it was almost impossible to get a telephone installed unless there was a military need for it, so the Argos were without a phone. As Harold tells the story, rather late one evening his downstairs neighbor, a British naval officer, rapped on the door of their apartment to tell them that they had a call on his phone; the neighbor apparently did not appreciate this, even though it was the only call for the Argos he ever received. When Harold, in some mystification, answered the phone, he discovered that I was on the other end of the line. He says that he never was able to learn how I had acquired their neighbor's phone number to contact them. The explanation, of course, is that I am Hungarian.[10] But as a consequence of that call, he and Mary arrived in Los Alamos in the early spring and, together with Cloyd Marvin, Jr., joined my group.

Mici's life during these years was extremely busy. Not only did she have Paul but also she had me, a husband who disappeared for weeks at a time and when he was home paid little attention to his attire or his surroundings. And although that was fully enough, she was also working at the laboratory. Because of her training in mathematics, she had, in effect, been drafted into the computations division. That group was headed by Donald Flanders—a mathematician with a scraggly beard whom everyone called Moll.[11]

In one way, Mici had a slight advantage over many of the other working wives at Los Alamos: We did not increase our family size. Paul provided a great enough challenge for both of us during that time. He was an outgoing, happy child, but busy and determined. One evening when we had guests, we allowed Paul to stay up later than usual. When Mici finally scooped him up and started to carry him off to bed, Paul said his first words. "No, no, no, no, no," he caroled, thus effectively answering our question as to whether he

---

[10] One commonly accepted definition is that a Hungarian is a person who enters a revolving door after you but exits ahead of you.

[11] Why that nickname? The reason given was that he had absolutely nothing in common with that more famous Flanders of English literature.

understood the meaning of that word. Paul also hated to sit in his high chair at mealtimes. He much preferred to stand in it, which was, as Mici pointed out, a risky perch. One night when he had assumed his lofty position, Mici and I matched him: We climbed onto our chairs, too. Paul sat down.

Whenever I went to Chicago on a liaison mission, I stopped and saw Eugene Wigner, who worked there until he transferred to Oak Ridge. On one visit, he told me that one of his former students from Berlin, Rolf Landshoff, was now teaching at a small college in Minnesota; he was about to get his citizenship papers, which meant that he would be eligible for clearance. Eugene planned to recruit him but kindly allowed me to make the attempt to get him for Project Y.[12] I managed to convince Rolf that living in the wilderness of New Mexico and working on a project that I couldn't describe would be more interesting than working on reactors. In November of 1944, he joined our group.

During the war, group sizes went up and down as projects were completed and new questions arose. Oppie had said that he wanted our group to come up with new ideas and new approaches. So we tackled a variety of questions. For instance, during the first twelve months or so, we began investigating von Neumann's suggestion that shaped charges may be a potential alternative to the gun and implosion methods of assembly, and we checked out several suggestions that Niels Bohr made.[13] My travels made it natural for me to gain new perspectives, and by virtue of running the colloquia, I was kept up to date on the current obstacles that could benefit from new ideas. In addition, we spent perhaps a third of our time on exploring rudimentary ideas about the fusion weapon, which was nicknamed the Super.

All in all, I think my group had about a dozen different people at different times. Its members included, among others, Geoff Chew, Stan Ulam, Stan and Mary Frankel, and Eldred Nelson. But the regulars were Kayski, Nick Metropolis, the Argos, Henry Hurwitz, Rolf Landshoff, and Cloyd Marvin, Jr.

Cloyd, who looked considerably younger than his eighteen years, was the baby of the group. But he was quick to learn and was a diligent worker.

---

[12] Rolf recently said that he thinks the telegram from us inviting him for an interview arrived within a day of his being sworn in as a citizen.

[13] Unfortunately, the suggestions that Bohr, Fermi, and Chadwick made all proved unfeasible. Although Johnny's idea of shaped charges failed to prove workable, his contributions, ranging from implosion, explosive lenses, and computers to many less obvious improvements in the mathematical work, made him the foremost (but largely ignored) scientific contributor to the development of the atomic bomb.

Henry Hurwitz, a former student of Bethe's, was our irreverent character. He decorated his memos with cartoons, scattered his belongings everywhere, and kept his wife's pet skunk in his office. (The last activity may explain why he had that space all to himself for a considerable time.)

Rolf, who was rather shy and quiet, ran afoul of his first office mate, Egon Bretscher, a Swiss-German who was working on the experimental side of the Super project. Because Egon had a somewhat similar accent, Rolf asked him one day whether he was German too, an inquiry that Egon took as an insult.[14] Rolf happily joined Henry and the skunk for the duration.

The newly wed Argos were, by nature, thoughtful and generous people and did much to contribute to the congeniality of our group. And everyone enjoyed Nick, a soft-spoken and charming young bachelor with a kindly sense of humor. Kayski, of course, was my steady right-hand man, taking over whenever I was away on trips.

A great deal of teaching had to go on as new people came to Los Alamos, not only because of the differences in their educational stages, but also because much of what we were working on involved information that had only recently been discovered. Because both Kayski and I enjoyed teaching, and because our Los Alamos "students" were able and unusually eager, we found our work enjoyable.

When the laboratory was in the planning stages, it appeared as though the thermonuclear weapon would receive a considerable amount of effort; for this reason, a cryogenics facility—to determine the cross sections of deuterium and tritium nuclei experimentally—was among the first buildings constructed at Los Alamos.[15] Egon Bretscher and Perce King spent the war years providing experimental cross sections for our calculations, which we did by hand.[16]

The work was laborious, and progress was understandably slow, but whenever we had the time, we kept the work on the Super (the original design of

---

[14] Rolf says that when he reported the incident to me, beginning, "I am afraid I stepped on Egon's toes," I responded, "Egon has big toes."

[15] Although positively charged nuclei repel each other, nuclei of various elements can overcome that repulsion with varying degrees of probability. The mathematical model representing that likelihood is called a cross section because a nucleus with a higher probability of being hit corresponds to a target with a larger cross section. Like most quantum mechanical calculations, cross sections include many assumptions and so must be checked experimentally.

[16] The calculations involved plotting the experimental cross sections as a function of energy against the theoretical distribution of energy. Combining those two factors produces a cross section that is a function of temperature rather than of energy.

a thermonuclear bomb) going forward. I had originally assumed that I would work exclusively on the thermonuclear device, but I found the redirection of my efforts towards the atomic bomb most agreeable because of the immediacy of its importance.

My work as a liaison to other projects took considerable time. Because I could not discuss the work at Los Alamos by telephone or correspondence, I made a trip East about once a month. Those trips, particularly the ones to New York, had some unexpected pleasures associated with them. Harris Mayer, one of Maria's two excellent students working on the opacity study, was responsible for some of those bonuses. Harris's father was a distributor of alcoholic beverages, which were hard to come by during the war under any circumstances, but particularly at Los Alamos. I have never developed much of a taste for liquor, but the wonderful scotch that I acquired from Harris on each visit made me popular with our friends back in Los Alamos.

There was another happiness connected with my visits. I had always liked Maria Mayer, but our friendship during the war years grew deeper. I am definitely Hungarian, but my ties to Germany are unusually strong for two reasons: the intense attachment to the German language and culture that my mother's family had and my seven happy and productive years in Germany. Maria and I not only shared common concerns for friends and families about whom we had no news but also felt a common nostalgia for the music and literature of Germany. During the war, anti-German feelings in the United States were strong. Few people bothered to differentiate between Nazism and anything else that originated in Germany. Maria hated Nazis but loved Germany, a feeling that I shared.

On one early occasion, during a visit to the Ureys, Maria wistfully mentioned that she had not seen an opera for a long time. As it happens, I, too, had missed attending the opera because Mici does not enjoy it. So I invited Maria to a performance of a light opera, *Die Fledermaus*. On other occasions, we attended some of Wagner's long, involved operas.[17]

There were other benefits to traveling. I often stopped at Princeton to talk with Johnny von Neumann. Characterizing Johnny is not easy. On the sur-

---

[17] Wagner tried to develop a new form of art and failed. He disregarded the limitations of theater and nonchalantly insisted at various times on a sailing ship, a dragon, and a cathedral on stage. He used motifs, patterns of music, as reminders of individuals or ideas, and thereby created a language that must be learned, which takes lots of time. Finding someone who also understands the language is always pleasant, but it was particularly so at a time when most people associated the language with bombast and an insane dictator.

face, he appeared formal and completely correct. One of the favorite Los Alamos recollections of Johnny is that when he went hiking, he wore a suit, a white shirt, and a tie. But intellectually he was far from formal. We formed a partnership in using trilingual puns on each other. Johnny used to assert that each pun would earn its author a thousand years in purgatory.

On a visit in the early summer of 1944, while I was explaining details of the Super's plan to Johnny, I first noticed a serious difficulty in the design. From the beginning, because of the losses from radiation, there seemed to be barely enough energy to keep the fusion reaction going. Much of the energy emitted was relatively low-energy light quanta. None of us had noticed during the the intensive Berkeley discussion or the two years following that those escaping photons will collide with far more energetic electrons and carry away much more energy than we had estimated.[18] It now looked as if a fusion reaction would be impossible. Johnny and I examined the problem briefly and set it aside for further thought.

Not much later, back at Los Alamos, Oppie was holding one of the regular meetings for the ten or so section leaders. I always felt uncomfortable at those gatherings. Johnny was in Los Alamos that day, so he also attended. When Oppie asked me, "What's new?" I mentioned that I had found a new difficulty with the original design of the Super. "But," I went on, "since I haven't thought it through yet, I would rather talk about it later." "No," Oppie said. "Talk about it now."

That arbitrary order particularly upset me because I was afraid that, in light of the new difficulty, work on fusion would be scrapped completely. I stood up and left the room. Johnny caught my eye on the way out and raised his eyebrows disapprovingly.

Within a few minutes, I agreed with Johnny. I didn't want to leave Los Alamos and I didn't want to cause trouble. I knew that my work as liaison and safety consultant and as a recruiter and symposium organizer was useful, and I certainly didn't want to slow down our bomb project. I began regretting my impulsiveness.

Oppie made a very nice gesture: He came to me after the meeting with the intent of resolving our differences. I began by apologizing for my rudeness and stating a dislike of the group meetings. "Okay," he said, "you don't want to

[18] I call the principle involved the inverse Compton effect. Compton studied collisions between high-energy photons and low-energy electrons, which result in the electrons' gaining energy. In a thermonuclear reaction, the reverse situation exists.

return to the meetings. You don't have to. I'll talk with you about your group's work by yourself." He may have been slightly unreasonable before, but now he was the more reasonable of the two of us. I gratefully accepted his offer.

A few weeks later, those difficulties were resolved. Most of the urgent theoretical work on reactors had been completed, so Fermi arrived at Project Y and was made a section leader. The Fermis were offered a house on Bathtub Row, but not wanting to be treated differently from the majority, they instead moved into one of the fourplex apartments. Oppenheimer turned the job of hearing my group reports over to Fermi. But first Fermi had to learn about our work in Los Alamos, so, for once, Fermi was my pupil. Needless to say, I never derived more pleasure out of teaching.

At Los Alamos, Enrico spent most of his time putting together a nuclear reactor, which was cooled by boiling water, just east of the laboratory in Omega Canyon. But even though he was not much involved in the work on the hydrogen bomb, he took a great interest (as always) in new projects, and listened to us and offered guidance in his usual ingenious way.

Like Bohr, Fermi was too famous to use his own name, and so he had been transformed into Mr. Farmer. By the time he arrived at Los Alamos, two experimental reactors (not counting the first model at the University of Chicago) had been built, one in the Argonne Forest outside Chicago under Fermi's direction, and the other at Oak Ridge, supervised by Wigner. One of my favorite stories about the wartime aliases concerns a visit that Enrico and Eugene (who had been renamed Wagner) made to the new site at Hanford, Washington.

Eugene is not only extremely polite but scrupulously honest. When he and Fermi presented themselves at the gatehouse and the guard asked their names, Eugene had considerable difficulty admitting to being Wagner. The guard was not about to admit a stranger speaking with an accent who couldn't seem to remember his own name, but Fermi solved the problem: "His name is Wagner as surely as mine is Farmer."

As the security officer had informed Maria and me, the construction of full-scale reactors in Hanford, Washington, began in late 1943. Unlike the Argonne or Oak Ridge reactors, the Hanford reactors were to be water-cooled. Because water absorbs neutrons, reaching the stage of criticality needed for a chain reaction was more difficult. The engineering responsibility for that tremendous construction project rested with the DuPont Company, and they did not assume the job lightly.

The wartime Hanford reactors were built to standards far different from those used today. Now, it takes five years to build a reactor according to plans based on well-proven designs.[19] The first prototype reactors on the Columbia River were built in less than eighteen months on the basis of a theory proposed by physicists that no engineer had thoroughly checked,

In his memoir, Groves makes clear the uncertainties of the project's success. He talks about his "extreme disappointment" when, having completed the construction of the Pentagon and expecting to be assigned to the European theater, he was instead put in charge of the army's effort on the Manhattan Project.[20] "What little I knew of the project," he says, "had not particularly impressed me." Others have said that Groves called the effort to build a fission weapon "a crazy Buck Rogers project."[21]

Groves had valid reasons for doubt, a significant one being that the bomb was to be made from materials that didn't yet exist in measurable quantities. Doubts also assailed the scientists at DuPont who were going to build the equipment to produce some of that material. Groves had to work hard to convince them that such a seemingly hare-brained scheme could work. It must have been a remarkable spectacle when one doubting Thomas (who was also a good soldier) persuaded a flock of doubting Thomases to carry out the presidential order. But that is the stuff of which the success of the Manhattan Project was made.

The DuPont representative, Crawford H. Greenewalt (who later became the president of the company), took a remarkably positive and imaginative approach. In planning the Hanford reactors, the Met Lab scientists insisted that only minimum-sized reactors were required. Making them as small as possible, they declared, would put them into production faster, thereby speeding up the collection of weapons-grade material.

Greenewalt, whom we called Greenie, was concerned that the project was moving too fast; he believed the reactors were risky even with the inclusion of the safety factors on which he had insisted. He settled for what he could get, swallowed hard, and never stopped protesting. But on the basis of his experience and conservative nature, Greenie insisted that the size of the reactors be increased. General Groves decided in Greenie's favor. The expanded

---

[19] In France, Taiwan, and many other parts of the world, only five years elapse between the time reactor construction is commissioned and the time production of electricity begins. In the United States, the same work takes ten years or more because of complicated, unnecessary procedures.

[20] Leslie R. Groves, *Now It Can Be Told: The Story of the Manhattan Project* (New York: DaCapo Press, 1983).

[21] Although it hardly seems possible to me, current readers may not know that Buck Rogers was the hero of a very popular science fiction comic strip.

reactors were constructed even though the scientists protested against the unnecessarily longer construction time mandated by their size.

Operations at low power levels seemed to bear out the theorists' predictions. But in September 1944, when the operators brought the first Hanford reactor up to full power, they noticed a peculiar phenomenon. After about an hour, the power in the reactor began to drop; a few hours later, the reactor had shut itself down. The next day, the reactor slowly began to function again. The shutdown and slow recovery was an upsetting problem.

The explanation was quickly identified. One of the radioactive fission products, iodine, decayed into radioactive xenon. Xenon, it turned out, was a fierce neutron absorber. At low power levels, the xenon had time to decay into harmless cesium before absorbing neutrons. But at high power levels, the only way to solve the problem was to destroy the xenon by providing it with extra neutrons. That meant more reactivity was needed, and Greenie, by cautiously building a bigger reactor than theorists wanted, had made it possible to increase the number of fuel rods and thus the power.

By the end of 1944, a modified version of the Urey diffusion separation process was in operation at Oak Ridge, and a plant using a third type of isotope separation, based on thermal diffusion, was nearing completion there. (The plant for this new type of enrichment was constructed in about three months.)

Earlier, when I was in New York in September 1944, my phone rang at six o'clock in the morning, which, because I had arrived late the night before, felt much earlier. General Groves, with whom I had never before had a personal conversation, was on the other end of the line. "Dr. Teller, we need you in Washington. Can you come down immediately?"

I did just that. Upon arrival, I was given the details of the new enrichment plant, including its plans, and of an accident that had occurred in an earlier installation in Philadelphia. The day before, a chemical explosion, caused by an operating error, had killed and injured some of the men working there; but in respect to fission reactions, the plant was perfectly safe.

In the afternoon, I was called into Groves's Washington office to make my report on whether a similar accident could occur at Oak Ridge. The general was sitting at the end of a very long table. I was surprised when he instructed me to sit on his right because quite a few dignitaries were in attendance. The group discussed the isotope separation facilities in interminable detail. Our general, who had rousted me from bed at an ungodly hour, appeared a little slumberous himself. At the end of my comments, he would occasionally open his eyes to say, "But, Doctor, isn't that only theory?" or,

"After all, that would need thorough experimental verification." I realized I did not enjoy his full confidence.

A colonel at the lower end of the table asked, "But couldn't it be that, just by pure chance, all the uranium-233 could go to one end of the apparatus and all the uranium-238 to the other, and that a fission explosion could then occur? Isn't that possible?" By that time, my patience had worn thin, and the perverse side of my sense of humor got the better of me. "Yes," I replied, "that is possible. It is just as likely that all the oxygen molecules in this room will collect under this table and leave us up here to suffocate."

General Groves, who had been napping again, opened his eyes. "But you admit that it might happen?" he asked. At that point, James Conant, the joint scientific leader of the atomic bomb project with Tolman, spoke up: "What Dr. Teller is implying is that such an event is impossible." Remarkably enough, Conant's comment established my credentials. From that point on, General Groves never again questioned my opinions. He even treated me with what was, for him, exquisite politeness.

On January 15, 1945, I celebrated my thirty-seventh birthday with a cake at Harold and Mary Argo's. Forty-five years later, the mystery of how they knew it was my birthday was solved when Harold Argo explained.

> Bob and Jane Richtmyer were good friends of Mary's and mine during the war. Mary's birthday was January 11, Jane's January 16, and mine January 20, so the three of us decided to have a joint birthday party. We scheduled it for the fifteenth and invited you and Mici too, without mentioning that it was to celebrate our three birthdays. So when the birthday cake was lighted and brought in, you were truly amazed and delighted, asking: "How ever did you know that today is my birthday?"

Without discussing it, they decided that I needed the celebration more than they, so they simply went ahead with the party; my question went unanswered until almost half a century later. The young people with whom I worked at Los Alamos were generous in many ways. In spite of the difficulties, I (and many others) consider the wartime years at Los Alamos the most wonderful time in our lives.

18

An End, a Beginning

1945

IN THE HISTORY of the twentieth century, 1945 was the watershed year. I realize in retrospect that the year also marked a turning point in my life. I cannot discuss those events without including some international events as I know them today.

By January, the war in Europe was moving closer to its end. A few days after my birthday (the 15th), the Red Army entered Budapest. But it was more than half a year, some weeks after the Third Reich collapsed, before we received news of our families. We did not know, and certainly could not imagine, what was going on in Hungary. Since then, I have heard and read a lot about those months of terror, but even today I cannot really imagine them.

Hungary, hoping for the return of its lost lands and anticipating a German victory, joined the Axis in late 1940. That necessitated a purge of the army, because in Hungary, a convert to Christianity was no longer considered a Jew. Under Hitler's standards, a person remained a Jew, regardless of religious beliefs, even if only one of his or her grandparents was a Jew. Beginning in 1940, all Jews were removed from their posts in the government, the military, and the schools and universities.[1]

Even with that change in Hungarian policy, until 1942, Jews from Poland and other neighboring nations were still fleeing to Hungary; and, until the spring of 1944, Hungarian Jews were free to live where they chose and not required to wear a yellow Star of David on their clothing. The

---

[1] From then on, conscripted Jews were assigned to military labor battalions, where they served without rights and with inferior clothing and rations. Tens of thousands died in those circumstances.

nightmare in Hungary did not begin until March 17, 1944, when Hitler, aware that Hungary was seeking a separate peace with the British and Americans, forced Horthy, the former admiral who had been the dictator of Hungary since 1920, to agree to Nazi occupation.[2]

I am glad to say that Hungary, unlike Austria, provided no welcoming speeches for the Nazis. But Hungary had a small but virulent anti-Semitic party, the Arrow Cross. Their emblem, a swastika with four arrow endings, was appropriate: Their methods of murder, cruder than Hitler's, made it possible to kill more than half of the 800,000 Jews in Hungary in a few months.

In the end, the Holocaust in Hungary was more openly vicious than in any other country. In Budapest during the grim days of December 1944, members of the Arrow Cross rounded up thousands of Jewish men, women, and children, and with no attempt to hide what they were doing, took them to the banks of the Danube, shot them with machine guns, and threw the dead and dying into the river. But in the countryside, a far larger percentage of Jews were killed; in the cities, a fair number of Jews were able to survive, helped in many cases by Gentile friends. The experiences of my own family are fairly representative.

From the beginning of March 1944, the entrances to the Palatinus, where my parents were still living (and every other building where Jews were allowed to live), were marked with a Jewish star. Periodically, the residents were herded into the courtyard, and a group of people taken away, purportedly to labor camps. In the beginning, the Arrow Cross soldiers as well as the Jews seemed to believe that there was a military purpose to the effort. On one occasion, a soldier in passing over my frail, elderly mother told her, "We don't need you."

By the summer of 1944, few young and middle-aged men had escaped the net. My sister Emmi and her six-year-old son, János, had watched in anguish as her husband, János's father, András Kirz, was taken away. Mici's brother Suki had similarly disappeared. As it turned out, both men had been taken to labor camps. Together with the other tens of thousands of Jews in the Hungarian labor camps, they were released in late fall—on the condition that they report to the authorities a week later. András walked back to Budapest, a journey of four days, and spent three days and nights with Emmi and János.

---

[2] Horthy could offer no resistance. The Hungarian army had been decimated on the Eastern Front. A joke from that period describes the situation. A Hungarian asks a Nazi: "How long would it take you Nazis to occupy Hungary?" "Six hours, if you resist." "What then?" asks the Hungarian. "Then," says the Nazi, "twenty-four hours for the welcoming speeches."

But he felt that he had to honor his pledge. So, too, did my gentle friend Suki. Their inability to believe in the nightmare that had transformed the civilized world sealed their doom. Both of them died in the Mauthausen concentration camp.

The roundups did not stop when the able-bodied men were gone. Emmi escaped once by hiding in the steam of the laundry room of her building. On another occasion, my father's barber warned him of a roundup in progress and hid him until it was over. An elderly neighbor of my parents, also a lawyer, fainted after he was selected to be taken away. But the Gentile doctor called in pronounced him dead, and ordered his "body" taken back to his apartment, where not much later the neighbor revived.

Emmi's apartment was destroyed by bombing in November. She and my parents, who were alarmed at the increasing frequency of the roundups at the Palatinus, tried to find a safer refuge. First they moved to an apartment house protected by the Swiss consulate, but there was room for them only in the courtyard. Then they found a home for widows of distinguished Jewish-Hungarian officers where they could stay indoors, but the government was using the widows' home as an auxiliary ammunition dump.

My parents returned to the Palatinus, but Emmi felt she had to find a safer place for János. She managed to get him into a Red Cross home for children.[3] But by then, Jews were being picked up on the streets, so Emmi couldn't return to visit her son. A few weeks later, a rumor circulated that the Red Cross home had been evacuated and that the Jewish children in the home had been returned to the ghetto. Emmi hired a Hungarian soldier to accompany her, took off her star, and returned to the Red Cross home. János wasn't there, and no one at the home had any information about where he had gone.

More rumors circulated: The children at the Red Cross home had starved to death; the children had died in an epidemic. Emmi abandoned all caution. She simply went back alone to the Red Cross home. This time, a kindly nurse told her that János had contracted chickenpox and had been moved to a hospital in the ghetto.[4] Emmi rushed to the hospital where she found

---

[3] Traveling to the Red Cross home by bus, they were caught in an air raid, and a bomb broke the bus windows. Still, she went through with her plan and left her terrified six-year-old son there for safekeeping.

[4] The nurse also said that János had given her a letter for Emmi. He had told the nurse that he would give her a reward if she sent the letter to his mother. When the nurse asked him if he really had a reward, he admitted he didn't. But, he assured the nurse, his mother would surely give her one in exchange for a letter from him.

János, gaunt, pale, and ragged. He remained silent until Emmi told him that he had to stay on until he was well. His pleas and tears convinced her. They left the hospital together.

By then, Jews were being taken from the ghetto daily, and my parents and Emmi had moved in with Emmi's mother-in-law. A few neutral countries had taken individual apartment buildings under their protection, and András's widowed mother had a very small apartment in one of them. By then, twenty-six people were living in its three rooms. Emmi added János; but rather than increase the crowding further, she left, eventually finding refuge in a school where she had taught. Miraculously, Emmi, János, and my parents survived until the Russians arrived a few weeks later.

The Soviet occupation ended the massacre of Jews but brought with it a new peril: general robbery and rape. At least that horror was temporary, and once again my family was fortunate. With the arrival of the Soviet troops, my parents, together with Emmi and János, had returned to their apartment in the Palatinus. When the Red soldiers arrived to pillage the apartment, my father, confined to bed by illness, was there alone. The soldiers, in loading up all the things of value they could find, even pulled the pillows from under his head. But they did not take his blankets.[5]

Mici and I, together with the rest of the world, knew little of this until much later. Some weeks after the war in Europe ended, we learned through the Red Cross that my parents, Emmi and János, and Mici's mother, stepfather, and two half-brothers were all safe in Budapest. Considering that more than half the Jews in Hungary were killed, that was good news. But many years passed before Mici's grief subsided enough that she could bear hearing Suki's name.

While dead and dying Jews were being shoved into the icy Danube near the ruined Chain Bridge, I was safe and comfortable in Los Alamos and thinking about how the plutonium bomb might be completed in the least time. The design at that time called for assembling the plutonium as a hollow shell around a neutron-producing device that would be activated by a strong shock. The plutonium sphere was to be surrounded by tamper, which served the dual purpose of reflecting the neutrons and holding the plutonium together long enough for the proper amount of neutron multiplication to occur.

---

[5] Hungarian humor described that period, too: A Russian soldier approaches a Hungarian peasant and asks, "What time is it?" The peasant sticks his pitchfork into the ground, looks at its shadow, and says, "4:00." The Russian strikes back his sleeve, looks at his collection of watches, says, "Correct to the minute," picks up the pitchfork, and leaves.

The tamper was surrounded in turn by a sphere of explosive lenses; these produced the spherical shock that imploded the tamper onto the central sphere, compressing it and the fissionable material and setting off the chain reaction.

The lenses appeared to work well. Ingenious experiments had been used to follow the course of the implosion inward, and the results were reassuring. Peierls and his group had completed their step-by-step calculations on the inward progress of materials during the implosion. Those calculations, based mostly on pure and experimentally unverified theory about the compressibility of matter, were extremely complicated. They could not have been completed in time except for the computers obtained on Johnny's advice.

But one serious doubt persisted. In the flow of any material, instabilities can develop. In a situation where a material of low density (the high explosives) attempts to push and accelerate material of higher density (the tamper and plutonium), small deviations from symmetry may grow very rapidly. That raises the possibility that the more easily accelerated lightweight material will make its way through the heavier layers and, instead of a simple spherical implosion, a complex mixing of layers may prevent the assembly of a critical mass of plutonium.

Unfortunately, the inner portion of the imploding material was to be the most heavily compressed, a result that would occur in the last phases of the implosion when experimental observation was not possible. Neither theoretical arguments nor calculations of the lateral movement and mixing could banish the concerns about that danger.

At this point, one of Oppenheimer's students, Robert Christy, pointed out that if we adopted a simpler plan, we would eliminate the difficulties. Instead of imploding a thin shell of plutonium, we could implode an assembly of the high explosive and tamper on a solid sphere of plutonium. With little movement of the plutonium, mixing would be practically impossible. The calculations showed that the converging power of the explosion, even in this conservative design, would produce enough compression for success.[6]

Early in 1945, General Groves's primary scientific advisor, James Conant, who had taken over from Briggs as head of the National Defense Research Board in early 1941, visited Los Alamos to obtain a comprehensive report on the modifications that would be involved in adopting Christy's proposal. I remember his visit distinctly because of one occurrence. When the meeting

---

[6] That simple, ingenious suggestion made at an earlier time would have saved a great deal of effort. But the work was not wasted because it later helped in producing improved designs.

ended, Conant and I sat silently for a moment after the others had left. I heard him mutter less to me than to himself, "This is the first time I have really thought it would work." That was the first indication I had of how little confidence those in the highest scientific quarters had in our work. I was slightly shocked.

Maria and her two able students had made real progress on the opacity study.[7] I felt sad that I could discuss so little of the project with Maria. I asked permission to invite her to Los Alamos so that she would have a complete picture of our work. In late spring of 1945, Oppie gave the okay.

Seeing Los Alamos through Maria's eyes, I realized what a wonderful and remarkable place it was, and my admiration of Oppenheimer's talents as an administrator deepened. A few weeks after she arrived, Maria got word that, with the end of the campaign in Okinawa, Joe was coming home. Stanley Frankel and I drove Maria down the canyons to Albuquerque. She had decided on the extravagant but speedy adventure of flying home; at that time, more than a half a century ago, neither Santa Fe nor Los Alamos had an airport.

By then, enough U-235 had arrived from Ernest Lawrence's calutrons, fed by the product of Urey's diffusion cascades, to build a gun-assembly weapon. Because uranium was in extremely short supply and the design of the bomb was so straightforward, the decision was made to use the bomb without testing it. The situation was different for the implosion device. Even with the improvements in design, there were too many unverified assumptions to warrant its use without testing. The experiment was scheduled for mid-July.

A few weeks before the test, General Groves arrived to address and encourage the senior people of the laboratory.[8] Groves told us how unhappy he had been when he was assigned to stateside work on the fantastic project now nearing completion. Then he said a few words more memorable for their spontaneity than for their intended effect of encouragement: "When this job is finished, with or without success, you will go back to work in your laboratories and not care much about what the result was. But my reputation depends on it."

---

[7] When that work was declassified after the war, Boris Jacobson and Harris Mayer received their Ph.D. degrees for their efforts on that interesting problem. As it turned out, the results had no bearing on the immediate effort at Los Alamos, but they later became quite important in the work on the hydrogen bomb.

[8] At thirty-seven, I was indeed among the senior people. The general may well have been the only person over forty-five in the room.

Years earlier, I had heard about a pep talk our general had given when he visited Ernest Lawrence's laboratory in Berkeley. At its conclusion, he turned to Lawrence and said, "Professor, I expect success. Remember your reputation depends on it." Nobel Laureate Lawrence never blinked an eye. But after the meeting, he took the general to his favorite watering spot, Trader Vic's, for dinner. There, after they had enjoyed a few Mai-tais, Lawrence turned to Groves and said, "You know, General, my reputation is made. It is yours that depends on the outcome of the Manhattan Project."

Groves apparently did not mind Ernest's comment. They became good friends. And Groves remembered Ernest's instruction about reputations. Those of us who had heard of Lawrence's exchange thought Groves's plea remarkably funny. But after I heard the story, I realized that our general could change his mind. I began suspecting, for the first time, that there might be more to the man than was reflected in Oppie's many derisive comments and stories about him.

In late June, not long after Groves's visit, I received a mimeographed letter from my friend Leo Szilárd, who was still in Chicago, where much of the bomb-related work had now been finished. Szilárd's letter was dated July 4.[9] He had addressed the envelope by hand but had neglected to fill in my name on the letter. The text of the letter read:

Inclosed is the text of a petition which will be submitted to the President of the United States. As you will see, this petition is based on purely moral considerations.

It may very well be that the decision of the President whether or not to use atomic bombs in the war against Japan will largely be based on considerations of expediency. On the basis of expediency, many arguments could be put forward both for and against our use of atomic bombs against Japan. Such arguments could be considered only within the framework of a thorough analysis of the situation which will face the United States after this war and it was felt that no useful purpose would be served by considering arguments of expediency in a short petition.

However small the chance might be that our petition may influence the course of events, I personally feel that it would be a matter of importance if a large number of scientists who have worked in this field went clearly and

---

[9] As my friend Charles Critchfield suggested, the fact that Szilárd's letter arrived before he wrote it "carries Hungarian thaumaturgy beyond the power over revolving doors."

unmistakably on record as to their opposition on moral grounds to the use of these bombs in the present phase of the war.

Many of us are inclined to say that individual Germans share the guilt for the acts which Germany committed during this war because they did not raise their voices in protest against those acts. Their defense that their protest would have been of no avail hardly seems acceptable even though these Germans could not have protested without running risks to life and liberty. We are in a position to raise our voices without incurring any such risks even though we might incur the displeasure of some of those who are at the present in charge of controlling the work on "atomic power."

The fact that the people of the United States are unaware of the choice which faces us increases our responsibility in this matter since those who have worked on "atomic power" represent a sample of the population and they alone are in a position to form an opinion and declare their stand.

Anyone who might wish to go on record by signing the petition ought to have an opportunity to do so and, therefore, it would be appreciated if you could give every member of your group an opportunity for signing.

War brings out an ugly side of human nature. Only those Americans who were born before 1935 can remember the fervor of the feelings in that period or the hatreds generated by the inhumanities and sufferings. I remember one Los Alamos scientist proposing that we not drop an atomic bomb on Japan until we could drop a dozen at the same time and thereby assure the complete defeat of the Japanese.[10] That plan struck me as excessive, but, until I received Szilárd's letter, I had not thought much about the alternatives to using the bomb.

The petition—which had been drawn up jointly by Szilárd and Papa Franck—drew attention to three further points: The atomic weapon would drastically change the relationship between nations; a demonstration prior to use in an attack might end the war without further bloodshed; the consequences of using the bomb without prior announcement would be of uncertain expediency and of deplorable morality. Those reasons made good sense to me, and I could think of no reason that those of us at Los Alamos who agreed shouldn't sign it.

---

[10] I shall not name that gentleman because it is clear that he later deeply regretted his suggestion. That same scientist eventually refused to work on weapons and became a disarmament activist.

But before I did anything, I felt I had to talk to Oppie. Because of censorship, he was probably aware of the materials I had received; and without doubt, on a topic such as this, nothing could be sent out of Los Alamos without his approval. I also wanted to talk to him because I respected his opinion. I arranged to meet him at his office.

Oppie's reaction when I asked about circulating the petition took me completely by surprise. He began talking about Szilárd and Papa Franck in a way that, until then, he had reserved for General Groves. Then he asked, "What do they know about Japanese psychology? How can they judge the way to end the war?" I had no ready answers. He went on, "The leaders in Washington, not individuals who happened to work on the bomb project, our political leaders—who include men like George Marshall, a man of great humanity as well as intellect—those are the people who should make such decisions."

Our conversation was brief. His talking so harshly about my close friends and his impatience and vehemence greatly distressed me. But I readily accepted his decision and felt relief at not having to participate in the difficult judgments to be made.

Today, half a century after these events, I have reached three conclusions about that important matter. First, Szilárd was right. As scientists who had worked on producing the bomb, we bore a special responsibility. Second, Oppenheimer was right. We did not know enough about the political situation to have a valid opinion. Third, what we should have done but failed to do was to work out the technical changes required for demonstrating the bomb over Tokyo and submit that information to President Truman.

Had we done so, President Truman would have had an alternative to dropping the bomb on Japan. The bomb could have been detonated during evening hours over Tokyo Bay at an altitude of 30,000 feet. Ten million Japanese would have seen the night turned to day. They would have heard a colossal clap of thunder. No one would have been killed in such a demonstration. We then could have announced that the next bomb would destroy a Japanese city. Emperor Hirohito probably would have surrendered, much as he did after Hiroshima was bombed. We in Los Alamos, familiar with the technical details of the atomic bomb, were in an unique position to submit such a report to the decisionmakers.

But in early July 1945, after Oppenheimer had convinced me that I should not take action in regard to the petition, I had to tell Szilárd what I had decided. I wrote to him the next day, and although my letter was not completely candid, it does reflect the feelings I had on leaving Oppenheimer's office. But knowing how strongly Oppenheimer had objected to the petition and wanting to remain on good terms with him, I didn't feel I could mention our meeting.

July 2, 1945
Dr. Leo Szilárd
P.O. Box 5207
Chicago 80, Illinois
Dear Szilárd,

Since our discussion I have spent some time thinking about your objections to an immediate military use of the weapon we may produce. I decided to do nothing. I should like to tell you my reasons.

First of all, let me say that I have no hope of clearing my conscience. The things we are working on are so terrible that no amount of protesting or fiddling with politics will save our souls.

This much is true: I have not worked on the project for a very selfish reason and I have gotten much more trouble than pleasure out of it. I worked because the problems interested me and I should have felt it a great restraint not to go ahead. I can not claim that I simply worked to do my duty. A sense of duty could keep me out of such work. It could not get me into the present kind of activity against my inclinations. If you should succeed in convincing me that your moral objections are valid, I should quit working. I hardly think that I should start protesting.

But I am not really convinced of your objections. I do not feel that there is any chance to outlaw any one weapon. If we have a slim chance of survival, it lies in the possibility to get rid of wars. The more decisive a weapon is the more surely it will be used in any real conflict and no agreements will help.

Our only hope is in getting the facts of our results before the people. This might help to convince everybody that the next war would be fatal. For this purpose actual combat use might even be the best thing.

And this brings me to the main point. The accident that we worked out this dreadful thing should not give us the responsibility of having a voice in how it is to be used. This responsibility must in the end be shifted to the people as a whole and that can be done only by making the facts known. This is the only cause for which I feel entitled in doing something: the necessity of lifting the secrecy at least as far as the broad issues of our work are concerned. My understanding is that this will be done as soon as the military situation permits it.

All this may seem to you quite wrong. I would be glad if you showed this letter to Eugene and to Franck who seem to agree with you rather than with me. I should like to have the advice of all of you whether you think it is a crime to continue to work. But I feel that I should do the wrong thing if I tried to say how to tie the little toe of the ghost to the bottle from which we just helped it to escape.

With best regards.

Yours,

E. Teller

Rereading the letter, I cannot really agree with the person, my earlier incarnation, who wrote it. I stand fully behind my strong statement against secrecy, but I would no longer say that helping the "ghost" escape was terrible at all. That was our job as scientists, a point that became clearer when I became aware of the great progress the Soviet Union had made on a nuclear explosive. The responsibility of scientists is to describe and demonstrate what is possible, to disseminate that knowledge as fully as possible, and, with everyone else in our democracy, to share the decisions that are necessarily connected with knowledge.

Szilárd's petition made an important point: We, the small sample of population who worked on and knew about the bomb, had a responsibility to consider and discuss that knowledge and to provide our perspectives. Indeed, the petition was an entirely proper way to communicate some of this knowledge to those who had to make the immediate practical decisions.

I knew that the censors would have Oppie review my letter. Wanting to be sure that my letter would be sent, and hoping to smooth over the upset of our previous conversation, I wrote him a note and attached my letter to Szilárd.

> Dear Oppi,
>
> You may have guessed that one of the men "near Pa Franck" whom I have seen in Chicago was Szilárd. His moral objections to what we are doing are in my opinion honest. After what he told me I should feel better if I could explain to him my point of view. This I am doing in the enclosed letter. What I say is, I believe, in agreement with your views. At least in the main points. I hope you will find it correct to send my letter to Szilárd.
>
> Edward

I did not know then that in the late spring of 1945, four scientists had been asked to serve as an advisory panel on the use of the bomb: Arthur Compton, from whose laboratory the petition originated; Ernest Lawrence from the isotope separation laboratory at Berkeley; Oppenheimer from Los Alamos; and Enrico Fermi, who had worked primarily on reactors during the war. Ernest Lawrence held out for a demonstration rather than use longer than the other panel members, but the panel finally submitted a recommendation for the use of the bomb.[11]

In the course of time, I became aware that when Oppenheimer had advised me that, as scientists, "we" should not participate in the decisionmaking, he had already acted contrary to his advice. The result was that I became convinced that, as scientists, we have a clear responsibility to participate in decisions by making new knowledge and new possibilities available for discussion.

There is little chance that the signatures I could have collected in Los Alamos would have made any difference. But had I done so, it is likely that I would have talked with Fermi—who was only peripherally involved in the bomb design—about the feasibility of a demonstration. Because of my position as head of the colloquia, I had considerable knowledge about most aspects of the bomb. In retrospect, I think that Fermi asked me a few questions that may have been related to that decision to use the bomb. I only wish that I had been more alert to instructing him on the technical possibility of a demonstration.

When Szilárd's petition arrived, my attention was on scientific, not political, questions. Several weeks before, when the test was being considered, Fermi revived a general question that, as I have mentioned, arose and was dismissed at the Berkeley conference in 1942: Could a nuclear explosion set in motion cataclysmic reactions in the atmosphere or oceans? That possibility, remote as it was, had to be conclusively investigated.

My group's work on a thermonuclear device was based on the idea that a very high temperature could initiate enough nuclear reactions in an appropriate fuel (specifically, liquid deuterium) to ignite the whole fuel. As we were the specialists on such reactions, we were given the task of answering the question in the most thorough manner possible.

The temperatures a fission bomb could achieve were considerably less than those required for fusion to occur in any but a carefully contrived, artificially produced situation. I decided that looking for a possible generalized reaction would be more meaningful if the higher temperatures achieved by a fusion explosion were also included.

---

[11] Arthur Holly Compton, *Atomic Quest: A Personal Narrative* (New York: Oxford University Press, 1956), p. 240.

The nuclei that are apt to react with each other (and thereby release a lot of energy) contain an unpaired neutron and proton. In general, such nuclei are quite rare. For example, deuterium, the heavy isotope of hydrogen, constitutes 1 part in 5,000 of hydrogen. The exception to that rule is nitrogen, which, containing an unpaired neutron and proton, is a conceivably reactive material. Given the increased energy, it was possible to theorize that the heat might produce a nuclear reaction in the atmosphere. Kayski, Cloyd, Jr., and I worked out the calculations. They demonstrated that such a cataclysm could not occur.[12]

But when we had completed our proof, Fermi insisted that we go one step further. All we had proved, he pointed out, was that such an explosion could not occur according to known laws of physics. But what presently undiscovered phenomena might exist that, under the novel conditions of extreme heat, might magnify the consequences and lead to an explosion? Considering that question occupied my time immediately before the test. I explained the possibilities I had considered and asked for suggestions from everyone who would listen to me.

The afternoon before the test, Oppenheimer sent a memorandum to everyone permitted to view the test of the implosion (plutonium) bomb, which was code-named Trinity. Because the test would take place before sunrise, we would be driven down in buses the evening before. Oppenheimer's memorandum contained advice about spending the night in the desert. Its most important message was, "Beware of the rattlesnakes!"

The technology used at Los Alamos was the most advanced in the world at that time, but the technology that served our comforts was not in the same category. That evening was one of the moderately frequent occasions on which the generator in Los Alamos failed. I left the laboratory well after sun-

---

[12] Those calculations, like all the work at Los Alamos, included a fair number of assumptions. Six years later, before the first fusion test was conducted, removing as many of those assumptions as possible became important. A most thorough theoretician, Gregory Breit, who was then working at Oak Ridge, tied down all the details, repeated the work, and obtained the same result.

In the late 1950s or early 1960s, Rand McNally, the grandson of the atlas publisher, wrote a paper suggesting that some of the data included in both Breit's paper and my own was wrong. Lowell Wood wrote a paper explaining why McNally was in error, and why the original paper was correct. As is the custom in the world of classification, McNally's incorrect paper was declassified, and Wood's correction was not. Sometimes it seems to me that the rule in classifying information is this: If it is wrong, it cannot be used by the enemy, so release it at once. If it is right, be careful and keep it secret.

down, and, as I was trying to find my way in the dark, I literally bumped into another person similarly engaged. It was Bob Serber.

Knowing that he was also going to the test, I asked him how he planned to deal with the danger of rattlesnakes. He said, "I'll take along a bottle of whiskey." Then I remembered that Bob was one of the few people with whom I had not discussed the question of what unknown phenomena might cause a nuclear explosion to propagate in the atmosphere. Because I took that assignment seriously, and even though officially the project had been completed, I proceeded to dish out the arguments and counter-arguments that we had considered. I ended by asking, "What would you do about those possibilities?" Bob replied, "Take a second bottle of whiskey."

Later that night, we boarded the bus that took us to the test site near Alamogordo in southern New Mexico. There were perhaps thirty of us in what was the secondary group, including William H. Lawrence, the science correspondent for the *New York Times*.[13] Our viewing site was about twenty miles from the tower that held the bomb. We were all fairly confident of success; someone had even organized a betting pool on the magnitude of the explosion. By the time I joined the pool, only the very low and very high explosive yields were open. I chose 40,000 tons, which was higher than the predictions. I thought that such a yield was far from impossible. (The actual yield was about half my estimate.)

The night seemed long and became even longer when the test was postponed. The problem causing the delay was rain—in the desert in July! Just a shade of pink had appeared over the mountains in the east when the shot was announced. We all listened anxiously as the broadcast of the final countdown started; but, for whatever reason, the transmission ended at minus five seconds.

We all were lying on the ground, supposedly with our backs turned to the explosion. But I had decided to disobey that instruction and instead looked straight at the bomb. I was wearing the welder's glasses that we had been given so that the light from the bomb would not damage our eyes. But because I wanted to face the explosion, I had decided to add some extra protection. I put on dark glasses under the welder's glasses, rubbed some ointment on my face to prevent sunburn from the radiation, and pulled on thick gloves to press the welding glasses to my face to prevent light from entering at the sides.

---

[13] The government invited Lawrence to represent the press at this historic occasion, after securing a promise that he would not publish this account until he was given permission.

For the last five seconds, we all lay there, quietly waiting for what seemed an eternity, wondering whether the bomb had failed or had been delayed once again. Then at last I saw a faint point of light that appeared to divide into three horizontal points. (It actually was the nuclear explosion and the luminous ring around it.) As the question "Is this all?" flashed through my mind, I remembered my extra protection. As the luminous points faded, I lifted my right hand to admit a little light under the welder's glasses. It was as if I had pulled open the curtain in a dark room and broad daylight streamed in. I was impressed.

A few seconds later, we were all standing, gazing open-mouthed at the brilliance. Then we heard a loud report. Bill Lawrence jumped and asked, "What was that?" It was, of course, the sound of the explosion. The sound waves had needed a couple of minutes to arrive at our spot twenty miles away.

The condensation cloud produced by the fireball slowly changed shape as it was blown in several directions by the winds. Eventually, it became a many-mile-long question mark. We returned to the buses with hardly a word. We knew that the next nuclear explosion would not be an experiment.

As the sun rose on July 16, some of the worst horrors of modern history—the Holocaust and its extermination camps, the destruction of Hamburg, Dresden, and Tokyo by fire-bombing, and all the personal savagery of the fighting throughout the world—were already common knowledge. Even without an atomic bomb, 1945 would have provided the capstone for a period of the worst inhumanities in modern history.

People still ask, with the wisdom of hindsight: Didn't you realize what you were doing when you worked on the atomic bomb? My reply is that I do not believe that any of us who worked on the bomb were without some thoughts about its possible consequences.

But I would add: How could anyone who lived through that year look at the question of the atomic bomb's effects without looking at many other questions? The year 1945 was a melange of events and questions, many of great emotional intensity, few directly related, all juxtaposed. Where is the person who can draw a reasonable lesson or a moral conclusion from the disparate events that took place around the end of World War II?

19

GIVE IT BACK
TO THE INDIANS

1945–1946

THE SUN WAS well up in the sky when our bus rolled up the slopes of the Los Alamos mesa. Mici, smiling, received me at the door: "Did you hear the news? A big ammunition dump in southern New Mexico exploded with considerable pyrotechnics. But no one was hurt." She obviously knew what had gone on even though I had not been allowed to tell her anything.

I lay down, but I was too excited to sleep. Finally, I went to my office. About eleven o'clock, young Mary Argo, eyes bright and shining, burst in: "Mr. Teller, Mr. Teller. Have you ever seen such a thing in your life?" An answer was impossible. We both laughed.

Junior scientists had not been invited to the test, but some of them knew a great deal about it. Determined not to miss the historic event, Mary and Harold had gone with a group of their colleagues to the top of Sandia Mountain, about fifty miles north of the test site. The shot was so long delayed that they had decided the test was a failure. The first nuclear explosion had gone off, unexpectedly, in all its brilliance, not long after they started down the mountain. Our laughter that day was not a response to the bomb but to our ridiculously inadequate reactions to it.

Work on the atomic bomb at Los Alamos was over; efforts in the Pacific were speeding up. About a week and a half after the Trinity test, the ship USN *Indianapolis* arrived at the staging island of Tinian in the Pacific, and delivered its precious cargo, the uranium-235 that had been painstakingly separated at Oak Ridge and Berkeley. Three days later, while on its way to join the invasion fleet, the USN *Indianapolis* was attacked by a Japanese submarine; it sank in shark-infested waters with the loss of hundreds of lives.[1]

The uranium bomb being readied was called Little Boy because it was slimmer than the plutonium device. The design, worked out during the first weeks in Los Alamos, was so simple that nobody felt the bomb needed to be tested before use. The other reason there had been no test was that, given the lengthy nature of the separation process, a test would have used up all the uranium-235 that could be made available during the likely duration of the war.[2]

Everything was ready by August 1, but the weather, once again, caused a delay. The bombing was finally scheduled for August 6. The *Enola Gay,* a specially fitted B-29, piloted by Paul Tibbets, took off before dawn. The crew included Los Alamos physicist Luis Alvarez and ordnance expert Deke Parsons, the ranking naval officer at Los Alamos, who armed the bomb. The yield of the uranium bomb dropped on Hiroshima on August 6, 1945, was similar to that of the device tested at Alamogordo.

President Truman promptly announced the bombing, calling the weapon, in a slightly imprecise fashion, an *atomic* bomb. (Nobody asked the obvious question: What in the world isn't made of atoms and isn't atomic?) The headline of our local newspaper, the *Santa Fe New Mexican,* read: "The Secret of Los Alamos Revealed." The article also reported on speculations about the purpose of Los Alamos; people had guessed it was everything from a factory making windshield wipers for submarines to a home for WACS who were unwed mothers.[3]

After the bombing, there was considerable jubilation at Los Alamos. One young enlisted woman, nicknamed the fifty-minute-WAC for her reputed ability to drive either of the important commutes (Los Alamos to Santa Fe or even Santa Fe to Albuquerque) in fifty minutes, had long been despondent

---

[1] I have a strong urge to see a meaning in that terrible disaster, but the only message I can read is that war is full of meaningless tragedies.

[2] Even an untutored General Groves would have had to admit that Ernest Lawrence's reputation was saved: Lawrence and his group delivered the material used in the first actual bomb. Separation by magnetic deflection was too clumsy and expensive a method for the mass production of uranium, but the method found continuing application in separating other isotopes for scientific use. And, to the surprise of many of us, that method was used in Saddam Hussein's attempt to make an Iraqi atomic bomb.

[3] In his *Memoirs* (Alfred A. Knopf, New York, 1990), Andrei Sakharov reports that "the peasants in the poverty-stricken villages nearby [the Soviet atomic bomb research center] . . . invented a highly original explanation for what was going on beyond the fence: a 'test model of Communism' was under construction."

over her assignment. On one of my trips to the airport, she complained, "When we all go home, my girlfriend will tell about driving ammunition trucks to the front in El Alamain. What will I have to say? I drove Mr. Teller to a place called Albuquerque!" Now, with the bombing of Hiroshima announcing the success of our project, the fifty-minute-WAC was smiling at last.

I was not. The colloquium that week was a viewing of the early pictures showing the destruction of Hiroshima. I remembered Szilárd's suggestions; the scenes were particularly troubling and I wondered whether such devastation had been necessary. Then, just three days later, on August 9, 1945, the plutonium bomb was dropped on Nagasaki. I remember telling Laura Fermi, "If this goes on, I want to leave."

But then, on August 14, the big news arrived: Japan had surrendered! The war was over. Celebrations, elation, and relief continued until late in the night. And I was fully as glad as everyone else. But I continued to regret that the bomb had not been demonstrated.

I felt that regret even more keenly when, a few years later, I read some official air force documents about the debates and decisions made in Japan just after Hiroshima.[4] After Okinawa fell to the Allies that June, the only question was how much longer the Japanese would fight before admitting defeat. As it turned out, the six-member War Cabinet that directed the Japanese war effort was split over how to proceed. Three members favored accepting the Allied demand for unconditional surrender, and three, led by General Anami, wanted to fight on in the hope of better terms for surrender.

At the beginning of the summer, Emperor Hirohito sent Prince Fumamiro Koniye to Moscow to try to offer terms for surrender. (The terms were practically identical to those accepted on August 15.) But the Soviets had no interest in facilitating negotiations, and no one responded to Hirohito's emissary.[5]

---

[4] *Summary Report (Pacific War)*, United States Strategic Bombing Survey (Washington, D.C.: Government Printing Office, 1 July, 1946). John Toland later put the material together in a beautiful and accurate work, *The Rising Sun* (New York: Random House, 1970).

[5] The U.S. Navy intercepted and decoded the message from Tokyo to the prince. But at that time, President Truman was at Potsdam, and the message never reached him. A tragic sequel occurred, when early in the occupation of Japan, Fumamiro Koniye was arrested as a war criminal and, unable to endure the shame, committed suicide. The navy generally opposed the use of the bomb without warning. Lewis Strauss, a Washington based naval officer during the war and the strongest single supporter after the war of developing the hydrogen bomb, devotes a chapter in his memoirs, *Men and Decisions* (New York: Doubleday, 1962), to the last days of the war and calls it "A Thousand Years of Regret."

The incredible destruction in Hiroshima on August 6 did not change a single vote in the divided War Cabinet. But that bombing did move the emperor to intervene. Disregarding his constitutionally limited role, he recorded a speech to be broadcast the next day; he asked the Japanese people to endure the unendurable: to surrender.

Followers of General Anami, upon learning of the recording, staged a palace revolution and seized the emperor. When General Anami, who venerated Emperor Hirohito, heard of their action, he ordered his adherents out of the palace. The emperor's speech was broadcast not long after Nagasaki was bombed. With the emperor's plea for surrender, the course of events was inevitable. The decision passed from the War Cabinet to the full Cabinet. Surrender was accepted, and General Anami went home and took his life.

President Truman considered a simple choice: to use the bomb or to continue the battle using conventional arms. The atomic bomb would speed the conclusion of the war and save hundreds of thousands from death in an invasion. He was also moved by the terrible conditions in Europe, where millions, if unaided, would not survive the winter of 1946. The war had to end, not only to prevent further loss of American lives, but also before proper efforts could be given to aid. I only wish that we at Los Alamos had provided the president with another choice.

Thinking that a course of events could have unfolded only the way that it did is reassuring but unjustified. I am convinced that each of us is a participant in creating the future. When we approach crossroads, our responsibility is great. I believe that the only way to learn from history is to consider what was and what might have been.

The first public awareness of atomic power could have been information very different from photographs of a city in ruins. It could have been the realization that modern science could stop a war without killing a single person. Such knowledge might have led to a more reasonable and stable world.

So many times I have been asked whether I regret having worked on the atomic and hydrogen bombs. My answer is no. I deeply regret the deaths and injuries that resulted from the atomic bombings, but my best explanation of why I do not regret working on weapons is a question: What if we hadn't? Those who question the morality of working in wartime Los Alamos seem to have forgotten that the Soviet Union of the 1940s was controlled by Stalin. Today, the Russian press rates Stalin's malevolence as almost as intense and dangerous as Hitler's.

As it turned out, the German atomic bomb project, the stimulus for our efforts, need not have been taken seriously. But an intense and serious effort, led by I. V. Kurchatov, had continued in the Soviet Union throughout the war. Four years after Hiroshima, the Soviet Union tested its first atomic bomb. It is a mistake (although a widespread mistake) to believe that if we had not "created" an atomic bomb, atomic bombs would not exist. Our work was significant because it gave the power of the first atomic weapon to Truman rather than to Stalin.

Another question, rarely posed, asks: What if we had the atomic bomb a year sooner? The easiest and least expensive method of separating isotopes, a method used throughout the world today, is based on a centrifuge procedure that Harold Urey proposed in 1940. General Groves chose the diffusion method instead. Karl Cohen, Urey's able assistant during that period, believes that Groves's decision delayed the atomic bomb by a year.[6]

If Dr. Cohen is right, atomic bombs of the simple gun design might have become available in the summer of 1944 and, in that case, would surely have been used against the Nazis. Atomic bombs in 1944 might have meant that millions of Jews would not have died, and that Eastern Europe would have been spared more than four decades of Soviet domination.

But those same bombs would have done irreparable damage to central Europe. Hitler repeatedly said that if Germany could not win, Germany deserved to perish. Unlike Emperor Hirohito, Hitler probably would not have surrendered under any conditions; far more people would have perished in the last year of the war. All the other events of Hitler's war together might not have inspired the horror and hatred such bombings would have spawned.

In the immediate postwar period, however, my concerns were not with the past but with the future. In September 1944, the Nazis began using a remarkable new weapon to bomb London: the first rocket to leave the earth's atmosphere. The V-2 rockets, weighing more than ten tons, were fired from launching pads in France into the stratosphere; minutes later, they reentered the atmosphere at great speed to strike their targets in England. The powerful new rockets gave notice that in the near future, no point on the earth would be more than minutes away from rocket attack. The prospect of combining rockets with nuclear weapons was terrifying. The importance of maintaining peace was rising exponentially.

My friend Steve Brunauer had spent the war years doing research for the navy. In the late fall of 1945, Commander Brunauer visited me in Los Alamos. He was writing a report on how atomic weapons would affect the navy. I do

---

[6] An account of how Groves's made his decision is available in Dr. Cohen's contribution to the British Royal Academy memorial tribute to Harold Urey.

not remember that I was pessimistic about the prospects for international co-operation at that time. I continued to write articles and give speeches advocating a world government for at least three more years.[7] But the report I wrote at Steve's request makes it clear that I was already giving considerable thought to less lofty but more practical means of keeping the peace. The stakes were high.

My report was lengthy and detailed. I discussed everything from rocket guidance systems and fuels to naval artillery, but a few comments indicate my particular concerns:

> It has been often stated that no defense against the atomic bomb is possible. I do not agree with this statement if taken too literally. . . .
>
> I assume that atomic bombs will be delivered by long-range missiles. The natural type of defense against such missiles seems to be jet-propelled homing projectiles. . . . Another possibility of defense would lie in interfering with the guiding radar waves in case the enemy should use guided missiles. In either type of defense, automatic release of the defensive missiles will be necessary because the time is likely to be too short for human decisions. . . . In addition to great strides in radar and in jet-propelled missiles, the possibilities just described will require very rapid calculating machines. These will act as a control mechanism both for releasing and guiding the defensive missiles. . . .
>
> I believe that practically for every offensive weapon it will be possible to devise a defensive one, but the new field opened up by the atomic bomb is likely to develop so rapidly that future offensive weapons will continue to outstrip the possibilities of defense. . . .
>
> Every time there is a radically new development in the tools of warfare, some old units and methods become obsolete. It has been stated that the atomic bomb will greatly reduce the importance of the navy. In my opinion, new developments in the navy will become necessary, but the overall effect of the atomic bomb will be to make the navy a much more important part of our national defense. . . . Even a small unit can launch rockets and atomic bombs. . . .
>
> It seems to me that underwater units of not too big a size (perhaps in the neighborhood of 1,000 tons) will be the appropriate ships of the future. Using small piles [the name then given to nuclear reactors] of power-producing units, these submarines can carry with them the energy needed for an indefinite period. Power-producing piles need not be heavy except for the necessary

---

[7] The idea, which envisioned a sort of United Nations with far greater powers, enjoyed some popularity at that time.

shielding, which must be used to protect personnel from the radiations that accompany the nuclear reaction. . . . A powerful navy would greatly add to the defense of our homeland against atomic bombs. Incoming missiles could be detected a thousand miles away at sea. Either home bases could be notified or defensive missiles could be launched from the naval units. . . .

In future developments we must not neglect offensive uses of the atomic bomb. We are at the very beginning of the development of atomic bombs, and there seems to be many ways in which these bombs could be improved. Such developments are likely to be so great that in the end they will probably thwart any method of defense. This, however, we cannot know for sure. Our only hope of facing future dangers in a realistic way is to explore the possibilities of improving atomic bombs. . . .[8]

In light of what I knew about the future of Los Alamos by then, my comments about research were optimistic. There were many unfinished projects when the war ended in August. Serious work on the hydrogen bomb had begun only in mid-July. The day after the test, Oppenheimer reorganized the laboratory, making Fermi and Bethe jointly responsible for the fusion bomb work. I was very happy with that arrangement. I had long hoped for a greater effort, and now the best people were working on the program. But the day after peace was established, Oppenheimer came to my office to tell me that "with the war over, there is no reason to continue the work on the hydrogen bomb." His statement was unexpected. It was also final. There was no way I could argue; no way I could change Oppenheimer's mind.

Beginning with his strange comment after the Trinity test (a quotation from the *Bhagavad Gita*, "I am become the Destroyer of Worlds"), Oppenheimer had seemed to lose his sense of balance, his perspective. After seeing the pictures from Hiroshima, he appeared determined that Los Alamos, the unique and outstanding laboratory he had created, should vanish. When asked about its future, he responded, "Give it back to the Indians."

An attitude—almost as thoughtless as the celebration when the Hiroshima bombing was announced—was growing among some of the higher ranking people at the laboratory: a revulsion against working for military

---

[8]I could not discuss the hydrogen bomb with anyone who did not have "TOP SECRET" clearance. Steve Brunauer, with his assignment to assess the future of the U.S. Navy, was cleared only for "SECRET" information. I devoted almost an eighth of this report to a discussion of the need for a more rational classification system.

purpose. The emotion seemed especially strong among those who had been most enthusiastic about using the bomb before the actual bombing. I began to worry about the prospects for peace. It would be secure for a few years because of the advantage the United States enjoyed from its current technical position. But what would happen when that edge disappeared?

Although I was already convinced that peace was most securely preserved when military power was held by free people, I, too, was looking forward to going back to civilian life. My job at George Washington University had been waiting for me for four years. The first house that Mici and I had ever owned was also waiting for us. But I had already decided on another, better prospect.

The University of Chicago had sponsored a great deal of work on the atomic bomb and wanted to continue nuclear research by collecting Manhattan Project scientists in a special institute led by Enrico Fermi.[9] In addition to Fermi, the university had signed up Harold Urey, James Franck, Leo Szilárd, our upstairs neighbor Cyril Smith, and Joe and Maria Mayer. The invitation to join my friends was too tempting to turn down.

One day in the fall, Oppenheimer caught up with me as I was walking to the laboratory and announced, "Touch me. I am no longer your director." An interim director had been appointed. Norris Bradbury, a Stanford physics professor called up as a naval reserve officer, had joined Los Alamos in the second half of the wartime effort. An experimental physicist, mild-mannered Bradbury proved a competent administrator under difficult circumstances. He definitely did not want to give Los Alamos back to the Indians. He asked me to stay on and take over Bethe's position as head of the theoretical division.[10]

Much as I wanted to go to Chicago, I did not immediately say no to Bradbury's offer. I desperately hoped that a lasting peace would be secured through international cooperation; but I feared that the survival of peace depended upon the ability of the United States to maintain the technological edge in nuclear weaponry. I was willing to stay if the work at Los Alamos would make a real contribution to peace.

Either of two programs could lead to important results. I would stay, I explained to Bradbury, if we developed fission weapons thoroughly—this

---

[9] After Fermi's death, the institute was named for him.

[10] Bethe was returning to Cornell. Eventually, George Placzek accepted the post, but he became ill and had to leave Los Alamos the following May; Robert Richtmyer became theoretical division leader, a post he held until Carson Mark assumed it about the fall of 1947.

would require, I estimated, a dozen nuclear tests a year—or if work on the hydrogen bomb became an essential part of the program at Los Alamos. Bradbury assured me that he would be happy to see either or both projects carried out just as I described. But, he explained, neither of the two efforts was likely. Given the popular mood, the government would be unlikely to provide more than the bare minimum of support for military research.

Unquestionably, had Bradbury indicated even the slightest inclination of being willing to fight for a thorough and ongoing program of development, I would have stayed on at Los Alamos—not because I particularly wanted to, but because no one else was willing. But Bradbury maintained a cautious approach, then and throughout his career as director.

I hoped that the laboratory might receive assistance from another quarter. Oppie had been a splendid director, and I had no doubt of his ability, given that success, to be heard in the political arena. I decided to talk with him before deciding.

After describing my conversation with Bradbury, I made my plea: "This has been your laboratory. Its future depends on you. If you tell me you'll work to enlist support for either a program on the hydrogen bomb or for vigorous development of the atomic bomb, I'll stay." Oppie immediately gave me his answer. "I neither can nor will do so."

My decision didn't take much longer. Without someone of stature to point out the reasons for maintaining as vigorous a program as possible, I saw little likelihood of meaningful work. The work at Chicago was too exciting to turn down. I told Oppie I would be leaving. I silently eased my conscience by deciding that I would return as often as I could to help out.

That evening, Deke Parsons gave a big party. Parsons, a naval officer, had served as part of the administrative team since the beginning of Los Alamos and had supervised the Hiroshima bomb from its earliest beginnings to its final arming. Many of us appreciated him especially for his instrumental role in replacing the goat trail up to the mesa with something resembling a highway. I remember the party celebrating his promotion to commodore and marking his farewell to Los Alamos.[11]

Oppie was also at the party. During the evening he drifted over to ask with a smile, "Now that you've decided to go to Chicago, don't you feel better?" I

[11] Parsons was among the last to hold the naval rank of commodore, which was equivalent to the army rank of a one star general. Today, a navy captain is promoted directly to (two star) rear admiral.

didn't feel better, and I said so, and added that I felt our wartime work was only a beginning. Oppie closed the subject: "We have done a wonderful job here. It will be many years before anyone can improve on our work in any way."

Around that time, Leo Szilárd, together with Trudi Weiss, the pleasant young Austrian physician who had been his girlfriend for many years, came to visit.[12] I was very anxious to see Szilárd again. I had not been in touch with him since I had written to him about the petition. As it turned out, he was not allowed to enter Los Alamos, even though he had worked on the Manhattan Project in Chicago throughout the war years.[13] Mici and I went to Santa Fe and visited with them there. Szilárd had put the failure of the proposal to demonstrate the bomb behind him. The future was his only concern now.

In the late fall, the departure of the wartime collection of physicists was further accelerated when a makeshift device, which had allowed a desert to become a laboratory, suddenly gave up the ghost. From the beginning, the two small canyon streams to the north and south of the mesa had been inadequate as a water supply for Los Alamos, and water had been brought in from more distant canyons by pipe. During the war years, Mother Nature kindly cooperated by giving us the ample protection of snow each fall before the onset of the first hard freeze of winter. But when peace arrived, that protection was suddenly withdrawn: The freeze came before the snow, and the water pipe froze. I still remember a photograph, captioned "Animal Heat," of a few GIs sitting on an exposed part of the pipe, to no avail.

So water had to be brought up by trucks, and we watched with growing anxiety as the level in the water tower fell. The commanding officer issued appropriate instructions, which ended with the memorable words: "Residents will not use the showers, except in an emergency." The residents caught on and left in droves. The members of my group began making frequent visits to Santa Fe for interviews.

---

[12] I may be the only person ever to have embarrassed the unflappable Szilárd. Although their relationship had always appeared to be one of devoted monogamy, Szilárd did not marry Trudi until some years later. Not long after that momentous event, I saw him at the Quadrangle Club of the University of Chicago and congratulated him, in all innocence, on his marriage. To my amazement, my unconventional friend blushed.

[13] I never learned what led to his exclusion. It did remind me of Oppenheimer's wartime comment to Charles Critchfield: "God protect us from the enemy without and the Hungarians within."

One of my last (infrequent) administrative acts was connected with that exodus. Rolf Landshoff had a beard, though not a particularly decorative one. He asked me whether he should go to his interview with or without it. I submitted that weighty question to a vote by the four female members of our group. The only one voting to retain the beard was Ellen Flanders, whose father had a similar beard. Rolf remains beardless to this day.

One of the questions being discussed during that period was the future development of atomic energy. Radioisotopes already available could play a wonderful role in medical diagnosis and biological investigations. The development of nuclear reactors would eventually contribute to raising the standard of living throughout the world by providing reasonably priced energy. But if the armed forces with their extreme secrecy measures continued to oversee atomic energy, progress on all those projects would proceed at a snail's pace.

Unfortunately, the first proposal to reach Congress, the May-Johnson Bill, suggested continued military control of all aspects of atomic energy. Worse yet, most of the leading wartime administrators, including Oppenheimer, supported the bill. Most scientists, myself included, felt that if the potential benefits were ever to be realized, oversight of that research had to be returned to civilian control.

Fortunately, a young senator, Brien McMahon, was responsive to the question. He set up hearings in Washington on the topic, and Steve Brunauer suggested my name to McMahon's committee as a possible witness. Thus it happened that I, a citizen for less than five years, was invited to make suggestions to members of Congress on a most important matter. I never considered turning down that honor, but the timing could hardly have been worse.

During the hectic (and secrecy-laden) war years, there had been no possibility of visiting Mexico, even though it was hardly a day's drive away. Genia and Rudy Peierls, having scheduled their return to England, decided it was one excursion they needed to take. Mici and I, although we were only going to Chicago, wanted to join them. The four of us had been planning a joint trip for some weeks before the congressional invitation came. There was no way to change it.

Understandably, Mici was not happy about the problem. Nor did I want her to miss the trip. Eventually, the Peierls came up with the perfect solution: Mici would invite Klaus Fuchs to be her traveling companion. He was a good friend of the Peierls, a good driver, and a polite, quiet, and courteous escort. Thus it was that Rudy, Genia, Klaus, and Mici set off for Mexico while I went off to Washington.

I recently reread the comments I made February 1, 1946, and was reminded of the truism that every author has just one book to write, no matter
how many times he writes it. In outlining the conditions that had to be established for successful work on atomic power, I once again began by addressing the need for effective defense:

> Among the fields of future work, I should like to mention first the defense
> against the atomic bomb. Such defense may not utilize atomic power. Yet in
> connection with the atomic bomb the feasibility of defense must be upper-
> most in our minds.
>
> It has been stated repeatedly that a satisfactory defense is impossible. I
> share this belief. Nevertheless, the difference between an unsatisfactory de-
> fense and no defense may be decisive.
>
> Devices may be constructed which destroy a considerable fraction of atomic
> missiles directed against us. It is extremely difficult but not impossible to
> develop fast-moving defense missiles which are automatically steered toward
> approaching projectiles. To accomplish this end, scientific and technical
> developments similar in magnitude and success to recent work in radar and
> jet propulsion would be necessary.
>
> In recent years development of aggressive weapons has outstripped the devel-
> opment of defense. The V-2 rocket and the atomic bomb are two instances of
> weapons against which, at present, no defense exists. The atomic bomb is in its
> earliest infancy, and even a moderate amount of work may improve it consider-
> ably. Future bombs may become less expensive, may be easier to handle, and
> they may have a much greater destructive power. I am convinced that it will not
> be very difficult to construct atomic bombs which will dwarf the Hiroshima
> bomb in the same way that the [atomic] bomb has dwarfed high explosives.
>
> In the near future, we can hardly expect that defensive measures will catch
> up with the means of aggression. Our present military advantage seems great.
> But the events of the last years show how quickly this situation may change.
> Only three and a half years of intensive effort were needed to make an atomic
> bomb. Unless the possibility of a future war can be eliminated, we are going
> to live in a world in which safety no longer exists.
>
> I do not know whether international developments will make further work
> on atomic bombs necessary. I share the hope that the atomic bomb, together
> with other weapons of aggression, will be eliminated. But if it should be de-
> cided that we renew work on the development of the atomic bomb, it must be
> pointed out that, under present conditions, we are not prepared to do so.

Among the peacetime applications, extraction of useful power from chain-reacting structures is first in economic significance. One must not expect any profound effects on our economic life in the near future, but specific applica tions may soon become important. One is production of energy in places which at present lack cheap power. Another is construction of smaller energy-producing units which will function for a very long period of time. It must be stated, however, that even these smaller units cannot be installed without a considerable weight of shielding, and they therefore cannot be used in cars or airplanes but only in fairly large-sized vessels. Progress toward all these ends has been, in the recent past, slow.

Use of radio-elements which are by-products of atomic power plants will have an extremely great influence in science, particularly in medical science. Work with these by-products will lead to a better understanding of living organisms, and the knowledge so gained will, in the end, help to save human lives. Progress in this direction has been practically negligible so far. In the past this was due to necessary wartime secrecy, which made it impossible to distribute the radio-elements among the men who could have made use of them. The publication of the Smyth report has changed this situation. The distribution of many radio-elements would disclose now no important secret and would result in no real danger since, in appropriately small quantities, these by-products are harmless. That the by-products have not been distributed and used in the last months is due, to a considerable extent, to the inertia of the administrative apparatus required for the distribution. I believe that these materials should be made available not only to scientists in this country but to scientists throughout the world. This would be a gesture which would cost us little and would bring us great returns in good will as well as in the advancement of scientific knowledge.

I went on to explain that weapons tests were of great interest to scientists as well as to the armed forces, and that an atomic bomb may be regarded as a scientific tool that allows us to find out facts of nature that cannot be found out in any other way. I discussed the need for public education on the topic of atomic science and the reasons that had contributed to the lack of interest among physicists in continuing work on projects related to military affairs; I mentioned the lack of freedom and autonomy in research, the lack of long-term government planning, and the overabundance of routine operations that crowd out research and development. I mentioned that money alone would not be sufficient to encourage scientists to return to government work. But most of my efforts, as had been true in my report to the navy, went to describing the harmful effects of secrecy.

> Pure scientific data—that is, facts concerning natural phenomena—must not be kept secret. If such secrecy is continued, it will warp the entire research activity of any man who is involved in work on atomic power. He either has to sever relations with the scientific world not involved in the development of atomic power or he has to acquire a split personality, remembering in certain parts of his work only certain parts of the information available to him.
>
> Furthermore, scientific facts cannot be kept secret for any length of time. They are readily re-discovered. If we attempt to keep scientific facts secret, it will certainly hinder us but will hardly interfere with the work of a potential competitor.
>
> The only secrets which can remain effective for a reasonable length of time are technical details of construction and industrial know-how. Indeed these things cannot be easily communicated except by actual collaboration. As an example, I may mention the construction of cyclotrons. In spite of the fact that full details have been published, everyone had the greatest difficulties in reproducing these instruments except those men who had a chance to learn directly from the original inventors.
>
> I believe that even if some secrecy must be maintained, it should be restricted to a few subjects on technical details. Secrecy regulations should be in large measure entrusted to the people who themselves engage in the work.

As it turned out, those topics—defense, nuclear energy, the medical and biological applications of radioactive isotopes, the scientific importance of testing, education, and secrecy—were the issues about which I would entreat, harangue, and reason for the next fifty years.

Enrico Fermi once told me (with hardly a trace of a smile) that I was the only monomaniac he knew who had several manias. The world had just lived through a period in which there was indeed something new under the sun. By February 1, 1946, I had established most of the topics that would constitute my several lifelong monomaniacal attachments.

From Washington, D.C., I went to Chicago. The postwar housing shortage there was terrible, a problem that affected our many Manhattan Project acquaintances who were coming to the University of Chicago: Cyril and Alice Smith, Enrico and Laura Fermi, Joe and Maria Mayer, Herb Anderson, Bill and Lorelei Libby, Robert Christy and his wife, Nick Metropolis, and

Bob Sachs.[14] Geoffrey Chew, Joan Hinton, Harold and Beverly Agnew, and several young people from my Los Alamos group—Mary and Harold Argo, Eldred Nelson and his wife, Stan and Mary Frankel, and Ellen Flanders—were arriving to complete their graduate degrees. For everyone, finding a place to live was a challenge.

Eventually, we found a solution for ourselves in the form of an enormous, well-built old home in a declining neighborhood well north of the university, which we rented jointly with the Christy family. I knew Christy mostly as the ingenious physicist who had come up with the simplified design for the plutonium bomb. Even though we lived in the same house, we didn't see a great deal of each other, but what I saw of him and his family, I enjoyed. The Christy family lived on the ground floor; we Tellers spread ourselves over the top two floors, far more space than we needed.

The house was only a fifteen- or twenty-minute brisk walk from the university, so during the six months we lived there, we welcomed parades of guests. Moll Flanders had stayed on in Los Alamos, so Ellen moved in with us.[15] The Fermis also lived with us for some weeks while they were looking for housing. Then Szilárd sent a friend (whom we didn't know) who stayed awhile. We had so many guests that our home was nicknamed the Teller Hotel. The only problem with our arrangements was that while the Christys had their own bathroom on the first floor, the one on the second floor served the Teller family and all the guests. Even today, Mici remembers that house as the one with the bathroom shortage.

In some ways, that period in Chicago bore a resemblance to the life I had enjoyed in Washington. It was fun to be back in an academic setting, to think about and discuss scientific questions with friends and students. But it was not the same. The world in 1946 was different in every way from the world of 1939.

---

[14] Sachs had been Maria's first graduate student at Johns Hopkins and had subsequently worked with me at George Washington. Bob later became the director of the Argonne Laboratory.

[15] I remember Ellen particularly because of her attire; bare legs and bare feet in sandals in the midst of a Chicago winter suggested that she was impervious to cold, but her often bright-blue legs told a different story.

20

INCOMPLETE ANSWERS

1946

THE SECOND MAJOR war in my lifetime had ended. Once again, central Europe was experiencing the bitter aftermath that is the natural consequence of war. Would this peace also contain the seeds of the next conflict?

War in the atomic age holds a new horror. I cannot imagine that anyone present at the Trinity test was confused about that; the danger of another war lent intense importance to healing the wounds of war and to building a cooperative, stable relationship among the nations of the world. The United States responded with a program unprecedented in history: Under the Marshall Plan, Germany and Japan, the defeated foes, were given aid for postwar reconstruction. That investment paid great dividends in easing bitterness and creating a more cooperative spirit in the decades that followed. It is unpleasant to imagine what those years might have held without the contribution made by the Marshall Plan.

A new era was underway, and the alumni of the Manhattan Project would play a considerable role, sometimes intentional, sometimes unintentional, in determining the shape that it assumed. Several misconceptions skewed developments in 1946. The best-known and most damaging was the assumption that American secrecy had successfully kept detailed information about nuclear weapons within Great Britain and the United States. A more subtle and less recognized influence was connected with the German atomic bomb project. Most of the people who could recount that story with authority are now dead. Knowing that the answers I offer are full of uncertainties, I feel that guesses are better than silence.

Speculation about the German effort to build atomic weapons, as the Szilárd-Einstein letter indicates, began in 1939. In May 1945, a special group, led by Colonel Boris Pash, completed their investigations of German nuclear-research sites. They found only a heavy water reactor, of good design, but still not operating! That discovery, unfortunately, contributed to the myth that only the United States had scientists gifted enough to design and build nuclear weapons, and consequently to the idea that keeping the scientific knowledge about the bomb secret would prevent other nations from producing similar armaments. My opinion, then and now, is that quite a different set of circumstances, not the least of them emotional, sharply limited the effectiveness of the German atomic bomb project.

Colonel Pash's race behind the lines in late April and early May resulted in the capture of Werner Heisenberg, Carl Frederick von Weiszäcker, Otto Hahn, and other leading physicists who had been working on the German atomic bomb project.[1] (The purpose of the raids was to prevent scientists and their work on reactors and atomic explosives from falling into Soviet, or even French, hands.) A few weeks later, these scientists were transported to a country estate, Farm Hall, near Cambridge, England, where they were held for the next several months. Their conversations at Farm Hall were secretly recorded. Almost fifty years later, the transcripts were declassified, and they have now been published.[2]

Heisenberg was the leading theoretician involved in the atomic bomb program, and by 1943, he had been made head of the physics department of the Kaiser Wilhelm Institute, where the work on the German atomic bomb was conducted. But the atomic bomb project had begun long before this time: Three groups of scientists had brought the possibility of a uranium bomb to the attention of officials in the army and in the ministry that oversaw the universities. By the fall of 1939, the army had taken over the Kaiser Wilhelm Institute for war work, and Otto Hahn and Werner Heisenberg were brought in to oversee the scientific research on fission. By February 1940, Heisenberg was already aware that an atomic bomb based on uranium-235 was possible, and not long after, Hahn and Strassman were attempting to produce a sample of element 94 (plutonium), believing that this element, which could be produced in a nuclear reactor, would also provide bomb material.

From about this time on the German work was conducted in a dispirited and slipshod manner; for that reason, I believe the idea of putting the power

---

[1] In addition, Erich Bagge, Kurt Diebner, Walter Gerlach, Paul Harteck, Horst Korsching, Max von Laue, and Karl Wirtz were taken into custody.

[2] *Operation Epsilon: The Farm Hall Transcripts.* (Berkeley: University of California Press, 1993). A more comprehensive book on the German atomic bomb project is *German National Socialism and the Quest for Nuclear Power 1939–1949* by Mark Walker (Cambridge: Cambridge University Press, 1989).

of an atomic bomb into Hitler's hands was consciously or unconsciously re-pellant to many of the scientists involved, but most especially to Heisenberg. They may have kept the institute running, thereby preventing the sacrifice of young talented physicists to the battlefield; Heisenberg may have reported the results of their work to Göring, and thereby kept his own lack of Nazi Party membership from becoming an issue; but I do not believe—and there is no evidence that suggests it—that Heisenberg actively pursued research on an atomic bomb.

On August 6, when Heisenberg and his colleagues—now interned at Farm Hall—were told of the bombing of Hiroshima, they did not believe it. At one point Heisenberg, talking with Hahn, said, "I still don't believe a word about the bomb, but I may be wrong. I consider it perfectly possible that they have about ten tons of enriched uranium, but not that they can have ten tons of pure U-235." Hahn responded, "But tell me why you used to tell me that one needed fifty kilograms of 235 in order to do anything? Now you say one needs ten tons!"

Although the estimate of fifty kilograms is high, it is not an unreasonable guess; but ten tons is an amazing statement from so gifted a scientist as Heisenberg. The error to my mind suggests that Heisenberg had been constructing mental barriers to making progress on the atomic bomb throughout the five years since he had seen the possibility of such a bomb. His deepest nature had turned away from solving the problem. Yet Heisenberg strove to be, and indeed was, excellent in every aspect of his life, from playing Ping-Pong to playing the piano, but most particularly in science.

The following morning, Heisenberg, now emotionally able to examine the problem, came up with the correct timing for the detonation of a bomb.[3] One week later, when after years of procrastinating Heisenberg had finally put his mind to work on the problem, he presented a lecture to his fellow detainees on how the American bomb worked; but he demonstrated his lack of previous effort by making a remarkable mistake, the same erroneous possibility that I had considered early in the Manhattan Project. He raised the question of whether at the relevant high temperatures, opacities allow radiation to leak out, thus diminishing the energy available for disassembling the bomb.

The mistake is natural, and I am pleased that I had come up with the same idea in 1942. The idea was generally disbelieved at Berkeley, but the issue

---

[3] *Operation Epsilon,* p. 91. "In order to produce fission in 10^{25} atoms, you need 80 steps in the chain so that the whole reaction is complete in 10^{-8} seconds."

was not settled until Maria Mayer and her colleagues in Chicago had demonstrated that opacities had no importance in the atomic bomb. But Heisenberg—who by 1940 had understood that bombs could be produced—didn't make the mistake until August 14, 1945; this strongly suggests that he had just begun thinking seriously about how to develop an atomic weapon.

I am not surprised. It is inconceivable to me that Heisenberg would ever have pursued such a purpose. He loved his country, but he hated the Nazis. He was deeply grieved by the Aryan laws Hitler enacted. He was incensed by the proscription of teaching "Jewish science"—any theory, such as Einstein's relativity, that had been developed by a Jew. In 1936, Heisenberg was even attacked in an official Nazi publication as being "a white Jew," and "Jewish in character." By 1938, his position had become so perilous that Prandtl, the prestigious head of the aeronautical institute in Aachen, had to intercede for Heisenberg with Göring.

Yet Heisenberg, still in disfavor and therefore at great personal risk, in 1942 tried to save the parents of Samuel Goudsmit (a Dutch colleague) from deportation to the concentration camps. In 1944, Heisenberg again bravely intervened when the Nazis were about to dismantle Niels Bohr's Institute and ship the instruments to Germany. Carl Friedrich, who was very close to Heisenberg, once told me that "Heisenberg died without regrets." To me, that statement makes it clear that Heisenberg never worked for the Nazis in the real sense.

This story is a different account from the one that Niels Bohr, Heisenberg's mentor and closest colleague, carried to Los Alamos in 1943.[4] Bohr claimed that Heisenberg visited him in Copenhagen after Denmark had been occupied by the Nazis. Bohr said that Heisenberg had told him that he was working on the bomb for Hitler and considered that a good thing to do. Bohr never moderated or modified his statement.

Most scientists at Los Alamos and elsewhere in the Western world accepted Bohr's simple story without question. But I was deeply troubled by it. Heisenberg was not only a brilliant physicist but also a man whose decency and fairness I had long appreciated. I could not imagine that he would support the Nazis willingly, much less do so enthusiastically, as Bohr's account suggested. How did the misunderstanding with Bohr occur?

---

[4] Bohr's escape, engineered by the Allies, began with a journey by small boat across the North Sea to Sweden and continued by military plane to England. During the flight, Bohr could not manage to get his oxygen mask to work properly. Although he lost consciousness and had to be revived, he was not badly hurt.

Any hope of resolving the differences between the two accounts must begin with an understanding of the difficulties each participant faced. Neither Heisenberg nor Bohr was popular with the Nazis. Heisenberg not only failed to subscribe to their goals and beliefs but also upheld Einstein's theories, proscribed as Jewish attempts to degrade German science. At one point, there was enough of that sort of evidence to convince Hitler that Heisenberg was a traitor who should be sent to a concentration camp.

Bohr also was in danger from the Nazis. Bohr's ancestry was half Jewish, and that put him at risk once Denmark was occupied. But Bohr became a symbol of resistance because he was the glaring antithesis of everything the Nazis stood for. So why, when Heisenberg knew that he himself was under suspicion and that Bohr was in open opposition to the Nazis, did he go to confide in his old friend and mentor?

The information I gathered leads me to believe that Heisenberg went to Bohr for moral advice. I also believe that the meeting with Bohr had two parts: the first in Bohr's magnificent residence, the Carlsberg Castle; the second in Bohr's garden. Indoors, Heisenberg, fearing that the Nazis had bugged Bohr's rooms, reported working for his country. Subsequently, while walking in the garden, Heisenberg explained that he was involved in the Nazi fission research project. But, there, according to Carl Friedrich von Weiszäcker, Heisenberg also passed along the suggestion that made his trip seem worth the risk: He added that he thought it would be impossible, fortunately, to build an atomic bomb in Germany; and that he hoped the British and American scientists would not succeed either. What did Bohr think could be done about the possibility of such a terrible weapon?

Why didn't Bohr report the second part of the conversation? The reason may be simple. Bohr was in deadly danger. Once Heisenberg said that he was working for his nation, Bohr may have stopped listening.[5] I believe there is a deep disagreement between Bohr's refusal to listen to Heisenberg's point of view and Bohr's general principles. Bohr was the embodiment of complementarity, the insistance that every important question has opposite sides that appear to be mutually exclusive; understanding of the question becomes possible only if the reality on both sides is acknowledged.

Bohr's theory applied to important questions in general, not just those formulated in physics. He often said that every eighteen-year-old should master

---

[5] Even under the best of circumstances, Bohr was never a good listener.

that idea, because without it, he or she would be incompletely equipped for life. Yet, Bohr failed to apply that principle to the conflict between Heisenberg's patriotism and Heisenberg's thorough unwillingness to help the Nazis. On the basis of his one-sided view, Bohr died without making a rapprochement with his most talented and devoted collaborator.

And so the irreversible effect of the war, and particularly of Hitler, was to produce a deep disagreement involving two of the century's most outstanding physicists. In this connection, the Farm Hall discussions are particularly significant. The transcribed evidence makes it clear that Heisenberg had succeeded in putting aside consideration of the physical details of the atomic bomb.

Bohr's influence in the postwar world did not stop with the damage to Heisenberg's reputation. Bohr loved paradoxes; in the exact science of physics, that turned out to be a virtue. In politics, paradox is overabundant, and exactitude is in short supply. Before the end of the war, Bohr had succeeded in telling both Roosevelt and Churchill his ideas about the path the development of nuclear energy should take: "Nuclear energy has made war impossible. Work on nuclear energy must be conducted on an international basis, and we should begin by sharing all of our knowledge with the Soviets." Churchill and Roosevelt had little faith in radical solutions and even less in Joseph Stalin. Their response to Bohr's suggestion was prompt and negative.

That failure, however, seemed only to spur Bohr on to greater efforts in gaining converts. He continued to expound his political theory within the scientific community: War in the nuclear age, because of its destructiveness, had become impossible. Therefore, scientists no longer should work on weapons.

Bohr's position reminded me of the statement Oppenheimer had made in our train compartment years earlier; that is, the time would come to oppose the military. Hearing the idea in a different context and in a more moderate form, I was less shocked—but I was still in thorough disagreement. In fact, I was more worried than ever. I disagreed with Bohr's solution, but I agreed that the most important task facing the world was to maintain peace.

Hopes that atomic energy would be equitably controlled through an international effort were formally addressed in the spring of 1946. A committee led by David E. Lilienthal and Dean Acheson came up with a comprehensive program for the international control of atomic energy. The plan seemed to merit the generalized hope of assuring that nuclear weapons would never again be used in warfare. Although Oppenheimer was not listed as an author, he had obviously played an important role in developing it.

This first proposal (which has come to be known as the Baruch plan because Bernard Baruch later submitted it to the United Nations) was a plan with reliable, workable controls. They involved five interconnected levels: mining of materials, refining, nuclear reactors, production of nuclear explosives, and, most important, free communication with all the people who could work on such projects. The most attractive feature of the proposal was that, instead of laying emphasis on prohibitions, it proposed international cooperation on all programs. Free exchange among the qualified scientists of all nations as they worked on common projects would be the means of uncovering emphasis given the military applications.

As I have mentioned, I had disagreed with Oppenheimer on whether the military (his position) or a civilian agency (my position) should direct the development of nuclear energy, a question that was still under heated discussion. Therefore, I was pleased to find that on the Acheson-Lilienthal report I could wholeheartedly agree with Oppie. I added my voice to the chorus of praise for the plan, in part by writing an article for a new journal, *The Bulletin of the Atomic Scientists of Chicago*.[6]

During my wartime stay in Chicago, I had met Eugene Rabinovich, a chemist then working with Papa Franck. When we met again after the war, we discovered that we both agreed on the importance of a journal that not only discussed the issues connected with the new technology but presented ideas about atomic science in language accessible to everyone. I promised to help with writing articles, should there be a need, and suggested that the magazine use a clock with its hands set at five minutes to midnight as a symbol of urgency. I was pleased when that emblem was adopted.[7]

I gave my article about the Baruch plan the title "A Ray of Hope."[8] The plan proposed open collaboration on all matters pertaining to nuclear energy; if the Soviets wanted to participate, they would have to abandon the requisite amount of their secrecy. In exchange, the United States was offering all the detailed information we had gained during the war years. At the time, the offer seemed generous.

---

[6] The journal later dropped the last two words of its title.

[7] I didn't then realize that future editors would move the clock to an earlier or later time, depending on their political opinions. Neither did I guess how one-sided a discussion the *Bulletin* would eventually present. In 1946, I was simply pleased to help gain a wider audience for the discussion of the problems related to atomic energy.

[8] Edward Teller, "State Department Report—A Ray of Hope," *Bulletin of Atomic Scientists*, I, 8 (April, 1946), 10, 13.

The Soviets' immediate response to the Baruch plan was to demand that, before further discussion occurred, the United States destroy its existing nuclear weapons. Although many months of discussions followed, they were to no avail. Not until 1950 did we learn why the proposal met with so little interest. Soviet espionage had already provided Stalin the secrets we were offering in exchange for open cooperation.

In the spring of 1946, hopes for the success of cooperative international control of nuclear energy were still high. The postwar period in the United States was full of the pleasures and excitement of demobilization. Not many scientists were willing to continue full-time work at Los Alamos. Given the shortage of staff, funds, and particularly of interest, it was clear that work on the hydrogen bomb had to be terminated. Several of us, including me, had left Los Alamos with the intention of returning on frequent visits to lend a hand. But because work on the hydrogen bomb was unlikely to be addressed in the near future, we thought it important to summarize what we knew at that point. In the late spring, 1946, I left the University of Chicago to attend a summary conference at Los Alamos.

For the reader to understand future events, I need to review the history of the work up to that time. My initial efforts on the suggestion Fermi made in 1941, that an atomic bomb might initiate nuclear reactions between hydrogen isotopes, had to deal with the difficulty that too much energy appeared as radiation; not enough energy was left for nuclei to overcome their mutual repulsion to approach each other and produce fusion.

Then, in the spring of 1942, when Konopinski and I were attempting to write up that finding, we discovered that, given a relatively slow transfer of energy into radiation, an equilibrium between particle motion and radiation could be avoided. Indeed, those first estimates, which considered the energy radiated a loss, indicated that the nuclei of the hydrogen isotopes would attain sufficiently high energies for a sufficiently long time to approach each other and react. That led to the optimistic predictions about the feasibility of the hydrogen bomb at the Berkeley conference in the summer of 1942.

The difficulty that occurred to me while I was visiting with Johnny von Neumann at Princeton during the war was that the radiation emitted would not simply escape; rather, it would be scattered by the fast-moving, energetic electrons. If the electrons, together with the nuclei, had been heated more effectively than the radiation itself, then, in such scattering processes, energy would be handed over on the average from electrons to radiation, particularly to the abundantly emitted low-energy, long-wave radiation. Thus, the electrons would cool, and more energy would escape in the form of radiation.

The electrons, having lost energy, would in turn extract more from the nuclei, a process that might slow the thermonuclear reaction to the point where the energy production by nuclear reactions could not keep up with the energy loss.

The design all of us were then considering called for a nuclear explosion to send a strong, very hot shock into liquid deuterium.[9] My group had been working on the calculations needed to ascertain the extent to which such energy losses would occur. The earliest hand calculations suggested that this difficulty, although very real, would not be decisive.

In the months following the end of the war, Johnny von Neumann helped make the best computing resources available to Nick Metropolis and Stan Frankel for their continuing work on those calculations. I barely heard about the results before I left Los Alamos, but they were available for the late spring conference. The question their calculations attempted to answer was: Would the processes give rise to increasing production of energy as the shock wave is propagated through a tube filled with liquid deuterium, given the energy loss from radiation and from collisions with electrons? Their answer was: Yes, and easily so.

As it turned out, those calculations, performed after most of the group, including me, had returned to other work, were flawed. As I recall, Fermi and Stan Ulam, a mathematician whom Johnny von Neumann had sent to work at Los Alamos during the war, raised doubts about them. Because the decision not to proceed with work on the hydrogen bomb had been made, neither I nor anyone else, to my knowledge, checked the calculations in any detail.

I remember that those of us at the conference concluded that a hydrogen bomb based on the ideas I have just described (a design nicknamed the Super) could be perfected fairly easily, although no one discussed the engineering details. One person definitely not of that opinion was Norris Bradbury. He maintained that a thermonuclear weapon could not be built within the foreseeable future.[10] The director of a laboratory has a great deal to do with

---

[9] The temperature that could be reached would be particularly high because, in the energy transfer between the dense material in the nuclear explosion and the much less dense material of liquid deuterium, high velocities would be attained, which translates into fast, disorderly motion of the particles (temperature).

[10] In Appendix A of Edith C. Truslow and Ralph Carlisle Smith, eds., *Project Y: The Los Alamos Story* (Los Angeles: Tomash Publishers, 1983), Bradbury is quoted as saying in a speech on October 1, 1945, that fundamental experiments to establish the feasibility of a Super should be undertaken, but "this does not mean we will build a Super. It couldn't happen in our time in any event."

whether a program is continued. It was clear to me that all meaningful work on the project had ended for the foreseeable future.

Phillip Morrison also participated in the conference. He had arrived at Los Alamos relatively late in the war, and he had never worked on the Super. Even so, he was greatly interested in the hydrogen bomb—as one of its opponents. In a detailed and eloquent section of the conference report, he described the horrible damage that such thermonuclear bombs could cause if used against the densely populated cities on the East Coast of the United States. The idea that there could be no defense against nuclear weapons was used to support a corollary: therefore, a thermonuclear weapon should not be developed.

Another participant at the conference deserves mention, although at the time, his presence was hardly noticed: Inconspicuous, agreeable, helpful Klaus Fuchs was still at Los Alamos. His extended stay to write reports was completely understandable and helpful. He had enjoyed full access to all the work that went on at Los Alamos, and he often talked in great depth with me and others about our projects; he made several impressive contributions during those discussions. He also extended my knowledge of various technical matters. So, of course, he joined the meetings.

Less than a year after the conference, Bradbury named a Canadian mathematician, Carson Mark, to replace Robert Richtmyer, with whom I had enjoyed working, as head of the theoretical division. Carson held the post until he retired thirty or so years later.

Carson, his wife, Kay, and their children (whose number increased steadily during the next few years) had arrived from the Canadian Chalk River atomic energy project just before the test; unfortunately, no one had sufficient time to incorporate him into any project until several weeks later. Carson, a man of good humor, understanding, and executive abilities, turned out to be an excellent choice as division leader. He was a real diplomat and was always pleasant in his dealings with people.

Carson and Kay extended a great deal of hospitality to the community throughout their years at Los Alamos. During the next five years, I would spend many pleasurable (but hardly profitable) evenings playing poker at their home. I have a distinct memory of Carson that dates from earlier that spring. A group of us were at a dinner party when the arrest of Alan Nunn May for espionage was announced. May had worked on the same Canadian wartime atomic energy program as Carson Mark. Carson could not believe that his countryman and former colleague could be a traitor. Klaus Fuchs was also part of the gathering that day. I remember because I was surprised that Fuchs, too, without saying a single word, seemed so very upset.

Forty-five years after that conference, I read Andrei Sakharov's memoirs and noted with interest that a few months after our conference, Lavrenti Beria, infamous head of the KGB under Stalin, first attempted to draft Sakharov to work on Soviet nuclear weapons.[11] Sakharov evaded the offer twice; but less than two years later, in 1948, he was drawn into the effort by two excellent senior scientists involved in the program, I. V. Kurchatov and Igor Tamm.

In spite of all the efforts of the security officers at Los Alamos, Fuchs had spied for the Soviet Union throughout the war years. During the war years and subsequently until the end of 1949, he provided vital technical and scientific information to Soviet agents; this information simplified and speeded the work on the Soviet atomic bomb. He undoubtedly informed the Kremlin of the post-conference status of the hydrogen bomb: that although the weapon was highly feasible, work on the project had been discontinued.

Seven years had passed since fission had been discovered. The world was a better world for being without Hitler. But there was still the fact of the atomic bomb. In counterbalance, the world was full of people believing in a better future and wondering, in their individual and often incompatible ways, how to help such a future become a reality.

[11] Andrei Sakharov, *Memoirs* (New York: Alfred A. Knopf, 1990).

21

AMONG
FRIENDS FROM HOME

February 1946–June 1949

M Y SEARCH FOR a way back to the great adventure of pure science began in earnest when I reached the University of Chicago in February 1946. For me, colleagues have always been one of the particular pleasures of science, and the companionship of three of my friends, Maria Mayer, Enrico Fermi, and Johnny von Neumann, figured large in my plans for a return to normalcy.

Maria was already an important person in my life. We had a great deal in common: love for the puzzles of science; memories of a world that for us had been irretrievably lost; and an unspoken, perhaps even unrecognized, commitment to preserving some of the values of those bygone days. Between 1944 and 1952, I wrote to her many times. Our friendship was such that I simply discussed whatever was on my mind. I was astounded to learn a few years ago that she had saved all my letters.[1]

I have in front of me her letter dated July 12, 1945. It begins, "It was nice to get a letter from you—even if you did have to mention the oranges." A few weeks earlier, when I had made a trip back East, we attended an official meeting in New Jersey together. Driving back to Leonia, Maria lost her way, and we landed in Orange, New Jersey. My next letter began: "Thanks for the oranges."

---

[1] My letters to Maria Mayer, which were particularly helpful in writing the chapters covering those years, are part of the Mandeville Special Collection Library, University of California at San Diego.

The reason for her inattention during that drive was that we had been theorizing about the origin of the elements. The discovery that the universe was expanding had been made several years before the war. That in turn gave rise to the idea that sometime in the distant past, the universe was born with one Big Bang, when all matter started moving away from a central point.

Matter can be described as being composed of light elements (those with a nucleus of fewer than twenty-seven protons), which constitute the majority of all substances in the universe, and heavy elements (cobalt through uranium), which are comparatively rare. Before the war, Hans Bethe explained the origin of the light elements, but no one explained how the comparatively rare heavy elements had come into being.[2] When I finally decided to come to Chicago, Maria and I agreed to work on the theory that neutronic matter, formed shortly after the Big Bang, might have been the source of the heavy elements.

But Maria's and my collaborative effort had hardly got underway before the summer of 1946 arrived; Mici and I, this time accompanied by Paul, reverted to the habits of our former academic years and once again became nomads. Felix Bloch, who had returned to Stanford after the war, invited me to teach summer school there, and I happily agreed.

Our weeks at Stanford were very pleasant. Norris Bradbury, formerly of Stanford and now the director at Los Alamos, rented us his home, a quiet and agreeable change from the Teller Hotel. The weeks passed quickly: I lectured, Paul played with the Blochs' sons, and Mici grew large with our second child.

The only noteworthy event during the period was a letter from Heisenberg, my first word from him in six years. But he said nothing about himself or conditions in Germany. He simply asked whether I would send him the *Physical Review* in exchange for some German publications. I promptly arranged to do so.

When we were almost ready to leave for the second part of our summer, which we would spend at Los Alamos, we had a long session with Felix Bloch, tracing our route from Palo Alto. Our baby was not due to arrive for six weeks, but Felix would have preferred to see us stay and gleefully predicted

---

[2] The two groups of elements also differ in that, among the lighter elements, the isotopes with the fewest number of neutrons are most abundant; among the heavier elements (which grow increasingly rare as their atomic weight rises), the isotopes containing the most neutrons are the more abundant.

the point en route, in the middle of nowhere in Nevada, where Mici's labor would begin. Fortunately, he was wrong.

On our arrival at Los Alamos, we found a few changes. A real sidewalk had appeared (in front of a new post office!) together with a sign that read: "Pedestrians shall use the sidewalk." That summer, the McMahon Bill passed: Los Alamos would be run by civilians. Soon after, the sign on the grass at Los Alamos was amended to: "Pedestrians please use sidewalk."

The housing was unchanged. The house assigned to us leaked, both through the chimney and through the windows. Because that summer was the wettest of the four we had spent there, Mici persisted in her appeals until we were granted a drier apartment, which happened to be kitty-corner from the Egon Bretscher family, whose children Paul especially enjoyed.

On August 31, Mici went to the hospital and delivered our wonderful daughter, Wendy. This time, we could send the joyful news to our families, but the prospects of a reunion were still far in the future. The Bretchers were a great help during Mici's recuperation. I have never been known as a morning person, and Paul, at three and a half, was already resourceful; but I don't recall, as rumor had it, that Paul served me breakfast in bed during Mici's hospital stay. I do remember singing my disconsolate son his favorite song when, not many weeks later, the Bretchers and their children left for England.[3]

About the time of Wendy's birth, Maria, for the first and only time in our many years of friendship, got angry with me. I much prefer to get along well with everyone, so when someone I care about is angry with me, I am truly and deeply in despair. In this instance, I was, unintentionally, the guilty person.

In examining the facts our theory had to explain, Maria noticed that those nuclei that had either 2, 6, 14, 28, 50, 82, or 126 protons or neutrons were far more abundant than nuclei with not very different proton or neutron numbers. (These were called the "magic" numbers.) If both the neutrons and protons were of a "magic" number, the isotope was particularly abundant.[4]

That seemed like a detail to me, but Maria thought that the regular and repetitious appearance of these abundances must have an interesting explanation

---

[3] We called the song "Sprinkles," Paul's approximation of the word *princess;* and although I don't know the song's origin, I still remember the words to all eight verses, probably because of the many renditions it received. I also remember the melody, but my singing voice now only approximates the notes.

[4] For example, lead-208, which comprises the vast majority of all lead, contains 82 protons and 126 neutrons.

in itself; whether it was connected with the origin of elements was not the issue. I persisted in disparaging her interest until finally she lost her temper.[5]

Fortunately, her displeasure was short-lived. And the work that Maria began that summer proved to be most important: It was the beginning of a detailed understanding of nuclear structure. It is not an overstatement to say that her shell model does for nuclei what the periodic table does for the chemical elements.[6]

Shortly after she published her work, three German scientists discovered the same facts independently. (There is no doubt of her priority.) In 1955, Maria published a book on theory of nuclear shell structure with the senior German author, J. Hans Jensen. In 1963, Maria, Jensen, and Eugene Wigner shared the Nobel Prize for work on that topic.[7]

During the summer of 1946, I spent some time working with Robert Richtmyer, who was then the leader of the theoretical division. He was concerned about the absence of any effort on thermonuclear research, and we came up with the first alternative design to the Super and performed a few related calculations. Bob insisted on calling that design the Alarm Clock: Given its simple and feasible nature, it should wake people up to the idea that work on a thermonuclear explosive ought not be delayed. Unfortunately, it did not rouse anyone.

Mici had made it clear from the beginning of the summer that she was not about to return to Chicago until we had more acceptable accommodations: Substandard housing in Los Alamos was preferable to the Teller Hotel. But

---

[5] Maria's theory became the shell model of the nucleus, which, contrary to Bohr's liquid droplet model, says that the neutrons and the protons, in first approximation, move freely throughout the nucleus. Bohr's model essentially said that the nuclear forces were of shorter range than the average nuclear radius, so only neighboring protons and neutrons affect one another. The question is not yet fully resolved.

[6] She found that in the nuclei, there is a very strong coupling of the angular momentum of the orbit and of the internal angular momentum (or spin) of the nuclear particles. Making the assumption of such a strong spin-orbital interaction, Maria explained the irregularities of the stability in the nuclei. What is more important, she gave a complete explanation of practically all of nuclear spectroscopy, including the regularities in the beta decay and gamma decay schemes.

[7] Maria remains to my mind in the first rank of theoretical physicists of the twentieth century. She received relatively little recognition, even after she received the Nobel Prize. That may have been because she was a woman; but I suspect that, more important, it may have been because she held opinions on politically sensitive questions that were not those of the closely knit group of theoretical physicists who dominate the style of physics, including appointments to the universities.

the housing shortage in Chicago remained severe. Finally, in late summer, Maria and Mary Argo located a little house for us on Ellis Avenue, which, though small, proved acceptable. We promptly bought it, but the renovations couldn't be completed in time for Mit i and the children to return with me in October. I shuttled back and forth until December, when at last we all reassembled in Chicago.

Maria and I resumed our work that fall and continued it for the next two years.[8] When, in the late spring of 1948, I received an invitation to the Solvay conference in Belgium, a prestigious gathering of physicists from around the world, I decided to present our theory.

I left for the conference early in September. Heading back to Europe for the first time in twelve years, I was very worried about the changes I might find. I went first to London, and Frederick Lindemann, the physical chemist whom I had met at Franck's home in Göttingen in 1933, kindly invited me to join him at his home in Oxford for lunch.[9] Our meal was simple. Three years after the end of the war, the food shortage remained noticeable. But the British humor was as excellent as ever: One of the other guests, a small smiling man, was introduced as the only Anglican bishop in the United Kingdom without a cathedral. (He had the responsibility for all of Oxford instead.) Lindemann had accompanied Churchill to the Soviet Union, and the bishop asked our host for his candid impression of Stalin.

Lindemann smiled at him and said, "A very nice man. If he were visiting here, he might say, 'What kind of nice bishop is this?'" Turning to the rest of us, Lindemann continued: "Churchill, at the table in Moscow, asked Stalin about General Blucher.[10] Stalin replied, 'Blucher?'" Here Lindemann paused, looked puzzled, then relieved, and went on slowly: "'Blucher! An excellent general. A very important man. A man of such importance should not be interested in women. If such a man were interested in women [here

---

[8] We postulated that most of the matter would turn into protons and electrons but that some would be left over as sizable lumps of neutrons in a state of as high a density as is encountered in atomic nuclei. We found good and satisfactory reason why, within such lumps, there would be a relatively small number of protons and electrons. The action of the electrons would make the surface of the neutron lumps unstable, and smaller lumps would continue to break off as more neutrons turned into protons and electrons. That was the process we theorized would eventually lead to the formation of the heavier elements.

[9] Lindemann was now Lord Cherwell, having been honored for his service as Churchill's science advisor during the war.

[10] Blucher was a Soviet general, most famous for his accomplishments during World War II in the Far East, whom Stalin executed.

Lindemann's voice rose], that man should be shot.'" Lindemann paused, as if Stalin were having a hard time remembering. He concluded his impersonation in a small surprised voice, "'He was shot.'"[11]

While I was in London, I went to the American embassy on some errand, and the scientific attaché there asked me whether I would go on to Göttingen after the conference and report back to him, in an informal way, on conditions at the university there. Beside dreading the changes I might see, the Nazi attitudes were fresh in my mind, and I was afraid I might meet considerable animosity and lawlessness.[12] But when I asked the security branch of the embassy to check with the AEC (Atomic Energy Commission) in Washington about it, they told me not to worry.

I was flown to Frankfurt, where I was provided with a military car and a driver, a very young American who spent his time in two states—asleep or lost. The roads were still torn up; even the Autobahn was not repaired yet. The young G.I. drove diligently but with less and less certainty of direction. After more than an hour of not knowing where we were, I insisted on checking with people in the vicinity. We then learned that in a mile or two we would have reached the Russian control post for East Germany.

Eventually, we arrived at Göttingen, and I arranged to see both von Weizsäcker and Heisenberg. My meeting with Heisenberg was brief. He said no more about his wartime experiences in person than he had in his letter. He thanked me for the journals I had been sending, and I left, saddened by his weary reserve.

I met Carl Friedrich in a small room full of law books. He was worried about his father, who had been charged with war crimes by the Nuremberg tribunal. That was the only time I ever saw Carl Friedrich upset. He said, "If the Americans had come in and shot every tenth German, I could have understood it. I could have called it justice. The Americans had every reason to be angry. But I cannot accept ex post facto laws. They have nothing to do with justice."[13]

---

[11] I thought that my opinion of Stalin was low enough, but Lindemann's account managed to lower it further. I would not want to have to decide whether this little story is most instructive about Stalin or Lindemann, or both.

[12] That concern was not uniquely mine. After my return, members of the AEC staff, and my friend Admiral Chick Hayward, voiced amazement that I had "risked" the trip.

[13] Carl Friedrich's concern was well founded. His father, who had been a friend of Canaris and of various members of the group that attempted to assassinate Hitler, could not prove that he had tried, through quiet moderation, to limit Hitler's insanities. Stationed in the Vatican for the last years of the war, he had also played a role in convincing the German commander not to conduct a battle for Rome, thus sparing that beautiful city from what would

I also saw Professor Eucken during that trip. Of all my old acquaintances, he was most changed. Deeply discouraged, both about the state of his country and his personal affairs, he committed suicide a year or so later. After seeing my old friends, I wrote to Maria:

> I feel sure that this is what German scientists need now more than anything: to be taken again as normal human beings. It is not necessary to avoid the subject of Nazism. One can even disagree with them quite violently. But it is wrong to act as though the only important thing in the world would be politics. I certainly should not like to be judged on the same standards by which most of the American scientists judge the Germans.

I had another lesson about the divisions that politics had produced in the scientific community on that trip. On a bus ride on the way to Brussels for the Solvay conference, I sat next to P. M. S. Blackett, a British physical chemist who had just completed a wonderful analysis of the intricate structure of water and soon thereafter won a Nobel Prize. Blackett was also a communist.

A few months earlier, Stalin had closed the roads connecting the Allied sector of Berlin with the free world, intending thereby to force its incorporation into Soviet holdings through starvation.[14] The airport in the Allied sector was grossly inadequate for the size and number of planes needed to supply the hundreds of thousands of people held hostage, but the costly struggle to maintain that island of freedom was continuing as we talked.

I had and have great respect for Blackett's scientific contributions, and I am much happier to agree with a colleague than to disagree. But I could not let his remarks about the rectitude of the Soviet blockade and the stupidity of the airlift pass without challenge. The upshot was that we ended up in a somewhat acrimonious exchange. Political discussions among scientists were no longer as calm and friendly as they had been before the war.

Maria's and my theory was received well at the Solvay conference; but later that fall when we discussed our work at the department seminar in Chicago,

---

surely have been irreparable damage. His conviction and sentence to seven years in prison was based principally on his writing "no objection" on an earlier order deporting Jews from France. He served eighteen months of his sentence before he was released because of ill health. He died a few weeks later.

[14] At the end of the war, the Allies had divided Berlin into sectors: American, British, and Soviet. The British merged their sector with that of the Americans.

we met with heavy criticism from Fermi. Unfortunately, the estimate of the strength of nuclear forces that had seemed acceptable to us turned out to be too large. Fermi kept pointing out that our postulated lumps of neutronic matter would not hold together. I was slow to realize that Enrico was right, but by the spring of 1949, I had to accept his arguments.

The real explanation of how the heavier elements are formed seems to be connected with big chunks of neutronic matter held together by gravitation. Maria's and my work was significant only as a precursor that described some properties of the neutron star.[15] The validity or lack of validity of a theory should not be connected, in principle, with strong emotions. The fact is that I was deeply disappointed in our lack of success.

Our work on the origin of heavy elements was one of my favorite projects during this period, but it represented a small part of my efforts. Like several other members of the physics department at the university, I spent a fair amount of time at the Argonne Laboratory, where, under Wally Zinn's leadership, the first postwar reactors were being planned.[16] Maurice Goldhaber, a German refugee who had earlier worked with Szilárd, was part of the Argonne staff, and we collaborated on a paper explaining the absorption by nuclei of gamma radiation in the range of 10 to 20 million volts.[17]

During these years, I also finished my first book, *The Structure of Matter*, which I wrote with Frank Rice of the Catholic University in Washington,

---

[15] For nuclear matter to hold together, the percentages of neutrons and protons must not be too different; for instance, the percentage of protons must be at least 30 percent. Higher percentages of neutrons may occur only if gravitation assists. Because gravitation is a weak force exerted over a long range, the objects that are formed tend to be very big compared to the nucleus. For example, material composed almost exclusively of neutrons will be stable (at very high densities), provided the radius is at least a few kilometers. Such objects are known as neutron stars.

In the mid–1960s, William A. Fowler described beautifully how neutron stars are formed from collapsing stars, or supernovae, which generate great quantities of neutrons. The heavy elements are formed not at the origin of the universe, but bit by bit as a supernova collapses. How the neutrons are divided between the neutron stars and the regions where the heavy elements are formed has not yet been completely clarified. The universe is 15 billion years old, but our solar system condensed a mere 5 billion years ago out of the remnants of a local supernova, which was also the source of the heavy elements on earth.

[16] Mici was also employed at Argonne during these years, working on an early computer.

[17] M. Goldhaber and E. Teller, "On Nuclear Dipole Vibrations," *Phys. Rev.* 74, 8 (November 1, 1948): 1046–1049. Goldhaber pointed out that between 10 and 20 million volts, practically all nuclei absorb and emit strongly. We concocted a model to explain the phenomenon, with all the protons going one way and all the neutrons the other.

D.C. We had begun the book in 1937, but with the interruption of the war, we didn't return to it until 1946.[18]

The University of Chicago was a busy place during these years. Beginning in the fall of 1946, students freed from wartime occupations and from overseas were flooding in. Bill McMillan, a chemist from the Columbia branch of the Manhattan Project, came to Chicago for postdoctoral work.[19] His wife, Nancy, became for a year the wonderful, resourceful secretary for the fourth floor, where Fermi, Maria, and I, along with many others, had our offices.[20] I remain grateful to Nancy McMillan for introducing me to travel itineraries; during the following five decades, I would have literally been lost without them.

I remember Nancy most fondly in connection with a paper I published with Enrico: We jointly dictated it to her.[21] Fermi didn't think that it would work, but the project went forward without a hitch. Enrico and I dictated alternately, and I saw nothing unusual in that; but Nancy was later complimented by many of her colleagues for having taken dictation simultaneously in two foreign languages.

---

[18] Francis Owen Rice and Edward Teller, *The Structure of Matter* (New York: John Wiley & Sons, 1949). Our explanation of what a big number is still pleases me. According to quantum mechanics and George Gamow, the electron in a hydrogen atom will eventually jump to a proton if it is close enough. Rice and I calculated that if the atom and the proton were one centimeter apart, the average time required for that jump to occur is $10^{100,000,000}$. What is interesting is that it doesn't matter whether that huge number represents seconds or years. The ratio between a second and a year amounts only to $10^{7.5}$, and adding 7.5 to an exponent of 100,000,000 makes a negligible change, particularly because the constants involved in the process aren't measured that accurately.

[19] Bill McMillan took up permanent residence at UCLA at the end of 1947, but we continued to work together and published a more detailed explanation of the paper I had published earlier with Brunauer and Emmett.

[20] Although Maria had an office on the fourth floor of the university physics building, because of a university rule about employing spouses (Joe Mayer was part of the faculty), she was paid only by Argonne.

[21] The paper in question appears in the literature twice (E. Fermi, E. Teller, and V. Weisskopf, "Decay of Negative Mesotrons in Matter," *Phys. Rev.* 71, 5 (March 1, 1947): 314–315; and E. Fermi and E. Teller, "The Capture of Negative Mesotrons in Matter," *Phys. Rev.* 72, 5 (September 1, 1947): 1–6).

They are actually the same piece of work. Fermi wanted to publish quickly to avoid being scooped. He then heard that Weisskopf had been working on the topic, too, and included his name as a courtesy. The later publication reflects our completed work. Bill McMillan and I wrote another paper on the production of mesons not long after I completed the paper with Fermi.

This is the story of that joint paper. The most popular topic in those days was subatomic particles, which were being found in cosmic radiation. A Japanese physicist, Hideki Yukawa, had postulated an extremely short-lived subatomic particle, which, through its emission by a proton or a neutron and its absorption by another, accounts for nuclear forces.[22] When a mesotron was discovered in cosmic rays, everyone assumed that it was the particle that Yukawa postulated.

About then, I read a paper by three Italian physicists that noted the meson could live a substantial time in proximity to the nucleus.[23] I realized that meant the particle in question could not fulfill the role assigned it by Yukawa's theory. I pointed that out to Enrico, and we decided to look into what the particle, which we called a mesotron, actually did.

It turned out that the particle that Fermi and I were discussing, which appears in cosmic rays, is not connected with Yukawa's proposed particle. The particle we considered slows down when in contact with the electrons around the nucleus. If it carries a negative charge, it falls into the nucleus, and even lives in the nucleus for a while before coming to the natural end of its existence. Another new particle discovered just as we published our paper is, as Yukawa predicted, involved in nuclear forces. Those particles proved to be the nuclear glue.[24]

Working with Enrico Fermi, as his friends and collaborators know, was stimulating, amazing, and altogether pleasurable. His inspirations about physics were not limited by the topic at hand. For example, during this time, I was greatly impressed by his theorizing (rightly or wrongly) that the systematic circulation of ocean currents (such as the Gulf Stream) may in the long run have an effect on the orientation of the rotational axis of the earth.

At the end of a qualitative discussion, Fermi would almost always complete the argument with relatively simple numerical calculations. He would then quickly extract the necessary references from various works at hand

---

[22] There is not enough energy available on the basis of $E = mc^2$ for such a particle to be emitted, but quantum mechanics allows energy of the amount Δe, to be "borrowed" for a period of time equal to 10^{-27} second divided by Δe. That time is so short that, even moving at the speed of light, the particle could travel less distance than the diameter of a nucleus. That accounts for the short range of nuclear forces.

[23] M. Conversi, E. Pancini, and O. Piccioni, "Disintegration of Negative Mesons," *Phys. Rev.* 71 (Feb. 1, 1947): 209–210.

[24] See page 261 in this chapter.

(which were, to a great extent, his own) all of which he had filed in his desk in an impeccably systematic way.[25]

Fermi and I had been friends since our 1937 cross-country trip, but during our postwar years, he shared reminiscences that astonished me. At the beginning of the century, Italy had no outstanding research centers, and when he was in his early twenties, Enrico felt left out of the great contemporary developments in physics. It seemed unthinkable that feelings of inferiority could have brushed Enrico's life! Yet, in his casual stories, I could hear that he had felt, as a young man, deeply separated from the group of physicists working in central Europe. Fermi was grateful to Paul Ehrenfest, the one physicist close to the center of the in-group who appreciated him and told him so.[26]

Not all my conversations with Fermi were serious. Once, during a visit to Los Alamos, a group of us, including Fermi, walked over to Fuller Lodge for lunch, chatting about flying saucers. Fermi asked me how probable I thought it was that we would have clear evidence within the next ten years of a material object that moves faster than light.[27] I replied, with considerable optimism, "About one in a million." Fermi contradicted me: "That's much too low. The probability is more like 10 percent."[28]

The conversation moved on to several other more down-to-earth topics during lunch. Then Fermi, famous for his non sequiturs, abruptly interrupted a discussion to ask, "Then where is everybody?" Everyone at the table burst out laughing. We immediately understood that he was asking about extraterrestrial life.

Fermi began as a theoretical physicist, but by the time I visited him in Rome, he was already making contributions in experimental physics that earned him his Nobel Prize. He devoted much of his time during the postwar 1940s to planning an accelerator, but he never lost his interest in theory. One of his important contributions on cosmic rays was stimulated when a Swedish physicist, Hannes Alfvén, visited the university in late 1948 or early 1949.

---

[25] In this, he differed from my friend Johnny von Neumann: Johnny carried all the necessary references in his head.

[26] Ehrenfest did not invent quantum mechanics, but he had the reputation of understanding it, or at least of explaining it, better than those who invented it.

[27] As science fiction authors have made obvious, the question is relevant because exceeding light velocity would make interstellar travel more feasible.

[28] That was Fermi's standard estimate of the probability of unlikely events: They had 10 percent probability of occurring, which explains the term *Fermi-miracle*.

Alfvén's ideas were connected with the fact that magnetic fields are tied down to matter if the conductivity is high enough.[29] I was very interested in that topic. Before the war, Dave Inglis and I had pointed out a problem related to the earth's magnetic field; the conductivity of the earth's core of liquid iron is only high enough to retain the earth's magnetic field for about 100,000 years. Why, then, does the earth's magnetic field persist?

Alfvén's answer is that in a conducting fluid, the lines of force characteristic of a magnetic field move along with the motion of the fluid. The core of the earth is partly fluid, conducting, and inhomogeneous. Gravity stirs the masses of different density and continues to concentrate the denser masses near the center of the earth. The resulting disorderly motion stretches and entangles the magnetic field lines, thus strengthening the field. Although additional field strength can occur in any direction, the rotation of the earth brings order into the magnetic field and results in the observed magnetization. That point was carried on by several people, but Alfvén's ideas provided the impetus.

Alfvén also stimulated speculations about cosmic rays, and the mechanism of interaction between cosmic ray particles and magnetic fields became a hot topic in the University of Chicago Institute for Nuclear Studies. I made an unsuccessful attempt at a theory about the origin of cosmic rays, but Fermi proposed a truly beautiful one. Particles, particularly protons, deflected again and again by magnetic fields in the galaxy, would gradually accelerate until they eventually obtained velocities quite close to that of light. He demonstrated that in a lifetime of the galaxy, then estimated at 2 billion years, the particles on the average would gain energy and velocity, producing in the end the distribution of velocities observed in the cosmic rays.

The Teller family also spent a good deal of time with the Fermi family, and one of my favorite memories dates from an Easter when Paul was four or five years old. Enrico enjoyed children and on that visit decided to engage Paul in a little reality testing: He asked Paul if he believed in Santa Claus. Paul gave a diplomatic response. Enrico, intending to strengthen his doubts, asked Paul how Santa Claus could possibly manage to deliver presents to each child throughout the world in a single night. I don't remember what Paul's reply was, but the conversation ended with the two of them deep in discussion about the possibility that, because the Easter Bunny was unemployed at Christmas, as was Santa at Easter, perhaps the two helped each other out during their busy periods. Enrico never cracked a smile.

---

[29] Alfvén later won the Nobel Prize for his essential contributions in plasma physics.

Fermi, Sam Allison, and I also shared a common concern: Given the connections between science and national well being, all students, not just future scientists and educators, should have at least a passing acquaintance with physics. But teaching our regular classes was a challenge, and many of us were needed as advisors on the multitude of atomic energy projects being developed under public and private auspices. Nonetheless, the three of us felt the general need strongly enough that we offered a course on modern physics for the layman, one of us in rotation giving the course each year.[30]

Teaching classes, working on my research questions (and everyone else's), and enjoying my students kept me reasonably busy. I remember a few students particularly well: Wally Selove, now a professor emeritus of the University of Pennsylvania in Philadelphia;[31] Murph Goldberger, longtime president of Cal Tech; Marshall Rosenbluth, internationally acclaimed expert on plasma physics; T. S. Lee, who was not my graduate student but who found a place under my wing; and C. N. (Frank) Yang, who is the only one of my students to win a Nobel Prize.

Yang began as the student of Robert Mulliken, a friend from my student days in Leipzig. Yang showed Mulliken a beautiful paper on normal vibrations he had written while he was studying in China, and Mulliken, remembering my work on the topic, tried to turn Yang over to me. I suggested a thesis topic that I still think was an excellent one: How will a nucleus disintegrate if given plenty of energy? Yang turned it down. China was still free, and he planned to return home when he had completed his studies. "Only practical experimental physicists," he told me, "not theorists, are needed there." So he deserted me and went to study in the experimental side of the department under Allison.

During that period, Kayski and I wrote a paper in which we made a plausible but, we noted, unproved statement about the relationship between angular momentum changes and the angular distribution of the products in a nuclear reaction involving deuterons.[32] Not long after our article appeared, Yang showed up in my office. "I can prove your statement," he announced, and went to the blackboard and proved it in a few minutes.

---

[30] Those lectures marked the beginning of a course that I taught several times over the next forty years or so.

[31] Wally later married Faye Ajzenberg, whom I also count among my friends.

[32] E. J. Konopinski and E. Teller, "Theoretical Considerations Concerning the D + D Reactions," *Phys. Rev.* 73, 8 (April 15, 1948): 822–830.

I had been hearing about Yang the experimentalist since he had left the theoretical physics department. Some of his colleagues considered his work a disaster. In fact, some wag produced the rhyme, "If there's a bang, it's Yang."[33] So I was being tactful when I said to him, "I've heard that your experiments are not going too well. Why don't you come back and try writing up your proof for a thesis?"

Frank hesitated a little bit, and then said he would try. A few days later, he reappeared with three sheets of paper. They did indeed supply the proof of the relationship, but so short a doctoral dissertation made me nervous. "That's very good," I said, "but why don't you add the proof for the relationship in the case of half-integer angular momentum values?" A few days later, Yang again showed up in my office. This time he was carrying an additional four sheets of paper. I was glad to see the increase and told him so. But, I explained, the custom in Chicago was that theses should be even longer than that. When he got to eleven pages a few weeks later, I said okay. He submitted them and was granted his doctorate.

Throughout his career, he maintained the same density of ideas per page, but his papers were longer because he had a great deal to say. Yang went on to make major contributions, and he and Lee shared the 1957 Nobel Prize in physics.[34] Four of the students I had during this period—Selove, Rosenbluth, Yang, and Lee—have remained my friends over all the intervening years.

During this early postwar period, international tensions were steadily worsening. At the end of the war, the Soviet Union had swallowed Poland and half of Germany. In 1946, the Soviet Union was supporting communist guerrillas in Greece. Communist forces were making gains in China. Stalin's demands had stopped the plan for United Nations control of nuclear energy. With that hope dead, an arms race seemed unavoidable. Strong communist parties were developing in Czechoslovakia, Hungary, and Romania.

I worried about my family. My parents were too old and frail to emigrate, but my widowed sister and her small son needed and wanted to do so. In the spring of 1947, I sent the necessary affidavits to Hungary, but we heard nothing further.

I was still troubled by the shorthandedness at Los Alamos and concerned that I had been wrong to leave when their needs were so great and the work

---

[33] Others in the department referred to him as the "Yellow Peril."

[34] They discovered that, in physics as in human affairs, there is a difference between right and left.

so important. I spent as much time at Los Alamos as possible and began recruiting others to come. It was not hard work. So many of my friends, including the Fermi and Mayer families, came to Los Alamos during the summers of 1947 and 1948 that the months seemed a sort of extended reunion.

Among those who returned in the summer of 1947 were the Cyril Smiths.
Although they were less concerned about Stalin's intentions than I, Alice, in
commenting on current attitudes, said she felt she was shivering in the drafts
of an open mind. I loved her way of expressing her doubt about her strong
opposition to more work on nuclear bombs.

Irving Langmuir, a pioneer in the field of physical chemistry, also came to
consult that summer. I enjoyed meeting him because the work that
Brunauer, Emmett, and I had done was based on his theories.[35] In 1947,
Langmuir was mostly interested in talking about cloud seeding; he talked so
much about the amount of damage done by a storm his seeding had caused
that I began to wonder whether he saw the technique as competition to the
atomic bomb.[36]

I also met Wernher von Braun during that stay. Von Braun, who had led
the Nazi V-2 rocket program, came to the United States after the war to
assist in developing a rocket program here. The immediate question that Los
Alamos needed answered was how much weight a rocket could carry. I went
to El Paso to find out.

Von Braun unintentionally enlightened me about more than rockets. Although his English was adequate, he spoke German with the colleagues he
had brought with him from Germany. He apparently thought I didn't speak
German and made disparaging comments in front of me. He was particularly
contemptuous of the quality of American rocketry. The gist of his remarks
was: We Germans know about rockets, but these Americans will never get

---

[35] That work had earned Langmuir the Nobel Prize in 1932. After the BET paper appeared,
I was criticized for not citing Langmuir's work, but at the time I thought it no more necessary
than mentioning Newton in connection with $F = ma$.

[36] Some years later, when I read *Cat's Cradle* by Kurt Vonnegut (New York: Delacorte Press,
1963), I remembered that Langmuir had told me that Vonnegut's brother was working with
him on cloud seeding. *Cat's Cradle* suggests the possibility that complicated structures of water molecules, which have a relatively simple arrangement in solid ice, can form a much more
complicated structure that is even more stable.

In the story, that structure is very unlikely to form on its own, but if a piece of it is put in
contact with water, the water will suddenly solidify. Vonnegut's story ends when some of the
new ice gets into the ocean, and the oceans throughout the world solidify. I, and presumably
Langmuir, like the story because, although it is probably impossible, we cannot prove it is
impossible.

anywhere unless we help them. (In later encounters, I noticed that von Braun had changed his attitude: His politeness approached perfection.)

The person I was always happiest to see and work with at Los Alamos was my friend Johnny von Neumann. Johnny was the most versatile and brilliant scientist I have ever known. His mind operated at speeds that suggested neural superconductivity. Once someone posed him the following problem: Two trains, each going thirty miles per hour, are approaching each other on the same track. When the trains are one mile apart, a super-fly, traveling at fifty miles per hour, begins flying from one train and back again to the other. How long a distance will the fly travel before it is crushed? Johnny gave the answer instantly. One of the physicists in the group asked, "How did you solve the problem?" Johnny said, "I summed the infinite series." The funniest part of the story is that he might actually have done so.

Johnny and I had a common concern about the international situation. With Stalin in the Kremlin, neither of us felt comfortable with doing less than we possibly could. In particular, Johnny was as much interested in the hydrogen bomb as I was.

The von Neumanns, like the Tellers, often came to Los Alamos not only during the summers but also at Christmas, when everyone stayed at Fuller Lodge. Johnny and I both loved to walk, and we made many treks together. One snowy afternoon, Mici had gone skiing. When Johnny invited me for a walk, I left the children with a babysitter. Paul protested that babysitters are no fun. We left anyway. By the time we were returning, Paul had figured out a better strategy. When he saw us, he stuck his head out the window and called down, "Daddy, if you come up now, I have a little time for you."

I understood what Johnny said in some of our discussions on those walks only after he had repeated it the third time. But Paul rarely had difficulty understanding Johnny, although on occasion he disagreed with him. We gave a birthday party for Paul during that winter visit, and among his presents was a set of toy blocks called Lincoln Logs. Johnny began building a house with them, and Paul joined him. The set of blocks was small, and it soon became clear that there were not enough logs to complete both houses. A hot argument erupted, Johnny claiming that Paul had to turn over his logs because he, Johnny, was the guest; and Paul adamantly claiming the opposite because he was the birthday boy. I don't recall who won.

In discussions with Johnny, which sometimes went beyond science and included literature, I was once rewarded with an accolade of Johnny's laughter. I remember that conversation with real pride. While we were ambling down Omega Canyon one summer day and discussing German literature, we discovered that we were both fond of Christian Morgenstern's poetry. One of his poems is a nonsense rhyme. "Das Grosse Lalula" begins "Kroklokwafzi? Sememeni!," which makes no more sense in German than in English When Johnny recited the first two words of that poem on our walk, I finished all three stanzas.[37] Johnny was awestruck. Of course, my feat is not so astounding when one knows that the poem Johnny quoted was the one that Carl Friedrich and I had spent an evening in Copenhagen "translating." The memory of a pleasurable "understanding" is more easily retained than gibberish.

Johnny and I were both very young students when quantum theory turned physics upside down. (He first talked to me about quantum mechanics in 1925.) Much later, on one of our walks in Los Alamos, Johnny complained that Niels Bohr's discussion of a measurement in classical physics was fuzzy and therefore unacceptable. This was disturbing because Johnny was the Euclid of quantum mechanics, having proved that there are no contradictions in it.

The complete difference of approaches of Johnny von Neumann and of Niels Bohr soon became clear to me. For Johnny, quantum mechanics was a new science, hardly related to classical physics. For Bohr, classical physics was the basis of understanding.

In quantum mechanics, the results of one measurement generally do not follow from the results of another measurement. One result merely gives

---

[37] *Das Grosse Lalula*

Kroklakwafzi? Sememeni!
Seiokrontro—prafriplo:
Bifzi, bafzi; hulalemi:
quasti basti bo . . .
Lalu lalu lalu lalu la!

Hontraruru miromente
zasku zes rü rü?
Entepente, leiolenti
klekwapufzi lü!
Lalu lalu lalu lalu la!

Simarar kos malzipempu
sitzuzankunkrei (;)!
Marjomar dos: Quempu Lempu
Siri Suri Sei []!
Lalu lalu lalu lalu la!

From Werke und Briefe: *Christian Morgernstern. Band III, Humoristische Lyrik* (Stuttgart, Urachhaus) 299.

probabilities concerning the next one. The relation is one of probability. Yet there is as clear and beautiful a set of relations between the quantum mechanical probabilities as in the relations between points and straight lines in Euclidean geometry.

A measurement in classical physics clearly specifies the relationship of itself to other measurements that may have been performed in the past or could be performed in the future. True, classical physics got into difficulties with the facts of atomic physics. But, as Bohr had pointed out, this could not lead to abandoning of classical physics; if we did, we would not know what we were talking about.

For Bohr, "reality" had an inherent, immutable, basic meaning. We cannot define reality because it is in terms of reality that everything is defined. A classical experiment is a part of the reality of classical physics. It needs no further definition. Only the limitations of the applications of classical measurements need to be discussed. For Johnny, ideas became satisfying, "real," when we defined their relations in a consistent manner.

Is there a bridge between Bohr and Johnny? I think there is. I am pleased to report Johnny accepted my explanation immediately. Most basic classical laws describe reversible processes, for example, the slow compression and heating of a gas that can be reversed to give expansion and cooling. But some processes are irreversible: the flow of heat (and energy) from a hot body to a cool body, or the end of the motion of an object that is dropped.[38]

A classical measurement is, as a general rule, an irreversible process. For example, in a Geiger counter, a great number of coordinated ionizations take place. The reverse of this process is, in principle, not impossible, but its probability is exceedingly low (much lower than one part in a billion). The result is that a classical measurement effectively wipes out the probability of coordinated occurrences that are explained by quantum peculiarities (such as the wave nature of particles). Such considerations are necessary and sufficient to avoid direct contradiction between a classical description and a quantum description.

In quantum mechanics, the situation is quite different. The past is definite and knowable. The future is uncertain and regulated by the laws of probabil-

---

[38] When an object hits the ground, it does not lose its energy, but it dissipates it into the disorderly motion of molecules, and the molecules will never organize themselves into the orderly motion to make the body rise again. The "never" should be replaced by the "hardly ever" of Gilbert and Sullivan's major general. But that "hardly ever" is not apt to arise before the end of the universe.

ity. We know about these processes through measurements which, as a rule, amplify quantum effects into readily observable quantities.[39] Amplification is always connected with the release and dissipation of stored energy in an irreversible way. A measurement in quantum mechanics, or a reaction in a living being, is never complete until an irreversible process has made it impossible to return to the quantum process that triggered the observation or result. In this sense, a classical measurement can demonstrate the action, laws, and probabilities of quantum processes while keeping these laws and processes separate from classical physics.

Later, during a train ride from Los Alamos to Chicago that Bohr and I made together, I told him of our discussion. Bohr did not agree. To his mind, I had explained the simple and obvious ideas of a classical measurement by the complex and derivative idea of irreversibility. Only Johnny was satisfied. Perhaps that was an obvious consequence of my abilities and limitations. In Hungarian, I am fluent; in Danish, I am inadequate. My written English (although improved by my collaborator) can be judged by the reader.

Returning to the description of events in purely "classical" terms, I remember a hike with Johnny one summer that has become part of Los Alamos folklore. The group that day included Maria and Joe Mayer; Nick Metropolis; Johnny; Foster Evans and his wife, Cerda (mathematicians who had recently joined the theoretical group); Stan Ulam (who had recently returned to Los Alamos); my son, Paul; and me. We were on our way to Lake Peak.[40]

When we reached the first meadow that day, no more than a mile along the way, Stan announced that he would wait for us there. The spot is still called Ulam's Landing. After about a mile and a half, five-year-old Paul noticed the distance and began to ask whether we could turn back. Nick tells me that I engaged Paul in a conversation about the merits and demerits of his idea that lasted until we were so close to our objective, the lake, that Paul

---

[39] The amplifier may be an apparatus or a person's own body, which can translate the perception of quanta of light into the raising of a hand. That process in our bodies is irreversible: A great number of phosphate molecules (called ATP) change their stored chemical energy with the contraction of a muscle.

[40] In retrospect, I can only imagine that Ulam joined our hike because of his great fondness for Johnny. Stan was not at all addicted to exertion, a characteristic so marked that it became a joke. Stan's disinterest in exertion extended to many activities. As I wrote to Maria later: "Just before I left Los Alamos, Stan Ulam told me that he wants to do some work. He wants to work himself, personally, not by proxy, as much as 2 hours per diem. I should have liked to know how Stan looks when he is working. No one ever caught him red-handed."

decided to continue; but I do remember carrying him on my shoulders for a good part of the way.

Johnny (who made the hike in his usual impeccable attire of a suit and tie) carried an enormous glass bottle of orange juice, which he assiduously resisted sampling until we had reached our destination. When we finally reached the lake, Johnny opened his bottle of juice, and Paul immediately asked for some. Johnny kindly handed him the bottle. Paul took a nice long drink and then turned the bottle upside down, dumping the contents into the lake. Johnny, with his long-awaited treat now a faint color by the shore, looked so upset that I feared I might lose both son (to murder) and friend (for murdering my son) in one swoop. But Johnny demonstrated his extreme tolerance and good nature: He managed a weak smile.

Back in Chicago in the fall of 1948, I became for the first time actively (though slightly) involved in politics. Stalin's dictatorship was now twenty-five years old, and, to my mind, had a terrible record. However, American congressmen, particularly those of the extreme right, seemed primarily interested in an imaginary danger: un-American activities; that is, supporting left-wing ideas in the United States. One of the members of the House Un-American Activities Committee was the congressman from Chicago, Richard Vail. Several of us at the university formed the Citizens Against Vail committee. What we actually did was try to gather support for his opponent, whose name was Barratt O'Hara. Although my role in the campaign was appropriately modest—it consisted mostly of baby-sitting Paul and Wendy while Mici went out canvassing voters with other faculty wives—I was considerably pleased when our man won.

I also wanted to see Truman elected. Earlier that year in a letter to Maria, I had written:

> Truman does not have Roosevelt's showmanship. He is clumsy, he has a gray background, and it is easy to ridicule him. But in every important issue Truman is right. He is right in his methods by which he wants to stop inflation, and he is right that the question of inflation is one of our most important problems. He is right in the plans to help Europe. He is right in the plans to stop Russia. He is opposed by the Republicans, and he is opposed by the so-called liberals, but he is right. He is probably the only man in Washington who cares more about right and wrong than he cares about elections.

My respect for Truman developed slowly but remains unchanged to this day.

Early in the presidential campaign, when left-leaning Henry Wallace came out in favor of rightist Robert Taft, I was reminded of the coalition of extremes that had brought Hitler to power. But a popular New York governor, Thomas Dewey, not Taft, won the Republican nomination.

On election night, I remember listening to the returns on the radio. The announcer was interviewing Mr. Gallup of the Gallup poll and asked, "Mr. Gallup, with more than 100,000 votes counted, do you see a trend developing?" Gallup gave a long explanation about how the effects of regional differences and socioeconomic factors made it impossible to predict with so few votes in. I listened throughout the evening, and the announcer repeated his question about every hour, with half a million votes, 1 million, 3 million, 5 million votes. Each time Gallup's answers grew shorter. Around 2:00 A.M., when about 35 million votes were in, I heard Mr. Gallup asked again whether he saw a trend. I don't remember now whether he did or didn't, but I went happily to sleep: All night, the vote had been running three to two in favor of Truman.

For some months before the election, I had been struggling with a decision about returning to Los Alamos. A test series in the Pacific was scheduled for the spring of 1951. There was a great deal of planning and work to be done, and early in the summer, Norris Bradbury asked me to return full-time to the laboratory as an associate director. I had written to Maria from Los Alamos, "As you had said, there is pressure for my staying here. I shall not stay unless there is very good evidence that by spending a year in Los Alamos, I can really do a lot of good." But in the fall of 1948, I had reached a decision: I would go back for one year.

The temptations of the ivory tower are many. My years at Chicago were similar to those in Washington—hours and hours filled with the pleasures of exploring the puzzles of science with friends. I wanted to be a normal physicist. I did not want to disagree with friends over anything. And only on a few occasions had political differences intruded. But my perspective on the affairs in Europe was different from those of most of my American-born colleagues. The situation brought on by the failure of the Baruch plan was so bleak that most of them either refused to think about it at all or pursued will-o-the-wisp hopes.

Nonetheless, making a break, relinquishing my role as a professor, was difficult. I did not realize fully how deeply my indecision was affecting me until I consulted a doctor; that summer, my leg had become very painful and I was generally not feeling well. He examined me thoroughly and suggested that I lose some weight. The several pounds I had recently gained were putting too much stress on my knee. Then he added, "I suspect that you are struggling with some decision. You won't feel better until you make it."

Los Alamos, with its small band of relatively inexperienced people, was working on problems that had momentous significance to continuing peace and freedom. There was no possibility of working on the hydrogen bomb, but innumerable other important problems needed to be addressed. I could not avoid the realization that my advice at Los Alamos was more useful than my work at the university. The contrast felt particularly stark: Research on particle physics, the prevailing area of study at the university, discouraged rather than challenged me. I found that particle physics made little sense; and although a great many physicists were willing to work on the problem, few were willing to work on weapons. At Los Alamos, my efforts would be directed to more concrete concerns, and I was ready to make the shift temporarily.

At Christmas in 1948, which we again spent in Los Alamos, I wrote to Maria about another reason I should return to Los Alamos for a year:

> A place where I have lived for a year or two is home for me. In Los Alamos, I know where every house has been built, who lived in it. I know, for instance, that the dog of Bob Davis is a much more permanent institution than the movie theater and considerably more ancient than the water tower. I think I have a right to feel at home and I do.

I spent some of the spring of 1949 in Los Angeles working with Bill McMillan at UCLA, and the rest of my time in Chicago closing down my work for a year's stay at Los Alamos. In June, I said my goodbyes and bundled the Teller family into the car and headed for Los Alamos.

But on the way, I stopped in Central City, Colorado, for a conference on cosmic rays and subatomic particles. That was the second time I made a real effort to involve myself in what had become the most popular subject in physics.

A year earlier, in the spring of 1948, I had attended a conference on cosmic rays held in the Pocono Mountains in the hope of becoming more deeply involved. The conference was pleasant enough socially. Oppie was there and was very cordial. I remember our meeting because it included, for the first and only time in my life, a lengthy session of drinking Tom Collinses.[41] But I gained no great enlightenment, then or later, on particle theory. The field

---

[41] But thinking back, I realize that Oppenheimer and I, in our many social conversations, never touched on my favorite topic, science. That is particularly puzzling because during this period, Lorelei Libby (whose husband, Bill Libby, had developed carbon-14 dating) threatened never to allow me to come to another party at their house. It seemed that when I was there, the men ended up in one room talking science, and the women were left unattended.

seemed to grow steadily more complicated. Bohr had attended that conference, and one of his remarks there summarized my half-conscious feeling about the state of research on that topic. Bohr said, "Particle work lacks a contradiction. Until one is discovered, there will be no progress."

He was not far wrong. For a considerable time, mesons merrily proliferated.[42] I remember the conference for two connected attempts that ended in futility: to become enthusiastic about elementary particles and to write poetry in English.

At the end of the Colorado conference, we had the traditional banquet, and for the occasion I wrote and recited a poem that owed a great deal to the Gilbert and Sullivan evenings I had enjoyed at the Critchfields' during the war.[43] I called it "The Meson Song," and it summed up my feelings at that time.

> There are mesons pi, and there are mesons mu.
> The former ones serve us as nuclear glue.
> There are mesons tau—or so we suspect—
> And many more mesons which we can't yet detect.
> Can't you see them at all?
> Well, hardly at all,
> For their lifetimes are short
> And their ranges are small.
> The mass may be small, and the mass may be large.
> We may find a positive or negative charge.
> And some mesons will never show on a plate,
> For their charge is zero, though their mass is quite great.
> What, no charge at all?
> No, no charge at all.
> Or if Blackett is right,

---

[42] One big step toward simplifying the theory came with the introduction of the quark, about fifteen years later. Quarks made it possible to explain the observed phenomena with a smaller number of different particles. In addition, quarks have properties that almost satisfy Bohr's request for a paradox: The charges are not multiples of the integer of a real charge, but a third of that charge. The real paradox is that quarks have never been observed singly. When they appear outside the nucleus, they always appear as three together (three quarks make a proton, a neutron, or a heavier particle called a hyperon) or else as one quark and one anti-quark (which can make up varieties of mesons).

[43] Except for the first two lines, I had completely forgotten the words to the poem; but on a visit to Hungary in 1990, an Hungarian physicist had a copy of it, which he shared with me.

It's exceedingly small.
Some beautiful pictures are thrown on the screen
Though the tracks of the mesons can hardly be seen,
Our desire for knowledge is most deeply stirred
When statements from Serber can never be heard
What, not heard at all?
No, not heard at all.
Very dimly seen
And not heard at all.
There are mesons lambda at the end of our list
Which are hard to detect and are easily missed.
In cosmic ray showers they live and they die,
But you can't get a picture—they are camera-shy.
Well, do they exist?
Or don't they exist?
They are on our list,
But are easily missed.
From mesons all manner of forces you get;
The infinite part you may simply forget.
The divergence is large, the divergence is small:
In meson field quanta there is no sense at all.
What no sense at all?
No. No sense at all.
Or if there's some sense,
It's exceedingly small.

In the intervening fifty years, I have seen many reasons to change my opinion, none of them completely convincing. The expense, the number of people involved, and the ingenious ideas have increased. Big physics is flourishing, but when in the 1980s I tried to return to theoretical physics, I still did not find the revolutionized particle field interesting.

During the intervening years, quarks—particles out of whose fractional charges protons and neutrons are built—had been recognized, and current efforts were attempting to deal with an abundance of new facts and a continuing scarcity of unifying ideas. I was more attracted to strange phenomena, such as high-temperature superconductivity and molecules made of sixty carbons in the shape of a polyhedron, than to the ultimate problems of physics and the universe. I do prefer problems with a solution that can be found within a lifetime.

22

THE REACTOR
SAFEGUARD COMMITTEE

1947–1949

IN LATE 1946, President Truman announced his appointees to the Atomic Energy Commission (AEC). The passage of the McMahon Bill had established that the board overseeing the development of the military and peacetime applications would be made up of civilians. David Lilienthal, who had worked closely with Oppie to draft the Baruch plan, was nominated as chairman. The nominee-commissioners were Admiral Lewis Strauss, a financier and philanthropist who had served in the navy during World War II; Sumner Pike, another financier who had served in the Office of Price Administration during the war; William Waymack, a former newspaper editor and deputy Federal Reserve Bank chairman; and Robert Bacher, a physicist who had replaced Ed Condon as Oppenheimer's second-in-command at Los Alamos.[1]

Although I was confident that each of the appointees was a bright man, it seemed to me that having only one physicist on the commission might not be the best arrangement. Bacher, like Condon, appeared to hold the political views of the majority of physicists at Los Alamos, but he seemed a much less independent and imaginative thinker than Condon. That worried me because the AEC had huge responsibilities in regard to the emerging science and its applications. The AEC was responsible for building up a nuclear arsenal, developing new weapons, and reorganizing and directing the laboratories—including those at Los Alamos and Oak Ridge and the facilities at Hanford—for

---

[1] Bacher had been Compton's assistant in the early 1930s, and then worked as Vannevar Bush's aide until coming to Los Alamos.

directing the development of nuclear reactors and the biological and medical applications of radioisotopes. Yet the new AEC members seemed to me far more noteworthy as domestic political figures than visionary scientific leaders.

I was worried about the attitudes Bacher might bring with him. The letter I wrote to Maria introduces the topic by saying, "You know that Graf Bobi is on the Commission." (*Graf* is the German title for a count, and Bobi was my unsuccessful attempt to spell Bobby. I was by then legally and in intent an American, but my spelling still had a way to go.)

> I wonder how good Bacher is—I mean for the particular job . . . he has a lot more detailed information about the facts of life than our previous bosses (Bush, Conant, and Tolman) had . . . but I fear that he may do a lot to strangle ideas. But he will listen, and he is thorough. Scientifically, we may have done worse by getting someone else. . . .
>
> Bacher is a great administrator. He loves organization charts, and he loves reports in proper shape, and he is completely devoted to priorities. In other words, he is a normal human being of the genus "manager."[2]. . . I wonder what Enrico will say.[3]

Eventually, the the shortage of technical expertise among the new commissioners was solved by appointing a General Advisory Committee (GAC) of scientists familiar with atomic energy. Headed by James Conant, the former civilian leader of the Manhattan Project, it was a diverse and excellent group: Oppenheimer, Fermi, Hood Worthington of duPont (who had helped build the Hanford reactors), Isidor Rabi, Cyril Smith, Lee DuBridge, and Glenn Seaborg. It seemed likely that most of the decisionmaking would rest with them.

But even more painstaking work was needed than the General Advisory Committee could accomplish. By June 1947, the GAC decided to appoint a subcommittee to take over the technical job of assessing the safety of nuclear

---

[2] In those days, I failed to appreciate the need for (and benefits of) well-organized administrators. Five or six years later, I began to be grateful for such orderly people.

[3] I don't remember what Fermi had to say on this occasion, but not many weeks later, *The New Yorker* wrote a complimentary article about the new commission. After reading it, I again wrote to Maria: "I wonder whether we do not oppose the Washington organization too strongly . . . I am glad of what the New Yorker wrote. I like the New Yorker, and I am quite 'class-conscious' as a scientist. In public, I would rather see every scientist praised. Even Bacher."

reactors. They suggested that John Wheeler, Joseph Kennedy, Richard Feynman, and I serve on it. The AEC took their advice.

Johnny Wheeler, of course, had been involved from the earliest beginnings of work on atomic energy and had worked on reactor design in Chicago. Joe Kennedy, an able chemist from the Manhattan Project, was chairman of the chemistry department at Washington University in St. Louis. Dick Feynman, the talented young physicist who had bedeviled the security people at Los Alamos, was then working at the newly established Laboratory of Nuclear Studies at Cornell.[4] I suspect I was chosen because of my wartime work on the safety of the Oak Ridge isotope separation plants. I was surprised and pleased when my three colleagues unanimously made me chairman of the Reactor Safeguard Committee (RSC) when we met for the first time.

But I was even more surprised by the way this first meeting began. Barely had we sat down when Joe Kennedy announced, "We are dabbling in what will always be considered the blackest of black magic. The day will come when people will want to string us up from the nearest lamppost."

In the fall of 1947, such an idea came as something of a shock. I was much more used to listening to Oppenheimer and Fermi, and to almost all concerned, talk about the great blessings that reactors would bring by providing low-cost energy. U.S. industries, too, were looking at the new technology as a bonanza. Certainly there were some reasonable concerns about radioactivity, but the common mood was one of general optimism about the benefits that nuclear power would bring.

Although I didn't initially agree with Joe Kennedy's perception, I didn't disagree with it, either. A reactor contains a huge amount of radioactivity. Its dispersal by a violent series of events would be dangerous. Even without Joe's comments, we were not light-hearted about the risks of nuclear energy. The usual industrial practices are to exercise caution and add safety measures when accidents occur. In the case of reactors, we agreed that such a policy was out of the question. If a flourishing nuclear industry was to be established, a major accident could not be allowed to happen.

By the end of our first meeting, we had decided that we had to identify in advance all possible malfunctions in each design and make sure that each reactor was built where there was the least possible risk of harm.

So when we began, our job looked impossible, but we were determined to succeed. As I recall, C. H. Giroux of the U.S. Office of Chief of Engineers

---

[4] His imaginative work later won him the Nobel Prize.

was considered for membership, but he withdrew after he attended one or two of our meetings. What we proposed to do, he asserted, was impossible.[5]

We needed more people to work with us. We invited three people to join our group: Manson Benedict, the excellent chemical engineer who had helped plan the wartime isotope separation plants; Benjamin Holzman, the colonel heading the meteorology department at the Pentagon; and Abel Wolman, a water contamination expert who headed the public health department at Johns Hopkins University.[6] Dick Feynman dropped out after the first meeting, so the six of us—Benedict, Holzman, Kennedy, Wheeler, Wolman, and I—set about trying to make reactors absolutely and completely safe.[7]

One problem we attacked immediately. In 1947, information about nuclear reactors was not only secret but also compartmentalized. Although all the people designing a specific reactor had security clearance and access to basic information, they could not share their findings with another team. We managed to convince the security people to change the way they applied the laws to those engaged in reactor engineering.

A little more than a year later, we invited everyone working on designs to attend our meetings when we were considering the problems connected with specific reactor designs and sites. That review amounted to a sort of final examination for those who had planned the reactor. Just as students are interested in hearing what the professor asks other students before taking their own examinations, so those planning reactors eagerly attended our meetings.

A bigger and more important problem was that no one on our committee had experience in designing reactors. It is hardly an exaggeration to say that nuclear engineers didn't exist at that time. About two dozen people were planning and building reactors, but they, too, were learning on the job. In addition, each was dedicated to his own design and could hardly be expected to provide unbiased criticism.

---

[5] Of course it was impossible, and we knew it. But the task was of great importance, and I had learned from Bohr not to be repelled by the impossible.

[6] Wolman provided his expert advice on the subject of reactor safeguards longer than anyone else. He also played an active role elsewhere in preventing water supplies from being contaminated by industrial wastes.

[7] George Weil, the AEC liaison, contributed to our group by acting as our secretary. And, in 1950, two more members: Fred Seitz, an excellent physicist (later president of the National Academy of Sciences), and H. L. Friedell, an expert in the medical effects of radioisotopes, joined the RSC.

Within a year, however, we came up with a way that not only eased our problem but fostered a good deal of positive and imaginative criticism. We asked that the planners submit, along with their designs, a description and discussion of the worst accident that each reactor could have. That encouraged designers to think especially hard about safeguards because the possibility of an accident would have eliminated a reactor from consideration.

We met for the first time in November 1947, in Schenectady, New York. The reactor we reviewed at our first meeting, like the one the GAC had reviewed earlier, truly represented an innovation: It was a fast breeder. In 1939, with little demand for uranium, only two major deposits had been discovered. Not much more had been found by 1946, when serious reactor development got underway. That led to the assumption that little high-quality uranium ore was available.[8] Because every reactor, regardless of its design, required a considerable amount of uranium, the prospects for the development of nuclear power seemed to depend on finding an alternative source of fuel, such as making fuel in the reactor itself.[9]

In 1947, almost everyone involved was trying to design a reactor that would maintain the fission process while producing plutonium, which is fissionable—in other words, a breeder.[10] Most reactors use slow neutrons, a speed at which they cause fission in U-235 most efficiently. But slow neutrons are often absorbed in the U-238 without producing fission or neutrons, which prevents breeding. Fast neutrons (with a velocity of more than 1,000 miles per second) are needed to make breeding in uranium practical.

Wigner and Fermi both knew that thorium, a common and widely distributed element, could also serve as reactor fuel, and that a thorium reactor

---

[8] In fact, the official history of the Atomic Energy Commission (see Richard G. Hewlett and Francis Duncan, *Atomic Shield: 1947–1952* [University Park, Pa., and London: Pennsylvania University Press, 1969], p. 29), which I perused while writing this chapter, claims that when the GAC first met, the stock of uranium ore seemed too small even to build a modest number of weapons.

[9] Even as early as 1948, the ore shortage had eased, and in the intervening decades, a great deal more uranium has been discovered. In addition, methods for the economic extraction of uranium from relatively poor ores have demonstrated that the fuel shortage is a nonexistent problem.

[10] That is possible because, when plutonium undergoes fission, it releases on the average slightly more than two neutrons. One could be used to continue the chain reaction and the second and the occasional third could be captured by uranium-238, which would then eventually become plutonium-239. (U-238 plus a neutron → U-239. The U-239 after two beta particle emissions → Pu-239.)

could produce U-233, which, like Pu-239, undergoes fission and produces two or occasionally three neutrons, making it possible to breed more U-233. (Th-232 plus neutron → Th-233 after two beta particle emissions→ U-233). And U-233 undergoes fission and produces more neutrons.

The thorium cycle has the advantage that it can be carried on with slow neutrons during ordinary operation. The reason that slow breeders based on thorium were not designed and built was that the amount of uranium needed to begin their operation was hard to obtain at that time. (Today, thorium breeders could extend the fuel supply necessary for global electrical power based on nuclear reactors into the next millennium.)

The fast breeders based on the uranium cycle place increased demands on safety systems. First, absorbing higher velocity neutrons requires far more massive control elements, which are more difficult to move. In addition, the coolant in a uranium-based fast breeder must be easy to circulate, but it cannot contain hydrogen (which would slow the neutrons). Sodium and potassium were chosen, but both of those substances react explosively with water or air, thus introducing a new set of dangers.

The reactor we reviewed at our first meeting was a fast breeder that had been developed by General Electric (GE) under the aegis of the AEC and was to use intermediate-speed neutrons to produce energy and more fuel simultaneously. The preliminary plans seemed safe enough, but the site chosen was only about twenty miles from Schenectady (to allow the researchers from GE easy access).

In assessing the consequences of a worst-case accident, we had to determine the quantity of radioactive materials that could be released, where they would be deposited (which depended on weather patterns, water systems, and topographical features for each site), and how many people could be affected. We mentioned that we would prefer the GE reactor in a more isolated location, but because we would be reviewing the plans again, we gave the site a preliminary okay.[11]

We met again in January, this time to consider a reactor that had already been given a preliminary go-ahead by the GAC: Walter Zinn's experimental fast breeder, which was planned for construction at Argonne National Laboratory. We found the reactor, designed to be operated at low power, safe enough when the amount of hazardous material allowed to accumulate was kept at a

---

[11] The reactor was built at that site, but it never went into service because it proved not to breed efficiently.

very low level. Given those circumstances, we noted, it seemed ten times less hazardous than the GE reactor. But even so, because the reactor was not that far from Chicago, we reserved the right to review our recommendations after the meteorological and water reports for the site were completed.

We also met in February, this time to consider another reactor for Argonne. My friend Eugene Wigner had given a hand in designing this reactor, which had originally been planned for construction at Oak Ridge. The current plan was to build the reactor near a city of 4 million people. Unlike Zinn's fast breeder, the high-flux reactor (so called because it was to provide a great number of neutrons, which would then be used to study the effects of neutrons and radiation on various materials) was to operate at much higher power (30,000 kw), would have more hazardous material in it, and would require facilities for reprocessing and waste storage. We didn't want to say no, but we couldn't say yes. As we had done in regard to the fast breeder, we delayed our report for the wind and water analyses.

In mid-June, we met to consider a different question: Could the exclusion area surrounding the Hanford complex of reactors be made smaller? During the war, a large area around the complex had been set aside in the interests of safety and secrecy. Three years after the end of the war, the farmers of the region (and the State of Washington, which missed the taxable income) began to inquire whether the exclusion area could be made smaller. The proponents of the idea could point to the long, successful operation of the reactors, the great care in operating procedures, and the high quality of the operating personnel.

We agreed that although all those things were true, the Hanford reactors, designed to produce plutonium, suffered from two serious defects. Eugene Wigner had already identified one difficulty, today called *Wigneritis*: Graphite, when used to slow the neutrons in a reactor operating at lower temperatures, accumulates energy.[12] We knew that the Hanford reactors could develop Wigneritis.[13] If overheating occurred during a malfunction,

---

[12] Graphite consists of carbon atoms tightly bound together in hexagonal structures arranged in planes. The high-velocity neutrons released by fission hit the carbon atoms so hard that the atoms are shifted out of their stable positions in the lattice and into perches between planes, where they store a great deal of potential energy. If the reactor continuously runs at a sufficiently high temperature, the carbon atoms gradually find their way back to a more stable place: in a vacancy in the lattice or at the ends of the planes. If the reactor runs at a lower temperature, which was the case with the Hanford reactors, the energy steadily builds up in the graphite.

[13] The proof—experimental studies—had not yet been completed; but eventually we were able to speed that effort.

the stored energy in the graphite would be released and further raise the temperature.[14]

In addition, the wartime Hanford reactors had a dangerous design defect: a positive void coefficient.[15] If water, used for cooling and moderating the speed of the neutrons, were lost from the reactor, the reactor would go critical almost immediately.[16]

At our meeting at Hanford, we formalized the guidelines for the two concentric circles that encompass reactor complexes. Our formula dictated that the first circle, excluding all people except those operating the reactor, have a radius of half a mile; and the second, limiting the population density, a radius of about five miles.[17] At Hanford, that second region included most of the fertile Wahluke Slope.

Two weeks later, we met for a fifth time. The reactor in question was to be constructed at Brookhaven National Laboratory on Long Island. Because it was to be used for research, it would have comparatively low power. Unlike earlier reactors, the Brookhaven reactor had an air vent between the two halves to its core, separating them by a matter of inches. We were concerned that if those halves were to shift in an earthquake, the reactor might pose a hazard to New York City.[18]

---

[14] Wigneritis is a troublesome problem, and subsequent reactors built in the United States avoided it. The first reactors built in England had a similar problem, and an accident at Windscale (now the Sellafield nuclear reprocessing plant) was the result of trying to release some of the energy built up by Wigneritis.

[15] The water used for cooling in a graphite reactor has two opposite effects on the fission process. First, because neutrons are slowed when they collide with a water molecule, the presence of water raises the efficiency of the fission process and the loss of the water decreases fission. Second, water also absorbs slow neutrons, and does so much more efficiently than graphite. The loss of water therefore increases the number of slow neutrons available for fission and speeds up the chain reaction. Which effect is stronger depends on the amount of graphite. The wartime Hanford reactors had a large amount of graphite, and water had a greater effect in absorbing slow neutrons than in increasing fission, so loss of water could result in prompt criticality.

[16] That is what happened in the Chernobyl reactor. By contrast, the wartime Hanford reactors were replaced by new reactors of an improved design in about 1953, and no other reactors with that design flaw were ever again built in the free world.

[17] We also suggested that commercial reactors be located in a region where there were no installations vital to the nation's defense.

[18] As a result of this question, safety shut-down systems responsive to earth movement eventually became standard equipment in reactors; and extensive earthquake-fault studies became requirements for reactor sites.

We suggested at once that two immediate shut-down devices should be included, and we also decided to make a thorough study of the earthquake potential on Long Island. When we explored that question at a later meeting, we asked a Jesuit priest from Fordham University to testify to our committee.[19]

The good father came to the AEC office in Washington, made his presentation, and politely answered all our questions at considerable length. Finally, a lull. The Jesuit straightened up in his chair and, as a parting summary, said, "Dr. Teller, I can assure you on the highest authority that there will not be a major earthquake on Long Island in the next fifty years." I am proud to report that we all managed to maintain straight faces until the door was firmly closed behind him. We acted on the father's highest-authority advice and recommended for the reactor.

In September 1948, we submitted our final report on the hi-flux reactor: We could not agree to building the hi-flux reactor at Argonne unless its power was cut back to the level of a research reactor, one-thirtieth of the level requested. We also submitted a preliminary report on the Hanford reactors. It said, in effect, that there was no possible way we could recommend a smaller exclusion region. We suspected that our decisions would be unpopular. Some of our colleagues even began calling us the Committee for Reactor Prevention.

While I was writing this book, I discovered just how unpopular we were when a Department of Energy archivist made the following memo available. Ralph Johnson, who was temporarily acting as AEC director of research, wrote in a note, dated September 30, 1948:

> Happenings in the past few months lead me to suspect that we are misusing the Reactor Safeguard Committee, with risk of embarrassing ourselves and them. . . . The Safeguard Committee, as I understood it, would feel responsible only for giving a competent technical judgment on a difficult and oftentimes fuzzy technical problem, and would not be expected to carry any of the responsibility that goes with the giving of advice, recommendations, approvals, or limitations. Specifically, it would feel no responsibility for safeguarding the

---

[19] The Jesuit order has long been known for its expertise on earthquakes. When Jesuit missionaries were first admitted to China, they studied earthquakes and developed a method of locating the epicenter with widely dispersed tremor detectors. By studying the delay time in recording the tremor, they could identify the area of the earthquake and report it to the emperor days before messengers arrived from the region. That unexplained ability, of course, added considerably to their prestige.

health and safety of the public, except a responsibility to make its estimates of risk to this health and safety as precise and as competent as such estimates can be. . . . On the other hand, the record is getting cluttered up with such words as "advice," "recommendations," "approvals," "limitations," and "criteria," which suggest quite a different role for the Committee. I suspect that the thinking is similarly cluttered up and that we stand to gain by reaffirming the original concept that the Committee will estimate some of the consequences for us, but will not be asked either to recommend or to decide. The Committee is so able, conscientious, and generally helpful to us that I should not like to see its activities turned into improper channels.

The authors of the AEC official history also report that at the October 19, 1948 meeting, the GAC "felt that the Teller group had exaggerated the consequences of a reactor accident and perhaps without adequate justification had retarded reactor development."[20] I still do not believe that the delays in developing energy-producing reactors were the result of what has proved to be an effective safety program.

One of the issues that we had raised repeatedly during those first months was the desirability of having a remote location where new designs could be tested thoroughly, even to the point of creating an accident so that we could assess the effects. Late in the fall, the AEC agreed to the plan, and by the spring of 1949, our committee had examined and approved two sites. The site near Pocatello, Idaho, was finally chosen, and construction of the fast breeder and the hi-flux reactor got underway.[21]

Not long before I left for the 1949 conference in England, a smiling Washington bureaucrat had registered a complaint with me as chairman of the safeguard group: "When will you get out of the brake department and into the engine department?" I believe that even then I had the suspicion that the engine department might not be a more comfortable place. Those of us on the Reactor Safeguard Committee were united in our determination, in our objectives, and in our vision. The situation in the engine department was apt to be quite different.

---

[20] Hewlett and Duncan, *Atomic Shield:* 181.
[21] Both operated safely and satisfactorily at that spot for many years.

23

TWENTY
YEARS TOO SOON

June 1949–January 1950

B Y THE TIME I returned to Los Alamos in the summer of 1949, the AEC had greatly improved the housing. For our proposed year-long stay, we were assigned a real house in a new subdivision that had been built west of the laboratory. The Mark, Taschek, and King families lived on the same block, and each had a daughter about Paul's age. Paul's relationship to them was not unlike mine to Lizi Grátz: Paul loved to talk, and the girls loved to listen. Our block was the farthest street up the gentle slope that led all the way to the ancient volcanic crater, so the children had a lot of space to play in and explore. Mici was very happy with our new arrangements.

The change in the laboratory that Norris Bradbury had effected during the first three and a half years he was director was impressive. In January 1946, when I had left, Los Alamos seemed close to extinction. By 1949, the laboratory had become a small, solid group of colleagues, working effectively together on simple, well-defined goals.

The first surprise I had had in the postwar period was that, when implosion bombs—the same design tested at Alamogordo and dropped at Nagasaki—were detonated on the Bikini atoll (in the Marshall Islands) in 1946, they replicated the previous yields. That our relatively crude wartime attempts had proved so reliable was impressive as well as reassuring. Many aspects of the bomb still needed modifying for safe handling and more efficient use of the expensive materials.

During the first postwar years, we also needed guidance about the nature of the bomb that the military wanted for our permanent arsenal. The designs of the first bombs reflected only our distrust of our calculations on implosion and the size of the current bombers. During the summer of 1946 or 1947, I was part of a planning group that met with military representatives in Albuquerque to ask what modifications the military thought would be most desirable. But no matter how we phrased the question, we received the same reply: The bomb was fine just as it was; it fitted the biggest airplane, and it had enough power.

Although the military men recognized the relationship between technology and national security, they were willing to allow a chance decision, made during wartime, determine the nature of weapons for the indefinite future. Flying back to Los Alamos after the meeting, Marshall Holloway, the plainspoken, almost curt experimentalist in charge of weapons development at Los Alamos, aptly summed up the conference: "I never knew it was so difficult to find a horse's mouth."

Los Alamos had gone ahead with the improvements it could readily identify: making the bombs smaller and using the still-limited supply of plutonium more efficiently. That was the main thrust of the work when I arrived in 1949; but in addition, there was going to be a major test series that would start in early 1951.

At some point in August, not long before I left for the reactor safeguard meeting in England, Bradbury invited me to attend a planning session together with Carson Mark, John Manley (the associate director), and other division leaders to plan the work for the coming year. Al Graves suggested resuming work on the hydrogen bomb, and Jack Clark agreed that seemed a good idea. I remained silent. I would work on whatever program the group judged most important.

I was happy to be crossing the Atlantic for the second time since the end of the war, and Mici and the children were happy to be staying in our new home on Forty-ninth Street. My traveling companion was to be Freddie de Hoffman. Freddie had come to wartime Los Alamos with his training in physics only partially complete. As a teenager, much against his parents' wishes, he had fled Czechoslovakia when Hitler took over. That decision led to his survival and gave him, perhaps justifiably, a strong sense of the correctness of his opinions. (Even he was no match for Szilárd in that regard, though.)

As a twenty-year-old, Freddie had worked on the Water Boiler with Fermi, and during that wartime sojourn, he had also developed the first theory of fluctuations in reactors with Dick Feynman. After the war, he completed his Ph.D. at Harvard, then took a post with the AEC. When he returned to Los Alamos earlier in the summer of 1949, he and I began some work together.[1] A few months later, Freddie had become my indispensable assistant, so I asked the AEC to let him accompany me to the conference on nuclear affairs. When the AEC agreed, we decided to travel to England on the *Queen Mary* (At that time, crossing the Atlantic by ship was less expensive than flying.) Although Freddie's overflowing energy made the voyage less restful than it might otherwise have been, I did enjoy his good company.

The section of the conference we attended was concerned with the safety of nuclear reactors. It was held at a pleasant spot on the Thames near Oxford. Klaus Fuchs, our acquaintance from Los Alamos, now one of the leaders of the British Atomic Laboratory at Harwell, was among the conference participants. The RSC had identified the problems that reactors could develop as Wigneritis, positive temperature coefficients, positive void coefficients, after-heat, xenon positioning, and operator error. Our joint discussions made it clear that, although we may not have thought of all the problems, the British had not thought of any we had overlooked.

The only distinct memory I have of our discussions was that at one point during our consideration of a reactor accident through sabotage, which I considered improbable, Johnny Wheeler remarked, "There may even be a traitor sitting here at this table." Klaus Fuchs was sitting right next to him. If he flinched, I didn't notice.

Toward the end of my stay, Klaus Fuchs invited me to his apartment. As it happened, when I arrived at his home I was so tired that I felt ill. Fuchs, always a thoughtful and considerate person, noticed and suggested that I stretch out on his bed. Thus it happened that I slept away most of what proved to be our last meeting. A few months later, the British arrested him as a spy for the Soviets.

Fuchs's espionage activities were publicized about four months later, when I was back in Los Alamos. The letter I then wrote to Maria accurately sums up what I had come to understand during the previous decade:

> You remember Klaus Fuchs? I never liked him very particularly, but Mici did. He was too reserved for my taste although he was always very nice. He must have been living under an incredible stress. Quite a few people here are furious at Fuchs. They feel personally insulted. I do not feel that way. We

---

[1] That paper, titled "Magneto-Hydrodynamic Shocks," was published in the *Physical Review* in 1950.

should have learned what kind of a system the communist party is and what kind of demands it makes on its members. Fuchs probably decided when he was 20 years old (and when he saw Nazism coming in Germany) that the communists are the only hope. He decided that before he ever became a scientist. From that time on his whole life was built around that idea.

People always do this: They underestimated the Nazis and they underestimate now the communists. Then the disaster comes, and then the same people who would not believe that trouble is ahead get very angry at individual communists or individual Nazis.

Actually, the damage that Fuchs has done is great. He surely gave away a lot, and by now I feel quite doubtful whether we can keep up with the Russians in the atomic race. But that is not all. The Fuchs case probably will give rise to great difficulties in making a sensible agreement with the British (and it seemed just around the corner). And finally, we can now confidently expect a witch-hunt.

Rereading that letter a half-century later, my feelings are unchanged. I neither defend nor excuse Fuchs's spying. I do not doubt that he was convinced of the justice of the communist cause. The Communist Party did not tolerate acts of conscience. His masters forced Fuchs to accept money—the largest payment was $400—which he neither needed nor wanted, in return for the information he passed along.[2] Fuchs's story is yet another example of the party's penchant to dehumanize the individual, to destroy every form of freedom.

Many have theorized that Fuchs's espionage was the reason the Soviets were able to develop nuclear weapons so rapidly during the postwar period. In 1992, conversations I had with Russian scientists confirmed that the information Fuchs had provided was of considerable help. But from what I have seen of the competence of Soviet scientists, I have reason to believe that they could have produced the weapons independently, once they knew that an atomic bomb could be produced.

---

[2] Fuchs served a fourteen-year sentence in Great Britain and was returned to East Germany, where he headed a research institute for many years. Those of his American colleagues who saw him during his later years reported that he appeared to be an isolated and lonely man. Fuchs did not live to see the end of the communist régime in Russia.

Even before Fuchs's betrayal became more widely known, tension between the United States and Great Britain was high. The British anticipated that we would share all the information on nuclear matters gained during the war. But that information was not forthcoming. Because the topic was so touchy by the time of the conference in 1949, I was disappointed to learn that Isidor Rabi, a GAC member attending another section of the conference, was saying that a British atomic bomb would be felt as a menace to the United States.

I was pleasantly surprised when, in the midst of those bad feelings, the former head of the British delegation to Los Alamos, now Sir James Chadwick, invited me for dinner at his home in Cambridge, where he was the headmaster of Caius College. It turned out to be a very small dinner party: Lady Chadwick, Sir James, and me.

Although my prewar experiences in London had led me to conclude that the famous British reserve was a myth, Chadwick fit the stereotype. His contribution to an hour-long conversation was usually no more syllables than could be counted on the fingers of two hands. So it was that during dinner, Lady Chadwick inquired about various mutual friends; I dutifully reported; and on rare occasion, Chadwick added a syllable.

This went on until we came to General Groves. I believe I began by reporting, with no regret, that our general had been eased out of power and was no longer formulating policy about atomic affairs. At that point, Sir James underwent a change both profound and unexpected and began delivering an impassioned lecture on the virtues of the leader of the Manhattan Project. He said in effect that Groves was the only person who had taken the atomic bomb project seriously; the scientists hadn't appreciated the urgency of the threat, having no experience with war; without Groves's leadership, the scientists would never have finished anything!

I contributed a surprised silence for a considerable time but finally was moved to interject: "Did you know that Groves was strongly opposed to the presence of the British at Los Alamos during the war?" "I knew," said Sir James. "But whenever any of the others, Conant, Oppenheimer, or whomever, promised me something, it didn't happen. If Groves promised me something, it was as good as done." I cannot remember the details of all his comments, but he continued in this vein for some time. When the evening ended, my host walked with me back to my hotel. His parting words made the surprising and puzzling evening even more so. "Please remember what I told you tonight. You will have need of it."

Chadwick never told me what need he had in mind. But before the new year began, I realized that he had known two facts that evening of which I was ignorant: that the Soviets had tested an atomic bomb, and that Klaus Fuchs had probably passed all his knowledge of nuclear weapons to the Soviets. Chadwick, who knew of my wartime work on the hydrogen bomb, also realized that, in light of his knowledge about Fuchs and the Russian bomb tests, I would want to pursue that development while many would counsel holding back. He provided me with something that I soon needed desperately: the knowledge that I was not quite alone in believing the United States should develop the hydrogen bomb. For that I am deeply indebted to him.[3]

After disembarking from my return voyage, I went on to Washington for a meeting at the Pentagon that had been scheduled before I left for England. Today, all I remember about the meeting was that it was rather long and dull—until the final sentence: "And, incidentally, what the president said today is correct." I did not know what the president had said, so as the others left, I went forward and asked. The answer was, "A few hours ago, President Truman announced that the Soviet Union has exploded an atomic bomb."

Until the fall of 1949, our intelligence community, most of the leading scientists, and general public opinion held that the Soviet Union could not develop an atomic bomb before the 1960s: The Soviets were at least twenty years behind the United States. There seemed to be a certain amount of sense to the idea that, during the ghastly battles conducted on Russian soil, they would not be working on something as difficult as developing an atomic bomb. A few of us, familiar both with totalitarian states and with such talented Soviet scientists as Lev Landau, were less optimistic.[4]

---

[3] Chadwick took the conversation seriously, for thirteen years later when I sent a copy of my book *Legacy of Hiroshima* (Doubleday, 1962) to him, he remembered it well. His thank you note read in part: "I am still optimistic about the final outcome. We have bought time—and thanks to you, more than I expected. I believe that the time is being used in the right way, tentatively and slowly perhaps, but some progress is being made. We are learning how to get along with each other's bombs, and in the end we may even learn how to get along with each other. I don't think that I agree altogether with your account of meeting in 1949 and of our conversation. I agree that I said what you report, but I hoped I had said something about the future as well as the past. But however that may be, I am very happy to know that some part of our conversation was helpful."

[4] Stalin had commented, on learning of the bombing of Hiroshima, "We shall have an atomic bomb, and we shall have even more." That prospect was so terrifying that many people seemed either not to think about it or to cling to the hope that the Soviets would prove even slower than anticipated.

In the AEC, it seemed that only Lewis Strauss was seriously worried about the Soviets.[5] Strauss, charged with protection in regard to nuclear affairs, took his job seriously. He was conservative, even to the point of not wanting to release radioisotopes to researchers overseas (a stance that was unpopular among members of the scientific community, including me). I learned years later that it was also Lewis Strauss who, when he learned to his shock that the United States had no means to identify nuclear explosions, insisted that the atmosphere (which would contain radioactive material from such an explosion) be sampled on a systematic basis. When Freddie and I arrived back in New York on the *Ile de France,* that surveillance system, established at Strauss's prompting, had been in service for about a year.

To say I was upset and shocked by Truman's announcement is an understatement. Almost instinctively, I thought of Oppenheimer. With his prediction about the rate of Soviet progress proved wrong, I imagined he would be working on some appropriate new effort. I called him to ask, "What do we do now?" His answer was abrupt: "Keep your shirt on." With great reluctance, I did.

The newspaper the next day, September 24, 1949, carried a picture of General Groves and his statement: "We shall stay ahead of them." Groves, too, had been part of the group who believed the Soviets would not have the bomb for twenty years. I feared that Groves's prediction that we would keep our advantage might not be accurate either.

I took the train back to Los Alamos, stopping for a day in Chicago to see Maria. When I reboarded the Chief, I discovered that John Manley, Norris Bradbury's director of research as well as the secretary of the GAC, was also taking the Chief back to the laboratory. As I later wrote Maria:

> He is a good listener, and the fact of the Russian bomb does not make me a less good talker. So we got along for several hours very well. It is still not clear to me whether I managed to stir him up. I do not think that I ever have seen John Manley excited. I do not know how the race of phlegmatics who populate this continent had managed to survive. Nor do I understand how they can put up with the Hungarian invasion.

---

[5] Two or three years after the war, I had given a speech at Temple Emanuel in New York City on behalf of a world federation. Afterwards, a sprightly gray-haired woman, who I now believe to have been his aunt, introduced herself and asked me (in a somewhat remarkable fashion) whether I thought her boy's decision to take a job with the newly formed Atomic Energy Commission was a good one. I assured her that I thought so, but at that time I would certainly have underestimated the number of beneficial programs Strauss would initiate.

I returned to Los Alamos feeling a great desire to do something to improve our situation but undecided about what it should be or how to do it. I had realized back in 1942 that once an atomic bomb was feasible, a thermonuclear weapon was scientifically the logical next step. I had little doubt but that the Soviets had been working on it for some time. But I also knew that without instructions from Washington to the contrary, work at Los Alamos would continue at its current leisurely pace. Oppie was the acknowledged and popular leader of the GAC. Given his comment to me, I had little hope that they would recommend accelerating work on the hydrogen bomb with the urgency required to stay ahead of the Soviets.

Nor did I hold out much hope that the administrators at Los Alamos would support a more vigorous thermonuclear program. Bradbury had never taken much interest in thermonuclear work. He had resisted the idea almost from the beginning on the grounds that it probably wasn't feasible; or if it were, it couldn't be realized for decades. Manley, who was impressed by Oppenheimer, was inclined to follow Oppie's lead. Carson Mark was more neutral, but in the face of the opposition he was unlikely to provide much encouragement. I could think of nothing to do.

In early October, Luis Alvarez called me: Could he and Ernest Lawrence see me in Los Alamos the next day? Luis had been at Los Alamos during the war and knew about my wartime research, and I suspected that was the topic he wanted to pursue. I would be very happy to talk with them, I replied. Before I had time to digest the implications of their visit, I received a polite call from Norris Bradbury: "Are Ernest and Luis coming to Los Alamos? Could John Manley sit in on the meeting?" Of course, I agreed.

In retrospect, it seems clear that the reasons for Bradbury's interest in Lawrence's visit were different from mine. I saw in Ernest Lawrence a capable and knowledgeable physicist whose views on the possible responses to the new Soviet threat were of great interest. Bradbury probably thought Ernest Lawrence more notable as an excellent and influential director of the Berkeley Radiation Laboratory, another national laboratory and a potential competitor for funds and prestige.

Not only was Lawrence a Nobel Laureate for his work on accelerators but he was an excellent administrator and an experienced and effective advocate of innovative scientific programs. Lawrence was a take-charge kind of person and a great recruiter. He had proved his ability to get things moving during the war: His accelerator program had provided the U-235 for the Hiroshima bomb.

The determination and diligence that enabled Ernest to set projects into motion and accomplish the desired result had not made him popular among the inner circle of the scientific community. Ernest, not at all reticent about taking a stand and acting on his beliefs, was worried about maintaining our military advantage. It is hardly an exaggeration to say that politically Lawrence and Alvarez were at opposite ends of the spectrum from most of the members of the GAC, a group with whom Bradbury and Manley appeared to be in firm agreement.

The meeting took place as scheduled. Manley joined us, mouth tightly closed, eyes and ears sharpened. During the next hour or two, I gave a slow and careful account of the status of the research. My comments were a summary, in effect, of the conference held in April 1946; for although some effort had been given to a boosted device—that is, a fission explosive enhanced by fusion—the project of developing a fusion weapon had been close to dormant for three and a half years.

I explained that although a fission explosion can ignite an expensive mixture of deuterium and tritium (a D-T reaction), fusing the cheap and readily available deuterium (a D-D reaction) was more questionable. The old and crucial question was whether, at the required temperature, there would be enough energy in the motion of particles to keep the fusion process going. The proposed solution was to consider the energy emitted as radiation as lost because it would not contribute to the fusion. Then, in about 1944, I had discovered that different kinds of radiation are emitted; if we allowed it to stick around, its effects would be harmful to the fusion process. It appeared necessary to allow the radiation to escape. That, in turn, required that the arrangement be made small. But if we made it too small, it would expand and disintegrate before it could react.

When I stopped talking, Ernest said simply, "In the present situation, there is no question but that you must go ahead." I felt a tremendous sense of relief and hope because it was highly probable that we could produce a fusion weapon. How such a weapon might change military affairs was unknown, but the changes were likely to be profound. Ernest's support meant that there was at least a possibility of our finding the necessary answers.

It was late in the day when we finished our talk. Ernest and Luis needed to leave for Albuquerque because they were going on to Washington the next day. Ernest suggested that I accompany him to Albuquerque, and I did so gladly. During our trip down in the small plane that provided service between the mesa and Albuquerque, we had a simple personal exchange about the importance of proceeding with work on the hydrogen bomb and about the necessity of my explaining the scientific possibilities to everyone who would listen.[6] He then managed to reinforce the last point in his unique and characteristic way.

Ernest took me back to his hotel room and, while he was preparing for bed, even invited me to come along to his bathroom where he proceeded to wash his shirt. (In 1949, a drip-dry shirt was something of a novelty.) He explained, "What you have to do now will involve a lot of traveling. This," picking up his shirt, "is the means that has made that kind of traveling possible. If you wash your shirt like so," here he scrubbed the collar and cuffs, "and hang it up to dry, you can wear it in the morning."

This was hardly a standard pep talk, but Ernest managed to convey to me, very effectively, the message that he thought the program was important, and that I had to be the person who promoted it. Lawrence knew that although an unwilling pupil cannot be taught, a willing one needs only to be shown how the task can be accomplished. His first instruction was on how to wash a shirt. That demonstration made a deep impression on me.

I returned to Los Alamos and thought about what to do next. Finally, I decided to give Bradbury a list of scientists who would be essential to the program if we were given a go-ahead. Oppenheimer had briefly assigned Fermi and Bethe to the thermonuclear project at the end of the war, and the most important thing, to my mind, was to get Fermi or Bethe to lead the program. Bradbury had not discouraged me from making preliminary inquiries, so I decided to go East for a few days.

I saw Fermi first.[7] I hoped very much that Fermi would head the work on the hydrogen bomb at Los Alamos, but Fermi made it clear that he would not be willing to do so. To my mind, then and now, developing the hydrogen bomb under him would have been by far the best alternative. Today, knowing

---

[6] As a slightly polemic aside, I should like to correct unreferenced statements in the record book of the official history of the AEC (Richard G. Hewlett and Francis Duncan, *A History of the United States Atomic Energy Commission: Atomic Shield, 1947–1952,* vol.2 [University Park, Pa.: Pennsylvania State University Press, 1962], p. 376). I did not discuss a heavy-water reactor program with Lawrence or Alvarez, either in our talks in Albuquerque or in Los Alamos.

[7] Fifty years after these events, I cannot begin to specify dates and places. However, contrary to reports in several histories of this period, I am convinced that I saw Fermi before I talked with Bethe. I suspect the erroneous accounts are based on Luis Alvarez's notes for the date October 24, read into the record at the Oppenheimer hearing. As I recall, I received his call after I had returned to Los Alamos following my trip East. My explanation of his account is necessarily incomplete. I cannot guess how Luis came to think I had seen Fermi at the airport, but I am certain I never met Fermi at an airport. If, as Oppenheimer's calendar suggests, I met with him on October 21, then I met with Fermi three or four days earlier, not on October 24, as Alvarez' note indicates.

the difficulties we encountered, I believe his guidance would have saved us a great deal of unnecessary work; better still, he would probably have found a way to avoid many of the disagreements that arose among the scientists.

I then went to Ithaca to visit Hans. To my great pleasure, Hans was willing to return to Los Alamos to work on the hydrogen bomb. (That was not surprising: Hans was always attracted to difficult problems that he believed could be solved.) Toward the end of our conversation, Hans received a call from Oppenheimer: Could he come to Princeton to talk with him the following day? In accepting, Hans mentioned that I was visiting. As a result, Oppie extended his invitation to me as well.

The next day in Princeton, Oppie greeted us both in a cordial manner. We discussed few details of the program, but we did touch on one related problem. To my delight, Oppenheimer announced, "If we do go ahead on the hydrogen bomb, we should proceed with much less secrecy than we had during the war." Bethe was shocked and disagreed strongly. He appeared to think that the greater the effectiveness of the weapon, the greater the secrecy that should surround it. For once, I was completely on Oppenheimer's side.

Earlier, I had told Hans of my suspicion that Oppie was opposed to work on the hydrogen bomb. Characteristically, Oppie did not state his own opinion but instead showed us a letter from Conant, who condemned the hydrogen bomb in strong terms. I remember only one phrase of it: Conant said it would be built "over my dead body."

Our meeting lasted less than an hour. After we left the office, Bethe turned to me and said, "You can be satisfied. I am still coming to Los Alamos." Less than a week later, when I talked to Bethe again, he told me that he had changed his mind. He did not give me an explanation.

The situation was clear. Neither Fermi nor Bethe was willing to take on the project. If there was to be research done on the hydrogen bomb in the United States, I would have to work on it with all my might. I found that reality particularly discouraging. I wrote to Maria about my troubles.[8]

Life is getting a little harder and it is more difficult to avoid mistakes. In fact I may have made one—a big one—when I last saw Fermi. That was the only time I got thoroughly frightened. I want to tell you more about it

Fermi did not tell me what the General Advisory Committee proposed. He did tell what his own ideas are. He said: "You and I and Truman and

---

[8] Unfortunately, I did not date my letters to Maria, but I believe I wrote this letter about the time the GAC was meeting. At that time, I was unaware of the dates of their sessions.

Stalin would be happy if further great developments were impossible. So, why do we not make an agreement to refrain from such development? It is, of course, impossible without an ultimate test and when that happens we shall know about it anyway."

I tried to keep my wits about me and I tried not to use strong words. I succeeded—partly. It was only too easy to point out to Enrico how greatly he has changed his mind. He used to be opposed to the Baruch-Lilienthal proposal because he did not trust the Russians. Now he is willing to consider an arrangement with no guarantees. "Yes, but what else can one do?"

It is clear that one cannot change Enrico's mind by a logical argument and I knew it. I tried to change the point of discussion. The worst of it was that I felt clearly: Enrico wants to be rid of the whole problem. (Why talk about it—why think about it?) At one point, I made the mistake to tell Enrico what is on my mind: That I have never been so frightened as I am now when I hear his argument of compromise. That I think a compromise is so dangerous that I never would participate or help in it myself.

In the end I made this much (or this little) progress: Enrico said he would change his mind if Truman told him so. He almost became friendly: "Don't hurry us, we may come around to your point of view."

There is only one difficulty in the world: Wishful thinking. It is unexpected that Enrico should succumb to it. (It would be good if no danger existed. It would be good to continue to do physics. Even if there is danger why should I of all people be the first to do something about it. Any argument which gives me the right to do nothing is a good argument. Any person who reminds me of the danger is a nuisance.)

Enrico does not know what I think of him. But, unfortunately—he has an inkling.

There was one minor point of interest in the discussion with Enrico. I mentioned that the Laboratory is unanimous in its desire for action. Enrico was surprised. He did not believe me. He had heard from Manley . . . that the Laboratory is deeply divided. When I came back to the Hill I mentioned this detail to three or four people. I began to believe that here is a fine chance for me to jump to conclusions and to make mistakes.

You said you wanted to know one thing: does Washington want to go fast . . . or does Washington plan to hold back. I have the answer now: Washington will try every substitute rather than decide to make an all-out effort. There are many indications which point to this conclusion. One indication is what Enrico told me. What I saw in Washington makes it quite clear that there are big forces working for compromise and for delay.

It is needless to ask you not to show this letter to anyone and not to tell anyone what I told you. But I do want you to know what the situation is and I think this may have an effect on what you may want to do.

In one thing I may have exaggerated. There are also forces which work for action. The fact of the Russian Bomb is one of them. There may be still a little hope that some responsible people will be influenced more by facts than by desires.

Would you let me know how things are coming? What happens to Szilárd's document? Do you have any indications of what goes on in Enrico's mind?

Now I have been back for a few days in this center of meta-stability: Los Alamos. I want to take a holiday from politics. I want to work. This is the only way in which I can keep up my spirits and also keep up the spirits of some people around me.

All this is not easy. To do things—that is no problem. To sit and wait—that I never learned properly.

Please write—even if there is nothing to write about. I need it.

Edward

I let this letter lay for a few days. Would you do two things? Please destroy it after you looked at it.[9] And please get something done so that it should be less easy for some people to sit on their antipodes. And, please, write.

Although I didn't mention it to Maria, during my meeting with Fermi I had received a phone call from John Manley. As best I can recall, after my visit with Bethe, I was going on to Washington to talk with Senator Brien McMahon, the senator who had sponsored the bill placing atomic affairs under civilian control. I believe that McMahon had called me at Los Alamos and asked me to come to his office, but it may be that I had an appointment—made before the hydrogen bomb controversy flared up—in regard to other matters.

Because Manley wanted to talk with me before I spoke to McMahon, I met Manley at the railroad station in Washington.[10] Without much of an introduction, he asked me to cancel my talk with the senator so that

---

[9] Maria was a woman of independent spirit. She did not destroy my letters even when I specifically asked her.

[10] Recently, I reread my sworn testimony given half a century ago on this incident and discovered a few differences between my present and past memories. In my testimony, I believe I misspoke in reporting some of the comments that I remember Manley's making at the train station as occurring during our earlier phone conversation. I recall that our phone conversation was brief. But in all other regards, my present memory is identical to my recollection in 1954.

McMahon wouldn't get the impression that the physics community was not unanimously opposed to the Super. I pointed out that the physics community was not unanimously opposed.[11] Manley insisted that I not go. He was an associate director of Los Alamos, so finally I said, "Okay. I'll call McMahon and explain that you've told me not to come." Manley then said, "In that case, you'd better go."

In retrospect, that meeting with Manley had a deep effect on me. At the time, I felt it was a terrible thing to demand unanimity where obviously there was none. Many years later, I realized how essential it was for me to stand up to him that day. The hydrogen bomb research was classified as top secret, so few people were allowed to know about it. Of those who did, none had worked on it for even a fraction of the nine years that were behind me. Those who had worked diligently for extended periods—Emil Konopinski was one—were even less well known than I for their early involvement in the project. My refusal to accept Manley's advice may have been crucial to injecting enough facts into the political pipeline that Truman was able a few months later to make a vital decision in regard to national security.

When I was shown into McMahon's office and before I could say anything, McMahon said, "Have you heard about the GAC report? It just makes me sick." I had no information about the report, and McMahon didn't enlighten me. I did not expect the GAC to recommend work on the hydrogen bomb, but I was surprised by the strength of McMahon's reaction.

The senator spent a fair amount of time asking me about the status of the hydrogen bomb research, the amount of work needed, and the probability that such a weapon could be developed. As the visit was ending, McMahon called in Bill Borden, the aide to the Joint Committee on Atomic Energy, which McMahon headed, and introduced him. McMahon said, "If you can't reach me, talk to Bill. He has my complete confidence."[12]

In November, back at Los Alamos, work was proceeding in its usual leisurely fashion. A test series was to be held in eighteen months, in the

---

[11] I do not believe that Los Alamos (the Hill, as we affectionately called our mesa) was deeply divided. Norris Bradbury was unenthusiastic about the hydrogen bomb, but I think that was a result of his interests and nature rather than because of his political or moral concerns. Fermi's comment was the first hint I had of the depth of John Manley's opposition, which I did not fully recognize until much later.

[12] Borden, a lawyer, impressed me as serious, well spoken, and more polished than McMahon; but, unfortunately, Borden lacked McMahon's political acumen. Four years later, after McMahon's death, that shortcoming led to the unnecessary and tragic Oppenheimer hearing.

spring of 1951. One of the candidates being considered for that series was a fission device that would attempt to use the neutrons from a small amount of fusion to improve its efficiency, a process nicknamed *boosting*. I was hopeful that such a test would be included for the useful information it would provide. But such a device, which would suffer from the same high costs and heavy weight as a fission weapon, could hardly be considered a hydrogen bomb. Work on the Super, except for preparing related calculations for the advanced computer that Johnny von Neumann was building, was at a standstill. But I could do nothing.

Weeks passed; and then one day, John Manley called me into his office to show me a copy of the GAC report. Because the report was highly classified, I could only read it in his presence. The majority report, signed by James B. Conant, Hartley Rowe, Cyril Stanley Smith, L. A. DuBridge, Oliver Buckley, and J. R. Oppenheimer, said, in part,[13]

> We base our recommendation on our belief that the extreme dangers to mankind inherent in the proposal wholly outweigh any military advantage that could come from this development. Let it be clearly realized that this is a super weapon; it is a totally different category from an atomic bomb. The reason for developing such super bombs would be to have a capacity to devastate a vast area with a single bomb. Its use would involve a decision to slaughter a vast number of civilians. We are alarmed as to the possible global effects of the radioactivity generated by the explosion of a few super bombs of conceivable magnitude. If super bombs will work at all, there is no inherent limit in the destructive power that may be attained with them. Therefore, a super bomb might become a weapon of genocide.

Then I was shown the minority report that Fermi and Rabi had signed. Having talked with Fermi only a short time before, I expected that it would at least be a more moderate view of the question. I read its conclusions:

> Any postwar situation resulting from such a weapon would leave unresolvable enmities for generations. A desirable peace cannot come from such an inhuman

---

[13] The final member of the GAC, Glenn Seaborg, was in Stockholm receiving the Nobel Prize at the time of the meeting. He had written a letter suggesting more emphasis on the hydrogen bomb, but that was not known at the time. The quotes that follow appear in the second volume of the official history of the AEC.

application of force. The postwar problems would dwarf the problems which confront us at present.

The application of this weapon with the consequent great release of radioactivity would have results unforeseeable at present, but would certainly render large areas unfit for habitation for long periods of time.

The fact that no limits exist to the destructiveness of this weapon makes its very existence and the knowledge of its construction a danger to humanity as a whole. It is necessarily an evil thing considered in any light.

Fermi's characteristic moderation was completely missing! I was shocked. I could only marvel at the gentle way he had expressed himself when we had talked on the same subject a few weeks earlier. The differences between the minority report and the majority report were difficult to identify. The arguments in the majority and minority reports followed in almost identical order, and I could find no difference in the lack of moderation.

The scientists on the GAC seemed to consider research, development, and actual use all the same thing. But what about the deterrent effect of weapons?[14] The few senior members at Los Alamos who had seen the report began to question why moderate progress—for instance, increasing the efficiency or power of an atomic bomb—was considered moral, but making progress on a new possibility was evil. It made no sense.

I was deeply upset, even apart from the danger of Soviet superiority, by the idea of stopping at a point of partial knowledge. There was no way to assess the military implications of thermonuclear weapons without knowing more about them. I was and am convinced that knowledge, in itself, is good. Being a scientist, that point of view was natural for me. And it was glaringly obvious that knowledge about fusion was ready for harvest.

Yet the gist of the GAC report seemed to say that if we did not pursue the program, the Soviets under Stalin would not proceed, either. I found that very hard to believe.[15]

My contract with Los Alamos ran out in the fall of 1950. I began to think about not returning to the University of Chicago. Mici didn't like the climate: Winters with small children and snowsuits seem particularly long.

---

[14] U.S. military policy during the following four decades was in fact based on deterrence; although the United States was involved in two wars during that period, they never escalated into widespread conflicts.

[15] As I mentioned in Chapter 20, by then the Soviet program was well underway. A year earlier, Josef Stalin had received an espionage report on the same Los Alamos summary conference that had ended the effort in the United States.

And my relationship with Fermi, one of the main pleasures of being in Chicago, seemed far less firm than I had supposed.

A few months earlier, at the instigation of Bill McMillan, I had received an offer for a professorship at the University of California in Los Angeles. I had neither accepted nor rejected it. But as I had written to Maria:

> There is no part of America left that is America except southern California. Everybody has his 10^6 $ scheme of making water, everything is different, everything is changing, and one has the comforting feeling that all persons within a 300 mile radius are really on leave of absence from a madhouse.

Why not enjoy myself? I sent a letter to UCLA: I was interested in joining them in the fall of 1950. In that frame of mind, I made another trip to the East Coast. The AEC commissioner, Lewis Strauss, had asked me to visit him in New York. I undertook the trip without much hope, but when I got there, Strauss seemed to be genuinely interested in learning all the facts. By the time I left, I knew that McMahon was not the only strong advocate of the program.

In January, the hydrogen bomb was even being mentioned in the press. The prospects for the United States' taking a more courageous stance looked more promising. I saw Oppie again at that time and, hoping that he had moderated his stance, asked, "If the president gave the H-bomb project the go-ahead, would you come back to Los Alamos?" He quickly advised me of my error: "Certainly not."

At the end of the month, word reached Los Alamos that Klaus Fuchs had been arrested: He had been spying for the Soviets since the beginning of the war. Within a day or two, on January 31, 1950, President Truman announced his decision:

> It is part of my responsibility as Commander-in-Chief of the armed forces to see to it that our country is able to defend itself against any possible aggressor.
>
> Accordingly, I have directed the Atomic Energy Commission to continue its work on all forms of atomic weapons, including the so-called hydrogen or super bomb.

In spite of the lack of parallel activity in the United States, Stalin had established the Soviet program and appointed Lavrenti Beria, the most infamous of all KGB leaders, to lead it. According to Sakharov's memoirs, slave laborers were used to construct the facilities for the project. Such a project was unlikely to be affected by diplomacy or world opinion.

What had convinced the president? Was it the influence of Senator McMahon? That of Lewis Strauss? Was it that Klaus Fuchs had provided the Soviets almost as much information about the hydrogen bomb as we had ourselves? Or was his decision based simply on his abundant common sense? Probably no one will ever know, but my bet is on the common sense.

The decision lifted a heavy weight from my mind. My letter to Maria describes how I felt:

> A few things I wanted to tell you and perhaps I did—but not clearly enough. I know now what I want and there is a reasonable chance that I shall get it. In any case, I want only one thing: To get out of this situation into which the atomic bombs—our atomic bombs and the Russian atomic bomb—has put us. I do not want to do anything else, and I do not want to think of anything else. I appear to be in a position where I can do a little more than most people. I do not even care very particularly whether I shall succeed. I simply want to do, in this one thing, what seems right to me. This is a big enough ambition and I am more satisfied than I have been in the last 35 years or so. I wonder to how many people it happens that they are set back where they have been before and that they get a second chance. I am now where I have been in 1939. I even see the rudiments of the mistakes that I am going to make—the same ones I made 10 years ago. But this time, I am going to try hard not to make the same mistakes. I never loved a fight. That is why I always was so bitter when I had to fight (or thought I had to). But this time I love the job I am going to do—I shall even love to fight if it must be. Whatever the reason is that I work at Los Alamos, it is not that I am scared.
>
> Thanks for everything. I never felt better starting a job, and I never needed more optimism than I need this time. Whatever help and whatever advice I can get from you—I need it. Not because I feel subjectively that I must have help but because I know objectively that we are in a situation in which any sane person must and does throw up his hands and only the crazy ones keep going.
>
> Edward

24

OUR DOUBTS
HAVE A FIRM FOUNDATION

1950

DURING THE LATE 1940s, the United States made a grand step toward peace. The Marshall Plan, together with assistance to Japan, laid the foundation of friendship with the enemies of yesterday. Those were courageous decisions. They were unprecedented. But during that period, the United States had neglected the development of arms.

During the postwar period in the Soviet Union, in spite of all the other needs of the country, Stalin had placed a high priority on the development of armaments. To me, Truman's decision to move ahead with the "so-called super bomb" was an acknowledgment that an arms race existed, and we would necessarily lose the race if we continued to do nothing. At the time, I believed my perspective—that given the Soviet emphasis on military power and the ability of their scientists, they were fully able to win an arms race—differed from that of most physicists.

My feeling about opinions within the scientific community was based on what I knew: the responses of Fermi, Bethe, Conant, Oppenheimer, and the reports of the General Advisory Committee. I was not particularly well informed. Even today, I seldom read nontechnical articles, and in 1950 I was isolated and busy at Los Alamos. Forty-some years later, having finally taken time to read the March 1, 1950, issue of *The Bulletin of Atomic Scientists,* I discovered that my opinion about my colleagues then was wrong, or at least incomplete.

Scientists gave a wide variety of responses to President Truman's announcement. According to the March issue of *The Bulletin,* the public debate began with an indiscretion made by Senator Edwin C. Johnson. In a televised discussion on November 1, 1949, the senator said: "Here's the thing that is top secret. Our scientists . . . have been trying to make what is known as the super bomb." Three months later, the president's decision was announced, and a month after that, the March issue of *The Bulletin* appeared.

The divergence of views in the scientific community was great. Only one conclusion appeared to have general support: It would be better to have less secrecy about the topic. The opinions offered by Albert Einstein and Harold Urey, both great scientists, reflected the depth of the disagreement.[1] Einstein claimed that "achieving security through national armament is . . . a disastrous illusion"; and Urey said, "I am very unhappy to conclude that the hydrogen bomb should be developed and built. I do not think we should intentionally lose the armaments race."

Einstein's views are of considerable interest, both because he had enormous authority and because he took an extreme position. He predicted the effect that working on weapons would have on society:

> . . . concentration of tremendous financial power in the hands of the military, militarization of the youth, close supervision of the loyalty of the citizens, in particular, of the civil servants by a police force growing more conspicuous every day. Intimidation of people of independent political thinking. Indoctrination of the public by radio, press, school. Growing restriction of the range of public information under the pressure of military secrecy.

Today, Einstein's error is obvious. But in the late 1940s and early 1950s, several events, ranging from the loyalty oath adopted at the University of California to the House Un-American Activities Committee hearings that questioned the loyalty of Edward Condon, among others, made such developments seem possible.[2] But although Einstein was right about the potential, he underestimated the resistance.

Einstein also offered a picture of the concrete dangers of the hydrogen bomb:

> The armament race between the USA and the USSR, originally supposed to be a preventive measure, assumes hysterical character. On both sides, the

---

[1] Harold Urey, "Should America Build the H-Bomb?" *Bulletin of Atomic Scientists*, 6, 19 (March 1950): 92–93; and Albert Einstein, "Arms Can Bring No Security," *Bulletin of Atomic Scientists* 6, 3 (March 1950): 71.

[2] As one of my letters to Maria, quoted in the last chapter, suggests, I also feared a "witch hunt," but I attributed it to different causes.

means to mass destruction are perfected with feverish haste behind the respective walls of secrecy. The H-bomb appears on the public horizon as a probably attainable goal. Its accelerated development has been solemnly proclaimed by the President.

If successful, radioactive poisoning of the atmosphere, and hence annihilation of any life on earth, has been brought within the range of technical possibilities. The ghostlike character of this development lies in its apparently compulsory trend. Every step appears as the unavoidable consequence of the preceding one. In the end, there beckons more and more clearly general annihilation.

A month later, Leo Szilárd elaborated the same point:

I have made a calculation in this connection. Let us assume that we make a radioactive element which will live for five years and that we just let it go into the air. During the following years, it will gradually settle out and cover the whole earth with dust. I have asked myself: How many neutrons or how much heavy hydrogen do we have to detonate to kill everybody on earth by this particular method? I come up with about fifty tons of neutrons as being plenty to kill everybody, which means about five hundred tons of heavy hydrogen.

Following Szilárd's statements, *The Bulletin* offered an editorial note:

David E. Lilienthal, recently retired chairman of the Atomic Energy Commission . . . said such pronouncements by the "new cult of doom" served no purpose—neither the intimidation of Russia, nor the building-up of international trust, nor the cool appraisal of our military security needs. Rather, he said, they only spread a feeling of "hopelessness and helplessness."

Many who contributed to the debate in *The Bulletin* discussed possibilities and needs in a less alarmist manner. But given the respect accorded Einstein, Fermi, Oppenheimer, and Bethe, all of whom made exceedingly strong statements about the dangers connected with the development of the hydrogen bomb, it is not surprising that their attitude eventually became the dominant one among physicists.[3]

---

[3] In his article in the next issue of *The Bulletin* (April 1950), Bethe, who at one stage had promised to work on it, called the hydrogen bomb "the greatest menace to civilization."

I also participated in *The Bulletin* discussion in March. In retrospect, it is clear that my article, "Back to the Laboratories," was too prosaic and too blunt to be effective in recruitment. However, the article did reflect my feelings and thoughts.

President Truman has announced that we are going to make a hydrogen bomb. No one connected with work on atomic bombs can escape a feeling of grave responsibility. No one will be glad to discover more fuel with which a coming conflagration may be fed. But scientists must find a modest way of looking into an uncertain future. The scientist is not responsible for the laws of nature. It is his job to find out how these laws operate. It is the scientist's job to find the ways in which these laws can serve the human will. However, it is not the scientist's job to determine whether a hydrogen bomb should be constructed, whether it should be used, or how it should be used. This responsibility rests with the American people and with their chosen representatives.[4]

I went on to point out the difference that a decade had made in the attitudes of military men and scientists toward the role of technology in warfare. In 1939, the colonel at the first meeting of the atomic bomb committee believed that wars were not won by weapons but by the justice of the cause. In 1950, I wrote:

Tempora mutantur. I have not met any skeptic like that colonel in army uniform in a long time. Today there is a discussion of the possibility of a new weapon; already it is considered a reality.

On the other hand, many of the scientists now think, "Peace is not won by weapons.". . . We must realize that mere plans are not yet bombs, and we must realize that democracy will not be saved by ideals alone.

Our scientific community has been out on a honeymoon with mesons. The holiday is over. Hydrogen bombs will not produce themselves. Neither will rockets nor radar. . . . This does not mean that we should neglect research or teaching. If we get to work now, it will be sufficient to have perhaps one quarter of the scientists engaged on war work. The load could be lightened by rotation.[5]

---

[4] Edward Teller, "Back to the Laboratories," *Bulletin of Atomic Scientists* 6, 19 (March, 1950): 72.

[5] Ibid.

I have not changed those views. But they are hardly inspirational and certainly did not persuade any scientists to postpone their academic work and move to Los Alamos to work on a project strongly opposed by most of the great names of science.

As for my personal plans, the only certain thing was that my work would not be finished in time to join the UCLA faculty in the fall. Among the first things I did in early February was to let the University of California know that I wanted to see the program at Los Alamos through to its completion. They generously agreed to postpone my starting date.

The staff at Los Alamos was still barely adequate to meet the challenges of the upcoming tests. If we were to continue fission work and at the same time move forward on a thermonuclear weapon, we had to have more scientists. I had some success with a few of the people who had been consulting at Los Alamos. Emil Konopinski (Kayski), who had been at the heart of my wartime group, returned almost at once, and the continuity he provided was invaluable.[6] In addition, Marshall Rosenbluth, one of my best students at Chicago, responded to the need. Now finished with his Ph.D. studies, he agreed to postpone his appointment at Stanford to join us at Los Alamos.[7] As soon as he was able to leave his current post, Lothar Nordheim returned as a full-time consultant to explore the consequences of his earlier work. And another important success came when I called Johnny Wheeler.

Johnny had just gone to France for a well-deserved sabbatical. I didn't expect him to be interested, but when I reached him by phone, he immediately responded, "Here you are supporting one end of the project and President Truman is supporting the other, but there is nobody supporting that clothesline in the middle. I had better take the next plane." And he did. As a wonderful bonus, he recruited two of his students, Ken Ford and John Toll, to come to Los Alamos with him.

I also called Oppenheimer, the head of the Institute of Advanced Studies at Princeton. The summer before, Oppie had promised the particularly fine theoretician I had recruited there, Conrad Longmire, that he could return

---

[6] Throughout the war years, Kayski had made sure that all the questions that came up were thoroughly explored and that our slowly accumulating knowledge was preserved in clear and usable documents. His contributions stretch from his inspired guess in 1941 that tritium would be more readily reactive to his steady work during the latter part of the program.

[7] During vacations, Marshall had spent some time on the mesa working on aspects of plasma physics, so he was also already familiar with some of the problems.

after spending a year at Los Alamos working on the upcoming tests.[8] This time, Oppie was proper rather than cordial in his response. He explained that he wanted to cooperate with the president's directive, so I was welcome to recruit at the Institute. He suggested several names, but none of them chose to leave the Institute.

In addition to those who came to Los Alamos, Maria Mayer finished the work on opacities at Chicago; Fred Hoyt worked on another part of our research at Chicago; Gregory Breit directed an effort at Yale on basic interactions of particles and radiation; and Johnny von Neumann supervised the computer calculations at Princeton. Their help, and the encouragement it provided, was deeply appreciated. But the problem of enough hands to do the work at Los Alamos was still not solved.

Norris Bradbury was skeptical about our chances for success and concerned about minimizing the effects that failure would have on the laboratory. Nonetheless, he tried to be cooperative. He gave me free rein to recruit from other projects within the lab. Jim Tuck shelved his favorite projects to devote himself exclusively to the urgent phase of the program; and a former member of my wartime group, Rolf Landshoff, returned to the work. Cerda and Foster Evans, a wonderful pair of mathematicians who had come to Los Alamos shortly after the war, devoted their energies to preparing important calculations for solution by computer. Geo Gamow had come to work as a consultant at Los Alamos the previous year and was interested in the Super project.[9]

The most enthusiastic recruit was Freddie de Hoffman, the young man who had accompanied me to England for the Reactor Safeguard Committee meeting. During the following eighteen months, I sometimes wondered

---

[8] As it turned out, Conrad never returned to Princeton. He became deeply interested in the problems studied at Los Alamos and today ranks among the foremost experts in weapons research.

[9] Geo's talents were ill-suited for much of the task. His lack of concern for details, whether they were in mathematics or in literature, was legendary. He wrote wonderful books explaining the ideas of twentieth century physics to the layman, but decoding his manuscripts wasn't easy. After his editor sent him a dictionary, Geo wrote back complaining that the book was incomplete: Why wasn't the word *eple* included? Try *apple*, the editor replied. Many people have difficulty with spelling in a second language, but Geo's problem was more deep-seated. Foster Evans said that when his wife, Cerda, hurt her leg, Geo autographed her cast—in Russian— and teasingly refused to translate. Bob Richtmyer, who had studied Russian briefly, offered to interpret. But he found the task particularly daunting, because, as it turned out, Geo couldn't spell in Russian, either. But Geo did contribute wonderfully amusing introductory lectures for the newcomers during this period.

whether I had recruited Freddie or he had recruited me. He was a demanding taskmaster; hardly a day went by that he didn't urge me to work faster. Having witnessed Hitler's successes, Freddie was well aware of what a dictator can accomplish. He was particularly concerned about our lack of action on the hydrogen bomb. Young, energetic, highly motivated, he was, for the following months, my daily prodder. It was my particular misfortune that my two "bosses," Norris Bradbury and Freddie de Hoffman, did not agree on any issue.

It is impossible to mention all the people whose diligence helped our effort. But during the first year of our work, my mainstays were Marshall Rosenbluth, Johnny Wheeler, Conrad Longmire, Emil Konopinski, and Freddie de Hoffman. Without them, the program could not have made such a vigorous start.

In addition to giving me general responsibility for the work on the Super, Bradbury put the laboratory on a six-day work week. Everyone was given a corresponding 20 percent pay raise. By the time Johnny Wheeler arrived, there was grumbling in the ranks. Wheeler, as the impartial newcomer, was asked his opinion. Johnny was suffering from jet lag and did not answer. The next morning, I met him for breakfast at Fuller Lodge. He told me that after he had got into bed, he picked up the Gideon Bible on his nightstand; it opened (he assured me with a solemn expression) to the commandment: "Six days shalt thou labor."

How did our efforts compare to Einstein's vision that the work would entail "concentrations of tremendous financial power in the hands of the military [and] militarization of the youth?"[10] The facts were that the AEC (a civilian agency) provided for an additional annual expenditure of approximately $100 million and a handful of eager, excellent scientists joined the project. Einstein, when talking about subjects other than his specialty, was able to be quite wrong; but he made his misleading statements in resounding language.

We needed experimental data about fusion. From Bradbury's point of view, we also needed an immediate, visible goal. He decided that in addition to the fission weapons already scheduled for testing in the spring of 1951 we should test the Booster, a device I had advocated for more than a year.

In an imploded fission bomb, the center is the hottest region. Materials containing deuterium and tritium placed there and compressed were likely

---

[10] See *The Bulletin* article quoted at the beginning of this chapter.

to undergo fusion, thus heating themselves further and generating a veritable flood of neutrons. Those would produce much more energy by causing fission in the surrounding atomic bomb material, thus boosting the original atomic bomb to a higher yield. That practical design was an advance on our original technology. The proposal to test it was accepted with almost no debate. From a technical and practical point of view, the Booster might have been as important as the hydrogen bomb; but it might have appeared less significant, because no controversy surrounded it.[11]

The Booster was not a true hydrogen bomb. A hydrogen bomb would use inexpensive deuterium as the fuel and a small amount of expensive tritium in the initial reaction. The problem was that calculations were our only basis for supposing that fusion would propagate in deuterium.

Up to this time, all the tests on nuclear explosives had been done on completed weapons. I proposed that the Eniwetok test series include something different and, by comparison, impractical: We should run a true laboratory-type experiment to see whether our calculations were correct, at least about the propagation of fusion in a mixture of deuterium and tritium. It was surely time we had some solid experimental evidence. The outcome of the test was far from a certainty; but if the experiment worked, it would tell us whether our theoretical calculations gave the expected quantitative results. Bradbury readily agreed.

The other need was to review the design of the Super. The calculations hurriedly completed in the spring of 1946 had been accepted without detailed criticism. Unfortunately, I had neglected to check them. The question that the calculations purported to answer—what volume or thickness of cryogenic deuterium would allow the fusion reaction to burn most of the fuel—was of utmost importance. The design of the Super was based on the expectation that an appropriate volume or thickness could be found.[12]

Johnny von Neumann had been working for more than a year on constructing an advanced computer that could provide a more reliable answer. By the time (early in 1950) Foster and his wife, Cerda, had nearly finished

---

[11] The Alarm Clock design, on which Richtmyer and I had worked during the summer of 1947, has another set of drawbacks; but it, too, is a feasible and workable design. Joe 4, the first thermonuclear device tested by the Soviets (June 1953), was of a closely related design.

[12] To review: If the system is too thin, it will disassemble. If it is too thick, collisions between light quanta and electrons will deposit too much energy in the form of electromagnetic radiation and leave too little energy in the form of the movement of particles, necessary for a thermonuclear reaction.

preparing the calculations for Johnny's computer, it was clear that the computer would not be operating for at least another year. Under von Neumann's direction, Foster and Cerda began to revise the calculations for use on other, simpler computers.[13]

Fermi had resumed consulting at Los Alamos. He had recommended against work on the thermonuclear device, but now that it was going ahead, he had an obvious interest in its status and wanted to guard against mistakes. His discussions with Stan Ulam gave rise to serious concerns about whether the earlier calculations had led to overly optimistic projections.

Stan Ulam, a mathematician from Poland, had worked for a time in my wartime group. Stan had left Los Alamos soon after the end of the war, but he returned a little more than a year later. He had originally come with my friend Johnny von Neumann's recommendation, but I found him difficult company. He seemed to think very highly of himself and expended much effort in demonstrating his cleverness (which was strange because his ingenuity was obvious). Although we had limited contact with each other during the war and postwar period, I had developed an allergy to him. His demeanor made it clear that his feeling about me was even stronger.

Stan could show great mathematical inventiveness. One such occasion occurred immediately after the war when he developed the Monte Carlo method.[14] Another major contribution began now. Ulam converted Fermi's estimates, qualitative discussion, and intuitions into a set of calculations. He announced the results of the first crude calculations in April: An appropriate volume or thickness of deuterium could not be found. The Super would not work.

I made no secret of my skepticism. Ulam's calculation involved a great many interlocking factors, and I strongly felt that the Super would work. Ulam rose to the challenge. He undertook, with the able help of Cornelius Everett, to prove the 1946 machine-calculations wrong. Thus a race began between the tortoise and the hare: Ulam and Everett performed necessarily simplified calculations with their pencils; and the best available computer, operated by Johnny and Klári von Neumann, churned out more detailed calculations.

---

[13] Johnny's second wife, Klári, whom I had known as my friend Nándi's girlfriend during my high school years, took charge of the computer run of those calculations.

[14] That method, employing a sampling technique, proved to be a useful tool for examining the interactions of a very large number of particles. It may be characterized by saying that it imitated the processes of statistical mechanics by inventing statistical mathematics. The fast computer, which made repetitive processes easily available, lent itself to this procedure.

Meanwhile, I had plenty of other things to worry about. With the Booster and pure fusion tests okayed, we had to decide the general nature of those experiments. The Booster test required making extensive calculations pertinent to the events of the explosion, designing the equipment to observe those events, and building the various devices needed to produce and record the event.[15] But at least the general outline for the Booster was in place. The fusion experiment was at a much earlier stage. We had not even determined a general outline of how to test whether an arrangement of the deuterium and tritium would undergo fusion.

To coordinate the complicated and interlocking activities required to meet the deadline only twelve months away, Bradbury set up a test-oversight committee that discussed the practicality of planned experiments, the allocation of resources, and scheduling. Because a family of fission and fusion weapons was to be tested, the committee became known (with a slight dissonance) as the Family Committee.

Darol Froman, the associate director, headed the committee, which usually had about ten participants. Froman was reasonably supportive of the effort on the Super. Dick Taschek, an experimental physicist on the committee—and my next-door neighbor and friend—was even more so. Another member, Eric Jetty, who was responsible for the low-temperature equipment, was neutral. Jetty and I remained comfortable colleagues throughout the period, occasionally playing chamber music together.[16] The only committee member who seemed generally opposed to the work was Marshall Holloway, who was in charge of manufacturing the necessary parts and equipment both for the tests and for the observations. He needed little encouragement to complain about the demands of the fusion experiment and to express strong doubts about the outcome. My collaborator Freddie de Hoffman, an frequent attendee of the meetings, disagreed and greatly enlivened the discussions.

The Family Committee met a few times each month, depending on how many questions were ready for discussion. Geo Gamow, Kayski, and I each came up with a plan for the thermonuclear experiment, a test named George

---

[15] Those are sizable problems in themselves. See Chapter 26, p. 323, for further explanation.

[16] Jetty, who was a large, rotund man, presented an interesting picture playing the cello. Among the pieces that we attempted was Schubert's Trout Quintet, written for piano, violin, viola, cello, and big bass. Although Jetty could easily have played the big bass, he had none, so we played the score rewritten for two cellos, violin, viola, and piano. We never reached the point where an audience would have approved of our performance, but we enjoyed the exercise.

shot. Each of our test designs had a different geometry and different requirements. The committee reviewed the experiments on the basis of their technical feasibility and, after discussions, decided on my plan. I had chosen a conservative design because I was very much afraid of failure: Given the number of eminent scientists trying to prove a hydrogen bomb impossible, a failure might well end the program.

I gave the responsibility for designing the Booster and calculating the details of its operation to Marshall Rosenbluth. Johnny Wheeler led the group that designed an arrangement that would enable us to observe the details of the D-T reaction. There was more than enough work to go around.

Stan Ulam repeated his predictions of failure with more and more assurance as the months passed. Given the uncertainties of ultimate success, Norris Bradbury grew increasingly worried about how Los Alamos would be affected if the tests were not conducted in a manner completely above reproach. He issued instructions that further planning and modifications on the design of the hydrogen bomb should not be pursued until planning and preparations for the test series were complete.

Those instructions were in direct contradiction to the style of research most comfortable for me. I hardly know how to think without exploring the ramifications along with the immediate problems. But Bradbury's instructions had some justification. I accepted his order, even though, given the early results of the Ulam calculations, I had concerns about the Super design.

By the end of July, terrible events were occurring elsewhere in the world. The cold war had become a hot war, the first war in the nuclear age. Communist troops had crossed the thirty-eighth parallel (the boundary established by the United Nations separating the free and communist regions) into South Korea. President Truman decided on military intervention. Fighting began within a week, and during the first months, news from the battlefield was not good. Many people thought it was the beginning of World War III. No one could predict how it would end.

In August, Mici and I went to Los Angeles, where Bill and Nancy McMillan helped us look for housing for the following year. We had sold our Ellis Street house in Chicago before coming to Los Alamos, so when we found a pleasant home for a modest price near the UCLA campus, we bought it. At least this part of my future appeared to be settled.

In spite of the problems and frictions, my life outside of the laboratory was pleasant. Even with the short weekends, I managed to spend a fair amount of time with my children and their friends, telling stories, taking them swimming, going to the movies, or, accompanied by Mici and the Wheelers, attending the Indian dances. I also enjoyed the poker games held at Carson Mark's home on Saturday nights. In 1989, Carson commented on those gatherings:

> Between the end of the war and 1951, some of us who were in the theoretical physics group played some poker . . . Nick Metropolis, Stan Ulam, George Cowan, Rod Spence, Tony Turkevich, Jim Tuck, Jack Calkin, Foster Evans, Freddie de Hoffman, John von Neumann when he was here, Edward, me— that was the group that played.
>
> This was a fairly talented group of people, good minds, and Teller and John von Neumann were among the best. Edward and von Neumann had a similar style: they both had a problem keeping their minds on the game. Every now and then they would make an outstanding mistake, a simply stupendous mistake. The evening's winnings was usually about $20, which was not very impressive, but winning was very important.

I do not want to disagree with Carson, but I think he exaggerates.[17] I was never, even in those circumstances, Johnny von Neumann's equal. In addition, according to the best of my most questionable memory, Stan Ulam should also be included in the group of us notable for our "outstanding, simply stupendous" style. The three of us all demonstrated our ability to lose money during those five-hour-long evenings. But the excitement and company were well worth it.

At some point during that summer, Stan Ulam and Cornelius Everett finished their calculations. Given Stan's enjoyment of other people's discomfort, I had not taken the earlier results very seriously, but I found the completed results more disturbing. They contradicted the results of the 1946 calculations and suggested that tritium would be needed throughout the entire volume of fuel if the reaction was to continue. The expense of such an large amount of tritium would make the design wholly impractical.

I was becoming truly discouraged, the more so for having been instructed not to think about what was now the most important problem of all to me: the design of the hydrogen bomb. Because I couldn't work on the design, I

---

[17] During the same interview in 1989, Carson recalled that on one occasion, having just offered his opinion on a question, he introduced me to his companions by saying, "This is Edward Teller. He always disagrees with me." He claims, probably accurately, that my immediate response was, "But Carson, I only disagree with you when you are wrong."

decided I might as well not get excited about the question until Johnny had the results from the electronic computer.

Under those circumstances, I was worried about a meeting scheduled in mid-September: The GAC, long notable for opposing the project, was coming to Los Alamos to review the program.[18] The prospects for an American hydrogen bomb looked bleak indeed, partly because of the scientific complications but equally because of the political ones.

Bradbury had other subjects to discuss with the GAC. A young physicist from Berkeley, Ted Taylor, had joined the lab at about the same time I had returned. We had been stuck in an airport together some months earlier, and Taylor had described his innovative ideas for nuclear weapons of lower yields. I was impressed, and, on our return, I did what I could to support his work.

By the time of the GAC meeting, Bradbury could report some interesting results from Taylor's work as well as from other fission work. But his report was focused on the Super and was so negative that it seemed an outright attempt to squash the project. Johnny Wheeler and I decided that an additional report was needed to balance Bradbury's negative emphasis. So we drew up and submitted a supplementary report that discussed the current situation in a very different tone.

When I reread our report more than forty years later, I was surprised at first to see that we had mentioned the possibility of a second weapons laboratory. But then I recalled our reason for doing so: Johnny Wheeler wanted to return to Princeton and continue his work there, which he later did. I went along with his proposal without giving it much thought. We said that if our test of igniting deuterium and tritium failed and proved our past calculations wrong (in other words, if we found clear evidence that thermonuclear reactions would not work), then Los Alamos would be capable of handling all the necessary work on nuclear explosives. But a successful test would open up a wide unexplored field of possible nuclear weapons. Then, we said, Los Alamos alone would not have the capability of answering all the important questions. Establishing a second laboratory might well become necessary.

---

[18] After I had left Los Alamos and a second laboratory had been established at Livermore, Bradbury asked Bethe to write a history of the hydrogen bomb effort, which Bethe did in May 1952. I disagreed then with many points in Hans's assessment, and I disagree now. On the effect of the calculations (which he called the Fermi-Ulam calculations) he commented that those "very logical steps in the program . . . would have led nearly every scientist to give up the thermonuclear program altogether." I had a different view. Ulam's calculations predicted failure by a hair's breadth. There had to be a way of improving the design.

In retrospect, I can imagine how offensive Bradbury found our statements. I was foolish to make them. At that time, my main hope was for the success of Los Alamos. I suspect that those comments explain the suspicions that Bradbury developed concerning my intentions.

Almost simultaneously with the GAC meeting, my plans for becoming a professor at UCLA changed. During the late spring, the regents of the University of California had demanded that each member of the faculty take an oath of loyalty to the government of the United States. When I heard about it, the requirement seemed superfluous. Of course you were loyal to the government if you chose to live in the United States. Indeed, an act of disloyalty can be a criminal offense. I had no objection to signing a meaningless oath. I had sworn that I had no plans to overthrow the government when I became a citizen.

But I was not looking at the problem in light of the current hysteria. An unreasoning fear of disloyalty, already present in 1948 when Ed Condon had been accused by the House Un-American Activities Committee and heightened in 1949 by the revelation of Klaus Fuchs's espionage, had been increased once again by the war in Korea. Some of the University of California's professors refused to sign the oath, and, when I thought more about it, I could understand their point of view.

Given the faculty's resistance, I was sure the university would recognize the damage the oath would cause and back away from the requirement to sign. But before the fall quarter began, I realized that my optimism was misplaced. In late August, the university fired all the tenured professors who refused to sign the oath. Among them was my friend Gian Carlo Wick, and several acquaintances whom I knew to be fine men.

As I learned more about the regents and how some of them maneuvered, I saw how offensive the affair was. At one crucial meeting, the radical regents (who wanted to expel those faculty members who refused to sign the oath) were in the minority. Their leader, Regent John Francis Neyland, voted against his convictions because, according to the rules of procedure, a positive vote gave him the right to reopen the issue at the next meeting, when the radical regents would again have the majority.

I also learned that on one occasion, Neyland used my name to strengthen his argument. The more reasonable and moderate regents argued that expelling tenured faculty members unwilling to sign the oath would make it more difficult for the university to recruit good people. Neyland then asserted that was not so in practice: Edward Teller was planning to join the university in spite of the oath controversy.

I could no longer wait and hope that the question would resolve itself properly. I wrote to my friends in Los Angeles that, although I had no personal objection to the oath, I did have strong objections to the expulsion of professors. Furthermore, having been quoted as approving the regents' behavior, I now had no way to clarify my position except to withdraw my acceptance.

My wonderful, patient friends at the University of Chicago, particularly Warren Johnson, saved the day for me. Over the next several weeks, they made it possible for me to arrange my return to my old position at the University of Chicago. We were also lucky in regard to the house we were buying in Los Angeles. The owner had died, and because the estate was not greatly inconvenienced by our withdrawing, the matter was easily settled.

There was one further problem. Ernest Lawrence had strongly supported work on the hydrogen bomb. Now that the Ulam-Everett results indicated the unworkability of the design, the hydrogen bomb project was in great need of Lawrence's continuing support. But Ernest Lawrence was also a strong proponent of the loyalty oath at the University of California. I knew he would be angry over my position; I could only hope that he would not withdraw his support.

My letter to Maria vividly describes what happened when we next met:

I do not know where I should start. So much seems to happen in a short time, and the world looks now different again.

You know that I planned to see President Sproul [then president of the University of California] and a few others before resigning, and so I went out to California. I did this mostly for the purpose, which, in another connection, you had recommended: To leave with good feelings. By and large I succeeded. There was one exception: Ernest Orlando Lawrence. Since the days of the Nazis I have seen no such thing. I had talked sufficiently gently and generally so that Lawrence did not attack me personally. But he did use threats and he was quite unwilling to listen to any point of view except to the one of [Neyland]. I felt somewhat sick when I left his office.

At least this made it quite clear that I have to resign from California. I decided to do this as quietly as possible. I do not want to get into any more fights. Even my fine talk with Lawrence I shall keep as quiet as is compatible with my indignation and my loquacious nature. To Sproul I sent a letter of resignation giving my full reasons. I asked him, however, to use it only if he expects that it will have a strong and good effect.

And now it would be good to come back to Chicago. It was good to hear from Sam [Allison] and from Warren [Johnson] that they expect me back. But in the meantime, the World is falling to pieces I think that this is it. There is still enough determination left in me that I should like to be in on the fight. But I am tired and I do not know how long I will last. I should desperately like to close my eyes tight and come back to Chicago and never again think of any event which need be localized closer to earth than a million miles.

Although I did not mention it to Maria, Luis Alvarez, wanting to prevent a real clash between Lawrence and me, interjected himself in our meeting. He remained silent while Ernest gave his opinion, and while I gave mine. But Luis's presence helped me temper my heat. I was deeply grateful to him, because, when I left, it was clear that Lawrence would continue his intensive support of the Super.

Lawrence invited me to his laboratory to report on our progress on the bomb. Naturally, I agreed to do so. Besides Lawrence, the group I addressed that day included Robert Serber—Oppie's friend who had attended the spring conference in 1946—Herb York, a very talented young physicist who was working on some of the planned observations for the Eniwetok shot, Luis Alvarez, and a few others.

I had little of basic interest to communicate. I told them about the test plans for the Booster and the D-T reaction, and about the variety of observations and experiments that would be made; but I told them in particular about the doubts concerning the use of inexpensive deuterium to fuel a bomb.

When I had finished talking, Bob Serber asked, "We've heard all those doubts and questions before. What's new?" "Now our doubts have a firm foundation," I said with a smile. The question would have bothered me more had it not corresponded so thoroughly with my own feelings. I had no idea at the time how helpful that foundation would soon turn out to be.

In late October, a double dose of bad news arrived. Johnny reported the results of the calculation he had run on the ENIAC.[19] They confirmed the Ulam-Everett calculations. The Super would not work. We had to begin again with a new design, assuming we were allowed to continue our work.

The probable success of a radically new development is not likely to depend exclusively on one approach. There were several possible methods of reaching the goal; for example, the Booster and the Alarm Clock. The

---

[19] The ENIAC (Electronic Numerical Integrator and Calculator), built in 1946 and located in Philadelphia, was the first electronic computer.

Booster would be tested, but it was not a true hydrogen bomb. At this point, we had given only one approach, the Super, much attention. The perils and needs of that situation remain clear in my mind to this day.

Then, about the same time, I received word from Hungary that my father had died on September 11. My mother and sister, both widows, and my nephew, now a boy of nine, were in a desperate position. As long as my father was alive, there was some hope that he would be able to marshal help from his large circle of friends and acquaintances to moderate their difficulties. Now they were alone. My attempts during the past three years to secure permission for them to emigrate had proved fruitless. Although the State Department had promised to do what it could for my family, they had suggested that I do nothing that would draw attention to them.

The Korean War became more threatening. The voices arguing for pacifism became more shrill. In October, an anonymous British author, calling himself Sagittarius, published a poem in *The Bulletin of Atomic Scientists*. The gist of his message—that Americans were behaving in too belligerent a fashion—prompted me to write a response. It was, I believe, the last time I wrote a poem.

I showed my efforts to Carson Mark, whom I could depend upon for criticism. Carson on this occasion went further than a simple critique. He helped me smooth it into such acceptable shape that I submitted it to *The Bulletin*, where it was published in January 1951.

> If to a poet a physicist may speak
> Freely, as though we shared a common tongue,
> For "peace in our time" I should hardly seek
> By means that once proved wrong.
> It seems the Muscovite
> Has quite a healthy, growing appetite.
> We can't be safe; at least we can be right.
> Some bombs may help—perhaps a bomb-proof cellar,
> But surely not the Chamberlain umbrella.
> The atom now is big; the world is small.
> Unfortunately, we have conquered space.
> If war does come, then war will come to all,
> To every distant place.
> Will people have the dash
> That Britons had when their world seemed to crash
> Before a small man with a small mustache?

You rhyme the atoms to amuse and charm us—
Your counsel should inspire, and not disarm us. [20]

In December, another review report appeared in regard to the hydrogen bomb. A committee, chaired by Oppenheimer, recommended that the fission effort receive more attention than the thermonuclear work. The opponents of the hydrogen bomb seemed once again to be gathering momentum.

During the late fall, which I remember as exceptionally beautiful that year, I thought often of one of my father's untranslatable sayings: "Majd lesz valahogy, mert még sohasem volt ugy, hogy sehogyan se lett volna." [*Things will surely turn out somehow, because it's never happened yet that they turned out no-how.*]

---

[20] Edward Teller, "To Sagittarius," *Bulletin of Atomic Physicists* 8, 1 (January 1952): 22.

25

DAMN THE TORPEDOES

November 1950–April 1951

A S I WRITE this, I am on my way home to Stanford from one of my fairly frequent visits to Los Alamos. It has developed into an attractive, intellectual, and remarkably homogeneous community. It is forever grateful to Oppenheimer for its fabulous location and its dramatic beginnings. It is also liberal in the sense that great differences of opinion are easily tolerated. The period I must now write about, the early 1950s, was a critical period in its development and full of controversy. It is impossible to look back to those times without some feeling of confusion.

Today, the Soviet Union has ceased to exist. I do not believe that the massive military spending and the expansionist policy in the Soviet Union in the second half of the twentieth century could have been contained if the United States had not used technology. Only advanced technology made it possible to provide the necessary military preparedness without the expenditure of enormous amounts of money. The work at Los Alamos was the starting point of an important portion of that technology. Yet, during this period, the question was raised as to whether a truly innovative effort in technology should be undertaken or avoided. The turning point came in the early 1950s. I was in the middle of those events.

In retrospect, neither Truman's decision to develop a thermonuclear weapon nor the variety of the scientists' responses to that decision are surprising. What I never expected were the difficulties and increasing doubts about the feasibility of the Super. In the fall of 1950, when Johnny von Neumann, with the help of his wife, Klári, completed the pertinent calculations on the ENIAC, those doubts were greatly reinforced. The calculations indicated that our design would not work.

Today, the shortcomings of those calculations are widely known. Most important among them is that reality proceeds in infinitesimal steps, but a computer operates in finite steps. That difference can be tolerated if the steps are small enough. But the early computers could not accommodate many steps, and, therefore, the steps were comparatively large. But, regardless of whether the calculations were conclusive, I now had a real reason to worry. The opposition to the Super shown in the General Advisory Committee had in no way abated. If we hoped to continue work on the hydrogen bomb, we needed what we did not have: a reliable design.

One of the questions I have often been asked during the past years is why I wasn't happy when the hydrogen bomb appeared not to be feasible. Hadn't I, like my colleagues, agreed in discussions, and even in print, that it would be better for everyone if the Super didn't work?

Motives are difficult to understand, even one's own.[1] There can be no doubt that having discussed, worked on, and worried about the Super for almost ten years, a part of me wanted it to work. Many find that desire, at the very least, improper. I understand that feeling. But I believe another motive also played a part in my point of view. The calculations showed that fusion failed only by a narrow margin. What if we had given up and the Soviets hadn't? What if they had succeeded?[2]

More than forty years later, I cannot determine exactly what role each of those feelings played. Perhaps I should have tried to analyze my feelings even as I was experiencing them, but I didn't. I can recall that I felt strongly, even desperately, that we needed to continue our research. I know that I would have been satisfied to leave the work in the hands of others. But had I abandoned the attempt, the chances for successful development during this period would have been exceedingly small. There was not the slightest question in my mind that I had to try. To say that I was committed is an understatement.

That was my state of mind on an afternoon in late November or early December 1950, when Carson Mark stuck his head into my office. By that

---

[1] Leo Szilárd claimed that a person never does anything unless he has two differing motives. That was certainly true for me in regard to this time.

[2] History has proved the validity of that argument. The development of the Soviet nuclear weapons program has now been described by reliable Russian sources. The Soviet atomic bomb was largely a copy of our implosion bomb, brought to rapid realization because of Fuchs's disclosures. But the development of the Soviet hydrogen bomb seems to have been completely independent of our own, and their test followed ours by a matter of months.

time, Carson had joined the ranks of those who sided with the General Advisory Committee. Ever since the negative results from the ENIAC had been reported, he had appeared to gloat over the results. (Perhaps he believed they proved that a hydrogen bomb could not work and he was therefore rightly jubilant.) The immediate purpose of his visit was to tell me about a conference that he and some other administrators had just had with an important visitor, an admiral. They had told the admiral that the Super was definitely not feasible and then had tried to explain some of the difficulties. Carson found it hilarious that the admiral's only answer amounted to: "Damn the torpedoes; full speed ahead."

Carson Mark made it a practice to needle me in a subtle manner. Until that moment, I had brushed off his teasing as harmless. But his ridicule of what he took to be the admiral's stupidity infuriated me. I knew that I would give him pleasure by showing my anger or trying to defend the admiral, so I remained silent. He took my lack of audible response for agreement and left. I expect he has forgotten the incident, but the flood of adrenaline he engendered in me had real repercussions.[3]

I began a review of every idea that had gone into planning for a hydrogen bomb, looking furiously for a possible mistake or new idea. When Fermi asked me in 1941 whether an atomic bomb could start a thermonuclear reaction, I said no. An atomic bomb would produce enough energy to heat the relevant atomic particles, but only part of the energy would be distributed to the particles. The rest would be distributed as radiation. And at those extremely high temperatures, radiation predominates. The alternative, using the radiation from an atomic bomb to heat a volume to the necessary temperatures, demands radiant energies that are not available.

In the midst of my mental review that afternoon, I suddenly realized that there was an easy way to avoid the difficulty I had described to Fermi: Particles carry energy in proportion to their number, but radiation carries energy in proportion to volume. If there were many particles and little volume, particles would carry most of the energy!

When we had first discussed a thermonuclear weapon at the Berkeley summer conference, we believed that materials in a solid state could not be compressed much beyond their natural density. Yet, as Johnny von Neu-

---

[3] Unfortunately, Carson passed away in the late 1990s, without my ever telling him about the role he had played.

mann and I had pointed out little more than a year later in connection with the atomic bomb, uranium, a metal, would be compressed many-fold in the course of implosion. Liquid deuterium is much more readily compressed, and such compression would make thermonuclear reactions possible after the energy transfers had reached equilibrium! The answer of how to design a thermonuclear weapon was simple and obvious.

Why hadn't I realized that earlier? The primary reason, of course, is that I believed I already had an adequate design for a hydrogen bomb. I became so fixated on that first, extremely difficult approach that it took an emotional shakeup to break me loose from it. I was already committed to the non-equilibrium Super in my mind when Johnny and I introduced the idea of compression into the atomic bomb work.

How did that first approach—the non-equilibrium Super—begin? When Konopinski and I were in Chicago in 1942, we realized that energy is communicated directly only to particles: A time, although exceedingly brief, will elapse before the energy is transformed into radiation. Thus, the first design for a thermonuclear bomb, the device that acquired the nickname of the Super, began. We would produce a situation where the high-energy particles give rise to thermonuclear reactions before the radiation was emitted. The most important condition in that design—the basis on which success depended—was to accomplish fusion before the energy transfer processes could come to equilibrium. From that moment on, avoiding equilibrium had been my dedicated goal. In principle, the design would work, but the calculations that had just been completed made the Super appear a failure.[4]

The effect of compression was repeatedly raised in subsequent discussions. To reach a qualitative understanding, I took into account only two effects: the reaction between two nuclei (which produces energy and imparts it to particles); and the emission of radiation, which reduces the energy available to the particles. Compression would speed up those processes by the square of the compression. Therefore, on the balance, compression would make no difference. Later, it turned out that the scattering of light by electrons also enhances the share of energy in radiation, so that process had to be taken into account. But that third process, depending on the collision of two entities, behaved like the previous two processes and varied with the square of the compression; therefore it didn't make any difference.

---

[4] Subsequent, more accurate calculations indicate that such pessimism was exaggerated. The approach could have been successful by a small margin: Success was feasible but difficult.

The argument would be completely correct if, in all relevant processes, only two partners were participating. But one process, the absorption of light, depends on the interaction of three particles. If an electron and a photon collide, the result is scattering. But if, in addition to the electron and photon, a nucleus is present, the electron can absorb the energy of the photon. The absorption of light is usually of minor importance, but it increases with the cube of the compression rather than the square, because three, rather than two, participants are involved. Thus, if the deuterium is strongly compressed, the absorption of radiation changes from a minor factor into a process crucial to a different and much simpler design, a thermonuclear reaction in equilibrium.

My mistake in neglecting that process was simple, great, and stupid! As Wigner had pointed out years before, stupidity is a general human property, and in regard to that year's work, I had proved that I possessed an appropriate share of it. But now it was clear what had to be done. For a substantial thermonuclear reaction to occur, the deuterium should be compressed.[5] Within a few more minutes, I realized that the deuterium could indeed be compressed by the energy produced in a fission explosion so that radiation will be reabsorbed and fusion can occur.

For years, I had been concerned about the transport of energy by radiation out of the atomic bomb. Maria had worked on the same problem throughout the war.[6] I already had reasonable estimates of how much radiant energy would leave the atomic bomb at various times, as well as an understanding of the manner in which the absorption and scattering of this radiation would occur in various materials. Therefore, the tools were available to evaluate how a considerable part of the fission energy could be transferred to a neighboring region. That energy then could be used to compress some deuterium. Thus, a thermonuclear reaction would occur under the easily calculated and controlled conditions where all forms of energy (radiation energy, material energy) are in equilibrium.

---

[5] Today, detailed discussions and internationally known efforts are devoted to the production of controlled fusion by means of extremely strong compression. This effort is known as inertial confinement fusion. The principle on which all advanced work is proceeding, not only in the United States and Russia but in Europe and Japan as well, is that at high densities, radiation is reabsorbed and, therefore, it is not useless. (These remarks are not relevant to the burning of D-T. The fast burning of D-T proceeds much more easily and can be performed in small quantities of D-T from which radiation can escape.)

[6] See Chapter 16, pp. 178–79.

Within an hour of Carson's derisive remarks, I knew how to move ahead—avoiding the torpedoes. Thus, almost at once, the new plan appeared to be ready. Many important details still had to be settled, and new calculations had to be completed, but the principles of the new plan would serve as the basis for the development for many years. I cannot emphasize enough that this development was unduly delayed. My single-minded focus on ideas formulated much earlier was an extreme case of mental inertia.

But what should have been a time of great relief and an immediate revision of the laboratory program was neither. Much of the speedy success in the development of the atomic bomb arose from Oppenheimer's immediate grasp of the validity and implications of a new idea, and from his ability to change course to accommodate its development.[7] Bradbury could hardly have been more unlike Oppenheimer in those regards, and Bradbury's edict—that no new ideas about the hydrogen bomb could be discussed until after the test plans were final—was still in effect. So the best I could do was to discuss my idea quietly with a few people.

I first went to see Johnny von Neumann, who agreed that the equilibrium approach seemed very promising. I also went over the plan with Freddie de Hoffmann, who was enthusiastic. But Darol Froman, who was then head of the Family Committee, would not really listen. I must assume that he did not understand the new approach because he had not understood the old one. Yet he was in charge of the development. Or, perhaps, I made a mistake in my presentation. I probably began my discussion by telling Froman, "I have a new idea." I should have started by emphasizing that I was stupid.

The impossibility of a serious general discussion created a sense of unreality. That feeling grew even stronger when, around Christmas, I went to an American Physical Society meeting in Pasadena. Lee DuBridge, the head of Cal Tech, president of the Physical Society, and a member of the General Advisory Committee of the AEC since its founding, was the after-dinner speaker.

Some weeks before, President Truman had declared a national emergency: Chinese forces had attacked the United Nations forces in Korea and forced a retreat. DuBridge began by saying that, after the attack, many physicists had asked him whether the time had come to take work on weapons more seriously. At that, I pricked up my ears. But the next sentence took a negative turn. According to the president of the Physical Society, all the discoveries that

---

[7]See Chapter 16, p. 175.

the nation needed had been made by 1945. Our job as physicists now, he said, was to make sure that those important discoveries were not misused. After the talk, I went up to DuBridge and tried to explain to him that some interesting and important work was going on at Los Alamos. He would not listen.

The preparations for the test at Eniwetok were proceeding rapidly, but some of the methods of measurement and a few other questions were so new that everyone agreed they needed to be verified beforehand. With great speed, the head of the Test Division, Jack Clark, made arrangements for such experiments to be conducted in Nevada. Finally, in a meeting on January 15, 1951, my forty-third birthday, the plans for the Pacific tests were formally accepted with agreement on every essential point. It almost seemed like a birthday present that, at last, the conditions of Bradbury's edict had been met.

At that point, I asked Bradbury for permission to talk about the design for the hydrogen bomb; I noted that it was a different approach and would require a new set of calculations and tests. Everyone was now free of former responsibilities, and I thought it an ideal time to get on with the new work. But Bradbury refused me permission again! He said that there was no point in discussing anything new until we had learned the results of the Pacific test.

I had known that Bradbury was unenthusiastic about the hydrogen bomb, but I could hardly believe what I was hearing. I was, to say the least, frustrated, and Bradbury recognized that his refusal had upset me. A day or two later, he decided to do something to improve our relations. He kindly extended me an invitation to accompany him to Nevada to look at the new test facilities there. It was an obvious effort on his part to smooth things over.

The trip was pleasant, and throughout it, Bradbury used every opportunity to offer me advice. He told me that I was taking everything much too seriously. "If you worried less," Norris kept repeating, "you would be more effective." After our day at the test site, Norris took me to see a striptease show at a nightclub in Las Vegas in the hope, I suspect, that it would help me follow his advice. I spent the evening as usual—worrying. What mistakes had I made in my relations with colleagues and administrators at Los Alamos? Would I be able to avoid such errors in the future? Most of all, how could I get the thermonuclear program under way with enough speed to stay ahead of the Soviets?

It would be easy to say that it was Bradbury who made the mistake at this point. But that would be only a part of the truth. I was not sufficiently aware of how much Norris wanted Los Alamos to succeed. Had I made more of an effort to put myself in his shoes, I might have understood that he was less uninterested in the hydrogen bomb than he was afraid that the program would fail and reflect badly on Los Alamos. What might have happened if I had emphasized that we (particularly, me) had made a serious error? I certainly wish that I had.

Not long after my visit to Nevada, Stan Ulam came to my office. He announced that he had an idea: Use a fission explosion to compress the deuterium, and it would burn. His suggestion was far from original: Compression had been suggested by various people on innumerable occasions in the past. But this was the first time that I did not object to it. Stan then proceeded to describe how an atomic explosive should compress several enclosures of deuterium through hydrodynamic shock. His statement excluded my realization of why compression was important, and it also included details that were impractical.

I told him that I had thought of something that might work even better: It would be much more effective to compress the deuterium with the help of radiation. To be strong, compression must be appropriately symmetrical. Continued symmetrical compression can be much more easily obtained if the energy is first distributed with the help of radiation. But Stan was not interested in my proposal and refused to listen.

Finally, to put an end to the discussion, I told him that I would write up both proposals, and we would sign it as a joint report. I have no idea whether Stan ever considered the extent to which compression would or would not help. But, having considered it so many times in the past, I never imagined that our joint report would be the first to discuss seriously the possibility of compression.

In that paper, I wrote down my new plan for the first time. I explained how it would work and why it was better to compress the deuterium through radiation. We both signed the report and, in spite of Bradbury's edict, I submitted it. Because I was now in open rebellion, although supported by Ulam, the next day I asked Freddie de Hoffmann to write a detailed description of how the transfer of energy from the primary fission explosion would compress the deuterium and produce a secondary thermonuclear explosion.[8]

By now, I had become extremely concerned about the lack of interest in the hydrogen-bomb work at Los Alamos. In April, I obtained an interview in Washington with the current chairman of the AEC, Gordon Dean. I hoped

---

[8]Freddie's finished report became the basis of the new design, but he submitted the report with me listed as the only author. I continue to regret that I allowed him to exclude himself from his rightful role as joint author.

that he would see the importance of my new plan and help promote new efforts to move our work at Los Alamos ahead. He listened patiently to my explanation of how I now believed a hydrogen bomb should be constructed, but he seemed unenthusiastic about what I had to say and preoccupied with other thoughts.

After I left his office, I found to my considerable dismay that the fly to my trousers had been unzipped. It looked as though my careless grooming had defeated my last hope for obtaining greater support for the hydrogen bomb project at Los Alamos. A few months later, after listening to me make an identical statement at the GAC meeting at Princeton, Dean said that he was astonished by how I had produced a brand-new idea on the spur of the moment!

Although I believed for years that my disarray was at fault, I will never know what had led to Dean's lack of focus during my first presentation. Having recently read documents that Dean and administrators at Los Alamos wrote during those months, I now see that at the time of my meeting with Dean, he and Bradbury were concerned with a completely different set of issues than I was.

The misunderstandings began with the memo Johnny Wheeler and I had written back in September 1950 that included the mention of a second laboratory. All I had in mind in that connection was to support Johnny Wheeler in his effort to establish an adjunct laboratory at Princeton; he wanted to continue his work on nuclear weapons there with the aid of additional physicists whom he might be able to recruit. [9] But what we had said had been interpreted as a request for a full-fledged second laboratory.

During the intervening period, Bradbury had been worried about that possibility and had tried to discourage the AEC chairman from considering it. Freddie de Hoffman, who later married Gordon Dean's administrative aide, Patricia L. Stewart, spoke frequently with Dean's office during that time, and he often mentioned my unhappiness with the lack of attention being given the hydrogen bomb project. But until I read Dean's diary, I was unaware that Freddie had relayed such information. [10]

When I asked for an interview, Dean had apparently expected to hear about my unhappiness with the administration at Los Alamos or about my

---

[9] The idea was eventually approved, and the Matterhorn Project was established at Princeton, where Wheeler and his group continued to work on the hydrogen bomb until 1953.

[10] Roger M. Anders, ed., *Forging the Atomic Shield: Excerpts from the Office Diary of Gordon E. Dean* (Chapel Hill, N.C.: University of North Carolina Press, 1987).

suggestions for a second laboratory. When I mentioned neither topic and talked exclusively about a new design for the hydrogen bomb, he was probably too baffled to pay much attention. Today, I suspect he was waiting for me to discuss administrative details and so ignored what he thought was the preface. He may never even have noticed my problem zipper.

For many years, I have been mystified by the plethora of statements suggesting that I began a campaign for a second laboratory during this period or at an earlier time. Not only do I not remember doing so, but I would not think it seemly for anyone in full-time employ of an organization, whether a government laboratory, a private company, or a university, to actively promote a competing institution.

During that period, I made a lot of mistakes because of simple lack of understanding. My only interest, and it was a passionate interest, was in the successful development of the hydrogen bomb. I failed to consider issues that might be affecting others. For example, I gave no thought to how Bradbury might feel about one of my office decorations in Los Alamos. I had learned a poem from Lewis Strauss and reported it to Freddie. Freddie made a copy, framed it, and hung it on my wall. It must have offended Norris. It read:

> *Providence,*
> *which looks after Drunkards and Children and Fools*
> *With silent miracles and other esoterica,*
> *Continue to suspend the customary rules*
> *And protect the United States of America.*

I find it hard to understand how Norris could have been so blind to the technological questions—and how I could have been equally blind to his organizational problems.

During those months I was moving diligently down the long road toward satisfying Niels Bohr's definition of an expert. As I have mentioned, Bohr defined an expert as one who, from his own painful experiences, has discovered all the mistakes one can commit in a very narrow field. But the politics of national laboratories was the field in which I was unintentionally a student. Unfortunately, four decades and innumerable errors later, I still cannot claim to be an expert. I have failed no doubt to make all the mistakes that are possible in the realm of politics and administration.

About March 1951, Johnny Wheeler, together with his able collaborators Bert Freeman, John Toll, and Ken Ford, left Los Alamos for Princeton, where

Johnny had permission to set up an auxiliary laboratory, the Matterhorn Project. With them went the new design for the first hydrogen bomb, which was to be tested in 1954 in the Pacific.

The calculations required to assess the function of a particular thermonuclear reaction are awe-inspiring in their complexity. Johnny had an excellent nucleus of a group, but he needed more workers if he was to complete the task in a mere twelve months. (This was the same sort of task that Fermi, Ulam, Bethe, Everett, and others had worked on in connection with the Super for two years without success at Los Alamos.) Wheeler found the climate for recruitment little different from what it had been a year earlier. He sent out hundreds of pleas with little result.

The Matterhorn Project, fortunately, had (like the Los Alamos hydrogen bomb project) the highest military priority in the country at the time. As a consequence, Johnny was able to request the transfer of a young army officer who had recently finished his advanced studies in physics, and then had been assigned to "baby-sit the embryonic stockpile of atomic bombs." Captain Carl Haussmann was more than a little bored with his assignment, so when John Wheeler called to inquire whether Carl would like to work on a subject of high national priority that couldn't be discussed over the phone, Carl's immediate response was loudly positive. A week later, Carl was working at Princeton. In addition, Walter Aron, David Layzer, Lawrence Wilets, John McIntosh, Ralph Bennington, Ed Frieman, Jay Berger, and a few others found the work and the environment stimulating enough to join the group.

The Matterhorn group attacked their formidable task with great determination and vigor. This small but excellent group not only completed the calculations for the *Mike* test—which verified the principles on which the new design was based—but also designed several further related weapons and performed at least the preliminary calculations for all the devices that Los Alamos tested in the Pacific in 1954.

John Wheeler credits the help that Marshall Rosenbluth provided in the early stages of their work. But I would note that the Matterhorn group also used every assistance they could get, including the new, rapidly developing computers. They used the Univac computers as they were being built on the floor at the Eckhart-Mauchley factory, as Livermore did the following year. Out of this early computer work grew a body of design tools for thermonuclear weapons, which Livermore eagerly started acquiring as soon as it was founded. Los Alamos failed to develop real enthusiasm for computers until several years later, a lag that proved telling during the 1960s.

26

PLEASURES IN THE PACIFIC, PERILS AT PRINCETON

April 1951–September 1951

THE NUCLEAR TESTS in the Soviet Union appear to have been executed in grim surroundings. Reading Sakharov's memoir, I formed the impression that the Russian physicist's strong negative feelings about nuclear explosives may have been related in part to the use of political prisoners as laborers at the test sites, and the lack of even rudimentary safety measures to protect them. The situation in the United States was very different. As a general rule, the spirit of the test-site workers—military men and laboratory employees—was excellent. And the surroundings in which the tests were conducted, although primitive, were beautiful rather than grim. That was certainly true of the tests held in the spring of 1951.

The test series scheduled for April and May 1951 had been the original reason for my return to Los Alamos. The thermonuclear test, the *George* shot in the *Greenhouse* series, had been the focus of my efforts for a considerable part of the year. *George* was an experiment rather than a test; its sole usefulness was to prove that our calculations were correct. The device had no military usefulness; the amount of tritium involved would have made it too expensive to be a practical weapon, and the device itself, because of the refrigeration required for the liquid deuterium, was much too cumbersome to travel as a single unit.

Because of my involvement in the *Greenhouse* series, I was invited to witness what we all hoped would be the first man-made macroscopic thermonuclear reaction. I felt confident that the test would be successful, but I still had enough misgivings to be excited about the event. Perhaps that explains how I happened to cut my thumb badly while shaving on the morning I was to leave. I wrapped it tightly so that it would stop bleeding. By the time I got off the little plane that had taken me down to Albuquerque, my thumb ached horribly: The bandage had cut off circulation and, combined with the effects of an increase in altitude, now felt like a medieval thumb screw. I had to go the Lovelace Clinic where, when my little wound was properly bandaged, my thumb felt fine. The next day, on the plane heading out over the wide waters of the Pacific, I felt liberated from the worries that had haunted me during the past months.

Our first stop was Hawaii. I still vividly remember the descent into the beautiful landscape of water and mountains, the clouds colored brightly by the setting sun. I even did some shopping voluntarily, for only the second time in my life. I happened into an exhibition of wood carving by the Swiss sculptor Fritz Abplanalp. His medium was driftwood, often charred, and for the most part from shipwrecks, that he collected on the beaches. I could not resist buying one of the smallest pieces, a little masterpiece measuring only ten by five by one and one-half inches. The second spontaneous purchase of my life, quite different from the first—an ancient concert piano—is a small piece of charred wood into which is carved, in relief, the beautiful profile of a woman.

The next day a military plane flew Freddie de Hoffman and me, together with quite a number of other participants, from Hawaii to the test site at the Eniwetok Atoll. After hours of uninterrupted ocean, I finally saw a little flat island less than a mile in diameter. Then I could make out rusting tanks and a great deal of ugly and forever useless military equipment sprawled on the beaches—remnants of the fighting that had taken place there less than ten years earlier. But it was not much longer before I began to appreciate the beauties of the setting.

My position as a visitor was a peculiar one. Everyone appeared to be afraid that I would insist on some important but impractical modification at the last moment. Therefore, everyone had come up with activities to divert me and make me feel happy lest I make some impossible proposition. It turned out that I was on my best behavior and made no new suggestions whatsoever. Instead, I enjoyed a truly wonderful few days of vacationing.

Even on the first day, I swam in the quiet lagoon, which was surrounded by the almost circular chain of little islands.[1] The contrast of the big waves outside the lagoon and the smooth lake of water inside was striking. I had

---

[1] Freddie did not enjoy swimming and looked at my attempts at exercise and recreation with faint disapproval.

taken along a snorkel so that I could lie flat on the water, face down, and look at the wonders below without having to come up for air. As I wrote to Maria, "I never felt so fishy in my life." Swimming not more than a hundred feet into the lagoon brought me to a group of coral reefs. The fish seem to cluster around those reefs like birds in a tree, except more colorful, more numerous, and, to human ears, completely silent. Some of them were always swimming from one reef to another, but their home seemed to be the corals.

The commanding officer at the test site, General Pete (Elwood R.) Quesada, was pleasant and amiable. He had brought his dog along, a small, friendly creature called Duchess, who wore a well-chewed security badge. Duchess, it turned out, was the solitary female among all of us at Eniwetok.

The next day, one of the pilots at the site took Freddie de Hoffman and me in a small open-cockpit plane to look at the tower that carried our experimental explosive object. I sat up front in the copilot's seat, and Freddie rode in the back. The pilot put on earphones. So did I. There was music. We took off. After a couple of minutes, I saw the pilot's right thumb poking in my direction. What did he mean? Earphones? Music? There was no verbal communication.

Then I noticed that he had taken his hands off the controls. So why shouldn't I touch mine? I did. Nothing happened. After a while, I noticed that the plane started to veer to the right, in the general direction of the seemingly endless empty ocean. Hesitantly and very gently, I applied pressure toward the left. The plane came back into line with the little islands.

I had never flown a plane before. Now I suddenly suspected that I might be an expert. I enjoyed being a pilot so much that I was almost sorry to surrender the controls for the landing. The experience had two consequences. Ever since, I have felt much safer flying in an airplane. After all, even I could make the thing behave. The other consequence was that when we got off the plane, Freddie's face had a noticeable green tinge. He obviously trusted me more with hydrogen bombs than with airplanes.

After we landed, we went up the tower and looked at the object that was to determine whether the calculations Johnny Wheeler and his group had made were trustworthy. The details of the equipment had been arranged by Herb York and Hugh Bradner, two of Ernest Lawrence's bright young men from Berkeley. The device appeared to be well done, and I had no reason for worry. To everyone's relief, I suspect, I offered no suggestions.

Two days later, the shot went off at mid-morning. It was a big explosion, impressive even from my position ten miles away. For the moment, the explosion told us essentially nothing. We knew that our questions had been answered. But to learn the answers, we had to gather samples from the various instruments and devices that had been collecting data near the explosion. The results would not be available until the next day.

One of my Los Alamos friends from the war years, experimentalist Louis Rosen, had volunteered to identify the fusion process.[2] A thermonuclear reaction between deuterium and tritium produces fast neutrons. They leave the neighborhood of the explosion and can be easily found a few hundred feet away from their origin. Such neutrons will bump into protons, and they will leave characteristic long tracks when captured on a photographic plate. Such a long track is unmistakable evidence of a thermonuclear reaction. Louis had decided to place glass plates coated with an emulsion at five locations, each about two hundred yards from the blast.

Ernest Lawrence had watched the event that morning, and in the afternoon he and I went out for a swim. There was not a hint that Lawrence remembered the strained interview we had had over the loyalty oath. It was clear that Lawrence was not a man who insisted on political conformity or harbored a grudge. In retrospect, I believe this was the first time I recognized Lawrence's uncommon generosity and selflessness, his way of taking wholehearted, enthusiastic pleasure in a good idea or a good piece of work, whether his own or someone else's.

The question on my mind since the amazing explosion that morning was: Did fusion occur or didn't it? In addition to the big explosion we saw, had there been a reaction between the tritium and deuterium? I expressed my anxiety to Lawrence by saying, "I believe it didn't work." Ernest's immediate, smiling reply was, "I bet you five bucks it did." I make about one bet per decade. This was my bet for the fifties.

The next morning, as I brushed my teeth, I saw my friend Louis next to me, similarly occupied. I asked him how his plates had fared, and he reported that they had all survived nicely. Then he added, "I saw one long proton track, but don't tell anybody until I have finished examining the photographic plates." Of course, I knew what he was talking about.[3]

---

[2] In the 1960s, Louis Rosen developed the Los Alamos meson production facility, a great contribution to scientific research. Rosen remained at Los Alamos throughout his career,

[3] Louis recalls the event a little differently. (We agree only that the other's version may be correct.) He remembers that our early morning conversation took place in his darkroom, where, he claims, I had come to see what results he was getting. He also reports that, on one occasion when I preceded him as a speaker, I was asked whether I had ever violated security voluntarily. I replied, he says, "Yes, but it was Louis Rosen's fault," and then repeated this story.

Ernest was taking a plane that morning for Japan. I could not share my feeling of great relief with anyone yet. But as I saw Ernest's jeep pull out, I ran after it and gave Ernest five dollars. His smile was as big as mine.

Within a few hours, we saw the whole picture. The experimental shot had succeeded in every important detail. Johnny Wheeler's calculations about thermonuclear explosions had been correct. The prospects for a weapon based on the Super design were once again good, but by now I was firmly convinced that the latest design, the report that Freddie de Hoffman had submitted in my name, was far superior. Now the proof existed that thermonuclear explosions were possible. It was high time to get on with the work.

But when I got back to Los Alamos, I found that the political part of the problem was unchanged. What I have to report now seems unbelievable, but it happened. Facts can be strange, and if they are, there is every reason to remember them.

We were scheduled to report on the hydrogen bomb program to the General Advisory Committee in early June. The meeting was to take place at the Institute for Advanced Studies in Princeton, then the high fortress of academia. I would have liked to report on our successful demonstration, but Bradbury had other plans. That report would be delivered by Carson Mark, who had been, and still was, a deeply entrenched skeptic of the project.

Johnny Wheeler and Lothar Nordheim—both of whom shared my point of view—were to be present. Johnny von Neumann would also be at the meeting; that reassured me. I would be there. But Norris Bradbury refused to allow me to report the new developments. He said his reason for that decision was his desire to allow me to speak freely!

Stan Ulam, who is listed as the co-author with me on the first written report of the new design (which also included his proposal for an alternate), chose not to attend. During the months following our joint report, Stan had repeatedly told people at Los Alamos and outside the laboratory that my new plan for the hydrogen bomb would not work. He did not discuss the matter with me.[4] I don't know why Stan changed his mind.[5]

---

[4] One of the mathematicians working on the new design claims that after several months of work, Ulam still did not understand the new design. He suggests that there was no claim that Ulam came up with the idea until after the Oppenheimer hearing.

[5] To me, the authorship of a paper does not mean a question of priority—it is a matter of responsibility. If I sign a paper, I am ready to stand up for it; if I don't want to stand up for it, I expect to have to explain why I changed my mind.

I arrived in Princeton before the meeting, so I decided to visit Oppenheimer. When I told him of the new approach and of my confidence in it, he seemed to listen with interest and understanding. But although I was certain that the hydrogen bomb project needed to move forward as rapidly as possible, I couldn't guess what Oppenheimer thought, or what the GAC would decide. I had considerable misgivings; his indifference led me to suspect that he opposed taking the next step.

At the meeting the next day, Carson Mark reported the details of the satisfactory confirmation of Johnny Wheeler's calculations in the test conducted at Eniwetok. He concluded his remarks by saying that, with the *Greenhouse* test, we had satisfied President Truman's instructions.[6] Carson did not mention the test's implications for developing the Super, nor did he mention the new, vastly simplified design. He made no mention of future work.

I was upset. To my mind, the omission was a flagrant misrepresentation of the current status of the hydrogen bomb project and, therefore, a disservice to the General Advisory Committee, which had the responsibility of understanding and of planning the work at the laboratories. To my mind, President Truman's directive would not be fulfilled until we had completed our research on a thermonuclear *weapon*, and there was no way the experiment just completed could be viewed as a weapon.

I asked to be heard, but Norris Bradbury immediately opposed my being allowed to make a statement; he said (correctly) that I could not speak for the laboratory. The situation was odd. Several people present—Johnny von Neumann, Nordheim, Dean, and Oppenheimer—had heard my proposal for the new design and the steps that I believed would lead directly to the demonstration of a fusion bomb.[7] They said nothing. Even Bradbury, although he had never paid attention to my proposal, could not have been completely ignorant of it. To my great and unexpected relief, a member of the GAC, Henry DeWolfe Smyth said, "Why don't we listen to Teller?"[8]

---

[6] Truman's actual words were that research would be conducted on "the so-called hydrogen or super bomb." In a strict sense, Carson may have been correct in his statement. The theoretical basis of the Super had been demonstrated as correct, although fulfilling the president's directive in such a literal manner seemed to me grossly insufficient. A thermonuclear explosion is not yet a thermonuclear weapon.

[7] Johnny Wheeler, who also had heard my proposal, had left the meeting before this exchange; as I recall, he went to pick up some results that were being completed by the Matterhorn group for his report later in the meeting.

[8] Smyth was the author of the famous Smyth Report, which described for the first time the basic principles involved in making an atomic bomb.

It was easy to make my statement brief. Carson Mark had just described how a large fission explosion could compress a mixture of deuterium and a relatively small amount of tritium and produce a thermonuclear explosion. I just pointed out that a much smaller fission explosion could, in a similar arrangement, compress a larger amount of deuterium and produce a hydrogen bomb. I had only to add a few words to anticipate obvious objections and to estimate appropriate orders of magnitude. I think I talked fifteen or twenty minutes.

Oppenheimer's response, which may have been the first one made at the table, was that my proposal was so "sweet" that it could not be rejected. With practically no debate, the GAC decided that Los Alamos should proceed to produce a thermonuclear bomb along the lines I had proposed.

The contrast between completely ignoring new possibilities and completely accepting them could not have been more striking. I should have been happy and satisfied by the acceptance of my suggestions in those academic surroundings. But I was much more bewildered than satisfied. The surprising events were so contrary to the attitudes present before the meeting that I still doubted future events. A part of me was waiting for the next disagreeable surprise to emerge.

A disagreeable surprise of a different nature arrived shortly after I returned to Los Alamos. My mother, my sister, Emmi, and János, now twelve, had been deported from Budapest to the remote rural village of Tálya and were not permitted to leave. That was terrible news; my sister had to support all three of them, and her prospects in the countryside for securing work as a translator—or any employment other than manual labor—were next to zero. János would not be able to keep up his school work. Worst of all, they would have no friends nearby to help them.

Yet there was nothing I could do to help them openly without risking even worse treatment for them. Emmi's best defense was to pretend that she had no connection to me. At one point, she was taken by the police for a three-day-long interrogation about me. But in truth, she knew nothing. Emmi wrote only to Magda Hesz in Chicago, our au pair from childhood, and Magda relayed the news to me. In her letters to Emmi, Magda wisely said nothing about me. I renewed my pleas to the State Department and to the Red Cross.

I was still hoping for a resolution to the thermonuclear program's administrative problems at Los Alamos. Reorganizing the laboratory for developing and testing the new design was, to my mind, a first order of business; but I could do little other than make suggestions. As the weeks passed, the status quo seemed to be a permanent. Bradbury behaved as if nothing had changed. He didn't mention anything pertinent to the hydrogen bomb program to me. If he had changed his mind about the value of the program, he gave no indication of it.

There was one bright spot in that sea of gray: One of Fermi's able young students, Dick Garwin, had come to work at Los Alamos for the summer. Given the lack of interest and enthusiasm, it was important to me that a paper be drawn up detailing how the New Super would work and addressing every conceivable doubt as to whether it would work. If its first test shot misfired, it was not at all certain there would be a second one.

I explained the overall scheme of the new Super to Garwin and asked him to draw up a concrete design, complete with dimensions. The design need not be a deliverable weapon, I said, but I did want as complete a proof of the principle as he could provide. Garwin produced just that. Thus, not long after the meeting in Princeton, the details of the plan for the hydrogen bomb were completed.

Garwin's paper was criticized up and down, but, in the end, it stood almost as he had written it. Marshall Rosenbluth and Conrad Longmire, possibly with the help of others, worked out the calculations and details of Garwin's proposal. Eventually, Hans Bethe looked it over, and he agreed that it was all right. So, in the end, Garwin's design remained unchanged.

But that was the only bright spot. In September, Norris Bradbury finally decided how he wanted to reorganize the laboratory to accommodate the program on the new Super. Ten months had passed between the time I had realized how to proceed with the more straightforward approach and the time the program based on the new ideas was finally going to begin. I was glad that the eventual decision was positive.[9]

Bradbury made a decision that gave me a less welcome message: The effort to complete the hydrogen bomb should be placed in the hands of Marshall Holloway. Holloway, who, as a member of the Family Committee, had created difficulties in connection with the hydrogen bomb at every turn. Somewhat negative in his approach to life in general, Holloway had not cooperated on any project pertaining to the Super. Bradbury could not have appointed anyone who would have slowed the work on the program more effectively, nor anyone with whom I would have found it more frustrating to work. Norris

---

[9] But I also felt that the right decision had won out by a hairsbreadth. For much of that period, it seemed equally possible that the work would be abandoned; had that happened, the decision could not have been reversed in an easy or obvious way.

had announced, in effect, that he did not care whether I worked on the project or not.

The next days were full of hesitation and personal decisions that I changed almost hourly. They were full of discussions with close friends. I finally came to a decision that I had hoped to avoid, but I could no longer ignore the experiences of the past twenty-three months. The uncertainties and lack of commitment to the thermonuclear program at last convinced me that depositing the full responsibility for the development of nuclear weapons in one laboratory was dangerous.

Los Alamos was not entirely at fault. Secrecy prevented the broad participation and informed criticism of the scientific community. The General Advisory Committee had proved in its June meeting that it was capable of producing a pleasant surprise. But reasonable progress must not be based on the hope of a surprise. Now that Los Alamos had become an established laboratory, it had all the advantages and disadvantages of such an institution. The advantage is technical excellence; the disadvantage is set ideas. A second laboratory would produce rivalry and thereby give impetus to innovation. It would be unseemly to advocate a second laboratory while working at Los Alamos, so I had to leave for that reason alone.

I decided to return to the University of Chicago. That decision was made easier because neither Bradbury nor Holloway wanted my collaboration in any case. I could probably provide as much assistance to the project during brief visits as I could by staying at Los Alamos.

For the better part of a year, Bradbury had mistakenly suspected that I wanted to create competition for Los Alamos. Now he and the events in which we all had participated convinced me that a second laboratory was a necessity.

Before I left Los Alamos, I had one last project that I wanted to complete. The computer that Nick Metropolis had built was now operating, and it was my last chance to work on it. So for the few days (and nights) just before I left, Nick, Marshall Rosenbluth, Marshall's wife Ariana, Mici, and I worked out and ran a program that used the repetitive application of probabilistic selection to describe a simple two-dimensional model of a liquid.[10]

---

[10] N. Metropolis, A. Rosenbluth, M. Rosenbluth, A. H. Teller, and E. Teller, "Equation of State Calculations by Fast Computing Machines," *J. Chem. Phys.* 21, 6 (June 1953): 1087–1092.

The paper that resulted from our work was the first practical application of the Monte Carlo system, a statistical procedure introduced by Stan Ulam with John von Neumann's help. In our model of a liquid, the loosely arranged molecules were represented by identical circular disks, they were not permitted to overlap or to interact further. The normal procedure would have been to give all the disks some initial velocities and then calculate their future positions, including elastic rebounds when the disks collided. Instead, we started with the disks' forming a regular, somewhat loose lattice in a regular hexagonal arrangement, each disk surrounded by six others but not touched by them. We then allowed the disks, one after another, to undergo a displacement selected by a random process. If that move led to an overlap, the disk was not moved from its original place. If it did not overlap, the move was completed. In either case, we went on to move the next disk.

The original regular arrangement of the disks was changed to a fluctuating density characteristic of liquids. It is easy to show that our result is the same one we would have obtained had we allowed the disks to have velocities and collide. There were no practical applications. We simply provided an example of how computers can give interesting results by simple repetitive operations. It was science just for fun.

27

The Campaign
for a Second
Weapons Laboratory

November 1951–July 1952

WE HAD SOLD our house in Chicago, which was too small for us, when we left for Los Alamos. In the late summer of 1951, I left Mici and the children in the newly built house we'd enjoyed for two years and went back to Chicago to look for a place to live. The housing situation had not improved much during our absence, and the city was locked in a muggy hot spell. After a discouraging search, I came across a nice apartment on the first floor of a three-story building on East Fiftieth Street near the university.

I arrived just as the owners, a middle-aged couple named Eckhaus, were finishing their lunch. The apartment for rent was their living quarters, and they planned to rent it complete with furnishings. I discovered almost immediately that Mrs. Eckhaus was far more eager to rent their apartment than her husband. When I mentioned that we had two small children, Mr. Eckhaus stretched back from the table in horror, obviously suffering from visions in which my children were dismantling his belongings. My heart sank. I mentioned that I was a friend of the famous Dr. Enrico Fermi and that he would surely provide a reference for me and my family. My claim produced only puzzlement: Who was Fermi?

Then Mrs. Eckhaus, observing that her husband was looking more disapproving with each passing second, said, "We must ask Maria." Maria, it turned out, was the tenant who lived on the second floor. She also seemed to be the fount of good judgment and the coordinator of peace and understanding in the house. Mrs. Eckhaus left and soon reappeared, out of breath.

"Maria knows him!" she announced in amazement. At once I was offered a seat at the table and a cup of coffee.

Presently Maria came downstairs. She was a pleasant woman and identified me as the person she knew. I had never before set eyes on her, but I decided not to mention that. I finished my coffee, and, to my relief, the arrangements for me to rent the apartment were promptly completed.

Maria then invited me upstairs to say hello to her husband. There the mystery was solved. Maria and her husband, Gerhardt Piers, were psychoanalysts who had emigrated from Vienna in the late 1930s. Trudi Weiss and Leo Szilárd were mutual friends and had given them a letter of introduction to me, which Maria handed over on that occasion. The Piers had two children whose ages were similar to those of our own children. The arrangements were ideal, and that meeting proved to be the beginning of our long friendship.

Although we now had a place to live, it took me several more weeks of commuting between Los Alamos and Chicago to tie up all the loose ends. Finally, around the first of November, Mici, Paul, Wendy, and I said goodbye to the lovely mesa and returned to university life in a great city. Our old friends, Joe and Maria Mayer, James Franck, and Enrico and Laura Fermi welcomed us back; and our new friends, the Piers, provided a further bright spot.

It was hard to leave Los Alamos. The theoretical framework for the new Super was complete, but there were unfinished problems connected with the upcoming test and the new design. Going back on visits is not the same as seeing day-to-day progress. But all in all, I felt confident that between Conrad Longmire and Marshall Rosenbluth, who would continue their efforts at Los Alamos, and John Wheeler's group in Princeton, who were handling most of the theoretical work for the future tests, the program would proceed on a sound scientific basis.

I decided that my first theoretical work in Chicago would be on the blast effects of the hydrogen bomb. Oppenheimer, Conant, and the others who had signed the GAC majority report had said, "If super bombs will work at all, there is no inherent limit in the destructive power that may be attained with them"; and Fermi and Rabi had claimed, "The fact that no limits exist to the destructiveness of this weapon makes its very existence and the knowledge of its construction a danger to humanity as a whole." It seemed important to investigate the nature of the effects of the extremely powerful new weapon that lay just over the horizon.

The results of my calculations differed markedly from the catastrophic predictions that had been offered. Instead of a steady increase in the blast with greater explosive power, the blast effects were limited. An explosion equivalent to 10 million tons of TNT (10 MT) would heat a mass of air a few miles in diameter to so high a temperature that the velocities of the air molecules would exceed the velocity at which molecules escape earth's gravitational pull. Thus, a chunk of the atmosphere, weighing perhaps a billion tons, would be blown into space. If one further increased the explosive power—for example, to an equivalent of 100 million tons of TNT (100 MT)—the main change would be that a mass of air of practically the same size would be blown away with three times the velocity.[1]

That is not to say that the destructiveness of the hydrogen bomb was not great. The effects at ground level of a 10 MT explosion would be the complete destruction of everything within an area of several miles in every direction. But the effects of an explosion ten times larger would not extend the ground effects to a significant extent.[2]

Contrary to the first guesses in the General Advisory Committee, the effects of increasingly massive explosives would not give rise to universal destruction, at least not in a simple and straightforward way. Very large explosives would be more expensive to produce and harder to deliver, but they would cause little additional blast damage. In other words, increasing the yield beyond the equivalent of 10 MT TNT would not increase the dangers of the hydrogen bomb. The blast effects of the thermonuclear bomb were huge, but they were limited. That argument remained valid, no matter how huge the explosion or how it was delivered.[3]

The most important of my activities during my return to Chicago was my effort to establish a second weapons laboratory. Science historically had moved forward because of openness, but research on weapons was conducted in strict

---

[1] In the course of time, military authorities, both in the United States and the Soviet Union, found that explosives equivalent to about one million tons of TNT (1 MT) are most cost-effective. The largest device ever exploded was near 100 MT. As Sakharov reported, the Soviets detonated it to intimidate the West, not because it would ever have served a direct military purpose. The hydrogen bomb became a truly dreadful menace not because it was unlimited in size but because it was inexpensive to produce and became available in great numbers.

[2] Although other claims of universal disaster were based on the effects of the radioactivity produced, not on the effects of shock, the destructive effects of radioactivity from individual bombs are less certain than the blast effects. To some extent, the amount of radiation released depends upon the manner in which nuclear weapons are detonated. A large portion of the radioactivity in exceedingly large nuclear weapons would be blown into space. Radioactivity is most effectively spread without the use of bombs, but radioactivity is not likely to be used as a weapon because it acts on friend and foe alike.

[3] Later, Lowell Wood confirmed those conclusions through more detailed considerations carried out in the new laboratory in Livermore.

secrecy. Because secrecy imposed limits on how many scientists were permitted to offer advice or criticism, and because those overseeing the program at the political level were not always knowledgeable about the possibilities, it seemed vitally important to establish a separate, second weapons laboratory, a competitive younger sibling to Los Alamos. Being less well established, a second laboratory would be more likely to support innovation. It would share the awesome responsibility for maintaining the military strength on which peace depended, and it would provide balance and the spur of competition for the Los Alamos program.

My thoughts on this question had become clear during my last few months at Los Alamos. Having seen that the nation's only weapons laboratory was motivated in a rather distant and abstract way by concerns about the safety of our nation, but in a real and substantial way by concerns about the good public relations of the laboratory, I felt I had to discuss my concerns openly.

My career as a "promoter" began at this time.[4] I cannot say that I enjoyed my new occupation, but it was far better than doing nothing but worrying. My memories of the conversations I had about the second lab are hazy at best. I am not even that sure I can list all the people I approached; but I do know that I spoke with Lewis Strauss, who had been a member of the original AEC committee. That conversation was our second.

Lewis Strauss was a courteous man with a deep-seated sense of decency. We had in common a firsthand familiarity with the ravages of World War I, and, as ethnic Jews, an acute awareness of some of the horrors of World War II. We both believed that peace was lost in the 1930s because the world's democracies disarmed themselves through neglect and negotiations. We were both convinced that the United States could help preserve peace only if it remained militarily strong.

All that had become clear during our first meeting in New York, when Lewis had invited me to talk with him about the hydrogen bomb. During that conversation, he had adopted a somewhat fatherly tone. In the second conversation, he adopted an even more pronounced paternal attitude. When I explained my concern about the necessity of a second laboratory, he told me

---

[4]Oppenheimer accused Ernest Lawrence and me of being experienced "promoters" in his October 1949 letter to fellow GAC member James Conant. At that time, the only important political figure with whom I had spoken to urge research on the hydrogen bomb was Senator McMahon. To my mind, a single visit to one individual does not qualify me as a promoter. In connection with the second laboratory, I earned the title: Over the next several months, I went to talk with everyone who would see me.

that he would do what he could to help. For all that, talking with Lewis Strauss always inspired a slight sense of awe in me. I was not all that sure of his support, and not long after that meeting, a dream I had reinforced that feeling; in it, Strauss told me he loved me like a brother-in-law.

When I returned, my friend Bill Libby, with whom I had worked during and after the war, was still at the University of Chicago, and we saw each other fairly often. Bill was now a member of the GAC. He was in full agreement that a second laboratory was a good idea; but, that fall, when the GAC had considered a second laboratory, he had not been able to sway anyone else.[5] Not long after learning those facts from Bill, I ran into Oppenheimer at a conference, and I decided to ask for permission to address the GAC. Oppenheimer agreed that I could make a presentation at the December meeting. But the odds appeared to be against me.

The meeting was to be in Washington, and I took the sleeper from Chicago to Washington. On the train, I had an unusual dream. Perhaps my conversations with the Pierses, who as psychoanalysts were always interested in dreams, affected its intensity, or perhaps it was merely an outgrowth of the feelings that had haunted me during this period. I dreamed that I was alone defending a position in a trench, similar to the ones that had so terrified me as a child in Budapest. Thereupon, my dream took a mathematical turn. I had only eight bullets for my rifle, and nine men were coming to attack me. I was in despair. There was no chance of my surviving.

Then suddenly, with the wonderful illogic of dreams, I felt elated instead of frightened. Nine men meant that there was a target for each of my bullets. Not one needed to go unused.

In the morning, I woke up with a pervasive sense of cheer. When I got off the train, I discovered the weather that day was most unusual. It was snowing heavily, and in Washington this means that traffic is at a standstill. I couldn't get a cab, so I trudged along through the snow from the railway station to the AEC office. Given my missing foot and unsteady balance, I barely made it, but that didn't bother me at all. I was aware of the absurdity of my dream. I recognized that the bullets in my dream were my polite arguments and that those arguments were not likely to penetrate their targets, but I was not at all concerned about firing them off.

---

[5] In October, 1951, the AEC commissioners met with the GAC and briefly considered the question of a second laboratory. AEC Commissioner Thomas Murray, a former mechanical engineer who was then a director of several corporations, was a dedicated advocate of a second weapons laboratory. I can claim no credit for his early positive stand.

I believe that the argument I presented that day was among the very best I have ever made. I was constrained, logical, and polite. And I was also correct about the attitudes of the GAC members: Their minds remained unchanged. Only Libby favored a second laboratory. Nonetheless, as I fought my way back to Union Station through the deep snow, I felt a peculiar satisfaction. Even if I had accomplished nothing, I had stood firmly in my place in the trench and faced my opponents.

Not long after that presentation, Mici complained for the first time about being left behind when I went on a trip. The incident is memorable because Mici, throughout our sixty-plus years together, almost always viewed my business trips with a disinterested eye. But during the early part of January, left in Chicago to deal with ice and snow and eight-year-old Paul and five-year-old Wendy, Mici was unhappy. I did my best to comfort her, but I also went off alone, with only a slightly bad conscience, to my first U.S. Air Force Scientific Advisory Board (SAB) meeting at sunny Cape Canaveral, Florida.

My friend Theodore von Kármán had played a most important role during the war in modernizing and accelerating the buildup of U.S. air power. During the course of that work, he had been asked to advise the Army Air Corps on preparing for the future. One of von Kármán's suggestions during the war had been to set up an advisory group of scientists. That group proved so helpful that after the war it was made permanent.[6] While I was still trying to find a way to stay at Los Alamos during the summer of 1951, von Kármán asked me to join the SAB; and in September, I accepted.

From its earliest beginnings, one of the SAB's most important roles was to oversee and provide direction for the research being conducted by the air force. Only five years had passed since Marshall Holloway and I had tried, unsuccessfully, to persuade air force planners to describe modifications to the atomic bomb that would better meet their needs. Now, the planners showed lively interest.

The current air force concern was with rockets. Towards the end of World War II, Theodore von Kármán had developed a liquid propellant research rocket at Cal Tech, which he named the Corporal.[7] Although that rocket had

---

[6] My service on the SAB continued until the early 1990s.

[7] During the test in which a modified version of the Corporal reached 80,000 feet, a general who was also observing the test asked von Kármán how much higher the Corporal could go. Von Kármán immediately replied, "Only to Colonel. Beyond that they don't work any more."

been much improved and others designed, in 1952 the range and accuracy of U.S. rockets was still limited. The air force was interested in the hydrogen bomb because the increase in explosive effects would help to compensate for the inaccuracy of the rockets.

In 1950, the air force had stepped up its efforts to bring more scientists and engineers into its ranks and had established a rotating civilian post of Air Force Scientist. Dave Griggs, a geophysicist on leave from UCLA, was at the January meeting as the Air Force Scientist. Dave had been one of the first employees of Rand Corporation, a Los Angeles company that conducted scientific research on contract to government departments and to private industry. We had worked together briefly on a problem in shock hydrodynamics at Los Alamos. He was thoroughly familiar with the attitudes there and thoroughly concerned about them.

As I look back, I think it would be fair to say that without Dave Griggs, Lawrence Livermore Laboratory would not have come into existence. He introduced me to many influential people and succeeded in developing a lot of friends for the idea. The Cape Canaveral meeting was chaired by a friend of Dave's, the famous General Jimmy Doolittle, an outstanding man, full of vitality, good humor, and common sense.[8]

Dave arranged for me to talk privately with General Doolittle outside the meeting. I briefed General Doolittle about the difficulties connected with the development of the hydrogen bomb and about the possibilities for a variety of thermonuclear weapons. He listened with a sympathetic smile, but at that time I never would have guessed the far-reaching consequences of that conversation.

Not long after the SAB meeting, I heard once again from Ernest Lawrence.[9] Ernest invited me to come to Berkeley to talk with him. I went, and on February 2, 1952, Ernest took me to view a site that he felt would be an appropriate place for the second weapons laboratory, a one-square-mile area near the little town of Livermore. During World War II, the site had served as an inland navy base for training pilots. After the war, the base was closed and sat idle until 1950; then Lawrence acquired the land as the site

---

[8] Doolittle had achieved fame as the pilot who led a bombing attack on Japan at the beginning of World War II, when the Japanese were still advancing rapidly throughout the Pacific region. A man of remarkable vigor, Doolittle was still making hunting trips in Alaska when he was in his late eighties. He passed away at ninety-six in 1993.

[9] According to Herb York's later account, Ernest had wanted to be directly involved in national defense ever since the Soviets had tested their atomic weapon.

for the materials testing accelerator (MTA) that he and Luis Alvarez had recommended in 1949.

The accelerator, designed by Luis Alvarez, would produce new materials—for example, plutonium from uranium-238 or tritium from deuterium; this led to the AEC acceptance of the project. Even though the base, some thirty miles east of Oakland, was a slightly uncomfortable commuting distance from Berkeley, Herb York and his group of about forty young people had used the infirmary there as their headquarters while they were working on the *George* shot of the *Greenhouse* test. At the time of my first visit, work on the accelerator was the only science being conducted there.

That evening, Ernest took me to dinner at Trader Vic's, his usual choice for discussing a really important project. Lawrence was enthusiastic about having a second laboratory at Livermore. He was sure he would be able to persuade several of his excellent young students and collaborators to join the project. Although it remained unspoken, Lawrence and I both knew he was influential enough to secure support when necessary, both from the University of California and in Washington.

I consumed a very tasty Mai Tai while Ernest explained that the much needed second weapons laboratory would be welcome as an extension of the Berkeley Radiation Laboratory. At the moment, one Mai Tai was not enough to convince me that this was a splendid offer, and I did not have a second drink. I agreed that I wanted to work in a laboratory that was devoted to developing thermonuclear weapons. Ernest suggested that I go to Washington to secure the authorization for such a laboratory. I pointed out that I had already tried, unsuccessfully, to convince the people I could contact there. Ernest told me I had to continue trying, and as it turned out, I soon had a chance to do just that.

Arriving back in Chicago, I learned that General Doolittle had understood my worries and the arguments for a second laboratory: He and Dave Griggs had arranged for me to meet with the Secretary of the Air Force, Thomas K. Finletter, in mid-February. When I began explaining my concerns at that interview, Finletter appeared cold, almost hostile; but within fifteen minutes, his interest picked up. He paid particular attention to one of my statements: Los Alamos has no competition, and the leadership in Los Alamos is sure that they can make no mistake under any conditions. I found out later that he promptly arranged a visit to Los Alamos to check whether I had exaggerated my description. Apparently, the result convinced him of the need for a second laboratory. He eventually stated that the need for a second laboratory was so great that the air force would establish one if the AEC would not.

But even Finletter's strong support was not enough to decide the issue. The crucial interview came when, because of Doolittle's and Finletter's recommendation, Secretary of Defense Robert A. Lovett agreed to see me. I arrived early for my meeting with the secretary, and as I sat waiting, Robert LeBaron, the chairman of the Military Liaison Committee of the AEC, passed by. LeBaron's office was nearby, and he asked me to come over and visit him while I waited. LeBaron personally favored a second weapons laboratory, but once we were in his office, he wasted no time in telling me that I was pursuing a lost cause. He said, "You might as well not bother going in. Lovett will never accept a second laboratory." That was hardly encouraging news, but I was not ready to give up.

My interview with Secretary Lovett went very well. As I remember our discussion, Lovett was interested in the technical arguments concerning the hydrogen bomb. That was remarkable because his background was not technical. He appeared to understand that the job was by no means beyond Soviet capabilities, that our further development of the hydrogen bomb was important, and that the art of making atomic explosions had only begun to be explored. But although he was courteous and interested, he made no commitment to a second laboratory while I was with him.

Not many weeks earlier, Lovett had recommended against a second laboratory, but shortly after this interview, he sent a brief note to the AEC recommending the establishment of a second laboratory. In his letter of positive recommendation, he did not mention his earlier opinion or why he had changed his mind.

A short time later, I made a final presentation, this one to Secretary of State Dean Acheson, Deputy Secretary of Defense Bill Foster, and the AEC chairman, Gordon Dean. Although I was honored to meet Dean Acheson at the time, I did not think of this meeting as particularly significant as far as establishing a second laboratory was concerned. I had the mistaken feeling that the question of the second laboratory had already been settled. Many years later, when I read Gordon Dean's office diary, I discovered that, even then, he still saw the problem as one of personal frictions. I met with Dean a few weeks later, but he was very successful in not giving me any hint of his views. Finally, in early June 1952, the AEC recommended the establishment of a second weapons laboratory. I still do not quite understand what combination of the presentations (if any) led Dean to change his mind.

In late 1951, I had begun considering the question of where such a laboratory should be located, under the mistaken assumption that the AEC had implicitly acknowledged the need for a second laboratory. One of my first ideas was that it would be easy and practical to set it up in Chicago. Argonne was nearby, and a vast pool of talented scientists was readily at hand. And I would not be separated from my close friends again. Enrico had found a wonderful house for us to buy, right next door to his own. It had belonged to the parents of one of his students, Dolores Bandini, and the bid that Mici and I submitted was accepted.[10]

I began talking informally about the possibility of establishing a second weapons laboratory at the University of Chicago with Thorfin Hogness, a professor of chemistry. Hogness had been involved in the wartime work at the university and was interested in helping establish a second weapons laboratory in the vicinity. Before our planning had gone very far, I broached the subject with Enrico.

Recently, I was asked how Enrico and I managed to maintain our friendship in view of our political differences. I do not believe either of us ever felt that such differences existed. We had both lived in Europe as young adults. We both preferred safeguards to simple trust when it came to international agreements. Enrico felt so strongly about that point that he had opposed the Baruch plan. Both he and Laura knew from direct experience the costs of war, and they were also intelligent and experienced enough to know that what appears to be a simple way toward peace may produce war. On these matters, our opinions did not differ. Our difference was mainly dispositional; it lay in Fermi's greater reticence, and in how we would have described our political responsibilities.

As a physicist, Enrico had been intellectually fascinated by the possibility of a hydrogen bomb since 1942. In 1947, although he did not defend a research program on such a device, he did make it possible for my contrary position to be heard. By 1949, facing an even more vigorous opposition to the program, he temporized (according to Gordon Dean's interpretation of the minority report), saying that an attempt should be made to negotiate a non-research-and-development agreement with the Soviets on the hydrogen bomb before attempting serious research in the United States.

But no one should be surprised to hear after having signed the minority report opposing work on the hydrogen bomb, Enrico would be working on that very project in Los Alamos less than a year later. During our only conversation on the political aspects of the hydrogen bomb, Enrico asked

---

[10] The Bandini house, like the house we purchased in Washington, D.C., and like the house we purchased in Los Angeles, was a house we owned but never lived in. We rented it out for a year and then, having decided to stay in California, we sold it.

whether I didn't agree that it would be better if it were impossible to make a hydrogen bomb. Of course, I agreed that it would be, but I was already fairly certain that such was not the case. I suspect that he was, too. Once the president made the decision that the work would go forward, Enrico was willing to cooperate. That did not mean he was enthusiastic about such a weapon. His work was primarily directed to finding errors in our program, which he did most effectively; he set the direction of the new calculations, completed by Stan Ulam, that were a great contribution to the final development.

But when I broached the idea of having a laboratory to work on the further applications of the hydrogen bomb in Chicago, Fermi disapproved of the idea. I had to respect Fermi's feelings. If I pursued such work practically under his nose, I knew he would continually have to make choices that would be difficult for him and for our friendship. Under those circumstances, rather than strain our friendship, I felt that I should not pursue the plans that Hogness and I had drawn up for a laboratory at the University of Chicago. If the laboratory could be located elsewhere, once it was established I could resume my life as a professor. I hoped that would be somewhere near Enrico.

While I was still trying to decide what to do next, Herb York came to see me; he brought a message from Ernest, who now seemed to be actively campaigning to have the second lab established as an adjunct of his Berkeley laboratory. Herb, who seemed embarrassed by his role, was trying to be delicate. Ernest wanted me to know, Herb reported, that if the University of California were chosen as the site, the new laboratory director would report to Ernest. I said that seemed like a good arrangement. Herb went on, tentatively, "Ernest would like me to be the new director." I immediately and sincerely responded, "That sounds like an excellent idea to me."

And it did. I much preferred to pursue new ideas that occurred to me and to support others' good ideas when I met them than to be involved in the day-to-day administrative affairs that confront directors. I saw York as a thoroughly able administrator. He had worked at Oak Ridge on the separation process during the war, he had headed the Berkeley group that had provided instrumentation for the George shot, and he had Ernest's approval. He did indeed prove to be a good administrator.

I thought it a typically forthright gesture for Ernest to tell me of his desire for York to head the laboratory before I made my decision about accepting an appointment there. York concluded by pointing out that the University of California wanted the laboratory, Ernest believed that they would get it, and I should come and help establish it.

That decision was one of the most difficult I have ever had to make. I had now been a citizen of the United States for eleven years, but my new country still provided me with many surprises. Not only was Chicago a hospitable center for immigrants but it was home to my closest friends—Maria, Enrico, Papa Franck, and our more recent good friends, the Pierses. Besides that, I felt very much at home with the larger circle of American colleagues I had in Chicago. While I had sojourned in Los Alamos, Chicago was the place where I was most content.

In California, my only friend from Europe was Theodore von Kármán. Although I was fond of him, we had never been close friends; and not only did he live in Southern California but he now spent a great deal of time in Germany. The only other person with whom I had spent any amount of pleasurable time—Bill McMillan—was four hundred miles away at UCLA. For me, there were few personal enticements for a move to Northern California. Nonetheless, I wanted the second laboratory to get off to as good a start as possible.

I had long been aware that Ernest was unpopular in the community of physicists because of his strong conservative political opinions. During the years of loyalty oaths and the McCarthy hearings, several friends and colleagues had made disparaging comments about the group of California scientists, headed by Lawrence, who supported the loyalty oath and who suspected that there were many communists in positions of influence. To put it mildly, his colleagues considered Lawrence a right-wing extremist. While I was pondering my dilemma, Enrico and Johnny von Neumann both came to me to talk about their concerns. They acted independently and spoke forcefully, and both offered me strong, unsolicited advice not to go to California. Their taking the initiative to warn me against a step they considered a terrible mistake—and the intensity of their arguments—took me by surprise.

I was particularly impressed by Enrico's statements. He was a reserved man, and it was unusual for him to show such emotion. But on this occasion, Fermi was adamant: I would be making an immense and awful mistake if I went to California. Those people, he asserted, are not like us. We think about science as science. They are political plotters. Enrico and Johnny both believed that if I went to California, I would be excluded from the community of physicists.

Enrico disliked the hydrogen bomb, but Johnny was strongly for it; so their arguments seemed to be based on their opinion of general sentiment among our colleagues. I am certain that their only motivation was friendship. I was strongly moved by their spontaneous concern for me and more than a little unsettled by it.

But I decided, somewhat unwillingly, that I had to go to California for a year to help start the new lab. I hated to leave my friends in Chicago. I still had reservations about working with Ernest Lawrence, in spite of the generosity and decency he had shown since our disagreement. And although I didn't want my colleagues to ostracize me as a political extremist, I couldn't, at that time, imagine that happening.

Come what might, I felt that I had to turn my deeply felt advocacy of a second laboratory into reality and see the hydrogen bomb through to a more mature state. And so I took yet another leave of absence from the University of Chicago; Mici and I rented our beautiful new home for a year, packed our belongings, gathered our children, and left for California.

28

THE NEW
WHEEL SPINS A BIT

———

1952–1954

EARLY IN THE summer of 1952, Mici, the children, and I had moved into a rental house on Alameda Avenue in the small community of Diablo, located at the foot of Mount Diablo in Contra Costa County. Until the laboratory was formally established, I worked at the Radiation Laboratory in Berkeley, where Ernest had made space for us. Planning went on throughout the summer.

At one point, Herb York showed me an organizational plan for the new laboratory that included groups to work on weapons tests, on computing, on the materials testing accelerator (MTA), on theoretical physics, and on controlled fusion—everything but a weapons design group. As I had been saying for months, the only reason important enough for me to leave my friends and my professional interests in Chicago was to work in a weapons research group that would provide friendly competition to Los Alamos.

When I asked why there was no weapons design group, Herb said that work on the hydrogen bomb was well underway at Los Alamos, therefore the main effort at Livermore should be given to research on controlled fusion. I liked our young director, and I knew he wanted to do well in his job. I did not want to upset him, but I was opposed to his plan. Without a program to develop the new possibilities of thermonuclear weapons, I could see no pressing need for a second laboratory.

Herb York wanted Livermore to become the lead laboratory in the effort on controlled fusion, a much less controversial program politically than weapons research. In contrast to fission reactors, a controlled-fusion reactor would release nuclear energy from relatively inexpensive fuel with comparatively little associated radioactivity. The project was important; but because it was not associated with military applications, many other groups through-out the world were interested in it.

I also believed that Herb grossly underestimated the difficulties involved in the project. Research on controlled fusion means dealing with the hydro-dynamics of a plasma. I had a thorough respect for the fearsome nature of hy-drodynamics, where every little volume does its own thing.[1] Plasma does not consist of molecules, like a gas, but of ions—heavy slow-moving positive ions—and light, rapidly moving electrons. Those, in turn, create and are coupled to electric and magnetic fields. For each little volume of plasma, sev-eral questions had to be answered: How many positive ions? How many elec-trons? How fast does each move on the average? What is the electric force, and what is the magnetic force acting on them?

The same complications occur in planning a thermonuclear explosion. But an explosion occurs in so short a time that many of the complicated phenom-ena have no chance to develop. Even so, it took a decade from Fermi's first suggestions of a thermonuclear reaction to the point (which occurred after the first full-scale demonstration of fusion) that the theoretical calculations for thermonuclear explosions were reasonably complete. I had no doubt that demonstrating controlled fusion would be even more difficult.[2] I suspected that Herb supported the plan to eliminate weapons research and place the emphasis instead on controlled fusion because he didn't want to get into a fight with Bradbury or with any other scientist.[3] (After all, he was young and without credentials.) I told Herb that I could not agree to his plan for the laboratory.

My disagreement with York was not a problem. Ernest understood my po-sition and made the decision: The laboratory would give emphasis to weapons design, but we would also devote effort to controlled fusion.[4]

---

[1] Mathematicians can predict the flow of matter as long as the volumes involved move in an orderly way. But even the hydrodynamics of air was (and to some extent still is) beyond the grasp of mathematics. Theoreticians in the nineteenth century proved that flying was impos-sible! In the twentieth century, they retreated to the statement that flying is impossible unless the air flow is confused and disorderly (turbulent). Hydrodynamics as a science remains un-charted water.

[2] Today, after decades of national and international support, no one can yet say whether work on controlled fusion is closer to its start or its successful conclusion.

[3] In retrospect, it seems to have been an early indication of Herb's leaning toward the ma-jority of politically active scientists who opposed work on weapons.

[4] The Sherwood Project, as it was called, pursued magnetic bottle fusion for three decades.

Not long after my talk with York, when AEC chairman Gordon Dean and Captain John T. (Chick) Hayward, a member of the AEC military liaison committee, were visiting Berkeley, we secured AEC agreement on the scope of the laboratory's mission: Weapons research, weapons testing, and controlled fusion would all be important programs at Livermore.

On September 2, 1952, the Livermore contingent moved to our new quarters. The site was still in a rather primitive state: Telephones were so scarce that only Herb York had a private line; the Livermore post office couldn't provide a post office box for the laboratory; and even with a staff of less than 150 people, there were hardly enough desks to go around. But there was plenty of enthusiasm, energy, and excitement in our new setting.

Ernest Lawrence had a managerial style that can be described, with only a little exaggeration, as gathering together a critical mass of self-reliant, talented young people, providing the physical resources they needed, pointing them towards a goal, and stepping out of the way. (The goal, as Ernest saw it, was to provide for the strength and well-being of the United States.) Someone once said that Lawrence's laboratories at Berkeley and Livermore had an organizational chart with a box at the top, which Ernest filled, and two thousand boxes under it, all reporting to him. Ernest was indeed interested in his young people's work and he was pleased when it succeeded.

Staff from the Berkeley Radiation Laboratory were recruited to Livermore; the materials testing accelerator program was also an important source of talent. The accelerator that Ernest and Luis Alvarez had built at Livermore was to have been the model for a full-scale version that would later be built in Kansas. When the MTA was planned in 1949, a shortage of uranium-235 was expected. The demand for uranium led to the discovery of sufficient uranium deposits in the United States and no shortage occurred. The original purpose for the accelerator had thus disappeared and its scientists were looking for new jobs.

For more than four decades, the directors of the laboratory were drawn from the pool of talent that was formed within the first year of Livermore's inception: Harold Brown, the third director, was among the youngest people at the laboratory when it began. Harold had earned his Ph.D. from Columbia University when he was twenty-one years old and had immediately joined the Berkeley lab; he transferred to Livermore when it opened. The next director, John Foster, who was only a few years older than Harold, was also recruited from the Berkeley lab when Livermore began. Mike May, who took over the directorship from John Foster, received his Ph.D. in physics at Berkeley in 1952. And the next director, Roger Batzel—who served as director for seventeen years—had taken his degree in chemistry under Seaborg at Berkeley and had then gone to work on the MTA program, where he stayed until early 1953. John Nuckolls, who replaced Roger Batzel as director in 1988, can almost be considered part of that group; John came to the laboratory in June 1955 from Columbia University.[5] Finding so many exceptional leaders among the first hundred people who joined the laboratory is a remarkable record. This group alone would have made the concentration of talent at Livermore striking.

Before the first year was over, Harold Brown and Johnny Foster had taken responsibility for the weapons design work. Harold was head of the group working on thermonuclear weapons (usually called the secondary), and Johnny Foster headed the fission devices group (the primary). Harold and Johnny were both able and ambitious young physicists, although their personalities were a study in contrasts. Harold was reserved, almost shy, a somewhat solitary young man. He was full of ingenious ideas and was sometimes impatient with those who didn't understand them right away, but he was cautious and thorough in planning his work. Johnny Foster was personable, full of encouragement for his colleagues, ready to delegate work, eager to get his projects under way, and equally ready to modify them to incorporate improvements. Both men did excellent work, and both made remarkable contributions.

Under Harold Brown's leadership during the next few years, work on the hydrogen bomb underwent reorientation. Originally, most people had considered the hydrogen bomb important because of its unlimited explosive yield. As I have mentioned, my recent work in Chicago indicated that around a megaton, the effectiveness of huge bombs begins to change. A megaton bomb would destroy an area several miles across. But bombs very much larger have little further effect. Therefore, huge weapons are of no military interest. In the end, the great military advantage of the hydrogen bomb turned out to be not the size of its explosion but the flexibility of its construction. The bomb material (deuterium) was cheap. That made it possible to optimize cost, yield, and weight. Harold Brown undertook the job of working out just what flexibility was possible. He was remarkably successful.

Johnny Foster worked on the construction of much smaller nuclear weapons (in the low kiloton range, equivalent to a few thousand tons of TNT). In this case, it turned out to be particularly important to change the

---

[5] Bruce Tarter, who became director when John Nuckolls retired in 1994, continues to provide able and enthusiastic leadership in that post as this book goes to press.

original design and make weapons small enough to be useful in defense against a massed tank attack. Johnny succeeded so well that eventually it was possible to make a nuclear weapon small enough to be shot from a gun. The availability of such weapons undeniably contributed to the fact that none of them have ever been used.

Many other people had roles that were less obvious, but hardly less important. In the spring of 1952, Ernest assigned Duane Sewell the task of helping Herb put the laboratory together. Because Duane had worked on the calutron at Oak Ridge during the war and at the Berkeley laboratory both before and after the war, he took over the engineering, operational side of the administration. To the great good fortune of the laboratory, Duane continued in that role, save for a few years during the 1980s, until his retirement in 1993.[6] His foresight in planning everything from the construction of new buildings to the organization of such disparate entities as the first engineering department and the security force must be credited for the smooth running of the laboratory and its minimum of internal problems after the first hectic and chaotic months.

Sid Fernbach was the man responsible for one of the most important, if least visible, laboratory programs. Sid was a theoretical physicist who had studied under Oppenheimer and Serber at Berkeley, finished his degree in 1951, and signed on at Livermore immediately after his postdoctoral year at Stanford. A reserved man, Sid was noted for his evenhandedness with the members of his group and for his own diligence. He saw the computer as an extremely important tool for theoretical physicists, a vision Johnny von Neumann had been promoting since the early years at Los Alamos. In addition, Sid had a bulldog-like tenacity in pursuing his goal of securing the most effective computers possible. It is not an overstatement to say that his vision guided the commercial development of computers during the next two decades.

Even before the Livermore laboratory began, I was convinced that computers were instrumental to success, and Sid held the same opinion. The problems we were trying to solve were too lengthy and complicated to be tackled by hand. We needed to have the best available computers and to develop new computer techniques. In that last regard, another mathematician who had been recruited from the Berkeley lab, Cecil (Chuck) Leith, Jr., should be mentioned. Chuck and Herb York had worked together on experimental physics

---

[6] He was appointed the Assistant Secretary for Defense Programs in the newly formed Department of Energy, and served in that post for about nine years.

problems at Oak Ridge during the war. Both of them returned to Berkeley for graduate work and continued working together on experimental physics problems at the Berkeley lab. Herb was a graduate student in physics with Emilio Segré, but Chuck was in mathematics. When the laboratory was set up, Chuck still had work to do on his Ph.D., but he became so caught up in the computing business that he set his studies aside and joined the laboratory.

Sid and Chuck were working on the computer program before the laboratory officially opened. They had gone out to the Eckhart-Mauchley plant in Philadelphia to oversee the final development of the laboratory's first computer, a Univac (Universal Automatic Computer), one of the first computers produced commercially. I joined them there to try out the Univac while it was still on the factory floor.

The calculations we wanted to do were needed to complete the details of Livermore's first weapon design. The Univac performed wonderfully until shortly before the work was completed. Then the computer broke down so thoroughly that there was no hope of our using it to complete the calculations in a timely manner. We had nothing but pencil and paper to assist us in that task, which sufficed, but that experience explains why our first computer at the Livermore site had a glass case standing on top of it, complete with a small hammer and the instructions, "In Case of Emergency, Break Glass." Inside the case was an abacus.

The value of the Univac, which arrived five months after the laboratory opened, can hardly be overstated. It was built with vacuum tubes—and located in the only air-conditioned area in the laboratory—and it had a memory of only a thousand words. But a little less than four years later, someone tallied the operations that had been completed on it. They were equivalent to the number of calculations that 440 people, working forty hours a week, fifty-two weeks a year, without any vacations or breaks, could have completed in a hundred years.

Being able to reach a more sophisticated stage of design without conducting tests in the Pacific and without using an additional staff of thousands for hand calculation was sufficiently cost-effective that computers were easy to justify in our budget. For many years, the Livermore laboratory would be the first to acquire any new generation of commercial computers. Two years after the arrival of the Univac, we purchased the first fully electronic computer that IBM produced, the 701. It had about 2,000 words of memory and was twelve times as fast as the Univac. In addition, it was the first computer that did not require an operator to supervise the calculation: The data and the program instructions were contained on punch cards.

We were also fortunate to have a wonderful theorist, Montgomery Johnson, working with us almost full-time during the next years. Montgomery, who was a year older than I, had been working in a navy research project on the East Coast, but he decided, correctly, that he could be of greater help at our fledgling laboratory. A kindly, quiet, approachable man, Montgomery helped with every problem, offering support and guidance to the younger recruits. He was an exceptional human being. The more I worked with him, the more I liked him. He remained my favorite collaborator until his death in 1984.

Another theorist who made great contributions to the laboratory's beginnings was Albert Latter, even though he didn't join the lab officially. Dave Griggs, whom I had met through the air force's advisory board, had worked with Albert at Rand Corporation, a research center funded in large part by the U.S. Air Force; Dave had convinced Albert and his brother Richard, also a theoretical physicist, to help get Livermore started. In addition to heading the theoretical division for the first year or so, Albert became my favorite chess partner.

The man who eventually became the head of the theoretical group, Mark Mills—an excellent older (in his mid-thirties) physicist—was a former student of Theodore von Kármán. Dedicated, hard-working, and reliable, Mills was a natural leader and was recognized as such shortly after his arrival in 1953.[7] He, like Sid Fernbach, quickly recognized the importance of computers to theoretical work and strengthened the work in that area.

A little later in 1953, another physicist (in his early thirties) elected to join us. Jerry Johnson, following his service in the Korean War, had gone to work for the AEC. While there, he became interested in the programs that we were pursuing at Livermore and wrote to Herb about a position. Two years later, Gerry was running the entire testing program at Livermore.[8]

---

[7] Mills was a friend of another postdoctoral student at Cal Tech, Weichang Qian, who was a Chinese citizen. At some point in the mid–1950s, Qian was going to be deported as a possible spy. Mills went down to Los Angeles to have dinner with him and discovered that he did indeed want information about nuclear weapons. Qian asked several technical questions about them during their meal together, all of which Mark evaded. Mark reported the conversation when he got back to the laboratory and told me the story as well, which led me to follow Qian's career. Once back in China, Qian quickly established himself as an outstanding physicist and eventually became head of the rocket program there. Although I can find no reference to it now, I believe Qian also contributed to the development of the People's Republic of China's first atomic bomb.

[8] Later, Gerry left the laboratory to become the Director of Navy Laboratories.

There was no shortage of young talented physicists, thanks in part to Art Hudgins, who took the responsibility for recruiting scientific personnel shortly after the laboratory was founded. The group of physicists who came from the Berkeley Radiation Laboratory either directly or via the MTA— Stirling Colgate, Dick Post, Bob Jastrow, Ernie Martinelli, Jack Peterson, and Art Biehl—provided a strong backbone of talent. Stirling, the Los Alamos Ranch School student I mentioned in an earlier chapter, had taken his Ph.D. in physics as an experimentalist; but in the end, under Montgomery's excellent coaching, he was converted into an exceptionally fine hybrid theorist-experimentalist. Dick Post, one of Ed McMillan's former students, did an excellent job of getting the work on controlled fusion underway.[9] Such a strong concentration of able physicists eventually led to a much broadened program; eventually, we came to think of ourselves as a sort of department of applied astrophysics.[10] From the beginning, and throughout the years to this date, Livermore has emphasized astrophysics and other branches of pure science in the recognition that great progress in applications cannot be made if science itself is neglected.

For me, the early months at the Livermore laboratory were strongly reminiscent of the spirit at Los Alamos in the spring of 1943. The physical plant was, to say the least, raw and disordered, and new, enthusiastic, ingenious but inexperienced young people were pouring in. I spent most of my time presenting seminars and introductory discussions explaining the fundamentals of weapons development to them.[11] But there was a big difference between 1943 and 1952. At Los Alamos, there had never been time to follow up most of the original suggestions for modifications and improvements. At Livermore, after settling in, examining some of those alternate designs constituted our first effort.

Understanding the scientific and technical considerations connected with fission and thermonuclear weapons is not easy. I remember that at one point, Harold Brown came to me with a proof that the hydrogen bomb wouldn't

[9] Five years later, Dick Post's magnetic mirror program, in an experiment led by Frederic Coensgen, produced what is believed to be the first fusion reactions from a magnetically confined thermonuclear plasma.

[10] See Chapter 33, page 430, for a description of Colgate and Johnson's work on supernovae.

[11] Jack Peterson, one of the first physicists recruited from the Berkeley Laboratory, recalled, "When the first group of people were assembled, no one knew the least first thing about bombs. I remember they locked up all of us newcomers in a big room in Berkeley, and Edward lectured us on how a bomb was designed. Everyone would sit around saying, 'Well, what do you know. So that's how it's done.'"

work. It took me about an hour to convert him into an enthusiastic believer (and, not much later, a significant contributor). When the familiarization process was complete a few months later, we turned our efforts to exploring come of the different approaches to making low-yield fission weapons.

During that fall, Ernest approached me with a proposal to stay for good. The University of California would be happy to have me join the faculty, and I could divide my time as I pleased between Livermore and Berkeley. I was hesitant, but Mici was vociferously on his side. Return to Chicago? With the winters and young children? Later that fall, I spoke with President Sproul. The loyalty oath was no more. The professors had been invited back. My only remaining concern now was being separated from my old friends.

The future of Livermore had come, more and more, to seem vitally important to the future. Finally, I called Thorfin Hogness, who had supported my plans in Chicago, and discussed the question with him. His answer was simple: "Livermore is your job. You must stay." That decision was not an easy one, but in the end, it was clear-cut. I was needed at Livermore; and, really, I wanted to stay. In spite of inconveniences, the spirit in the laboratory in those early days was one of high enthusiasm and good fellowship. I decided to submit my resignation to the University of Chicago, this time for good. I would become a professor at the University of California the following fall.

In October 1952, preparations for the *Mike* test were almost complete; this test would verify the principles on which the new hydrogen bomb was based. Norris Bradbury kindly invited me to attend the shot that took place on the Eniwetok atoll on November 1, 1952. But it was only eight weeks since the lab had opened its doors, and we were still trying diligently to prepare for our own first tests a few months later. I could find no justification for taking enough time off just then to observe a test in the Pacific, but I was very anxious to learn the results.

Dave Griggs came up with a solution. He told me that one of the seismographs at Berkeley was able to detect the shock waves that a successful test would produce, even though the test would be conducted above ground. He worked out the intensity of the shock wave and the amount of time it would take to travel to California and told me what to expect.

At the appropriate time, I sat down in the dark in front of the proper seismograph in the basement of the geology building and watched a luminous spot on a screen. I soon realized that the spot appeared to be jiggling; only by holding a pencil point on it could I correct my eyes' natural jitter. I watched the now steady spot while the time of the shot in the Marshall Islands came and went. About a quarter of an hour later, precisely when

Dave told me it should occur, I saw the dot on a seismograph screen do a little dance. The compression wave from the explosion had spent that time traveling to the coast of California.

I watched a few minutes more because I wanted to be sure my hand hadn't moved in anticipation at the appointed time. Then I took the film from the seismograph and had it developed. The tracing was clear, big, and unmistakable. It was the size that Dave had predicted. The proof was in my hand. The new approach had worked.

Ernest Lawrence had come down to the geology department to get a report of the news. He warmly congratulated me on the success. I was glad, both for the success of the shot and for Ernest's congratulations. But I felt that congratulations were too much. A failure would have been a heavy blow. The success meant only that I could turn my attention to other matters.

I decided to send a telegram to my friends at Los Alamos. Because I would be sending it through Western Union, I had to find a way to convey the information without violating security regulations. I addressed my message to Elizabeth Graves, the physicist-wife of Al Graves, both of whom had worked diligently on the hydrogen bomb since its inception. My message in full simply said: "It's a boy."[12] I was later told that my message was understood immediately. And in spite of the time needed for the shock wave to arrive, and for me to have a conversation with Lawrence, my message was the first indication of success Los Alamos received. All my delays added up to less time than it took to send a classified telegram from the Pacific.

From the beginning of the work on the hydrogen bomb, Johnny Wheeler had been dedicated, unselfish, and outstandingly productive. After I had received a somewhat detailed report of the test results (and after the Livermore tests had been prepared), I decided to go to Princeton to tell Johnny about it and thank him personally. His friendship, then and now, has been a source of great pleasure.

After I had arrived in Princeton, Oppenheimer invited me to his house that evening for a drink. As we sat in his living room, Oppenheimer commented that now we knew the test device worked, we should find a way to use it to bring the Korean war to a successful conclusion. I was astounded and asked how that could be done. Oppie explained that we should build a duplicate device somewhere in Korea and force the communist troops to concentrate nearby so that detonation of the device would wipe them all out.

---

[12] In the mid–1990s, I mentioned that wire at a public meeting and was criticized for its sexist tone. The questioner asked, "If that bomb had not worked, you would have wired 'It's a girl'?"

During his tenure on the General Advisory Committee, Oppie had complained in a letter (to James Conant, I believe) that the Super, if it could be built at all, couldn't be taken to a target by oxcart. Here was the same scientist who had expressed moral reservations about conducting research on a weapon as destructive as the Super now suggesting the test device be used; and the device was so huge and clumsy that a hundred oxcarts would barely get it to a target! Oppenheimer's suggestion left me speechless. I did not reply to the proposal but simply said, "I don't want to think about that."

I put the incident out of my mind until several weeks later. On the last day the lab was open before Christmas in 1952, I received a phone call from Oppenheimer. He asked if I remembered our conversation in Princeton.[13] I assured him that I did. He then explained that he just wanted me to know that he had found a way to get his suggestion to President-elect Eisenhower.

For me, there has always seemed to be an enormous difference between knowledge about (and possession of) an extremely powerful weapon and the use of that weapon. Oppenheimer seemed not to differentiate them. In working on the hydrogen bomb, I had been concerned that the United States have as much knowledge about its unique qualities as possible, whatever their applications or lack of them. I had few doubts that the Soviets would aggressively pursue this research. Looking at weapons in general, I had not thought of the hydrogen bomb as designed for battlefield use, except possibly in an extreme crisis. I could not understand Oppenheimer's behavior.

One very happy consequence came out of my November visit to Princeton, however. I convinced Johnny Wheeler to bring his group of people out to visit our lab, which he did about a month later. Johnny's Matterhorn group was officially disbanded in the spring of 1953, and one of his young colleagues from the project, Carl Haussmann, decided to join our new laboratory. Carl was a West Point graduate, a captain on loan from the army to the Matterhorn project. The casual organization of the laboratory and the enthusiasm of the staff at Livermore led him to arrange to serve out his tour of duty at Livermore. Several of his Matterhorn colleagues—among them Larry Wilets, Howard Greyber, and Dick Levee—also joined the Livermore laboratory.

We were happy to have a recruit with a little experience even if it wasn't directly applicable to our first task. We had come up with a design for a relatively low-yield nuclear weapon that minimized the amount of nuclear material needed. It became the basis of our first tests, which were held at the

---

[13] Because his call came on an open line, neither of us could name the device in question.

Nevada Proving Grounds in the spring of 1953, barely six months after the lab had begun operation. We were interested in a smaller weapon, not only because of the scarcity of bomb material but also because we wanted to be sure there would be a minimum of fallout from our test.

When the dust settled from the first of our shots, we saw that the lower portion of the tower on which the explosive was mounted was undamaged. We certainly had not intended the explosion to be that small! The second test destroyed the tower, but it was a much smaller tower. The Los Alamos contingent could hardly laugh loudly enough.

We were, indeed, embarrassed. The best that could be said was that we did gain instruction about which of our assumptions were wrong. Yet today, it strikes me as a remarkable achievement that our small group of novices, after scarcely six months of effort, working in an old barracks and an old hospital building under the most primitive and trying conditions, were able to design, fabricate, build, and test any devices at all.

And although those early tests failed, they laid a strong foundation for the work that followed. Barney Rubin and his engineering group had manufactured the critical parts of the first test device. Eventually, the engineering group developed the capability of producing more accurate parts than could be produced on commercial equipment. Livermore went on to develop a tool that, directed by computer and using lasers to make measurements, can mill to an accuracy of a few millionths of an inch.[14]

Among the other novices who became experts in that failed effort were Wally Decker and Jim Bell; they came up with a structure of practically no weight that was able to hold a fair amount of weight in a precisely adjusted position. (Wally also put together the detailed procedure for the step-by-step assembly of the parts of the devices.) From the beginning, Pat Kilpatrick designed flawless electrical systems, and Ken Street and his group, which included Roger Batzel and Ed Fleming, performed the diagnostic radiochemistry of the tests perfectly. Art Biehl contributed a great deal to understanding what was wrong theoretically. Although obvious success had eluded us, not one of them was daunted.

In the summer of 1953, Mici and I sold the house next door to the Fermis' in Chicago and bought a house in the Berkeley hills. As I described it to

---

[14] That equipment machined the secondary mirror on the Keck telescope. Because it is guided by a computer, the machine also can produce a mathematical surface, such as an ellipse. The field has been taken over by commercial efforts, but the original work was done at the Livermore laboratory.

Maria Mayer, it was "a wonderful white elephant with big grounds (all weedy so it can't get any more), with columns, a huge living room, and a beautiful view. It is just north of the physics building. We are planning to stay in the house for e^3 years." [15]

But in my next letter, I complained:

> I am no longer a physicist but a gardener. Today I spent several hours cutting grass and weeding. This is most satisfying and interesting. Clearly the purpose of cutting grass is to encourage the grass. Offhand, it would seem that cutting is a somewhat remarkable way of encouragement, but in reality it must be a very good way. . . .
>
> The weeds are even more interesting. While pulling them out, I understood for the first time the deep satisfaction that can be derived from lofty moral principles as applied to less lofty individuals. Of course, the difference between a weed and a good kind of grass is merely a matter of convention, but this does not diminish one's enjoyment when one succeeds to remove the evil together with its deep root. (It is a pity that dandelions are weeds. O'Henry has a nice story in which dandelions occur without any mention of their non-Aryan origin.) It is also a pity that sometimes when you remove a weed, you also remove some grass—at least I do. Finally the sharp instrument used in weeding sometimes cuts the finger. In all these respects the fight against weeds and against immorality are similar.
>
> To show that I am consistent: My desk is as clean as my lawn. All my correspondence is answered. I have started a new existence. Whether there will be time for physics is doubtful.

Irrespective of my complaints, I loved our house on Hawthorne Terrace. The Brickweddes came out for the summer. Ferdinand helped at the laboratory, as he had the previous year, and the whole Brickwedde family helped us to get settled in our new home. But there was no denying the fact that I missed my old friends, particularly those in Chicago, very deeply. [16]

---

[15] Rereading my letter decades later, I was astounded at how close we came to fulfilling my prophecy: We stayed twenty-three years, rather than the twenty of my estimate.

[16] Some of them did come to see us. I remember a visit that Leo Szilárd made when Wendy was about eight years old. During his stay, Mici, Leo and I often spoke Hungarian, and at one point, Leo asked Wendy, in English, if she wanted to be a mother someday. Wendy responded mournfully that she couldn't be a mother. When asked why not, Wendy explained that Mici had never taught her the secret language that mothers and fathers speak, so she wouldn't be able to talk with her husband.

In the fall of 1953, I began teaching quantum mechanics at the university. Much to my pleasure, two years later, the son of Herman Mark, the man who had introduced me to the subject, came to the Berkeley campus as a postdoctoral student and became my teaching assistant.

In 1934, the Mark family had left Karlsruhe and returned to their home in Vienna. But by 1938, they knew they had to flee. Herman took all the money he could raise and bought platinum wire (which he could do because he was a chemist) and fashioned the wire into coat hangers, which he then painted black; in this way, the family nest egg migrated with the Marks in their baggage, holding up their winter coats. It was fortunate they were able to carry assets with them, because during the next three years, they fled from Italy to Switzerland to France to England. They finally emigrated to Canada, and then, in 1941, to the United States.

When I had left Karlsruhe, Hans Mark had not yet been born. He came to the United States when he was about twelve, and in 1954 had just completed his Ph.D. in experimental physics at M.I.T. Hans wanted to strengthen his background in theoretical physics, and his father told him that real mastery of a subject comes with teaching it. I was happy to serve as the bridge in quantum mechanics between the two Marks. The following year, Hans began a joint appointment to the Livermore laboratory, which he held for the next twelve years. Hans then went to work at NASA, and then served as chancellor of the University of Texas system for several years. Hans, a very thoughtful and kind person, remains one of my close friends to this day.[17]

At the Livermore laboratory, during much of 1953 and early 1954, we were concentrating on getting ready for our first thermonuclear test; this was to occur in the Pacific during the tests (the *Castle* series) scheduled for early spring. The principles of the new Super, tested in the 1952 *Mike* shot, had been incorporated into a true, deliverable weapon, which Los Alamos would test during the same test series.

Because the *Mike* test had obliterated the island where it was exploded, testing the New Super would probably damage the several permanent facilities on the Eniwetok atoll. It was decided that the *Bravo* shot would take place at Bikini, an uninhabited atoll about 180 miles east of Eniwetok. But

---

[17] I also had two graduate students during these years, a lovely young woman from England, Ann Auriol (nee Ross) Bonney, and a young man from Germany, Hans Peter Dürr, who became Heisenberg's successor at the University of Munich. I last saw Hans Peter on a trip to Germany in the mid–1980s.

when the *Bravo* shot was fired in late February 1954, the weapon proved to be more than twice as powerful as Los Alamos had estimated. It released an explosive force equivalent to more than 10 million tons of TNT; to this day, it remains the largest explosive the United States ever detonated.

That might not have been so serious, but the weather conditions at the time of the test were also misjudged. Radioactive fallout landed on three inhabited Marshall atolls east of Bikini and on a Japanese fishing boat in the vicinity. The three islands were evacuated, but not before 250 islanders and 28 American servicemen were exposed to fallout.[18]

No one was aware of the presence of the fishing boat, and the twenty-three Japanese fishermen were unaware of the nature of the white dust on their vessel. They made no attempt to rid themselves of it. When they returned to Japan two weeks later, they were all suffering from radiation sickness, and one of the fishermen died six months later.[19] That accident had consequences that went far beyond the lives of the unfortunate people who suffered directly.

Livermore's turn to fire its first thermonuclear test arrived in early April. Although we had worked out a novel design for a weapon that was to be tested in two stages, the first part failed. We had experienced two failures with our fission weapons. Now our first thermonuclear test didn't work. Three failures in a row! We were chagrined, to say the least. I had not gone out for the shot, but, like everyone else who had worked on the plans, I participated in the heated postmortem discussions as we tried to understand our error.

The only bright spot in Livermore's misadventure was that Stirling Colgate's diagnostics for the test had worked perfectly. Not many hours after detailed information from the test arrived back in Livermore, Montgomery Johnson was able to explain our failure. (That Montgomery was able to do so in such a short time was a remarkable accomplishment.)

When Ernest Lawrence appeared at the laboratory the next day, I could see that he was deeply disappointed. He sat quietly at the back of the meeting room and gave his support by his nonjudgmental presence while the rest of us worked out the details of the problem. As we rode back to Berkeley together, Ernest asked, "What's the matter? Aren't the people at the lab any

---

[18] A considerable number of those evacuated from the closest atoll developed radiation sickness. Up to 1982, one death (in 1972, and a case of leukemia) had resulted among the 278 islanders irradiated.

[19] Two other fishermen died: one twenty years later and the other twenty-five years later, of liver disease that may have been associated with the radiation.

good?" I told him that they were excellent and hard-working as well. But mistakes happen, particularly in new ventures.

Then I told him the good news—Colgate's observations were excellent and Montgomery Johnson had already identified our mistake—and some bad news. According to those observations, the second installment of our test would also fail. But, I pointed out, we could save a considerable amount of money if we canceled the remaining test. (Holding the test meant waiting for good weather in the Marshall Islands before firing the shot.) "Would you," I asked Ernest, "please just call off the second shot?"

Ernest immediately replied, "I will not. Herb York and Harold Brown need to be convinced to call it off. You take the first plane out to the Pacific and see if you can convince them." I appreciated that approach. Ernest wanted Herb and Harold, the people in charge, to know that he considered them completely responsible and still had confidence that they were able to make the correct decisions, even in the face of our failures.

I did take the first plane out and, upon my arrival, almost at once confronted Herb York. At first, he would not believe my arguments, which were, of course, Montgomery Johnson's arguments. But a half hour later, he was convinced. Then the two of us went to see Harold Brown. Harold was more hard-headed, and, even though it was now a two-against-one discussion, it took a full hour to convince him. But finally, he did call the shot off.

After the three failures, many people in the weapons group were talking about looking for employment elsewhere, and not altogether humorously. To me as well as to the young people, it seemed far from unlikely that the weapons program might be closed down. We were all discouraged. When Duane Sewell and I were reminiscing about that period recently, he recalled a story that helps to explain why our new laboratory kept its enthusiasm in spite of repeated failures. As Duane recounted it:

> After everybody got back from the Pacific, a group of us were meeting in Herb York's office. We were all kind of down and worrying about, my gosh, we have had this failure and what do we do. We were concentrating on the failure. Ernest came to the meeting about five minutes after it had started, walked in with his usual vigor and boyish-type of presentation and sat down. I still remember the first words he said: "Well, what did we learn?"
>
> It wasn't a question about the failure but what did we learn from it? And immediately people started thinking, well, we learned this, and we learned that, and after a few minutes, everybody had forgotten about failure. It was

what did we learn and how we were going to build on that. I saw that as a major turning point in the maturity of this organization. It was just that little thing.

Later, I heard Ernest make a statement to people in the Berkeley Laboratory: "Look, you had a certain number of successes in a row. That says to me that you are not taking enough chances. You are not moving ahead as fast as you can. If you were, there would be a few failures along the way."

Perhaps in Ernest's eyes we became too conservative, because that was our last test failure. We established a "pre-mortem" committee to replace the postmortem one. Those groups were made up of people who had not been directly involved in planning the experiment. From that time on, such a group met before a test was to be fired and went over every last detail. That made our tests incomparably more reliable. The wheels of our Livermore enterprise stopped spinning, took hold, and moved us forward in a satisfactory manner.

29

OTHER NUCLEAR AFFAIRS

1949–1955

M Y EFFORTS ON the Reactor Safeguard Committee (RSC), beginning
in 1947, had gone on during my postwar years in Chicago, and then in
Los Alamos, and had continued through my early years in California. The
several concerns that simultaneously occupied me during those years—the
pursuit of a true hydrogen bomb, the establishment of a second laboratory,
the modification of weapons to meet the new needs of rocket delivery, and
the development of safe electricity-generating nuclear reactors—suggest a
justification for Fermi's having called me a monomaniac with several manias.

During those years, I learned that serving in either the engine or the brake
department was apt to produce political complications. Perhaps knowing
how to express one's opinions less forthrightly may make it possible to avoid
some criticism; but, then again, critics are available for every position. I saw
the first clear evidence that our work on the RSC was viewed with displeasure during the fall of 1951, not long after my return to Chicago. The decision we had made at our meeting in late September 1950 was particularly
bothersome to the AEC: We had refused to change our minds about the
problems of the Hanford reactors. Those water-cooled, graphite-moderated
reactors, built during wartime, had several safety problems.

Today, water-cooled reactors are commonly in use throughout the United
States and Europe; they are easy to operate and very safe.[1] In this design, if

---

[1] See Chapter 15, p. 154. Using water for cooling in the reactor has two effects on the fission process: It moderates (lowers) the energy of the high-velocity neutrons produced by fission, which makes those neutrons more likely to be captured by uranium-235, thus enhanc-
ing fission; and the water absorbs neutrons, effectively removing them from capture by
uranium, and thereby slowing the fission process.

water is lost, the fission process slows down because uranium is ineffective at capturing high-velocity neutrons. But reactors that are both water-cooled and graphite-moderated can have a particularly dangerous flaw. The Hanford reactors that were built during the war, like the reactors later built at Chernobyl, contained so much graphite that water had no further effect in slowing the neutrons. Therefore, loss of water in the cooling system of the wartime Hanford reactors resulted in the capture of fewer neutrons and thereby increased the fission process. In such a reactor, if one pipe loses water, the neighboring pipes overheat, which converts the cooling water to steam, thereby forming a void in the cooling system, which in turn increases the fission, thus producing more heat and more steam—a situation that continues until the reactor explodes.[2]

The wartime Hanford reactors shared a further danger with Chernobyl-type reactors: There was no containment vessel. In case of an accident at Hanford, the adjacent Wahluke slope, undeveloped land used as a buffer zone, was likely to be contaminated. The AEC had operated the three Hanford reactors at a moderately low power level for six years without problems. They asked, therefore, to be allowed to develop the Wahluke slope and to raise the power level at which the Hanford reactors operated. At our meeting in September 1950, for the first time in our history, the RSC turned the AEC down. We recommended against increasing the power level at which the Hanford reactors ran and against shrinking the uninhabited area that surrounded them.

We were not directly overruled, but in the fall of 1951, the AEC appointed a new committee, the Industrial Committee for Reactor Location Problems (ICRLP). Their first task would be to review the question of the Hanford reactors and the Wahluke slope exclusion zone. By way of explaining why it was assigning a similar function to another committee, the AEC stated that the new committee would serve to "balance the technical and scientific aspects of reactor hazards, as developed by the Reactor Safeguard Committee, against the non-technical aspects of reactor locations." In other words, the AEC hoped that the new committee was composed of people more practical and cooperative. (The Washington bureaucrats saw me at that time as a pure theoretician, opposed to nuclear reactors.)

---

[2] The RSC recognized that danger, called a positive void coefficient, before 1949, and information about that design flaw was disseminated throughout the world by 1955.

Although the RSC had been accused of being the committee for the prevention of nuclear reactors, that was hardly the case. We had remained absolutely committed to the highest safety standards, but several new reactors were under development. The test site that the RSC had recommended was opened in Pocatello, Idaho, during the summer of 1949. The construction of three test reactors got underway almost immediately.[3] One of them was the prototype of a reactor to power submarines.

I remember meeting the naval officer—then Captain Hyman Rickover—who was in charge of the project. He introduced himself by saying, "I am Captain Hyman Rickover. I am a dope." I raised my eyebrows, and he calmly continued, "Yes, a dope—D. O. P. E.—Doctor of Pile Engineering." Rickover, who had earned that title at Oak Ridge soon after the war, had every reason to be proud of his expertise.[4] Rickover was firmly committed to a submarine force that would operate almost silently and would be able to do so for more than a year at a time. That required nuclear power. The navy was enthusiastic about the project, but not so enthusiastic about Rickover's attitude. A considerable amount of pressure was brought to bear on Rickover to relax standards in the design of the reactor and in the training of the crew. Rickover put his career on the line and stood firm.

The safety record of the U.S. Navy nuclear-powered submarines stands as a monument to Rickover. In the summer of 1960, Admiral Rickover took me, together with the members of the current safeguard committee and General Alfred D. Starbird, for a short trip on the USS *Patrick Henry;* not much later, the submarine would be armed with Poseidon missiles, thereby providing the sturdiest leg of our triad of deterrence.[5] I was impressed by the excellent performance of the reactor operators and by the new reactor. In fact, once it was fully designed, everyone was confident of its excellence: Construction of

---

[3] The first reactor built and tested at the Pocatello site was the fast breeder designed at Argonne by Walter Zinn, which went into operation in December 1951. The third, as I recall, was a boiling-water reactor, also designed at Argonne.

[4] Some years later, I was introduced to the newly elected governor of Georgia, Jimmy Carter. As he shook my hand, he said, "I am particularly glad to meet you. You are the one man who scared the one person of whom I was afraid." It took me three seconds to figure out whom Carter meant. Rickover headed the navy training program for nuclear engineers that Carter had entered (but did not complete) after his graduation from Annapolis. I particularly appreciated Carter's compliment.

[5] The warhead for the Poseidon missile, designed at Livermore, is discussed in Chapters 33 and 34.

the submarine began at the same time the prototype reactor was being built for its test.[6]

I believe that the RSC submitted only two negative reports: the one on the Hanford reactors, and the other on a small model of a reactor that had been built at Argonne as part of the Nuclear Energy for the Propulsion of an Aircraft (NEPA) program.[7] Strange as it may seem today, neither of the safeguard committees was asked for a view on the safety of putting a reactor in an airplane; but because airplanes do occasionally crash, we of the RSC thought the program tantamount to insanity.[8] But as we hadn't been asked, there appeared no way for us to affect the program that was the most likely to produce an accident.

The design of the NEPA reactor, which had been built at Argonne, included several safety interlocks, including one that prevented entry to the reactor chamber when the reactor was operating. But the reactor had recently developed a problem and shut itself down. The researchers operating the model couldn't figure out what was wrong, so they manually overrode the interlocks and entered the reactor chamber. Then, when they still could not figure out what had caused the problem, they pulled the control rod out by hand! The reactor, of course, went critical. Fortunately, a final safety measure then went into effect and shut the reactor down. By that time, the researchers had received such a high dose of radiation that they showed signs of radiation sickness.[9]

That incident had occurred shortly before our meeting to review the NEPA reactor. Although not foolproof against fools, the NEPA reactor was a

---

[6] The keel of the first nuclear-powered submarine, the USS *Nautilus*, was laid in June 1952, and the prototype reactor was successfully tested at Pocatello about six months later. The *Nautilus* put to sea, on schedule, at the end of 1954.

[7] The reorganized committee, the Advisory Committee on Reactor Safeguards (ACRS) submitted a third negative report in 1955 on the Enrico Fermi breeder reactor, which was to be located near Detroit. The AEC overruled the ACRS, and the plant was built, but it never went into service.

[8] The NEPA project died for lack of funding about 1960, but it was not the most overly enthusiastic proposal made during the era when atomic power was popular. In 1957, when I was no longer active on the ACRS, I volunteered a comment to *The Lamp*, the magazine published by the University of California, about a proposed nuclear locomotive: "I think such a machine is a most ingenious solution of the question how to combine minimum utility with maximum danger. Trains in the atomic age will no doubt be electric."

[9] As far as I know, in the years following their exposure, none of the researchers showed signs of illness that was related to their irradiation. Hard as it is for laymen to believe, the percentage of people who are irradiated—even at high doses of prompt radiation—and later die from a related cancer is very low.

workable design. Given our concerns about reactors in the air, we were not unhappy to note that we could hardly be expected to claim the reactor was safe in light of the recent accident.

The RSC uncovered one design defect. The reactor had been designed at Oak Ridge and had a far greater amount of water for cooling than was required, which led to its being called the swimming pool reactor. It was considered particularly safe because, if the water increased in temperature, the rate of fission would decrease. In other words, the swimming pool reactor had a negative temperature coefficient; if the heating continued long enough, the reactor would shut itself down.

But we were not convinced that the swimming pool reactor was altogether reliable. We asked to have a model constructed at the reactor test site, and we then designed an experiment where all the control rods were removed at once. That, of course, was not an approved procedure for operating a reactor, but our suspicions were confirmed: The swimming pool reactor blew up. The heat transfer between the fuel elements and the water was too slow to accommodate the sudden change in reactivity. Before the water got hot enough to increase the neutron speed and decrease fission, the fuel elements got so hot that the steam explosion destroyed the reactor. The experiment had proved the value of having a test site. No one was injured, and the cost of the demonstration was a tiny fraction of the costs that would have been incurred had the development proceeded.

In the period before 1952, the RSC had one final concern that we discussed but never fully resolved: whether the material that was used to clad the uranium fuel—for instance, zirconium—might react with the water being used for coolant if rapid heating occurred. Under those conditions, the material might melt or even vaporize; and if the water also heated, a very rapid reaction producing hydrogen might occur.

Walter Zinn was adamant in his opinion that the oxide formed over time on the material would protect it adequately from contact with the water, no matter how much heating occurred. Testing materials under the appropriate conditions was not only extremely difficult to arrange but impossible in terms of the time required for a realistic appraisal. The issue was dropped, although it arose again under less auspicious conditions at the time of the Three Mile Island accident.

Another safeguard was also introduced, I believe, around this time: the containment vessel. This thick-walled concrete enclosure of the reactor was a second line of defense against the dispersal of radioactive material in the event of an accident. When Walter Zinn introduced this idea, he had already worked out the costs of adding such a structure to the reactor.[10] I would have preferred to see reactors built a few hundred feet underground, but I had not calculated the costs of such a program. As a result, Zinn's proposal was adopted.

When the AEC formed the second safeguard committee (the ICRLP) in the fall of 1951, they named as the chairman C. Rogers McCullough, an excellent Monsanto scientist who had been working on reactor design at Oak Ridge since World War II. Almost immediately, McCullough asked the AEC for some time so that his committee could acquaint itself with the issues. When his request was granted, he asked me for permission to sit in on all the RSC meetings; I was delighted to grant it. McCullough attended our meetings for almost a year.

Then, in late 1952, the ICRLP submitted its report on the Wahluke slope problem: They were even more determinedly negative than we had been. I could not help but feel relieved. But I also felt it was pointless to have two committees doing identical work. I asked the AEC to form a single combined committee and to appoint McCullough as its chairman. I volunteered to continue to serve on the committee, but I was happy to resign as chairman because I was feeling the time pressures of multiple roles.

In January 1953, Dwight D. Eisenhower was inaugurated as president.[11] In June, AEC chairman Gordon Dean resigned, and President Eisenhower appointed Lewis Strauss the new chairman. Later that month, the AEC finally decided to merge the two reactor safeguard committees.[12] I happily turned over the chairmanship of the somewhat enlarged committee, which was renamed the Advisory Committee on Reactor Safeguards (ACRS) to Rogers McCullough, but I stayed on as a committee member for two more years.

In late August 1953, the atmospheric surveillance system picked up debris from a Soviet thermonuclear test. The Soviets had detonated a mixed fission-fusion device, similar to the Alarm Clock design that Richtmyer and I had worked on during the summer of 1946. The Soviets were making rapid progress, indeed, but with two competing laboratories in the United States, and with seemingly unanimous support from the AEC, I was not worried.

---

[10] The Soviets did not adopt containment vessels because of the extra cost involved.

[11] During the previous November, the Livermore Univac computer, still on the factory floor, was borrowed by the television networks to predict the election results. With 7 percent of the vote in, the Univac predicted an Eisenhower landslide. The results were not used because most polls predicted that Stevenson would win. When the final vote was in, the Univac-generated prediction was discovered to have been within a few electoral votes of the actual results.

[12] Replacements for the Hanford reactors, which had been such a source of concern, were under construction by then.

About the same time, journalists were becoming impatient for more information about the development of our hydrogen bomb. I was concerned about the effect of publicity about my work on my family in Hungary. My mother, Emmi, and Janós had recently been allowed to return to Budapest. Hungary was allowing a few Jews to emigrate to Israel, and I was hopeful that they might be among them. It was impossible for me to guess how much of their earlier trouble had been caused by my efforts on the hydrogen bomb, but I had no doubt that my being involved in weapons work would not endear my family to the communists in Hungary. I had asked the State Department for help in getting them released, but my concerns seemed small in comparison to the other problems the State Department faced, and the means at their disposal to help anyone in Hungary were far from adequate.

Thus, I was upset when the columnist Joseph Alsop called me at Livermore to tell me that he planned to use my name in a book he was writing about Oppenheimer. Lewis Strauss helped to keep my name out of Alsop's book, but the following month, *Time* planned to mention my name, this time in connection with an article on Lewis Strauss. Once again I called on Strauss for help, and once again he gave it. He also put me in touch with two people in the State Department. They received me kindly whenever I appeared at their office doors, and in the early fall, when I pointed out that the list of the last group of emigrants from Hungary to Israel was being drawn up, they said they would do what they could to get my mother, Emmi, and Janós on it; but those efforts came to nothing.

In October, as a member of a newly reorganized Advisory Committee on Reactor Safeguards, I attended a second U.S.-Britain conference on reactors, this one held at the Chalk River facility in Canada. We reported on the NEPA reactor accident that had occurred at the Argonne Laboratory. There had also been a small accident at the Chalk River facility, although I no longer recall the details of it. We spent considerable time examining the ways in which foolproof shutdown devices could be constructed. Unfortunately, we could not discuss the swimming pool reactor incident at the conference because all the reactor test experiments were still classified.

I had already discussed the need for more openness in regard to information about reactor safety with Lewis Strauss, and I decided to renew my arguments the next time I saw him. That occasion came in early December 1953. Uncharacteristically, Strauss was late in arriving, and when he did appear, he was visibly shaken. Asking me to say nothing about it to anybody, he told me that he had just come from a meeting with President Eisenhower. The president had demanded that Strauss investigate Oppenheimer and suspend his clearance pending the results of the investigation

As I have mentioned, throughout the late 1940s, national concern about Soviet espionage had been increasing. The House Un-American Activities Committee (HUAC), which had been formed before the war, began to examine those on the political left. Linus Pauling was refused permission to travel abroad, and Ed Condon's job at the Bureau of Standards was in jeopardy.

In the early 1950s, the nation learned that in addition to Klaus Fuchs, a couple in New York City, the Rosenbergs, and Mrs. Rosenberg's nephew, an army technician named Greenglass who was stationed at Los Alamos, had passed information to the Soviets during the war. Following that revelation, the issue of loyalty became even more highly charged. The loyalty oath controversy in California was just one example of the concern. By 1951, a senator from Wisconsin, Joseph R. McCarthy, had brought a new and frightening dimension to the proceedings as the leader of a militant anticommunist movement. His accusations, in retrospect, were little more than smear and innuendo, but they were widely publicized and stirred up a great deal of political controversy. Many innocent people suffered.

Strauss seemed as opposed to smear campaigns as I. He feared that taking action against Oppenheimer would appear to be another form of McCarthyism. He deeply hoped that some way could be found to avoid it. I later learned that he had offered Oppenheimer the option of resigning from his consulting positions so that he could avoid confrontation.

Strauss also told me that the president would soon make a speech about nuclear reactors that would make me very happy, and that some of my frustrations with the secrecy surrounding the topic might soon be eased. Indeed, within a week, Eisenhower announced a program that proposed international cooperation on nuclear energy.

In March, Strauss wrote to tell me that James Shepley of *Time* wanted to feature me in an article. I still hoped that I would not receive publicity about my role in weapons research because of the precarious situation of my family in Hungary. Lewis had explained to Shepley my reasons for not wanting such an article and assured me that if Shepley called, he would behave in an honorable and fair manner. As I recall, Shepley did not reach me at that time, which was just before Livermore's first major test in the Pacific.

The article that *Time* published was disastrous. It erroneously gave all the credit for the successful development of the hydrogen bomb to the Livermore laboratory.[13] I immediately tried to correct the impression in a letter to the editor that I wrote from Eniwetok:

> What you would find here are people from two laboratories working together effectively and in friendship. Of these two laboratories, Los Alamos Scientific Laboratory is senior in every respect. You mention only the junior partner, the Livermore Branch of the University of California Radiation Laboratory, with which I am connected, and which works under the direction of Dr. Herbert York. You gave to our Laboratory the kind of publicity which is most welcome to a new organization; but you do not mention the great accomplishments with which Los Alamos is starting its second decade of existence. I should like to convey to you that the spirit on this island is a spirit of cooperation, modesty and awe in face of the forces of nature, which we are trying to explore for the defense of our Country to the best of our ability.

Unfortunately, my efforts to heal the growing breach with Los Alamos were not successful. My letter to the editor attracted little attention.

Coming back from the Pacific test site after canceling the Livermore shot, I rode in an airplane piloted by General Curtis LeMay. During part of the trip, General LeMay turned over control of the plane to his copilot and came back and played poker with us. I was invited to join the game and did so. The general attended closely to the immediate situation, a desirable trait in pilots; by contrast, theoreticians are inclined to let their minds wander, and, as usual, mine did. As a consequence, I not only lost money but also a considerable amount of the general's respect.[14] During the game, General LeMay mentioned that there would be a closed hearing about Oppenheimer's clearance. That was when I learned that the proceedings against Oppenheimer were indeed going forward.

---

[13] *Time,* "The Atom: The Road Beyond," 12 April 1954, 21–24.

[14] General LeMay's piloting, like his poker playing, can be characterized as vigorous. I particularly remember the landings, which were followed by the most extraordinary deceleration I have ever experienced.

30

THE
OPPENHEIMER HEARING

April 12, 1954–May 6, 1954

L EWIS STRAUSS DID not have his way. Oppenheimer did not withdraw. On April 12, 1954, the Atomic Energy Commission (AEC) assembled the personnel board—chairman Gordon Gray, president of the University of North Carolina and former secretary of the Army; Ward Evans, professor of chemistry at Loyola University, Chicago; and Thomas A. Morgan, former president and chairman of Sperry Rand—and the hearing began. The next day, the *New York Times* published the questions that the AEC had sent to Oppenheimer, together with Oppenheimer's replies.[1] I should have availed myself of that information, but I was convinced that I understood the charges and had made up my mind not to pay attention to questions regarding Oppie's left-leaning associations.

I had heard that Oppenheimer had been sympathetic to communist causes during the prewar period, and everyone knew that Oppie had friends on the far left; at Los Alamos during the war, he often had complained because he wasn't allowed to see them. This was neither surprising nor, to my mind, alarming. The charges concerning Oppenheimer's employing active members of the Communist Party at wartime Los Alamos were hardly noteworthy, either. I had long known that David Hawkins, the historian at Los Alamos, was extremely liberal. Again, the issue seemed of little significance.

The question of Oppenheimer's friend Haakon Chevalier also failed to arouse my interest. The story I had heard was much the same as the statement

---

[1] James Reston, "Dr. Oppenheimer Suspended by A.E.C. in Security Review: Scentist Demands Record," *New York Times,* 13 April 1954, sec. 1, 15–18.

Oppenheimer had published in the *New York Times* in answer to the AEC charges:

> I know of no attempt to obtain secret information at Los Alamos. Prior to my going there, my friend Haakon Chevalier, with his wife, visited us on Eagle Hill, probably in early 1943. During the visit, he came into the kitchen and told me that George Eltenton had spoken to him of the possibility of transmitting technical information to Soviet scientists.
>
> I made some strong remark to the effect that this sounded terribly wrong to me. The discussion ended there. Nothing in our long-standing friendship would have led me to believe that Chevalier was actually seeking information; and I was certain that he had no idea of the work on which I was engaged.

I knew that Oppenheimer's friend Chevalier, a French professor, had lost his position at the University of California, probably on account of his communist associations. But so had many other people who I was certain were loyal Americans and who had fewer communist ties. It had occurred to me that Haakon and Barbara Chevalier might well have been the professor and his wife who were present at Oppenheimer's home the night Mici and I had had dinner there. Certainly that man had been politically on the far left, and equally certainly, he seemed to be a harmless and thoroughly loyal American. Given a friendship of the nature that Chevalier and Oppenheimer had, I could well imagine how Oppenheimer would try to protect his friend.

I thought the charges involving the development of the hydrogen bomb were worthless. Many others of most impressive credentials had opposed that development out of motives that I considered misguided but certainly not treasonous. All those charges arose from Oppenheimer's opinions, and opinions hardly make one a security risk. The case appeared baseless. Oppenheimer was extremely influential: His work as a physicist, his contribution in bringing quantum mechanics to students in the United States, his extraordinary service during the war years, and his personal charm and prestige had won him many loyal admirers both inside and outside the scientific community. All that made his point of view persuasive, but it violated no security regulation that I knew of. It seemed to me that a reasonable board would dismiss the charges.

Had I read the charges as they were printed in the *New York Times*, I would still have casually dismissed them. Oppenheimer's former fiancée, Jean Tatlock; his wife, Kitty; and his brother and sister-in-law, Frank and Jackie Oppenheimer, had all been active members of the Communist Party. A large group of organizations to which Oppenheimer had belonged were characterized as subversive; he had also been associated with several Communist Party officials, had attended various Communist Party functions, and had contributed $150 every month to the Communist Party, making the last such payment in April 1942. (At that time, $150 was a considerable amount of money, even for someone as wealthy as Oppenheimer.)

The charges also alleged that various officials of the Communist Party had made statements indicating that although Oppenheimer was a party member, he could not be active in the party at this time and his name should be removed from the party mailing list; in other words, that he should go underground. I suspect that even the degree of Oppenheimer's involvement would not have affected my feeling that he was innocent of sinister activity.

Ernest Lawrence and Luis Alvarez came to talk to me about Oppenheimer. Like me, they had been called to testify. During the war, Ernest had recommended Oppenheimer to lead the effort at Los Alamos. He was now strongly convinced that Oppenheimer's clearance must be denied. Both men pointed out the thorough involvement Oppenheimer had had with communists. No one could dispute that the extent was unusual. They also pointed out the several decisions that had worked against national security in which he had played a leading role. They argued that national well-being made it necessary for him to lose his clearance.

I was not outspoken about my disagreement with them. I particularly needed Ernest's support for the Livermore laboratory at that time, given our recent (and third) test failure. In addition, I knew I wasn't likely to be able to change either of their minds. From them, I learned that Kenneth Pitzer and David Griggs had also been asked to testify. In all, some forty people were called.

Ultimately, Lawrence, in spite of his strong opinion, did not testify, because he was having a severe ulcerative colitis attack. Why did I testify? In retrospect, the answer is simple and obvious: because I was demonstrating my fulsome quantity of that general human property, stupidity. While I had shown a great deal of it during 1950 when I was working on the Super, on this occasion I believe I showed more.

I was in basic agreement with what Lawrence and Alvarez said about the negative effects of Oppenheimer's activities in recent years. My disagreement lay in the fact that I firmly believed that there was no reason for his erroneous opinions to affect his security clearance. I was not disturbed by his involvement with communists. Being a communist in the 1920s and 1930s was hardly uncommon among intellectuals and reflected little more than a strong streak of idealism. Oppenheimer's connection with communism could be easily explained on such a basis without connecting him to espionage. Rather, I saw (and continue to see) Oppenheimer as a man of unusual emotional needs.

In May 1952, while I was still at the University of Chicago, an FBI agent had interviewed me and asked in vague terms about any knowledge I might have concerning Soviet espionage or pro-Soviet activity at Los Alamos. I said that I had no information. Then the FBI man became more aggressive. "What about Julius?" he asked. I was baffled by the question. "I don't know any Julius," I replied. "But of course you know him," was the rejoinder. "Julius Robert Oppenheimer."

It is strange, but that is the detail that stands out most clearly in my memory, probably because it was the first time that I heard what the *J* in J. Robert Oppenheimer stood for. The agent went on to ask me in detail about Oppenheimer's role in connection with the hydrogen bomb.

As far as I was concerned, the advice of the committees Oppie had chaired had come close to shutting down the program on several occasions, first after the war, then after the first Soviet atomic bomb test, and then a year later when the calculations suggested that the Super design would not work. Most recently, Oppenheimer had opposed a second laboratory that was intended to refine the new weapon as rapidly as possible. "But," I added pointedly, "it is improper to think of a man as a spy because of his opinions. There is nothing subversive about giving advice, no matter how much I disagree with the advice."

The agent then questioned me about the motives that might underlie Oppenheimer's recommendations. I assumed that Oppenheimer's opposition arose from moral values, that the horror of the bombings in Japan, which he had recommended, had turned him into a pacifist. (This was before his suggestion that the test design of the new hydrogen bomb be used in Korea.) Or, I suggested, perhaps he opposed the hydrogen bomb out of misplaced pride about the device he was responsible for producing. But neither of these, I repeated, had anything to do with disloyalty. The agent went away, neither pleased nor completely unhappy.[2]

---

[2] Reading the FBI agent's report about thirty years later, I found in it the statement: "Teller states he would do almost anything to see subject separated from the General Advisory Committee because of his poor advice and policies regarding national preparedness." I feel confident that the quote is not accurate. I no doubt made it clear that the effects of Oppenheimer's behavior worried me. But I knew at the time that the agent wanted a negative statement about Oppenheimer from me, and I recall trying to be limited and specific in my comments.

Ernest Lawrence, me, and Herb York, about 1957.

Genevieve Phillips, Harold Brown, and me in my office at Livermore, about 1960.

Mark Mills, Harold Brown, me, and John Foster socializing at the
Missile Test Center in Florida about 1957.

Lewis Strauss
and I talking
after we had
received
honorary
degrees.

Glenn Seaborg, then chairman of the AEC, me, Mici, and President Kennedy, who was about to award me the 1962 Fermi Prize.

(Photo courtesy of the White House, reprinted with permission)

My daughter, Wendy, and me at a party at our home, about 1962.

The University of California Department of Applied Science faculty in 1963. (L to R) Mike May, Harold Furth, Mongomery Johnson, Berni Alder, John Killeen, Roy Bainer, me, Wilson Talley, Richard Borg, Albert Kirschbaum, and Richard Post.

Werner Heisenberg and me at a theoretical physics conference in Faldefing, Germany, 1965.

(Photo courtesy of Presse-Foto Townes Leybold, reprinted with permission)

Geo Gamow, in a photo he gave me in the 1960s, holding a cat, about which he has written "Spinor or Scalar?"

Governor Ronald Reagan and Mike May at a press conference at Lawrence Livermore Laboratory in November 1967.

Lowell Wood, John Nuckolls, and me at the laboratory before the "War Criminals" protest on November 22, 1970.

Harold Agnew, telling me something in his agreeable but definite style, at Los Alamos in the early 1970s.

Former Vice President Nelson Rockefeller greeting Roger Batzel as he arrived in Livermore in 1977, to dedicate Fannie and John Hertz Hall.

Sharing a quiet moment at my retirement party with Eugene Wigner
in 1975.

Helen Hertz Hexter presenting the second Hertz Prize in 1977 to Greg Canavan with me looking on.

Talking with Sid Fernbach at his retirement party in 1979.

(Photo courtesy of the Lawrence Livermore National Laboratory, reprinted with permission)

Hans Bethe, offering a lecture in Los Alamos in the early 1980s.

Carl Friederick von Weizsäcker and me on a hike in the Bavarian Alps in 1981.

Mici and me in Vienna in 1981.

(Photo courtesy of Ernst von Fuchs, reprinted with permission)

At Hoover with Judy Shoolery working on a manuscript in about 1983.

Andrei Sakharov and me at the Center for Ethics and Public Policy banquet, 1988.

Roger Batzel, retiring as director of the Lawrence Livermore National Laboratory, in 1988, with John Nuckolls, the incoming director, and Carl Haussmann, another of the early and great contributors at the laboratory.

The July 26, 1988, White House briefing on Brilliant Pebbles. Those I can identify are: next to me, Lowell Wood; and slightly behind him, John Nuckolls. General James Abrahamson, military director of the Strategic Defense Initiative Organization is across the table in uniform and seems to be looking at Vice President George Bush. President Ronald Reagan is at the far right, and the model of a Brilliant Pebble (shrouded) occupies the center of the table.

With Herman Mark, my professor from Karlsruhe, and his son, Hans Mark, in 1991 in Austin, Texas, where Hans was chancellor of the University of Texas.

In 1994, at the Russian weapons research center Chelyabinsk-70, me posing with the largest-ever Russian hydrogen bomb.

Ambassador Pal Tar presenting me with the Hungarian Star of the Order of Merit, one of Hungary's highest decorations, in 1994.

At Ames Research Center in November 2000.

When Oppenheimer was formally charged, I found myself in the distressing position of being the only person who could speak with authority about the positive expectations that had been held for the hydrogen bomb and about the obstacles the hydrogen bomb program had suffered over the years. But if I did so, I would seem to be supporting the idea that a person's opinions, if wrong, could disqualify him for a security clearance. I was in sore need of someone to talk to and missed my Chicago friends very deeply during this period.

A few days before I was to leave for the hearing, Charter Heslep of the U.S. Information Agency came to see me about Eisenhower's Atoms for Peace proposal. I had known him only in an official role, but he was the first face connected with the AEC that I had seen since I had begun considering the Oppenheimer hearing. I hoped for some information about the hearing, but I also wanted the AEC to know that I thought the proceedings were a terrible mistake.

I was certain that Oppenheimer would be cleared. I thought the only good that could come out of the affair would be that the testimony might demonstrate the degree to which Oppenheimer's advice was wrong-headed. I went over all the incidents where I felt his advice had worked against national well-being. Perhaps I hoped that by pouring out my thoughts to an impartial witness, I would reach some new insight and clarity. But I did not.

Earlier that year, I had seen Oppenheimer at a physics conference on the East Coast. He had asked me whether I believed he had done anything "sinister." I assured him I did not. He then asked me if I would talk with his lawyer, Lloyd Garrison, and I agreed. Eventually, I did see Garrison and the co-counsel, Herbert Marks. I don't recall just when our meeting took place. At the time of the interview, I was only vaguely aware of the charges; some were related to Oppenheimer's opposition to developing the hydrogen bomb and some were related to his and his family's involvement with communists. I was unaware of the complexity of the charges related to Chevalier—that when Groves had pressured Oppenheimer to name the spy that Oppenheimer had mentioned earlier to security officers, Oppenheimer had given the name of his friend Chevalier.

As soon as I seated in the office, Oppenheimer's lawyers asked me whether I was familiar with the accusations against Oppenheimer. Because I felt that the interview was a waste of time given my personal conviction that Oppenheimer had done nothing sinister, I somewhat inaccurately told them that I was familiar with the charges. Consequently, they did not mention the Chevalier incident. Rather, they devoted all their efforts to convincing me, indirectly, that Oppenheimer's actions in regard to the hydrogen bomb were innocent of disloyalty. In consonance with them, I had already made up my mind about this. For the half hour or more that I was with them, they described the magnificent contribution that Oppenheimer had made in wartime Los Alamos and emphasized that Oppenheimer's work had demonstrated his great dedication to his country. They mentioned nothing I didn't already know and believe.

At one point during that interview, I was tempted to interrupt the lawyers in hopes of gaining insight into Oppenheimer's beliefs, but a misguided sense of courtesy kept me quiet. They mentioned none of the essential charges that had to do with Oppenheimer's past. I left unimpressed with their comments and without having changed my mind: I would testify that Oppenheimer was a loyal citizen.

I went out to the East Coast shortly before I was scheduled to testify. I had decided to offer the best testimony that I could for Oppenheimer. But I also felt that I had to testify, if asked, about the development of the hydrogen bomb. No one else had been consistently involved in trying to bring that program to completion. I spent the night before the hearing with Johnny Wheeler, who was in Washington for a meeting. As he describes it, I spent the evening pacing his hotel room floor and worrying about how best to make my statement without creating doubt about Oppenheimer's loyalty.[3]

The following day, April 28, 1954, I arrived at the building where the hearing was being held. By that time, there had been eleven days of testimony. I arrived early, which was unusual for me. While I was waiting to be called, Roger Robb, the attorney for the AEC, came to the room where I was waiting and asked me, "Should Oppenheimer be cleared?" Without hesitation, I replied, "Yes, Oppenheimer should be cleared." Robb then proposed that I read a short section of the testimony that Oppenheimer had given.

At that time, the proceedings of the hearing were secret. For a moment, I thought about saying no to Robb. But then I remembered that I had listened

---

[3] An historian from the Smithsonian, Gregg Herken, kindly supplied me with a copy of a handwritten letter I sent to Lewis Strauss; in the letter, I said that had I met with the AEC attorney, Roger Robb, the night before the hearing. When I wrote to Strauss, I was very upset and I was careless in describing the details of the meeting. Had I talked with Robb before I met with Wheeler, a trusted and fair-minded friend with as high a security clearance as my own, I surely would have discussed with him the information Robb had given me. Wheeler remembers my talking with him that night but recalls no mention of my interview with Robb, which, if it occurred, would have occurred shortly before I saw Wheeler. I therefore continue to believe my vivid recollection that Robb approached me a few minutes before I was called to testify.

to Oppenheimer's lawyers for more than half an hour. Having given them that much time, I thought it would be fair to read the material that Robb wanted me to see.

The section that Robb showed me contained the following portion of Oppenheimer's sworn testimony, describing an event that took place during the Los Alamos wartime project:[4]

[Robb]: I think your first interview with Johnson was quite brief, was it not?

A: That is right. I think I said little more than that Eltenton was somebody to worry about.

Q: Yes.

A: Then I was asked why did I say this. Then I invented a cock-and-bull story.

Q: Then you were interviewed the next day by Colonel Pash, were you not?

A: That is right.

Q: Who was he?

A: He was another security officer.

Q: That was quite a lengthy interview, was it not?

A: I didn't think it was that long.

Q: For your information that was August 26, 1943.

A: Right.

Q: Then there came a time when you were interviewed by Colonel Lansdale.

A: I remember that very well.

Q: That was in Washington, wasn't it?

A: That is right.

Q: That was September 12, 1943.

A: Right.

Q: Would you accept that?

A: Surely.

Q: Then you were interviewed again by the FBI in 1946; is that right?

A: In between I think came Groves.

Q: Yes. But you were interviewed in 1946; is that right?

A: That is right.

Q: Now let us go back to your interview with Colonel Pash. Did you tell Pash the truth about this thing?

---

[4] *In the Matter of J. Robert Oppenheimer: Transcript of Hearing before Personnel Security Board, Washington, D.C., April 12, 1954, through May 6, 1954* (U.S. Government Printing Office, 1954), p. 137.

A. No.

Q. You lied to him?

A. Yes.

Q. What did you tell Pash that was not true?

A. That Eltenton had attempted to approach members of the project—three members of the project—through intermediaries.

Q. What else did you tell him that wasn't true?

A. That is all I really remember.

Q. That is all? Did you tell Pash that Eltenton had attempted to approach three members of the project—

A. Through intermediaries.

Q. Intermediaries?

A. Through an intermediary.

Q. So that we may be clear, did you discuss with or disclose to Pash the identity of Chevalier?

A. No.

Q. Let us refer, then, for the time being, to Chevalier as X.

A. All right.

Q. Did you tell Pash that X had approached three persons on the project?

A. I am not clear whether I said there were 3 X's or that X approached 3 people.

Q. Didn't you say that X had approached 3 people?

A. Probably.

Q. Why did you do that, Doctor?

A. Because I was an idiot.

I was amazed and confused by what I read. According to Oppenheimer's sworn testimony, he had made up a "cock-and-bull story" and told it to a security officer as fact. But Oppenheimer had not just lied to the security officer; if he was now telling the truth, he had lied in such a way that he put his friend Chevalier in the worst possible light![5] Oppenheimer had first made up a story that someone called Eltenton had approached an intermediary who had contacted three men on the Manhattan Project to gain information about the work on the atomic bomb. Then he had claimed that the intermediary was his friend Chevalier!

---

[5] Oppenheimer's testimony on the Chevalier incident can be found in the hearing transcript on pp. 10 and 129–147.

Why in the world would Oppenheimer do that? He had not protected his friend, as I would have expected, but in fact had accused Chevalier of making three approaches to three different people on the Manhattan Project! What possible motives could underlie such behavior, which he now admitted were lies? And how could he now claim there was no reason except idiocy?

The portion of transcript that Robb showed me was a tremendous shock. That Oppenheimer had communist friends and relatives I did not consider important. That he had accused a close friend of espionage—without any justification or explanation except stupidity—seemed to me inexcusable. I could find no way to make sense of Oppenheimer's betrayal of his friend. I was certain of only one thing: Oppenheimer was not an idiot! But as to what sort of person he was, I could no longer guess.

Oppenheimer was a scientist whose behavior was unlike that of most of my colleagues and acquaintances. Most of the outstanding scientists I have known, with the possible exception of Heisenberg and his musicianship, had no other particular field of excellence. But Oppenheimer, like Johnny von Neumann, one of his great contemporaries whom I knew well, applied his talents in many fields. Yet the two men were remarkably different.

Johnny von Neumann worked on and made outstanding contributions to the fields of mathematics, physics, economics, and history, and to the development of atomic bombs and computers. Johnny's motive was straightforward: He used his brain for the sheer pleasure of exercising it. He thoroughly enjoyed many aspects of life, but his deepest joy lay in intellectual activity.

Oppenheimer was a first-rate physicist and an exceptionally talented administrator; he also had a genuine interest in politics. He was, I believe, dedicated to his profession and unusually ambitious for its success. In collaboration with I. I. Rabi, he established the study of quantum mechanics in the United States. Oppenheimer was deeply discouraged when so many excellent physicists were unable to find work during the Depression. He learned Sanskrit and studied French literature. But the motives behind his behavior and the sources of his pleasures and sorrows were difficult to discern. I spent some time reviewing the several earlier occasions we had spent time together. My previous interpretations of those experiences now were called into question.

As the reader knows, my first real acquaintance with Oppenheimer began in the summer of 1942, when he invited me to spend several weeks in Berkeley at a conference to work on the theory of the atomic bomb. I was pleased by the warmth of his invitation. His sense of urgency seemed to match my own. At the conference, our preliminary discussion led us all to believe that the theoretical problems standing in the way of an atomic bomb were straightforward. That Konopinski's and my suggestions about a fusion weapon became the focus of the summer conference was to a great extent Oppenheimer's doing because as chairman, he had directed our discussions.

My impression was—and still is—that Oppenheimer had vigorously pursued the idea of a hydrogen bomb at that time because he was engaged by a novel idea and wanted all the details explored. It was the only time that he and I discussed physics with the kind of dedication, excitement, and focus that I have enjoyed with my colleagues throughout my life.

Toward the end of the conference, Oppenheimer talked to Arthur Compton, the scientific leader of the Manhattan Project. Afterwards, Oppenheimer told us that he had emphasized the great possibilities that nuclear explosions opened up and had used the hydrogen bomb as an example. He said he had argued that constructing an atomic bomb and looking into its further scientific ramifications required a separate laboratory. This was how the motivation for establishing Los Alamos was described to us at the conference.

Throughout the Berkeley conference and for some weeks afterwards, my relationship to Oppenheimer was cordial. He invited Mici and me to his home for dinner. During dinner, which included another couple from the University, Oppenheimer voiced the opinion that it would be impossible to defeat Hitler without the use of an atomic bomb.

There was no doubt that Hitler's successes during that time indicated that something almost miraculous was needed to stop him. But I was struck by the absoluteness of Oppenheimer's statement and by the unhesitating way he mentioned using an atomic bomb. Szilárd, Wigner, and I had a shared vision of needing the bomb to *deter* Hitler's use of such a weapon rather than to use it ourselves.

I returned to Chicago in late August 1942, and underwent a minor operation from which I was slow to recover. I was still something of an invalid when Oppenheimer arrived in Chicago in the fall. By that time, plans for Los Alamos had advanced, and Oppenheimer was recruiting scientists in the Chicago area. I remember one of the arguments he used in his recruiting speech because it disturbed me. He recalled the years of the recent Depression when a good physicist he knew had been obliged to work in a filling station to earn a living. He then pointed out that if we succeeded in making the atomic bomb, such indignities would never again happen to physicists.[6] He

---

[6] Today, I am tempted to spin out this idea in a manner that is quite probably exaggerated. If physicists pursued the atomic bomb for the purpose of earning a more secure and respected position for themselves, then we may be rightly asked to feel guilty about the entire enterprise.

made the statement before a group of people, and I remember keeping my peace with some discomfort. The atomic bomb seemed to me, and to many other refugee-scientists, pertinent to more important issues than unemployment among physicists.

During this period, my feelings about Oppenheimer were happy and friendly. He was an excellent physicist, he was engaging company, and he was exceedingly pleasant to me. So it was nice to be able to arrange to share a compartment on the train when we were were going to Washington. I had an infected finger, and Oppenheimer, in addition to all his other talents, was very skillful in bandaging it.

The setting, as I mentioned in Chapter 15, remains clear in my memories because of my surprise at the exchange that followed. Oppenheimer made some derogatory remarks about General Groves. He then said in effect: "In the present situation, we must cooperate with the general, but the time will come when we will have to stop working with the military."

I had the strong impression that Oppenheimer was talking about some form of civil disobedience; but I could not imagine that anyone of good will and intelligence would find it necessary in this country. I could not imagine myself voluntarily breaking the law while living in the United States.[7] Even today, I find the idea of civil disobedience in a democracy wrong. I am the son of a lawyer, and I continue to believe that civilization, the ability to live by means other than brute force, depends on discourse and consensus to change laws, not on individual disregard for lawfulness. In my comment that day to Oppenheimer, I expressed my disagreement in a far less emphatic form.

Looking back on that conversation, I believe that from that moment on Oppenheimer was no longer interested in having a close relationship with me because he had discovered that we held different political values. That seems to have been a far more important matter to him than it was to me. It was only later that I began to wonder whether my startled statement (something to the effect that I couldn't imagine doing so) was enough to lose me his respect.

When I was working on the mesa, my admiration for Oppenheimer's organizational abilities grew steadily deeper, as did my gratitude for the many ways he helped me find an effective role at Los Alamos. On the one hand, he systematically encouraged the gathering of good people in Los Alamos; on the other, he encouraged constructive work even if it was conducted outside

---

[7] In 1942, civil disobedience did not enjoy the level of acceptability it developed during and following the Vietnam War.

Los Alamos. He fully supported my attempts to understand the behavior of radiation in nuclear explosives even though that appeared to be of no immediate use for our short-term goals.

My first unresolved disagreement with Oppenheimer came in late June 1945 in connection with the question of whether the atomic bomb should be demonstrated to the Japanese before it was used. I was shocked and hurt by the terms he used to describe my friends in Chicago, James Franck and Leo Szilárd. His sudden decision to terminate further work on the hydrogen bomb about six weeks later when Japan surrendered was even harder to understand. But even in that case, he seemed solicitous of my well-being. He did not simply tell me his decision; he did his best to persuade me that abandoning the work was the wisest course.

Not much later, Oppenheimer made his second great contribution: the development of a practical plan for international control of nuclear development. The Acheson-Lilienthal report, which served as the foundation of the Baruch plan and was presented to the United Nations in 1947, was based on Oppenheimer's suggestions.[8]

Through the end of 1949, I had little but respect for Oppenheimer. I had been upset when I learned of what appeared to me his duplicitous conduct in regard to Szilárd's petition. Oppenheimer had instructed me not to circulate it because, he said, only political leaders, not scientists, had the expertise to make such decisions; but he, as a scientist, had already provided his (opposite) advice on the same question. Nonetheless, I was able to set the incident aside in consideration of the contributions he had made.

I had been hurt and somewhat mystified by the first sign of his hostility, which came in 1949, when I called him after hearing about the Soviet atomic bomb.[9] Oppenheimer's brusque comment, "Keep your shirt on," made it clear that he didn't want to share his thoughts with me, that he had

---

[8] Bernard Baruch added teeth to the report by proposing that the security of all participants should be supported by measures of enforcement that would not be subject to any veto. The plan would have made possible a world in which there would be no threat of nuclear attack. In the United States, the plan had widespread bipartisan support. Unfortunately, the Soviets refused to consider any plan for international control of nuclear weapons unless all U.S. nuclear weapons were destroyed beforehand. See Chapter 20.

[9] It should be clear from the previous that between 1945 and 1949, I did little work on the hydrogen bomb. I think that was reasonable because to act differently would have been futile. Oppenheimer's opposition to the hydrogen bomb was so strong that I knew it would be a waste of time to try to counter it. That fact tended to make my decision easier and spared me unnecessary frustration.

decided I must be trying to move in a direction opposite to his own. When I made that phone call, I was sincerely looking for his advice and was open to any he had to offer. But after I had considered the question on my own for a few weeks, particularly after talking with Ernest Lawrence, I reached a conclusion different from Oppenheimer's. Our different political views on the issue should have been resolved by an open objective debate that involved the nation. That, unfortunately, was not the case.

During the time I was working on the hydrogen bomb, what little contact I had with Oppenheimer was superficial and reflected no encouragement or interest on his part. I suspected, and so several people (ranging from Freddie de Hoffman to Senator Brien McMahon) reported, that he was actively working to close down the program. Every report he was associated with during that period suggested that other work was more important than the hydrogen bomb project. Yet I still respected him enough that when I was struggling over my decision to go to UCLA in the fall of 1950, I discussed the loyalty oath with him and the action I should take.

After the successful test in 1951 and with the new hydrogen bomb design presented at the Princeton meeting that followed, Oppenheimer gave up his opposition to the further development of the hydrogen bomb. His opposition to establishing a second laboratory eventually proved of little account. Consequently, I had given little further thought to what might have motivated him in the past. I simply concluded that I could not understand a man as complicated as Oppenheimer.

Now I struggled to understand how, according to his own sworn testimony, Oppenheimer could be asked to pass information to the Soviets, not report the request for several months, and then report it but lie about the request or requests, and then involve his good friend in a manner that increased the sinister appearance of his friend's actions. None of the motives I could imagine seemed reasonable, but neither did Oppenheimer's explanation that so peculiar a series of events occurred because he was "an idiot."

Outside the hearing room, Robb asked me again, "Would you still say Oppenheimer should be cleared?" My answer was, "I don't know." With that, I was taken into the hearing room. In short order, I was sworn in, told of the existence of perjury laws, and the questioning began. It proceeded rapidly.

In retrospect, I have wondered how I would have reacted had I heard a different account on the day that I visited with Oppenheimer's lawyers, one that included a mention, and perhaps the explanation, of Oppenheimer's lying to security officers at Los Alamos. Unfortunately, neither Oppenheimer nor his lawyers gave me any indication of the depth of his problems, and my shock left me unsure that I could trust my convictions about Oppenheimer. Certainly, before seeing his sworn testimony, I would have believed it impossible that he could be involved in such events. My confusion is evident in my testimony.

> [Robb]: Dr. Teller, may I ask you, sir, at the outset, are you appearing as a witness here today because you want to be here?
> A. I appear because I have been asked to and because I consider it my duty upon request to say what I think in the matter. I would have preferred not to appear.
> Q: I believe, sir, that you stated to me some time ago that anything you had to say, you wished to say in the presence of Dr. Oppenheimer.[10]
> A: That is correct.

Robb then asked me to describe my academic background briefly, and when I had done so he asked:

> Q. Dr. Teller, you know Dr. Oppenheimer well; do you not?
> A. I have known Dr. Oppenheimer for a long time. I first got closely associated with him in the summer of 1942 in connection with atomic energy work. Later in Los Alamos and after Los Alamos I knew him. I met him frequently, but I was not particularly closely associated with him, and I did not discuss with him very frequently or in very great detail matters outside of business matters.
> Q: To simplify the issues here, perhaps, let me ask you this question: Is it your intention in anything that you are about to testify to, to suggest that Dr. Oppenheimer is disloyal to the United States?
> A: I do not want to suggest anything of the kind. I know Oppenheimer as an intellectually most alert and a very complicated person, and I think it would be presumptuous and wrong on my part if I would try in any way to analyze his motives. But I have always assumed, and I now assume that he is loyal to the United States. I believe this, and I shall believe it until I see very conclusive proof to the opposite.
> Q: Now, a question which is the corollary of that. Do you or do you not believe that Dr. Oppenheimer is a security risk?

Time seemed almost to be standing still. I had been prepared for this question and, before reading Oppenheimer's testimony, would have vouched

---

[10] Oppenheimer was in the room throughout my testimony and cross-examination.

without a second thought for his being no security risk. Now I was truly bewildered by his behavior, and my answer reflected that confusion.

> A: In a great number of cases I have seen Dr. Oppenheimer act—I understood that Dr. Oppenheimer acted in a way which for me was exceedingly hard to understand. I thoroughly disagreed with him in numerous issues, and his actions, frankly, appeared to me confused and complicated. To this extent, I feel that I would like to see the vital interests of this country in hands which I understand better and therefore trust more.

In retrospect, I should have said at the beginning of my testimony that the hearing was a dirty business, and that I wouldn't talk to anyone about it. I should have remained disengaged, but I didn't do that. I had an odd conviction that if the government asked one to testify, one should do so.

But my most glaring error was that I did not reveal that Robb had shown me Oppenheimer's testimony about Chevalier. As a result, everyone assumed that my testimony was meant to accuse Oppenheimer for his opposition to the H-bomb. My comments were only meant to question his behavior in regard to Chevalier, but my statement could have referred with equal ease to Oppenheimer's opposition to the hydrogen bomb. By using general terms, I made it impossible for anyone to distinguish what I meant to criticize. By talking about Oppenheimer's behavior as a friend I had produced the impression that I was talking about Oppenheimer in regard to the hydrogen bomb.

I even reinforced that idea. Following my testimony, which had taken about an hour, I was cross-examined, first by Oppenheimer's attorney and then by Dr. Gray, who eventually asked about my earlier statement:

> I believe you testified earlier when Mr. Robb was putting questions to you that because of your knowledge of the whole situation and by reason of many factors about which you have testified in very considerable detail, you would feel safer if the security of the country were in other hands. . . . That is substanially what you said.

I agreed, and Dr. Gray went on:

> I think you have explained why you feel that way. I would then like to ask you this question: Do you feel that it would endanger the common defense and security to grant clearance to Dr. Oppenheimer.

I then repeated my error:

> I believe, and that is merely a question of belief and there is no expertness, no
> real information behind it, that Dr. Oppenheimer's character is such that he
> would not knowingly and willingly do anything that is designed to endanger
> the safety of this country. To the extent, therefore, that your question is di-
> rected toward intent, I would say I do not see any reason to deny clearance.
>
> If it is a question of wisdom and judgment, as demonstrated by actions
> since 1945, then I would say one would be wiser not to grant clearance. I
> must say that I am myself a little bit confused on this issue, particularly as it
> refers to a person of Oppenheimer's prestige and influence. May I limit myself
> to these comments?

In the aftermath of Oppenheimer's loss of clearance, most people came to believe that because I had made that comment, my remark must have referred
to Oppenheimer's behavior in relation to the H-bomb.

At the very least, I wish that my later testimony had clarified those first
ambiguous remarks. Unfortunately, it did not.[11] Instead of giving an ambiguous answer, I wish I had made clear the simple facts: that I had arrived
intending to testify for Oppenheimer's clearance irrespective of his opinions
on the hydrogen bomb; that Robb had showed me the section of Oppenheimer's testimony concerning Chevalier; and that, as a result, I was so mystified by Oppenheimer's conduct that I could no longer clearly recommend
for his clearance.

Had I simply stated that the transcript Robb had shown me of Oppenheimer's testimony on the Chevalier case had left me feeling so confused that
I no longer trusted my own evaluations, I believe the results would not have
been different for Oppenheimer, although such a testimony would have
made a great difference to me: I would have had the satisfaction of revealing
all the information I had that had a bearing on the case. Instead, for the second time in three years, I proved not only that stupidity is a general human
property but that I possessed a full share of it.

---

[11] See Appendix I for a complete transcript of my testimony.

31

SEQUELAE

June 1954–February 1955

WHAT I HAD done was done. What remained were the consequences. On June 2, the Gray Board voted, two to one, not to reinstate Oppenheimer's clearance, and Oppenheimer asked the commissioners of the AEC to review the decision. In mid-June, the transcript of the testimony at the hearing was published, a book almost 1,000 pages long. On June 29, the commissioners, in a vote of four to one, upheld the decision of the Gray Board. The leader at Los Alamos when the first atomic bomb was built had been told in effect that his government did not find him trustworthy enough to allow him to continue working on its affairs.

How can such a decision be understood? The evidence—the testimony and hundreds of pages of supporting documents—is complex and confusing. It is not likely that there will ever be a simple and accurate answer as to why Oppenheimer lost his clearance. The Oppenheimer affair had a deep influence on attitudes in our nation and changed my life irreparably. For this reason, I feel justified in discussing the hearing in some detail.

Let me begin by saying that the right decision would have been for President Eisenhower, having been informed of the situation, simply not to have asked Oppenheimer to serve further as an advisor on questions regarding nuclear topics. Even if Oppenheimer had then volunteered comments, they would have had little effect. I blame the president for not finding the courage to take responsibility in this matter.

I must also say that Oppenheimer's actions can be explained only if one realizes that his motives went beyond simple questions of truth and its proper consequences. No single perspective can provide a reasonably complete description of the Oppenheimer case, but an examination of the evidence from three views of it—those of Bill Borden, Haakon Chevalier, and the scientific community—may at least explain why many of its contradictions can never be completely resolved.

Oppenheimer's security clearance was challenged in 1954 because of Bill Borden, the man I had met in 1949 as the legislative aide to Senator McMahon. Borden, a graduate of Princeton and of Yale Law School, was straightforward, well-spoken, and courteous. As a pilot based in England during World War II, he was returning from a mission when his plane was passed at extremely high speed by an incoming German V-2 rocket. From that time on, his concern for American military preparedness never wavered.[1]

McMahon made Borden the executive director of the Joint Congressional Committee on Atomic Energy (JCCAE) which, like the General Advisory Committee (GAC) of the AEC, was a powerful voice in drawing up nuclear policy. Borden and McMahon had similar aims. They were eager to see the civilian uses of atomic energy realized and were committed to having the military requirements of the nation met. Throughout the years that Borden served as the administrator of the JCCAE, he found Oppenheimer giving advice completely at odds with the programs the JCCAE wished to pursue. Borden thought the situation particularly alarming when the GAC repudiated research on the hydrogen bomb.

Over the years, Borden developed a deep-seated distrust of Oppenheimer and began considering the possibility that Oppenheimer might be disloyal. Hearsay has it that for some time the senator and other members of the JCCAE dissuaded Borden from pressing his ideas; but Senator McMahon, Borden's mentor, died in July 1952. That fall, the Republicans the won the elections and took over the leadership of the JCCAE, appointing Senator Prescott S. Bush (the grandfather of President George W. Bush) to fill the vacancy left by McMahon. Borden, a Democrat, lost his job in May 1953; in November, having left Washington to go to work for Westinghouse Corporation, he wrote a letter to J. Edgar Hoover, director of the FBI. Borden, in his letter to the FBI, pointed out that

As chairman or as an official or unofficial member of more than 35 important Government committees, panels, study groups, and projects, [Oppenheimer]

---

[1] The event so impressed him that after finishing law school he wrote a book (William Liscum Borden, *There Will Be No Time: The Revolution in Strategy* [New York Macmillan, 1946]) on the changes in strategy that the technologically novel weapons would bring.

has oriented or dominated key policies involving every principal United States security department and agency except the FBI.

Borden went on to note that at the time of Oppenheimer's first security application in April, 1942:

He was contributing substantial monthly sums to the Communist Party; his ties with communism had survived the Nazi-Soviet Pact and the Soviet attack upon Finland; his wife and younger brother were Communists; he had no close friends except Communists; he had at least one Communist mistress; he belonged only to Communist organizations, apart from professional affiliations; the people whom he recruited into the early wartime Berkeley atomic project were exclusively Communists; he had been instrumental in securing recruits for the Communist Party; and he was in frequent contact with Soviet espionage agents.

In May 1942, he either stopped contributing funds to the Communist Party or else made his contributions through a new channel not yet discovered; in April 1942 his name was formally submitted for security clearance; he himself was aware at the time that his name had been so submitted; and he thereafter repeatedly gave false information to General Groves, the Manhattan District, and the FBI concerning the 1939–April 1942 period.

He was responsible for employing a number of Communists, some of them nontechnical, at wartime Los Alamos; he selected one such individual to write the official Los Alamos history; he was a vigorous supporter of the H-bomb program until August 6, 1945 (Hiroshima), on which day he personally urged each senior individual working in this field to desist; and he was an enthusiastic sponsor of the A-bomb program until the war ended, when he immediately and outspokenly advocated that the Los Alamos Laboratory be disbanded.

He was remarkably instrumental in influencing the military authorities and the Atomic Energy Commission essentially to suspend H-bomb development from mid–1946 through January 31, 1950; he has worked tirelessly, from January 31, 1950, onward, to retard the United States H-bomb program; he has used his potent influence against every postwar effort to expand capacity for producing A-bomb material; he has used his potent influence against every postwar effort directed at obtaining larger supplies of uranium raw material; and he has used his potent influence against every major postwar effort toward atomic power development, including the nuclear-powered submarine and aircraft programs as well as industrial power projects.

From those facts, Borden concluded that

> more probably than not, J. Robert Oppenheimer was a sufficiently hardened
> Communist that he either volunteered espionage information to the Soviets or
> complied with a request for such information . . . and has since acted under a So-
> viet directive in influencing United States military, atomic energy, intelligence,
> and diplomatic policy.

Hoover passed Borden's letter on to President Eisenhower. He could hardly
do otherwise with charges that could create such a damaging political situation. Hoover must also have been aware that Oppenheimer's security record
was open to question. During the course of the hearing, Colonel Boris Pash,
the officer who worked on security for the Manhattan Project, testified that
Oppenheimer had received his first security clearance in late July 1943, thirteen months after it was requested, and only because General Groves had demanded that Oppenheimer be cleared "without delay, irrespective of the
information which you have concerning [him]" on the grounds that Oppenheimer, who had then been leading the effort at Los Alamos for almost six
months, was "indispensable to the program." In 1947, when Oppenheimer,
now a national hero and chairman of the GAC, was again cleared, the review
was not particularly comprehensive.

Given the recent outcry, led by Senator McCarthy, over communists in
government offices, President Eisenhower may have felt it essential, after
Borden's letter, to clarify the question. It is interesting to note that Eisenhower did not assume responsibility for initiating the hearing until June 30,
1954, by which time conspiracy theories about how Oppenheimer had come
to lose his clearance were already well developed.

Borden wrote to me on June 21, 1954, seven weeks after my testimony
and a week before Eisenhower's announcement. His letter said in part:

> By this date you will perhaps have learned the details about my own part
> in the Oppenheimer case. Before the testimony was published I had talked
> to Ken and heard from him that some of your colleagues are tending to
> blame you for precipitating the hearings. This news struck me as pecu-
> liarly ironic because I have felt concern lest you yourself feel that my letter
> to the FBI, which Dr. Smythe told me did precipitate the case, goes too far.
>
> If such is your reaction, I would just like to say to you that I think
> each point in my own position can be documented to the satisfaction of
> an impartial judge. The information on which I rely goes well beyond
> what I have so far seen in surveying the published hearings.

The present letter is for you only, and I'd appreciate your not showing it to anyone.[2] However, you are certainly most free to point out that you and I were not in communication about the case prior to the writing of my FBI letter, and indeed that we had never discussed Oppenheimer from a security standpoint. You are also most free to point out that Dr. Oppenheimer and his four lawyers had two-and-one-half days in which to decide whether or not they would cross-examine me and they declined this opportunity. Finally, as you know, my own political sympathies happen to lie with the Democrats (in matters outside the field of atoms, that is—in the atom business I certainly have as much cause to feel grateful for the contributions of Republicans as Democrats). Also I revere the memory of Brien McMahon, and I still take an exceedingly dim view of Mr. McCarthy.

Your own testimony enhances my admiration, if that were possible— and it's not, for the moral courage which you have always brought to bear upon issues in the program. My heart really went out to you, Edward, in that moment before you were to appear. You may not find it easy to live with some of your colleagues these days (although publication of the testimony should help you with them), but you certainly can live at ease with your own conscience.

Naturally I am anxious about the effect of the case upon scientists in relation to Government work. In fact, I spent almost as much time worrying about this as about the details of the case before sending my FBI letter. In weighing the danger of having a probable subversive continue to orient our national policies against the danger of "alienating our scientists," it struck me that the former is the greater threat. It also struck me that someone had to take the first unequivocal step toward belling this cat and that I was the logical nominee, not only because I knew more about the cat than others so far as I could tell but because I am outside the scientists fraternity. Thus the "blame" for this action would not have to be focused by the fraternity members upon one of their own number.

I replied to Borden on July 9, after I had returned from a meeting at Los Alamos. What had been done was done. In the interests of not making Borden feel worse, my comments were muted.

As I indicated to you when we last saw each other, I do not really believe that you are right about Oppie. I know, of course, that you know more than I do

---

[2] I tried without success to locate Bill Borden to ask for his permission before publishing this letter. I hope that I am right in assuming that half a century later, he will not mind.

and you also know that I trust your judgment. I am just bewildered and also personally very greatly hurt by this case. I am sure that our work has suffered and is going to suffer, but you may be right that all this is really necessary.

One of the results of the controversy is that my name has been dragged into the press to an extent that I now feel certain that the Hungarian authorities are perfectly aware of the connections which I hoped to keep secret. I therefore have no longer any additional worry about my name being publicly mentioned.

I am sure you understand that however much I disagree with your letter that opened up this case I am thoroughly convinced that you did it because you felt that this was the correct thing to do. I also feel a great personal gratitude to you, both for your continued help in the years when we were trying to accomplish the same thing and for your friendly words which come to me at a time when I hear a great number of hateful words coming from people who used to be close to me.

To my mind, Borden's view was simplistic. The heart of a democracy lies in the individual's freedom to doubt and criticize his government. Today, it is hard to realize that the communist program in the Soviet Union appeared to most thoughtful people at one time or another during the 1920s and 1930s as a wave of the future. The difference among those of us who considered that possibility seriously was merely the detail of when and why we finally rejected that system. Did we say no to Marx, or to Lenin, or did we only give up our illusions when confronted with Stalin's horrors?

The historian-novelist Arthur Koestler, whose book *Darkness at Noon* had such an effect on me during my wartime years at Los Alamos, rejected communist ideology only after devoting decades of his life to working for the Communist Party throughout the world. Oppenheimer's pro-communist past can be judged only in the context of the generation that confronted the evils of fascism and the suffering brought about by an unusually severe economic depression. A well-motivated anticommunist position was not reached easily or quickly. Certainly, a sympathetic attitude toward communist ideology should not be judged as necessarily incompatible with loyalty to the United States.[3]

---

[3] Conversely, as AEC Commissioner Thomas Murray pointed out in his concurring decision, the word *loyalty* has its root in legality, so the extent to which an idealist communist respects the law does indeed have a place in evaluating his fitness to be privy to secrets and decisions of the gravest importance.

This leads me to discuss the second point of view, that of Haakon Chevalier, Oppenheimer's contemporary and close friend. Chevalier espoused communist ideology in 1932. As far as I can tell, Chevalier remained true to those ideals throughout his life. Chevalier's friendship with Oppenheimer, which began in 1937, remained strong until mid–1954, when the transcript of the hearing testimony was published. Eleven years later, Chevalier published his fourth book, *Oppenheimer: The Story of a Friendship.*[4] His view of the Oppenheimer hearing provides a completely different perspective, one that I find more convincing than Borden's.

As I explained in the last chapter, discovering the immense gulf between Oppenheimer's public statement regarding the Chevalier affair and the deeply incriminating responses he gave to the security officers upset me deeply. It seems practically certain that Oppenheimer was indeed a fool, but only in the sense that great cleverness can turn into its opposite.

Haakon Chevalier offers this explanation in *Oppenheimer: The Story of a Friendship:*[5]

Is it not possible, therefore, that when Oppenheimer told his fanciful story, and the security agents recognized it for what it was, they then first made the check that would assure them that it was without foundation, and then allowed him to build it up, to wind the noose ever tighter around his own neck, until they knew, and he also knew, that they had him? He was already highly vulnerable because of his record. Army Intelligence in its memoranda makes it clear that it was acutely aware of Oppenheimer's driving ambition, his determination to let nothing stand in the way of his carrying the work of the project through as its director to a successful conclusion and of thereby earning the renown that would be the reward of his achievement. Having now committed this terrible blunder—what General Nichols, ten years later, was to call a "felony" in violation of what was then section 80, title 18, of the United States Code—he had made himself their prisoner. That story would continue to hang over him like a sword of Damocles. They knew it was a lie, and he knew it was a lie. And because he is so exceptionally bright, he probably knew that they knew. They could count on him always to support government policy in any issue that

---

[4] Haakon Chevalier, *Oppenheimer: The Story of a Friendship* (New York: Braziller, 1965). He had earlier published two novels, *The Man Who Would Be God* (1958) and *For Us the Living* (1949), and a scholarly analysis, *The Ironic Temper: Anatole France and His Time* (1932).

[5] Chevalier, *Oppenheimer*, pp. 170–172.

might come up relating to the use of the bomb and any future arrangements regarding the awesome power of the atom.

Beginning in the the Nixon administration (and through the next fifteen or twenty years), I served on the president's Foreign Intelligence Advisory Board, which reviewed the information gathered by the CIA and the Defense Intelligence Agency. Dr. Gordon Gray sat on that same advisory board with me. We became well acquainted during our tenure, and eventually we discussed the Oppenheimer case. Dr. Gray told me that his original inclination had been to clear Oppenheimer. "The Chevalier affair," Gray told me, "changed my mind."

I believe Dr. Gray. Even before his comment, and in spite of all the views to the contrary, I suspect that neither Oppenheimer's opinion on the hydrogen bomb nor my ambivalent testimony had much to do with the decision of either the Gray Board or the AEC.

But what was the evidence regarding the Chevalier affair? Colonel Boris Pash, who worked on the security arrangements for the Manhattan District, was among the witnesses testifying at Oppenheimer's hearing.[6] According to Pash's testimony, on August 25, 1943, about six weeks after Oppenheimer's clearance had come through, Lyall Johnson, the security officer at Berkeley, had asked Oppenheimer to come to his office to discuss one of Oppenheimer's former students, who was suspected of being a communist. Something Oppenheimer said that day so alarmed Johnson that he called Pash; the following day, Pash and Johnson asked Oppenheimer to return, and they then tape-recorded their conversation with him. The transcript of that interview was introduced in evidence at Oppenheimer's hearing.

At the time of the interview, Pash was aware of efforts being made through the Soviet embassy in San Francisco to gather information about the wartime research efforts. Apparently, Oppenheimer had mentioned something pertinent in the previous interview, and when asked about it again, he stumbled through an explanation:[7]

I have no first-hand knowledge that would be, for that reason, useful, but I think it is true that a man, whose name I never heard, who was attached to the Soviet consul, has indicated indirectly through intermediary people concerned

---

[6] *In the Matter of J. Robert Oppenheimer: Transcript of Hearing before Personnel Security Board, Washington, D.C., April 12, 1954, through May 6, 1954.* (U.S. Government Printing Office, 1954), pp. 808–831.

[7] Ibid., pp. 845–853.

in this project that he was in a position to transmit, without any danger of a leak, or scandal, or anything of that kind, information, which they might supply. I would take it that it is to be assumed that a man attached to the Soviet consulate might be doing it but since I know it to be a fact, I have been particularly concerned about any indiscretions which took place in circles close enough to be in contact with it.

Piece by piece, under further questioning, Oppenheimer added:

> The approaches were always to other people, who were troubled by them, and sometimes came and discussed them with me; and that the approaches were always quite indirect so I feel that to give more, perhaps, than one name, would be to implicate people whose attitude was one of bewilderment rather than one of cooperation. . . .
>
> Now there is one man, whose name was mentioned to me a couple of times—I don't know of my own knowledge that he was involved as an intermediary. It seems, however, not impossible and if you wanted to watch him it might be the appropriate thing to do. . . .
>
> [Eltenton] talked to a friend of his who is also an acquaintance of one of the men on the project, and that was one of the channels by which this thing went. . . .
>
> The form in which it came was that an interview be arranged with this man Eltenton who had very good contacts with a man from the embassy attached to the consulate who was a very reliable guy (that's his story) and who had a lot of experience in microfilm work, or whatever the hell.

The story that the security officers finally elicited was that "5, 6, 7 months ago," an intermediary from Eltenton made approaches to three members of the Manhattan Project, two from Los Alamos and one from Oak Ridge, at three different times within a week of one another.

Having provided information of what seemed to be a thorough-going espionage attempt, Oppenheimer was repeatedly questioned by security officials until all the information came out. During a second interview at Los Alamos three weeks later, Oppenheimer provided the names of people he knew to be communists or fellow travelers but refused to name the intermediary. Finally, in December 1943, at General Groves insistence, Oppenheimer named Chevalier as the intermediary.

Whether Oppenheimer told General Groves at the same time that he had invented the story of three approaches will never be known. Oppenheimer suggests that he did. At the time of his testimony, Groves could not remember exactly what Oppenheimer had said. The telegrams sent following their conversation report that "Oppenheimer states in his opinion Chevalier engaged in no further activity other than three original attempts."[8]

The story that Oppenheimer reported in 1954—that Chevalier, having been approached by Eltenton, reported the conversation to Oppenheimer, who then told Chevalier that idea was treasonous—does not quite match Chevalier's version. Chevalier claims that Oppenheimer recognized that Chevalier was telling him about his conversation with Eltenton in all innocence, simply because Chevalier wanted no harm to come to Oppenheimer in his work. Chevalier points out that Eltenton was a mutual acquaintance, and both he and Oppenheimer knew that Eltenton was naive and foolish rather than subversive. And, Chevalier asks, if Oppenheimer had suspected that Eltenton was seriously attempting to spy, why didn't he report their conversation immediately?[9]

The wartime relationship between the United States and the Soviet Union was ambiguous. Oppenheimer's relationship with his friend Chevalier was just as ambiguous. My own strong distaste for ambiguity in friendship may be excessive. Unfortunately, those feelings exist, and they deeply affected my testimony.

The scientific community had still another perspective on the Oppenheimer hearing. Happenstance as well as the events themselves played a role in its development. The decision of the Gray Board, by virtue of being the first announced, was received with greatest interest. Gordon Gray and Thomas Morgan had voted to deny Oppenheimer clearance; Ward Evans had voted to reinstate it. The text of the majority decision ran to 25,000 words and was at best repetitious, discursive, and convoluted; Evans's minority report was about eight paragraphs long. All three men agreed that twenty-two of the twenty-three charges related to Oppenheimer's communist ties were true.[10] Their division occurred over their view of the Chevalier case, and over the twenty-fourth charge, which pertained to the hydrogen bomb.

---

[8] Ibid., p. 153.

[9] Chevalier, *Oppenheimer,* p. 145.

[10] The exception was the charge that a Communist Party meeting was held at Oppenheimer's house.

The majority findings seemed to fault Oppenheimer for his lack of enthusiasm in supporting the hydrogen bomb project after President Truman's February decision. Gray and Morgan found Oppenheimer's conduct "disturbing"; Evans found that "if his opposition caused any people not to work on it, it was because of his intellectual prominence and influence over scientific people and not because of any subversive tendencies."[11]

Although Gray and Morgan discussed the Chevalier case in even greater length than the hydrogen bomb, when the *Bulletin of Atomic Scientists* published the Gray Board Report, they omitted the majority findings related to the Chevalier case. The *Bulletin* explained: "Since space does not permit the reprinting of the allegations in full, we have selected only Allegation 24 which deals with the H-bomb controversy as that being most significant in the 'Findings' of the Board."[12] The editors' emphasis is understandable enough: The letter that Oppenheimer's lawyers sent to the AEC requesting a review, published in the same issue of the *Bulletin*, hardly mentions the Chevalier case. Oppenheimer's lawyers directed their arguments almost exclusively against the findings related to the hydrogen bomb.

In his minority opinion, Ward Evans gave impetus to the idea that idealism—a preference for negotiations over preparedness and an opposition to work on weapons as immoral—lay behind Oppenheimer's actions:

First [Oppenheimer] was in favor of [the hydrogen bomb] in 1944. There is no indication that this opinion changed until 1945. After 1945 he did not favor it for some years perhaps on moral, political or technical grounds. Only time will prove whether he was wrong on the moral and political grounds.

In that way, Oppenheimer came to be seen as having been barred from security clearance because of his political and moral views.

The idea that Oppenheimer was opposed to further work on nuclear weapons on moral grounds introduces an irony. The transcript of the hearing strongly suggests that Oppenheimer was not invariably opposed to the use of nuclear weapons: I. I. Rabi testified that in the early 1950s Oppenheimer had been talking about "preventive war," a euphemism for destroying the Soviet Union before it could develop a sufficient arsenal to be a threat to the United

---

[11] "American Scientist Declared Security Risk: Report of the Special Personnel Security Board," *Bulletin of Atomic Scientists* 10, 6 (June 1954): 243, 249–254.
[12] Ibid.

States.[13] Chevalier, true to the humanist tradition, viewed Oppenheimer's suppression of the Franck Report and his role in recommending the use of the atomic bomb without warning as greater betrayals than Oppenheimer's conduct toward him.[14] My own experiences with Oppenheimer, in connection with the Franck-Szilárd petition and after the *Greenhouse* test, support the view that Oppenheimer was not opposed to the use of nuclear weapons.

I can think of only a few people who worked on the atomic bomb at Los Alamos with the conviction that it should be used. In all the years that followed, I did not meet a physicist or military man who thought that nuclear weapons had any purpose other than deterrence. To my mind, in a democracy, using nuclear weapons is an issue entirely different from that of working on their development. Research on nuclear weapons has provided the United States with the ability to deter the use of nuclear weapons throughout the past half century.

Unfortunately, the scientific community came to believe, as Einstein had predicted four years earlier, that working on weapons would result in

> close supervision of the loyalty of the citizens, in particular, of the civil servants by a police force growing more conspicuous every day . . . [and the] intimidation of people of independent political thinking.[15]

For more than four decades, well-qualified scientists whose contributions would have been of great value have tended to avoid weapons work. I suspect that at least part of that unwillingness arose because of their misunderstanding of the Oppenheimer hearing and of security regulations.

What I had in mind when I said Oppenheimer's actions seemed confused was not Oppenheimer's opinion about the hydrogen bomb but his contradictions and admitted lies in his testimony about his friend. During the postwar

---

[13] Rabi, one of Oppenheimer's longtime friends, made the statement to defend his claim of having a great depth of knowledge of Oppenheimer's beliefs, (*In the Matter of J. Robert Oppenheimer,* p. 470). "I certainly reserve the right to my own opinion on this, because I am in the possession of a long period of association, with all sorts of minute reactions. I have seen his mind work. I have seen his sentiments develop. For example, I have seen in the last few years something which surprised me, a certain tendency of Dr. Oppenheimer to be inclined toward a preventive war. Nothing went all the way. But talking and thinking about it quite seriously. I have to add everything of that sort. All sorts of color and form my own opinion."

[14] Chevalier, *Oppenheimer,* pp. 195–204.

[15] Albert Einstein, "Arms Can Bring No Security," *Bulletin of Atomic Scientists* 6, 3 (March 1950): 71.

period, anyone who lied to security officers about his past when applying for an original clearance, who deliberately lied again in connection with a subsequent event, and who then refused to answer the security officers' questions about that event would surely lose his clearance. But during wartime, the situation was different: Oppenheimer's privileged position sheltered him from the consequences of his behavior.

The wrong decisions that Oppenheimer made during the war did not come under close scrutiny until 1954. As I have already mentioned, I believe that the real wrong decision in this matter was Eisenhower's decision to hold the hearing. Oppenheimer's offenses were in the past, and Oppenheimer had made great, well-known contributions. It is true that more recently he had given advice about the need for research on the hydrogen bomb, about the bomb's feasibility, and about the second laboratory that worked against the nation's ability to deter war. Had Eisenhower simply decided not to use Oppenheimer as a consultant in the future, the president would have avoided what appeared to be both the unfair persecution of a public hero and the capstone of witch-hunts. The controversy that surrounds the hearing to this day would not have occurred if Eisenhower has made a wiser, more logical decision.

The sequela that most occupied my mind during this time was my own pain. It may be hard for someone who has not left his homeland, language, and culture behind to appreciate the profound impact the events that followed had on me. Twice before, I had been forced to relinquish the familiar—first my homeland, then Germany, a country where I could speak my second language and was familiar with the culture; and then even the continent of my birth. In my new land, everything had been unfamiliar except for the community of theoretical physicists. Nineteen years later, I was passably acquainted with my adopted country's customs, language, and attitudes. But the community of my fellow scientists was the only place that afforded me complete comfort, and had done so since my arrival. Now, at forty-seven, I was again forced into exile.

A letter I received from a physicist in Iowa, whom I do not remember meeting, illustrates the response of the scientific community:

> Sir: Your testimony before the review board has been most disturbing to me and many other physicists. Your statement that you would feel more secure if Oppenheimer's influence were eliminated from the AEC seems to indicate that your ideal of security is a state where you would be running the show surrounded by a bunch of yes-men.

In my opinion the consequences of our decisions in the field of nuclear weapons are so far reaching that these decisions should be under constant review. The opinions and the arguments of dissenters should not be eliminated by discrediting these dissenters. In fact you should feel more secure by the very fact that men with convictions dare to disagree with you. If we ever get to a state of uniform agreement then would be cause for anxiety.

You are probably not aware what price you will pay for helping to eliminate the foremost opponent to your H-bomb project. First, you have lost the confidence and respect of many of our leading scientists in the country. Second, the curse of public disgrace will very probably fall some day on you, too. This is a historical law. You will doubt that now, but you will remember my prediction when you get there.

I do not think this letter will make a speck of difference in your attitude, but I do think you should know how I and many of my colleagues think about this. I hope you will forgive me for being so candid.

J. M. Jauch[16]

Such a response was understandable. My testimony reads as though I felt that Oppenheimer's judgment on the hydrogen bomb was a major objection to his continued security clearance. Within days of the Gray Board decision, speculation began on the underlying reason that Oppenheimer had lost his clearance. Every major newspaper writer promoted a different idea—the army was behind Oppenheimer's fall, or Lewis Strauss was, or Ernest Lawrence, or I.

The first appearances, to most people, suggested that the hearing was no more than a device to keep Oppenheimer from influencing atomic energy policy because of his judgment on the hydrogen bomb. My activities, both in pursuing the research and in testifying to those events, seemed to have been the only reason that Oppenheimer's stand on the hydrogen bomb had been discredited.

I had contributed to the development of the hydrogen bomb. Because top-secret classification had been imposed on that topic from the earliest days of its consideration, access to technical facts was limited to hardly more than a hundred people. The number of scientists whose voices reached the political arena was even more limited. Among those doubly selected few, I was literally

---

16 The letter is one of several in my personal correspondence from this period; it will be placed in the Hoover archive on publication of this memoir.

the only one who stood for the necessity of the development and the feasibility of the objective.

To the extent that the hydrogen bomb had any bearing on Oppenheimer's clearance, I must acknowledge that my testimony was damaging. But this fact remains: In spite of my ambiguous and fumbling testimony, I never wanted Oppenheimer's opinion on the hydrogen bomb to count in the decision on his security clearance, nor did I believe that doing so was justified.

The exile I was to undergo at the hands of my fellow physicists, akin to the shunning practiced by some religious groups, began almost as soon as the testimony was released. My recollection of that painful period is general rather than specific: I was more miserable than I had ever been before in my entire life. To refresh my memory, I reviewed the collection of Lewis Strauss's correspondence with me sent from his archives. In it, I came across a "memo to file" that Strauss had written on June 23, 1954. Apparently, about a week after the transcript of the testimony was published, I attended a meeting in Los Alamos. Lewis's memo reads:

> Dr. Luis Alvarez called to tell me that he felt very much concerned about Dr. Teller. He said that Dr. Teller was now in Los Alamos with his wife and was being given very rough treatment there. For instance, he said Dr. Rabi was there the day before yesterday and refused to shake hands with him. Alvarez said he thought Dr. Teller was very low in his mind and it would be an act of kindness for me to call him and encourage him.
>
> I called Teller who confirmed what I had heard from Alvarez. I told him that Rabi was calling me this evening and that I would give him hell. He besought me to do nothing of the sort. "I have made up my mind that I can take the gaff. I am no longer interested in anything except truth. I have complete confidence in the fact that my friends will eventually come to the conclusion that in telling what I believe to be the truth, I have done the cause of science in the service of my country the best that I could."

I do not recall Rabi's refusing to shake my hand. I think that this may have been another occasion, like the one involving my visit to Fermi in 1949, where Alvarez got the substance right but the details wrong. My letter to Maria, written about this time, reflects my recollections more accurately.[17]

---

[17] In the interests of clarity, I have corrected my spelling, which was unusually poor on this occasion.

Thanks for the graphs. The one thing I should like to do is to look at them. But this is impossible. Montgomery Johnson is doing it. He is wonderful. I have 43 minutes/per week for physics. The rest:

I came back from Los Alamos a few days ago. I was there for two weeks. I felt like Daniel in the lions' den. After some time you learn to distinguish the lions (here I had to interrupt. I am now back in Los Alamos for some 18 hours) by their growls. And as you see I am now back in the lions' den. The second time it takes no less courage.

I got so that I can guess what a man is going to say. And I begin to believe that I can guess what he thinks. It is not a nice experience.

The worst of them is Rabi. He never was my friend but now he is terrible. Tomorrow I have to give a report. He will be there to heckle me. I hope I shall not lose my temper. This is not much but it is something.

Last night I dreamed that there was a Raven and I did not dare to go to sleep because he may pick out my eyes. Please translate Raven into German.[18] I found this amusing because the Raven started to smile and I slept quite well.

I am reading the hearings. If it would not involve me so deeply I should find it interesting. I send you an extra copy. Please keep it and read it. If you already have one give it to someone who is interested. I do not know what people will think but they should know the facts.

I am ducking newspaper men. It is not easy and not fully successful. . . .

I remember a conversation a long time ago about backbone. I seemed to get along fine without one. Now there seem to be some growing pains. I also wonder whether it is growing in the right direction.

The media had become particularly interested in me. Perhaps their interest arose because of the intensity of feeling that the Oppenheimer case had generated, or perhaps my attempt to stay out of the news (because of my family in Hungary) made me seem unusual, or perhaps my role in the development of the hydrogen bomb was the cause. But for whatever reason, during the summer of 1954, I received a great deal of attention from the press.

Robert Coughlan, a journalist from *Life* magazine, was writing an extensive article about me. He was a pleasant and intelligent man, and I finally agreed.[19] As it turned out, our last interview was held during the late summer

---

[18] *Rabe* is the German word for raven.
[19] Robert Coughlan, "Dr. Teller's Magnificent Obsession," *Life*, 6 September 1954, pp. 61–69.

meeting at Los Alamos that Alvarez mentioned to Strauss. One of my friends later told me that Coughlan's friendly presence there was like pouring salt in an open wound: I was resented because I was receiving media attention and because I was suspected of trying to vindicate myself. At the time, I was oblivious to the implications. My sole concern was to make sure that all the statements I made to Coughlan were accurate.

Coughlan came up to my room in Fuller Lodge during the afternoon. Our interview ran later than I had hoped, so by the time Coughlan and his group were leaving, many of the participants in the conference were already assembled for a picnic on the terrace outside the dining room. The first person I spotted was Bob Christy, with whom we had shared a house for a year. I hurried over, reaching out to greet him. He looked me coldly in the eye, refused my hand, and turned away. I was so stunned that for a moment I couldn't react. Then I realized that my life as I had known it was over. I took Mici by the arm, and we returned to our room upstairs. Our last exile had begun.

32

THREE FRIENDS

___

August 1954–August 1958

Not everyone shunned me. Szilárd recognized the right of dissent.[1] Perhaps even more important, agreeing with the majority had always made him uncomfortable. Eugene Wigner and Johnny von Neumann seemed to believe that I had done the right thing; they even seemed embarrassed by my predicament. Fermi didn't care whether I was right or wrong— he simply wanted to help me heal the schism. Maria Mayer, Harold Urey, Lothar Nordheim, Johnny Wheeler, Papa Franck, Richard Courant, Emil Konopinski, Nick Metropolis, Harold and Mary Argo, and many others judged me innocent of bad motives. But those friends were far away, and many others who knew me less well—or not at all—saw me as a villain.

I continued to hope for a way to clarify my actions and beliefs. Thus, in early July, after a suggestion from Johnny Toll, I decided to issue a statement:

> Some people have misinterpreted my testimony in the hearings of Dr. J. Robert Oppenheimer. I, therefore, make the following statement:
>
> I was asked to testify at the hearings and was asked to give my full opinion on Dr. Oppenheimer's advice. It was my duty to do so.
>
> In my testimony I did not imply that the right to disagree should be limited. I consider that right as essential in a free society. That my testimony in this connection should have been misinterpreted is a matter of greatest concern to me.
>
> I am happy to see that in its determination of Dr. Oppenheimer's clearance the Commission reaffirmed explicitly his right to voice his opinion.

___

[1] Although we held opposite views on almost every political issue after 1947, our friendship never suffered.

Before giving it to the press, I decided to show it to Lewis Strauss, whose political acumen I respected. He passed my letter on to Roger Robb. Neither man
was encouraging, and the more I thought about it, the less I believed that my
statement would help. It might even stir up further anger. Perhaps, if I did
nothing more, the furor would subside. So I didn't publish my statement. In
the middle of September, the accusations against me grew markedly worse.

Two years earlier, I had risked my relations with my Los Alamos colleagues when I had worked to establish a second weapons research laboratory.
Trying to forestall resentments, I had emphasized the need for competition
in a highly secret field, and I had also tried to give credit to Bradbury for the
contribution he had made in keeping Los Alamos alive after the war. Although Bradbury wasn't happy to see a second laboratory established, within
two years he appeared to have accepted Livermore's existence with reasonable
grace. He also seemed to welcome my continued visits to Los Alamos.

All that changed with the publication of a book by two reporters from
Time magazine, James Shepley and Clay Blair.[2] Their book, titled *The Hydrogen Bomb*, made it appear that Oppenheimer was a spy, that Bradbury was at
best incompetent, that the AEC was ill informed and bureaucratic, that
Hans Bethe did not want to work on the hydrogen bomb because government pay was low, and that I was singlehandedly responsible for building
the hydrogen bomb.[3] I believe I had been interviewed by the authors, but I
had no control over their comments, and I certainly had not suggested the
perspective that they took. But many who were already angry with me over
my testimony decided that the authors were parroting my views.

By the time I read the book, the authors had been severely criticized. Although Shepley and Blair were wrong in many perspectives and specifics, the
framework of their account and their underlying concerns about national security did have some validity. Borden had attacked one man, but Shepley
and Blair attacked everyone. Their book was a gross exaggeration. Enough
people were already contradicting them with such enthusiastic fervor that I
didn't need to add my voice.

---

[2] James R. Shepley and Clay Blair, *The Hydrogen Bomb: The Men, the Menace, the Mechanism*
(New York: D. McKay, 1954).

[3] The book contained large and small mistakes about me as well as about others. For example, the authors reported a meeting between Bill Borden and me at which Borden promised to make the second laboratory a reality. I do not recall such a meeting; and more to the
point, such a promise would have been of little importance.

The flaw of the Shepley-Blair book that I felt forced to address was the statement that no one but I had contributed to developing the hydrogen bomb. Instead of criticizing the book, I decided to write an account of the hydrogen bomb that would give credit to the many people who had worked on the program. I was hopeful that such an article would bring some sanity to the current discussion, provide a common ground of agreement about the history of the development, and allow me to mend some of my sorely tried friendships with people at Los Alamos.

Ernest Lawrence agreed that publishing my own account of the development was a good idea, and for that purpose he offered the services of his wonderful senior secretary, Paula de Luca, to take my dictation. When she had finished typing my rather lengthy description, I asked her for her opinion of it. She suggested just one change. I had told her to call the article "The Hydrogen Bomb." She noted that the title, when combined with "by Edward Teller," sounded just a little immodest. I took only a moment to come up with a more accurate title for my article, "The Work of Many People."[4]

Not long after completing the first draft, I received the worst news I had had that year: Enrico Fermi was dying. Not quite seven years my senior, Enrico had turned fifty-three on his birthday that fall. He seemed in the very prime of life. But on his return from a summer trip to Europe, he had been diagnosed with cancer. Surgery indicated that metastases had spread so widely that nothing could be done. He was about to be released from the hospital to go home to die. I arranged to fly to Chicago at once.

Because of the incredibly rapid development in physics during the ten years between 1920 and 1930, some of my older friends were already well-established scientists when I began my studies. That in turn led to their being important and helpful to me professionally as well as personally. Fermi was such a friend.

---

[4]Paula did a little more for me: Together with Rosie and Stirling Colgate, she introduced me to the idea that there were two political parties in the United States. At the time, I was, like most immigrants, a Democrat. After my grasp of political realities had improved, Paula gave me two small carved onyx figures, a donkey and an elephant. Seeing the figures, now in my Hoover office, reminds me not of politics but of the German humorist Wilhelm Busch. Born in the 1830s, Busch wrote and illustrated whimsical, sometimes satiric rhymes, which today are considered the forerunners of comic strips, especially his *Max und Moritz*. His poem of the alphabet included illustrations of two dissimilar animals with each letter. The animals seemed chosen at random, except in the case of the letter *E*. There, his choice seems prophetic: "Der Esel ist ein dummes Tier; Der Elephant kann nichts dafür." (The donkey is a stupid beast; The elephant's to blame? Not in the least!)

In 1954, I was still uncomfortable when I disagreed with my friends. In 1950, when Fermi and I had disagreed on the issue of the hydrogen bomb, I had begun to question myself, to wonder whether I was giving too much importance to the development of the bomb. My worry about the correctness of my determination, which had steadily grown during those three years, increased my sensitivity to the criticism that followed the Oppenheimer hearing.

In addition, I had failed to take Fermi's strongly worded advice about my move to California. The wisdom of his perspective was now fully apparent. Political divisions within the university at Berkeley were sharp, and little tolerance was shown to those of opposite views. And, of course, Oppenheimer had been highly regarded at the university, which further exacerbated the divisions within the physics department. Yet, in the instance of my pursuing work on the hydrogen bomb and of seeing a second weapons laboratory established, Fermi had known that I felt the work was too important for me to refuse it. His response had been only sympathetic concern. Losing Fermi at a time when I was so greatly in need of friendly counsel was particularly hard.

Enrico was still in the hospital when I arrived, and Laura was standing by his bedside. Laura was not only intelligent; she was also wise. I could see that she was grief stricken, but it was also clear that she would not allow her grief to be a burden to Enrico. As I entered the room, Enrico said with a smile, "Isn't this a dirty trick on me?" My reply was heartfelt, "Yes, it is, and it's a dirty trick on the rest of us, too."

Fermi did not want to talk about himself, and he immediately changed the subject. Knowing that the harsh attacks on me had continued, he asked me how I was doing. Even as he lay facing death, he was concerned about my problems. I had brought a draft of "The Work of Many People" with me, intending to work on it during my trip. When I told Fermi about it, he insisted on seeing it.

Laura left us alone. Fermi read the draft very carefully without commenting. After half an hour, he asked me, "What reason would you have not to publish this?" I explained that I couldn't see any reason not to, but after all the criticism, I was so confused that I no longer was sure what to do. Enrico advised me strongly and insistently to publish it. About then, Laura came back, and seeing that Enrico was tired, I took my leave.

That visit proved to be the last I had with him. Our meeting was characteristic of his generous nature. He had almost all the good traits that a friend could have. From our first meeting twenty-two years earlier, he had proved himself open-hearted, good-humored, and alert to others' needs. He was vitally concerned with what was happening to any one of his many friends until the very end of his life.

Fermi was not a particularly religious man and was not at all scandalized that some of his students and younger colleagues called him "The Pope," a reference to Fermi's seeming infallibility. He often teased about mystical beliefs: When a rather ragged old man, from whom we asked directions on our way to Canyon de Chelly during our 1937 motor trip, advised us strongly against going there, Fermi said that he was a holy man sent by God to warn us. But Fermi was not in the least deterred from getting to the canyon.

Fermi and I both lacked formal religious beliefs; therefore, my first thought on hearing that he had died seemed peculiar. But I felt that I could not hope to find a more sympathetic presentation of my case to God than the one Fermi would present.

Enrico's pleasing disposition was not connected with a sense of false modesty. He was thoroughly realistic about everything—scientific problems, human failings, his own abilities. After working for a short time with Johnny von Neumann, Enrico told one of his collaborators (I believe it was Herb Anderson), "Johnny von Neumann is more clever than I am, just as I am more clever than you," a remark that had the impact of the unexpected as well as all the clarity for which Fermi was famous. Indeed, clarity and ability to organize and complete work were the properties that made Fermi a prominent scientist in an unusually productive period.

Fermi's was the first of three deaths that all occurred in less than four years; each left me feeling increasingly destitute and isolated. In retrospect, the deaths of those friends seem tied to the particularly bleak and difficult period of my life that began with the Oppenheimer hearing. The three men were as different as it is possible to be. They had been born in different countries; they might as well have been from different planets. Their combined loss left a hole in my life that could never be repaired.

During the remainder of the fall, I circulated copies of "The Work of Many People" to other friends. Although I accepted Fermi's advice about publishing it, I was still too uncertain of myself to do so without first obtaining a variety of critiques. I had already asked my friend Montgomery Johnson for his opinion, and I widened the circle of readers to include many others. Among them was my friend Teddy Walkowicz.

I had met Teddy at the first meeting of the U.S. Air Force Scientific Advisory Board. Teddy, knowledgeable about scientific and technical matters, was then an air force colonel assigned to the board. Personable and spirited, he soon befriended me. Like Dave Griggs, he did his best to put me in touch with people whose concerns about national security were similar to my own. Ultimately, he and his wife became good friends of Mici's and mine.[5] A few years after we met, Teddy left the air force and became a economic consultant to the Rockefeller Family Trust, which was administered by Laurance Rockefeller.

Teddy, now living in New York, was enthusiastic about the article. He also seemed best placed to help me get the article published. I wanted it to have as wide a circulation as possible, but even more important, I didn't want it much changed in tone. Over the next few months, Teddy approached several magazines, ranging from the *Saturday Evening Post* to the *Reader's Digest,* all without success. Finally, I arranged to have it published in *Science,* the magazine of the American Association for the Advancement of Science. When it appeared the last week of February 1955, I felt I had done all that I could to heal the schism.[6] At that time, I did not believe the breach was intractable.

Neither did I dream that two years later, my friend Johnny von Neumann would be dead. Shortly after my article appeared in *Science,* Johnny was appointed an AEC commissioner. That was good news. If anything, Johnny was more worried about Soviet progress in military technology than I. Johnny had been a strong supporter of the hydrogen bomb ever since learning about it on his first visit to Los Alamos in 1943. He also had been supportive of the second laboratory and had made time to come to Livermore to help out as a consultant.

As far as I know, Livermore's otherwise well-oiled security system worked smoothly with only two exceptions, and one of them was on John von Neumann's first visit.[7] Given Johnny's contributions to the secrets being

---

[5] My favorite memory of Teddy's wife involves an occasion on which, at her request, I spoke to the student body of a Catholic high school about physics. In the questions that followed, one student asked me whether I thought there was life elsewhere in the universe. I replied, "I doubt that we are the only mistake that God has made," and then stiffened, realizing that such a remark might be inappropriate given the setting. Teddy's wife, who was standing near me, quietly reassured me: "Don't worry. Catholics have a sense of humor, too."

[6] In the article, I even went so far as to give Stan Ulam credit for suggesting compression, although I had come to that realization weeks before Stan discussed it with me. His contribution that day was that, by his interest, he freed me from Bradbury's dictum not to pursue other designs. Still, I had no objection to the white lie in the article if it soothed ruffled feelings. Somewhat later, after it had become clear that Los Alamos intended to rewrite history, I was asked to sign the patent application and swear that Ulam and I had originated the design. Because months after the calculations had begun on the new device Ulam still didn't understand my design and claimed it would never work, I felt justified in drawing the line at perjury. I refused to sign, and as a result, that patent has never been submitted. I suffered a financial loss of $1, the standard remuneration for a classified patent.

[7] Gregory Breit's first visit was the other. Both men were temporarily refused entry. No two people could have been farther from being security risks.

protected, the situation was ludicrous. But the only consequence of the mix-up was that Johnny and I had a few extra hours to spend on other topics.

I cannot remember what we discussed that day, but the subjects Johnny enjoyed ranged from history to weather prediction to game theory. Johnny was interested in any topic that offered him a chance of seeing a new relationship. Perhaps the most striking example of that quality is the book he wrote with Oskar Morgenstern, *Theory of Games and Economic Behavior*.[8] The rather peculiar but substantiated conclusion of that work can be summarized in a simple statement: The optimal behavior in a zero-sum game is to have no strategy at all.[9] As mentioned earlier, Johnny often played the zero-sum game of poker at Carson Mark's. He consistently lost at poker throughout his life, a point his friends never failed to emphasize after the publication of this book.

Beginning in 1943, our main topic of conversation was the design of nuclear explosives. Johnny quickly realized that an atomic bomb might induce a thermonuclear explosion in a variety of ways, and from the beginning, he had shared my concern that such modifications be thoroughly investigated. The second-most-popular topic was the closely related subject of computers.

During the early 1950s, Johnny began thinking about an idea that is still popular today. He wanted to design a wireless computer where the information was carried by light impulses rather than by electricity via wires to vacuum tubes or semiconductors. The question he posed was how one could induce a beam of light to stimulate a component of the computer in response to the result obtained by another component. I suggested using some of Einstein's very early ideas about stimulated emission. My idea, which turned up later in some of our correspondence, describes a laser and anticipated that invention by several years. But, of course, an idea is unimportant unless one develops it.

Johnny's contribution to the early development of electronic computing machines, both to the theory and to many of the details of implementation, can hardly be overstated. I believe that of all the inventions of the twentieth century, the one with the most lasting influence may be the computer, and

---

[8] John von Neumann and Oskar Morgenstern, *Theory of Games and Economic Behavior* (Princeton: Princeton University Press, 1944).

[9] According to the book, in any zero-sum game, one should take all the known facts into account and make decisions accordingly. But that still leaves some choices open; some decisions outside the context of fact must be made. At that point, the best strategy is to have no strategy. One should make final choices at random. If one employs a strategy, no matter how ingenious, one's opponent will eventually figure the strategy out, take it into account in his decisions, and thereby win.

Johnny von Neumann was its prophet. Like Fermi, he had practically no enemies. Like the other scientists from Hungary that he knew well, he had only one ambition, and that was to see his ideas succeed.

Johnny von Neumann, like Fermi, seemed more my senior than our four years' difference in age would suggest; again, this was because Johnny was already making outstanding professional contributions by the time I was beginning my university studies. Nonetheless, growing up in the same place at approximately the same time did provide us with strong ties and many common understandings. Like me, he had chosen to marry a girl from Budapest—in fact, he outdid me in that adventure and married (albeit successively) two girls from Budapest.

His first wife, Marietta von Kövessy, although not particularly striking in appearance, was an exceptionally nice person with a lively wit that withstood all adversity. She bore John's only child, a daughter, Marina, who eventually became an economist. Marietta claimed that she had to divorce Johnny because, although she knew she was superior to him in every other field, she could not be sure that she was his superior in mathematics, and she couldn't tolerate that![10]

Mici and I had known Johnny's second wife, Klári, from our youth. She had been the girlfriend of my boyhood friend Nándi. Klári was one of the great Hungarian beauties, but I never enjoyed her as much as I did Marietta. Klári, a mathematician, had contributed to the original calculations on the first hydrogen bomb design. Klári and Johnny both enjoyed entertaining in their home at the Institute for Advanced Studies in Princeton, and I managed to see them almost every time that I was on the East Coast.

In the fall of 1956, a little less than two years after Fermi's death, I had a phone call from Carson Mark, head of the theoretical division at Los Alamos. Carson was one of my most outspoken critics in Los Alamos, but he did not allow his opinions to affect his social conduct: He was never less than polite to me, and on this occasion he was kind. Carson knew that Johnny and I were close, and as soon as he learned that Johnny had been diagnosed with cancer, he promptly let me know.

Johnny had not been a great one for physical exercise, but he was at least average in being energetic and active; yet early that autumn, he had managed

---

[10] After the divorce, Marietta married a member of the nuclear energy team in Brookhaven and served as a highly placed secretary-administrator at the laboratory. It may be said, with only a little exaggeration, that for several years she practically ran the laboratory.

to break a collarbone during a routine movement. That first surprising sign of trouble led to diagnosis: Carson reported that the break was the result of metastasized cancer.

Hearing that terrible news, I took the first opportunity to go East. Johnny was being treated at the Walter Reed Hospital near Washington, D.C., and I visited him and Klári there.[11] Their greeting made it clear that I was unusually welcome. Johnny wanted to continue our technical discussion and was particularly eager to have me return for more visits. I soon figured out why. Prostate cancer is apt to invade not only the bones but also the brain. In the past, Johnny had used me, perhaps even more than his other friends, as a sounding board. He was always far ahead of me, but I was not so far behind that explaining his idea to me would have bored him. After all, every Hungarian enjoys talking and explaining.

Over the next months, I probably visited Johnny in the hospital on ten occasions. I made my best efforts to provide a little lightness. I had long been Johnny's partner in making puns in three languages: English, German, and Hungarian. Other puns were obviously one-dimensional. But most unfortunately and painfully, whether pursuing puns or scientific topics, it slowly became clear that Johnny was no longer ahead of me. That discouraged him, and caused me anguish, although, of course, neither of us ever mentioned it. As long as he could, Johnny wanted to try, again and again, to exercise his brain as he had done before his illness. He pursued ideas very nearly until his death in February 1957.[12]

That deep, practically monomaniacal devotion to the thinking process is what set Johnny von Neumann apart from everyone else I have ever known. He was a mathematician, mathematics being the purest form of verifiable, precise thought. Man apparently may become addicted to anything—even to constructive, ingenious thinking. I believe that if a mentally superhuman race ever develops, its members will resemble Johnny von Neumann.

---

[11] A man from the security office of the AEC was always in the room for all of Johnny's waking hours. Because John's mind was affected, the officer remained in the room whenever Johnny had visitors to make sure that Johnny did not inadvertently disclose classified information. The officer, who appeared to be assigned for the duration, was extremely considerate and tried to be unobtrusive.

[12] After Johnny died, Klári remarried an extremely nice and considerate physicist, Carl Eckhart. Klári died by drowning not long after that. Their home was near the ocean, and she often swam at night. Perhaps an ocean wave carried her away. But others have suggested that Klári had learned she had cancer and decided not to experience what she had watched Johnny go through.

I had now, in less than three years, lost the comradeship of the scientific community and my two closest friends and advisors. But that horrible period was not yet over: Eighteen months later, Ernest Lawrence was dead.

My inclusion of Lawrence's death as a great loss should not be taken to mean that I found his friendship comparable with those I had with Fermi and von Neumann. Fermi and von Neumann were truly outstanding scientists, and they were also men of considerable emotional depth and complexity of thought. As natives of another continent transplanted to the United States, we had shared a common culture and many common understandings. I spent innumerable happy hours in conversations with each of them.

My relationship with Ernest Lawrence was quite different. Lawrence was, perhaps, the first physicist to be involved in projects that today fall under the heading of Big Science. He was also one of the most successful practitioners of that craft. Ernest's success can be laid to one of his distinguishing characteristics: He liked to get things done. He was a great organizer, a man who had an acute sense of what was important and what was nonsense. Even more to the point, he was endowed with the uncommon virtue of being unselfish and unemotional in his collaborations; that helped him turn the things he considered important into realities.

Perhaps the bond that was most important in our relationship was our mutual concern about the defense of the United States. As Duane Sewell pointed out in a conversation we had in 1994, "Ernest was very good at a kind of grand strategy planning—how a particular program would fit into national needs. He was very concerned about that. He started experimenting with separation of uranium long before World War II started, when he converted the thirty-seven-inch magnet into a calutron. As a result, the first uranium-235 was separated on that magnet in Berkeley."

Ernest had another characteristic, again one that served his basic purpose of getting jobs done: He was particularly astute in assessing people. He could talk to someone for ten minutes and decide, with considerable accuracy, whether that person was strongly motivated and knew what was needed. He did not want to know much more. That was enough for him to give the person a fair try. And I think that his willingness and his eagerness to select effective people and support them was the strength of his organizational capabilities. Many of the men who worked under Lawrence consider him a great motivator. I appreciate that quality less because I did not need much motivation. And for the most part, the people he gathered around him didn't seem to need a lot of motivation.

In most respects, Ernest and I could hardly have been more different. As I mentioned earlier, he was the quintessential American, confident and courageous, boyish in his pleasures, ethical and straightforward in his conduct. On a few occasions, we disagreed strongly on political questions. But I respected Ernest and appreciated his many contributions to his country. And I think Ernest, in the end, liked me, too.

I suspect that Ernest liked me largely because, like himself, I was more interested in national defense than in my personal well-being. I believe that our both wanting to do the job simply because it needed to get done was the basis for our friendship. We shared the quality of being willing to risk our personal reputations by pointing out what we thought could and should be done. We were willing to try to set people and programs in motion in the interests of national defense.

As I have mentioned, Ernest Lawrence was an excellent organizer and administrator, equally good at identifying administrative talent and scientific ability. From the beginning, he divided those two aspects of the laboratory's work because he did not want scientists to be bogged down by administrative duties. Wally Reynolds was responsible for seeing to the operational side of things, but he did not interfere with the essential things that were being attempted in science; however, Lawrence had no patience when scientists involved in research spent time on operational matters. Lawrence's appointment of Duane Sewell to oversee the operational affairs at Livermore was at least as important as his choice of York.

By 1958, I had come to appreciate Ernest Lawrence deeply as a forceful and courageous leader. Throughout the years of work on the hydrogen bomb and on the issue of the second laboratory, he had helped me in a most remarkable and effective way. That assistance had continued in a more broad-based manner during the mid-1950s.

A story I heard after the event provides an apt illustration: On that instance, I had made a proposal (which one, I can no longer remember) to Senator Hickenlooper, a particularly important member of the Joint Congressional Committee on Atomic Energy. Hickenlooper had listened carefully but with a scintilla of doubt in his eyes. I was later told that soon after my presentation, he asked Ernest Lawrence, "Can you really rely on Teller's opinions?" Lawrence's reply was, "I could not really say so. When Teller objects to an idea, he is quite often wrong. But if he tells you something can be done, he is right without any exception." I have my doubts that Ernest was completely honest in either part of his statement, but he could not have made a stronger recommendation for the purpose of bringing Hickenlooper over to my side (and his). Ernest was an effective and loyal ally on matters of national defense.

When I started work in California, some disagreeable symptoms that I had experienced as a student returned in an aggravated form. The physician I saw diagnosed it as a case of ulcerative colitis, a disease of the lowest part of the digestive system, which seemed to be aggravated by worry. In those days, I spent a considerable amount of time in the Berkeley offices of the Lawrence Radiation Laboratory. Soon after the diagnosis, Ernest sat down with me in my office. On no previous occasion had we had a conversation on personal matters. But I had gone to the physician who was also treating Ernest.

Ernest advised me to take the physician's advice very seriously. He spoke of his own case of colitis, which he had contended with for many years. He stressed the fact that colitis, if not taken seriously, resulted in death. He reminded me that his colitis had been too severe for him to risk testifying during the Oppenheimer hearing. He urged me to take regular vacations, to avoid unnecessary stress, and, in the event of a severe attack, to set aside every other activity until it was under control. Unfortunately, Ernest did not follow his own advice carefully enough.

He participated in political decisions. In some instances, he took me along and asked for my advice during the negotiations. There could be no question that his own emotions were often deeply involved.

During the second half of the 1950s, sentiments against further development of atomic weapons became ever more pronounced. In Geneva, the United States was negotiating with the Soviet Union about cessation of nuclear tests, and Ernest had been invited to participate in those negotiations. He asked me whether I wouldn't take his place; I felt strongly moved to help him, but I saw absolutely no way I could do that. I felt that cessation of testing would develop to our disadvantage and saw no room for compromise. In the end, Ernest decided to go himself. Indeed, he made this decision enthusiastically, believing, as he started, that he could accomplish something. During the negotiations, which he found frustrating and disappointing, he became violently ill, ran a high fever, and had to be flown back to the United States.

I visited him at what was then Stanford University Hospital, a building that later became the Hoover Pavilion. He felt somewhat better. Like Fermi, he was much more eager to talk about my problems than about his own.

By that time, the first director of Livermore, Herb York, had been called to Washington to fill the important, recently created job, Director of Defense Research and Engineering (DDR&E). A few months earlier, because of the controversy involving nuclear testing, I had taken over the directorship with the understanding that I would serve only until Mark Mills could take over. Unfortunately, Mills died about a month later. I was most eager to discuss with Ernest who my successor should be, and Ernest was equally eager to recommend that Harold Brown take over the directorship from me when Brown was a year or two older. I gladly agreed.

Soon after my visit, the doctors decided that they had to remove the lower section of Lawrence's digestive system, a difficult operation that I also had to undergo a little more than three decades later. Ernest was very discouraged and was convinced that he would not survive the surgery. He was right. His condition going into the operation was so poor that he survived only for a day or two.

When Ernest died, I was just fifty years old. For me, Fermi, von Neumann, and Lawrence had each filled a role similar to that of an older brother. They were guides and counselors as well as friends. They approached science in completely different ways; and in politics, their approaches were not only different but also, in several instances, antagonistic. Nonetheless, I looked to each of them for advice and assistance in a way that I more clearly understand now than I did at the time.

In the subsequent years, I have had other friends and other helpers, but I have never had one who could take the place of any of these three. Losing them, I could say, was the last and most painful stage of growing up.

33

DOWN TO EARTH

———

1955–1958

A T SOME POINT during the 1980s, when my grandson Eric was attending Stanford, he insisted that I go to see the movie *ET* with him. I am very fond of Eric, and I have never had much ability to refuse my children's requests, much less a grandchild's, so eventually we went. The movie told a simple story about the troubles that a creature from another planet encounters on earth. My grandson, my son, and my editor-collaborator all claim that the film character ET and I have more in common than our initials.[1]

Theodore von Kármán was the first to suggest that he and I, and other émigrés from Hungary in the 1930s, had an extraterrestrial origin. A curious preponderance of Hungarians played highly visible roles before and during World War II: Theodore von Kármán, the tireless advocate of U.S. Air Force preparedness and the founder of the Air Force Scientific Advisory Board, made great contributions to the aeronautics of U.S. planes; Leo Szilárd, the first to envision the atomic bomb and the initiator of the action that brought the need for its development to the attention of President Roosevelt; John von Neumann, who, as one of the foremost mathematicians of the century, made fundamental contributions to work on the atomic bomb and the hydrogen bomb and developed the necessary computational resources for the development of such weapons; and Eugene Wigner, whose work on symmetry was fundamental in applications of quantum mechanics and whose work on nuclear structure was most helpful, played a leading role in reactor design. As

---

[1] Perhaps it is our bewilderment over some human behavior; or perhaps all nonagenarians can be considered extraterrestrials of a sort: Surely the world we live in bears little resemblance to the world we entered.

the reader knows, I was also active in several of these affairs. People therefore asked: What is it about Hungarians?

Von Kármán, the oldest member of the group, gave the secret away: He admitted that we were Martians.[2] We had settled first in a little-known country in central Europe, he explained, so that we could assume a reasonable approximation of human behavior and have a credible explanation for our accent.

My own explanation of the seeming preponderance of Hungarians in defense work was that we were all survivors of a shipwreck. The history of Hungary during the twentieth century provides a fairly complete illustration of the lack of military prowess and its perils. When Hungary was defeated in World War I, the country was stripped of half of its citizens. It then became a dictatorship, first of the extreme left, then of the right. Defeated again in World War II, it became a captive colony of a less-developed but more powerful totalitarian régime. Those events cost hundreds of thousands of Hungarians their lives; and those left alive lost their freedom. Small wonder that emigrant Hungarians, with both their lives and their freedoms safe, were eager to secure the survival of their hard-won life raft.

The word *Martian* has its root in Mars, the Roman god of war; because I have spent the longer—if not better—portion of my professional life in one or another type of defense work, the description of me as a Martian has some ring of truth. And as a Martian, in spite of my personal pain during the 1954 to 1958 period, those years held some deep satisfactions for me. Of all the things I have done in my life, I am most proud of my role in the establishment and work of the Livermore laboratory.

In many respects, I was an anomaly at Livermore in 1955. The several hundred staff members were uniformly young, spirited, and vigorous. In the end, their mood proved contagious. Until 1958, airplanes collected samples of radioactive materials from clouds formed by U.S. nuclear tests in the Pacific. The deposits, gathered on filter papers, were placed in lead-lined carrying cases and flown back to Livermore as quickly as possible. The chemists then dissolved the filter papers with very hot, powerful reagents and analyzed the test debris qualitatively and quantitatively to determine how successfully the device had operated.

During those years, dissolving the filter papers meant placing them in beakers and heating them on hot plates; the chemists worked in glove boxes

---

[2] He also insisted that Zsa Zsa Gabor was one of the group. I know that he would have claimed she contributed to the morale of the war effort. Today, my secretary has a plaque hanging in her office, reputedly a replica of one that hung in a Hollywood studio during the 1940s. It reads: "Being Hungarian is not sufficient. You must also be talented."

in a building without air-conditioning. Such a task required great commitment. Ed Fleming, an energetic, personable chemist who joined the laboratory during the summer of 1955 (and made many contributions throughout his long career at Livermore), still recalls the physical misery of those summers. He claims that on Labor Day 1955, Livermore reached 114° F.

The weather in the valley at that time was hot and dry; and so, when a wing was finally added to the chemistry building in about 1958, the radiochemists, according to Ed Fleming, pointed out that the low humidity was affecting their experiments. They were hoping for air-conditioning, such as the computing people enjoyed. The chemists got their cooling, but it was provided by evaporative coolers, a system whereby air is blown through a wet filter. In this way, they exchanged intolerable heat with low humidity for intolerable humidity with slightly decreased heat.[3]

Livermore was an informal place. Aloha shirts, shorts, and sandals were common (and sensible) attire for several months of the year. Yet during these years, when unhappiness with the working conditions would have been fully justified, no one complained.[4] The dedication and spirit at Livermore was remarkable. Because many of the scientists commuted to Livermore in the early days, the laboratory set up dormitory rooms with bunk beds for those who needed to snatch a few hours sleep in the midst of a major project. Director Emeritus Roger Batzel, who was then assistant group leader for chemistry, recalled (with typical understatement): "We worked hard, with long hours. Sometimes our wives wouldn't see us for two or three days."

As I have mentioned, John Foster joined the lab in 1952. Originally, he worked on the controlled fusion program led by Dick Post. But after about nine months, Art Biehl, who up to then had been working on the small weapons program, suggested to Herb and me that John Foster might be a good person to take over the group. Although John was not immediately enthusiastic about the idea, Art's judgment was validated in early 1955, when the first of John's small weapons designs was tested in Nevada.

---

[3] Director Emeritus John Nuckolls joined the lab as a physicist in Harold Brown's design group during the summer of 1955 and was given what had been the ladies' room of the infirmary building for his office. He, too, recalls, "No air-conditioning, temperatures over a hundred degrees most days. It really was a young person's game."

[4] Roger Batzel added, "It was a really stimulating place to work. There was an administrative structure in the chemistry department, but it was certainly a very loose one. Everybody participated, everybody pitched in. Ken [Street, the group leader] did, I did. There were no exempt people when it came to doing the job. We simply ignored any administrative structure. We all felt responsible for seeing that the work got done."

When I was talking recently about those days, I was amused to hear John Foster describe the pre-mortem review committee (which examined the design before it was tested) as the "murder board." To a young group leader under scrutiny, I expect it did seem that way. John then recalled an approach of the board that I had forgotten.

> It was the task of the murder board to take the position that it didn't work. What's more they would visit that view on us: "This thing failed! Now tell us why." So you couldn't say, "But it didn't fail!" They were saying, "We have run the experiment, and it failed."[5] They didn't convince us that it wasn't going to go off, but they scared us enough that we did adjust it. So when we tested it, it had more power than we had intended.

Even if the device was not exactly as John had intended, John's device was Livermore's first successful test. The rest of the story, although John now is embarrassed by his youthful impulsiveness, illustrates the supportive role that Ernest Lawrence played during the last five years of his life.

> When I saw that [the test device] went off and it was clearly a high yield (even though I had never seen one of these things before), I went downstairs and called Professor Lawrence! Here I am, a kid out on the testing ground [in Nevada], and I decide I'm going to call Professor Lawrence. These things go off very early in the morning, so, obviously, he was in bed asleep. However, he acted as if he were already awake. I said, "I just wanted to tell you that it went off, and it's fine." He said, "I'll be right there."
>
> Now Professor Lawrence was in Berkeley. But somehow he got on an airplane and got out to the testing grounds around ten o'clock in the morning. Here I am, this kid, and I have Ernest Lawrence, Edward Teller, and Herb York walking around the parking lot talking about what did this mean and what should we do next.
>
> Weeks afterwards, I began to consider what Herb York must have thought when I came upstairs and said to him, "I called Professor Lawrence and he said he'll be right here." What outrageous behavior, actually outrageous!

I can't speak for Herb York, but I know that Ernest and I found nothing outrageous about John's behavior. We agreed that he was a wonderful young

---

[5] That approach sounds suspiciously like the technique the Reactor Safeguard Committee used on the reactor designers.

man who showed every promise of making major contributions to the nation. And he did.

Johnny von Neumann aided all the young weapons designers when he repeated the detailed work he had done at Los Alamos for our Livermore computer, working out the code relevant to thermonuclear reactions in such a way that a computer could perform the task. While Johnny von Neumann began the work and helped in its modification and expansion, the theorists at Livermore—Sid Fernbach, Chuck Leith, Carl Haussmann, Harold Brown, John Foster, John Nuckolls, and Roland Herbst (who joined the lab in mid-1954)—had soon developed Livermore's computer capabilities to the point that they were the most advanced in the nation.

In 1956, Johnny von Neumann was awarded the second Fermi Prize, given by the Atomic Energy Commission for contributions to the development of atomic energy.[6] His citation read: "For his scientific contribution to the the ory of fast computing machines and for his original contributions to their design and construction. More than anyone else, he foresaw the important and necessary role they would play in the control and use of atomic energy and to the general advancement of the arts and sciences for the benefit of mankind."

During that time, Johnny was concerned that the Soviets were about to combine their missile expertise with a nuclear weapon, thereby gaining a dangerous advantage. So he not only helped our weapons designers but also worked toward developing intercontinental ballistic missiles (ICBMs).

Under Theodore von Kármán's shepherding, the first rocket for military purposes, the Corporal, which had a range of about seventy-five miles, became operational about 1953. The system of missile guidance improved markedly in the mid-1950s, and by 1956, the Atlas, a long-range, liquid-fueled rocket, was being developed under the able direction of Colonel Benny Shriever, whom I had met as a member of the Air Force Scientific Advisory Board. But rocketry in the United States was hardly out of its infancy.[7]

---

[6] Enrico Fermi received the first award two weeks before his death in 1954. A year later, the AEC decided to make it an annual award and named it in his honor.

[7] By this time, Theodore von Kármán was seventy-five years old, but he had not lost his interest in life. He received an honorary degree from Northwestern University in 1956, and I saw him shortly afterwards in Berkeley. I asked about the ceremony, and he told me that hundreds of bright-eyed students received their bachelors' degrees, a few dozen received their masters, and a few got their doctorates. "Only I got an honorary degree," von Kármán said. "After the ceremony, the president of the university asked me if I was satisfied. I told him no. I would have much preferred to receive the bachelor's degree." Von Kármán, who died in 1963, remained, like Johnny von Neumann, a bon vivant to the end.

In 1955, Admiral Arleigh Burke had decided that the navy as well as the air force needed technical advice. Submarines powered by nuclear reactors were entering active service, and the new models under construction promised to be even better. The great advantage of a nuclear-powered submarine is its range, which, because the submarine needs to refuel so rarely, is limited mainly by the amount of time a crew can spend aboard without relief. Burke was looking for ways to increase the effectiveness of the submarine fleet.

The study session, which was called the Nobska conference after the nearby Nobska lighthouse, took place the following summer at Woods Hole, Massachusetts. In all, more than fifty people participated in the two-week-long meeting, including two of my old friends from the navy—Chick Hayward, who was then an admiral working in the Pentagon, and Hyman Rickover, who was also now an admiral—and Ivan Getting, whom I had met when he became chief scientist of the U.S. Air Force Scientific Advisory Board. Burke had also invited a group of scientists from Los Alamos, among them Carson Mark; and a group from Livermore that included Johnny Foster and me.

At some point during the conference, I suggested that we might be able to develop a nuclear warhead small enough to be carried on a missile that could be fired from a submarine. Carson Mark immediately claimed that it could not be done. We debated that possibility for almost half an hour before Burke put an end to it: "Stop this nonsense and tell me what can be done." Appreciating the combination of Livermore's talented young physicists and our recent advances, I made a concrete proposal (which remains classified): For a certain amount of money and in five years' time, Livermore could produce a lightweight thermonuclear weapon of a certain small size, suitable for transport by a small long-range missile and powerful enough to be effective.

Then Carson Mark made a tactical error. The navy might not have awarded a contract if Carson had stood by his earlier statement that the job could not be done, or said that I had exaggerated by a factor of ten, or said that such an undertaking required further study. But Carson offered an estimate. His cost estimate was higher, the explosive power was less, his estimates of the size and weight of the weapon were greater, and he added a couple more years to the development time. Burke then said, "All that doesn't make much difference. The important thing is that you now agree that it can be done. However, since Teller has promised us more, let him do it."

The results of that decision proved important to the development of the nation's defense and to the fledgling Livermore laboratory. The Nobska conference led in the development of a triad of nuclear deterrence—strategic bombers, land-based missiles, and submarine-based missiles. Before the collapse of the Soviet Union almost forty years later, the effectiveness of the air bases and the missile silos came under question because they could have been wiped out by a Soviet surprise attack; but, because of the difficulty of finding a submarine, the deterrent effect of submarine-based missiles remained uncompromised to the end of the cold war.

When I returned to the laboratory after the meeting, Harold Brown, the head of the thermonuclear weapons design group, let me know he was deeply worried that I had promised more than Livermore could deliver. He doubted that we could produce such a weapon in the next decade. As he pointed out, "I'm the person who has to make good on your estimate!" I did my best to reassure him, but he was still worried. Nonetheless, the young team of workers in his and John Foster's divisions took hold of the challenge with all their considerable energies.

One personally pleasant outgrowth of the Nobska conference was that, in the summer of the following year, I went to sea, an adventure that provided a sort of apprenticeship in naval affairs. Like most people, I was thoroughly impressed by the aerial powers demonstrated during the recent war. That led to my having some serious doubts about the efficacy of aircraft carriers, which seemed to me to be easy targets in comparison to the submarines, which were becoming more and more difficult to track. I voiced my opinions to my friend Chick Hayward. Chick strongly disagreed and apparently didn't stop talking about my mistaken opinions. In August 1957, Ernest Lawrence and I were invited to spend a few days on the flagship of our Mediterranean fleet.

Our host, Admiral C. R. (Cat) Brown had a well-developed sense of humor.[8] He was also serious about demonstrating to us that although an aircraft carrier was more expensive than a submarine, it was also more effective. I remember being taken out on another vessel that had been assigned as part of a group to intercept the carrier. I added my uninformed ingenuity to their ingenious informed efforts, but we—and all the other searchers—failed in the assignment. That, of course, led to considerable cheerfulness aboard the carrier on our return trip to port.

At the farewell party before we left the ship, I received a most unusual gift. During my stay on his ship, I had talked with Admiral Brown about

---

[8] A year before, tensions in the Middle East had been close to the boiling point. During the summer of 1956, Egypt had seized the Suez Canal and closed it to Israeli shipping. In the late fall that year, when Israel attempted to regain control of the canal militarily, Admiral Brown had received notice that his fleet was being placed on alert. A story still being recounted when I arrived on board stated that the admiral wired back, "I am now on alert. Whose side am I on?"

my concern that so few of our servicemen spoke a foreign language. I asserted (and still believe) that the ability to communicate with people of other lands would give our military a new dimension of effectiveness; but the admiral found my idea decidedly impractical. He presented me with a suit of armor (made of cardboard) bearing the name "Don Quixote."

When I was back in Livermore, I dictated a letter to the admiral and sincerely thanked him for all I had learned and for the pleasant time. I had recently hired an excellent secretary. When I told her to sign my letter "Edward Don Quixote Teller," she raised her eyebrows and asked, "Edward Donkey what?" (My accent in Spanish apparently provides about the same distortion of the language that it does in English.)

My new interests were mingled with the old. By 1955, the reactor safeguard committee had several accomplishments to show for six years of oversight. We had identified the hazards that could arise from the operation of reactors. We had warned against design defects, such as positive void coefficients, positive temperature coefficients, and Wigneritis. We had enumerated the source of accidents, including component or materials failure, earthquakes, sabotage, and human error. We had suggested safeguards to reduce and control such accidents including mechanical means, chemical means, and containment vessels. (However, we had overlooked the need for establishing standards for operator training.) We had examined reprocessing and the problem of waste disposal, although, at this writing, those recommendations have not yet been enacted. We had established a pattern for evaluating reactor sites in terms of meteorology, water systems, earthquake faults, and soil stability that stands largely unchanged today.

The chairman of the Advisory Committee for Reactor Safeguards (ACRS), Rogers McCullough, was a courageous leader, fully committed to the responsibility of insuring that U.S. nuclear reactors would operate without harming anyone. On April 15, 1955, I wrote to Rogers:

Dear Rogers,

I feel that the time has come for me to retire from the Committee. No person can be effective when serving too long on the same committee. New people and new ideas are required. An additional reason is the change in the situation now taking place. The main problem before the Committee at present is raised by the participation of industries. This is a problem of the utmost seriousness. . . . Since I know for certain that I am not able to give the proper amount of time and work to this problem, I feel the proper and honest procedure is to retire. . . .

... I feel that the problems which we are now facing are right now in the best possible hands. More specifically, I am sure that what YOU are doing is done as well as it possibly can be done. I feel sure that the good influence which the Committee exercised in the past will be exercised in a wider field in the future, and that the work of the Committee will go down as one of the really constructive forces in the atomic energy field. ...

Yours very sincerely, Edward

Having resigned, I got more deeply involved in the industrial side of reactors. Consulting with private companies taught me a lot, but in most cases my short visits did not produce significant results. The one exception was the work I began in the summer of 1956 with Freddie de Hoffman.

Freddie had stayed on at Los Alamos when I left, but after a few years, he decided that he could accomplish more in industry. He went to work first for General Dynamics, and later, with the help of John Jay Hopkins, head of General Dynamics, he began his own company, General Atomic. When Freddie asked me to help, I did so. I recall the day when we drove around in Southern California and found a beautiful site a few miles north of San Diego, not far from La Jolla. Then and there, Freddie talked about the location of the circular central building that was to be surrounded by buildings housing the various projects.

I suggested that one of his first projects should be the construction of a small foolproof reactor. I had been dreaming about and wishing for such a reactor for some time. The problem is by no means an easy one because fools are extremely ingenious in conducting their folly; this has been demonstrated over the years both in the Three Mile Island accident and at Chernobyl. The objective I had in mind was to produce a reactor that could be used in hospitals to produce short-lived radioactivities for diagnostic procedures and treatments, and in universities for research.

Freddie's immediate objection to such an installation was that reactors are dangerous unless handled by real experts. "All right," I said, "let us construct a reactor that is safe even in the hands of a young graduate student." So Freddie called together a group of people to plan a small, very safe reactor. The result was the Triga reactor.[9]

---

[9] The name is an acronym for its purposes—Training, Research, and Isotope (production)—and its maker—General Atomic.

The first successful design was due primarily to the suggestions of Freeman Dyson, a physicist friend from Princeton, whose practical proposals are as ingenious as his theoretical work. The Triga is a uranium reactor, well enriched in uranium-235, the fuel homogeneously dispersed in zirconium hydride and cooled by water. The Triga—like the Swimming Pool reactor designed earlier at Oak Ridge—has a negative temperature coefficient; that is, a rise in temperature produces a decrease in neutron multiplication, thereby shutting down the fission reaction.

But the Triga avoids the problem of the earlier design by modifying the fuel element so that the fuel rod itself has a negative temperature coefficient.[10] The hydrogen in the zirconium hydride in the fuel element, when heated, transfers energy from the protons to the fission-producing neutrons that had been slowed down. The temperature increase of those thermalized neutrons decreases their ability to cause fission. All that took place promptly in the fuel element itself, without having to wait, as in the Swimming Pool reactor, for the energy to diffuse from the fuel element to the cooling water.

Some years later, I watched with satisfaction as control rods were rapidly withdrawn from an early model of the Triga reactor. The reactor gave an audible pop, and then became inoperable; after half an hour, the fuel rods had cooled and were again at the proper temperature to allow fission. But, as we already knew, the Triga posed absolutely no danger from exploding steam or anything else. We had proved that if more energy developed than could be carried away by the cooling water, the fuel elements, because of the higher temperature, would stop releasing energy, and the Triga would shut itself down before any damage could be done.

The Triga ultimately turned out to be quite profitable. Over the next decade, General Atomic produced and sold more than seven dozen Triga reactors to hospitals and research centers, both domestically and internationally. Not one has ever malfunctioned, even when operated by students.

But the best thing to come out of that summer project for me personally was my introduction to Genevieve Greteman, who served as the secretary to our Triga group. I seem to be helpless without a good secretary. I cannot

---

[10] The temperature increase causes the uranium nuclei to move faster. The nuclei then not only undergo fission but also absorb neutrons. Neutron absorption in nuclei occurs only at specific narrow energy ranges (called lines), a phenomenon called *resonance*. Temperature motion of the nuclei effectively broadens those regions. The fuel rods of the Triga were designed to cause more neutron absorption and less fission when heating occurs.

locate papers or books, I forget what tasks (other than theorizing) I need to complete, and I cannot commit the English language in understandable form to paper. Most people think the last job is connected with stenography, but in my case, shorthand is unnecessary: I do not think that fast. A much more important requirement, as far as I am concerned, is that my secretary be able to read my mind. That is obviously an acquired characteristic, although a predisposition to it may be innate.

In those days, it was helpful if my secretary could drive and at the same time take mental notes. Much of the time that I had available to work with my secretary seemed to occur while I was traveling between offices or between office and airport. Although I persist in claiming to be an acceptable driver, I have found that my secretaries seemed less distracted if, when we were talking, they drove rather than I. Gen was able to meet all those requirements.[11] I was happy (having asked Freddie if I could do so) that when I asked Gen to join the laboratory staff, she accepted. I did not know at the time that I was shortly to become director in Livermore, but I know now that without Gen, I could not have managed.[12]

Most of my visits to Southern California during these years involved visiting my friends Bill Libby, Bill and Nancy McMillan, Albert Latter (who had taken himself and his fine chess skills back to the Rand Corporation), and Dave and Helen Griggs. The McMillans have a favorite story about one of those visits, which I had forgotten until they recounted it. During my stay,

---

[11] Gen was working for me by the time I wrote to Admiral Brown. She continued to work for me at the laboratory for the next ten years, but when her daughter was born, she left for several years. She came back to work for the Hertz Foundation to help Mici with the California program; not long after that, she returned to Livermore, where she continued to work as an administrator to the associate director for physics, and then as assistant to the director. She is now officially retired but continues to help out a few hours a week. Throughout its existence, Livermore has owed a great debt of gratitude to Genevieve Greteman Phillips.

[12] For some years in California, I had three offices: one in the physics department at Berkeley, one at the Berkeley Radiation Laboratory, and one in the old barracks building at the Livermore facility. Ruth Brockett, who had been my secretary at Los Alamos and then at the University of Chicago, was my first secretary at Livermore. The young recruits at Livermore provided a steady stream of company, in part because Ruth always had a pot of coffee available; but in larger measure, I suspect, they came because of Ruth's supportive, kindly nature—which I, too, enjoyed.

Ruth retired after a few years, and in mid-1955, Paula de Luca, Ernest Lawrence's able assistant, was temporarily taking care of my needs in Berkeley (in addition to taking care of Ernest's office), and Joan Jaffrey had left her administrative job to help out in my Livermore office. Both women were anxious to return to their regular posts.

the McMillans together with their daughter Janet and I often had dinner together at Taix. The restaurant served family style at tables for six—three on each side. Bill recalls that on one occasion

> The seating arrangement was that Janet, who was four or five, sat next to Nancy on one side of the table, and Edward sat across from Janet, and I was next to him. He and I were talking about the Thomas-Fermi equation of state, when a skinny man and a very buxom woman joined us. The man sat next to Nancy and didn't say anything, but the woman who sat next to me immediately started talking.
>
> You could tell from her conversation that she was an astrologer. She had to know everybody's birthday. Janet, being a friendly puppy, responded at once, and Nancy talked with her, too. The woman, however, wasn't satisfied. She kept nudging me: "When's your birthday?" After a while, I told her my birthday, but she couldn't get Edward's attention. So finally, she leaned way over the table—getting out of her chair so she could get a straight shot at him—and said, "Hey, bushy eyebrows, when's your birthday?"
>
> Edward said, "January 15," and went back to our conversation. But she wasn't dismissable. She said, "Well, that would make you a businessman. On the other hand, you look like an artist." Without any hesitation, Edward said, "Ma'am, in my profession, I combine those two talents. I am a pickpocket." Silence reigned at her end of the table for a considerable time.[13]

I don't recall the incident, but a sense of nonsensical fun did prevail when we got together socially, so I have no reason to contradict Bill's memory.

During these years, I became a closer friend of Dave Griggs, a geophysicist at UCLA, whom I had first met on the Air Force Scientific Advisory Board. Dave, because of his personal convictions, had testified strongly against Oppenheimer, and following the hearing had been accused by the media of having had a malicious role in bringing about the Oppenheimer hearing. I knew Dave as a different kind of person from the man those articles described. Forthright and brusque, Dave was a man whose personal standards of honor were extremely high. We were well-matched chess partners, and I enjoyed my visits with him and with his charming and lovely wife, Helen. Dave, an excellent geophysicist, made considerable contributions to our work, as the next chapter will show.

---

[13] Bill added, "The woman never got the joke, but she was not offended. After dinner, when she lit up her cigar, she offered one to Edward and me and invited us to come see her some time."

International political events during these years also had a resonance in my personal life. During the mid-1950s, President Eisenhower, whose policies I generally liked, committed what seemed to me a terrible mistake. He often talked publicly about pushing back the Iron Curtain, but he laid no plans to accomplish that goal. Hungarians, taking his words at face value, felt encouraged to revolt; when they did, they were not supported. For several days in early November 1956, freedom fighters trapped in the radio station in Budapest pleaded for help against the tanks and armed forces of the Soviet Union that had rolled into Budapest. No help ever came. The Hungarian revolution ended with its bloody suppression.

The Hungarian uprising did have one positive consequence for my family. My sister Emmi's son, János Kirz, like thousands of other young students, escaped to the West in the aftermath. He made his way first to Vienna, where my childhood friend Lizi Grátz took him into her small apartment— together with more than a dozen other young refugees—until we could arrange for him to come to Berkeley and live with us.

I was happy that he was, at last, where my sister and mother had longed for him to be—safe in the United States. Within a few months, János, then nineteen, had begun to ready himself for enrollment at the University of California, and had endeared himself to thirteen-year-old Paul and ten-year-old Wendy. To my eye, he had adjusted rapidly and easily to the actualities of American life.[14] I only hoped that my mother and sister were not missing him as badly as I suspected they were.

I took great interest at that time in the discovery of anti-protons in Berkeley. They are related to protons in the same way as positrons are to electrons. It became at once obvious that any material we know of could also become available as anti-matter, although matter and antimatter could not coexist. I concluded that no antimatter could be found in our galaxy. But could one consider an anti-galaxy?

My thoughts had a more immediate effect on literature than on physics. In December 1956, *The New Yorker* published a letter (in the "Department of Amplification") that I had written.[15]

---

[14] Years later, he told me that he had spent a great deal of time during his early months looking everywhere to find unemployed, hungry American workers! The Soviets had an excellent program of science instruction, which János demonstrated, but I was kept blissfully unaware of the effectiveness of their political indoctrination.

[15] *The New Yorker*, December 15, 1956, pp. 164–166.

To the Editors, *The New Yorker*
Dear Sirs:

In a recent issue of the *New Yorker*, I found the following poem describing the meeting of Dr. Edward Anti-Teller with an imagined person differing from Anti-Teller only in the sign of the charges carried by the particles of his body.

Perils of Modern Living

A kind of matter directly opposed to the matter known on earth exists somewhere else in the universe, Dr. Edward Teller has said. . . . He said there may be anti-stars and anti-galaxies, entirely composed of such anti-matter. Teller did not describe the properties of anti-matter except to say there is none of it on earth, and that it would explode on contact with ordinary matter.—*San Francisco Chronicle.*

> *Well up beyond the tropostrata*
> *There is a region stark and stellar*
> *Where, on a streak of anti-matter,*
> *Lived Dr. Edward Anti-Teller.*
> *Remote from Fusion's origin,*
> *He lived unguessed and unawares*
> *With all his anti-kith and kin,*
> *And kept macassars on his chairs.*
> *One morning, idling by the sea,*
> *He spied a tin of monstrous girth*
> *That bore three letters: A.E.C.*
> *Out stepped a visitor from Earth.*
> *Then, shouting gladly o'er the sands,*
> *Met two who in their alien ways*
> *Were like as lentils. Their right hands*
> *Clasped, and the rest was gamma rays.*[16]

The meeting, as described, is interesting, and tempts me to offer some scientific details.

---

[16]Right and left are reversed in an anti-universe, so if the meeting had proceeded that far, Anti-Teller and I would have been alerted to the danger of clasping hands by noting that we were extending the wrong hand.

I do not believe that Anti-Teller lives in our galaxy, since it is unlikely that there are any anti-stars or anti-planets in our milky-way system. On the other hand, anti-galaxies may exist. The main questions are how to get there and what to expect on arrival. (I shall not worry about space travel. Every child knows that it is feasible.)

The distance is somewhat of an obstacle. Light takes more than a million years to travel to the next spiral nebula. Fortunately, Einstein has shown that a million years will seem like only a few years if one travels fast enough, and so an explorer might arrive during his lifetime (though not during the lifetime of his friends whom he left behind on earth). As he approaches the anti-galaxy, he will be attracted by anti-gravity. Gravity and anti-gravity are one and the same thing. Here some may disagree, but upon second thoughts they will find they are wrong.

As the traveler enters the anti-galaxy, his ship will be bombarded by anti-particles. This bombardment will heat the spaceship. He must not crowd the speed limit (which is the speed of light) or his ship will melt. Furthermore, the resulting radiation will kill him before he has penetrated as much as one-millionth of the anti-galaxy. But let us not give up; Anti-Teller may live near the edge of the anti-galaxy.

At a distance of about two hundred miles from the surface of Anti-Earth, the intruder will surely be killed by the annihilation radiation that is produced as the space ship begins to dip into the anti-atmosphere. Only a miracle, or an unexpected development in biophysics, can save him. Before he gets down to an altitude of a hundred miles, the spaceship will collapse, and nothing can save him.

But let us arrange a meeting between Anti-Teller and Teller on a truly neutral ground: in space. If they are appropriately dressed (anti-space suit and space suit respectively) and if they carefully avoid the escape of any anti-molecules or molecules, they may approach without danger. They can see each other without trouble because light and anti-light are the same. Upon contact, however, a violent explosion will occur. Parts of Anti-Teller and Teller will produce an assortment of ephemeral particles (known as mesons, hyperons, and anti-hyperons) and a great number of more stable products such as nuclear fragments, anti-nuclear fragments, electrons, positrons, neutrinos, anti-neutrinos, and gamma rays. The remainder will fly apart in opposite directions as vapor and anti-vapor. All this will happen faster than anti-thought, which is probably the same as thought.

In spite of this inauspicious prospect, I was pleased that the *New Yorker* mentioned me. Come to think of it, only Anti-Teller was mentioned by name in the poem, but I am confident that somewhere in an anti-galaxy, *The Anti-New Yorker* devoted some pleasant lines to

Yours Sincerely,

Edward Teller

The author of the poem, identified only as H.P.F., was Harold P. Furth, an astrophysicist who had joined the theoretical group about this time to work on the magnetic fusion program. Harold had written the poem to tease me; but after doing so, he began to worry that I would be offended and signed the poem only with his initials. I thought Harold's poem was delightful, and as I enjoyed pointing out to him, because *The New Yorker* pays by the word, my not-nearly-so-clever two-cents-worth earned me several times as much money as he had made.

The members of the magnetic fusion group and the other theoreticians in the physics group during those years were uniformly outstanding: Al and Richard Latter, Bob LeLevier, Ernie Martinelli, Stirling Colgate, Montgomery Johnson, Mark Mills, Nick Christofilos, Harold Furth, and Dick Post, to name a few.[17] Nick Christofilos was a most welcome addition to the laboratory. An incident connected with our first meeting with Nick illustrates the not-always-serious effects of secrecy.

Nick Christofilos had been working independently and without clearance on magnetic fusion and had come up with an interesting innovation. We invited him to talk to us after a morning meeting at the Berkeley laboratory. The gathering was held in a big lecture hall equipped with electrically-operated blackboards. During lunch, the room had been specially sanitized for Nick's arrival: stray paper collected, wastebaskets emptied, the blackboard scrubbed so that no trace of previous work remained.

---

[17] One of the most remarkable papers produced by the physics group was a correct description of the working and effects of a full astrophysical explosion, known as supernova. Stirling Colgate and Montgomery Johnson outlined the sequence of events that occur in a star with a mass considerably in excess of that of the sun, when all the thermonuclear fuel near the center of the star is exhausted and the star collapses. It was already recognized that under those circumstances, the great concentration of gravitational energy in such a star starts a peculiar chain of nuclear reactions that eventually result in the production of the heavy elements. The novelty in Montgomery and Stirling's work was their recognition that a shock wave, taking its origin in the center of the star and accelerating as it spread into the less dense regions of the star, was the first step in producing cosmic rays. That work is still cited as one of the more important papers in our current understanding of the universe.

Because of classification rules, we were allowed to listen to Nick, but we were not allowed to comment, even to the extent of telling Nick whether what he was proposing was old or new.[18] Nick took our silence in his stride and, writing industriously, soon covered the blackboard with his work. When he started to erase it, someone said, "Just push that button and another board will come down."

The underlying board had been overlooked by the security people and was covered with calculations related to one of the high-security projects currently going on. There was a sharp intake of breath as Nick, oblivious to what had happened, set to work erasing the board. He was joined in his effort by one of the security people, who worked even more industriously. Nick joined the magnetic fusion group at Livermore not long afterward.[19]

As the incident shows, a great many physicists in a great many places, many of them enjoying complete freedom of discussion, were working on controlled fusion at that time. I had repeatedly argued that the topic should be declassified. Lewis Strauss disagreed. Then, in about 1957, I. V. Kurchatov, a good Soviet physicist and the former leader of their atomic bomb project, came to England and reported experiments and results identical to our own. I asked Lewis, "What are we keeping secret?" Lewis finally gave in and allowed us to present our work at the Atoms for Peace Conference in 1958.

In the fall of 1957, the Soviets launched the first unmanned space vehicle, Sputnik, a striking demonstration of their abilities in rocketry. (They also announced, almost simultaneously, that they had intercontinental ballistic missiles, which Sputnik had made obvious.) Interestingly enough, Livermore was the only facility in the United States that had a computer code in place capable of tracking Sputnik's course. The advent of Sputnik gave a real impetus to our own rocketry program. Suddenly, the concerns that we Martians had been describing were realities. The emotional climate changed overnight. In mid-November 1957, *Time* ran an article about American physicists that featured me on the cover.

---

[18] Nick presented an interesting approach, but the technology necessary to put it into practice was not available until two decades later.

[19] Nick's ingenuity was once again demonstrated when some of the ideas he discussed that day so convincingly were incorporated in the Strategic Defense Initiative work. Ed McMillan and Luis Alvarez proposed an electron-beam weapon during the 1950s. Although I funded the E-beam research during my term as director because money for it was available, I was not enthusiastic about its possibilities. In the 1980s, Nick's idea of using short bursts from the electron beam to hammer one's way through the atmosphere proved very useful.

A few days later, I was giving a speech in Kansas City. During my speech, I praised Truman's determination in withstanding communist aggression following World War II. After my talk, one of the organizers of the meeting mentioned that Truman was in Kansas City celebrating his seventieth birthday. "Would you like to meet him?" he inquired. I said that I would. So the next day, former President Harry S. Truman and I got together and had a lengthy conversation about several general topics; in the midst of our talk, Truman told me a story about trying to raise money for his memorial library in Independence.

When Truman had talked with representatives from the tobacco industry, they volunteered a considerable gift if he would write a short statement about tobacco that could be used publicly. He claimed he wrote: "Tobacco is an example of the fair cultural exchange between the Europeans and the Native Americans. The Indians gave the Europeans tobacco, and the Europeans gave the Indians syphilis." Truman concluded, "The tobacco industry never made their promised gift."

About this time, I became involved in yet another project. Public television was undergoing expansion, and the first public station in the Bay Area of California, KQED, had just begun broadcasting. In those days, I was excited about the potential improvement that television could bring to public education about science and often said so. The station soon asked me to collaborate on just such an effort. As a result, I offered a program on the atom in 1955; and then, beginning in January 1958, I offered a series of twelve programs based on my undergraduate Physics 10 course that was carried by an additional thirty public television channels.

Although the first program showed me playing Bach's Prelude and Fugue in C Major, most of them—complete with a few students and laboratory pieces—consisted of me discussing the surprises of twentieth-century physics. Relativity had made the time at which an event occurs dependent on the motion of the observer and thereby had made future and past somewhat similar to right and left. I went on to quantum mechanics, which describes atoms and their components not as particles alone or waves alone but as having properties of both. Without describing the formalism, I tried to point out the novel nature of our understanding of atoms and the universe. People commented favorably on the program, but I obviously underestimated the difficulty of presenting those ideas in a way that they could become widely understood.

While work on my television program was going on, I had a second postwar meeting with my dear friend Carl Friedrich von Weizsäcker, this time in the United States. He visited me in Berkeley, and we spent much of our time together debating. I believe we both enjoyed the exercise in spite of our different conclusions. A quarter of a century earlier, Carl Friedrich and I had enjoyed many political discussions. Of course, in the intervening period, I had become a somewhat different person. A similar statement can be made about Carl Friedrich. Carl Friedrich had hated the Nazis, yet he now was actively looking for ways in which the German government could help rehabilitate former Nazis. He had also hated the Soviets, yet he was now looking for ways in which the free world could get along with them.

Strangely, almost paradoxically, our friendship remained unchanged. We had always disagreed in a friendly manner; now we just disagreed about new subjects. One such disagreement was about nuclear weapons. Carl Friedrich, who had been assigned to the German atomic bomb project during World War II, now felt that all work on nuclear weapons should stop. I was in the middle of such work and was about to take an active part not only in the technical aspects but in the politics of preserving the work itself.

After hours and days of discussion, Carl Friedrich appeared to come around to my point of view. I am grateful to him for the opportunity to clarify in my own mind why I wanted to do the very thing upon which I was embarking. Plenty of American physicists shared Carl Friedrich's opposition to nuclear weapons, but none understood my point of view, or forced me, in a patient way, to explain my reasons.

I remember that one of my technical arguments was that the work on nuclear weapons of low yields (less or much less than a thousand tons of TNT equivalent), could be decisive in deterring a conflict that would otherwise be fought primarily with tanks and airplanes. That argument had the most effect on Carl Friedrich, and that fact had a real influence on my thinking.

About that time, Nikita Khrushchev, then premier of the Soviet Union as well as head of the Communist Party, proposed an informal test ban that would be in effect while negotiations for a more permanent test ban treaty were worked out. In spite of a few highly publicized liberal reforms in the period following Stalin's régime, the Soviet Union had remained a tightly controlled, secretive, totalitarian state. The dangers of a treaty with such a nation were obvious to me, and I talked almost incessantly about the topic for many months.

But mine was not the majority opinion. Finding a way to prevent the release of radioactivity to the atmosphere had become so important to some people that they were calling for a ban on all testing of nuclear explosives. The presence of even minute amounts of radioactivity in the atmosphere is easy to detect, so for atmospheric nuclear explosions of a significant size, the methods of detection appeared to be adequate. Test-ban proponents claimed that underground tests could also be detected on seismographs because they cause effects similar to earthquakes. The tests could be distinguished from natural earthquakes by their sharply timed energy release and, of course, by their unusual location. Given the nature of muffling, I thought those arguments incomplete.

The current director of the laboratory, Herb York, leaned considerably toward approval of such a treaty. The issue never came to a head between us as Herb left to become Director of Defense Research and Engineering (DDR&E) at the Department of Defense in Washington, D.C., on March 1, 1958.

Herb's resignation from Livermore presented a further problem. As I have mentioned, there were several candidates for director—headed by Mark Mills, who was then head of the theoretical division. All the candidates were young and somewhat untested. Mills was motivated, and, as Roger Batzel later described him, "a very intelligent doer." Mills did things methodically but quickly. As Mills was young and without much experience as an administrator, I reluctantly suggested to Ernest Lawrence (just before his final illness) that I take over as laboratory director for a few months until Mills was ready to take over.

The tests that were scheduled for the Pacific that year in April had assumed steadily increasing importance: Because of the likelihood of a test ban, they might be the last tests that we would run for many years. All the tests were extremely important to fulfilling our promise to the navy. Dedicated and scrupulously responsible, Mark Mills went out to the Pacific to oversee the test preparations in early spring.

On April 7, 1958, he died when the helicopter carrying him to an atoll where one of the tests was to be held crashed in shallow water. The two pilots and the other passenger escaped, but Mark drowned. It was a terrible loss to all of us as well as to his family.

In June, I, too, went to the test site at Bikini to watch another test. The setting was as lovely as ever, the test went well. One of the laboratory people rescued a pair of giant clam shells from the depths for me (they still stand in my yard at Stanford); and I swam and enjoyed a great many barbecues on the beach. But the quality of my life was different from what it had been.

I wrote to Maria about this time:

> It was good to talk to you, even for a few microseconds. Of course it was terrible of you not to contradict me when you said nothing to my statement that I am no longer a physicist. The more so, because it is true.

I have acquired strong habits. I am doing something all the time, without being in a hurry (at least I am not always in a hurry). And what I do is mostly *not* thinking. I just try to do what is best under the circumstances, and mostly it is fairly obvious what is best—at least given all the things I did before. . . .

I do not know whether it is possible to go back to physics. From my own point of view, it is the greatest challenge. Of course there are so many physicists these days, and I am—as I said—not ambitious to compete. I will have to see how much fun I get out of it these days.

Paul has been working on me. He wants me to get back to physics. He sees quite exactly that nowadays when I come home for dinner I do not declare that I cannot be disturbed.

The world is strange. I find no difficulties with teen-agers and none with administration in Livermore. I only have something of a feeling of unfinished business.

But I also feel that I do not want to quit the fight about nuclear explosives. A writer (Don Robinson) and I have discussed the possibility of a book called (perhaps) *How To Be an Optimist in the Atomic Age*. If I write it, more people will be mad.

One thing is clear: there is not time enough between planes (and do come to California).

That letter could serve as the synopsis of the story of how a Martian came down to earth.

34

THE DIRECTORSHIP

1958–1960

A FEW YEARS AGO, Freeman Dyson's son, George Dyson, paid me a visit in connection with his own interesting new book, *Darwin Among the Machines*.[1] Like his father, he is thoughtful and literate. He kindly brought along a transcription he had made of a letter that Freeman had written to his parents in the fall of 1958, following a visit to the Livermore laboratory.

> Livermore was wildly exciting. The days I was there were the last days before the test-ban went into effect, and they were throwing together everything they possibly could to give it a try before the guillotine came down. Everyone was desperate and also exhilarated. Edward Teller, who is head of the Lab talked to me quite a lot about his plans. He was in very good spirits and pressed me with invitations to come and work for him. There are so many wild ideas and enthusiastic people at this place, I almost felt sorry to come back here at the end of the week.
>
> A lot of the talk at Livermore was about cheating the test-ban. We found a lot of ways to cheat which would be quite impossible for any instruments to detect. The point of this is not that the Livermore people themselves intend to cheat, but we are convinced the Russians can cheat as much as they want any time they want, without being found out.

The circumstances surrounding Freeman's visit were these: Early in the summer of 1958, the news arrived that President Eisenhower and Premier

---

[1] George B. Dyson, *Darwin Among the Machines: The Evolution of Global Intelligence* (Cambridge, Mass.: Perseus Books, 1997).

Khrushchev had agreed that an interim ban on testing would begin on November 1, 1958, and would continue for the duration of the negotiations on a permanent test ban treaty. My family and I were on a brief vacation in Yosemite, but I hurried back to help with work on the last permitted tests.

The test ban made fulfilling our commitment to the navy at the Nobska conference (to develop warheads small and lightweight enough to be fired from submarines) less certain. We had several new designs, but only testing could determine whether they worked. The Livermore laboratory went on a six-day week to complete as many tests as possible for the fall tests because we might not be able to test again for a considerable time.

As it turned out, a design under Carl Haussmann's direction provided the explosive suitable for Polaris missiles; but Carl did not receive immediate accolades for this accomplishment. Recently, he recalled an incident that I had forgotten. On the day of his test in the summer of 1958, the AEC General Advisory Committee was meeting at Livermore. Carl, who was then in his early thirties and not completely self-assured, described the test to what he saw as an august body and then gave an estimate of the yield.

That day, his group had conducted a little sabotage. In the past, when the group gave Carl an estimated range of yields, he had submitted only their highest yield estimate. That usually resulted in the test's giving a lower yield than predicted, which made it appear that something had gone wrong with the device. Unbeknownst to Carl, the group gave him an upper limit estimate on that test that was really their lower limit. That way, they felt, no one could assume that anything had gone wrong with the device.

When Carl reported back to the AEC committee, he had to tell them that the test gave twice the yield he had predicted. Carl was embarrassed, particularly when one of the committee members implied that Carl really didn't know what he was doing.

But I was delighted with the test result. Carl and his team had designed a device with capabilities that would more than fulfill the promise I had made to the navy at Nobska. As I told Carl after the meeting, I'd much prefer that people do too much rather than too little. The contribution that this work made to our nation's ability to deter attack cannot be overestimated.

On a completely different testing question, I had had a brief but decisive conversation with Herb York, the outgoing director. Herb felt it was important to do a high-altitude test, and so we did one in the 1958 test series. The test shot was hundreds of miles away from the Hawaiian Islands, but it disabled the electrical system there with a pulse of electromagnetism (EMP). That was the first clear evidence we had for the existence of that phenomenon.

Although I had volunteered to be director of the Livermore laboratory in early spring 1958, it was not a position I had wanted. Being director meant I had to give up teaching at Berkeley.[2] The only class I could fit into my schedule as the director was my Physics 10 course. Because it had achieved some popularity on campus, I felt it important to continue the course.[3] With such a light teaching load, I had to vacate my Berkeley office in the physics department.

I also had to resign my membership in the General Advisory Committee of the AEC (a post I had assumed only recently), which bothered me less. But in addition to these things, I had to give up an interesting and financially beneficial invitation to do consulting with the Rockefeller Family Trust.[4] In short, I had to sharply curtail my activities.

But most important, I do not enjoy administrative work, and I never imagined that I could run the laboratory effectively. I took the directorship because I felt it important that the laboratory have as effective a spokesperson as possible to explain the importance of continued testing to our national defense. The weapons laboratories, Los Alamos and Livermore, had a natural interest in testing: It connected our work with reality. But because Los Alamos was rather moderate in support of further tests, the second laboratory had to do the bulk of the work in presenting the consequences of a test ban.

I had two reasons for my strong support of continued testing. The first, hardly ever mentioned, is that testing has the obvious purpose of increasing knowledge. Throughout my life, I have had a strong conscious and unconscious addiction to knowledge. Suppressing knowledge seems to me (and this holds at present more than ever) wrong and impractical. Obviously, knowledge

---

[2] I was involved enough in educational issues that I was asked to give the keynote address at the White House Conference on Education in 1959.

[3] In 1959, my son, Paul, was about to graduate from high school, and he came to my Physics 10 lectures at Berkeley. Paul didn't want to be criticized for being too scholarly, so he persuaded two friends to take the course with him. I had begun teaching Paul relativity theory when he was five or six. I showed him the moon and told him it was so far away that light takes more than a second to travel from it to us, and nothing can travel faster than light. Paul asked, "Why?" I told him that was a complicated story that I couldn't tell him right then. Paul was properly brought up, so he didn't ask again until breakfast the next morning. I fed him little bits and incomplete answers, never too much at one time, and he understood the theory of relativity by the time he was twelve. The first lecture in Physics 10 starts with relativity. I came to the point of saying, "Two events that are simultaneous to one observer need not be simultaneous to another." Paul nudged his neighbor and asked, "Do you believe that?" His friend answered, "No, but I don't think *he* is to be blamed for it."

[4] I did continue my work with Nelson Rockefeller, which I will describe in the next chapter.

can be used and misused. But prevention of misuse, I firmly believe, must be kept separate from limitations on knowledge. Those who believe that we are not yet ready for some knowledge consider themselves members of a world aristocracy that is ahead of everyone else in its value judgments. Some of the horrible events of the twentieth century may appear to justify their opinion. Nonetheless, I cannot help opposing aristocracy and elitism, whether they be an elite of nobility, race, money, morals, or even knowledge itself.

The second, practical, and obvious reason to oppose test limitation is the difficulty of enforcing such a limitation and of checking whether the limitation has been violated. But my point of view was not that of the majority of politically active scientists; nor was it the public's view, given the multiplication of alarmist statements about ill effects from the small amounts of radioactivity that had accumulated in the atmosphere as a result of nuclear testing.

The public perception of radioactivity is easier to understand in retrospect. At the time of the Hiroshima bombing, millions of people learned all at once that a new, extremely powerful weapon existed and had killed almost 100,000 people, several thousand of them by an unknown disease, radiation sickness. One would have expected immediate worldwide fear and revulsion. But World War II had killed 50 million people, and the atomic bomb brought a speedy end to that war. The result was a feeling of relief that overrode all other sentiments.

But in the following years, objections to everything associated with radioactivity—from weapons to reactors—kept increasing and spreading.

Antinuclear feelings came to a peak first with the 1954 *Bravo* test at the Bikini atoll. The crew of a Japanese fishing vessel, which was in a proscribed area, was exposed to considerable radiation; and one man died shortly after his return to Japan. (This was the worst accident in the history of U.S. testing.) That one death appeared to have made a deeper impression on the American public than all the casualties in Hiroshima and Nagasaki. That sounds absurd, but it isn't. The death of many thousands of people goes beyond the imagination. A great disaster becomes something abstract. An individual tragedy is real.[5]

---

[5] One should notice another, more remarkable, circumstance. In spite of the deaths from the atomic bombings, and the death of the fisherman on the *Lucky Dragon,* the Japanese are now in the forefront of nuclear engineering. They are building excellent nuclear reactors. We are not. It is perhaps impossible to completely understand the motivation of individuals; is it any easier to understand the motivation of nations?

The concern about the effects of any amount of radiation grew rapidly from this point; eventually, even the tiny amount of radioactive material circulating in the atmosphere became a grave concern. Claims were made that atmospheric contamination from testing had led to an increased incidence of cancer, and lawsuits were filed. Yet, the only basis for those claims was the exaggerated fear of radiation. The annual amount of radiation received from atmospheric nuclear testing at its highest level (in 1963) was 13 mrem.[6]

That dose did not occur at once, in what is called a prompt dose, but over the course of a long period.[7] The amount of radiation that accrued as a result of nuclear testing at its peak can be compared to that received by an individual who for a year has a luminous dial clock in the house (9 mrem) and cooks on a gas range (6–9 mrem).[8]

But such facts did nothing to change public opinion. A great outcry for the cessation of nuclear testing was underway. Shortly after I became director, in the spring of 1958, I was involved in a debate with Linus Pauling on the nuclear test ban. I had known of Pauling for many years because of his work in applying quantum mechanics to chemistry.[9]

When I was in Chicago after the war, the State Department denied Pauling a passport on the grounds that he was a member of many left-wing organizations. Some of his friends asked me to sign a letter they had written on his behalf. Although I did find him politically on the far left, that did not seem like a good enough reason to deny him a passport, so I signed the letter. His thank-you note introduced me to the relativity theory in politics. Pauling said, "Thank you for writing on my behalf. An absurd statement—that I

---

[6] A mrem is a dose of one-thousandth of a roentgen-equivalent in man. New terminology for discussing the dosage of ionizing radiation was adopted in the late 1980s, and Sievert (Sv) has replaced those terms. To estimate the size of these measures, exposure to 5 Sieverts of prompt (single dose) radiation is usually fatal. The proportionality of damage for doses between 5 and 0.2 Sieverts is well established. For exposure between 0.2 Sieverts (20,000 mrem in the old terminology) and the natural background radiation everyone experiences (around 0.01 Sieverts or 1,000 mrem), there is no reason to assume damaging effects.

[7] The following comparison, therefore, contains the assumption that a long-term dose is not very different in effect from a prompt dose of the same size.

[8] These figures about commonly occurring radiation exposure are drawn from a report by the National Academy of Sciences, *The Effects on Populations of Exposure to Low Levels of Ionizing Radiation* (Washington, D.C.: National Academy of Sciences, 1980). Burning gas, oil, or coal releases naturally occurring carbon-14, which is radioactive; the luminosity of watch and clock faces are produced by radium, a radioactive element.

[9] See Chapter 13. Pauling is equally famous for his work on the health effects of megadoses of vitamin C, which he began around this time.

was a left-winger—was made about me. As you well know, I am a middle-of-the-road moderate."

Pauling was the leader of a movement that claimed that fallout from the atmospheric tests was killing people and damaging future generations. That claim was made on the basis of a theory that there is no lower limit to the amount of radiation that causes damage—that the probability of damage is directly proportional to the amount of radiation received, no matter how small.[10]

The survivors of the bombing of Hiroshima and Nagasaki were heavily irradiated, and they have been closely examined for the late effects of that radiation. In an attempt to assess hereditary damage, their children have been studied for more than forty years. Such damage might be seen through a change in the number of pregnancies spontaneously terminated, in the infant mortality rate, in the mortality rate to date, in the cancer rate of their children, in the sex ratio among children of exposed mothers, in the growth and development of the survivors' children, in protein (recessive) mutations (studied through electrophoresis), in the balanced structural rearrangements of chromosomes, and in excess sex chromosomes.[11]

An immense and thorough-going study found no evidence of genetic damage in the children of the atomic bomb survivors in spite of the large prompt doses of radiation the parents had experienced. In fact, as a result of this study, researchers have increased their estimate of the amount of radiation in a single dose that doubles the natural occurrence of mutation: That value is now given as between 1.7 and 2.2 Sv (170,000 mrem and 220,000 mrem) of single exposure radiation, which makes it obvious that the .00013

---

[10] The leading geneticists of the 1950s, Thomas H. Morgan and Hermann I. Muller, had carried out extensive radiation studies on the chromosomes of fruit flies. The extension of their findings with fruit flies to human genetics resulted in the statement contained in the first report to Congress (National Academy of Sciences, *The Biological Effects of Atomic Radiation*, [Washington, D.C., 1956]): "Any radiation which reaches the reproductive cells causes mutations that are passed on to succeeding generations."

[11] James V. Neel and William J. Shull, eds., *The Children of Atomic Bomb Survivors: A Genetic Study* (Washington, D.C.: National Academy Press, 1991). The book is a description of the studies that were conducted on 31,150 children, one or both of whose parents were exposed to more than 0.01 Sv of radiation at the time of the atomic bombings, and on a suitable comparison group of 41,066 children, whose parents were not exposed to excess radiation. The book also includes several past papers of importance and a discussion of the inferences that can be drawn from the studies.

Sv from atmospheric testing, accumulated over a year, is highly unlikely to have caused genetic damage in humans.[12]

In the 1950s, the theory of cancer causation held that a single molecule in the body hit by radiation could cause cancer. There is no doubt that exposure to large amounts of radiation, such as the atomic bomb survivors experienced, causes an increase in leukemia; and in the case of some other specific types of cancers, doses down to approximately 0.2 Sv were also associated with an increase.

Today, cancer causation is known to be extremely complicated, involving many factors. Some researchers even suspect that radiation in small amounts may contribute to a decrease in the incidence of some specific types of cancers.[13] Although the evidence of somatic effect from small doses of radiation is not as clear-cut as that of genetic effect, the relationship between small amounts of radiation and the incidence of cancer is highly improbable.

In 1958, it was still possible to claim that all amounts of radiation, no matter how small, caused damage. Pauling did so, frequently and vigorously. The chancellor of the University of California, Berkeley, at that time, Clark Kerr, differed from me in his political philosophy, but he was friendly towards me. He pointed out that Pauling and I, both faculty members, were leading proponents on opposite sides of the question and suggested that we publicly debate the question. Pauling and I agreed, and eventually our debate was held on KQED.[14]

Our discussion did nothing to moderate Pauling's ideas. He collected thousands of signatures from scientists of countless backgrounds in support of a test ban. His campaign was successful enough that no political figure

---

[12] Neel and Shull, *Children of Atomic Bomb Survivors,* pp. 431–450. Also published as an article: J. V. Neel et al., "The Children of Parents Exposed to Atomic Bombs: Estimates of the Genetic Doubling Dose of Radiation for Humans." *American Journal of Human Genetics* 46, 6 (June 1990): 1053–1072.

[13] Sohei Kondo, *Health Effects of Low-Level Radiation* (Madison, Wisc.: Medical Physics Publishing, 1993); Bernard Cohen, "Problems in the Radon vs. Lung Cancer Test of the Linear No Threshold Theory and a Procedure for Resolving Them," *Health Physics* 72, 4 (1997): 623–628. K. S. Nambi et al., "Further Observations on Environmental Radiation and Cancer in India," *Health Physics* 59, 3 (1990): 543.

[14] There is a somewhat humorous postscript to my exchange with Pauling. During the summer following our debate, my family and I went to Mount Hood in northern Oregon. One day I took Paul, who was then sixteen, and Wendy, who was fourteen, for a hike in the surrounding woods. The trails in the woods were good, but in the marshy meadows, they disappeared. In those areas, our course was determined mostly by the rocks sticking out of the water far enough to keep our feet dry. At the other side of a meadow, there was always a search

could effectively resist the public demand for cessation of atmospheric tests. Nonetheless, I continued to do my best to present the counter-arguments.

In about 1956, on one of my trips to Southern California, Dave Griggs had mentioned that an explosives expert with the Byrd polar expedition discovered that if a kilogram of explosive was buried in deep snow and detonated, the hot gases ran out into the snow and were quenched so thoroughly that no sound escaped and the snow above didn't even show a bulge. He suggested that a cavity might muffle a nuclear explosion equally well.

On the next visit, I gathered a group of my friends—Albert Latter, Ernie Martinelli (who by then had left Livermore to join Albert at Rand Corporation), Bob LeLevier, Dave Griggs, and Bill McMillan—to discuss the idea. Some doubted the efficacy of a cavity to muffle the shock.[15] Others suggested that the effectiveness of retaining energy in the cavity could be further enhanced by providing methods of energy absorption in the cavity. Such methods could be as simple as the evaporation of droplets in an artificial fog or lining the cavity with soot to lower the heat.

The idea of muffling was important in regard to verifying compliance in the Soviet Union of a test-ban agreement. Someone else suggested that an underground nuclear test near an earthquake-prone region, held in readiness for a long time and triggered by a natural earthquake, may not modify the earthquake sufficiently to be discovered and identified as a weapons test. That argument seemed to me somewhat far-fetched and impractical, but the possibility that a cavity could muffle a nuclear explosion remained extremely

---

to find the beginning of the trail in the woods. We took a five-hour hike and then made slow progress returning to camp. The sun set. Rather than get lost in the woods, I decided we should sit down and wait for rescue.

Two groups came out looking for us. They could hear each other hollering, but they were making such a din that they couldn't hear us. But eventually, they found us and led us back. As it happened, the next day was Labor Day, and there was an unfortunate scarcity of news. Media people kept calling all day, and I kept repeating our story. (Finally, Paul asked, "Why do you keep repeating the same old story? It would be more interesting if you told some different ones.")

Not much later, Linus Pauling was hiking along the beach near cliffs and had to be rescued after he was trapped by the tide. I called to offer my sympathies, and began by saying, "Well, here we two physicists are, in trouble again, and needing to be rescued." Pauling didn't take kindly to my comment. "It's not so funny as you think," he snapped, and went on to detail his peril.

[15]Hans Bethe had discounted the idea completely; but when he was eventually moved to do the calculation himself, he discovered that we had been too conservative by a factor of more than two.

important. I thought it likely that if tests were carried out in a cavity of sufficient size, more energy would be retained in the cavity and less would go into seismic effects resembling an earthquake. Eventually, I decided that we should do a test contained in a cavity to see whether the muffling actually occurred.

Dave suggested that such a test would also be a good time to gather further geological information about the composition of the earth's mantle by announcing the test time so that geologists could observe the speed at which the signal arrived. And, of course, such a test would have the advantage of containing all the radioactivity within a chamber where it could do no harm.[16]

A nuclear weapons test we ran in the fall of 1957 confirmed our feelings that underground testing would be hard to detect. The Rainier test was fired in a tunnel in Nevada and was the first completely contained underground test. We then conducted studies via drill holes over the following six months. After fifteen months, when the radiation had decayed to levels that allowed for physical examination, we were able to establish the phenomenology of underground explosions in detail.

Geologists, notified in advance of the test, gained many new insights by tracing the shock wave produced by the explosion through the mantle of the earth. The instrumentation designed to register the test information in a completely new manner worked well. Our questions were answered in the Rainier test—muffling does occur, and underground testing can yield information about weapon design and about the composition of the earth. This line of testing made possible the evolution of safer nuclear testing procedures. More important, the Rainier test was crucial to the upcoming negotiations with the Soviets. But by the time it was possible to continue testing underground, the test ban was a well-established popular movement.

Another outgrowth of my Southern California visits was my second book, *Our Nuclear Future*, which I wrote with Albert Latter.[17] By 1957, public distress over the dangers of radiation had outdistanced all reasonable assessment. Until reports of injuries and deaths from the atomic bombings in

---

[16]One outgrowth of these conversations was that Albert Latter worked out a system for generating electricity by repeated small thermonuclear explosions in a cavity. So far, it is the only concrete proposal for generating commercial electricity from thermonuclear energy. I believe that it might have been worked into a safe, practical system; but the necessary studies were not carried out because the idea of repeated explosions generated enough opposition that the development was abandoned.

[17]Albert Latter and Edward Teller, *Our Nuclear Future* (New York: Criterion Books, 1958).

Japan were published, radioactivity had been discussed almost exclusively by a small group of physicists. In 1945, the horrors of war were so recently experienced that the new danger of high, prompt (immediate and single) doses of radiation, while frightening, did not attract much attention. But as the years passed, the injury and death of people miles from the detonation site caused by invisible radiation activated fears: Radiation became the stuff of nightmares. The public response to the injuries connected with the Bravo test was highly emotional and spread to even the tiny increase of radioactivity that had arisen from atmospheric testing.[18]

Albert Latter and I decided that a book might help the general public better assess the nature of radioactivity and the risks connected with it. After all, the phenomenon of radioactivity had been part of man's natural environment from the beginning of human history. Our book discussed the types of radiation, the natural and perpetual sources of such energy, and the extremely small, probably undetectable effects of low doses received over an extended period, together with some of the issues connected with nuclear energy in general. Unfortunately, our book had little or no effect on public opinion.[19]

At the laboratory, I was adopting the advice Herb York had given me shortly before he left: "Leave as many of the details of the job as possible to other people. Delegate!" Had I not followed his advice, my directorship would have been a failure. The first and most productive thing I did was to arrange for Duane Sewell to take responsibility for all the operations—from personnel recruiting to engineering, from support services to building maintenance.

Duane had served as operating manager since the laboratory had opened, but what I had in mind for him amounted to some increase in his duties and responsibilities: I wanted his advice about practically every decision I had to make. Duane claims that I said, "I want you, Duane, to tell me, Edward, what the right decision is, when I make decisions. I want you to give me guidance in the administrative area on how to be a proper director. Tell me when I need to take action. When I don't need to be involved and you can do it, you go ahead and do it." Duane was cautious and conservative, so although asking his advice was easy, following it was sometimes much more

---

[18] At the peak of testing (1963), the radioactivity rose to 13 mrem. See Chapter 38, pp. 493–94.

[19] By contrast, Neville Shute's novel *On the Beach* (New York: W. Morrow, 1957), although it was based on a huge overestimate of the damage done by residual radioactivity from a nuclear war and dramatized the fate of the last human survivors, gained a wide readership, was converted into a movie, and had immense and far-reaching effects.

difficult. In retrospect, I am glad that I did listen to him. His assistance was present in every accomplishment we had during these years.

Duane handled the administrative work and laboratory operations, but others supported work on the technical program. Among the scientific and technological leaders at the laboratory were two young men: Harold Brown and John Foster. During my tenure as director, I became much better acquainted with both of them as I collaborated with them in solving the problems that were then under consideration. John Foster was in charge of fission weapons. Basically, those were of the old type in which I was less interested, but John continued to provide new and ingenious twists. Specifically, he and his group proposed designs of quite low yields. The size of the devices was decreased, as mentioned in Chapter 28, to a fraction of their former size.[20]

In June 1960, John Foster was awarded the first Ernest O. Lawrence Memorial Award for his work. The award, which includes a gold medal and a monetary award, had been established by President Eisenhower the previous year to recognize scientists who have made outstanding contributions to the development, use, or control of atomic energy. Because it is awarded by the Department of Energy, it is one of the few scientific prizes that can be awarded to those whose work is classified. It is of interest to note that to date, twenty-two Livermore staff members have received the Lawrence Award.[21]

I found that Johnny Foster had a simple and straightforward approach to everything in the world. He appeared to be unsophisticated, but he was precise and perfect in details. In the course of the years, he became better and better. I now consider him one of the most sophisticated people I know. He does not love sophistication for its own sake, but his brand of sophistication—being calm and unruffled in every situation—is the best of all kinds: It is based on experience and necessity.

Harold Brown was in charge of the fusion weapons; that is, further development of the hydrogen bomb. He was also on the senior technical advisory group established by the navy to oversee the development of the navy's ballistic missile system. And not long after I was appointed director, I brought

---

[20] Fission explosives, of course, are equally important as a source of energy to compress the secondary or fusion explosives in the hydrogen bomb.

[21] Other Livermore scientists who have received the Lawrence Award include Herbert York, John Nuckolls, Michael May, Thomas Wainwright, Seymour Sack, Charles A. McDonald, Jr., Willliam Lokke, John Emmett, B. Grant Logan, Lowell Wood, George Chapline, George Zimmerman, Peter Hagelstein, Robert Laughlin, Thomas Weaver, Joe Gray, Wayne Shotts, Richard Fortner, E. Michael Campbell, John Lindl, and Charles Alcock.

Harold into the director's office to help me run the laboratory. Brown did an excellent job of carrying out plans, and we worked most harmoniously for the next two years.

In November 1958, the interim ban on testing went into effect. Without the reliability established by testing, it was not easy to continue meaningful and challenging work on novel designs. The Eisenhower administration announced that the two laboratories should remain ready for testing because of the possibility that the Soviet Union would resume testing. I decided that during this period, Livermore should strengthen its design tools and make as much use of our computers as possible.

We had excellent computers, and talented people to exercise those tools. We took all the wartime Los Alamos designs that were available to us, all the Livermore designs, and all the new ideas, and spent the moratorium using the computers to examine those designs. And we developed much more powerful computer programs, called codes, that were able to make two-dimensional rather than one-dimensional calculations. Within a few years, we knew a great deal more about the Livermore and the Los Alamos designs.[22]

One other development transpired during this period. Chuck Leith was the champion calculator on the computer when I was director, but he grew tired of working on weapon design codes and wanted to tackle something difficult but useful. Chuck wanted to work on weather prediction, and I encouraged him to take on the problem. His work became one of the first climate simulation codes, and it eventually became an excellent program. Unfortunately, it also led to his leaving Livermore a few years later to work at the National Center for Atmospheric Research; it was fifteen years before he returned to Livermore.[23]

As director of the Livermore laboratory, I was supervised by the AEC, and General Alfred D. Starbird was my direct superior. I was periodically called to Washington for an all-day AEC meeting. On one such occasion, I discovered suddenly that I couldn't move half my face. General Starbird thought I had suffered a stroke and insisted that I see a doctor immediately. Fortunately, it turned out well; all I had was Bell's palsy, an inflammation of a facial nerve.

---

[22] That was fortunate, for, as the next chapter will tell, the Soviets broke the interim agreement on August 30, 1961, giving us one day's notice that they were resuming testing.

[23] Leith is now retired, but he continues to stop in and visit us.

I returned home to Mici wearing a patch over my eye because my eyelid was immobile. "With whom have you been fighting?" she immediately asked. "A senator," I replied, which on at least one occasion would have been true, though only in a figurative sense. Eventually, electric treatments stimulated the nerve, and today the only evidence of this experience is a slight droop in my right eyelid.

Perhaps the most surprising event of the two years I spent as director was that I received a royal visitor. In late 1958, Queen Frederika of Greece was visiting the United States and decided that she would like to visit our newly established and still somewhat primitive facility. I was pleased, but Gen Phillips, ordinarily as calm a person as I know, was truly excited. She planned the refreshments, refurbished my office (which consisted mainly of clearing off the surfaces of my desks and tables), and generally tackled the impossible task of making Livermore look nicely appointed.[24] Queen Frederika arrived and proved to be a most charming and attentive guest. I do not recall that she was particularly interested in any scientific presentation we made, but we all enjoyed making them and receiving her lovely smile.

A more important business that got underway during my directorship was a program called Plowshare. In 1945, those of us working on nuclear energy expected that it would be applied in three broad fields. The first, of course, was its application to military weapons. Another, which Fermi and Wigner were already pursuing during the war, was to supply energy through the generation of electricity. The third logical application was in civil engineering, the use of nuclear explosives to dig harbors and canals or to stimulate gas or oil production through explosions. The use of nuclear explosives rather than conventional explosives provides considerable advantages in cost, time, and manpower.

Harold Brown was the first person to become really excited about the possibilities of the last application. By the spring of 1956, Harold had seen that

---

[24] In most regards, Gen succeeded beyond my wildest imagination, but she did run into an insurmountable problem. The administration building was still in one of the old original buildings of the naval base, and the ladies' room was a small dingy bathroom that was tacked on when the more commodious bathrooms were converted to offices. Only major remodeling, which was definitely not in the budget, could have fixed that room. Finally, Gen decided to fill it with flowers from her own and her friends' gardens and hope that, should the queen visit that corner, she would not notice its shortcomings. Gen's efforts were defeated when a plumbing problem made the room unusable, but Queen Frederika and her party never knew.

further development of nuclear weapons would eventually make smaller, cleaner explosives possible. He had begun planning a conference with Los Alamos scientists early in the following year to discuss using nuclear explosives for civil engineering. At the Nobska conference, someone in the Los Alamos contingent asked whether the upcoming conference meant that we wanted to "beat our swords into plowshares." There was no small amount of condescension in that (as well as many other comments emanating from our colleagues on the mesa), but on this occasion I felt strongly about standing up to it. After I. I. Rabi had made a similar comment to Harold Brown, we decided to call our proposal Plowshare.

The Rainier test had provided a good deal of information pertinent to using nuclear explosives for excavation. The explosion had produced a hole 110 feet in diameter; it was lined with molten rock that imprisoned much of the radioactivity in an all but insoluble form. The cavity had collapsed and the porous rock around the cavity had formed a chimney of rubble 400 feet high.

Some radioactivity escaped into the water-permeable rubble. That radioactivity was watched for years, but long before it could reach any living thing it would have decayed. Thus, Rainier had demonstrated that nuclear explosives could break up large quantities of rock and that the cavity would contain almost all the radioactivity.

The Plowshare project was funded just after I assumed the directorship. In retrospect, given the steadily increasing public hysteria over radiation, we should have given up without beginning. But even in 1958, only a few people could have guessed how the technique of using nuclear explosives for civil engineering would fail to develop.

Milo Nordyke was part of the Plowshare program from its inception, and a recent talk with him filled in many details about the beginnings of the program that I had forgotten:

> The AEC made the decision to go forward with the Plowshare project to build a harbor in Alaska (which was named the Chariot project) in April, and in July, several people from the lab went up to see what the people in Alaska thought about the idea of carrying out a field experiment there to demonstrate the ability of nuclear explosives to build a useful harbor. The study suggesting the first site was a very preliminary effort; it indicated that there were coal resources near there, so the harbor became associated with the idea of coal mining. As a result of a longer study, it became obvious that there were coal resources, but they were a long way away. So the project was scaled down to a much smaller harbor.

I remember little about my first trip to Alaska, but I remember the second in some detail. By 1959, the plan was to create a usable harbor in the far northwest coast of Alaska at Kotzebue, near Cape Thompson. Because the region has a low population, only a small number of people would have to be relocated temporarily for the nuclear shots.

I set out to inspect the site in June 1959. My first impression of the Alaskan coast from the airplane was memorable. I have flown over that region several times since then, but I have never seen the coastal mountains with their fjords in such splendor. All this was rendered more dramatic by a recent earthquake. We could see debris in the fjords even from the plane.

The earthquake had shaken loose a part of a glacier inside the fjord, thereby creating a huge wave that had stripped the vegetation from the sides of the fjord.[25] We noticed similar parallel lines at higher altitudes on the sides; they told us that the recent event was not unique because each line had a bigger growth of trees on the high side.

We stopped in Juneau and in Anchorage and found rather less than the expected opposition to the project. On the flight to Fairbanks, I noticed smoke breaking out from under the snow, which still covered the ground. I was told that the smoke was from huge forest fires that had burned out of control; the hot ashes were still smoldering under the snow cover. In Fairbanks, the smell of smoke was everywhere and inescapable.[26] During our short stay in Fairbanks, I received an honorary doctor's degree from the University of Alaska in a pleasant, relaxed ceremony.

From Fairbanks we went on to Kotzebue, an Eskimo village north of Nome; from there, our group flew along the coast to the site where the Chariot harbor was to be located, and then on to Point Barrow, where the coast turns to the east. At that time, the Alaskan oilfields had not been discovered, but had the harbor been completed, it would have made a shorter pipeline possible.

The discussions of the proposed harbor naturally included considerations of the project's effect on the local fauna.[27] That environmental study, which began in 1958, eventually grew to be the largest, most elaborate study since

---

[25] We were also told the story about a couple on their honeymoon who were canoeing in the fjord when the earthquake occurred. The flood picked them up and deposited them, safe but thoroughly scared, far out in the ocean, where they were later rescued.

[26] I am still wondering whether and to what extent remnants of similar forest fires may have contributed to the formation of Alaskan coal deposits.

[27] Worries about the caribou had not then reached the level that they did in connection with the construction of the Alaskan pipeline. I had occasion to return to Alaska in June

the Lewis and Clark expedition.[28] It laid the foundation for the many environmental studies that have become commonplace today.

The Chariot project produced the first full fledged environmental study, but it did not produce a harbor because the economic advantages were too slight to warrant the expense. The government did show interest in the feasibility of using nuclear explosives in connection with building a second sea-level Panama Canal, thought to be necessary to accommodate a future increase in world shipping. Work began on that study in 1959, but eventually the project was abandoned because of the absence of a compelling need for a second canal. Plowshare projects then branched out in other directions, which are discussed in Chapter 38.

Later, during the Kennedy presidency, the bad relations between the United States and the Soviet Union grew worse: The competition between the Soviet Union and the United States for leadership in weaponry continued, but, in addition, a true arms race began. Yet the cost of military expenditures was kept on the whole at the level of about 8 percent of the gross national product, less than one-half of which can be ascribed to this competition. Thus, the United States was successful in deterring war for the cost of a fraction of its total economic activity.

This unprecedented situation was possible because we relied more on ingenuity than on material armaments. I am proud of the contribution that the Lawrence Livermore Laboratory made during these years. In the end, my directorship was a success only in so far as I steered the laboratory through the obviously difficult transition period at the beginning of the test ban.

In June 1960, when matters appeared to be stabilized, I tendered my resignation, and Harold Brown took over as director. Perhaps the best part of leaving that office was that I no longer had to be so careful about voicing my opinions. As director, any statement I made had to be guarded, because to some extent my words were considered to be the policy of the laboratory.

My opposition to a test ban continued long after I resigned. The opposite point of view had widespread support, and I am somewhat astonished that I was at least partially successful. Continued testing was essential to our effort

---

1987. Work on the North Slope was flourishing and so were the caribou, which had multiplied impressively near human habitation. Because the caribou's two enemies—fires and polar bears—were limited near the settlements, the caribou had benefited. As for the pipeline, I even saw a caribou snuggling up to its warm side.

[28] The finding that strontium from nuclear test fallout was being picked up by caribou and concentrated in their milk was a result of the studies done for the Chariot project.

to stay ahead in the Cold War. The Soviets were at all times ahead of us in terms of the great numbers of weapons they had amassed. We had to compensate by supplying high-quality technology, and that required an emphasis on knowledge.

I owed my partial success on the test ban question, I believe, to the fact that common sense appeals to politicians and people in general. But much to my personal sorrow, my stand contributed further to the barriers between myself and many of my former colleagues.

35

A FEW LESSONS IN
POLITICAL AFFAIRS

1955–1960

THE WELL-BEING of the Livermore laboratory was always at the fore-front of my thoughts, but until 1958, it did not occupy all my time. In addition to my academic responsibilities at the university and my work at the Berkeley and Livermore laboratories—and my occasional activities in Washington—I was involved in consulting with Nelson Rockefeller.

In about 1954 or 1955, my friend Teddy Walkowicz introduced me to Nelson Rockefeller. (Teddy knew Nelson Rockefeller because of his work as a consultant to the Rockefeller Family Trust.) Nelson had held some ap-pointed offices in the Roosevelt and Eisenhower administrations, and at the time I met him I believe he was undersecretary of the Department of Health, Education, and Welfare, and also a special advisor to President Eisenhower on foreign affairs.

Nelson was committed to a career in public service (rather than politics) and, being a conscientious man, he was undertaking an assessment of the needs of the nation to prepare himself for political office. I was honored when Nelson asked me to join the study group, even though that meant foregoing my inter-est in being a consultant to the Family Trust, an invitation that Laurance Rockefeller had issued. I considered the work of the study group an important and interesting project. And so it proved. Nelson's study group provided me my first real (although not necessarily fully realistic) introduction to the world of American political thought.

In one respect, Rockefeller was the most unusual political figure I have known. All politicians in my experience listen to advice. Some of them listen carefully, most listen selectively. Rockefeller was the only public figure I have ever met who actively participated in the formation of advice. He set up committees and presided over them. He listened to all sides. He was fully aware not only of the answers to important problems but of the detailed reasons that led to judgments, agreements, or disagreements.

Our meetings consisted of the fifteen or twenty of us sitting around a table, with Nelson leading our discussion.[1] Most of the initial presentations of issues were given by Henry Kissinger, a young man whose family had fled Germany in 1938 and who had just completed his Ph.D. studies at Harvard. I was not tremendously impressed with Kissinger at the beginning of this study, but by the time we had finished, I had revised my opinion. Eventually, we became friends.

I was on two of the study panels. One was on national security. Detlev Bronk, who was then head of the National Academy of Science and president of Rockefeller University, was also on that panel, and so were Teddy Walkowicz and Laurance Rockefeller. Laurance was quieter and more passive than Nelson. He was also more concerned with the practical aspects of life than with the political. The other panel was on energy. Two acquaintances from the Atomic Energy Commission, Carrol Wilson and Gordon Dean, were on the panel, as was John Flossbery (who left the panel when he received an appointment to the AEC). I was also on the overall panel, and Nelson attended all those meetings.

The Rockefeller committee considered everything from economics to defense; the purpose, quite clearly, was to prepare Nelson to enter the race for president. Nelson, as chairman, was a pleasant, effective, and courteous leader. Our discussions always ran smoothly; and, on most occasions, he promptly acknowledged anyone who wanted to offer a comment.

On one occasion, when I tried to mention something, Nelson did not acknowledge me. When we adjourned for lunch a quarter hour or so later, Nelson asked me to join him and explained to me in almost embarrassing detail why he had not given me the floor. He told me that the topic of the moment—to give considerably more authority to the Armed Forces Chief of Staff—was especially urgent and that he had had to give preference to those whose expertise had particular relevance to the question. I was amazed that he felt it necessary to explain his actions to me, and I decided that it was in large part occasioned by his well-developed sense of politeness.

---

[1] The Prospects for America study group was administered by a distant descendant of Abraham Lincoln's mother, Nancy Hanks.

The only idea I introduced to that study was the feasibility and benefits of carrying out civil defense. I had been concerned about the question since 1945, and eventually Eugene Wigner convinced me of its great potential for saving lives. I presented the facts about the requirements for protection in the event of nuclear attack, and Nelson Rockefeller took a thorough interest in what I had to say. Indeed, following his election as governor of the state of New York in 1958, he continued to advocate a civil defense program for many years but with little success.

I remember distinctly a dinner that was held for several of us committee members in Nelson's home in 1957. The first Mrs. Rockefeller was the hostess, but she seemed so aloof that her behavior almost amounted to rudeness. I was surprised by the extreme contrast in personality and deportment between Nelson and his wife on that occasion. I was not surprised when I learned, not much later, that the Rockefellers were getting a divorce.

At that time, I did not fully realize the national importance of that event. A year or two after my work on the study group was over, I saw Nelson again. He was a changed man. The best brief description would be to say that he was not all there. I then began to connect facts: Nelson could not run effectively for the presidency in 1960. He was not in a state to do so because of his marital difficulties. In addition, he had become a less suitable candidate because no previous president had been divorced. This failure and its reasons I consider a real tragedy.

I tend to blame many of our politicians for being too ambitious. I cannot blame Nelson for not being ambitious enough to allow his political career to interfere with his private life. Nelson later married a charming and wonderful woman, Margaretta Murphy (nicknamed Happy), with whom he had a second family. Why was that considered inappropriate? Why did that make him a less suitable candidate for the presidency? Some of our presidents have been forgiven for much greater deviations.

In 1958, Nelson was elected governor of New York. At that point, the study was almost completed, so Laurance Rockefeller took over and saw the project through to book form.[2] Many of the recommendations of that study were adopted by the next president, John F. Kennedy, in his New Frontiers program. Kennedy even made one of the foreign policy panel experts from Nelson's group, Dean Rusk, his secretary of state. Unfortunately, Kennedy did not pursue Nelson's foreign policy recommendations as they pertained to

---

[2] *Prospects for America: The Rockefeller Panel Reports* (Garden City, N.Y.: Doubleday, 1961).

the Western Alliance, the Soviet Union, or Latin America, a region in which Nelson Rockefeller had specialized.

I completed my work on the Rockefeller study in early 1958, and I was about to begin consulting with Laurance, who, as head of the Rockefeller Family Trust, was interested in investing in (among other industries) small, technically adventurous young companies; but when I accepted the position of director at the Livermore laboratory, that became impossible. I stopped almost all my consulting work with the exception of the safe nuclear reactor (Triga) that I had been working on with Freddie de Hoffman.

In the spring of 1959, a controversy arose concerning my friend Lewis Strauss. Strauss had resigned as chairman of the AEC, and his replacement was working effectively. President Eisenhower then nominated Strauss to the cabinet post of secretary of commerce. At that time, the Senate usually approved such a nomination automatically. But Lewis had offended a powerful Democratic senator, Clinton Anderson, from New Mexico. Anderson's effectively organized opposition proclaimed that Lewis was too conservative, believed nuclear weapons testing was safe, and opposed science.

Lewis asked me to testify about his so-called opposition to science, and I did my best to respond to the charges against him. I mentioned the splendid job he had done in supporting basic scientific research as head of the AEC, his role in establishing the Office of Naval Research, and his interest in instituting the metric system.[3]

If anything, the anger and bitterness over the Oppenheimer hearing had increased among the politically active scientific community. Niels Bohr had tried with all his power to clear Oppenheimer and continued to resent what he felt was Strauss's unfair treatment of Oppenheimer. At one point, Bohr told Strauss, in effect, "You have your rules, but to a great man like Oppenheimer, rules do not apply." Many other scientists, particularly those in the Federation of American Scientists, felt similarly.

My testimony for Strauss was of little help. During the following discussion period, the unrelated question of my contributions to the hydrogen bomb (as compared to those of Stan Ulam) became one of the main topics. In the end, Lewis's nomination was defeated by a slim majority of three votes. I, in turn, was bitterly and publicly attacked by Drew Pearson, a popular political columnist of that period.

---

[3] The government did encourage the introduction of the metric system during the early 1960s, but public unwillingness to change doomed the effort.

The brunt of his argument was that I, a government employee, was consulting with industry and being paid for it.[4] He demanded that I stop consulting, and, most particularly, that I resign as an advisor to Freddie de Hoffman's company, General Atomic. Following that attack, I did stop consulting with Freddie, although with regret.

Having resigned my consulting with General Atomic, I went to Southern California less frequently, but I still visited a new friend there fairly often. Teddy Walkowicz had introduced me to Floyd Odlum; at the time I met him, he was chief executive officer of Atlas Corporation and had played an instrumental role in the development of the first Atlas rocket. Without his imaginative leadership, it is doubtful that rocket development would have begun in a timely fashion.

During the war, Odlum had also been active in Washington as the director of the Office of Production Management, although he was simultaneously serving as chairman of the board of RKO Radio Pictures in Hollywood. His foremost interest was in the well-being of his nation's defenses. By the time I came to know him well, Odlum was most notable as a financier, having gained his expertise, he claimed, "in the School of Hard Knocks."[5]

Floyd Odlum's wife was hardly less impressive than he: Jackie Cochran was an internationally known early aviator and had been a pilot in Europe during World War II. After the war she went far—in the cosmetics industry—towards matching her husband's financial success. In spite of these and later exposures, I never really learned much about high finance, probably because finance is not as simple as theoretical physics.

By the 1950s, the Odlum-Cochrans had established a beautiful ranch in the desert not far from Indio, California. Both Floyd and Jackie were gregarious and hospitable people. During the late 1950s and early to mid-1960s, Mici and I and the children visited them there a few times each year. In addition, they insisted that, whenever Mici or I needed to recuperate following an illness or surgery, we do it there. I could say that the Odlums contributed

---

[4] Although as director of the Livermore laboratory, I was an employee of the University of California and could freely consult, I had dropped most of my consulting roles save for my work on the Triga reactor.

[5] Odlum had some interest in science, at least to the extent of trying to learn about the age of the universe. I told him it was 2 billion years old, which was the estimate thought to be correct in the mid–1950s. A few years later, after the original measurements were further refined, I had to tell him that the universe more probably started some 10 or 20 billion years ago. Odlum was shocked, either by the lack of accuracy in the science of astronomy, or, I am afraid, by my lack of reliability as a scientist. But our friendly relationship survived.

to my directorship through their good attentions to my health and well-being. We availed ourselves of their kind offer on two or three occasions.

We could not, of course, express our gratitude in monetary terms, but I made (involuntary) contributions of moderate size by losing gin rummy games that I played with Jackie. She enjoyed the games even more than I. Wendy, because of the stables, and Paul, because of the huge swimming pool, also looked forward to our visits, so there are family memories of several happy relaxing vacations at the ranch.[6]

My memories of the setting are indistinct save for the clear impression that everything at the ranch was oversized, even the dates on what seemed to be thousands of palm trees. The main hall and dining room of the house were almost but not quite big enough to serve as a football field, and the crossbeams were timbers of a most impressive size. While we were visiting, we stayed in one of several charming, comfortable, and unassuming guest houses on the ranch, and we were never without other company in addition to the Odlums. One of the many attractions of the Odlum ranch was a remarkable array of visitors, among whom Theodore von Kármán frequently appeared.

The Odlums enjoyed organizing friendly competitions in various subjects where none of us had much expertise. One that I remember involved producing a painting. The Odlums provided the equipment, but we were required to provide the talent. Actually, I quite enjoyed myself because I had recently brought a tiki, a sacred object of rather indeterminate form, from Hawaii. I could paint its representation with little fear that the other guests might comment about its lack of resemblance to reality.

On another occasion, after 1960, former President Eisenhower and his wife Mamie were among the guests.[7] At the dinner table that night, Mamie Eisenhower was seated next to Theodore von Kármán, and Mici was seated across from her "Uncle Theodore." During the meal, Mamie apparently found von Kármán less than stimulating company; as a consequence, Uncle Theodore began speaking to Mici in Hungarian, which in itself bothered Mici, who considered that a breach of etiquette.

But what he was saying bothered Mici even more, because he was making somewhat unflattering comments about Mamie Eisenhower's personality and

---

[6] Wendy loved animals, and when she was in high school, we got her a horse on the condition that she take care of it. We secretly hoped that the horse would encourage her to go to school in Berkeley, but her love for her horse proved less than her devotion to education: She abandoned her horse and went to Radcliffe.

[7] Although I had served on Eisenhower's Presidential Scientific Advisory Board, I do not recall any of the questions I was asked to address, and I had never met the president before this occasion at the Odlums.

appearance. Mici, blushing furiously, tried to kick him under the table, but failed, which only delighted von Kármán. Eventually, either Mici adopted my trick of ignoring the tormentor, or Uncle Theodore tired of his game, because no one else at the table except the three of us seemed to notice anything unusual going on.[8]

Still another visitor whom I met at the Odlum ranch, Tom Lanphier, was involved in matters of some import. The advent of Sputnik, as I have mentioned earlier, inaugurated an era of concern about the missile technology the Soviets possessed; this came to be known as the "missile gap." I heard much about the problem of Soviet excellence in rocketry and space vehicles from Floyd Odlum, who was seriously concerned about our slow progress. His concern was shared by Tom Lanphier, who was a frequent visitor at the ranch.

During World War II, Lanphier had been a fighter pilot in the Pacific theater. U.S. intelligence people had broken the Japanese communication code and had found the flight that Admiral Yamamoto was making. (Yamamoto was the admiral who planned the attack on Pearl Harbor.) Tom Lanphier flew out and shot down the admiral's plane. That event, combined with an excellent previous record, had made Tom a war hero and a public figure.

After the war, Tom went to work for Convair Corporation, and in the subsequent period, he became increasingly concerned with what seemed to him a lackadaisical American approach to the development of rocketry. During the late 1950s, I listened to Tom on several occasions. We even had a joint speaking engagement: I talked about nuclear weapons, and he about the missile gap. When we talked, I believed his statements, although I did not permit myself to get involved in the controversy.

The event I particularly remember occurred at the end of 1959. Tom, on account of his war record, had access to President Eisenhower. He was determined to put before the president his concerns about Soviet superiority in rocketry and space, a subject that can be discussed more acceptably today. Even though he was working on his farewell address, Eisenhower received Lanphier. The president resented Tom's appeal, mistaking it for a request for more money for the corporation. Eisenhower's farewell address reflected his apparent annoyance with Tom's impassioned plea.

---

[8] On another occasion in the 1960s when we were at the Odlums, Theodore von Kármán told me that I had really made it. "Why do you say that?" I asked. "Because it is now possible to trade ten Teller autographs for one Elvis Presley," von Kármán reported. In January 2000, another Hungarian, George Marx, pointed out that in an Internet survey in Hungary on "the best known and most respected living Hungarian," I ranked third, following former Premier Kádár and current President Göncz. At ninety-two, I am honored by the company, and I am especially pleased to be living.

The incident had two unfortunate consequences. One was that as soon as Tom left, Eisenhower wrote into his address the phrase "military-industrial complex." Opponents of appropriations for military defense still call upon those words to gain an advantage today. The other unfortunate consequence was that Convair was embarrassed and Tom was fired.

But one truly joyful event occurred during those somewhat difficult years. During the fall of 1958, I saw my friend Leo Szilárd again. Over dinner, Szilárd began talking about the Pugwash conferences (meetings of scientists from the United States and the Soviet Union) that he was helping to organize. He urged me to visit the Soviet Union so that I could dispel some of what he felt were my erroneous ideas about that country.

I told him that I had no interest in visiting the country that was denying emigration visas to my elderly mother and my sister, Emmi. My mother was long past the age where she could be gainfully employed, and my sister was only occasionally employed as a translator; they were being kept in Hungary for no good economic reason and against all humanitarian considerations since my nephew had escaped to the United States two years earlier. Szilárd promised to look into the question.

I expected to hear no more about either my travels to the Soviet Union or about my family in Hungary. But I underestimated the importance the Soviets gave to maintaining good relations with Szilárd. At the next Pugwash conference, Szilárd went to the leader of the Soviet delegation and asked why my mother and sister could not obtain exit visas. The leader retorted, "Hungary is an independent country. We have nothing to do with their exit policies in Moscow." A few hours later, the Hungarian delegate to the Pugwash conference came to Szilárd, who raised the same question. I don't know what transpired then, but a few weeks later, my sister, Emmi, and my mother received emigration visas.

They made their way to Vienna, Austria, where they were welcomed by Yoshio Fujioka, my old friend from my days in Leipzig, who was then serving as Japan's representative to the International Atomic Energy Agency. Once again, Lizi Gratz, my friend from childhood days, provided a temporary safe haven for the refugees. And in mid-January 1959, my mother and Emmi at last arrived safely at the San Francisco airport. For the first time in twenty-three years, the Teller family was reunited.[9]

---

[9] My mother lived to the age of ninety-four, and when I wrote this, Emmi was still living. Much to my sorrow, Emmi passed away on April 29, 2001, after a short illness. She had helped me recall incidents and names from our childhood and had recounted again her painful memories of the Holocaust in Budapest and had looked forward to the publication of this book. Her death, together with Mici's less than a year before, has been a terrible loss.

36

THE TEMPERATURE
OF THE COLD WAR RISES

1960–1965

U NTIL 1959, WHEN I reregistered so that I could vote for Nelson Rockefeller in the primary, I, like most immigrants, had been a Democrat. In this, I was confirmed by my association with an outstanding Democratic senator, Henry (Scoop) Jackson of Washington. He took a detailed interest in our work on defense. Among my memories about him, the most dramatic—if not the most pleasant—was when he invited me for lunch in the Senate Dining Room. It was in the late 1950s, and in the middle of lunch another senator came by. We stood up, and Scoop made the introductions. Senator Jack Kennedy smiled sweetly and fulfilled the ritual of bestowing a compliment: "I read so many nice things about you in the Shepley-Blair book, *The Hydrogen Bomb*."

That book was a great embarrassment to me. It was unabashedly full of praise for me and unrestrainedly full of criticism for Oppenheimer.[1] I felt it highly unlikely that Kennedy was unaware of the controversy surrounding the book. If he was familiar with the heated criticism, his comment was, in effect, a subtle insult. At best, he assumed that I would be flattered by Blair and Shepley's improper exaggerations. I reacted instinctively with a quotation from Gilbert and Sullivan's *The Gondoliers:* "The things they have related, they are much exaggerated, very much exaggerated. Scarce a word of it is true."[2]

Kennedy smiled a second time (a little less sweetly), and said, "I'm happy to have met you," and ended our encounter. As Scoop and I sat back down,

---

[1] See Chapter 32, p. 405.
[2] The only slight defense I offer of my impolite behavior is that at least I reproduced my words as mere recitativo.

Scoop said, "You know, he may be your next president." I replied, "I'd rather that you would be." Scoop went, "Shhh!"

I should have recognized Kennedy's comment as a simple attempt to be pleasant. That first incident typified my interactions with Kennedy: Throughout the following years until his death in November 1963, our relationship continued to be prickly. I do not know why Kennedy brought out a spontaneous rudeness in me. I do not think I normally behave like that, and I like to believe that I am courteous in most of my dealings with people, and particularly with political leaders. This was only the first of a few occasions when I could not restrain an involuntary urge that I seemed to get around Kennedy: To shoot off my mouth, thereby shooting myself in the foot.

The contrast between Jack Kennedy and Nelson Rockefeller is interesting. Kennedy wanted badly to be president. Rockefeller wanted equally to be a good president. Kennedy got what he wanted. Rockefeller did not. Of course, it is less difficult to become president than to be a good president. Both of them gave the problem of nuclear war maximum attention. Kennedy hoped to solve the problem by imposing a test ban; Rockefeller, by strengthening defense.

In the spring following Kennedy's inauguration, a group of us were invited to Washington to discuss the plans for a permanent test ban. In addition, I was asked to serve on the science advisory committee headed by Jerome Wiesner. I agreed, but I was rarely asked for my opinion and cannot think of one occasion on which it was reflected in the policy adopted.

Several things were in flux during this period. Harold Brown, who at that time had been director of the Livermore laboratory for barely a year, resigned to take over the post of Director of Defense Research and Engineering in Washington (DDR&E). The question of succession had a wonderful solution: Johnny Foster took over as the director at Livermore. Over the following four years he proved to be a splendid administrator.

During this time, tensions between the United States and the Soviet Union were intensifying. Fidel Castro had joined Cuba to the communist bloc of nations, and the United States had received a flood of Cuban refugees. In April 1961, Cuban refugees, with tacit support from President Kennedy, attempted to overthrow Castro by force. The Bay of Pigs invasion proved a fiasco, and the Soviet Union pledged Cuba its support against all attacks.

The Soviet Union, which had announced its possession of intercontinental ballistic missiles (ICBMs) about the same time it had orbited Sputnik, was continuing to demonstrate its superiority in rocketry: Yuri Gagarin and Ghermin Titov orbited the earth while Alan Sheppard and Gus Grissom had to be content with flying up into space and coming straight back. But while the Soviets were flying in outer space, citizens in East Germany (as well as in Cuba) were fleeing to the West. The German exodus occurred through Berlin, and in mid-August 1961, the East Germans decided to close the route. They erected a wall around Berlin. Kennedy, after hesitant behavior in his meeting with Khrushchev in Vienna, went to Berlin and tried to reassure the West Germans with his remark, "Ich bin ein Berliner." Unfortunately, he and the other millions of Berliners were ineffective in solving the problem. The blockade continued.

Within two weeks, a further shock occurred. On August 30, while negotiations of the test ban treaty were in full session, Khrushchev announced that the Soviet Union would withdraw from the interim test ban agreement. The following day, September 1, 1961, the Soviet Union began the most powerful test series the world has ever experienced. Within the next eight weeks, the Soviet Union conducted thirty-one tests, ten of them in the megaton range, one of them—the largest explosive ever detonated—of more than 60 MT of explosive power.

As I have mentioned, there is no military advantage to such a weapon.[3] The main advantage to testing so huge a weapon was the psychological effect it had on the people of the free world. The test series did have one unforeseen consequence: It began the conversion of the Soviet Union's foremost weapons designer, Andrei Sakharov, into the Soviet Union's foremost dissident. At a meeting when the preparations for the test series were begun, Sakharov sent a note to Khrushchev protesting the tests, pointing out that "breaking the moratorium would lead to a new round in the armaments race."[4] Khrushchev responded by reading Sakharov's note to the assembled scientists. He then announced:

---

[3] See Chapter 27.

[4] Part of Sakharov's motivation for his protest to Khrushchev was not the breach of faith involved in resuming the tests during negotiations for a permanent treaty; rather it was Sakharov's impression (based on well-publicized speculations) about the hazards of low-level radiation: "Beginning in 1957 (not without the influence of statements on this subject made throughout the world by such people as Albert Schweitzer, Linus Pauling, and others) I felt myself responsible for the problem of radioactive contamination from nuclear explosions. . . . Each series of tests of a nuclear weapon . . . involves tens of megatons; i.e., tens of thousands of victims."

Many people still share Sakharov's concern about radioactivity in the trace amounts. The belief arises from the no-threshold theory, which holds that, because large amounts of radiation are undoubtedly damaging and moderate amounts are proportionately less damaging, even miniscule amounts must produce damage. Contrary evidence is presented by the experience of populations living in regions of China, Brazil, and India, where naturally occurring radioactivity is present in amounts that expose the inhabitants to doses of about 0.2 Sv per year. In many instances, families have lived in those regions for generations without sustaining identifiable damage.

This does not in any way lessen my admiration for his courage in arguing against the dictatorship in Moscow.

Sakharov is a good scientist. But leave it to us, who are specialists in this tricky business, to make foreign policy. Only force—only disorientation of the enemy. We can't say aloud that we are carrying out our policy from a position of strength, but that's the way it must be. I would be a slob, and not Chairman of the Council of Ministers, if I listened to the likes of Sakharov.[5]

Not surprisingly, within three years, Andrei Sakharov was no longer working on weapons for his country.

The United States intelligence services had claimed throughout the previous three years that a Soviet attempt to mount even a small test series would be observed long before its actualization. They were mistaken. The Livermore laboratory had little more than discussions by way of test preparations when, hours after Khrushchev's surprise revelation, we received orders to resume testing.

As the reader already knows, putting together a test series is a laborious and lengthy affair. Livermore went back to a six-day work week, which for many people involved almost round-the-clock employment. We had taken the precaution of making some preparations in case the Soviet Union withdrew from the gentlemen's agreement. Our preparations were limited to those tests that, in our opinion, had the greatest chance of being permitted. In particular, we were not permitted to proceed with some important details of the preparation lest they appear to be evidence of bad faith on our part.

We resumed testing with two small kiloton devices in late September 1961, but we had not prepared for atmospheric tests. The tests we could get ready were hardly of the importance or quality that longer, unrestricted planning makes possible. And it was with the 1961 test series that the Soviet Union took the lead in nuclear weapons research.

In the spring of 1962, President Kennedy visited Berkeley and met with some of us from Livermore. On that occasion, I took the opportunity, while waiting for the events to get underway, to make a remark to the president about the extent of the misinformation circulating about the great dangers of small doses of radioactivity. I was about to point out that some evidence indicated that amounts of radiation in slight excess of background radiation might be beneficial. Before I could do so, the president interrupted me to observe, "Dr. Teller, if you are trying to convince me that radiation is good

---

[5] Andrei D. Sakharov, *Sakharov Speaks* (New York: Knopf, 1974).

for me, you will fail."[6] In this case, as in many others, Kennedy demonstrated more talent as a politician than as a scientist.

Perhaps the most memorable event of the Kennedy administration was the Cuban missile crisis. I remember clearly when I heard about it: I was on the Queen Mary on my way to France.[7] Like almost everyone else, I was alarmed.

The interpretation of the outcome remains a puzzle to me. We obtained the withdrawal of missiles from Cuba in part by the announcement of a strong policy of preventing delivery of missiles through a naval embargo. But normalization of relations was reached at the heavy price of promises to tolerate a communist régime in Cuba and to withdraw U.S. missiles from Turkey and England. Although I cannot consider the result a victory for the United States, the claim is made, with great emphasis, that the Soviets considered the denouement a defeat they were determined should never be repeated.

I must admit that all my tactical and untactful blundering did not seem to affect the president. On December 3, 1962, President Kennedy awarded me the Fermi Prize, which at that time carried with it an award of $50,000, for my "contributions to chemical and nuclear physics, for leadership in thermonuclear research, and for efforts to strengthen national security." I was deeply honored.

I was also deeply gratified to discover the following year that as a recipient, I was allowed to offer a nomination for the Fermi Prize. I, like countless other scientists, was saddened by the onus that the security hearing had cast over Robert Oppenheimer, who had indeed provided unparalleled leadership at Los Alamos during the war years. I also hoped that government acknowledgment of Oppenheimer's great service would help to heal the schism that had developed in the scientific community. Therefore, I used my newly acquired position as nominator to submit Oppenheimer's name for the 1963 Fermi Prize, which, to my delight, he received that year. Unfortunately, the schism persisted without change.

The ceremony at which I received the Fermi Prize in 1962 was a gala occasion; many notable political figures attended, including Glenn Seaborg, who was then head of the AEC. Given my past history with the president, my politically astute friends were concerned lest I inadvertently spoil the occasion.

---

[6] The question raised that day remains unsettled. The reason, in part, is that evidence for favorable effects of small doses of radiation are not easy to document, nor have many scientists been able to acquire research funds for such studies. See Dixy Lee Ray with Lou Guzzo, *Trashing the Planet* (Washington, D.C.: Regency Gateway, 1990), and note 12, Chapter 34.

[7] I was on my way to a NATO meeting concerning collaboration on missile-carrying submarines.

Harold Brown, who was then Director of Defense Research and Engineering, asked me to send him my acceptance statement so that he could review it. I dutifully sent my statement to Harold, and he approved it. (I no longer remember whether that was with or without modifications.)

In spite of their good efforts, my friends did not succeed in turning me into a politically polished person. As President Kennedy handed me the medal, he asked me about the proposed Plowshare plan of a second sea-level canal across the Panama isthmus.[8] My response to the president was truthful but inexcusable: "It will take less time to complete the canal than for you to make up your mind to build it."

I hope I am mistaken in my recollection of my remark and that I conveyed that thought in a less direct manner. My interactions with President Kennedy were the low point in my career as a diplomat. During the intervening years, I have not changed my mind about unnecessary concerns for minute doses of radiation or about the frustrations of trying to work through the bureaucratic obstacles resulting from misplaced concerns. But I deeply regret my disrespectful behavior in the presence of the head of our government.

In the spring of 1963, the negotiations with the Soviets had progressed to the point that a test ban agreement that would ban all atmospheric tests was being considered. President Kennedy, through Jerome Wiesner, his science advisor, invited me to the White House to discuss the topic. I was privileged to see Kennedy in his famous rocking chair, face to face. In a brief conversation, I stated the most important reason for opposing such a ban: Since the age of missiles began, we had had the opportunity to conduct one test series in the atmosphere, which had been done in 1962.

Our 1962 test series had left us convinced that the amount of knowledge we needed was far greater than the knowledge we possessed about how nuclear explosives could be used in ballistic missile defense. Some of the Soviet tests of 1961 and 1962 appeared to have been directed at missile defense. I agreed that underground testing was far preferable to no testing; and underground testing negated the issue of atmospheric contamination and allowed us to continue to improve our deterrent force.

---

[8] The unwillingness of political leaders to take a stand on the importance of the Panama Canal program and on the minimal risks of the potential radioactivity had slowed the program greatly. The hyperbole in the popular press about the risks of exposure to radiation had met with silence from political leaders since 1956, when Adlai Stevenson had espoused an extreme position on the risks of exposure to radiation. Political timidity and the lack of economic benefits had effectively cancelled the plans to build a harbor in Alaska.

President Kennedy had heard me out courteously if somewhat noncommittally. When I was leaving, the president came with me to the door of his office, where he asked me, "How many weapons were there in the stockpile at the time of the first Berlin crisis? Too few to risk their use?"

I was shocked because of the implications his question raised about his willingness to use nuclear weapons. I replied, truthfully but incompletely, that at that time I had no need to know how many weapons were in the stockpile and had no factual knowledge on that highly classified subject; but I went on to say that we should not have used nuclear weapons unless in retaliation against a nuclear attack.

I wondered whether the president was trying to discover my point of view or whether he seriously considered using nuclear weapons. In all likelihood, he questioned me about the stockpile to evaluate my character.

Some months before the moratorium went into effect in 1958, I received a nudge toward thinking about the possibility of missile defense. Air Force General E. E. Partridge invited me to visit the Strategic Air Command Center in Colorado Springs, Colorado. The massive stockpiling of nuclear arms by the Soviet Union and the United States started around this time. The difficulties of trying to hit a series of missiles traveling at hypersonic speeds made defense seem hopeless. But the extreme difficulty of a problem is no excuse for ignoring it, especially if the problem is of grave importance.

Exploring the amazing underground installation with General Partridge, I learned that an incoming missile would be observed by radar approximately twenty minutes before it struck its target in the United States. "However," General Partridge observed, with some frustration, "there is nothing more that we can do, other than to issue a warning."

There had been a few scattered and poorly coordinated attempts at instituting a civil defense program, so the warning would have saved some lives. General Partridge obviously felt this was far too little, and I think it highly probable that he had invited me to visit so that he could encourage me to worry about that problem as well. Partridge was successful. In that setting, his words brought home to me the importance of being able to take action to protect the nation in the event of a nuclear attack. From that point onward, I have had a deep and abiding interest in active defense.[9]

---

[9] Even so, I was not a full convert to the advisability of active defense for another few years.

For the first time, I began talking with my colleagues at Livermore about the means by which a missile might be intercepted. One idea soon looked quite promising. If an interceptor could come near the attack missile, a nuclear explosion of appropriate size could incapacitate the explosion mechanism in an enemy warhead.

To the general public, detonating nuclear weapons over one's own country is an absurd idea. But I knew, not only from theory but also from personal experience, that if the explosive was detonated five miles above ground, the effects at ground level would be minimal.

In the early 1950s, I once sat on the glass bottom of an observation plane, flying over southern Nevada, watching for the explosion of a nuclear device with a yield equivalent to a few kilotons of TNT. When it was set off, I almost missed it. Apart from a brief flash, it looked as if a pebble had been dropped in a clear pond and stirred up a small amount of mud. The shock wave, which arrived about half a minute later, was so slight that I could barely feel it over the normal bumpiness of the flight.

A shock wave becomes stronger as it travels upward and weaker as it travels downward. Thus, detonating a small defensive nuclear explosive to intercept and destroy an incoming multimegaton missile is by no means an absurdity. Little or no sound from such an explosion would be heard at ground level. Detonation at 25,000 feet might alter or form clouds of the sort seen in the wake of a jet airplane. A nuclear device detonated at five miles of altitude would not stir up dust and debris and would produce no more than a tiny fraction of the radioactivity of a ground burst. (The observation plane I rode in did have to veer out of the path of the subsequent mushroom cloud.)

The glimmer of that idea was much in my mind in 1963, when I testified to the Senate that even a limited test ban would impede our development of active defenses against nuclear weapons. Atmospheric tests were the way that we could best find out how to destroy an approaching nuclear missile. The atmospheric test ban made testing this possibility much more difficult. In addition, the proposed test ban treaty would produce even greater bureaucratic difficulties for the development of peaceful uses for nuclear explosives under the Plowshare program.

In 1959, I had met a medical radiologist, Dr. James R. Maxfield. At that time, Maxfield was president of the American College of Nuclear Medicine (ACNM), a group to which John Lawrence, Ernest Lawrence's brother, belonged. John asked me to offer a memorial tribute to Ernest at an ACNM conference that was being held in the Rocky Mountains. I agreed. After my talk, Maxfield invited me on a day-long hiking excursion to some nearby lakes. The day proved to be the beginning of my many decades-long close friendship with J. R., as he is affectionately known.

During the 1960s, Maxfield was active in political affairs, serving as an advisory board member of the Southern Governor's Conference and on the Texas Governor's Radiation Study Committee. I discussed the testimony I was planning to give on the atmospheric test-ban treaty with many friends. When J. R. heard that I was going to testify, he strongly recommended that I not do so, because, with Kennedy's strong support, the treaty would probably be ratified no matter what points I brought out. He pointed out that the principle of retreating when the battle is lost makes good political sense. Nonetheless, I testified against the treaty.

It was a day-long affair with my text given in the morning and questions and answers occupying most of the afternoon. On the whole, I was satisfied that I had done my best to present the other side of the treaty. But I was also certain that I had changed few minds. When, thoroughly tired, I arrived back at the hotel, I got a call from Dr. J. R. He had heard that my testimony was being widely discussed and asked whether I would be willing to take the next plane to the Southern Governors' Conference, which was going on at that time in Arkansas, to present my comments to them.

The thunder and lightening flashes going on outside my hotel room at that moment were making it difficult to hear or concentrate while I was talking. As I told J.R., the storm was so spectacular that I doubted that planes were flying. Besides that, I was exhausted. J.R. was undeterred. "Take the train," he said, "and I'll meet you at the station in Arkansas."

A few hours later, I was asleep on a train; it seemed only a brief time before the porter roused me. There was J. R. at the station to inform me that Kennedy had sent a message to the governors in protest of my speaking on the grounds that it would be a one-sided presentation because no one was there to present the other side of the issue. I thought this a strange situation because the president himself had come out strongly in support of the treaty. If anything, the shoe was on the other foot. I did not speak at the governors' conference.

Nonetheless, I felt the presidential protest had a greater element of flattery in it than anything I had yet received from that quarter. Again, I must confess that, in retrospect, I see some merit in Kennedy's action. If I had objections to the treaty, why hadn't I voiced them more strongly when I saw him earlier that year? As Maxfield had predicted, the Limited Test Ban Treaty was ratified and went into effect in late 1963.

Having resigned as director, I became a technical consultant to the Rockefeller Family Trust. That work proved to be most agreeable: It involved listening to ingenious people present the plans and projects of fledgling companies and then advising Laurance of my opinion about their chances for success.

One enterprise that I had found most interesting was the newly formed company called ThermoElectron, headed by a wide-awake Greek scientist-businessman, George Hatsopoulos, whom I immediately liked. (We subsequently became friends, a relationship which has proved lifelong.) The purpose of the company was the direct conversion of energy at the high temperature of several thousand degrees into an electric current.[10]

My advice about ThermoElectron resulted in the one clear and significant service I offered Laurance Rockefeller. He seemed unconvinced that Thermo-Electron was a good enterprise; I was able to assure him that the company had good and competent leadership. Indeed, it did turn out to be a profitable enterprise for the Rockefeller family.

Just as the work with Nelson had provided new political insights, the work with Laurance provided me with glimpses of the world of finance. My education in international affairs also grew, in part because of my friendship with George Hatsopoulos.

Hatsopoulos, like me, felt a strong tie to his native land; but, unlike me, he could visit it freely and help to rebuild its fortunes after World War II. This led, ultimately, to our taking a trip to Greece in July 1962, where we cruised the Mediterranean on a much smaller ship than an aircraft carrier.

We began in Athens, where we visited an institute of atomic studies. We then sailed through the Isthmus of Corinth, which connects mainland Greece with the Peloponnesian peninsula, on our way to Ithaca, the home of Odysseus, near the entrance to the Adriatic.

On a later trip with Hatsopoulos, in 1970, we visited the deposed Queen Frederika of Greece, who was then living on an island in the southern Adriatic Sea. She proved to be just as lovely and gracious as she had been during her earlier royal trip to Livermore. After that agreeable visit, we ended our excursion in Delphi. My main interest was not in visiting the site of the

---

[10] The principle was simple enough. The apparatus consisted of a metal with a high melting point, such as tungsten, from which the high temperature caused the emission—one might say, the evaporation—of electrons. Crossing a small distance in a conducting gas, they would be deposited on a metal of low surface temperature. From there, the electrons could return via electric wires to the hot tungsten, thereby closing the circuit. The efficiency of the energy conversion exceeded 10 percent. That does not appear particularly high, but the simplicity of the arrangement, which contained no moving parts, made it a promising enterprise.

Delphic oracle, justly famous for its ambiguities, but in seeing the mountain from which Aesop was hurled to his death.[11] I greatly enjoyed being able to fit the lovely scenery with the long-told stories.

During this period, a trip to another region that was new to me came about because of a physicist I had met at two or three physics conferences in the United States, Yuval Ne'eman. He sought me out and invited me to Israel. At first, I paid little attention, having at that time limited interest in the country.[12] But Yuval is the kind of person to whom I cannot say no. The events connected with the hydrogen bomb and with Oppenheimer had separated me from most of my earlier friends among the American physicists. Given my continuing isolation, new friends in the community of physicists were particularly important.

Yuval is a native-born Israeli whose family has lived in Jerusalem for generations. He was just eighteen years old at the time of Israel's war of independence, during which he served as a soldier. Subsequently, he stayed with the army as an intelligence officer and took an engineering degree from Israel's first academic institution, the Institute of Technology in Haifa.

When he was in his thirties, he was sent to London as a military attaché. In that role, he managed to get thoroughly bored. To make his time in London more interesting, he took up theoretical physics and, relatively late in life, became one of the true leaders in that endeavor. In the 1970s, he played an eminent role in the advances in the theory of quarks.[13]

I cannot describe Yuval as a man with a double personality, because he, like the quark, is triple: soldier, scientist, and politician. He founded a political party (Techiya), served in the Knesset (Israel's parliament) and eventually served three times as a cabinet member. He is a lively, multidimensional man, and I enjoy talking with him. From the first, he had urged me to come to Israel; eventually, probably at his instigation, Tel Aviv University invited me to give a few lectures, which I did in the late fall of 1965.

---

[11] The reason for his execution was that many Greeks recognized his tales as a justified (and therefore intolerable) criticism of their moral standards.

[12] That situation changed completely after my first introduction to the country. In the following years, I made many more trips to Israel.

[13] Quarks, in groups of three particles, make up the not-so-elementary particles called protons and neutrons. I believe that Murray Gell-Mann should have shared the Nobel Prize for their discovery with Ne'eman.

One of the great problems of Israel, and indeed of the entire Middle East, is the shortage of water. Before I left, I had called Lewis Strauss to learn more about Eisenhower's Atoms for Peace plan (which was really the Strauss plan) to build reactors for use in desalinization. The source of reasonably priced electricity would make water available both to Arabs and Israelis, and thus aid the prospects for peace in a highly unstable region. Unfortunately, at the end of my trip, I had to report to AEC Chairman Glenn Seaborg that the project did not appear to be practical.

At that time, Israel already had a functioning reactor at Dimona in the Negev desert region. The Israelis made no attempt to hide its presence from me, but neither did they appear interested in having me see it or discuss it. I am sure that at that time Israel was worried that China might arm Egypt with nuclear weapons. Considering the number of wars with Egypt that followed, the world can only be greatly relieved that this did not occur.

Yuval arranged for me to be introduced to Israel by a most interesting person, Admiral Ben Nur. The admiral had been among those who fought for Israel's independence. In an act of great courage, he had swum to an enemy ship anchored offshore and planted the explosives on its side that destroyed it. The admiral provided me an excellent tour of his small country and introduced me to the major sites and regions.

During this trip, I met with the Israeli military leader Moshe Dayan. He proved to be a remarkable mixture of success and failure. In 1965, when I met him, he was out of government, out of office, and working on a fishery. During the conversation, one of our group brought up the Sinai campaign, then nine years in the past. Would Mr. Dayan tell us about that? He did. I do not remember his exact words, but this was the gist:

> At the end of the fighting, we let the prisoners go except for a relatively small number of general officers, whom we kept in Israel and showed around, hoping they would learn something about us. As they went through a kibbutz, one of the Egyptian generals noticed the Israeli general who had captured him. The Israeli general was sitting on a three-legged stool, milking a cow. The Egyptian went past without averting his eyes, but then he came up to me and asked in a low voice, "Why was your general court-martialed?"

That was the end of Dayan's report on the Sinai campaign.

The most exciting meeting of the trip personally was seeing my favorite cousin, Ily, whom I had last seen in 1936. She had spent the terrible war years in the part of Hungary that became Romanian. Less than a year before I visited, she had managed to emigrate to Israel with the remaining fragments of her family. For the first time, she was looking into the future with real hope and with the humor she had never lost. When I asked her about Israeli politics, her brief answer was, "We have our troubles: The Messiah won't come, and Ben Gurion won't go."

Israel, I discovered, is a remarkable phenomenon. Although it remains an island in a sea of hostility, it is also an exemplar of the benefits of technological progress, a beacon of hope for improvement of the quality of life for all the peoples of the region.

While I was learning more about different regions of the world, I was continuing my apprenticeship in national affairs under the tutelage of Nelson Rockefeller. The most vivid memory of my work with him during the late 1950s and early 1960s is that I was confronted with environmental questions for the first time.

In this relatively early period, Nelson Rockefeller was a thoroughly interested environmentalist. Questions such as pollution from automobiles, the sad state of Pittsburgh (at that time), and the widespread pollution of Lake Erie were of great concern to him. Indeed, they deserved his interest.

In 1964, Nelson again ran in the Republican presidential primaries. I was concerned about the development of a split in the Republican Party into a right and left. Those of the right were, to my mind, wrong in matters of internal affairs, most especially on the civil rights issue. They were also wrong in their isolationist orientation. I thought it important to try to counter their increasing power within the party. Unfortunately, not enough people felt the same way. Nelson once again lost the nomination, this time to Barry Goldwater. Rockefeller continued as governor of New York, and in 1965, he faced the first major crisis of his tenure.

By coincidence, I witnessed the crisis as it occurred. I do not remember what brought me to New York City, but I was in a taxi heading toward Manhattan by way of the Triborough Bridge when the taxi driver said, "Look at that!" "What's the matter?" I asked. "The lights have gone out," he replied. Arriving at the hotel, I had to climb several flights of stairs to reach my room, but fortunately, the telephones were still working. The moon was still shining, so I decided to go for a walk. I have a vivid memory of how friendly the people in New York City were.

A power failure in an Ontario, Canada, plant had caused the blackout of parts of eight states. The temporary failure of electric power from Canada led to steeply increasing demands on domestic sources, including a major station in New York City, which I believe was called the Ravenswood station.

Unfortunately, Ravenswood was temporarily closed down; when called on for compensatory electricity, it could not respond. The demands on the system led to a shutdown of generators, and the entire system was knocked out completely. A widespread blackout ensued that lasted for many hours.

It struck me that the basic reason for the blackout was only to a small extent a lack of power. To a greater extent, lack of information caused the blackout. The operators were ignorant of the status of the generators throughout the system. Had they been fully informed, they would have made other arrangements, which included accepting a more temporary blackout affecting a much smaller area.

It is quite difficult to be informed of all the details of an extensive system of electric power generators mutually supporting one another. But by the mid-1960s, the problem could have been easily solved by computers that reported the minute-by-minute status of each power generator to a computer available to the operator-dispatcher. He would then have been currently informed and could even have asked the computer to determine the consequences of the decisions he considered. The seemingly complex problem of making electricity available was within the technical possibilities of that time. Nelson gave me the opportunity to make those recommendations publicly. Unfortunately, they were not adopted at that time.[14] Instead, plans were made for a hydroelectric station to be built at Storm King Mountain.

My involvement with the Storm King project did not occur directly because of Nelson Rockefeller but because I had become knowledgeable about the problems of the energy supply of New York City. The hydroelectric power station planned near West Point was based on a reservoir that would be created near Storm King Mountain. The electricity that would be generated by discharging water from the lake would insure New York against future blackouts. Nonetheless, environmentalists objected.

Because I felt strongly that the planned hydroelectric station was fully justified and would cause minimal damage to the environment, I decided to volunteer to campaign for the plan. Nelson readily gave his permission, so together with two friends, I appeared at public meetings on the topic to answer questions.[15] The attorney representing the environmentalist cause was Herbert Marks, who had been part of Oppenheimer's defense team at the hearings.

---

[14] Fortunately, the damage from this particular blackout was not terribly great. A second blackout some years later resulted in rioting and destruction.

[15] The two friends, who will be introduced in the next chapter were Lowell Wood and Harry Sahlin.

One of the questions Marks put to us was particularly easy: What financial interests did we have in the project? The answer was: None. Later, I learned that after our testimony, several witnesses who were to testify against the project withdrew, perhaps in part because they were uncomfortable about having to answer the same question. Nonetheless, the reservoir project was defeated.

Those early experiences in environmental protection gave me a foretaste of something that was to grow into an important international issue. A quarter of a century ago, I was converted from a person who approved most efforts for improving the environment into one who looks at environmentalists' arguments with some skepticism.

To close the chapter where it began, I need to return from my travels during this period to the Livermore laboratory. In 1965, Johnny Foster followed in Harold Brown's footsteps and accepted the post of Director of Defense Research and Engineering in Washington. Mike May, an émigré from France, and a computer expert, assumed the post of director; he carried on most competently during the following six years, a period when the emphasis nationally was on developing treaties to limit the development of weapons technology.

Although the politics of the Cold War dominated these years (1960 to 1965), some developments were more encouraging than others. The western democracies were learning to be cooperative partners rather than rivals. For the first time in four hundred years, France and Germany signed a treaty of cooperation. In addition, at the prompting of Leo Szilárd, the United States and the Soviet Union (in the aftermath of the Cuban missile crisis) established a permanent, ever-ready telephone link, a hot line, between the White House and the Kremlin. And Livermore responded to the increased Soviet efforts to intimidate the free world by developing the warheads for the Poseidon, Spartan, and Minuteman missiles, thereby continuing its tradition of providing strength for a nation committed to peace.

37

EDUCATING
INVENTIVE ENGINEERS

───────

1961–1975

DURING THE FIRST half of the 1960s, I spent a great deal of time and effort on issues pertaining to education. My daughter, Wendy, was then in high school, and Paul was entering college, and I was somewhat disturbed by some of the current practices. In addition, I was a teacher, and it was during this period that I apparently caused the University of California to come under investigation by the California legislature.[1]

But my primary concern was with a different subject. In early 1963, I described it rather succinctly in a letter I wrote to Henry Kissinger (who was advising Nelson Rockefeller):

> In the field of pure science the United States is in a leading position. . . . In pure engineering we have a considerable number of competent men. . . . There is, however, an intermediate field on which the demands are the greatest and the supply in the United States is minimal. This is a field which lies between pure science and traditional engineering. You may describe it as inventive engineering or you may instead call it applied science. The two expressions really mean the same thing.
>
> A few institutions like M.I.T. and Cal Tech are doing a good job in this field. Even these are deficient in many respects, and there can be no doubt that our total educational effort in this area is insufficient. As a consequence of this

───────

[1] It seems that 1,000 students were unable to get into my Physics 10 course, and many of them (or their parents) complained to their legislators. The problem could not be resolved easily. The lecture hall held only six hundred seats, and once those were filled, conventional classroom practices, if not the laws of physics, prevented more bodies from occupying the same space.

deficiency, the billions of dollars spent on defense, on space, and on improving our industrial products are wasted to a considerable extent. I would guess that a hundred thousand really competent men in the field of applied science could improve our production by an amount somewhere between ten billion and one hundred billion dollars per year. . . .

The reason [for the shortage] is that applied science occupies a position of no man's land between pure science and engineering. The pure scientists look down upon it as an effort that is boring and unworthy . . . of a person who is interested in basic truths. On the other hand, our engineers are trained in a traditional manner emphasizing the use of handbooks and the exploitation of past experience rather than discoveries. The pure scientists underestimate the great intellectual stimulation that one can derive from working on applied science, and they are wrong in assuming that pure research is intrinsically more valuable than applied research. On the other hand, the workaday engineers fail to recognize the most eminently practical values that recent basic discoveries can generate.

That concern motivated me in two major undertakings: the establishment of a university-level educational facility at the Livermore laboratory and the reorganization of the Hertz Fellowship awards.

The Berkeley Radiation Laboratory, despite being constrained by issues of clearances and governmental regulations, had long been successfully integrated into the University of California, Berkeley. It had served as a marvelous training ground for physicists who, as a result of their connection with the Berkeley laboratory, entered their chosen field with a considerable head start on their productivity.

Although the Livermore laboratory was thirty miles away, it had grown during the decade since its founding into a tremendous research center, and in 1961 it possessed a pool-type nuclear reactor, a ninety-inch cyclotron, one of the world's most advanced digital computers, a considerable number of contained-plasma machines, molecular and electron beam apparatus, and many other instruments of great usefulness for research and development.

In addition to exceptional equipment, Livermore also possessed an outstanding group of scientists—a splendid potential teaching staff.[2] Recognizing the

---

[2] Even today, the list of laboratory employees who, in 1963, were eager to teach part-time seems impressive: Berni Alder, Stewart Bloom, Richard Borg, Stephen Brush, David Dorn, Sidney Fernbach, Harold Furth, Walter John, Montgomery Johnson, Allan Kaufman, John Killeen, Albert Kirschbaum, Cecil Leith, Michael May, Richard Post, Richard Stuart, and Richard von Holdt.

wealth of educational resources in the Livermore laboratory, I began a campaign to put them to more comprehensive use.

At that time, the curriculum I proposed was somewhat unusual: All the general science courses would emphasize application. The graduate studies would initially consist of a core of engineering, mathematics, and physical science courses; advanced students would specialize in nuclear chemistry, physical chemistry, computer technology, materials science, or plasma physics. The faculty would include Livermore researchers, who would dedicate a portion of their time to instructing students and supervising the research of graduate students, thereby exposing the students to the most recent research in their field of interest.

I approached UC President Clark Kerr about establishing such a school at Livermore. He was encouraging, so we pursued the idea further. We quickly discovered that the professors, especially those in the history department, were unhappy to think that students would receive a university degree at Berkeley but fulfill their course requirements at Livermore. With President Kerr's encouragement, we tried various modifications to make the plan more palatable, all without success.

During this period, I won a valuable ally, Ralph W. Chaney, who was a distinguished emeritus professor of paleobotany at Berkeley. I no longer remember how he came to espouse our cause, but Ralph was as distressed as I that Livermore's great potential for contribution should go untapped. Because he had a great deal of experience in educational projects as well as in administrative affairs, he was a wonderful resource person. I particularly enjoyed his sense of humor. In his garden in Berkeley, he had planted representatives of plants from all the various geological periods. He said that his purpose in this was to befuddle paleobotanists who, in the far future, might excavate the site.

While I was teaching a class in the fall of 1961 in the Berkeley department of nuclear engineering, I met another man who played an important role in founding the Department of Applied Science.[3] I was allowed to have a graduate student as a teaching assistant for my course; among the students I interviewed from the department was Wilson K. Talley.

Wilson's recollection of our interview differs from my own. He asserts that I stood him up at the blackboard for fifteen minutes to explain the difference between a shock wave and a sound wave, to jot down the Rankine-Hugoniot

---

[3] At that time, Tom Pigford was chairman of the department and Hans Mark was an associate professor.

equations, to sketch a Hugoniot adiabat, and to provide a mathematical instability to go with a physical instability. Wilson adds:

> I wonder where I would be today if, even once during that fifteen minutes, I had answered one of those questions correctly. I believe that Edward felt he had never seen anyone with more room for improvement and took me on as a personal challenge to his skills as a teacher. I remain today his greatest failure.

Those comments are to my mind a gross misrepresentation of what went on. Wilson, even at that time, was an able and talented man. Indeed, he has been a friend since that meeting and has over the years collaborated on two books with me, the first of which we began that year.[4]

Wilson would take notes of my lectures on the constructive uses of nuclear explosives and bring them to my house where we would go over them. At the end of the year, he typed them up, and they became the first three chapters of our book.[5] It was a collaborative effort: In addition to the four chapters Wilson and I wrote, Jerry Johnson, who headed the test division of the laboratory and oversaw the Plowshare experiments, and Gary Higgins, a radiochemist at the laboratory who was working on the earth-moving, petroleum, and mining aspects of Plowshare, each added a chapter. It was finally finished in 1967 and became a moderately popular textbook in nuclear engineering classes.[6]

Although I enjoyed teaching the course on the peaceful uses of atomic explosives, I was frustrated. If only the Livermore laboratory could be included in a partnership arrangement with the university, all the results of the experiments we were conducting under the Plowshare program would be available to students and would greatly enrich their understanding. After almost two years of trying unsuccessfully to work things out with the Berkeley administrators, I decided to approach another school. I would try to set up a collaborative arrangement between Livermore and the University of California at Davis, geographically the next-closest campus to Livermore.

---

[4] The second book, *Conversations on the Dark Secrets of Physics*, which includes my daughter, Wendy, as a third author, began with the notes of my Physics 10 class. It was published in 1991 by Plenum Press, and has been translated into Korean, German, Italian, and Hungarian.
[5] Edward Teller, et al., *The Constructive Uses of Nuclear Explosives* (New York: McGraw-Hill, 1968).
[6] I published other books during this period; among them was *The Legacy of Hiroshima*, which I wrote with a professional writer, Allen Brown.

The small town of Davis, California, is located about sixty miles from Livermore. John Foster, who was then the director of the laboratory, was a strong supporter of the idea of a graduate division at Livermore, and he agreed that we should widen our search. Ralph Chaney and I drove over and approached the UC–Davis chancellor, Emil Mrak. We had learned enough by then to limit our request to graduate students (rather than trying to include undergraduates). Chancellor Mrak was interested in the idea, but once again some of the professors balked at the thought that others might be teaching their students.

The Davis campus was trying to build its new College of Engineering, then headed by Roy Bainer. Dean Bainer was enthusiastic about the idea of adding Livermore's resources, and more productive negotiations began. This time, after many more months of negotiations, including some with the AEC, we overcame all the obstacles: The Department of Applied Science (DAS) would be established at Livermore and would be part of the College of Engineering, University of California, Davis. Classes would be conducted at both locations, with Livermore's pool of talent contributing as lecturers and supervisors of graduate students.

Today, the arrangement is intact. DAS is the first and most comprehensive use of a national laboratory for graduate student education and research. DAS has granted more than two hundred Ph.D.'s, and almost an equal number of master of science degrees.[7] The doctoral candidates have chosen their advisors from either the faculty on the Davis campus or from any of several hundred researchers at the Livermore National laboratory. In addition, because of the unique advanced equipment and the specialized advisors available, no Ph.D. candidates working on an experimental thesis have ever suffered the (all too common) discovery near the end of their research that their thesis project has been scooped by a student at another school.

Much as I dislike administrative tasks, I found that if the DAS was to get off to a successful start, I had to become an administrator once again. I became chairman of the DAS and held the post for the first two and a half years of its existence. The department in Davis hired one full-time employee, my recently

---

[7] About one-third of those graduates are employed at DOE laboratories, and half of those are at Livermore. The deputy director of Livermore (Bob Kuckuck) is among them. Ted Gold, former director of Sandia, is also a DAS graduate, as is Lee Buchanan, the deputy director of the Defense Advanced Research Projects Agency (DARPA). Several more of the many outstanding DAS graduates are mentioned later in this chapter and in note 22.

graduated teaching assistant, Wilson Talley, to instruct their enrollees. The university added a half-time vice chairman, Al Kirschbaum (who had formerly headed the nuclear reactor program at the laboratory), to serve on the Livermore campus. A trailer was brought in to house the administrative office, and two rooms in the old Barracks building were designated to serve as classrooms.

We welcomed the first group of eighty-one students—twelve of them full-time, the rest employees of the laboratory interested in finishing their advanced degrees—in the fall of 1963. One of those students stands out in my memory: Richard A. Van Konynenburg is still at Livermore laboratory today. Rich had just finished his undergraduate degree at Davis in agricultural and mechanical engineering and had won a Sloan Fellowship to pursue graduate studies at Cornell. Dr. Bainer sent Rich to talk to me. Rich knew little about physics, but after I had talked with him, I had no doubts about his abilities. I convinced him to switch to DAS, and he quickly proved himself an outstanding student.

Rich recently shared some of his reminiscences of that time in a letter to my collaborator:

> I think all of the students found the classes very challenging. I certainly did. Dr. Teller went out of his way to help us by instituting weekly help sessions in which we were invited to raise any topic with which we were having difficulty. At the first session, no one raised any questions. This was not because we understood everything in the lectures. Rather we were all aware that the future of the Department was hanging in the balance of our performance, and that the standards for grading would probably be high since the Department would have to prove itself to the University. We suspected that not all the students would pass, and none of us wanted to fail. Therefore, we weren't very interested in displaying our ignorance to each other in the presence of Dr. Teller. Dr. Teller seemed disappointed at the lack of response, and we collectively resolved that next time we would have some questions ready.
>
> The following week, a student raised his hand and told Dr. Teller that he had a problem understanding something in Dr. Michael May's class in electromagnetic theory. It was some kind of polynomial, but he couldn't understand what Dr. May was saying, nor could he find it in the textbook. Further discussion revealed that the topic in question was Legendre polynomials. Dr. Teller wrote the word on the board, and the student immediately recalled seeing it in the textbook.
>
> At the next meeting of the electromagnetic theory class, Dr. May opened the class by saying, "Edward tells me that you have a problem with my pronunciation of Legendre." He wrote the word on the board. Then he said,

"Legendre is a French word. I am French. Edward is Hungarian." That was the end of the matter.

I should add that not all the later questions raised in my study group were settled as easily.

Like many of the students from the early days of DAS, I recall the Christmas parties that Mici and I held at our home in an effort to help the students—who were at a most unusual campus in its beginning stage—to develop a sense of community. But I had forgotten about the Picnic Days at Davis until Rich reminded me of the 1965 DAS float. Like the Christmas parties, Picnic Days were intended to develop cohesiveness, but in this instance, the cohesiveness we were hoping for was with the Davis campus, where Picnic Day—which included a parade of floats and an old-fashioned picnic (provided by the faculty)—was the major event of the year.

Rich remembers in detail the first float the DAS students built. It was titled "Our Cousins—the Livermorons," and featured Ted Eller, Barry Boson, Cousin Sherwood (Sherwood was the name of the magnetic fusion program), Molly Molecule (dramatized by our only coed, who was a good sport), Cousin Plowshare, and someone holding a "fission pole." Rich notes, "We didn't win any prizes, but Teller Tech, as the students called it, was at least represented."

The following year, with the enrollment up to thirty-four full-time graduate students and thirty-two attending part-time, the Davis campus hired another part-time instructor, one of Willard Libby's recent graduates from UCLA, Carl Jensen. The following year, 1965, when the department had grown to sixty-five full-time and twenty-eight part-time graduate students attending, the university hired two more half-time faculty members for the Davis campus: George Sauter, who had recently finished his studies in the Berkeley Department of Nuclear Engineering, and one of Willard Libby's recent graduates in geochemistry, Lowell Wood.

Both men were excellent, but my friendship with Lowell Wood has been one of the more important relationships in my life. He has become a sort of auxiliary son.[8] I first became acquainted with Lowell when I lectured at UCLA in 1959. I was struck from the beginning by Lowell's irreverence. He was fond of his professor, but he openly called Bill Libby "Wuffle," a phonetic form of Libby's initials, W. F. L. For a physicist, Lowell is exceptionally

---

[8] Lowell has supplied me with the father-son controversies that my gentle son, Paul, failed to provide.

well educated in biology and the humanities. He admits that I know more about Hungarian history than he does, but he claims that that is the only area where I can beat him.

At any rate, during the years that Lowell was in graduate school, we met whenever I visited UCLA and discussed his thesis work on solar and interplanetary physics. We would then go on to an ever-widening list of topics. Lowell recalls that during that time he had clashed with my friend Bill McMillan, who was then chairman of the Department of Chemistry at UCLA. As a result, Lowell had been banished from the Chemistry Department. Consequently, we held our talks in the hallways outside the laboratories. Others attended these discussions, which would often start in the afternoon and run on late into the evening. I often took Lowell to dinner at a little French restaurant nearby; there we would continue talking until the restaurant closed. I found Lowell a most engaging and refreshing companion.

I was particularly happy at the finish of his graduate studies that Lowell accepted a part-time position at Davis, which was combined with a part-time consulting appointment at the Livermore laboratory. Together with another young physicist from the laboratory, Harry Sahlin, he also joined the team that was examining the electrical supply in New York for Nelson Rockefeller. A year or two later, Lowell began collaborating with John Nuckolls on fusion micro-explosion studies, and with me on two studies— one modeling supernova explosions and the other examining the conditions under which thermonuclear detonation waves can propagate in matter.

I enjoyed working with Lowell as a collaborator, but I had little time left for contemplation or research.[9] These were busy years for me. In 1960, when I had resigned my position as director of the Livermore laboratory, the University of California named me Professor of Physics at Large. The position enabled me to teach at any of the campuses of the university, and proved to be convenient in connection with establishing DAS. During 1963 and 1964, I taught two classes on the Davis campus (Production and Use of Nuclear Energy, and Structure of Matter, which was an introduction to quantum mechanics), and a further course at Livermore (Statistical Theory of Equilibrium and Transport Phenomena). This meant a great deal of commuting back and

---

[9] I also found it hard to keep up my music, although it was during this time that I was invited to play with the Ruth Quartet, which was based in Los Angeles. We gave one performance during the noon hour at UCLA, and we played well. Some of those in the physics department who opposed my work on weapons came to the concert. One of my strongest adversaries came up afterward and said with a warm smile, "If only you had stayed with music."

forth over the sixty-mile stretch between the two campuses (as well as the thirty-mile commute from Berkeley to Livermore most days). Fortunately, Gen Phillips was willing to accompany me or even drive me when the need arose, so I was able to do most of my office work while traveling.

During those years, I also taught Physics 10 at Berkeley, at UCLA, and at Rice University (in 1961). My stay in Houston for the Rice lectures was pleasant. I had met Oveta Culp Hobby—who was at this time president and editor of the *Houston Post*—through Nelson Rockefeller. She kindly invited Mici and me to stay in her home during the time I gave the physics appreciation course at Rice University because she was going to be out of town for those eight weeks.

We did so, and I particularly appreciated Oveta's library. She had many classics with which I was not familiar, and I read Plato's *Republic* for the first time during my stay. Although I applauded Plato's courageous defense of Socrates, I discovered that I not only disagreed with Plato about atomic theory but I thoroughly disagreed with his elitist ideas about government. I was shocked that a book advocating a centralized government administered from above, much on the lines of totalitarianism, was so highly recommended to young people. Eventually, I incorporated some of my thoughts in a lecture series I gave at University of Missouri in 1963, which was later published as a small book, *The Reluctant Revolutionary*.[10]

When Lowell joined the faculty, Carl Jensen was able to take over my quantum mechanics class at Davis. Carl didn't want to provide the lectures himself; instead, he would videotape the lecture I gave to the Livermore students, then drive back to Davis with the tape and show it to his class there. He would answer questions from the students and leave the tape available for them to review. Not surprisingly, at the end of the year, many more of his students than of mine placed in the top half of the class on their exams. I am happy to note that making lecture tapes available for student review has become a common educational practice.

By 1967, Lowell was bringing his best and brightest students at Davis into the laboratory for summer work. Over the course of time, he has, beyond a doubt, introduced more exceptionally talented young people to the work at Livermore than any other person. He accomplished that in part through his activities in the Department of Applied Science, but also because he became involved in another project, the Hertz Foundation Fellowships, which was developing during this same period.

---

[10] Edward Teller, *The Reluctant Revolutionary* (Columbia, Mo.: University of Missouri Press, 1964).

I became involved in the Hertz Foundation because, one day in the late 1950s, my friend Floyd Odlum took me to meet John Hertz, one of his old acquaintances who had left the bulk of his considerable fortune for educational purposes. Well before the turn of the century, Hertz and his family came to the United States from Austro-Hungary. He received his education in the public schools of the United States and went into business, where he founded, among other enterprises, the Yellow Cab Company and the Hertz Rent-A-Car enterprise. At our first and only meeting, which took place about a year before he died, Hertz explained to me that he felt deeply grateful to the United States and had in 1948 established a foundation, named after his wife and him. He asked me to join the board of advisors.

At the time I began meeting with the board, Edwin L. Weisl, a lawyer who had aided in setting up the foundation, was chairman of the board. Floyd Odlum was president, and among the other board members were Paul and Helen Hertz Hexter (Hertz's daughter and son-in-law), Harry Wyatt (of the Chicago law firm D'Ancona, Wyatt, Flam & Riskind), Herman Kahn (a partner in the investment firm of Lehman Brothers), and Allen Hunter (an investment advisor who managed the foundation's funds). I managed to have another scientist, Lawrence Hafstadt (vice president for engineering at General Motors) added to the board not long after I joined.

The foundation had one arm that functioned under the title of the Bay Area Pilot Project.[11] It awarded talented high school students scholarships for undergraduate work in science and mathematics. But the main effort went to awarding scholarships to undergraduate students studying engineering. These scholarships were given on the basis of college records and recommendations.

The only distinguishing characteristic of the Hertz scholarships at that time was that they were given to students who intended to become engineers. Hertz believed, correctly I think, that there was great value in applying the concepts of science through engineering. Engineers are, by definition, people whose work is dedicated to making people's lives easier; or, as people used to say, whose work is dedicated to progress.

In about 1960, a few of us on the Hertz board started to feel that ours was just another foundation whose efforts did not make much of a difference and that something more effective was needed. I then proposed a radically different

---

[11] For several years during the late 1960s and early 1970s, Mici ran the Bay Area Pilot Project, assisted for part of the period by Gen Phillips. Eventually, Mici found the job too time consuming and turned the work over to Hans Mark. Because of changes in college assistance programs, by 1997 the Bay Area Pilot Project had almost ceased distributing funds.

approach: Give several fellowships of the highest monetary value possible to students interested in working for a Ph.D. in engineering.

This was an unusual proposal. Students able to qualify for doctoral studies could easily get high-paying jobs in industry; even the maximum stipends we would be able to offer could not begin to compete with those salaries. Nonetheless, some students might be willing temporarily to accept less money in exchange for the privilege of developing their talents fully.

The selection of students able to fulfill the unique challenges of being imaginative engineers could not be made in the standard fashion. I recommended that grades and written recommendations be used only to eliminate candidates who were not in the running. But we also specified that candidates with some indication of excellence who were working under the handicap of foreign birth or who were economically disadvantaged should not be eliminated if their written records were not up to the highest standard.

That would leave us with a few hundred candidates. We would then select the best among them through personal interviews conducted by at least two separate interviewers. To emphasize the novel character of the procedure, we proposed to call the awards Fellowships in Applied Science rather than Fellowships in Engineering.

I continue to be astonished that my radical suggestions were accepted. I believe they were accepted only because most of my fellow board members did not realize what a true departure my proposal was. But because it was accepted, I found myself in the position of having become responsible for conducting the interviews, a time-consuming and demanding task.

In 1962–1963, the first group of applicants for Hertz graduate fellowships, about thirty of them, was interviewed, and I interviewed each one of them. After that, I do not think a year passed in which I conducted a full hundred interviews; although for several years, I don't think I was ever far short of that. Eventually I persuaded colleagues from Livermore, Berkeley, and other places to help me.[12]

Over time, many of my friends and successors adopted the style of the interview I conducted; thus it has become a part of the tradition of the Hertz Foundation. Early in the interview, I would ask the student what his main interest was and what field or fields he wanted emphasized in the interview. I had no

---

[12] Many board members were chosen from among those who assisted in the interviews: Arthur Kantrowitz, Hans Mark, Jack Boyd, Wilson Talley, Lowell Wood, and Jay Davis. Several former Hertz Fellows also serve on the current board: Greg Canavan, Richard Miles, Tom Weaver, and Tom McCann.

interest in finding out what the applicant didn't know. I was trying to find out in what respect he or she might be outstanding. I then tried to pose questions of real interest, even of considerable difficulty, in the field of the student's choice. If a student showed an interest in computers, I would ask how to find errors in the results of a computer. Those telling me that they wanted to work on aircraft got a chance to tell me how it came about that, during flight, the pressure under the wing was greater than the pressure above it.

I thought all students should be able to answer certain questions. One short question was: How big is an atom? Another question was: If you are engaged in a game of heads or tails with a stake of a penny a throw and persist for a thousand throws, how much do you expect to win or lose?[13] The answer is connected with the simplest facts of statistics, and it was surprising to see how many good engineering students had no clue. I did not consider that a serious shortcoming. I would offer some general suggestions and see how far each one could reason.

Why did I ask that question? Science is the search for phenomena that can be predicted with certainty. In applied science, random events and mistakes become important and must be dealt with in a commonsense way. An application fails if errors and random events exceed the limits of tolerance. Therefore, if one wants to do something practical, one must have a feel for the probable as well as for the certain, because certainty in applications falls short of the complete answer.

I also often asked a question about the Oort paradox. I asked this question to see how the candidate reacted to a novel question, and to evaluate the extent of his or her general information. Consider the light produced by all the stars. The light that reaches us from a star is proportional to $1/R^2$, where R is the distance of the star from the earth. Consider the stars in spherical shells of equal thickness. The number of stars is proportional to the thickness of the shell and to the area of the shell, which increases as R^2. To get the total light, we multiply R^2 by $1/R^2$. Thus the light is proportional to the thickness of the shell. Why don't we get infinite light from the stars?

The answer is that the stars we see are almost all in the Milky Way system; their number is not infinite. Take, as the radius of the first shell, a few light years of thickness. One star gives 10^{-10} times the light of the sun. The radius

---

[13] The simplest answer would be ten dollars if you lost or won every toss. It is almost no exaggeration to say this would never happen. The probability of winning or losing more than a dollar (three standard deviations from the mean) is about one-tenth of 1 percent.

of the Milky Way is approximately 50,000 light years. The light received from all those stars should add up to little more than 1/1,000,000 the light of the sun. There are other galaxies, but they are far distant and widely spaced; although we get some light from them, it is small. Furthermore, the universe is finite in size and is expanding. Therefore, the light we receive from distant stars is shifted to the red and the energy is reduced. The more inventiveness the student showed when he or she did not have a precise answer, the more I was encouraged.[14]

The question that to my mind provoked the most revealing response was the one I asked the applicant to ask me—about any topic. Some students would ask about a personal matter or about some of my experiences. Others would ask about career opportunities or about the Hertz Foundation. But some, and I was eager for such a response, would ask me a technical question. I liked it best when students posed questions from their own fields of interest.

To my mind, the interview was only in part concerned with what the student knew. The main point was to discover where the student's interest lay, and whether his curiosity would lead him to work really hard to find the answer. The opportunity to ask a question was simply a starting point to find out how the applicant felt about his field and his future.

We awarded our first Hertz Fellowships in Applied Science in 1963. Rich Van Konynenburg received a fellowship in 1963 and was one of the first recipients to use it at DAS. (At this time, Hertz Fellows could study at Cal Tech, M.I.T., the University of Chicago, the University of California, or at the Department of Applied Science at Livermore.[15]) Six more Hertz Fellowships went to students who chose to study at DAS in the following two years;

---

[14] Forty years before these interviews, I prided myself on being able to pass examinations a little more effectively than was justified by my knowledge. I remember that once in Karlsruhe, I was being examined on the composition of the atmosphere. I responded that it was made up of nitrogen, oxygen, and rare gases. Which rare gases and in what proportions? I was asked. I didn't know, but I went on talking as if I did. "There is helium and argon," I announced. "If helium predominates, the atmosphere would be less dense. If argon were more abundant, the reverse would be true." While I was answering, I was watching the faces of my examiners closely to determine which was the correct answer. When I spotted it, I did not go on; instead, I waited for them to ask me, "Well, which predominates?" And I responded as if I had known all along, "Why, of course, argon does." Now I was on the other side of the table, fully aware of the advantages the examinee had over the examiner.

[15] Today, the Hertz Fellowship may be used at any of thirty-one schools, including the eight University of California campuses, and Harvard, Yale, Princeton, Cornell, University of Wisconsin-Madison, University of Illinois-Champagne/Urbana, University of Washington, University of Texas-Austin, and Johns Hopkins University.

among them, Mike McCracken (who is today a leader in modeling atmospheric systems), Margaret Fulton Fels (who is a senior scientist in the Center for Energy and Environmental Studies at Princeton), and Greg Canavan, whose contributions will be described in this chapter and in Chapter 40.

As I recall, at one board meeting, Eddie Weisl and Paul and Helen Hexter suggested that I might be having an inordinate amount of influence on the Hertz Fellowships.[16] I felt that I was in an untenable position and immediately began to take steps to disentangle myself from conducting the interviews.

By the time I had made an inroad on distributing that responsibility to others, Eddie Weisl had died, and Floyd Odlum had become both chairman and president. Not long thereafter, Wilson Talley was elected to the board and was almost immediately elected president, a job he kept until ill health forced him to retire in 1998.[17] When Floyd and Wilson convinced me that the Hertz Foundation needed me to continue interviewing, I did so—although to a lesser extent—until the late 1970s or early 1980s.

Paul and Helen Hexter went to great lengths to repair the breach that had occurred.[18] They began to send me beautiful monogrammed ties for my birthday and continued to do so until Paul Hexter died. Those ties enable me to claim to be the only person openly designated as an extraterrestrial before the initials became popular. As it turned out, part of the rift occurred because Paul Hexter was interested in spending Hertz funds in other ways. One of his suggestions, which we adopted, was to give awards for excellent accomplishments in engineering.

The first award of the Hertz Prize was made in 1966 and went to Ali Javan and Theodore Maiman, the two men who developed lasers.[19] (Charles Townes, together with Nikolai Basov and Aleksander Prokhorov, received the 1964 Nobel Prize for developing the concept of lasers.) President Lyndon Johnson, a friend of Eddie Weisl's, presented the award to Maiman and Javan at the White House.

In 1976, Paul Hexter also suggested that the Hertz Foundation give matching funds to the University of California to construct a permanent

---

[16] Other board members have subsequently told me that the underlying problem was that Weisl and others felt that John Hertz's focus on engineering was too narrow.

[17] A year later, John F. Holzrichter, a former Hertz fellow and an employee of Lawrence Livermore's National Laboratory, became president of the Hertz Foundation.

[18] Paul Hexter was extremely successful as a breeder of race horses, and eventually he left his money to the foundation.

[19] Unfortunately, a priority fight developed between the two of them, and they were not on speaking terms when they received the award.

building to house the classrooms and offices of the DAS at Livermore. Before that, the department had conducted its affairs in temporary buildings. The present building, named in honor of John and Fannie Hertz, was dedicated in 1977. Nelson Rockefeller kindly came and gave the dedication address.

On that occasion, a second Hertz Prize was awarded, this one to a particularly eminent former Hertz Fellow, Greg Canavan. Greg had arrived at the DAS–Davis campus in 1965 following his graduation from the U.S. Air Force Academy. He had won an AEC fellowship, but it was good for only three years. Hertz can claim him because we gave him a fellowship for his final year of study.

Greg did some outstanding work on shielding missiles against laser radiation while he was in the air force, part of which was later published in the open (unclassified) literature.[20] It was for this work that he was awarded the Hertz Prize. A few years later, he resigned from the air force and joined the Los Alamos laboratory.

By January 2000, the Hertz Foundation had awarded 963 fellowships. Today, Hertz fellowships represent at least one-half those given in the field of applied science in the United States. Much of the other half is awarded by the National Science Foundation. At present, the Hertz fund supports about a hundred graduate students each year at a cost of about $2.25 million. The average fellow is funded for about four years, although some take five.

The Hertz fund began in 1948 with about $3 million. In the past thirty-five years, it has spent about $40 million. It currently has about $38 million left. I believe this to be a truly respectable accomplishment.[21]

---

[20] G. Canavan, "Breakdown of Deuterium with a Ruby Laser," *Proceedings of the IEEE* 59, 4 (April 1971): 187–188; "Theory of Laser Target Interaction in the Presence of a Shielding Plasma," *Proceedings of the Fifth Department of Defense Conference on Laser Technology* 1 (May 1972): 72–75; "CO_2 Laser Air Breakdown Calculations," *Proceedings of the VII International Quantum Electronics Conference, IEEE Journal of Quantum Electronics* 9, 1 (January 1971): 154; "Focal Spot Size Dependence of Gas Breakdown Induced by Particulate Ionization," *Proceedings of the XXV Gaseous Electronics Conference: Applied Physics Letters* (April 1973); Rensselaer Polytechnic Institute, "Laser Absorption Waves in the Atmosphere," *Proceedings of the Third Workshop on Laser Interaction with Matter* (August 1973); and "Electron Cascade Theory of Laser-Induced Breakdown in Pre-ionized Gases," *Journal of Applied Physics* 44, 9 (September 1973): 4224–4225.

[21] Much of the credit for this financial accomplishment belongs to Allen Hunter, who for most of those years managed to earn 16 percent per year or better on the Hertz funds.

Today, Hertz Fellows are playing important roles in a multitude of technology advances. Some have made a considerable contribution at the Livermore laboratory. About 35 of the 1,200 Ph.D. scientists currently employed at the laboratory are former Hertz Fellows.[22] Hertz Fellows as a group have come to constitute one of the nation's outstanding resources, just as John Hertz had hoped.

---

[22] Upon discovering that the ten brightest people working on SDI were former Hertz Fellows, an author writing about the Strategic Defense Initiative drew the conclusion that Hertz Fellows were mainly employed in weapons laboratories. Had he investigated thoroughly, he would have discovered that the ten brightest people working on the fifth-generation computer were also Hertz Fellows—among them Danny Hillis (founder of Thinking Machines); T. J. Rogers (founder and CEO of Cypress Semiconductor Corporation), Nathan Myhrvold (vice president of research for Microsoft), and David Tuckerman (whose micro-channel cooling process is important not only for microprocessor chips but also for solid state lasers). The same situation exists in connection with biological technology—for example, DAS graduate Eric Altschuler designed software manipulation of EEG patterns that allows people to think of a letter of the alphabet and have a computer print it; Robert Howard has refined the U.S. Navy Diving Tables; and DAS graduate David Galas, former coordinator of the U.S. program on the Human Genome, now is president of Darwin Molecular. Astronomy and space research have also benefited: Hertz Fellow and former Astronaut Byron Lichtenberg founded a company that assembles packages for the Shuttle and other launch vehicles; Tim Axelrod has contributed to the identification of the missing matter that is not observed directly but noticed by its gravitational effect in the universe; Christopher McKee is head of Space Sciences at Berkeley; and Bill Press is the former chair of the Astronomy Department at Harvard. Hertz Fellows are also providing leadership in government: Robert Hunter was the head of the DOE Office of Energy Research during the Reagan administration; DAS graduate Paul Nielsen is a brigadier general in the U.S. Air Force; Colonel Ellen Pawlikowski is currently the assistant director in the Office of the Assistant to the Secretary of Defense for Atomic Energy; and Amy Alving was the 1997–1998 White House Fellow and a special assistant to the secretary of commerce. Unfortunately, space does not permit me to list all the outstanding Hertz Fellows.

38

UPHILL

─────

1964–1972

FOR ROUGHLY A decade, beginning about 1962, I was deeply concerned about three issues. The Plowshare program, now four years old, was making wonderful technical progress, but the combined effects of the fear of low-level radiation and the lack of political leadership was making commercial applications increasingly unlikely.

Second, the chance for the people of South Vietnam to live in freedom was being lost, and with the fall of South Vietnam, the freedoms of the people of Cambodia and Laos were also likely to disappear. At the same time, student protests throughout the world transformed universities from havens for considered discussions to little more than arenas for mob action.

Finally, after many decades of neglect, the effort to develop an antimissile defense system was launched with considerable promise, only to be abandoned once again in spite of my best efforts to prevent its demise. Reviewing that period today makes me feel as if I, a one-footed man, spent my time struggling uphill against a heavy wind.

Between 1961 and 1973, the Livermore laboratory developed sharply modified explosive devices that provided great earth-moving ability at small cost while producing a minimal amount of radioactive residue. Those devices were used in the United States on three occasions. The Sedan Plowshare demonstration produced an impressive crater in the desert at the National Testing Grounds almost the size of Meteor Crater near Winslow, Arizona. The crater from the Sedan experiment has become a national monument, but the technique was never turned to more practical ends, such as building a harbor or a canal. Another of our tests demonstrated the production of a huge cavity in a salt deposit near Carlsbad, New Mexico.

Three further tests were conducted in connection with increasing the production of gas wells by breaking up the shale. The wells proved more productive. One of them, the Gasbuggy stimulation in 1967, carried out near Farm-ington, Utah, increased gas production by a factor of six; the 1969 Rulison test, performed near Grand Valley, Colorado, increased well production by a factor of ten to fifteen; the 1973 Rio Blanco test near Rifle, Colorado, used three explosives simultaneously to stimulate gas production, but was disap-pointing because there was little gas in the formation. Rio Blanco was the last test conducted under the Plowshare project.

At the time of the Rio Blanco test, I heard that Armand Hammer was try-ing to stimulate oil production using conventional (and therefore more ex-pensive) explosives. After breaking up the oil shale, he planned by some un-specified means to heat the oil shale, thereby liquefying the oil for easier pumping. Hammer's operations were located in the mountains overlooking the Great Salt Lake in Utah, and he took me by helicopter to inspect the site. (I remember that last fact clearly because I was so preoccupied with Ham-mer's exaggerated claims that for once I forgot to be concerned about the performance of the helicopter.)

Hammer bragged that his methods would produce oil from oil shale at the cost of a mere $2.15 a barrel. The estimate of $2 per barrel seemed a terrible exaggeration and the fifteen cents a plain impertinence. The project seemed to me unlikely to succeed at all. Hammer's project has remained unrealized, but I do not know whether it failed because of its economic costs or for tech-nical reasons. I do know why the Plowshare oil and gas stimulation effort failed: Popular misconceptions about the dangers of low-level radiation made it impossible to assess risks and rewards in a reasonable manner.

The hearing held in Washington, D.C., in connection with the Rulison test, which used an exceptionally clean nuclear device to break up gas-bearing rock, illustrates the problem of using the Plowshare program. The test proto-cols, meticulously worked out by Jerry Johnson, were conservative and safe and there was little concern about them; but the gas would pick up a minus-cule amount of radiation, and this did raise concern.

The concerns were so unreasonable that they might have been comical un-der other circumstances. Ed Fleming, who was working for the Department of Energy at the time, testified at a hearing in May 1973. His frustration with his failure to correct prejudices by offering facts is obvious in a story he recounted:

> A lady in a dirndl dress from Aspen, Colorado, made an emotional and highly
> determined plea: She did not want that gas to be pumped into her house as
> she didn't want to expose her two young children to that radioactivty. She

didn't want the Rulison gas to be pumped, and she certainly did not want the gas from a whole field that had been developed by nuclear explosives pumped into her lines.

After the hearings, I went back to the office and calculated the amount of extra radiation she and her children would receive under a couple of scenarios. One proposal at that time was to burn gas from the previous Rulison gas stimulation shot in Colorado, and another was to burn gas from a completely developed Rio Blanco field.

The lady and her children lived at an altitude of about 7,900 feet. The cosmic radiation received at that altitude is much greater than at sea level. The gist of the calculation was that if she were to have Rulison gas pumped into her house, all that would have to happen to compensate for the increase in radiation that she and her children would receive was to have the house settle about four inches. If the entire Rio Blanco field was developed she would have to move down hill approximately 100 feet to avoid any extra exposure.

The explanation of Ed's finding is fairly straightforward. Human beings during their evolution and existence have been exposed to radiation from outer space. In addition, many naturally occurring radioactive substances exist in the earth's crust, and many have been incorporated in the structure of plants and animals. Like cosmic radiation, these substances have always provided and continue to provide small doses of low-level radiation.

The effects, if any, of this ever-present radiation are hard to determine because they are so small; but there is no doubt that cosmic rays of a certain ionizing power will have similar effects to those of any other radioactive substance that gives rise to the same ionizing power. The human body is not differently affected by the residual radioactivity in Plowshare gas and the radiation it receives from natural sources.

Cosmic rays lose some of their ionizing power as they pass through the atmosphere; therefore, the lower the altitude, the less cosmic radiation one receives. The lady from Aspen clearly did not understand this fact. Children living in the mountains of Colorado not only receive considerably more cosmic radiation than those in other parts of the nation but also receive an increased amount of radiation from the radioactive elements present in Colorado's soil and rock. Yet, for unknowable reasons, the incidence of cancer in Colorado is lower than in other states. Ed's measure of the amount of additional radiation present in the gas as a result of using nuclear devices in the gas field—an increase equivalent to the cosmic radiation one would receive by living at an altitude a few feet higher—describes the extent to which the

Livermore laboratory succeeded in providing clean explosive devices. Nevertheless, ignorance and prejudice prevailed. The Plowshare gas was never used, and Rio Blanco was the last Plowshare test.[1]

I am hopeful that someday, given a better-informed public and a balanced concern for the environment and the economic well-being of people, a Plowshare gas-stimulation program may be put into effect. But I do not expect that nuclear explosives, even though they are considerably less expensive than conventional explosives, will soon be used for any constructive purposes.

Today, the opponents of economic progress require that every new activity guarantee the absolute absence of all possible negative health consequences. Proving that such a demand has been met is, of course, impossible. Fear of innovation has increased to the point that this emotionally charged sentiment has successfully blocked several new developments. One can only wonder whether the greater number of people in our nation who live in reduced circumstances is related to this unreasoning anxiety.

The Soviet Union had a parallel program to Plowshare that came to an end only with the 1989 test-ban treaty. The Soviets' program was at least twenty times more extensive than our own. Many of their results are in use today; for example, the water reservoir in Chagan, Siberia, and the industrial waste storage facilities in the Bashkir Republic and in the Sovkhoz and Orenburg oil fields.

The Soviets also used nuclear explosives successfully to extinguish four gas well fires.[2] In addition, they executed a series of explosions that made possible the study of the geological structure of the earth's crust throughout the Soviet Union. Using a technique similar to that of the Plowshare program, they used nuclear explosives to stimulate five oil fields and two gas fields. (Unlike the Plowshare program, the Soviet wells remain in production today.) The Soviet program also successfully used nuclear devices to break up

---

[1] Small nuclear explosives with lower residual radioactivity could also be used to generate low-cost electricity. In about 1974, Al Latter and Ernie Martinelli suggested that detonating in an underground cavity containing water would generate steam that could drive generators. But by then everyone was convinced that Plowshare projects would not be realized in the foreseeable future.

[2] Sealing a runaway gas or oil well fire is a difficult operation when the fire is so far out of control that nothing is left at the surface except a huge pit of fuming and flaring gas. The conventional technology for stemming a well does not suffice in such cases because there is nothing at the surface that can be used to seal the well. The Soviets drilled an angled shaft into the ground nearby so that a detonation at the bottom of the shaft crushed the well at great depth, shutting off the escaping gas and thereby suffocating the fire.

ore for mining. The radiation in the mine continues to be below the low level designated as permissible.[3]

Unfortunately, the test that we needed to put the Plowshare mining plan into practice was never conducted. The Russian test experiment produced a cavity that collapsed, leaving behind a chimney of rubble that did not breach the surface. This chimney of broken-up ore was then mined. (The mining of important metals, such as copper, is much easier when the ore is broken up. Furthermore, the mining operations can be replaced by pumping down an appropriate acidic reagent, dissolving the copper, pumping the liquid to the surface, and then processing it, thus sparing the region the disturbances caused by conventional mining.)

Our program, by comparison, was limited at best. Not all the difference can be laid to public concerns over radioactivity. In the United States, the industries involved had to pay 90 percent of the costs of the gas stimulation experiments, and few companies had so much funding. When the few pioneering firms who did pay for the experiments discovered that even a tiny amount of increased radioactivity was unacceptable to the public, the industrial sponsors gave up the work.

The civil engineering projects in Plowshare fared no better. Between 1961 and 1974, several projects were studied for the use of geographical engineering, the largest being the aforementioned study of a sea-level canal across the Isthmus of Panama. I was actively involved in three other studies: building canals in Israel and in Southeast Asia, and excavating a harbor in Australia. In the latter cases, I made personal expeditions.[4] Although the projects never came to fruition, the plans seemed important at the time. In addition, this work introduced me in a thoroughgoing manner to other parts of the world.

My first trip to Australia in 1966 was suggested by my Texan friend radiologist James R. Maxfield, for purely personal enjoyment as far as I knew. The Australia with which I became acquainted on that trip had (at least in

---

[3] The Soviet program involved about 125 devices. It was not without some failures. In the most serious case, nuclear explosions in a salt cavity with an overlying water table led to radioactive contamination of artesian wells in the region. Foreseeing all the difficulties that may arise when developing a new technology is hard (although exploding a nuclear device under an overlying water table seems questionable to me as an armchair observer). But on the whole, far more advantages than disadvantages—economically and ecologically—accrued from the Soviet program.

[4] As the reader will recall, I also made two trips to Alaska in the late 1950s in connection with the construction of a harbor there. In only one case, that of the sea-level canal across or near Panama, was the importance and the interest in a Plowshare project sufficiently great that it did not seem I could add information by visiting and offering public lectures.

my imagination) great similarities to the United States during the early nineteenth century: a sparse population and breakneck progress.

While we were there, Dr. J. R. suggested that Mici and I visit his Australian friend Lang Hancock, whom he thought we would enjoy. Lang Hancock was ideally suited to my vision of a nineteenth-century American. Although he resembled a stereotype of the pioneering man of the early West, Hancock was also a man of great wealth. He discovered and developed one of the world's richest iron ore deposits in northwestern Australia.

I do not know whether a project to establish a harbor there first came up in our conversation because of remarks by Maxfield, Hancock, or myself. But Lang was extremely interested. His great problem was how to move his product. He flew us up north to the Hamersley Range where his extensive mines were located. If Australia had been divided into equal halves, north and south, the northern portion would have held only about 1 percent of the population. To say that the region was undeveloped is hardly sufficient. It was a truly empty land, and therefore was almost totally without a transportation system. Hancock's holdings, though close to the ocean, had no available harbor; the water for miles out into the ocean was too shallow to allow ships to approach.

Hancock turned out to be a steady and strong advocate of a Plowshare harbor. I made a second trip ten years later and further discussed the project.[5] But the idea never developed strong support in the Australian government.

One further personally rewarding friendship grew out of my second trip to Australia. I stopped to give a lecture at the Royal Melbourne Institute of Technology and met a young Texan who was currently a professor of physics there. Robert (Bud) Budwine and his pleasant wife, Christine, were interested in coming back to the United States because of the health problems of their young daughter. I suggested that Bud check with the laboratory in Livermore, where the personnel office was always looking for talented young physicists, and Bud did. Some months later he joined the laboratory.

---

[5] I returned to Australia on yet another occasion, in the 1980s, at the invitation of Gina Hancock Rinehart, Lang Hancock's daughter. Gina was especially interested in the early diagnosis of breast cancer, a disease that she suspects has an increased incidence in Australia. The Lawrence Livermore laboratory had done some work on self-administered techniques for early detection, which I described on that visit. I also addressed the Parliament. That trip also provided me my most recent opportunity to visit Mici's younger half-brother and his wife and to see my old friend Marta Levy Fisher and her husband. Visiting old friends may be possible only by circumnavigating the globe, but I continue to feel fortunate that so many of our friends and family did survive the terrible cataclysms of the twentieth century.

Bud has proved his friendship to me in many wonderful ways. Especially during the 1980s, when I seemed beset with one health problem after another, Bud was a mainstay during my hospitalizations. On a few occasions, he and Chris also traveled with Mici and me to international scientific conferences held in Erice, Italy, thereby easing many of the burdens of making overseas trips. Unfortunately, Bud later developed health problems of his own and took an early retirement from the laboratory.

The second of my overseas Plowshare projects involved Israel and also depended on a private initiative. Israeli physicist Yuval Ne'eman, the friend who had suggested my first trip to Israel, urged me to return the following year (in 1967). He wanted my help in evaluating the possibilities of a north-south canal between the Red Sea and the Dead Sea. The amount of radiation released by cratering for a canal, although small, is not insignificant to populations in the immediate vicinity. Because Israel is a small and densely populated country, temporary evacuation was not an option. The Plowshare part of the canal plan was discarded and replaced by conventional high explosives. I did return to discuss the modified project on many subsequent occasions, the last for this purpose in 1984. During those years, I discussed the project with scientists and political leaders, among them Prime Minister Eshkol and Prime Minister Golda Meir. (I particularly enjoyed Prime Minister Meir for her sense of humor.)[6]

Eventually, I came to support the idea of the canal strongly for two reasons. One is that the Dead Sea is rapidly drying up because all the sweet waters that formerly flowed into it are now being used in agriculture. If the Dead Sea dries up, it will leave an unproductive salt desert; harvesting the various salts it contains will be impossible. That would destroy a flourishing industry. A second practical reason to stop the drying process by supplying water from the Red Sea is that supplying such water would make it possible to generate electricity. The water level of the Red Sea is about 1,300 feet higher than that of the Dead Sea. A dam constructed on a connecting canal could supply a considerable portion of the electricity needed by Israel.

This project, the long canal between the Red Sea and the Dead Sea, has been replaced by another. Yuval and others have advanced the idea of an east-west canal through the southern portion of Israel to connect the Dead Sea

---

[6] Although my sample of women leaders in government is remarkably small (Golda Meir and Dixy Lee Ray), I believe that just as female astronauts have a real advantage (they provide all the benefits of their male counterparts in lighter packaging), so female leaders may have an advantage in the amount of determination and directness they possess—as well as in their sense of humor.

with the Mediterranean. There are good arguments for this shorter route, which, in the main, traverses level ground. Even including the tunnels (through the few mountainous areas near the Dead Sea), such a canal would still be economically feasible if conventional explosives were used.

The third overseas project was in Southeast Asia. It arose in considerable part from the initiative of a retired U.S. Air Force general living in Hawaii, Edwin F. Black. The proposal was to build a canal by cutting through the thinnest part of the Malay peninsula; that would have shortened the sea route between the Middle Eastern sources of oil and Japan. In the absence of such a canal, large oil tankers do not merely have to go around by way of Singapore but have to go farther south to find a passage of sufficient depth.

On three occasions, I made extended visits to that region of the world. I visited the proposed site in Thailand as well as Singapore, Indonesia, and Japan. In Thailand, I learned that the country's history is a remarkable exception to the colonial past of that region. The people of that rapidly developing nation are proud of the proof they give that Western ideas and industry can be imported without the vehicle of colonization. I also enjoyed visiting Indonesia and returned there to give a lecture series at the Bandung Institute of Technology in 1975.[7]

In the case of the proposed canal across the Kra peninsula, the government in Thailand appeared to be quite willing to proceed as fast as or faster than the government of the United States was willing to go. The Thai government considered it feasible to evacuate 100,000 people for the explosions (four dozen explosions would have been required) because of the incidental benefits of building the thirty-mile-long canal. They expected that new communities along its route would receive economic benefits from the sea traffic flowing through the canal.[8]

One of the personal benefits of the Kra Canal project were the friendships I developed with General Black and with a Chinese financier, K. Y. Chow, who lived in Thailand. Chow was a splendid example of a successful and peaceful Chinese invasion along the western shores of the Pacific. Although China went communist, the emigrating Chinese demonstrated the advantages of capitalism with remarkable success.

---

[7] The Mitre Corporation, which had long employed me as a consultant, kindly sponsored those lectures, later publishing them as a small book, *Nuclear Energy in the Developing World*.

[8] The other benefit would have been the control of the movement of guerrillas down the Malay peninsula.

At the time of my visits in 1973, I received a somewhat negative impression of the promise of the Kra Canal, particularly during discussions in Tokyo at the end of the trip. It became clear that the enterprise was expensive enough that it would not pay for itself until the first decade of the twenty-first century. At that point, I expected that the exports from the Middle East might not be sustained because of the depletion of oil and the development of nuclear energy.[9]

Although the United States stopped funding the nuclear excavation program in 1971, interest in the program continued in other countries. In 1977, Anwar Sadat, the president of Egypt, became interested in a project to connect the Qatarra Depression (a region about 160 feet below sea level that constitutes about 15 percent of the surface area of Egypt) to the Mediterranean Sea.

At its closest point, the depression is about forty-three miles from the sea; turbines placed along a channel connecting the two would produce a high multiple of the amount of electrical power generated by the Aswan Dam for more than sixty years. In addition, the project would produce a harbor to the west of Alexandria, and the lake formed would provide jobs in farming, fishing, industrial development, and tourism, as well as provide for oil exploration with floating drill rigs.

The costs of using conventional explosives to excavate would be approximately six times greater than the nuclear option. John Toman, one of the chief scientists involved in several Plowshare programs, claims that this is the most feasible nuclear excavation project ever proposed. The isolation of the western desert is such that only 150 people would need to be temporarily relocated while the excavation work was completed.

Unfortunately, President Anwar Sadat, the most important proponent of the project, was assassinated shortly before the feasibility studies (funded by West Germany) were completed. This project is the only Plowshare program that is not quite dead, and articles supporting the project still appear occasionally in Egyptian newspapers.

During the same period that I was making these trips, the United States was rapidly becoming a divided nation. The turmoil and internal division plaguing the country, for the most part, were over the war in Vietnam.[10] By

---

[9] I was, of course, wrong. Japan now does generate much of its electricity with nuclear reactors, but the increased use of automobiles has balanced the savings in oil consumption.

[10] The other issue producing violence concerned the civil rights of black people, particularly their right to vote in the southern states. I was not even peripherally involved in that fight; but, of course, my sympathies lay with the disenfranchised.

1968, the controversy was fierce. President Lyndon Johnson chose not to seek reelection.[11] Nelson Rockefeller failed to win the Republican nomination, but Richard Nixon, a more mainstream Republican than Barry Goldwater, did manage to do so. Nixon was elected and immediately demonstrated his acuity by recruiting Nelson's principal advisor, Henry Kissinger, to serve as his national security advisor (and later his secretary of state).

I had met Nixon on several occasions during the Eisenhower administration when he was serving as vice president, and although I would have preferred a Rockefeller presidency, I found Nixon's presidency, particularly with Kissinger in a strong advisory position, a hopeful development. In many ways, that proved true. During the Nixon administration, ties within the western alliance were repaired and strengthened, a rapprochement with China was instituted, and détente, built on a realistic appraisal of our military position vis-à-vis the Soviet Union, developed.

Other reasonable programs were planned, particularly an effort to repair the environment in instances where industrial wastes had been improperly handled. Nixon adopted a program of environmentalism similar to the one that Nelson Rockefeller had developed. My friend Wilson Talley, who had taken a position as a White House Fellow during these years, was working as the special assistant to the secretary of health, education, and welfare. As such, he was one of the four people who put together the plans for the Environmental Protection Agency.[12]

The Nixon administration made some contributions to domestic affairs and outstanding contributions in foreign relations, but it was unable to rectify the problem in Vietnam. Stupid decisions were no longer made, but that conflict continued to go poorly. Even in retrospect, I do not know how we should have answered the hard questions posed by this conflict.

As mentioned in Chapter 31, I joined the President's Foreign Intelligence Advisory Board in 1969, but I was never involved in policymaking regarding Vietnam.[13] However, my perspective on that conflict is still clear to me. The United States grew up using the independence of world politics that its geographical position afforded it. After the Civil War, the country engaged in a relatively short imperialistic period. When that was over, the nation became

---

[11] The extent to which this was due to the unpopularity of the war or to his health problems can only be guessed.

[12] The agency was not formally created until October 1980.

[13] During the Nixon administration, Mici and I also attended a White House dinner for the president of Finland.

isolationist. That attitude persisted until President Wilson led the country into World War I and was immediately resumed at that war's termination. When I came to this country in 1935, the U.S. policy of isolationism was providing great help to Hitler.

Isolationism may have been more appropriate in the case of Vietnam, but stopping communist aggression was also important. Had the United States been successful in defending freedom in South Vietnam, the people there (as well as those in Cambodia and Laos), like the people in South Korea, might have enjoyed the following decades with development and prosperity.

To my mind, the point at which the war in Vietnam became truly hopeless was the assassination of President Diem at the beginning of the war in 1963. At the request of President Diem, President Kennedy had sent 17,000 advisors to Vietnam by that time. The United States knew of the plans to assassinate Diem but did not warn him. Syngman Rhee of South Korea, like Ngo Diem, was accused of abusing power. The free people of South Korea promptly got rid of him when the battle was won. Even though Diem was less than ideal, the situation might have been remedied had freedom survived. In the face of our prior knowledge of the assassination attempt, our silence seems to me a breach of faith. And after that, we supported the murderers.

The Kennedy administration acted in the belief that only the presence of Diem was preventing the peaceful cooperation of North and South Vietnam. But the communists wanted to rule the entire country. The war became inevitable, and our participation less clearly justified. There was no easy way to extricate ourselves, nor to demonstrate our good intentions to the Vietnamese people.

As a world leader, the United States had committed itself to a war that it little understood and was not well prepared to fight. The United States needed to live up to the obligations it had assumed. Failure to do so makes it impossible for a nation to be viewed as a reliable partner.

In addition, the assistance that Secretary of Defense Robert McNamara provided the South Vietnamese lacked forethought. Little attention was paid to the special needs of the situation. For example, the Vietnamese soldiers were of short stature and slight build, but instead of sending the M-16 rifles, which are smaller and lighter, McNamara sent the larger and heavier M-1 rifles. They proved to be almost impossible for the Vietnamese to use.[14] I believe that dur-

---

[14] Robert McNamara was eventually replaced, and under the subsequent process of President Johnson's Vietnamization program, M-16 rifles were made available.

ing this early period, the people of South Vietnam lost whatever confidence they had had in the United States. Once that happened, the only solution was to disengage in the speediest and least dishonorable manner possible.

By 1968, when Nixon assumed the presidency, the nation was fully involved in the war, with almost half a million young Americans being forced to deal with the miseries of that conflict. Within a year, Nixon had withdrawn about a quarter of the U.S. forces and had negotiated a cease fire. In spite of these sensible actions, young people who had worked themselves up to a fever pitch of emotion continued their violent protests.

When Ho Chi Minh broke the cease fire agreement, Nixon attempted to cut the guerrilla supply lines. That led to a renewal of the war for another year; but finally, in Nixon's second term of office, a permanent withdrawal was achieved through negotiations carried out by Secretary of State Kissinger. Within a few months of the signing of the agreement, the communist forces were victorious. Twenty years later, Vietnam still has a communist government and is among the poorer nations of the world. Everything about this war was tragic.

Student agitation during these years steadily increased. I found it more and more difficult to teach my classes or to give public lectures. I would be interrupted continuously by questions and remarks shouted from the audience to the point that it became impossible to continue. Eventually, the situation grew so severe that I could not even begin to speak.

I remember, for example, a meeting of the American Association for the Advancement of Science, where Margaret Mead was the chairman of the session. Mead was a soft-spoken and distinguished anthropologist, but even with all her experience in working with people of diverse backgrounds, she proved unable to gain her end of enabling me to speak. I do not believe that the two of us agreed on politics, but we did agree on freedom of speech, which suffered sorely during this time.[15]

A more dramatic incident took place in late November 1970. The Free Speech Movement at Berkeley had been joined by several other organizations—the Red Family, Scientists and Engineers for Social and Political Action (SESPA), Students for a Democratic Society (SDS)—that equaled or surpassed the original body in their ability to agitate. One or several of those groups decided that they should form a commission to investigate "war crimes." In mid-November, I received a letter inviting me to attend a meeting to defend myself.

---

[15] It is ironic that one of the first protest groups at UC-Berkeley called itself the Free Speech Movement.

In particular, I was accused of promoting the use of nuclear weapons in Vietnam. Fliers and posters that were circulated attributed the following quote to me:

> We can win the hearts and minds of men. If the people of the world really want freedom, and if our nuclear forces can stop massed communist manpower, I am convinced that our victory would be assured in any limited war.

The comments in question may be mine; if they are, they refer to the European theater, not to Vietnam. The problem of how to counter the massive Soviet tank forces had long been a problem for NATO. The European nations (and the United States) were unwilling to commit the exceptionally great funds that would have been required to counterbalance the Soviet tank force with tanks. When small nuclear weapons were developed, it became possible to provide a deterrent to a Soviet tank attack by means of arming NATO forces with tactical nuclear arms.

If I made the remark quoted above, I would have made it earlier when tactical nuclear weapons were being considered as a deterrent to the European theater, where Soviet troops and tanks vastly outnumbered the defending NATO troops. Separated from its context, the remark can be interpreted as promoting a limited war. My intention was wholly the contrary. My point was that arming our far-less-numerous forces with tactical nuclear weapons would negate the effect of the massive Soviet buildup of troops and tanks; with defeat assured, the Soviets would never mount the attack. I would never have made such a statement about Vietnam. Since the end of World War II, nuclear weapons have served their purpose extremely well. That purpose is deterrence. The hydrogen bomb, it should be remembered, has never been used in combat, and there is reason to hope that it never will be. The people of the world may have matured (and been educated) to the point that the folly of using nuclear weapons to attack another nation is clear. The folly of using nuclear weapons in Vietnam could hardly be exaggerated. Only in the most unreasonable of times could such an unreasonable interpretation of my comment gain credence.

Not only was it a horrible idea for humanitarian reasons, it was wrong for every tactical reason. To begin with, even the smallest nuclear weapon is never useful in guerrilla warfare. In Vietnam, we were fighting guerrilla forces; the North Vietnamese were fighting organized forces. The North Vietnamese were supported by China, which had nuclear weapons by then. The use of nuclear weapons against the North Vietnamese would have immediately invited the retaliatory use of nuclear weapons against our own troops, who were much easier targets. It would have been sheer madness to use nuclear weapons in Vietnam.

Trying to explain to the agitated students (and some faculty members who had even less of an excuse for their behavior) that my position had been misrepresented would have been futile. I comforted myself with the knowledge that I was in distinguished company. The other "war criminals" to be tried included the president of University of California, Charles Hitch; the chairman of the AEC, Glenn Seaborg; the director of research and development for the Defense Department (and former director of the Livermore laboratory), John Foster; the current director of the Livermore laboratory, Mike May; and the current director of Los Alamos, Harold Agnew.

During this unreasonable time, the value of nuclear weapons as a deterrent to war was not at all appreciated, as can be seen by the fact that, with the exception of President Hitch, the main offense that we "war criminals" had committed was that we had been involved in research on nuclear weapons. Yet, following World War II, I knew of no one in nuclear weapons research who did not believe that the purpose of his or her work was to prevent the use of such weapons by assuring the strength of our deterrent forces. That remains true today.

Some of my friends were concerned about the potential for violence against me. I was the nearest and most accessible of the "war criminals." Earlier in the year, someone had painted—on our house and on the sidewalk in front of our house—the message "Edward Teller War Criminal." On another occasion, someone painted the same slogan on Gen Phillips's car, which was parked at the house while she worked on the Bay Area Pilot Scholarship program with Mici. We were an easy target if someone wanted to harm us physically.

On several occasions, my friends urged me to stay overnight in the laboratory, which is a guarded facility. When the war criminals trial was publicized, the people in the security office at Livermore (and several of my friends) wanted to protest to the chancellor and demand that he cancel the meeting. I felt that canceling the meeting was the wrong thing to do from every point of view. However, I did not object when the security office asked the Berkeley police to provide whatever protection they could.

After failing to convince Mici and me to leave town for that night, two of my friends from the laboratory, Lowell Wood and George Chapline, decided to attend the meeting themselves. (Given their appearances, there was little chance that they would be singled out of the crowd as my friends.)

The meeting took place in the Pauley Ballroom on the campus. Charles Schwartz of the physics department had been active in sponsoring the meeting, and he was among the speakers that night. Although several hundred people were present, only the core group of perhaps 150 people was really stirred up. Eventually, one of them proposed burning down my house.

At that point, Lowell Wood and George Chapline left the meeting to come and warn Mici and me. The remaining core group began heading to my home at the same time. Lowell and George knew the neighborhood well, and, taking the back streets, reached my home first, approaching it through the backyard.

The first thing that Mici and I heard was a ruckus outside the front door. When Mici opened it, she discovered Lowell, George, and a policeman with his gun drawn. She immediately said, "Officer, please let Professor Wood come in." The policeman stood aside, somewhat reluctantly, for Lowell. George Chapline didn't make it inside until he had attracted Mici's attention with the plaintive plea, "Me, too?"

In the meantime, the police had stopped the main body of demonstrators a few blocks from our home. They burned an effigy of me there and then went on a spree at the university, where they broke two doors at Cory Hall and numerous windows in California Hall, the administrative office building. Mici and I—and our house—were untouched.

Lowell and George had never before seen such violence. They insisted we move somewhere farther from the campus (our house on Hawthorne Terrace was about a ten-minute walk from the center of campus). After a bit of arguing, Lowell remembered that I was much too stubborn a person to give up under duress. Another set of friends became involved at that point. Within a few days, Gen Phillips and her husband, Paul, heard that the chief of police in a neighboring town had a six-month-old puppy who had been trained to be a fierce watchdog. The police chief had taken a position in another city and was moving to an apartment without a yard. He generously offered to give us the dog, whom he had named Shah.

So Shah came to inhabit our fenced yard. Although he grew into a large muscular dog, he proved to have a dual personality. Shah could be fierce, as he demonstrated when he persuaded an unwise intruder to scramble up a tree in the garden. But when Shah was with us in the house, he was convinced that he was a lap dog. This was particularly hard on Mici, whom Shah almost outweighed.[16] Fortunately, the great excesses in behavior at Berkeley ended within a year or so of our acquisition of a protector.

---

[16]Our companionship with Shah was short-lived. Five years later, I retired, and we sold our house on Hawthorne Terrace. I would have liked to take Shah along to our new home at Stanford,

Throughout that difficult period, the University of California never wavered in its support for the Los Alamos and Livermore laboratories. Many government laboratories had affiliations with universities. The University of California was different in that it had the responsibility in the area of nuclear defense and nuclear weapons technology, which during this time was extremely unpopular. Considerable pressure was put on the university to give up its affiliation. Fortunately, the University of California did not withdraw. The relationship with the university allows people in the weapons laboratories to have points of view that are independent of current political views. That is important to the people in the laboratories, and it is good for the nation.

Throughout the Vietnam War, the national weapons laboratories went on operating in a normal, productive manner, although with some changes. At the Livermore laboratory, Michael May resigned as director, and Roger Batzel, a chemist who had worked at the laboratory from the earliest days, replaced him. In addition, the Berkeley and Livermore laboratories, which until 1971 were known conjointly as the Lawrence laboratories, became independent entities, and Livermore became the Lawrence Livermore Laboratory.[17]

At Los Alamos, Norris Bradbury stepped down in 1969 after more than two decades as director. The new director was my longtime friend Harold Agnew, who had worked on the Manhattan Project in Chicago and had been one of the earliest arrivals at Los Alamos. Harold made it plain, shortly after he took over, that he would appreciate my returning more frequently to consult at Los Alamos. I was happy to do so and continued that practice for as long as I could travel. Although a few people at Los Alamos, particularly some of the theoreticians from the 1950s, continued to believe that I had in some way betrayed Los Alamos by working to establish a second weapons laboratory, the majority of the physicists at Los Alamos were ready to resume working together for the common good.

Under Harold Agnew's directorship, Los Alamos developed strongly, acquiring new facilities and new techniques. Within a year or two, the two laboratories were equal competitors enjoying a friendly rivalry. The situation I had envisioned in 1951 had finally come to pass. Although I regret the rancor that developed over the second laboratory, I am glad that the

---

but it had a tiny yard. I felt that although Shah was attached to us, he was even more attached to his territory. The new owners promptly made friends with our dog and offered to let Shah stay on. He spent his remaining years peacefully with them.

[17] The final name change came in June 1980 when the laboratory assumed its present name, the Lawrence Livermore National Laboratory (LLNL).

Livermore laboratory was in existence during those seventeen years. Rapid developments in nuclear weapons and ballistic missiles took place during that time. Livermore's work assured the development of the sturdiest leg of the triad on which our deterrent ability rested—the submarine-based Polaris missile. That a portion of our retaliatory force would survive a surprise attack guaranteed that the Soviets would never find it advantageous to attempt a first strike.

Another deeply desired development began during this period. By 1967, the Livermore laboratory was working on developing a ballistic missile defense system. The system was based on high-acceleration missiles carrying nuclear explosives. If the interceptor could reach the vicinity of the incoming missile, the detonation of the nuclear device it carried would disable the firing mechanism of the nuclear weapon on the enemy warhead.

Both Los Alamos and Livermore had been directed to work on developing nuclear warheads for use in stopping incoming weapons.[18] Livermore built a specialized weapon (producing a large quantity of x-rays and having a high explosive yield) called the Spartan, which was intended to destroy incoming thermonuclear missiles at high altitude, outside the earth's atmosphere. Los Alamos's defensive missile (which had a much smaller yield and produced mainly high-energy neutrons) was intended to destroy incoming missiles at low altitude, just before they were to detonate over their targets.

One difficulty of ballistic missile defense is that it requires extensive, expensive, vulnerable radar installations to locate the incoming missiles. Shielding radar against both the shock wave and the electromagnetic pulse that the explosion of a large warhead produces is a formidable problem. The system was far from perfect, but we had at least made a start. We began working on a test of those devices, which was to be conducted underground on an island in Alaska.

In about 1966, W. Glenn Campbell, then the director of the Hoover Institution on War, Revolution and Peace, located on the Stanford University campus, invited me to visit there. (We had met during the time when I, as director of the Livermore laboratory, was reporting to the regents of the University of California, a board on which Glenn served for many years.) Glenn thought I might enjoy exchanging ideas with some of the scholars and visitors at Hoover. He was right, and I visited on a few occasions.

---

[18] The defensive system was first called the *Sentinel* ABM (Anti-ballistic Missile) system and later renamed the *Safeguard*.

During one of them, Glenn introduced me to a movie star and former labor leader who was politically active in Southern California, Ronald Reagan. (Glenn, who is notable for his acerbic humor, introduced us by saying, "Ron, I want you to meet a man attached to that well-known communist Nelson Rockefeller.") I was most impressed by Reagan's relaxed manner. The only thing that he obviously worried about was being late for his wife. He addressed all other problems with straightforward ease.

Reagan was elected governor of California in November 1966. Shortly after he moved into the governor's mansion, I went to Sacramento and invited him to become the first governor of California to visit the Livermore laboratory. Much to my pleasure, Governor Reagan agreed to pay a visit to the laboratory and arrived on November 22, 1967. Mike May, who was director at that time, organized a tour of the laboratory and a discussion of a few of the larger current projects. The test of the ballistic missile defense system warheads was being readied at the laboratory, and several scientists made a two-hour-long presentation covering the progress and deficiencies of the ballistic missile defense system and explaining the difficulties of testing an aerial system underground.

What we told the governor was not simple, but he listened carefully and asked perhaps a dozen salient questions. Those questions made two points clear: The topic was quite new to the governor, and he understood the essence and importance of what we were discussing. When the briefing was finished, I knew that Reagan had listened; I believed that he understood; but I had no idea whether he approved of the work or not.

We had a pleasant lunch following the presentation. The conversation centered on the troubles Governor Reagan was experiencing, including the criticism he was receiving for a comment he made about redwood trees. By the end of the luncheon, the governor had more friends than he had had at the beginning. But no mention was made of the defense system that was so much on my mind. Fifteen years later, I discovered that he had been very interested in those ideas.

In 1969, President Nixon was willing to support the deployment of the antiballistic missile system, possibly along the West Coast. The advantages of such a deployment were two-fold: Further development would be conducted to assess the costs of a larger system, and the defense itself would offer some protection. Henry Kissinger, then the National Security Advisor, contributed to that decision. Not long after it was announced, Kissinger phoned me to say, "We are supporting the idea of ballistic missile defense, but the objections to it are mounting. You must go on the road and defend it." So I did just that at every opportunity I had.

In June of that year, I was invited to speak at a conference of media people that was held in Glacier National Park. The weather was lovely, and the setting one of exceptional mountain beauty. Before the speeches were to begin, I decided to take a walk and was joined by several other people attending the conference. One of my companions introduced my speech that afternoon. He mentioned our little hike and then went on:

> About a hundred yards from the lodge, Dr. Teller picked up a big stick. I asked what it was for and he said: For protection against bears.[19] I protested that a stick wasn't effective enough against bears. I know, he replied, but I hope the grizzly bears don't. Dr. Teller will now talk about ballistic missile defense.

That, unfortunately, was an excellent summary of the state of effectiveness of our ballistic defense system.

Later that year, the Senate approved the deployment of the defense system by the margin of one vote. The decision was made to use the system to defend our retaliatory missiles. Yet work on a nationwide system to protect against ballistic missiles had hardly begun when it was stopped. In 1972, the ABM treaty limited the number of sites that could be protected by antimissile defenses to two, and a protocol signed two years later limited it to one! The Soviets defended Moscow with their system, and in 1975, the United States deployed the two types of defensive missiles in North Dakota to defend our retaliatory missiles there.

Thus the policy of Mutually Assured Destruction (MAD), initiated during the previous decade, a policy under which the United States virtually offered its unprotected citizens as hostages to an accidental or intentional attack by missiles armed with nuclear warheads, was formalized. The theory held that should an intentional attack occur, the United States would retaliate with the missiles that remained undamaged. Leaving aside the moral bankruptcy of this extremist policy, its basis in reason was also suspect.

The MAD policy was initiated to save the financial costs required to counter the great preponderance of the conventional forces—tanks, planes,

---

[19]Because of my artificial foot, I have always found a walking stick helpful, but when I was younger, I didn't like to admit to weakness. When I reached the age of eighty-five, I discovered that I had more frailties than strengths and gave up my attempts to appear robust. I now carry my walking stick everywhere. I am especially fond of the one that my son, Paul, gave me. It is almost as tall as I am.

and personnel—of the Soviet Union. The policy claimed that by concentrating on retaliation and ignoring defense, the United States could provide security for its citizens.[20]

In fact, it had the opposite effect of making a first strike by the Soviet Union seem more attractive. The Soviet Union had a larger territory than the United States, a lesser concentration of its population in urban centers, and well-programmed civil defense. The Soviet Union would have suffered far less than "assured destruction" following a first strike, particularly if the U.S. land-based missiles had been destroyed in an initial attack.

Nevertheless, the MAD policy became formalized as our national policy with the signing of the Anti-ballistic Missile Treaty in 1972. That treaty was followed in 1974 with a protocol that limited the number of defended sites to one. Our defensive system in North Dakota, even though it was in compliance with the treaty, was decommissioned a year after it was installed, in 1976, on account of budget constraints.

Living in times of unreasonable behavior always produces sorrow, but some of the sadness that entered my life during this period was simply a result of personal losses. In 1959, my friend Leo Szilárd, who tried above all else to be a reasonable person, had developed what was considered terminal cancer.[21] But, true to character, Szilárd did the unexpected: He did not die.

Most patients feel a little bit of awe, and occasionally even a trifle fearful, in their dealings with their doctors. With Szilárd, the situation was reversed. Szilárd took control of his medical treatment (again reminding me of why he had acquired the nickname The General) and demanded that the detailed courses of radiation treatment that he and his wife, Trude, had worked out be administered; and when they were, he gave his physicians no indication of his satisfaction. In the process, though, he was thoroughly cured, although his recovery took the better part of a year in the hospital.

I visited him and Trude on several occasions. Trude was a physician by training, and Leo worked out his radiation therapy with her advice. But during this year, she also served as Szilárd's secretary and general factotum. She almost never left his side. His hospital room had become his office, and the hospital solarium his receiving room. The hospital telephone lines during this period were tremendously overburdened by the multitude of calls he

---

[20] President Kennedy introduced the policy, but the treaty limiting defense was signed under President Nixon.

[21] As I recall, the cancer was located somewhere in Leo's digestive tract, perhaps his stomach.

placed and received. When Szilárd was declared ready to leave, Trude said that the hospital was even more relieved to be rid of Szilárd than Szilárd was to be rid of the hospital.

During the period of his recuperation, Szilárd managed to write a book, *The Voice of the Dolphins*, a most delightful fantasy about human folly contrasted with the reasonable behavior of the dolphins.[22] I still enjoy rereading it and only regret that Szilárd wrote nothing else like it.

In the latter part of his life, Szilárd had become interested in biology, and following his illness, he was invited by Jonas Salk to form an institute in La Jolla. He worked there for only a few years. In 1964, he died in his sleep of a heart attack. The ranks of the Martians had again been depleted.

But an even more painful loss followed. After Maria Mayer won the Nobel Prize for recognizing and explaining magic numbers, she was invited to teach at the University of California, San Diego. She invited me down occasionally, and two or three times I gave lectures. Just before she won the Nobel Prize, she had developed a neurological illness, which left her unable to speak clearly. Eventually, she partially regained her ability to talk, but I had continuing difficulty in understanding what she said. She spoke most clearly when she was rested. I remember that when I gave my first lecture in San Diego after her illness, she made a nice three- or four-minute introduction of me, clearly and with no errors. But that evening, I couldn't understand her at all. After I had asked her to repeat herself twice, I didn't want to ask her again, so we didn't talk much that evening.

Early in 1972, a friend called to tell me that Maria was dying. I went down as soon as I could. She lay in the hospital bed and didn't make a sound. I am not even sure whether she recognized me. I sat with her for almost an hour, occasionally offering comments that I hoped she could hear. But she never responded. She died a few days later.

I can never think of Maria in the period following her illness without great sadness at my own stupidity. A few months later, I was talking about Maria with a mutual friend, Bernd Matthias, and I mentioned that I had missed talking with Maria during her last few years.[23] Bernd told me that he had had no difficulty talking with her. I was puzzled. Presently it turned out that he spoke with her in German. I had been speaking in English.

---

[22] Leo Szilárd, *The Voice of the Dolphins and Other Stories* (New York: Simon & Shuster, 1961).

[23] Matthias fled Nazi Germany to Switzerland, and after the war emigrated to the United States. An able physicist, he worked in San Diego, and ended his career working at Los Alamos. He was also an excellent poker player who consistently beat me.

Today, neuropsychologists have demonstrated that languages learned at different ages are stored in different parts of the brain, and Maria's German was undisturbed by her disease. Maria and I had stopped speaking German together during the war years; since then, I had become so accustomed to conversing with her in English that I didn't think about trying her native language.

Our last meeting was sorrowful, but not because we couldn't talk: Even when words were no longer working well, I always felt that in some way we managed to understand each other. Our last meeting was painful because it clearly was the last.

39

CHOICES,
CRITICAL AND OTHERWISE

———

1973–1979

NELSON ROCKEFELLER WAS a wonderful example of a statesman, which is not the same thing as being a politician. Throughout his life, he consciously improved his breadth of knowledge and his grasp of the nuances present in important issues. That Nelson Rockefeller failed to win the Republican nomination for president in 1960 was a tragic loss for the nation. I believe that Rockefeller might well have beaten Kennedy.

Had that been the case, we might have avoided the Cuban missile crisis and the exacerbated tensions of the cold war. The unfortunate war in Vietnam (had it even taken place) would have taken a different course; furthermore, we would not have alienated our European allies by excluding them from Soviet-American negotiations. The 1960s might have been a greatly improved decade had Nelson been in the White House, but he was not. Nelson had lost his chance because of complications in his personal life.[1]

Nelson attempted to gain the nomination again in 1964 against Goldwater and in 1968 against Nixon. Nixon had not been particularly popular as Eisenhower's vice president, but when Ike was out with a heart attack, Nixon had performed well. That positive performance gave Nixon the advantage.

In about 1973, Nelson, still governor of New York, organized a Commission on the Role of the Modern State in a Changing World to consider the policies that New York should adopt for the future. President Nixon learned

———

[1] He lost the nomination, as I have mentioned, largely because he was divorced. In subsequent elections, he faced the additional onus of having remarried. It may be useful for the Republican Party to learn from the Democrats and give more emphasis to their candidates' leadership qualities and less to their personal lives.

of the commission and asked Nelson to broaden the study to consider the course the nation should follow. Nelson accepted the task, and, in 1973, resigned as governor of New York to direct the commission, which was renamed The Commission on Critical Choices for Americans. Nelson asked me to participate, and from August 1973 to mid-1975, I did.

I worked most of the summer of 1974 at Rockefeller's estate, where I was housed in a small but pleasant cottage on the grounds. Mici started to spend the summer there with me because the children were now grown; but aside from the occasional evenings when we joined the Rockefellers for dinner, she had little to do. She might even have adapted to that circumscribed life, except that one evening at the Rockefellers, the dinner entree was kidney pie. Eating food so un-Hungarian was more than she could tolerate; she went home, and I flew back to Berkeley to visit her on weekends for the rest of the summer.

I worked on two related topics. One pertained to national security and was concerned with the military aspect of international relations. The second was energy and technology, which, as we saw it, were the underlying forces that would determine the continuance of peace. Johnny Foster, who at that time had just left his post as Director of Defense Research and Engineering in Washington to serve as the vice president of energy research and development for TRW, and Hans Mark, who was then a NASA deputy director, also worked on that sub-panel.

The subject of energy sources and technologies was particularly timely and important because meetings of Nelson's commission overlapped the OPEC oil embargo, which generated energy shortages and raised the price of oil markedly. Throughout the time of the study, the embargo not only affected the economic strength of the free world but also caused great hardship throughout the developing world.

Norman Borlaug also served on the commission. He had introduced new strains of cereal crops that greatly increased the yields per acre. The new crops required the use of nitrogen-rich fertilizers, which need energy for their production. Many farmers in the developing world had recently replaced working farm animals with small tractors. Thus, the oil embargo had a two-fold negative economic impact on the developing world: The new fertilizers required energy, and the new farm machinery required fuel.

These questions were not new to me. I had been concerned with the question of energy supply since the late 1960s. In 1971, I was awarded the Harvey Prize by the University of Tel Aviv. The lecture series that I offered in connection with that award was on the topic of energy—its sources and the relevant technologies (solar, wind, geothermal, and nuclear, as well as increased domestic production of gas and oil).

During the summer of 1974, I spent a great deal of time discussing nuclear reactors, both those in current service and those of a new super-safe design. I also reexamined the licensing process in the United States. Worries about radioactivity coupled with the demand for increased government supervision had given rise to regulations that lengthened the construction period by several years and thereby dramatically increased the cost of such electricity.[2] By listening, arguing, encouraging, and having our results published, Nelson did what he could to develop a reasonable energy policy for the United States. But even he could not prevail over the mounting prejudice against nuclear energy.

Nelson not only invited me to join the project but he accepted my recommendations of several other people to serve on the commission. In addition to inviting Hans Mark and Johnny Foster to serve on the study, Nelson asked Wilson Talley to take over the organizing role that Henry Kissinger had held during the previous study.[3] I also recommended Johnny von Neumann's daughter, economist Marina von Neumann Whitman. Nelson accepted this last recommendation with particular enthusiasm.[4]

But the unexpected bonus of my commission work was in the new friends I made. I got to know Henry and Clare Booth Luce. Henry was the publisher and editor-in-chief of *Time* magazine, and Clare, who was a former member of the House of Representatives and had been ambassador to Italy, was an author knowledgeable on many topics. They were both charming and interesting people, and I enjoyed my visits with them in Phoenix and later in Hawaii. I also met Karl Bendetsen, president of Champion Paper Company.[5]

I also acquired a dear friend through my work with Nelson—Dixy Lee Ray. Dixy Lee Ray had been a fine environmentalist long before such an activity became popular. A former zoology professor at the University of Washington,

---

[2] The report of my work for Nelson's commission appeared as the first chapter in the fourth volume, *Power and Security*. The series was titled *Critical Choices for Americans* (Lexington Books, D.C. Heath & Co., 1976). Five years later, I published an expanded study of the energy question under the title *Energy from Heaven and Earth* (San Francisco: W. H. Freeman, 1979).

[3] Wilson, however, is more scientist than politician. His subsequent appointment was not to secretary of state but to chief scientist for the EPA.

[4] As time went on, it turned out that Marina and I disagreed on almost every issue. However, in true Hungarian style, our relationship stayed agreeable.

[5] Ten years later, Clare, Karl, and I would again serve on a panel together: General Danny Graham's High Frontier.

she made her home on Fox Island, in Puget Sound, where she lived content-edly in the midst of a remarkable menagerie. Dixy left her beloved Washing-ton state for what she considered the far less desirable eastern city of the same name when she accepted Nixon's invitation to head the Atomic Energy Com-mission. Dixy did not serve on the Critical Choices commission but occasion-ally visited with Nelson when the commission was meeting.

A widely circulated story asserts that when James Schlesinger, the outgo-ing AEC chairman, took Dixy to meet President Nixon, she brought along her dogs. Schlesinger, who was rarely seen without his pipe, was appalled and asked, "Do you think the president likes dogs?" Dixy's instantaneous re-sponse was: "Do you think the president likes pipe smoke?" Whether the story is true or apocryphal, it accurately reflects Dixy's independent spirit, her devotion to her dogs, and her thorough-going dislike of tobacco.

I had my first lengthy conversation with Dixy because of the unfortunate fact that Nelson's wife, Happy, unexpectedly had to have surgery for cancer. Therefore, Nelson couldn't keep his luncheon date with Dixy and asked me to stand in for him. I had a delightful time, and Dixy became a good friend.

Dixy and I touched on several topics over lunch that day, one of them the question of whether the increased level of carbon dioxide in the atmosphere could cause significant global warming. (That topic then as now was a re-search interest at the Livermore laboratory.) We also discussed the AEC, which had just been dismantled, and we discussed the upcoming elections.

After lunch, both of us were going to the airport, so we rode together. Dixy told me about the agreeable meetings she had had with two women heads of state, Indira Ghandi and Golda Meir. "But," she said, "you must be careful about these ladies. Like mother bears, they could be dangerous if you hurt their cubs." After a pause, I said, "Dixy, I want to tell you something that is a little impertinent, and you may not speak to me again." "Go ahead." "You wouldn't make such a bad mother bear yourself." Dixy was silent for a little while. Finally, she said, "Yes, that is impertinent, but I will talk with you again."

Dixy did not become president of the United States, although she would have done a better job in that role than some of those who have served in the interim; nonetheless, she did become governor of her state of Washington. She made a good Democratic leader and accomplished a lot, including the proper and safe handling of nuclear reactors. Dixy was always reasonable and always spoke out strongly in defense of facts, even in cases when the facts ran counter to popular opinion. I much admired her style, but that style did not help her become one of the mother bears. After she retired, she remained outspoken and active and published two excellent books.[6] She died a few years ago, and I continue to miss her.

Toward the end of the meetings of Critical Choices for Americans, I was having dinner with Nelson, together with Hans Mark, Bill Ronan (who was then Nelson's chief advisor), Bill Baker, and Laurance Rockefeller. President Nixon had just resigned. I, of course, cannot reproduce the conversation verbatim, but the following exchange is an approximation of what took place. Laurance turned to Nelson and asked, "What are you going to do when President Ford asks you to be the vice president?"

Nelson seemed thoroughly shocked by the idea and immediately responded, "I will never be vice president. I don't want to be a fifth wheel. I am not willing to waste my time in that sort of a role," and he continued with other similar comments. When he quieted down, Laurance, who was politically shrewd, responded: "But, Nelson, it is going to happen. You are available. You are from the right part of the Republican Party." Nelson denied that Ford would ask him and repeated all the reasons he did not want to be vice president.

The conversation then turned to other topics, but as we were leaving the table, Nelson said, "Laurance, dammit, you're right. I am going to be vice president. Let's all go into the study, and you fellows tell me what I am going to accomplish while I am vice president. It can't be much, because a president won't tolerate his vice president stealing the show, but there surely must be something worthwhile that I can do in two years."

Of course, Nelson was asked by President Ford to serve as vice president.[7] During his term, he accomplished the two tasks we suggested that night: He reestablished the position of science advisor, which President Nixon had abolished, and he established a commission that examined and reorganized the intelligence service. He did not run for reelection as vice president.[8] A few years later, in January 1979, Nelson died.

---

[6] Dixy Lee Ray with Lou Guzzo, *Trashing the Planet: How Science Can Help Us Deal with Acid Rain, Depletion of the Ozone, and Nuclear Waste (among other things)* (Washington, D.C.: Regnery Gateway, 1990); Dixy Lee Ray with Lou Guzzo, *Environmental Overkill: Whatever Happened to Common Sense?* (Washington, D.C.: Regnery Gateway, 1993).

[7] When Nelson was appointed vice president in December 1974, he left the commission, and Laurance assumed responsibility for the publication of the studies.

[8] Ford was defeated in his bid for election. A few weeks before the vote, President Ford, in a press conference, made the remarkable statement that Poland was a free country and reaffirmed that statement explicitly when questioned by a reporter. The next day, I saw Nelson in his office and asked what could be done. Nelson had no answer. Ford's unfortunate statement alienated millions of Americans of East-European descent and cast doubt on his ability to conduct an effective foreign policy. In my opinion, it cost him the election.

Perhaps the most important thing I learned from Nelson was respect for a peculiar aspect of the American Revolution. The changes that our revolution engendered have been uniquely full and long-lasting. I believe the idea that made this possible is contained in the *Federalist Papers*. The standard revolutionary slogan is: Trust me. The slogan of the American Revolution was: Trust nobody. Limit the powers of government. The government should do only those things that are absolutely necessary and that cannot be done by anybody else. Of course, that remains excellent advice.

During the years the commission was in session, I was approaching the compulsory retirement age for government employees. I did not much like the idea—I am not naturally a retiring person—but I am a law-abiding citizen, and if the government says go, I do so. In any event, I did not expect retirement to change my life dramatically. The laboratory would probably continue to employ me on a consulting basis for one-third time, which was only slightly less time than I had worked during the previous five years or so. I would also still serve as a professor at the University of California, albeit emeritus, and continue to give occasional lectures on the various campuses of the university, and I would continue to do consulting work with industry. In some ways, I even looked forward to my retirement. As an employee of the federal government and of the State of California, I had to make sure that what I said was attributed only to me, a private citizen, and not to the laboratory.

In 1973, I accepted an invitation from Edward Rozek, director of the Center for the Study of Democracy and Communism (CSDC) at the University of Colorado in Boulder, to offer a lecture series, which I called "The Miracle of Freedom."[9] Since the mid-1960s, I had noticed a growing pessimism among the public about science and technology. I firmly believed (and continue to believe) that the attitude was largely based on misinformation. I mentioned to Rozek that I wished there were a center devoted to correcting misconceptions, thereby introducing a balancing force to the pessimism. Such a center could serve as a sort of clearing house of scientific fact and scientific best guesses and help the public distinguish between those ideas and pure hokum. Rozek was excited about the idea and suggested that we convert the CSDC into just such a center and call it the Edward Teller Center for Science, Technology, and Political Thought. I was pleased by his enthusiasm,

---

[9] The four lectures were later published in pamphlet form, and I drew on one of those lectures in my discussion of the Vietnam War in Chapter 38.

and we both set about seeing whether financial support was available for such a center.[10]

Among the friends I called on was a man I had met through Jim Maxfield, Arthur Spitzer. Spitzer was born in Austria and managed to survive World War II in Europe. Penniless, he worked his way to the United States in 1951; he came to California, where he became first a part-owner of a gas station, and eventually the owner and president of Digas Company, which managed a chain of gas stations throughout the country. When Digas was purchased by Tesoro Oil, Arthur became a wealthy man. He also firmly believed that the freedoms and opportunities provided by his adopted country could be assured only if the United States maintained scientific and technological leadership. Arthur agreed that creating greater scientific literacy and informed scientific policymaking was worthy of his best support.

But the project to begin the center was hardly underway when, perhaps because the center was to be named for me, a virulent attack began against it. I suspect that two groups with different ideologies were involved. This period was the height of the cold war; at that time, people like me—who were outspoken about Soviet abuses and the excellence of the Soviet military machine—were seen as working counter to the cause of peace and freedom. Second, several physicists on the University of Colorado faculty, most particularly Ed Condon and Julius London, were still furious with me over my testimony in the Oppenheimer hearing.

The coalition was successful enough to force a vote of the regents on whether Frederick Theime, the president of the University of Colorado, who had supported the establishment of the center, should be asked to resign. Their effort failed to remove him or to ban the center, which was established in April 1973.

Unfortunately, this first success was not enough. To be effective, a research center requires a great deal of money and single-minded, dedicated leadership. Much as he wanted the center to succeed, Professor Rozek also had a great many other responsibilities. Although my friends raised almost half a million dollars, Professor Rozek was unable to raise funds from other sources. Arthur Spitzer and several other board members attempted to reorganize the center, but they failed and withdrew their support in November 1974. On their advice, so did I, although with regret.

---

[10] In the late 1980s, another friend, General Neil Beer, made another attempt to establish such a center, this time at The George Washington University. Unfortunately, once again, there was insufficient financial support.

Early the next spring, Glenn Campbell invited me to come to Hoover and give a lecture for the Hoover Fellows. There was nothing particularly unusual about this. I had met Glenn, who was a regent of the University of California, in 1960, when the University named me Professor of Physics at Large. I remember the meeting because Glenn asked me where I was when I was not at large, a question that continues to stump me. I had also had dinner with him and his charming wife, Rita, at John Lawrence's house once or twice, had worked with him on various election committees, and had visited Hoover on a few other occasions. This time a new development followed my talk. Glenn asked me to become a Senior Research Fellow at Hoover.

The idea was not entirely new. At the height of the student protests at Berkeley, my friend Hans Mark had approached Glenn (without my knowledge), hoping that an invitation to join Hoover would result in my moving away from Berkeley. Glenn broached the idea informally, and I explained that I would not be moving until I retired. Now retirement was only a few months away. The position Glenn offered was for one-third time, which accorded with my plans. I accepted with thanks.

I already knew a few of the Hoover scholars. I had worked with Martin Anderson on Rockefeller's Critical Choices Commission during the previous two years. And I also knew Marty's pleasant wife, Anneliese, who was also a Hoover Fellow. I knew Sidney Hook through his work at Columbia during the late 1960s and because I had written articles for his journal, *The New Leader*. I also knew Darrell Trent (who later became deputy transportation secretary under President Reagan) and Dick Staar (who in the mid-1980s became an ambassador to arms control talks in Geneva).

At the time I joined Hoover, I wasn't quite sure how well I would fit in: I was a scientist, not a political scientist. And I was in no way an economist, which seemed to be the predominant breed. I was not invited to join either of the two divisions at Hoover—domestic studies or international affairs.[11] I eventually realized that my concerns were groundless; Hoover Institution, which has been a valued base of operations for a quarter of a century now, is an interesting and congenial environment.

Perhaps it is a symptom of aging, but it seems to me that since 1960, political attitudes and statements have tended toward extremes, and organizations have come to consist of like-minded people talking louder because they

---

[11] Years later, I learned that Milton Friedman, who joined Hoover at about the same time as I, was similarly unattached. I was told that we should take it as a compliment that our interests were too broad to fit one category.

are of one voice. By contrast, the Hoover Institution is one of those rare places where contrasting points of view lead to reasonable and sometimes productive discussion.

In several ways, the Hoover Institution is more of an ivory tower than the university in which it is housed. Hoover is remarkably unaffected by the political fashions that seem to sway university administrators and faculty. That independence is, in part, an outgrowth of the wisdom of its founder, President Herbert Hoover, who insisted that the institution have its own separate trustees. The independence that Hoover Institution enjoys is also due, in part, to the remarkable man who served as its director from 1960 to 1994, W. Glenn Campbell. Under his leadership, the endowment of Hoover Institution rose from $2 million to almost $130 million dollars. Glenn's successor, John Raisian, has ably continued the policies of tolerance and excellence that Glenn established.

The reality of Hoover Institution is that it provides a home for dedicated and often highly distinguished scholars of several varieties of political opinion. No one I have known at Hoover stands at a political extreme; my Hoover colleagues tolerate other political opinions so long as those opinions do not infringe on the free expression of ideas. At various times during my tenure, Hoover Institution has been attacked as being "reactionary." To my mind, the description of Hoover offered by the British journal *The Economist*, which called Hoover "a right-leaning think tank" and ranked its facilities and scholars as "the finest in the world," comes far closer to describing the reality.[12]

For Hoover Institution to be perceived incorrectly seems almost fitting: Its founder, Herbert Hoover, is also wrongly perceived by most Americans. Hoover, as a visit to the Hoover Tower Museum demonstrates, was an outstanding humanitarian. His work on behalf of the starving peoples of Europe, during and after the World War I, saved hundreds of thousands of lives. His efforts in that same period to preserve the historical records of the Kerensky Republic in Russia made it possible to return some of those documents to their nation of origin in 1990. Although Hoover is blamed for worsening the Great Depression, he was not at fault. The uncooperative Congress during his administration, rather than his policies (which, had they been enacted, would have eased its severity), should receive the blame. I count myself most fortunate to be affiliated with the institution that is Herbert Hoover's legacy.

---

[12] *The Economist* in the December 21, 1991–January 3, 1992 issue.

In June 1975, I retired from Lawrence Livermore National Laboratory. For almost a year, not much changed. It seemed no harder to commute across the Bay in one direction than in the other. Eventually, though, I found myself spending more of my time at Hoover and decided to move to the Stanford campus.

Leaving the house in which you have lived for twenty-three years is difficult. In the midst of the chaos and confusion, some of the cartons of books that were intended for our move—including copies of his books that Geo Gamow had inscribed and given me—were lost.[13] I have not missed anything except those books (which I had intended to give to my grandchildren), so it was a good move. Because Mici found our new house unsatisfactory almost before she had unpacked the boxes, we moved to another house on campus a few years later, this one reminiscent of our old home in Berkeley. Mici spent the last twenty years of her life there most contentedly.

After retirement, I spent much more time on the road, speaking at various functions, consulting with industries, serving on committees and boards, and when asked, testifying in Washington, D.C. I remember in particular giving testimony to the Office of Budget Management on March 27, 1979.

At that time, Duane Sewell, one of the founding administrators at Livermore, had temporarily taken a post in the Department of Energy (DOE). Because he remembered Greg Canavan from his time as a graduate student at the Department of Applied Science in Livermore (Greg was one of our most outstanding graduates), he offered Greg a job.

Greg had returned to the air force after completing his graduate studies, but his eyesight was no longer good enough for him to qualify as a pilot (his long-held aim). Instead, he went to work at the U.S. Air Force Weapons Laboratory in Albuquerque, and in 1975, he was promoted to the Defense Advanced Projects Agency (where he was working when he won the Hertz Prize). After he had served a year as a White House Fellow, he decided to leave the air force. Duane immediately hired him as head of the inertial fusion program at DOE.

In early 1979, Greg was concerned that the Office of Budget Management (OMB) might not fund the laser program for inertial fusion, which has proved to be an important program. He asked me to help by adding my testimony.

He was correct in suspecting that the fusion program was not a favorite of the OMB. I spent the better part of the afternoon answering questions and

---

[13] A physics professor from Berkeley (who shall remain nameless) bought them at a used bookstore and then wrote to tell me that he had them.

strenuously arguing for the cause. At the end of the day, I was exceedingly tired. Jim Maxfield, my Texas doctor friend, was traveling with me on that occasion, and he pointed out that many seventy-one-year-old people get tired after a busy day. I went to bed.

The next day I woke up feeling exhausted, but almost at once I received some disturbing news: One of the nuclear reactors at the Three Mile Island plant in Pennsylvania had a serious problem. I forgot about being tired. For the next three days, feeling worse and worse, I worked hard trying to understand what was happening in the reactor, considering what steps might be taken to ameliorate the problems, and wondering what more the Reactor Safeguard Committee could have done to prevent the accident.[14] On the third day, when the size of the problem was evident and the worst of the damage over, I was hospitalized with a heart attack.

The heart attack proved to be mild, but it did curtail my activities for some months, and it made my Hoover office more important to me.[15] During my recuperation during the summer of 1979, I accepted several writing projects, including a long essay for a book Hoover was publishing. I was at the same time working on two other books. That was how I came to hire an editor, Judy Shoolery, who has been my collaborator on most of the writing I have done since that time.[16] My recuperation, fortunately, went smoothly. I say fortunately because I was about to become involved in one of the most important projects of my life.

---

[14]The severity of the accident was the result of operator error. When a valve failed to shut properly, the operators manually overrode the safeguard system. No one was injured in the accident, but the reactor was destroyed. Exposure outside the plant was minute, and occurred when a small amount of contaminated air was vented during the clean-up period.

[15]I have been fortunate during the last quarter century in my staff both at Hoover and at Livermore. My first Hoover secretary was Ann Fogle, who had served that role at the Commission on Critical Choices and moved to California to help me set up my Hoover office. Elizabeth (Wolfrom) Ashby capably filled that role when Ann left, and Patty (French) Shaw took over from Liz and remained my secretary for sixteen years until she remarried. At present, Patsy Pemberton, formerly one of my readers, fills that post. At Livermore, Tolly Williamson was my secretary for almost a decade, and for a few years Shirley Petty filled that role until she was promoted. Joanne Smith then joined my staff and continues, ably and agreeably, in that post to this day.

[16]The first book that resulted from our joint efforts was *Pursuit of Simplicity* (Malibu, Calif.: Pepperdine Press, 1980); and the second *Better a Shield than a Sword* (New York: Free Press, 1986).

40

STRATEGIC DEFENSE

1980–1992

IN DECEMBER 1945, in my report to the U.S. Navy, I emphasized the need for defense against atomic weapons. During the summer of 1951, I attended a conference in Pasadena, sponsored by the air force, for a few weeks.[1] Among the topics under consideration were low-yield nuclear weapons and strategic defense. The study that eventually came out of the conference recommended for tactical nuclear weapons and against trying to pursue strategic defense.

Even at that early date, the development of intercontinental rockets was on the horizon. The obstacles to developing defense posed by a combination of rockets and nuclear weapons seemed insurmountable. Then, in 1961, as I mentioned earlier, following a tour of the Strategic Air Command facilities outside Colorado Springs, General Partridge convinced me that I should at least consider the problem of defense seriously. That in turn led, in 1967, to the Livermore laboratory's developing and testing the effectiveness of using nuclear explosives to counter incoming missiles. Governor Ronald Reagan was introduced at that time to the idea of a ballistic missile defense system.[2]

In 1980, Ronald Reagan ran for president. I campaigned for him, making speeches around the country and serving as the chairman of Hungarian-Americans for Reagan. Martin Anderson, one of my friends at Hoover, also worked hard on Reagan's campaign. He was with Reagan during a tour of

---

[1] That conference was called the Vista Project. I believe that I was involved through the Rand Corporation, where my two friends, Dave Griggs and Albert Latter, worked.

[2] Although the defensive system—on which both Los Alamos and Livermore had worked—was technically significant and was deployed at an ICBM field, it was decommissioned in 1976 for lack of funding.

the same Air Command Center near Colorado Springs that I had visited in 1961. Although its name had changed, its purpose had remained the same.[3] It would direct defensive military operations should the United States be attacked. Although almost two decades had passed since my visit to the center, the possibilities for defense against an incoming missile remained unchanged: There were none.

The center was, and is, impressive. It is isolated inside a large chamber deep inside the mountain, the entry heavily reinforced and protected. Although the Air Command Center was effectively impervious to attack at the time of my visit, twenty years later it had become vulnerable. The difference lay in the Soviet SS-18 intercontinental ballistic missile (which dwarfed any U.S. missile) that had recently been incorporated in the Soviet arsenal. If a single SS-18 warhead struck within a few hundred yards of the command center, it would obliterate it. That was one of the first things Reagan learned on his visit.[4]

Anderson reports that after leaving the Air Command Center, Reagan reflected on the dilemma a president would face in case of a missile attack. His only options would be either to direct our ballistic missiles to be fired in a counterattack or to do nothing except absorb the attack. President Reagan saw both alternatives as bad. "We should have some way of defending ourselves against nuclear missiles," he told Anderson.[5]

President Reagan has been accused of making instantaneous decisions—shooting from the hip. His speed in getting off his shot was certainly not in evidence in regard to strategic defense: Sixteen years followed his introduction to the subject at Livermore, and four of them passed after his apparent decision following his tour of the Air Command Center. But on March 23, 1983, President Reagan became a most determined advocate of ballistic missile defense. I do not know how President Reagan arrived at his decision, but I can describe my own involvement in promoting protective defense.

In January 1981, Richard Staar, one of my friends at Hoover Institution, asked me to read a manuscript he had received from Daniel O. Graham, a recently retired army general. Although I was pleased to find that General Graham was promoting strategic defense, he had linked his plan to one that would collect solar energy in space, convert it to microwave energy, and beam it back to antennas on earth for conversion into electricity for common

---

[3] Today, the Air Command Center is called the North American Aerospace Defense Command.

[4] Martin Anderson, *Revolution: The Reagan Legacy* (Stanford, Calif.: Hoover Institution Press, 1990).

[5] Ibid., p. 83.

use. I doubted the economic feasibility of the plan, and I suspected that the public would not readily accept such a novel technology.[6] Because I considered ballistic missile defense the most important topic, I wished he had presented it independently of the exotic commercial energy proposal.

A more important problem lay with Graham's design of the defense system. The first priority for successful defense is that the defensive system be less expensive to deploy than the means for circumventing or destroying it. Graham suggested space-based platforms containing forty to fifty defensive units of guided missiles and a few manned space-based units that would coordinate and control the defensive devices housed in the platforms. Such a system of manned platforms would be expensive to deploy and maintain. Because of the ease in identifying the platforms, it would be much less expensive for an enemy to shoot them down than for us to deploy and maintain them. I agreed with him completely about the need for strategic defense, but I wished he would be less specific and simply call for using all new technologies that seemed practical.

By 1981, the prospects of detecting, discriminating, tracking, and destroying incoming missiles were greatly improved. One promising technology on the horizon involved the use of lasers to detect incoming missiles.[7] Guided defensive antimissile rockets, popped up from submarines once a missile attack was observed, were also a possibility. New and far more powerful lasers were becoming available that might make it possible to construct a system capable of destroying missiles in the boost phase.

General Graham had been effective in drawing public attention to strategic defense. He had helped found an organization, High Frontier, to promote space-based defense and had gathered an impressive list of supporters. Among the founding members of High Frontier were Karl Bendetsen, Joseph Coors, William Wilson, and Jack Hume, four of President Reagan's close friends and advisors. By the summer of 1981, I had joined High Frontier in the hope that I could assist the group in submitting an optimal technical proposal for strategic defense. Unfortunately, there were several topics that I could not discuss at that time.

One of them involved work at Livermore that I had followed closely. In the mid-1970s, laser development had proceeded to the point where scientists

---

[6] A sizable, vocal group in the Western world has become fearful about the potential effects of new technologies; for example, electric power lines, microwave ovens, and, as mentioned earlier, all applications of nuclear energy.

[7] It is hard to protect radar equipment against the destructive electronic effects of a nuclear explosion. Nuclear fireballs, even at high altitudes, are effectively opaque to most radar signals.

began considering the possibility of producing an x-ray laser. At Livermore, my friend Lowell Wood and two of the talented young people that Lowell had brought into the laboratory, George Chapline and Peter Hagelstein, were working on the problem.[8] While examining George's design before its test, Peter came up with a novel suggestion that became the second part of a test held in late 1980. Both designs worked. X-ray lasing had been demonstrated for the first time.

To appreciate the technical progress involved, one must understand a little about lasers and their history. A laser is a device that produces a high-intensity, precisely directed beam of electromagnetic energy of uniform wavelength.[9] The shorter the wavelength emitted, the more energy the laser can produce. The same properties of lasers that make it possible to put a great amount of intensity into a beam make it possible to transfer energy with little dilution from one limited region to a similarly limited region at great distance.

The first demonstration of lasing occurred in the 1950s, when Charles Townes and Arthur Schalow harnessed microwaves (which are short-wave radio waves) to produce a maser. Infrared lasers (which harnessed the next shorter electromagnetic wavelength) were developed in 1960. In the following years, lasers employing steadily shorter wavelengths and having an increasing variety of applications were developed. The x-ray laser is the shortest wavelength laser that is practical. An x-ray laser, driven by a nuclear explosion, could in principle provide an effective instrument for ballistic missile defense.[10]

---

[8] Lowell Wood has attracted an impressive number of talented people to the Livermore laboratory. Part of that can be attributed to Lowell's brilliance and energy, but another factor is the collegial environment he created within the group that he managed, O (as in omega) group. The O group achieved critical mass in about 1975, and its achievements during the following fifteen years were significant. In addition to George Chapline, O group included Rod Hyde (who is largely responsible for a novel rocket propulsion system), Curt Widdoes and Tom McWilliams (who were instrumental in developing the supercomputer S-1), Larry West, Joe Nilsen, Jack Marlow (who developed the blue-green laser system, which vastly improved communication with submarines), and Peter Hagelstein (who, like Chapline, was working on the design of an x-ray laser).

[9] The phenomenon of light emission (which is the opposite of light absorption or casting a shadow) occurs naturally when atoms return to a lower energy state; for example, when a very hot metal glows. In 1916, Einstein suggested that light emission may not occur only in a spontaneous manner but also may be induced by an incident beam of light. The challenge is to get atoms to prefer a higher energy state (which is called a population inversion). If a population inversion is produced, then, with an additional stimulus, a high-intensity, precisely directed light beam (of a specific frequency) can be produced.

[10] Longer-wavelength x-ray lasers using the powerful research laser system developed for the study of controlled fusion were demonstrated at Livermore a few years later.

Not being able to talk publicly about that and other new possibilities for strategic defense was frustrating. The American people, whose lives and well-being were concerned, were out of the decisionmaking chain because of secrecy. And it was likely that the president himself knew far too little about the new developments.

In mid-1981, George A. (Jay) Keyworth had been appointed White House science advisor. Not much later, he organized a White House Science Council and invited me to serve on that board.[11] As of mid-1982, the subject of the new strategic defense technologies had not been discussed.

That is not to suggest that Jay was not an excellent science advisor. I had suggested him as a candidate when Martin Anderson, who was then assistant to the president for policy development in the Reagan administration, asked me for a recommendation. I had become acquainted with Jay, a young scientist at Los Alamos, while I was consulting at the laboratory during the 1970s. I was impressed by his combination of enthusiasm and sound scientific instincts.

When my longtime friend Harold Agnew retired as director of Los Alamos in about 1980, I asked Greg Canavan to recommend Keyworth to the search committee. But Greg misunderstood my Hungarian-style pronunciation. He thought I had said Gibberth and diligently sought such a person at Los Alamos; when he failed to find him, nothing came of my suggestion. The misunderstanding proved fortuitous. Having not been chosen as director, Keyworth was available to be considered for the position of presidential science advisor in 1981.

A presidential science advisor contributes informed scientific and technical opinion about policy proposals only after they are formulated, and strategic defense was not a national policy. There appeared to be no way to call attention to the advances.

I was therefore willing to discuss the topic of secrecy with Bill Buckley on his PBS television show *Firing Line*.[12] During that interview, which aired in late July 1982, I said,

> From the time that President Reagan has been nominated, I have not had a single occasion to talk to him. . . . I have talked to people to whom I am close

---

[11] My fellow members were both illustrious and interesting. Chaired by Sol Buchsbaum of Bell Laboratories, the White House Science Council included Harold Agnew, John Bardeen, D. Allan Bromley, George Cowan, Edward David, Donald Fredrickson, Edward Frieman, Paul Gray, Robert O. Hunter, Jr., Arthur Kerman, and David Packard.

[12] My friends Teddy and Lois Walkowicz introduced me to Bill (William F.) Buckley during the early 1960s, and I have long appreciated the forum his program provides.

and who in turn are close to the president. I did not make an unreasonable request that I should talk to the president in person. . . . I have tried what seemed reasonable to me to get action [on recent developments related to strategic defense]. . . . I am deeply grateful for any opportunity to speak about these things.

A few weeks after my interview with Buckley, I heard from the White House. The president would soon be making a definite appointment with me to discuss defense prospects. The meeting was finally scheduled for 2:30 P.M., September 14, 1982.

That thirty-minute meeting was far less successful than I had hoped. Quite a sizable group was assembled in the president's office: President Reagan, Vice President Bush, Judge William Clark, Attorney General Edward Meese, Jay Keyworth, and Sydell Gold, a National Security staff member responsible for nuclear matters. I did my best to present the information about the developments in defense in a nontechnical manner and to emphasize the timeliness of making an effort to pursue research on strategic defense. But Ms. Gold injected so many questions and caveats that I felt discouraged about the conference.

Lowell Wood and Greg Canavan were both in Washington at that time, and we met shortly after my meeting with the president. Their recollection is that my mood was bleak: I had had my chance, and I had failed to convey to the president the gist of the information and the potential that it held. With their encouragement, I asked Jay Keyworth, now President Reagan's science advisor, to establish a study group within the White House Science Council to review the technical basis for strategic defense. Jay agreed and asked Sol Buchsbaum to head the group, which included me as one of about six members.

We worked diligently throughout the fall of 1982. We listened to detailed presentations in government and industrial laboratories all over the country. Our final report, issued in January 1983, favorably assessed the technical prospects for strategic defense. I believe the report was then provided to the president.

Later that month, when I was in Washington, D.C., for a meeting with Secretary of Energy Donald Hodel, I ran into an acquaintance, Admiral James D. Watkins, who invited me to lunch. At that time, Admiral Watkins was Chief of Naval Operations, the senior officer of the U.S. Navy. The work on the x-ray laser was new and had received little exposure even in high-security circles, so I discussed that development with him. I later learned that the admiral did not like the nuclear nature of the laser but was impressed that I was optimistic about strategic defense.

At that time, the Joint Chiefs of Staff were attempting to deal with the problem of increased vulnerability of U.S. silo-based missiles (from the new Soviet missile SS-18). The solution was not readily apparent. The best and most widely discussed proposal (the MX system) had not gained much support; it called for removing the missiles from their silos and moving them about on a rail system, a process that would make them more difficult to target. After our luncheon, Admiral Watkins, who had been hearing recommendations to consider strategic defense from others as well, convinced the Joint Chiefs to support a long-term shift in policy when he pointed out that strategic defense was both militarily and morally sound.

The recommendation of the Joint Chiefs of Staff was presented to the president in early February. I saw Watkins about that time at a tribute to Admiral Rickover, and he spoke with me briefly, telling me that he thought something good might come of our talk.

On March 20, 1983, I received a call from the White House: Would I please attend a dinner with the president on the evening of March 23? I canceled my appointments, scrambled to make flight reservations, and arrived on time at the White House. That evening, President Reagan made an eloquent plea for strategic defense:

I have become more and more deeply convinced that the human spirit must be capable of rising above dealing with other nations and human beings by threatening their existence. . . .

Wouldn't it be better to save lives than to avenge them? Are we not capable of demonstrating our peaceful intention by applying all our abilities and our ingenuity to achieving a truly lasting stability?

I think we are. Indeed, we must. . . . Let me share with you a vision of the future which offers hope. It is that we embrace a program to counter the awesome Soviet missile threat with measures that are defensive. . . . What if free people could live secure in the knowledge that their security did not rest upon the threat of instant U.S. retaliation to deter a Soviet attack, that we could intercept and destroy ballistic missiles before they reached our own soil or that of our allies?

I know this is a formidable task, one that may not be accomplished before the end of the century. Yet, current technology has attained a level of sophistication where it is reasonable for us to begin this effort. . . .

I call upon the scientific community of our country, those who gave us nuclear weapons, to turn their great talents now to the cause of mankind and world peace, to give us the means of rendering these nuclear weapons impotent and obsolete.

Those wonderful words moved me deeply. For more than twenty years, I had believed that peace would be far more secure if we had a ballistic missile defense system. Not only would such a system provide a humane alternative to retaliation, but also, by making the success of a first strike uncertain, it would add to the stability of peace.

Many in the scientific community had been invited to listen to President Reagan's speech; among those attending were Hans Bethe and Victor Weisskopf. Both had worked on the atomic bomb, and both considered strategic defense impractical. President Reagan's plea did not change their minds. Unfortunately, like many of their colleagues, they thought the policy of mutually assured destruction, inaugurated in the early 1960s, a better, more stable policy. That retaliatory stance had been taken because it was cheaper to counter the buildup of Soviet ground forces by adding more missiles to our arsenal than to increase our own ground forces.

Not long after announcing the Strategic Defense Initiative (SDI), President Reagan offered to use the defenses that were developed to protect all nations from missile attack. As a result, several nations joined the research effort. By the end of the Reagan administration eight years later, Germany, Israel, the United Kingdom, the Netherlands, Italy, and Japan were involved in SDI research.

Support for SDI in the United States was less than wholehearted. I believe that part of the problem was a lack of understanding of what constitutes effective ballistic missile defense. Immediately after the president's speech, Secretary of State George Shultz, with whom I was acquainted, asked me, "Can this system be 100 percent effective?" My response: "Against the largest attack that the Soviets can mount? Probably not."

My answer leads to another unasked question: Is it better to destroy 90 to 95 percent of the missiles in a massive attack or to have no defense against them? Critics of strategic defense proclaim that if even one missile escaped the defensive system, the damage would be unacceptably great. Such critics seemingly refuse to consider how much more unacceptable the damage would be if all attack missiles reached their targets.

Among the score of research projects that were undertaken in the first eighteen months of work on SDI, the x-ray laser was the most controversial. President Reagan had made it clear that he wanted the strategic defense system to be non-nuclear. Consequently, work on that laser was not emphasized.

A variety of other programs—ranging from lasers and other beam weapons to rockets to computers to kinetic energy devices—were being pursued at the national laboratories and in industry. In June 1985, twenty-seven months after work on strategic defense was announced, I reported to President Reagan that we had progress on several technologies, but no overall approach to a strategic defense system. That was discouraging news because some had expected to deploy a defense system within a few years. Yet the realities suggested that such deployment was likely to require more than a decade of work—as the president had suggested in his speech.

Jay Keyworth resigned his post as the president's science advisor in January 1986; he was replaced by William R. (Bill) Graham, who had formerly been an administrator at NASA. A few months after Graham assumed his job, he began warning that congressional support for SDI was weakening. By the fall of 1986, the political situation was painfully clear. A group of friendly congressmen and political advisors, including Jack Kemp, Rudy Boschwitz, Jack Courter, and Eugene Rostow, summoned Lowell Wood, Greg Canavan (as representatives of the SDI effort in the two national laboratories) and me to a meeting in Washington. They told us that even though SDI was little more than three years old, its political future was in doubt: Progress on strategic defense was being made too slowly.

We then jointly wrote a letter to the president asking him to continue his support; but we knew the pressures on him to abandon SDI during the upcoming summit in Reykjavik, Iceland, would probably be particularly great. (President Reagan had staunchly defended SDI at the first summit meeting with the Soviets, which was held in Geneva.)

The Strategic Defense Initiative, from the outset, had been anathema to the Soviets. That has always puzzled me because the Soviets had long favored establishing strategic defenses. The Soviets had installed a strategic defense system around Moscow in the mid-1970s; and in 1981, they modified and improved it. In addition, they were exploring the possible defense applications of large-scale lasers, one of which was installed at Sary Shagan. Yet, as soon as President Reagan announced a research program on strategic defense, they protested vigorously.

Mikhail Gorbachev had become premier of the Soviet Union in 1985; during the next few years, he instituted programs of liberalizing reforms. He moderated the harshness of Soviet human rights policies, freed many political prisoners—including Andrei Sakharov and Anatole Shchransky—and eased the censorship of news and literature. His policies appeared to be aimed at assuring the free world that it had much in common with the

Soviet Union—there were no threatening problems; peaceful coexistence could be the order of the day.

At the Reykjavik summit in October 1986, Gorbachev tried hard to dissuade Reagan from pursuing strategic defense. He pointed out the reforms that had been carried out and suggested that further liberalization could occur. The problem, he said, was that SDI was making improved relations impossible. If the United States would discontinue its research on strategic defense, a sharp reduction in Soviet missiles might be possible.

The Soviet concessions were attractive. Little progress was then apparent in the SDI program, but President Reagan was firmly committed to providing strategic defense. It was his responsibility as president, he told Gorbachev, to protect and defend the American people; that meant continuing to work on strategic defense.[13]

Both publicly and privately, I had wholeheartedly and actively supported the Strategic Defense Initiative—and this was not lost on the Soviets. On December 8, 1987, President and Mrs. Reagan held a reception and dinner at the White House in honor of the Gorbachevs, who were in Washington to discuss how best to reduce the intensity of the Cold War. The Reagans included me among the guests.

During the before-dinner socializing, I spoke briefly with Raisa Gorbachev, who was polite if distant. I don't remember whom I was talking to later, but our conversation went on so long that I was among the last to go through the receiving line. President Reagan was standing next to Premier Gorbachev and introduced me to him, saying, "This is Dr. Teller." I put my hand out to shake hands, but Gorbachev stood unmoving and silent. Reagan then repeated to Gorbachev, "This is the famous Dr. Teller." Gorbachev then said, with his hands at his sides, "There are many Tellers."

I was momentarily shocked and hurt. I did not look upon shaking Gorbachev's hand as a particular honor, but I was willing to do so because expressing animosity over another's political views is inappropriate, especially at a social event. My response was, "There are, indeed, many Tellers." I then turned and left the receiving line.

I had a bit of digesting to do before I sat down; by then I had realized that by leaving the line I had failed to greet Mrs. Reagan, an unintended

---

[13] Many, including Gorbachev, now see President Reagan's firm support of SDI as pivotal in the eventual collapse of the Soviet Union. See Ken Adelman (U.S. Director of the Arms Control Agency during the Reagan administration), "The Real Reagan," *Wall Street Journal,* 5 October 1999, p. A28.

discourtesy. At dinner, I was seated between Raisa Gorbachev and Jeane Kirkpatrick. Much as I enjoy and appreciate Jeane Kirkpatrick, the conversation at our end of the table was not lively.

When I was back home in California, I called Bill Graham and told him of my experience. I asked him: Should I write an apology note to Mrs. Reagan for failing to greet her, or should I not call attention to the incident? Bill assured me that my behavior had caused no offense, and I let his assurance end the matter.[14]

By November 1986, as the congressional leaders had told us, domestic support was ebbing away, in part for lack of a workable plan for an integrated defensive system. Lowell Wood, Greg Canavan, and I had met informally about once a month since SDI had begun to discuss and debate the various ways of providing defense. At our gathering for breakfast in early November, Greg proposed that we take a closer look at the kinetic energy system. That project, which had acquired the nickname Smart Rocks, called for predeployed arrays of explosive devices that would scatter projectiles into the path of a rising attack missile.

An intercontinental missile moves at about four miles a second. The satellite carrying the Smart Rocks would be orbiting at five miles a second. (For comparison, a bullet has the velocity of about one-half mile a second.) The great amount of kinetic energy converted in the collision would destroy the attacking missile.

I objected that once again we were looking at predeployed stations in space, which are cheaper to destroy than to deploy. Greg countered that the satellites could be made very small and therefore would be hard to find. He added that he had in mind a satellite with its own propulsion, sensing system, and decoys. The components of such a satellite—microprocessors and rockets to power the device—were small, light, and increasingly inexpensive. A constellation of a few thousand such devices could defend the Northern Hemisphere.

By the end of that breakfast, Lowell looked unusually interested. Although neither Greg nor I realized it, Lowell, with encouragement from Jack

---

[14]I have come to regard the incident as a great compliment. I received a few others from the Soviet Union. The earliest came in 1964, when the Polytechnik Literature Press in Moscow published a book (in Russian) by M. Vilenskiy, titled *Your Enemy Teller.* The next came on the occasion of my receiving the National Medal of Science in May, 1983. *Tass,* the Soviet news agency, said, "This priest of science . . . one of the most rabid nuclear maniacs . . . blinded by militarism and rabid anti-Sovietism, has always placed the results of his work at the Pentagon's service." I am a little proud that my efforts to protect freedom, and to extend it to those behind the Iron Curtain, were noticed.

Hammond (who headed the SDI directed energy program) had been investigating those possibilities for several weeks. He went back to Livermore and redoubled his efforts to prove or disprove the practicality of a small autonomous rocket that would detect Soviet missiles in the boost phase and wait in orbit to scatter destructive pebbles in the path of the attack missile.

The design Lowell and his colleagues developed during the next ten months converted me. The Smart Rocks, in Lowell's hands, had become Brilliant Pebbles.[15] Each satellite would measure less than forty inches and weigh about 120 pounds. Only about a fifth of the defensive devices would come within range of a specific missile launch at a specific moment. But those in range, if the command from Earth were given, would be capable of identifying the missile launch, moving into appropriate position, and firing projectiles into the path of the attack missile.

In October 1987, Lowell and I made a presentation of the system concept and design to General James Abrahamson, who had ably headed the SDI effort since its inception. Abrahamson gave the project a preliminary okay, and work continued at a furious pace. When we first started work on strategic defense, we believed that great force would be necessary to stop attack missiles. We came to realize that we could substitute precision and tiny computers and do the job even better.

On July 26, 1988, Lowell and I presented a briefing for President Reagan and Vice President Bush in the White House.[16] At last, we had a plan for a cost-effective, thorough-going defense system that could be in place by the mid-1990s. Such a system could provide protection for all nations in the Northern Hemisphere against both short- and long-range missiles. A few weeks later, President Reagan successfully fought off congressional reduction of the funding for the development of Brilliant Pebbles. A safer, more stable peace appeared within reach.

Vice President Bush was elected president in 1988 and assumed office in January 1989. The following November, the Berlin Wall fell, and, one by one, the Warsaw Bloc nations declared their independence. By the end of

---

[15] The word *pebble*, which is used in the biblical story of David and his slingshot that brings down the giant Goliath, seems particularly appropriate. The comparatively small Pebbles were designed to destroy incoming missiles tens of meters long. They were brilliant because they contained far greater sensing and computing abilities than their antecedents, the Smart Rocks.

[16] Three of my good friends, Director W. Glenn Campbell and Senior Fellow Martin Anderson of Hoover Institution and Director John Nuckolls of Lawrence Livermore National Laboratory, also attended the briefing.

1991, the cold war had ended, and the U.S.S.R. had ceased to exist. More than 300 million people had gained their freedom. After four decades of fear and tension, the Cold War had quietly and bloodlessly ended.

No one would have predicted those events in 1981, when President Reagan began his term of office. When, in 1982, he called the Soviet Union "the evil empire," he was called reckless and impolitic for the statement. Yet none of his critics offered a more factual or descriptive phrase. What, after all, should we call a government that swallowed its near neighbors, that dispossessed and starved to death millions of its subjects, and that imprisoned millions in concentration camps (from which they did not return) for the political crime of thinking independently?

In retrospect, it is clear that President Reagan's policies, drafted to address the domestic economy and to protect freedom internationally, also played a role in bringing an end to the Soviet system. For example, during his term in office, President Reagan was able to gain a three-fold reduction in the price of oil in the international market. He accomplished this in large part through negotiations with Saudi Arabia. Reducing the price of oil greatly benefited the U.S. economy. At the same time, the Soviet Union, which exported oil, found the price reduction detrimental.

President Reagan also devalued the U.S. dollar by 25 percent to increase domestic exports, a program that was notably successful. The same devaluation hurt the Soviet economy because many Soviet exports had dollar-determined prices.

The Soviet Union planned to construct a natural gas pipeline to Western Europe. Had the pipeline been completed, Western Europe would have become heavily dependent on the Soviet Union for its energy. Dependence on external sources of energy—as the United States learned in 1973—is full of perils, not only because of damage to the economy but also because of political pressures that energy suppliers can bring to bear. President Reagan negotiated with our European allies to scale down the pipeline project. In the end, the pipeline was only one-half the size of the original plan. As a result, Europe depended less on Soviet energy and contributed far less hard currency to the Soviet treasury, which was then straining to support its huge military budget.

President Reagan also supported those who resisted the Soviet Union's political oppression. The Soviet Union poured great amounts of money into keeping control in three nations: Poland, where the oppressive puppet government was attempting to put down the labor movement headed by Lech Walesa; Afghanistan, where the Soviet Union sent troops to support the unpopular communist government; and El Salvador, where a communist government was supported with Soviet military supplies. In each of those cases, President Reagan provided assistance to the resistance movement. In the end, in each case, the resistance succeeded.

But perhaps the greatest pressure on the Soviet Union came from the Strategic Defense Initiative. With the advent of Brilliant Pebbles, the SDI effort began to emphasize electronics, miniaturization, and computers—technologies in which the United States had a large advantage. The Soviets held advantages in nuclear and missile technologies. We spent a few billion dollars a year on all aspects of nuclear explosives, but the Soviets spent the equivalent of several tens of billions of dollars each year—obtained from a much smaller economic base. A successful ballistic missile defense would negate the Soviet Union's huge investment; and to compete in the requisite technologies, the Soviets had to spend substantially more than they could afford.

In pointing out the policies that President Reagan pursued, I do not mean to detract from the deep-seated cause of the collapse of the Soviet Union: The many peoples within that empire were responsible for its overthrow. But had President Reagan pursued another course, they might well never have had the opportunity to free themselves.

President Bush, like President Reagan, had an excellent grasp of the importance of strategic defense. On February 7, 1990, he came to the Lawrence Livermore National Laboratory to review the Brilliant Pebbles program, thus becoming the first sitting president to visit a national laboratory. His address to the staff of Livermore thanking them for their lengthy and effective efforts to maintain peace was deeply appreciated.

Not much later, President Bush proved particularly effective in handling a Middle East crisis. In mid-1990, Iraq invaded Kuwait. When negotiations with Iraq failed, President Bush worked within the United Nations to find a unifying plan to counter Iraqi aggression. After a careful and slow military buildup, and after unifying the opponents of the Iraqi aggression, the United Nations mounted a concerted attack. The U.N. forces sustained few casualties, but the Iraqi forces suffered a relatively rapid collapse. Saddam Hussein, the Iraqi leader, was forced to capitulate and agreed to withdraw from Kuwait.

During the war, Hussein launched several short-range missile attacks against Israel. Those attacks (like the missile attacks Hussein mounted during the Iran-Iraq war) re-emphasized the need for missile defense. In March 1992, the Pentagon formally adopted the Brilliant Pebbles system and planned to begin its deployment in 1996. The estimated cost of a sufficient number of Brilliant Pebbles to protect the Northern Hemisphere was $2 billion; another $1 billion would establish them in their orbits.[17]

President Bush proved to be a thoughtful and courageous supporter of strategic defense throughout his term. Following his defeat in the 1992 elections, the strategic defense program was sharply scaled back, and much of it effectively terminated.

As I write this memoir in 2000, the United States—and every other country—is as vulnerable to missile attack as it was when I began concentrating on the problem in 1961. The risk of missile attack has not abated. The availability of missiles has become more widespread, as has the supply of weapons-grade nuclear materials. Rogue nations—North Korea, Iraq, and Libya—and the instabilities in the former Soviet Union (which still possesses the largest arsenal of nuclear missiles in the world) perpetuate the peril. The lack of strategic defense gives small powers a chance to do great damage.

The two world wars of the twentieth century have demonstrated the importance of the role that the United States plays in preserving freedom. Today, the need for international stability is greater than ever. Realization of the importance of ballistic missile defense is growing, but at too slow a rate.

Boost-phase defense such as Brilliant Pebbles would destroy missile launches in the acceleration phase. Not only are the missiles most vulnerable then but decoys have not yet been deployed. Boost-phase defenses would destroy the missiles before conclusive data about the intended targets could be gathered. Such a defense system would automatically protect not only the United States but all nations in the Northern Hemisphere from missile attack. If all nations were safe from aggressive missile attack, world peace unquestionably would be much more secure.

To my mind, the vision of future possibilities that President Reagan brought to the White House was unique among the presidents of this century: He initiated intensive work on strategic defense and planned and executed programs that eventually brought freedom to millions and ended the fifty-year-long threat of massive nuclear war. He fully comprehended dangers that the majority of Americans are not fully able to face. In this respect, Reagan's ideas were not popular, but he succeeded in tempering their

---

[17] The Pentagon also noted that there would be $8 billion in other, largely administrative costs, to develop and deploy Brilliant Pebbles, operate the system for ten years following its deployment, and then decommission it.

unpopularity by employing his remarkable sense of humor. The result was sorely needed action on strategic defense but incomplete appreciation of the still-present dangers.

President Reagan honored me with the Medal of Science and with the Citizen's Medal. The second award was made on January 18, 1989, as the president was leaving office. Perhaps a dozen of us were so honored, including President Reagan's former press secretary, Jim Brady, who was crippled in the assassination attempt on Reagan.

Instead of reading the citations, Reagan said, "I have now been in office for almost 3,000 days. On this occasion, I want to tell you a story about a cantankerous old woman. She went to a judge and said, 'Your honor, I want a divorce.' 'How old are you, madam?' 'I'm ninety years old.' 'How old is your husband?' 'He's ninety-two.' 'How long have you been married?' 'Seventy-three years.' 'Any children?' 'Yes, your honor. Six children, and they are all well; twenty-six grandchildren, five great-grandchildren, and one more coming.' 'Madam, do I understand you rightly, that you want to be divorced?' 'Yes. your honor. Enough is enough.'" Reagan added, "I'm going home soon, as are most of you. Enough is enough."

At the time, I found his remark puzzling, but what happened during the following months clarified his remark as gentle advice. Few of President Reagan's appointees and advisors held the same positions with President Bush. Reagan—anticipating our feelings at being replaced—was telling us not to mind.

Reagan was serious about his goals, but he did not appear to take himself too seriously. His sense of humor was a form of modesty that I admire. Under his leadership, the mood of the nation was transformed from discouragement and defeatism into vigor and determination. I suggest that in a democracy—which is unavoidably imperfect—a sense of humor may be among the most important qualities a leader can possess.

Turning the program of strategic defense into a reality, technically and politically, will require more of the spirited leadership that President Reagan exemplified. In my opinion, the ideal president of the United States must fill two important roles: The first is to respond to the will of the people; the second is to inform and lead the American people in the direction that will help minimize the dangers of a rapidly changing world. Such a leader is a national treasure.

41

OTHER ISSUES—
PUBLIC AND PRIVATE

———

1980–1990

THE 1980S HAD two encouraging aspects: Under Reagan's leadership the mood of the country became positive and forward-looking, and the issue of strategic defense was addressed seriously. Unfortunately, the last issue led to yet another political controversy. The result of my taking a strong positive stand was that a sizable part of the opposition to the project concentrated on me.

For the first thirty-five years of my life, I cannot remember any unpleasant disagreements with my colleagues. Most people got along reasonably well with me, and no one charged me with slighting my collaborators, or tried to discredit me as a scientist, or suggested that I was evil. In those days, I could not have imagined that scientists would indulge in such behavior. Such are the pleasures of being uninvolved in political controversy.

The doubtful wisdom of old age and experience have replaced those pleasures. I have been involved in three political controversies: the question of whether to develop the hydrogen bomb; the question of whether to establish a second weapons laboratory; and the question of whether to develop strategic defense. On all three questions, my position differed from the majority of politically active scientists. In the first two cases, my point of view prevailed. The third case, that of developing and deploying a strategic defense system, is still in doubt.

As I look back at this last controversy, I feel I may have made a mistake in ignoring the harshest personal attacks. I had hoped that my lack of response would make it easier for my critics and opponents to collaborate on the

Strategic Defense Initiative (SDI). Instead, I may have made my support of the program less effective. Because missile defense is still under consideration, I will belatedly offer a few comments.

An article, "Comments on The History of the H-Bomb," written by Hans Bethe in 1954 and published in *Los Alamos Science* in the fall of 1982, opened a barrage of criticism.[1] Two articles based on Hans's "Comments" gave his accusations emphasis.[2] By February 1983, the commentary had become extreme.[3] I slowly realized that opposing a program might be done not by presenting the perspectives and facts that argue against an issue, but by attempting to undermine the credibility of the people who are arguing for it.

In his introductory paragraph, Hans states that his article "was written in some anger about certain events of 1953–1954," that is, the Oppenheimer case and articles and the Shepley-Blair book pertaining to it. He first tells his version of our conflict during the work on the atomic bomb and then goes on to criticize my supporting full-scale work on the hydrogen bomb in 1949–1950:

> Nobody will blame Teller because the calculations of 1946 were wrong, especially because adequate computing machines were not then available. But he was blamed at Los Alamos for leading the Laboratory, and indeed the whole country, into an adventurous program on the basis of calculations which he himself must have known to have been very incomplete. The technical skepticism of the GAC on the other hand had turned out to be far more justified than the GAC itself had dreamed in October 1949.[4]

---

[1] Hans Bethe, "Comments on The History of the H-Bomb," *Los Alamos Science* 3, 3 (fall 1982): 43–53.

Hans, who consulted at Los Alamos intermittently during 1950 and 1951, writes an account of the the hydrogen bomb's development that is different from the one I have presented in this memoir. I have not commented on those differences because I can say nothing further that will resolve this disagreement.

[2] Phillip Boffey, "Teller Faulted on Bomb Calculations," *New York Times*, 13 November 1982; and William Broad, "Rewriting the History of the Hydrogen Bomb," *Science* 218, 19 (November 1982): 769–772.

[3] Samuel H. Day, Jr., "Hans Bethe's Silent Whistle," *The Progressive* 54, 2 (February 1983): 29–31.

Mr. Day began his article: "For the many who follow the politics of nuclear weaponry, and especially for those who follow the politics of nuclear weaponry from a liberal perspective, the news was exhilarating: 'Have you seen the November issue of *Science*?' one of them wrote to me. 'I am delighted. Teller looks more and more like a madman—erratic, obsessed . . .'"

[4] Bethe, "Comments," p. 47.

Work on what Hans calls Method A ended in November 1951, when Johnny von Neumann's calculations pointed to its failure. Hans had pointed out earlier in his article that I invented two other designs:

> Method B was invented in 1946, Method C in 1947. . . . However, at that time, there seemed to be no way of putting Method B into practice. Method C [the boosted fission design] . . . seemed quite promising from the start. . . . Between January and May 1951, the new concept was developed. (This I shall call Method D.)[5]

Hans goes on to comment:

> The new concept was to me . . . about as surprising as the discovery of fission had been to physicists in 1939. . . . At that time concentrated work on any likely way of releasing nuclear energy would have led nowhere. Similarly, concentrated work on Method A would never have led to Method D. . . . By a misappraisal of the facts many persons not closely connected with the development have concluded that the scientists who had shown good judgment concerning the technical feasibility of Method A were now suddenly proved wrong, whereas Teller, who had been wrong in interpreting his own calculations was suddenly right. . . . One of the dangerous consequences of the H-bomb history may well be that government administrators, and perhaps some scientists, too, will imagine that similar miracles should be expected in other developments.[6]

I would point out that such "miracles" are by no means rare. Andrei Sakharov was already working on the Soviet hydrogen bomb in 1948, and he came up with a similar "miracle" quite quickly. Another fact should be considered: Although the occurrence of "miracles" cannot be guaranteed by whole-hearted work on a government-supported project, the absence of "miracles" can be guaranteed if the program is never initiated.

Work on thermonuclear weapons is complicated to conceptualize and describe, and accurate descriptions of it are still highly classified. I have described my role in the development of thermonuclear weapons as fully as is allowed. I can only point out that during the 1970s, when more powerful

---

[5] Ibid., p. 48.
[6] Ibid., p. 49.

computers became available, some of my original ideas were reexamined. As it turned out, Ulam's calculations, as well as Johnny von Neumann's, were based on incomplete assumptions. As Hans Mark and Lowell Wood wrote in 1988,

> Remarkably enough, all of Teller's earlier thermonuclear explosive designs and proposals were subsequently shown to be feasible—in experimental demonstrations.[7]

The flaw in Bethe's observation is the suggestion of absolutes: This is wrong, that is right. The main point is that the new approach was easy and practical.

Hans's political attitudes had an important bearing on his article. As he says in the last paragraph of his article:

> In summary I still believe that the development of the H-bomb is a calamity. I still believe that it was necessary to make a pause before the decision and to consider this irrevocable step most carefully. I still believe that the possibility of an agreement with Russia not to develop the bomb should have been explored. But once the decision was made to go ahead with the program, and once there was a sound technical program, I cooperated with it to the best of my ability.[8]

Even knowing that Bethe has a strong political dislike of strategic defense, I continued to hope that he would work on SDI after it became national policy. And indeed, on two occasions in 1984 and 1985, Hans came to Livermore and reviewed the work on the x-ray laser. During his visit in the spring of 1985, he praised the work on that project; but when some of those who overheard his comments repeated them more publicly, Hans wrote to the director of the Livermore laboratory asking him to make it clear to all concerned that "I still think that SDI is a fantasy. And a dangerous one."

As I wrote Hans at that time,

> I have to assume that at the end of our last meeting your favorable statements were colored by your desire to be kind and pleasant. If this is indeed so, you cannot blame anyone else in case you have been misunderstood.
>
> All of this is most unfortunate and the worst part of it remains that our national effort, which could do a lot towards stability and continued peace, is

---

[7] Hans Mark and Lowell Wood, eds., *Energy in Physics, War and Peace: A Festschrift Celebrating Edward Teller's 80th Birthday* (Dordrecht, Boston, and London: Kluwer Academic Publishers, 1988).

[8] Bethe, "Comments," p. 53.

being impaired. You have looked in detail only into the x-ray laser as far as SDI is concerned, or so it seems to me. It also seems to me that in this one field where you spent at least some time our differences have diminished. You continue to condemn the many parts of SDI to which, as far as I know, you have paid less attention. . . .

This letter was written with perhaps exaggerated optimism in regard to the possible influence of reason. Even if reason can no longer give rise to action, it may still help by putting past events into some kind of proportion and in diminishing further difficulties in the future. Of course, our mutual opposition on this important issue is a fact which as long as it exists can in no way be ignored or be kept quiet.

There was only one further unpleasantness involving Hans during the SDI controversy. In January 1987, while he was being interviewed on television, Hans made a derogatory comment about me and then wrote to apologize:

I had prepared a much better [remark], which was not insulting. But the interviewer would not take it, but provoked me into the one that came over the air. I should know better, but they still get the better of me.

Because Hans and I are no longer traveling much, it is not likely that we will meet again. But, just for the record, I would still enjoy his company. We share a lot of history, and the private Hans Bethe is a different sort of man from the public one. Perhaps the same can be said of me.

This period also held some pleasurable events. In about 1980, Eugene Wigner told me that I would enjoy the Majorana International Affairs conferences, which are usually held in late summer in Erice, Italy. Antonino Zichichi, an Italian physicist who works at CERN (the European Community Research Center for Physics), organized those meetings and invited physicists from both sides of the Iron Curtain. Each year, a scientific topic of political importance was chosen, and because there were a wide variety of political perspectives among those attending, the discussions were lively and informative. I decided that the next time I was invited I would attend.[9]

---

9 The conference is named for Etiore Majorana, one of Enrico Fermi's most outstanding students. I must have met him when I was in Rome in 1932, but today I have no memory of such an occasion. In 1939, Majorana left on a ferry heading for Sicily; but he never arrived and was never seen again. Whether he jumped, fell, or was pushed overboard, no one is ever likely to know. The institute established in his memory has grown steadily over the years, and now sponsors conferences, mostly on physics, year-round.

Erice is a small town on the northwest corner of Sicily. It lies at the top of a mountain 1,800 feet high. Its ancient monastery now serves as the residence for participants of the Majorana conferences. Myth holds that Odysseus met the Cyclops at this site, and the large rocks that lie offshore are supposed to be those that the blinded Cyclops threw at Odysseus and his men when they were making their escape.[10]

I first attended the conference in 1981. After that conference, I visited with the dear friend of my youth, Carl Frederich von Weizsäcker. We even managed a few modest hikes in the Bavarian Alps. As always, his company and conversation refreshed my spirit.

C. N. (Frank) Yang, my former student, celebrated his sixtieth birthday at the next year's meeting, a pleasurable event that I was happy to attend. In addition, Piotr Kapitsa, who had worked with Rutherford in the 1920s at Cambridge, was also there.[11] Kapitsa at that time was in his late eighties, and so frail that he could hardly speak; nonetheless, it was a pleasure to see him attending a physics conference in the free world.

I believe that the scientist who accompanied Kapitsa was his son. At any rate, the companion was a pleasant man; although he was a communist, he seemed temperate and reasonable. During the conference, we had a debate on some question that was moderated by a man from England. Before the debate began, the moderator went over the introductory remarks he planned to make. When the moderator said that he planned to identify me as the "father of the hydrogen bomb," I objected. (I have always considered that description in bad taste.) The moderator persisted, and my opponent spoke up: "I have always found it preferable to follow the wishes of the person I am to introduce." I was amused to see a Russian teaching an Englishman manners.

Another participant from the Soviet Union with whom I spent considerable time talking was Evgenii Velikhov, who was then president of the Soviet

---

[10] We read the Odysseus story in Latin class when I was a gymnasium student. I recall my teacher explaining that the Cyclops, because he had one eye, had no depth perception, which explained why his stones missed their target. I objected that the Cyclops had been blinded by Odysseus. My teacher responded, "Well, that too."

[11] Kapitsa was called back to Russia in 1934 and was not allowed to leave again until 1966. As I have mentioned, in the late 1930s, Kapitsa used his influence to have Lev Landau released from prison. Their collaboration on magnetism and low-temperature physics led to Kapitsa's receiving the Nobel Prize in 1978. During World War II, Kapitsa refused to work on the atomic bomb (and for a short time suffered house arrest as a consequence). Nonetheless, his contribution to wartime defense was considerable: He developed an inexpensive method of separating oxygen from air, thereby greatly improving steel manufacturing.

Academy of Sciences. Velikhov, like many scientists in the former Soviet Union, was as active politically as scientifically. When I asked him about Andrei Sakharov, he made a slighting, even scornful comment, whereupon our personal relationship took on a sour note. (I had long been impressed by the moral courage shown by Soviet dissidents, particularly Sakharov.) Nonetheless, at the Erice meeting the following year, Zichichi, Velikhov, and I signed a joint proposal of cooperation on scientific matters pertaining to the prevention of nuclear war and defense against the effects of nuclear weapons.

Following the 1982 conference, I had two further adventures. First, I was among a small group of people granted a papal audience at the Pontiff's summer residence, Castel Gondelfo.[12] Pope John Paul II in his remarks apologized for the bad treatment that Galileo had received.[13]

The 1983 conference included a great deal of discussion of President Reagan's proposal of the Strategic Defense Initiative. In spite of great differences of opinion, the exchanges on the topic were cogent and reasonable. Each of the several Erice conferences that I attended was marked by civility and openness. I cannot say whether that pleasant situation was the result of the delightful setting or of Dr. Zichichi's careful organization; in any event, I enjoyed these sessions very much because they reflected the collegial nature of science.

The 1980s was also a period during which I met several remarkable Russian dissidents, among them, Avital Shchransky. Mrs. Shchransky called on me at my Hoover office to ask my help in freeing her husband, a mathematician who had agitated for the observation in the Soviet Union of the Helsinki Accords on human rights. As a result of my conversation with Mrs. Shchransky, I wrote a few letters. Although my effort seemed futile at the time, Mrs. Shchransky's campaign generated a lot of support and a great many letters; within a few years, the Shchranskys were reunited in Israel.

In 1985, I had a lengthy conversation with Elena Bonner, a dissident of note in her own right but more famous as the wife of Andrei Sakharov. That meeting came about through John H. (Jack) Bunzel, a colleague and friend at Hoover. Jack is remarkable: As president of San Jose State University, he

---

[12] I no longer remember whether the audience was arranged by the conference leader, Antonino Zichichi, or by my friend Bill Wilson, who was then ambassador to the Vatican. I actually spoke with the pope in 1993 when he came to the Majorana conference in Erice; I also offered him the report of our conference, which was on the interception of meteorites.

[13] The punishment that Galileo received (house arrest), considering his ridicule of his former friend, Pope Urban VII, seems less harsh when all the facts are known. The story is included in my book, *Pursuit of Simplicity* (Malibu, Calif.: Pepperdine Press, 1981).

weathered the tumultuous protests of the 1970s without losing his good humor. I enjoy talking with him, not only to get a different but reasonable perspective (Jack is a thoughtful Democrat), but also because he knows more good stories than almost anyone I know.

Jack asked me whether I would be free to meet with Elena Bonner, who had been allowed to visit the Bay Area (to receive medical attention, I believe) and had indicated an interest in talking with me. To obtain her visa, she had to promise not to engage in political activities in the United States, so my visit had to be kept very quiet. (Andrei Sakharov was not allowed to accompany her.)

I went to the apartment in San Francisco where she was staying, and we talked for more than an hour. Bonner began by saying that she thought that there were similarities between her husband and me that went beyond our roles in designing thermonuclear weapons. She thought that our espousing unpopular political positions led to our having been excluded by a majority of our colleagues. She went on to explain her concern that the American physicists who were closest to her husband included many who had ostracized me. She was also unhappy that those scientists seemed not to realize that their sympathy with the far left gave them the appearance of supporting Soviet military stances.

I mentioned my acquaintance with Evgenii Velikhov and the agreement for cooperation we had signed. Bonner counseled me to be very careful in my relationship with him, because, she said, he might succumb to governmental pressure.

We also talked about the Sakharovs' daily life in exile in Gorky. Her description suggested that after more than two decades of persecuting Sakharov, the Soviet government had begun to moderate its treatment of him. Although Sakharov still lacked the freedom to travel, he was now enjoying better treatment. In their Gorky exile, they had a fairly pleasant apartment and a car for their personal use. Save for the KGB's dirty tricks—slashing the car's tires, spoiling its locks, and similar vandalism—they were largely left alone.

I suspect that Sakharov, by virtue of having been a hero and having received several of the highest Soviet prizes, was too famous, both inside and outside his country, to punish as severely as some other dissidents were. He was deprived of his vocation, his friends, and many of his comforts but at another level, he was protected. Had he died in Gorky, the communists would have been shamed. A few years later, Mikhail Gorbachev released the Sakharovs from exile, knowing that his action would gain him international approval.

I also had the pleasure—and the frustration—of meeting and talking with Sakharov himself at the end of 1988. The Ethics and Public Policy Center, a group dedicated to supporting U.S. human rights policy, was honoring me at a banquet, which included about four hundred guests, in Washington, D.C. Sakharov came to the hotel where the banquet was being held, and we met in private for about fifteen minutes. I began by talking for a minute or two about the advantages of siting reactors underground. Sakharov immediately and completely agreed with me. But he then launched into a diatribe against the Strategic Defense Initiative that lasted more than ten minutes.

Rather than confront him with his misconceptions, I tried to change the subject to one on which I thought we might agree and talked about ways to prevent the proliferation of nuclear weapons; but a minute or so later, our time together was up, and a photo session ensued.

Sakharov had told me at the beginning of our chat that he would be unable to attend the dinner, but that he would like to offer a few comments before the banquet began. Doing so, he began with a few friendly remarks about me, and then launched an even more vehement attack on SDI than he had offered me in private. As soon as his talk was concluded, he was whisked away.

The banquet organizers asked me to address the issues that Sakharov had raised about SDI; so at the end of the banquet, I did. I noted that Sakharov had been cut off from all work of a classified nature for more than twenty years, that his sources of information were limited, and that he couldn't possibly know the technical details of the U.S. program. The incident was unpleasant, but it did not diminish my basic appreciation of Sakharov. His forthright statements about Soviet work on nuclear weapons helped educate Americans about the nature of the Soviet government.

At the end of the decade, Sakharov (posthumously) and I even shared in a prize: the Etiore Majorana Erice Scienza Per La Pace. The award is made for practical suggestions of how to promote international cooperation. In 1990, the prize money ($1 million) was split into three awards: I received one and Victor Weisskopf received one; the third, a posthumous award, was shared by Andrei Sakharov, Paul Dirac, and Piotr Kapitsa.

In choosing the recipients of almost all prizes, the recommendations of one's colleagues are important, and one of my strongest supporters for the Majorana Prize, it seems, was my almost-student, T. S. Lee. After World War II, Lee had come from China, like my student Yang. Not only had their education been acquired in a foreign country, but it had also been eked out under wartime conditions. When the University of Chicago questioned the lack of prerequisites in their applications for admission, I defended them, and both men appreciated that.[14] The University of Chicago made the right decision about them because Lee and Yang won the Nobel Prize for their collaborative work.

I was deeply grateful when I learned of Lee's efforts on my behalf. And I do wholeheartedly support international cooperation and collaboration; I believe it is the most important activity we can pursue to assure lasting peace. My final chapter will discuss the three programs involving international cooperation—underground automated nuclear reactors, weather observation, and protection from meteorites—that I believe will yield the greatest benefits to all people.

[14] As I recall, I vouched for the scientific abilities of both men and noted the radical differences in the breadth of the arts and cultural requirements in China. I pointed out that the distinguished members of the admissions committee probably could not qualify for admission as undergraduates in China.

42

HOMECOMING

1990–2000

IN THE FALL of 1988, I received a phone call from Budapest, from a man named George Marx, who introduced himself as the president of the Eótvós Society, Hungary's equivalent of the American Physical Society. He invited me to visit Hungary.[1] Like every other exile, I had dreamed of seeing my home again. Unlike many other exiles—my friend Eugene Wigner, for example, who visited after the liberalization of the Hungarian communist government—I had stayed in place on the other side of the Iron Curtain.

That was not simply by choice, as the following incident indicates. In 1975, the Minta Gymnasium in Hungary organized a reunion party of my graduating class. My childhood friend Nándi Keszthelyi and another acquaintance from my graduating class telephoned from Budapest to invite me to come, adding in jest, "If you don't accept our invitation, we shall tell Gröger and Martos how you are behaving."[2] We exchanged a few pleasantries, but I declined the invitation. A few days later, two security officers arrived at

---

[1] Marx also told me the following story about János Kádár, the longtime communist premier of Hungary. It was glasnost time in the Soviet Union, and Mikhail Gorbachev called Kádár to Moscow and said, "Comrade Kádár, you are getting older. You should look for a smart young man to replace you." Kádár replied, "I tried, but they all turned out to be dull." Gorbachev said, "Let me show you an efficient technique for judging candidates." Gorbachev then called in Shevarnadze and asked him, "If someone is the son of your father and mother but is not your brother, who is he?" Shevarnadze answered, "He is me!" Kádár was impressed. He went back to Budapest, called in Miklos Nemeth, and asked, "If someone is the son of your father and your mother, but is not your brother, who is he?" Nemeth answered, "He is me." Kádár shook his head, "No, you are wrong. He is Comrade Shevarnadze."

[2] Gröger and Martos were, respectively, the Latin and the physical education teacher at the Minta; both had been sticklers for discipline and occasionally meted out memorable punishment.

my office in Livermore to inquire about the identities of Gröger and Martos. Until my homeland was free of communist rule, I would not see it again.

But when George Marx phoned me, communist rule in Hungary was ending. On December, 1, 1990, after more than fifty-four years, I arrived in Budapest to spend a weekend.

The effect of being in Budapest again was almost overwhelming. I was conscious at all times of the familiarity and comfort of all my surroundings. I was once again at home. On the day before my departure, the Hungarian Academy of Sciences made me an honorary member. I could hardly believe the warmth of the ovation that I received. For almost the first time in my life, I found giving an acceptance speech difficult: I could scarcely talk for the multitude of emotions I was feeling.

Of course, having seen Hungary, I wanted Mici to see it, too. A few weeks later, in late January 1991, Mici and I went for a two-week-long stay. We visited all the familiar spots in Budapest—our old homes, our schools, and Freedom Park, where the same clock looked down on sweethearts as it had on Mici and me sixty years before. Some things appeared to have changed: The Palatinus looked smaller and less elegant than I remembered it, and the streets looked a little shabby; but the people's enthusiasm and spirit was completely familiar.

During our stay, we went to Debrecen, where I gave a lecture to several hundred students at the university and was warmly received. We also visited Mátrafüred, where Mici and I had spent time together on our "separate" vacations when we were young. It is a such great pleasure to see the familiar surroundings of one's youth after an absence of more than fifty years. It is an even greater pleasure to see those places with the sweetheart who shared them originally. Mici and I were aware of our immense good fortune. Our native land had survived a terrible nightmare, and we were able to see that it was recovering.

That trip was the last one that Mici's health permitted her to make. She had successfully fought a bout with breast cancer and one with a brain tumor (and with the mood-altering medications following the surgery), but lung disease was a more formidable opponent: It claimed her life on June 4, 2000, at the age of 91. I cannot overestimate how much her steadfast love and support sustained me for seventy-six years (sixty-six of them as my wife).[3]

---

[3] Mici did not like formalities, so, in accordance with her wishes, no funeral services were held. Instead, I invited friends and family members to the house where we exchanged our memories of Mici, beginning with my sister Emmi, who talked about Mici in her early teens. We all recalled her indomitable and generous spirit. She gracefully weathered through determination the many difficulties life placed in her path, and she relished the joys.

Today, I depend on a crew of kindly women. Patricia Weible and her staff provide care at home. My secretary at Livermore, Joanne Smith, and my secretary at Hoover, Patsy Pemberton, arrange my schedules and correspondence. Judy Shoolery and Gen Phillips (both of whom are now retired) continue to work occasionally on special projects with me. Being a nonagenarian is not altogether as easy as it sounds. But in spite of my infirmities (arthritis in my legs and macular degeneration are the most troublesome), I am not about to stop working; I still have many projects to complete and an infinite number of problems to address.

My first and second visits to Hungary, and the five later trips that I made to my homeland (the last in October 1996), were not made exclusively for personal pleasure. After my first phone conversation with George Marx, I had given talks that were broadcast on Hungarian radio and had written an article on nuclear reactors for the physics journal *Fizikai Semle*. Eventually, I was asked to assess the safety of the Soviet-built nuclear reactors at Paks in Hungary after reviewing a documentary. The director of Paks at that time, Pónya József, and I spent the second day of my first trip examining the Hungarian reactors—which are second-generation pressurized water reactors and among the safest commercial reactors in the world.

After my tour of the facility, I asked how the integrity of the steel reactor vessel was monitored. As was true for every question I asked, the staff had an immediate answer: The vessel was made by the Czech Skoda Works (which has set a high standard in manufacturing steel for half a century). Pieces of identical steel have been placed in the core of the reactor, where they undergo heavy neutron bombardment. Those pieces are removed and examined periodically, thereby making it possible to anticipate deterioration of the containment vessels. The completeness of this answer was indicative of the excellence in the training, knowledge, and expertise of the staff at Paks.[4] The design of the Paks reactors is excellent, and so are the operating standards. I was happy to make a public statement to that effect.

Although I would not say that anxiety about nuclear matters is absent in Hungary, I do feel that a more sensible appraisal exists there, probably because of the excellence of Hungarian science education. On a later visit to Hungary, I met Esther Tóth, a science teacher at the Lauder Institute, a

---

[4] A year later, France offered a loan to Hungary to build reactors there that would generate electricity for sale to neighboring countries. The loan would be repaid from the revenues so derived. Because any accident, no matter how insignificant, would cause truly enormous damage to the French nuclear enterprise, that offer represented a strong testimony to the performance of the engineers at Paks.

private gymnasium.[5] In Hungary, students in their last year of gymnasium study are taught nuclear science during the spring. Many gymnasia have acquired Geiger counters (which monitor the level of radioactivity in the immediate area) in addition to the usual science classroom equipment.[6]

I enjoyed a story Esther told. Her students had completed their studies on radioactivity about a month before the day on which a cloud of radioactive material from the Chernobyl accident was to pass over Hungary. The students arrived early that morning, eager to turn on the counter and monitor the level. The background radiation usually produced about forty clicks a minute, but when the students took the count that morning, the clicks came at three times that rate. Everyone was impressed. Then a student pointed out that they hadn't even opened the windows yet, so they immediately flung them open. The rate of clicks promptly went down to thirty-six clicks a minute. The school had been closed for the weekend, and the Geiger counter had been registering the build-up of radon (a naturally occurring radioactive gas released from the stone of the building) during that time.

Outside the Soviet Union, the increase in radioactivity from the Chernobyl accident was never significant. It never rose above an amount that people regularly encounter during daily life or an airplane flight. Yet in the period after the accident, abortions in western Europe rose by 50,000. There was no rise in the abortion rate in Hungary. The usual number of healthy babies were born in Hungary over the months following the Chernobyl accident, thanks to Hungary's excellent science education. The unnecessary loss of 50,000 potential lives elsewhere in Europe was the result of ignorance, not the Chernobyl accident.

Esther Tóth also conducted an interesting survey in a village of about 2,000 residents in the Mátra Mountains. About a quarter of the homes in the village contained high levels of radon, enough to expose the residents to two to four times more radiation each year than workers in Hungarian nuclear power stations are permitted to receive.

Esther and her students went from house to house placing devices to measure and track the amount of radon present inside; the amounts varied depending on whether the foundation of the house was cracked (which increases

---

[5] Esther, like George Marx, has become a friend whom I have seen not only on subsequent visits to Hungary but also on several occasions in the United States.

[6] In the early 1980s, parts for Geiger counters could be purchased inexpensively from Russian soldiers. Students built the Geiger counters and later attached to them whatever simple computers the schools had.

radon buildup) or whether the residents preferred ventilation over savings in energy costs (which decreases it). The homes were ranked on a scale of one to four, depending on whether the residents had less than the usual amount of radiation exposure per year or a great deal more.

Then the students obtained the full health histories of the residents from their doctors. With a long-term measurement of the amount of radon present in the house and complete medical records for the inhabitants, it was possible to correlate the cases of cancer with the radon level in the house. What was interesting about the results was that they showed a U-shaped curve—higher rates of cancer occurrence at the low and high rates of exposure in the village, and lower than expected rates in the middle ranges. The data on a few hundred people suggested an induced immune response at moderate levels of radioactivity.

I asked Esther whether she planned to continue the project. She said she would enjoy doing so but had no funds for it. I asked her to figure out the cost of extending her study; and when she did, a Hungarian environmental group, on the occasion of my next birthday, gave her the $3,000 she needed. Esther and her students eventually extended their observations to 9,000 homes in two hundred villages. Her final paper refined and confirmed the pattern she had found earlier. I am impressed by the quality of science education in Hungary.

During my several visits in Hungary, I gave many lectures, and I often received compliments on my beautiful Hungarian. I attribute that praise to the practice I have had over the years: I sustained my connubial happiness through Hungarian, and that language served as my first defense when Mici was displeased with me.

I greatly appreciate my warm reception in Hungary and the kindness so many of the leading scientists have shown me; most especially I appreciate the generosity of George Marx, who has become a dear friend. I was given many awards and two honorary professorships (at Eötvös University and at the University of Debrecen). President Árpád Göncz presented me with the Order of Merit.[7] Former Prime Minister Gyula Horn, who opened Hungary's borders to East German refugees, was my host during my last visit. My reception in Hungary has made me feel much like a hero. I greatly appreciate these kindnesses. I am happy to see that Hungary has made the transition to democracy in a most promising way. I am proud of my homeland.

---

[7] On another occasion, I received the Bene Meritus de Hungaricum Fama Augenda award for increasing Hungary's fame.

In August 1991, I again attended a summer conference in Erice, as did Evgenii Velikhov. During that conference, a group of communist military leaders kidnapped Mikhail Gorbachev in the hope of restoring the Communist Party to power. The Russian delegation at Erice sat glued to the television set throughout the day. Velikhov and I were supposed to have a meeting with Nino Zichichi, but when he was delayed, I joined Velikhov in front of the television.

The news broadcast at that point was showing crowds of people, their fists upraised, in the streets of Moscow. I asked Velikhov what was going on. His reply was to the point: "They don't like the new government of the military coup." Velikhov was clearly on Gorbachev's side. Before the outcome of the situation was known, Velikhov gave a courageous press conference in support of Gorbachev; he stated that the Russian people had had enough of communist government.

Within twenty-four hours, the coup failed. If the hardliners had won, Velikhov and his family, who were with him at Erice, would have had difficulty getting back into Russia. But the peoples of the former Soviet Union and the Warsaw Pact nations opted for freedom and democracy. The lengthy Cold War had ended peacefully and with almost no bloodshed. The next year, I would meet Velikhov within a free Russian republic.

The transitions to democracy in the former Iron Curtain countries have not been simple. I remember being in Hungary during the campaign for the first presidential election. I was horrified to discover that twenty-seven candidates were on the ballot for president. How could a democracy function effectively without compromise, cooperation, and coalitions?

Upon my return to the United States, I asked some of my friends at Hoover about the origin of the two-party system. The upshot of the discussions was that such a system had evolved slowly over centuries. The new democracies in the former Soviet Union and its client states have had less than a decade to work out the proper functioning of their governments; for this reason, I am encouraged enough to be hopeful about their future. I also firmly believe that the United States, the European community, and the prosperous democracies in the Far East should find ways to strengthen ties with these developing democracies, politically and economically.

In August 1992, I made my first trip to Russia, accompanied by Lowell Wood. Evgenii Velikhov, who is the head of the Kurchatov Institute, invited me to visit his laboratory, which is located just outside Moscow. The institute includes the home of the late I. V. Kurchatov, who led the atomic bomb project in the Soviet Union and who was a senior scientist on the hydrogen

bomb project. Velikhov organized a pleasant reception for me in the Kurchatov home, now a museum. During that gathering, I was invited to play the
grand piano, which had belonged to Madame Kurchatova. I did and can report that the piano, made in Germany, is a very nice instrument.

Later, Velikhov, Lowell, and I were driven to Dubna, a little town about
ninety miles north of Moscow, for a conference on global environmental
monitoring. There, representatives from Kazakhstan, the Ukraine, and Russia, together with a delegation from the United States, discussed the possibility of collaborating on a space-based global system to monitor pollution
and developing weather conditions, including the measurement of wind velocities and temperature. Both the United States and the former Soviet
Union had initiated independent programs to develop a global observation
system. The Soviet effort had emphasized the capability of their rockets to
lift heavy loads, and the U.S. program had stressed the improvement of instrumentation and cost-effectiveness. Collaboration on a monitoring system
would use the complementary strengths.

Although discussions during this conference showed that the technologies
available would not be sufficient to monitor the spread of pollution—a problem that particularly concerns the Russians—improved weather prediction
seemed to have several promising technical aspects. The discussion of that
idea had begun in Erice a few years earlier and has continued to the present.

In the 1950s, weather could be predicted with fair reliability for two days
into the future; today, accurate weather predictions can be made five days in
advance. Considering the great improvements that have been made in computers in that interval, everyone agrees that we should do better—for the
short-term and long-term benefits. In the long-term particularly, we need to
understand the severe climatic changes that occurred in the past (and may
occur in the future), such as the Ice Ages, and we need to understand and
evaluate greenhouse warming.[8] The limiting factor in all instances is the
availability of information about the state of the atmosphere around the
globe. At present, we have little or no information about current weather
conditions over large portions of the ocean and in less-developed regions of
the world.

Lowell Wood and Greg Canavan have proposed a program that could contribute greatly to changing this situation. They suggest putting 1 billion
small floating spheres into the atmosphere together with a few hundred

---

[8] Greenhouse warming is the warming of the atmosphere that occurs in carbon dioxide-
laden greenhouses. A similar warming of the earth's atmosphere could theoretically occur.

satellites that would send out electromagnetic pulses in various directions. The spheres would then reflect back to the satellite by means of attached corner reflectors made of three mutually perpendicular planes.[9] Following the location of the spheres would make it possible to measure wind velocity. Making the spheres of metals that reflect differently at different temperatures would make it possible to obtain reasonable estimates of temperature.

If the spheres could be manufactured at one cent each, they would contribute only a small fraction of the cost of the program, estimated as being less than 1 billion dollars a year. Although that cost seems high, the economic advantages resulting from the program would be a hundred times greater. Agriculture would benefit by planting and harvesting at optimal times. Fuel costs for long-range air flights could be minimized by adjusting the flight course to the wind pattern. And, even more important, timely warning about catastrophic weather conditions would minimize damage and save lives. As the 1992 Dubna conference suggested, international collaboration on global weather monitoring could bring considerable long-term benefits to everyone in the world.

After I had returned to Moscow from Dubna, I was invited to the Ministry of Atomic Energy to meet Yuli B. Khariton, a weapons research physicist four years my senior. Dr. Khariton is not well known in the West, but he proved to be one of the more remarkable Russian scientists I have met.

Khariton was the founding director of the first Soviet nuclear weapons laboratory at Sarov in 1942, and he served as director for the following fifty years. I find it difficult even to imagine the obstacles he had to overcome during the Stalin era, when Beria oversaw the nuclear research program. Yet Khariton successfully preserved the safety and well-being of his scientists, and, at the same time, maintained the scientific integrity of his laboratory, Arzamas-16.[10] He has earned the deep respect of the Russian scientific community for his imagination, courage, and firmness of character.

Khariton was an excellent physicist, and between 1926 and 1928, he worked at the Cavendish Laboratory under Ernest Rutherford and James Chadwick. In the early 1930s, he abandoned his research and turned to the study of explosives because he was concerned that Nazi Germany might attack the Soviet Union. When fission was discovered in 1939, Khariton and

---

[9] The spheres, made of thin metal, would be distributed horizontally at distances of ten to twenty miles and vertically at distances of two to three miles.

[10] When Kurchatov was the head of the atomic energy program, which began in February 1943, Khariton supervised the development of an atomic weapon.

his long-time collaborator, Y. B. Zel'dovich, analyzed and conjectured the processes that take place in fission and formulated the prerequisites for a nuclear explosion, much the same work that was conducted independently and almost simultaneously in the West.

In 1949, the scientists of Arzamas-16 successfully tested the first Soviet atomic bomb, based, at Stalin's insistence, on the design plan Klaus Fuchs and others had stolen from Los Alamos. It is now known that the success of that test led Stalin to cancel his plan to purge the physics community. Khariton also led the work on the Soviet hydrogen bomb and served as director to Andrei Sakharov and Y. B. Zel'dovich.

In 1995, I decided to nominate Khariton for the Enrico Fermi Prize.[11] Not only do I believe that Khariton's scientific work fully merited this award, but I also believe that it is critically important to reincorporate the scientists of the former Soviet Union, separated for almost half a century by the cold war, into the international scientific community.

A similar situation existed in the German scientific community at the end of World War II. Although the Marshall Plan was highly effective in helping enemy nations recover economically—and the international community of democratic nations readily incorporated them—the scientific community healed much more slowly.

Few of my American colleagues supported my nomination of Khariton, and I suspect that several of them did not even approve of it.[12] I continue to believe that it is crucial that we, as a scientific community and as a nation, solidify friendly cooperation between Russia and the United States. Not only is it the right thing to do for humanitarian reasons but, in the case of the scientists of the former Soviet Union, it is also in our self-interest to do so.

I returned to Russia in the fall of 1994. On that occasion, I attended a conference held at Chelyabinsk-70, the second-founded weapons research center in the former Soviet Union. Like Lawrence Livermore National Laboratory, Chelyabinsk was founded to provide competition to the first weapons laboratory at Sarov.

---

[11] The Fermi Prize is awarded by the U.S. Department of Energy for contributions to "the development, use or control of atomic energy." Several foreign nationals, Bennett Lewis of Canada, Rudolf Peierls of England, and Lise Meitner, Fritz Strassmann and Otto Hahn of Germany, had received the Fermi Prize before I nominated Khariton.

[12] The question is now moot. The Fermi Prize is given only to living recipients, and Khariton died in December 1996. His life stands as a unique example of making important technical contributions under exceptionally difficult circumstances.

The Chelyabinsk laboratory is located in the southern Ural Mountains, and although pollution causes many problems in the surrounding highly industrialized regions, Chelyabinsk is quite attractive. Set on a lake in the midst of forested rolling hills, it has a resident population of about 40,000. I was received with great hospitality. I signed innumerable photographs showing me standing next to a model of the largest nuclear device ever tested.[13] Everyone I met was extremely kind, and I thoroughly enjoyed my two-week stay.

The purpose of the conference was to discuss the effects of meteorite and comet impacts on earth, and the possible means of avoiding such impacts. Interestingly enough, although catastrophic meteorite strikes are rare, many meteorites enter the earth's atmosphere every day, and more sizable meteorites (25 to 75 meters in diameter) strike the earth once every 100 to 1,000 years.

In 1908, the year I was born, a meteorite of about 50 meters in diameter struck Tungusta, a remote—and fortunately, uninhabited—region of western Siberia. The meteor came in on a tangential orbit and exploded about 8 or 10 miles above the earth's surface, just south of the Arctic Circle. Probably the meteorite was composed of loosely bound material, and, as it penetrated the atmosphere, friction generated enough heat to cause it to explode. The force of that blast leveled the forest for more than 1,000 square miles.

At lengthy intervals, a huge meteorite or asteroid strikes the Earth, an event that has massive consequences.[14] About 65 million years ago, an asteroid impact left a crater approximately 120 miles in diameter in the jungle near the Yucatan Peninsula in Mexico. That impact, suggested originally by Walter Alvarez and later discussed and publicized by Walter and his father, Luis Alvarez, probably caused the extinction of the dinosaurs. Scientists estimate that at the same time, 90 percent of life on earth perished and two-thirds of all species were exterminated.[15]

The scientists attending the conference at Chelyabinsk agreed that the more frequent medium-sized impacts and the infrequent large impacts are both important. When the probability-weighted damage of all these impacts

---

[13] That explosive, part of the 1961 Soviet test series, had an explosive yield equivalent to about 100 MT of TNT.

[14] An iron meteorite about the same size but far more solid than the Tungusta meteorite struck the earth near Winslow, Arizona, about 50,000 years ago. The crater it produced is about 1,200 meters in diameter and about 200 meters deep.

[15] It is thought that the impact stirred up enough dust to exclude most of the sunlight over the surface of the earth for a considerable period, thereby reducing plant growth, starving herbivores, and, in turn, decimating carnivores.

is considered, meteorite strikes appear to be about as damaging as earthquakes or hurricanes. The practical point is to prevent the great damage caused by large or massive meteorites.

U.S. military forces, having prepared to see incoming missiles at great distances, have observed many meteors that penetrated the atmosphere but did not reach the surface of the earth. Meteors of a few hundred feet in diameter or more can be observed at great distance. With modern computers, their orbits can be predicted accurately, and warnings of collisions can be offered years in advance (and many months in advance for smaller meteors).

An interesting and potentially beneficial program would be to observe sizable meteors from close quarters as they near the earth. Such a program could be based on Clementine, the device that discovered water on the moon.[16] Knowing the mass, velocity, and composition of a meteor is essential to predicting its effects.

It would be valuable to have a system that could intercept a sizable meteor on collision course with the earth. An explosive, detonated an appropriate distance below the meteor's surface, could expel material from the meteor and either alter its course or break it up. In most cases, conventional explosives would produce a sufficient blast. The only practical way to assure that we could deflect a meteor is to conduct experiments on them by interacting with meteors that pass between the earth and the moon. The experiments should be carried out, of course, when the meteors are beyond their closest approach to earth.

When a large meteor disintegrates, its fragments ionize the high atmosphere. There will be an outward motion, which in the temporarily conducting atmosphere will carry magnetic fields with it. The magnetic lines continue all the way down to the magnetic poles on the surface of the earth. It would be interesting to observe the brief changes of the magnetic fields near the poles.

According to geological evidence, the north and south magnetic poles of our planet have switched perhaps a little more frequently than once in 1 million years. When a switch occurs, is the earth less protected from cosmic rays, and therefore, mutation rates are temporarily higher? This is an interesting question.

I think that learning cooperatively with other nations how to prevent damage from meteor impact—becoming knowledgeable enough to prevent a globally catastrophic natural disaster—would be a worthwhile way to begin the new millennium.

---

[16]Lowell Wood and his collaborators developed Clementine at Lawrence Livermore National Laboratory.

EPILOGUE

I N THE HISTORY of physics, there have been three great revolutions in thought that first seemed absurd yet proved to be true. The first proposed that the earth, instead of being stationary, was moving around at a great and variable speed in a universe that is much bigger than it appears to our immediate perception. That proposal, I believe, was first made by Aristarchos two millennia ago at the Greek center of knowledge in Alexandria.[1] It took more than a millennium and a half before Copernicus offered a substantial proof, Galileo and Kepler further developed and enlarged the theory, and Newton turned it into a scientific fact. It has changed our outlook on the universe in a manner that is deep and thorough yet not deep enough.

The next two revolutions in thought occurred during my lifetime. In the early part of the twentieth century, the theory of relativity and the science of quantum mechanics came into existence. Relativity seems absurd because it challenges our idea of time; it points out that we can't talk about time independently of space. This concept goes far beyond our ability of immediate perception. The other novel development, quantum mechanics, disproves the mechanistic and predictive structure of our universe that was assumed true and concludes that in predicting the future, we can make statements only about probabilities.

Relativity and quantum mechanics have introduced the need for great revision in human thought. Thoroughly changing one's mind about the nature of the physical world requires considerable time and effort. Widespread recognition that our physical world is organized along the principles of relativity and

---

[1] Remarkably enough, the name Aristarchos in Greek means *best beginning*.

uncertainty rather than by absolutes and determinism would, I believe, contribute a great deal to the prospects for the future. But for most people, even for many intellectuals, these novel ideas remain incompletely absorbed, a source of uneasiness.

The changes in technology during the twentieth century have been as great as those in science: Transportation, communication, medicine, agriculture, and the instruments of warfare have altered the lives of people across the globe. The rate of change can be seen in the contrast of the military instruments in use at the end of the Napoleonic Wars with those in use a century later, when the first convulsion termed a *world war* ended. In 1815, weaponry included the battleship and the cannon, and wars were fought with fewer than 1 million men. In 1918, weaponry included machine guns, high explosives, railroads, the telegraph, trucks, airplanes, and primitive tanks. Battles had been replaced by trench warfare. The number of people involved reached into the tens of millions. Little more than twenty-five years later, dive bombers, radar, the telephone, computers, missiles, jet airplanes, and nuclear weapons played a role in a war that was fought throughout the Northern Hemisphere and involved most of the nations of the world. Technology has interconnected the world and made it much smaller.

I have no solutions to the world's future problems, but I can identify two great obstacles to solving them: ignorance and fear. The fear engendered by the rapid changes in warfare dominates many people's attitudes toward science and technology. Automobiles, airplanes, and space travel, control of innumerable diseases, decreased infant mortality, longer life span, almost instantaneous communication across the globe, world peace that has lasted for more than half a century—these are part of the good news of technology. But that good news has not captured the public imagination in the same way that the dangers of nuclear weapons have.

As the new millennium begins, the world remains divided into those who have and those who do not have. Poverty—which destroys and pollutes people's spirits as well as the environments in which it occurs—will be addressed, one way or another, during the coming century. I believe that most people now agree that the problem of overpopulation faced by many developing nations will be solved only when a decent standard of living and the survival of children is assured in all parts of the world. It is also worthy of note that people who control their own governments, whose lives and freedoms are secure, are less likely to engage in violence and warfare.

During the next century, the people of the developing world will want and need a several-fold increase in energy consumption. Alternative energy sources, such as wind power and solar energy, are not quantitatively significant.[2] Meeting global energy needs by an increased use of fossil fuels will not only increase atmospheric carbon dioxide (which may be involved in causing climate changes) but also may lead to the exhaustion of an economic coal supply.

Misplaced fear and ignorance about the physical world threaten the future. For example, fear of nuclear energy, a technology introduced in connection with a powerful weapon, has forestalled the development of this energy source. The economic and ecological consequences of that circumstance are still in the future.

The misinformation and scare tactics that the media has used in reporting events connected with nuclear energy, coupled with a lack of adequate science education, has made it impossible for most people to make intelligent decisions about what constitutes a danger, a risk, or an unimportant change in a natural phenomenon.

Almost half a century has passed since the first nuclear reactors were constructed, and during that time, only three large-scale accidents have occurred: the Windscale accident in Great Britain in 1957, the Three Mile Island accident in the United States in 1979, and the Chernobyl accident in the Soviet Union in 1986. The first two accidents harmed no one. The third, which involved a fire as well as dispersal of radioactive material, caused almost fifty immediate fatalities, and its long-term effects may cause as many as a few hundred more deaths. Yet media reports of the Chernobyl accident predicted hundreds of thousands of deaths.

The Chernobyl accident, like the Three Mile Island accident, was caused by operators turning off built-in safety systems. But although the Three Mile Island reactors were inherently safe, the Chernobyl reactors were not. Once out of control, the Chernobyl reactors proceeded on an accelerating course to meltdown and explosion.

The total number of deaths resulting from the Chernobyl accident is similar to the number of lives lost in the crash of a large jet airliner. One can only wish that people would apply just one-tenth of the objectivity with which they assess the risks of air travel to the risks of nuclear energy. One of the difficulties of this suggestion is that everyone recognizes the pleasures and gains

---

[2] Despite the passage of almost three decades of committed government support, such sources are able to provide only 3 percent of U.S. electrical energy. Today, 70 percent of the electricity in France, 40 percent of the electricity in Japan, and about 20 percent of the electricity in the United States is produced by nuclear reactors.

of air travel; few people recognize the great benefits that electricity brings to their lives.

A revision of reactor design, which sets to rest the current public misperceptions, may accelerate the availability of energy in developing nations and thereby reduce the great differences extant today between wealth and poverty. I believe four issues need to be addressed: the containment of nuclear material in case of an accident must be guaranteed; the operation of the reactor must be radically simplified to the extent that it becomes close to automatic; the fuel must be inaccessible for military use; and the disposal of spent fuel must be simple and reliable.

My suggestion in regard to the first issue is to place nuclear reactors 300 to 1,000 feet underground, in loose earth. In such a location, neither accident nor earthquake could result in a considerable amount of radioactivity's being released on the surface. I think that the public misapprehension of risk can be corrected only by such a clear-cut measure as underground siting.

The operation of reactors can be greatly simplified by constructing reactors with a negative temperature coefficient. Such a reactor would operate more vigorously when heat was extracted and, conversely, would heat up and shut itself down if little energy was extracted. The natural laws of physics rather than the care exercised by human beings would regulate the operation of such a reactor.

In addition, because of its underground containment and the absence of operators, the possibility of obtaining nuclear materials for weapons from the reactor would be sharply reduced. Obtaining nuclear materials from a buried reactor not intended to be accessible to human operators would be both expensive and conspicuous.

The disposal of waste products would also be greatly simplified. At the end of its useful life, when the reactor had exhausted its fuel, the system would shut down, and the remaining radioactive materials would be allowed to decay harmlessly in the buried reactor.

The reactor I envisage here would be a series of breeder reactors. The first would be based on uranium, and the subsequent members of the chain would be thorium breeder reactors.[3] By making the series of reactors longer

---

[3] Thorium is much more abundant than uranium and supports a chain reaction in much the same manner as uranium. (See Chapter 22.) To initiate a thorium chain reaction, a surplus of neutrons is necessary; these can be provided to the first thorium breeder in the series by a uranium-fueled reactor. The active thorium breeder is then able to provide neutrons to start the reaction in the next thorium breeder.

or shorter, a planned operational time of half a century could be extended or reduced. Thorium is sufficiently abundant in nature that it can provide nuclear energy for many thousands of years into the future.

A further interesting point is that such a system would be cost-effective. What may be even more important, it would operate safely even in regions where reactor expertise is hard to obtain. My proposal has not been worked out in detail. The point I am making is that using an approach different from most of the current proposals may hold real promise for public acceptance.

Other examples besides that of nuclear energy illustrate contemporary fears and extreme conservatism in regard to novel technologies; for example, fear of and resistance to cloning and genetically altered crops. These fears seem to be spreading among those who have most benefited from the advances in science and technology.

As I write this in the summer of 2000, genetically altered crops are being discussed by the news media because of the opposition they have incurred. Historically, plant breeding has made possible the growth and prosperity of the human species. That it can be done more quickly, more reliably, and more deliberately should be encouraging news. New crops that have better yields, or better resistance to plant disease, or require less pesticide treatment, or require less fertilizer, or are easier to transport in good condition would seem to offer great advantages. But many people in western Europe, and some in the United States, are refusing to eat them. Apparently, much of the anxiety connected with the introduction of genetically altered crops pertains to fears that the preliminary studies may have overlooked some possible hazard.[4]

Fear—of hunger, of disease, of natural disasters, of one's neighbors—has been justified throughout human history. Fear of science and technology, which have empowered humans since the beginning of history, is the height of folly. The world—and all the people who lived during the first half of the twentieth century—suffered grievously from two world wars. But although the second half of the twentieth century was full of tensions and anxieties, it was a period of comparative peace and prosperity. The Cold War was unique. It was won by the existence, not the use, of a new weapon, and without the loss of life. In the closing decade of the twentieth century, the most powerful

---

[4] As mentioned earlier, proof of a negative is hard to obtain. See National Research Council, *Genetically Modified Pest-Protected Plants: Science and Regulation* (Washington, D.C.: National Academy Press, prepublication copy April 2000).

totalitarian empire ended without bloodshed. As the new millennium dawned, the spread of democracy gave reason to hope for continued peace.

But tribalism—otherwise called ethnic tension—continues to generate conflicts, and the remaining totalitarian régimes continue to threaten world peace. Ongoing development of science and technology in the democracies of the world is essential. If democratic people are unwilling to harness the power of new knowledge, political power will shift to power seekers who may serve selfish needs rather than the needs of their communities.

I do not believe that the problems of our smaller world can be solved by one world government, although I once saw that as a hope. I now think it would be too easy for a world government to abuse its power. I also do not suggest that peaceful coexistence should be accomplished by the homogenization of all people, for I believe that homogeneity could lead to a devaluation of the individual. I do see the tentative beginnings of unification going on in the European Union as hopeful. I hold opposite views about the increasing power of the Green Party and similar environmental groups.

Sensationalist reports in the media propagate fear of change. It is harder to recognize that the development of technology can have (and has had) a positive effect on our environoment. No pollution is more destructive of the natural environment than the pollution of poverty. Only through fighting poverty by development can we halt and modify the blight that poverty creates.

Although the first half of the twentieth century was marked by terrible wars, the second half has proved that former enemies can become friends. On my ninetieth birthday, I celebrated with about two hundred friends—some from Hoover Institution, the Livermore and Los Alamos laboratories, some from other parts of the United States, and still others from Hungary and Israel. On that occasion, four scientists from Chelyabinsk sent me a letter wishing me a happy birthday on behalf of all the scientists of the Russian Federal Nuclear Center; the letter said in part:

> [The period after World War II] was a very dramatic period of world history, world nations and states. At the same time, in spite of deep and controversial social processes, the world was restrained from a devastating Third World War. There is the hope for the wisdom and maturity of people . . . .
>
> There is strong reason to trust now, that Humankind will not use these great discoveries for evil. There is a great hope that they will and should be used by wise future generations for the benefit of the people. . . . We have found many points where our efforts could be joined for the benefit of all people, and we hope that we all together . . . will win [through scientific] collaborations.

Those sentiments, and the fact of their expression, seem, in themselves, a source of hope.

During the last half century, the United States has been a leader among the nations of the world in many respects; but perhaps, most importantly, by illustrating that people who have no historical common background can cooperate for the good of all. Children whose grandparents were immigrants a hundred years earlier are considered thoroughly American. In the rest of the world, the residency requirement for acceptance is several centuries. Yet, in comparison, our composite society functions politically in an exemplary manner.

People throughout the developing world want to be Americans for the economic benefits they will gain. But the greatest advantage of being American is the separation from old ideas and attitudes. Being American means taking on a spirit of cooperation aimed at securing mutual benefits. Americans possess little that is as valuable as that political attitude.

The United States was protected during its early years by its geographic isolation. Today, the geographic isolation of any nation is illusionary. Unfortunately, human attitudes and political institutions have not yet fully acknowledged the global interconnectedness. The American attitude of acceptance and cooperation needs to flourish in all parts of the world, and if world peace is to continue, the nations of the world must learn to cooperate for mutual benefit.

If we truly hope to live together as free people in peace, we must learn to act at a considered pace, with moderation and tolerance, and, as nations, we must provide practice in working together cooperatively for the benefit of all.

Science and technology provide many opportunities to do so—programs that will increase human safety from natural or political disasters.

In this era of missiles and nuclear weapons, the possibility of sudden and massive attack makes it essential to replace warfare with international cooperation. International agreements that limit or forbid activities are less likely to have positive outcomes than cooperative efforts. For example, trying to limit the amount or type of energy that nations use is likely to create economic hardship and to engender resentment. Working together on positive programs to increase energy supplies makes for friendship and good feelings between nations, and it provides the benefits of energy to everyone.

Perhaps my preference for conducting shared activities rather than instituting prohibitions arises from personal feelings and belief. I take pleasure in activity; I believe that there is no other way in which to enjoy life in a consistent manner. I hate doubt, yet I am certain that doubt is the only way to approach anything worth believing in. I believe in good, an ephemeral and elusive quality, and I also believe in evil: It is the property of all those who are certain of truth.

The human spirit can thrive only if we acknowledge imperfection. To perceive imperfection in others is easy but sometimes mistaken. To recognize imperfection in oneself is obviously difficult, but this ability is an important part of one's own excellence. We can strive to have fewer flaws, but we must acknowledge how imperfect we remain. It is difficult for imperfection to serve as the basis of collaboration between people. Yet as history shows, acknowledged imperfection can be a remarkably solid foundation for human cooperation.

I firmly believe that reasonable planning for the future requires an understanding of the past. I have written about the events I have experienced as honestly and completely as my memory allows. I hope that this account may thus contribute to understanding the past and thereby provide hope for the future.

IN THE MATTER OF
J. ROBERT OPPENHEIMER

Transcript of Hearing before
Personnel Security Board,
April 12, 1954 through May 6, 1954.

Examination of Edward Teller, pages 709–727

Mr. Gray: Dr. Teller, do you wish to testify under oath?

Dr. Teller: I do.

Mr. Gray: Would you raise your right hand and give me your full name?

Dr. Teller: Edward Teller.

Mr. Gray: Edward Teller, do you swear that the testimony you are to give the board shall be the truth, the whole truth, and nothing but the truth, so help you God?

Dr. Teller: I do.

Whereupon, Edward Teller was called as a witness, and having been first duly sworn, was examined and testified as follows:

Mr. Gray: Will you sit down.

Dr. Teller, it is my duty to remind you of the existence of the so-called perjury statutes with respect to testifying in a Government proceeding and testifying under oath. May I assume that you are generally familiar with those statutes?

The Witness: I am.

Mr. Gray: May I ask, sir, that if in the course of your testimony it becomes necessary for you to refer to or to disclose restricted data, you let me know in advance, so that we may take appropriate and necessary steps in the interests of security.

Finally, may I say to you that we consider this proceeding a confidential matter between the Atomic Energy Commission, its officials and witnesses on the one hand, and Dr. Oppenheimer and his representatives on the other. The Commission is not effecting news releases with respect to these proceedings, and we express the hope that witnesses will take the same view.

Direct Examination

By Mr. Robb:

Q: Dr. Teller, may I ask you, sir, at the outset, are you appearing as a witness here today because you want to be here?

A: I appear because I have been asked to and because I consider it my duty on request to say what I think in the matter. I would have preferred not to appear.

Q: I believe, sir, that you stated to me some time ago that anything you had to say, you wished to say in the presence of Dr. Oppenheimer?

A: That is correct.

Q: May I ask you, sir, to tell the board briefly of your academic background and training.

A: I started to study in Budapest where I was born, at the Institute of Technology there, chemical engineering for a very short time. I continued in Germany, first in chemical engineering and mathematics, then in Munich for a short time, and finally in Leipzig in physics, where I took my doctor's degree.

After that I worked as a research associate in Goettingen, I taught in London. I had a fellowship, a Rockefeller fellowship in Copenhagen.

In 1935 I came to this country and taught for 6 years at the George Washington University, that is, essentially until the beginning of the war.

At that time I went to Columbia on leave of absence, partly to teach and partly in the very beginnings of the war work in 1941–42, as I remember, and then I participated in the war work. After the war I returned to teach in Chicago at the University of Chicago, which also was interrupted with some work for the AEC, and now for the last year I am at the University of California in Berkeley.

Q: Dr. Teller, you know Dr. Oppenheimer well; do you not?

A: I have known Dr. Oppenheimer for a long time. I first got closely associated with him in the summer of 1942 in connection with atomic energy work. Later in Los Alamos and after Los Alamos I knew him. I met him frequently, but I was not particularly closely associated with him, and I did not discuss with him very frequently or in very great detail matters outside of business matters.

Q: To simplify the issues here, perhaps, let me ask you this question: Is it your intention in anything that you are about to testify to, to suggest that Dr. Oppenheimer is disloyal to the United States?

A: I do not want to suggest anything of the kind. I know Oppenheimer is an intellectually most alert and a very complicated person, and I think it would be presumptuous and wrong on my part if I would try in any way to analyze his motives. But I have always assumed, and I now assume that he is loyal to the United States. I believe this, and I shall believe it until I see very conclusive proof to the opposite.

Q: Now, a question that is a corollary of that. Do you or do you not believe that Dr. Oppenheimer is a security risk?

A: In a great number of cases I have seen Dr. Oppenheimer act—I understood that Dr. Oppenheimer acted—in a way which for me was exceedingly hard to understand. I thoroughly disagreed with him in numerous issues and his actions frankly appeared to me confused and complicated. To this extent I feel that I would like to see the vital interests of this country in hands which I understand better, and therefore trust more.

In this very limited sense I would like to express a feeling that I would feel personally more secure if public matters would rest in other hands.

Q: One question I should have asked you before, Dr. Teller. Are you an American citizen, sir?

A: I am.

Q: When were you naturalized?

A: In 1941.

Q: I believe you said that about 1941 you began work on the atomic bomb program.

A: I don't think I said that. Certainly I did not intend to say it.

Q: I will rephrase the question. When did you begin to work on the atomic bomb program?

A: That again I am not sure I can answer simply. I became aware of the atomic-bomb program early in 1939. I have been close to it ever since, and I have at least part of the time worked on it and worried about it ever since.

Q: Did you work during the war at Los Alamos?

A: I did.

Q: When did you go there, sir?

A: In April 1943.

Q: What was the nature of your work there?

A: It was theoretical work connected with the atomic bomb. Generally speaking—I do not know whether I have to go into that in any detail—I was more interested by choice and also by directive in advanced development, so that at the beginning I think my work was perhaps more closely connected with the actual outcome or what happened in Alamogordo, but very soon my work shifted into fields which were not to bear fruition until a much later time.

Q: Will you tell the board whether or not while you were in Los Alamos in 1943 or 1944, you did any work on or had any discussions about the so-called thermonuclear weapon?

A: Excuse me, if I may restate your question. I got to Los Alamos in early April 1943. To the best of my recollection, although I might be wrong—I mean my date might not be quite precise—I left at the beginning of February 1946. Throughout this period I had very frequent discussions about thermonuclear matters.

Q: Will you tell us whether you ever discussed the thermonuclear method with Dr. Oppenheimer?

A: I discussed it very frequently indeed with him. In fact my discussions date back to our first association in this matter, namely, to the summer of 1942.

Q: What was Dr. Oppenheimer's opinion in those discussions during those years about the feasibility of producing a thermonuclear weapon?

A: This is something that I wish you would allow me to answer slightly in detail, because it is not an easy question.

Q: Yes, sir.

A: I hope that I can keep my answer in an unclassified way. I hope I am not disclosing a secret when I say that to construct the thermonuclear bomb is not a very easy thing, and that in our discussions, all of us frequently believed it could be done, and again we frequently believed that it could not be done. I think Dr. Oppenheimer's opinions shifted with the shifting evidence. To the best of my recollection before we got to Los Alamos we had all of us considerable hope that the thermonuclear bomb can be constructed. It was my understanding that these hopes were fully shared by Dr. Oppenheimer.

Later some disappeared and perhaps to counterbalance some things that might have been said, I think I have made myself some contributions in discovering some of these difficulties.

I clearly remember that toward the end of the war Dr. Oppenheimer encouraged me to go ahead with the thermonuclear investigations. I further remember that in the summer of 1945, after the test at Alamogordo it was generally understood in the laboratory that we are going to develop thermonuclear bombs in a vigorous fashion and that quite a number of people, such as the most outstanding, like Fermi and Bethe, would participate in it.

I also know that very shortly after the dropping of bombs on Japan this plan was changed and to the best of my belief it was changed at least in good part because of the opinion of Dr. Oppenheimer that this is not the time to pursue this program any further.

I should like to add to this, however, that this also thoroughly responded to the temper of the people in the laboratory, most of whom at that time, understandably and in consonance with the general tempo of the country, wanted to go home.

Q: Did you have any conversations with Dr. Oppenheimer at or about September 1945 about working on the thermonuclear?

A: We had around that period several conversations and in one of them, to the best of my recollection, Oppenheimer and Fermi and Allison and I were present. Oppenheimer argued that this is not the time at which to pursue the business further, that this is a very interesting program, that it would be a wonderful thing if we could pursue it in a really peaceful world under international cooperation, but that under the present set-up this was not a good idea to go on with it.

I perhaps should also like to mention that to the best of my knowledge at that time there was a decision by a board composed of several prominent people, one of them Dr. Oppenheimer, which decided in effect that thermonuclear work either cannot or should not be pursued that it at any rate was a long-term undertaking requiring very considerable effort. To my mind this was in sharp contrast to the policy pursued a short time before.

But I also should say that this sharp contrast was at least in part motivated by the fact that in Los Alamos, there was a crew of exceedingly able physicists who could do a lot and at the end of the war were trying to get back to their purely academic duties, and in this new atmosphere it might have appeared indeed hard to continue with such an ambitious program.

One member of the board which made this decision, Fermi, and who concurred in that decision, told me about that decision and told me that he knew that I am likely to disagree with it, and asked me to state my opinion in writing. This I did, and I gave my written statement to Oppenheimer, and therefore, both the opinion that the thermonuclear bomb at that time was not feasible, and my own opinion that one could have proceeded in this direction are documented.

Q: Did there come a time when you left Los Alamos after the war?

A: That is right. As I mentioned, I left in February 1946. May I perhaps add something here if we are proceeding in a chronological manner?

Q: Yes

A: Perhaps if I might interject this not in response to one of your questions.

Q: That is perfectly all right, sir.

A: I would like to say that I consider Dr. Oppenheimer's direction of the Los Alamos Laboratory a very outstanding achievement due mainly to the fact that with his very quick mind he found out very promptly what was going on in every part of the laboratory, made right judgments about things, supported work when work had to be supported, and also I think with his very remarkable insight in psychological matters, made just a most wonderful and excellent director.

Q: In that statement were you speaking of Dr. Oppenheimer's ability as an administrator or his contribution as a scientist or both?

A: I would like to say that I would say in a way both. As an administrator he was so busy that his purely scientific contributions to my mind and in my judgment were not outstanding, that is, not insofar as I could see his original contributions. But nevertheless, his scientific contributions were great by exercising quick and sound judgment and giving the right kind of encouragement in very many different cases. I should think that scientific initiative came from a great number of other excellent people whom Oppenheimer not let alone but also to a very great extent by his able recruiting effort he collected a very considerable number of them, and I should say that purely scientific initiatives and contributions came from many people, such like, for instance, von Neumann, Bethe, Segre, to mention a few with whom I am very closely connected, and very many others, and I cannot begin to make a complete list of them.

Q: Coming back to a previous question, Doctor, you say you did leave the laboratory in January, 1946?

A: I believe February 1946, but it might be the last days of January. I do not remember so accurately.

Q: Would you tell us whether or not before that happened you had any conversations with Dr. Bradbury and Dr. Oppenheimer about the question of whether you should leave or not?

A: I had several conversations.

Q: Would you tell us about those conversations?

A: Of this kind. I am not at all sure that I can mention them all to you. One was to the best of my recollection in August of 1946, at which time the laboratory was still apparently going at full tilt. Dr. Oppenheimer came to see me in my office.

Q: You said August 1946?

A: August 1945. Thank you very much for catching this mistake.

He had a long conversation with me from which it became clear to me that Dr. Oppenheimer thought that the laboratory would inevitably disintegrate, and that there was not much point in my staying there, at least that is how I understood him. I had been planning to go to Chicago where I was invited to go, and participate in teaching and research work, which I was looking forward to. Then somewhere during the fall of 1945, I believe, Bradbury asked me to take on the job of heading the Theoretical Division.

I was very much interested in seeing the continuation in a vigorous manner, and in spite of my desire to go back to academic work, I considered this very seriously. I asked Bradbury about the program of the laboratory and in effect I told him—I certainly do not remember my words—that I would stay if 1 or 2 conditions would be met, not both, but one of them. Either we could continue with the fission program vigorously and as a criterion whether we would do that or not, I said let us see if we could test something like 12 fission weapons per year, or, if instead we would go into a thorough investigation of the thermonuclear question.

Bradbury, I think realistically, said at that time that both of these programs were unfortunately out of the question. I still did not say no. Oppenheimer was going to come and visit the laboratory shortly after, and I wanted to discuss it with him

I asked him or I told him that Bradbury had invited me, and asked him whether I should stay. Oppenheimer said that I should stay and he also mentioned that he knows that General Groves is quite anxious that I should. Then I mentioned to him the discussion with Bradbury. I said something to this effect. This has been your laboratory. This is your laboratory. It will not prosper unless you support it, and I don't want to stay here if the laboratory won't prosper.

Q: If what?

A: If the laboratory will not prosper. I think I said, I know that there can be no hard and fast program now, but I would like to know whether I can count on your help in getting a vigorous program somewhere along the lines I mentioned established here.

Again I am sorry I cannot quote any literal reply by Oppenheimer, but my recollection of his reply was that it meant that he is neither able nor willing to help in an undertaking of this kind. I thereupon said that under these conditions I think I better leave the laboratory.

Oppenheimer's statement was that he thought this was really the right decision, and that by leaving the laboratory at that time, I could be of greater service to the atomic energy enterprise at a later period.

I remember having seen Oppenheimer the same evening at some party. I forget in whose house it was. He asked then whether having made up my mind, I don't feel better, and I still remember that I told him I didn't feel better. But that was where the matter rested at that time.

I think this tied in more or less with my general impression that Oppenheimer felt at least for 1 year after the laboratory that Los Alamos cannot and probably should not continue, and it is just as wise and correct to abandon it.

I am exceedingly glad that due to the very determined action of Bradbury, who was not deterred by any prophecies of this kind, the laboratory was not abandoned, because I am sure had that been done, we would be now in a much worse position in our armament race that we happen to be.

Q: Do you recall any remark by anybody to the effect that the laboratory should be given back to the Indians?

A: I heard this statement attributed to Oppenheimer. I do not remember that he ever said so in my hearing.

Q: Thereafter, you did in fact leave Los Alamos, Doctor?

A: I left Los Alamos, but I did go back very frequently as a consultant.

Q: When you went back as a consultant what was the particular problem you were working on?

A: Actually I have been working on quite a number of problems as required. I, of course, continued to be very much interested in the thermonuclear development, and I did continue to work on it, as it were, part time. This however, at that time was a very minor portion of the enterprise of the laboratory. I would say that on the average between 1945 and 1949, a very few people worked on it steadily. I would not be able to say whether this number was 3 or 4 or 5 or 6 out of a thousand or more than a thousand in the laboratory. But his was the order of magnitude, and therefore popularly expressing and crudely expressing the state of affairs, in spite of my working there and in spite of some reports being issued, I can say that the work was virtually at a standstill.

Those were also the years when after some initial hesitation, the testing program was resumed. I understand that this resumption of the testing program was encouraged by the General Advisory Committee on which Oppenheimer was the Chairman. I was also a little bit involved in planning the first extensive test after the war. I don't mean now the Bikini test, but the following one, which I think was called Sandstone. So I would like to say that even the fraction of the time, which was considerably less than one-half, which was one-third, it perhaps was not even as much as one-third, I was spending at Los Alamos. Perhaps one-third of my time went into Atomic Energy Commission work, and this was divided between thermonuclear work and other supporting work for Los Alamos, and work on an appointment which I got on the recommendation, I believe, of the General Advisory Committee, on the safety of reactors.

So I would say that of my own time a really small fraction has gone into thermonuclear development during those years and that altogether the effort was very, very slow, indeed.

Q: You were familiar with the effort that was being put in at Los Alamos in respect of thermonuclear?

A: I was.

Q: Doctor, let me ask you for your opinion as an expert on this question. Suppose you had gone to work on thermonuclear in 1945 or 1946—really gone to work on it—can you give us any opinion as to when in your view you might have achieved that weapon and would you explain your opinion?

A: I actually did go to work on it with considerable determination after the Russian bomb was dropped. This was done in a laboratory which at that time was considerably behind Los Alamos at the end of the war. It is my belief that if at the end of the war some people like Dr. Oppenheimer would have lent moral support, not even their own work—just moral support—to work on the thermonuclear gadget, I think we could have kept at least as many people in Los Alamos as we then recruited in 1949 under very difficult conditions.

I therefore believe that if we had gone to work in 1945, we could have had the thermonuclear bomb just about 4 years earlier. This of course is very much a matter of opinion because what would have happened if things had been different is certainly not something that one can ever produce by any experiment.

Q: That is right.

A: I think that statements about the possible different course of the past are not more justified but only less hazardous than statements about the future.

Q: Doctor, it has been suggested here that the ultimate success on the thermonuclear was the result of a brilliant discovery or invention by you, and that it might or might not have taken 5 or 10 years. What can you say about that?

A: I can say about it this. If I want to walk from here to that side of the room, and you ask me how long it takes to get there, it depends on the speed I am walking with and in what direction. If I start in that direction I will never get there, probably. It so happened that very few people gave serious thought in this country to the development of the thermonuclear bomb. This was due to the fact that during the war we were much too busy with things that had to be done immediately in order that it should be effective during the war, and therefore not much time was left over.

After the war the people who stayed in Los Alamos, few and discouraged as they were, had their hands full in keeping the laboratory alive, keeping up even the knowledge of how to work on the simple fission weapons. The rest of the scientists were, I think, equally much too busy trying to be very sure not to get into an armament race, and arguing why to continue the direction in which we had been going due to the war would be completely wrong. I think it was neither a great achievement nor a brilliant one. It just had to be done. I must say it was not completely easy. There were some pitfalls. But I do believe that if the original plan in Los Alamos, namely, that the laboratory with such excellent people like Fermi and Bethe and others, would have gone after the problem, probably some of these people would have had either the same brilliant idea or another one much sooner.

In that case I think we would have had the bomb in 1947. I do not believe that it was a particularly difficult thing as scientific discoveries go. I do not think that we should now feel that we have safety as compared to the Russians, and think it was just necessary that somebody should be looking and looking with some intensity and some conviction that there is also something there.

Q: Is this a fair summary—

A: May I perhaps say that this again is an attempt at appreciating or evaluating a situation, and I may be of course quite wrong, because this is clearly not a matter of fact but a matter of opinion.

Q: Is this a fair summary of your opinion, Doctor, that if you don't seek, you don't find?

A: Certainly.

Q: Do you recall when the Russians exploded their first bomb in September 1949? Do you recall that event?

A: Certainly.

Q: Will you tell the board whether or not shortly after the Russians exploded their first bomb in September 1949 you had a conversation with Dr. Oppenheimer about the thermonuclear or about what activity should be undertaken to meet the Russian advance?

A: I remember two such conversations. One was in the fall and necessarily superficial. That was just a very few hours after I heard, returning from a trip abroad, that the Russians had exploded an A-bomb. I called up Oppenheimer who happened to be in Washington, as I was at that time, and I asked him for advice, and this time I remember his advice literally. It was, "Keep your shirt on."

Perhaps I might mention that my mind did not immediately turn in the direction of working on the thermonuclear bomb. I had by that time quite thoroughly accepted the idea that with the reduced personnel it was much too difficult an undertaking. I perhaps should mention, and I think it will clear the picture, that a few months before the Russian explosion I agreed to rejoin Los Alamos for the period of 1 year on leave of absence from the University of Chicago.

I should also mention that prior to that Oppenheimer talked to me and encouraged me to go back to Los Alamos and help in the work there. I also went back to Los Alamos with the understanding and with the expectation that I shall just help along in their normal program in which some very incipient phases of the thermonuclear work was included, but nothing on a very serious scale.

I was quite prepared to contribute mostly in the direction of the fission weapons. At the time when I returned from this short trip abroad, and was very much disturbed about the Russian bomb, I was looking around for ways in which we could more successfully speed up our work and only after several weeks of discussion did I come to the conclusion that no matter what the odds seemed to be, we must at this time—I at least must at this time put my full attention to the thermonuclear program.

I also felt that this was much too big an undertaking and I was just very scared of it. I was looking around for some of the old crew to come out and participate in this work. Actually if anyone wanted to head this enterprise. One of the people whom I went to visit, in fact the only one where I had very strong hopes, was Hans Bethe.

Q: About when was this, Doctor?

A: To the best of my recollection it was the end of October.

Q: 1949?

A: Right. Again I am not absolutely certain of my dates, but that is the best of my memory. I can tie it down a little bit better with respect to other dates. It was a short time before the GAC meeting in which that committee made a decision against the thermonuclear program.

After a somewhat strenuous discussion, Bethe, to the best of my understanding, decided that he would come to Los Alamos and help us. During this discussion, Oppenheimer called up and invited Bethe and me to come and discuss this matter with him in Princeton. This we did do, and visited Oppenheimer in his office.

When we arrived, I remember that Oppenheimer showed us a letter on his desk which he said he had just received. This letter was from Conant. I do not know whether he showed us the whole letter or whether he showed us a short section of it, or whether he only read to us a short section. Whichever it was, and I cannot say which it was, one phrase of Conant's sticks in my mind, and that phrase was "over my dead body," referring to a decision to go ahead with a crash program on the thermonuclear bomb.

Apart from showing us this letter, or reading it to us, whichever it was, Oppenheimer to the best of my recollection did not argue against any crash program. We did talk for quite awhile and could not possibly reproduce the whole argument but at least one important trend in this discussion—and I do not know how relevant this is—was that Oppenheimer argued that some phases of exaggerated secrecy in connection with the A-bomb was perhaps not to the best interests of the country, and that if he undertook the thermonuclear development, this should be done right from the first and should be done more openly.

I remember that Bethe reacted to that quite violently, because he thought that if we proceeded with thermonuclear development, then both—not only our methods of work—but even the fact that we were working and if possible the results of our work should be most definitely kept from any public knowledge or any public announcement.

To the best of my recollection, no agreement came out of this, but when Bethe and I left Oppenheimer's office, Bethe was still intending to come to Los Alamos. Actually, I had been under the impression that Oppenheimer is opposed to the thermonuclear bomb or to a development of the thermonuclear bomb, and I don't think there was terribly much direct evidence to base this impression on. I am pretty sure that I expressed to Bethe the worry, we are going to talk with Oppenheimer now, and after that you will not come. When we left the office, Bethe turned to me and smiled and he said, "You see, you can be quite satisfied. I am still coming."

I do not know whether Bethe has talked again with Oppenheimer about that or not. I have some sort of a general understanding that he did not, but I am not at all sure that this is true.

Two days later I called up Bethe in New York, and he was in New York at that time, and Bethe then said that he thought it over, and he had changed his mind, and he was not coming.

I regretted this very much, and Bethe actually did not join work on the thermonuclear development until quite late in the game, essentially to put on the finishing touches.

I do not know whether this sufficiently answers your question.

Q: Yes, sir. Then, Doctor, the record here shows that on October 29 and 30, 1949, the GAC held its meeting, and thereafter reported its views on the thermonuclear program. Did you later see a copy of the report of the GAC?

A: I did.

Q: Would you tell us the circumstances under which you saw that.

A: Immediately following the meeting, the decision of the General Advisory Committee was kept very strictly confidential. I have seen at least one member of the committee namely, Fermi, who in spite of our very close relationships and the general support of my work in Los Alamos and his knowledge of my almost desperate interest in the undertaking, said that for the time being he just could not even give me an indication of what is happening except from the general tenor of his remarks it was clear that whatever decisions were reached were not terribly favorable to a crash program.

I sort of understood that some kind of action or discussion was under way which can proceed properly only if it is kept in the very smallest circles. This also, of course, became known in Los Alamos, and caused quite a bit of worry there.

After the passage of a little while—and I do not know how much time, but I would say roughly 2 weeks—the secretary of the General Advisory Committee, Dr. Manley, who also was associate director in Los Alamos, returned to Los Alamos. He called me into his office and showed me both the majority and minority report of the General Advisory Committee, and in showing me these reports, he used words which I at least at that time interpreted as meaning that Oppenheimer wanted me to see these reports, which I thought was kind. My general understanding was that these reports were also shown to something like half a dozen or dozen of the senior people in the laboratory.

At any rate, the contents of the report were known without my telling it to people. It was just public knowledge among the senior people practically then and there. Of course I was just most dreadfully disappointed about the contents of the majority and minority reports, which in my eyes did not differ a great deal.

I also should say that in my opinion the work in Los Alamos was going to be most seriously affected by the action of the General Advisory Committee, not only as an official body, but because of the very great prestige of the people who were sitting on it. Therefore, it seemed to me at that time, and it also seems to me now entirely proper that this document should have been made available in Los Alamos.

Q: Doctor, in what way did you think that the work would be affected by the [GAC] report?

A: I would say that when I saw the report, I thought that this definitely was the end of any thermonuclear effort in Los Alamos. Actually I was completely mistaken. The report produced precisely the opposite effect.

Q: Why?

A: Immediately, of course, it stopped work because we were instructed not to work, but it gave people in Los Alamos much greater eagerness to proceed in this direction and from discussion I had in Los Alamos in the following days, I gather the following psychological reaction:

First of all, people were interested in going on with the thermonuclear device because during the war it had been generally understood that this was one of the things that the laboratory was to find out at some time or other. It was a sort of promise in all of our minds.

Another thing was that the people there were a little bit tired—at least many, particularly of the younger ones—of going ahead with minor improvements and wanted to in sort of an adventurous spirit go into a new field. However, I think the strongest point and the one which was a reaction to this report was this: Not only to me, but to very many others who said this to me spontaneously, the report meant this. As long as you people go ahead and make minor improvements and work very hard and diligently at it, you are doing a fine job, but if you succeed in making a really great piece of progress, then you are doing something that is immoral. This kind of statement stated so bluntly was not of course made in the report. But this kind of an implication is something which I think a human being can support in an abstract sense. But if it refers to his own work, then I think almost anybody would become indignant, and this is what happened in Los Alamos, and the result was that I think the feelings of people in consequence of this report turned more toward the thermonuclear development than away from it.

Q: You mean it made them mad.

A: Yes.

Q: Doctor, in the absence of the President's decision of January, would that anger have been effective?

A: No.

Q: Let us go back for a moment—

A: There is no doubt about it. The laboratory just could not put aside a major fraction of its effort on a program of this kind unless we were going to be instructed to do it. Actually, I am pretty sure the anger in a way would have been effective in that more people would have been willing to put aside a little part of their time and worry about it and think about it, and so perhaps it would have been a little effective. But I think that still would have been a very slow and painful progress and probably even now we would be just nowhere.

Q: Dr. Manley has submitted an affidavit here to the effect that he showed you those reports as a result of an impending visit to Los Alamos by Chairman McMahon, Chairman of the Joint Congressional Committee on Atomic Energy. Would you comment on that, and tell us just what it was that Dr. Manley said that gave you the impression that it was Dr. Oppenheimer who wanted you to see the report and tell us whether or not Dr. Manley's remarks were susceptible of the interpretation that it was Chairman McMahon who wanted you to see them?

A: I must say this is possible. To the best of my recollection, I was even struck at that time by these words—Manley said something of that kind, that our Chairman, or the Chairman, I don't know which, sends his regards and wants you to see this. Now, this is to the best of my recollection, and I don't remember that Oppenheimer's name was mentioned. At that time I interpreted this as meaning that it was the Chairman of the General Advisory Committee—this is Oppenheimer. I am quite sure that Manley did not say explicitly that it was McMahon, and to refer to him as simply Chairman would seem to me to be a little remarkable. However, Manley has been showing this document to quite a few people, and perhaps in repeating the phrase a few times parts of the phrase got dropped off. I interpreted it at that time as meaning that Oppenheimer wanted me to see the document. I think it is not excluded that it was Senator McMahon who wanted me to see the document; and if Manley says that, then it must be so.

Q: Did you know Senator McMahon?

A: Yes.

Q: Let me ask you whether or not in that conversation with Manley he mentioned Senator McMahon by name.

A: To the best of my memory, no. I do remember that Senator McMahon came out shortly afterward. I believe I heard about his visit only later, but I might be mistaken.

Q: On the subject of Senator McMahon, will you tell the board whether or not you had proposed to see Senator McMahon about the thermonuclear matter.

A: I did.

Q: When was that?

A: This was quite shortly after the meeting of the GAC.

Q: Did you see him?

A: I did.

Q: Did you have any conversation with Dr. Manley before you saw him?

A: I did.

Q: Tell us about that.

A: I had two conversations with him; the one which I think is more relevant, and which certainly strikes more clearly in my mind, was a telephone conversation. This was after the meeting of the General Advisory Committee. I was on my way from Los Alamos to Washington. The main purpose of my visit was to see Senator McMahon. On the way I stopped in Chicago and saw Fermi in his office. It was at that time that I got the impression which I mentioned to you earlier. During my conversation with Fermi, Manley called and asked me not to see Senator McMahon. I asked why. He said that it would be a good idea if the scientists presented a united front—I don't know whether he used that word—I think what he really said was something of this kind, that it would be unfortunate if Senator McMahon would get the impression that there is a divided opinion among the scientists, or something of that kind. I said I had an appointment with Senator McMahon and I wanted to see him. Manley insisted that I should not. Thereupon I made the suggestion that I would be willing to call up Senator McMahon and tell him that I had been asked not to see him, and for that reason I would not see him.

At that point Manley—I don't know whether I said to Manley that I had been asked by him or whether I would just say I had been asked—and thereupon Manley said, "All right; you better go and see him." That was essentially the contents of my discussion with Manley over the phone.

When I arrived in Washington, Manley met me at the station. I had already the feeling from the discussion with Fermi that at least Fermi's private feelings were not for a crash program. I knew what was in the wind, but I did not know what the decision was. Manley had originally in Los Alamos agreed that we should proceed with the thermonuclear weapon. At least, that was my clear understanding.

He received me on the station with these words, "I think you sold me a gold brick." I remember this particularly clearly, because my familiarity with the English language not being excellent, I did not know what he meant, and I had to ask him what a gold brick is, which he proceeded to explain.

Q: What did he explain, Doctor?

A: A brick covered with gold fill which is not as valuable as it looks.

Q: What did you understand him to refer to?

A: To the thermonuclear program, which, in my opinion, was what we should do, what would be the effective way for us to behave in that situation. Manley implied that in the discussions of the General Advisory Committee another proposal emerged, which was much better, much more hopeful, a better answer to the Russian proposals—excuse me, to the Russian developments—he, however, would not tell me what it was. I was a little mystified. I then went to see Senator McMahon. He did not tell me what was in the report of the General Advisory Committee, but he used some very strong words in connection with it, and did so before I had opened my mouth, words to the effect, "I got this report, and it just makes me sick," or something of that kind.

Q: What was your purpose in seeing Senator McMahon?

A: May I say very frankly I do not remember. One of my purposes, I am quite certain, was a point not connected with the thermonuclear development. It was this, that at some earlier time—I am not sure whether it was a year or earlier or when—Senator McMahon was in Los Alamos at the time when I was visiting there. I had an opportunity to talk to him. Senator McMahon asked me to talk with him, and he asked me what I thought would be the best method to increase effectiveness of Los Alamos. I made a very general remarks at that time, which I do not recall, but I remember very clearly that Senator McMahon asked me a question, which I answered, and the answer to which question I regretted later. It was whether the salary scale in Los Alamos was adequate.

Later, when I got a little bit closer back and talked with people, I felt that I had given the wrong answer and I wanted to correct this, and therefore I wanted to see Senator McMahon. However, by the time I actually went to see him, the thermonuclear discussion had gone, as I have indicated, to a point where it was perfectly clear to me that I wanted to talk with him about that question and certainly even by the time I left Los Alamos and before Manley's telephone conversation, I fully hoped to discuss this matter with him because by that time it was quite clear to me that this was one of the very important things that was going on in Los Alamos. This is to the best of my recollection. But I am not at all sure. It may even be possible that I had seen Senator McMahon about another matter at an earlier time. I believe, however, that all this took place in the same conversation.

Q: In January 1950, the President decided that we should go ahead with the thermonuclear program. Do you recall that?

A: I do.

Q: After that decision was announced, did you go to work on the thermonuclear?

A: I most certainly did.

Q: Was the program accelerated?

A: It was.

Q: What was done in general to accelerate it?

A: A committee was formed which for a strange and irrelevant reason was called a family committee.

Q: Who was on that committee?

A: I was the chairman and there were a number of people representing various division in the laboratory, and this committee was in charge of developing some thermonuclear program and within a very short time this committee made a number of proposals directed toward some tests which were to give us information about the behavior of some phenomena which were relevant.

At the same time I exerted all possible effort and influence to persuade people to come to Los Alamos to work on this, particularly serious because theoretical work was very badly needed.

Q: What was done in respect of the number of personnel working on the thermonuclear? Was it increased, and if so, how much?

A: It was greatly increased. As I say prior to that there was at most half a dozen people working on it. I am not able to tell you how many people worked on it really full time. I am sure I didn't work on it full time although in that time the major portion of my effort was directed toward the thermonuclear work. I believe that Los Alamos has prepared an official estimate in response to a question, and that would be, I think, the best source of how many people worked on the thermonuclear program at that time. I would guess, but as a very pure guess, and I should not be surprised if that document would disprove me, that the number of people working on the thermonuclear program increased like 10, 20, or perhaps a little more percent of the laboratory's effort. Perhaps it was close to 20 percent. I might easily be mistaken.

Q: At all events it was a very large increase.

A: It was a very large increase. As compared to the previous one it was just between standing still and starting to go.

Q: Did you at or about that time, that is, shortly after the President's decision, have any discussion with Oppenheimer as to whether or not he would assist you?

A: I had two discussions with him, but one was shortly before. I would like to quote it a little. Actually the time when President Truman made the announcement I happened to be in Los Angeles and was planning to stay there, in fact had accepted an appointment at UCLA which I at that time had to postpone at any rate because I saw this in the paper. You see, I was not going to stay in Los Alamos much longer, and the fact that there came this announcement from President Truman just changed my mind. Prior to the announcement, preceding it perhaps by 2 or 3 days, I saw Dr. Oppenheimer at an atomic energy conference concerning another matter, and during this meeting it became clear to me that in Dr. Oppenheimer's opinion a decision was impending and this decision would be a go-ahead decision.

At that time I asked Oppenheimer if this is now the decision, would he then please really help us with this thing and help us to work, recalling the very effective work during the war. Oppenheimer's answer to this was in the negative. However, I also should say that this negative reply gave me the feeling that I should not look to Oppenheimer for help under any circumstance.

A few months later, during the spring, I nevertheless called up Oppenheimer and I asked him not for direct help, but for help in recruiting people, not for his own work but for his support in recruiting people. Dr. Oppenheimer said then, "you know in this matter I am neutral. I would be glad, however, to recommend to you some very good people who are working here at the Institute," and he mentioned a few. I wrote to all of these people and tried to persuade them to come to Los Alamos. None of them came.

Q: Where were those people located?

A: At the Institute of Advanced Study in Princeton.

Q: There has been some testimony here that a scientist named Longmire came down to Los Alamos to assist you with the cooperation of Dr. Oppenheimer. Do you recall whether he came down there before the H-bomb conference or afterward?

A: I should like to say first of all that Dr. Longmire did help in the H-bomb development and helped very effectively indeed. I should say helped in fission work and in the thermonuclear work, and is now one of the strongest members of Los Alamos. He came before all this happened. I remember that I tried to get him on the recommendation of Bethe some time early in 1949. I also remember that a little later in the spring or early in the summer I learned—I think it was in May—that Longmire had declined an invitation to Los Alamos, and I also learned that the salary offered him was some 20 percent less than the salary I had recommended. I thereupon talked with the appropriate people in Los Alamos, and I got them to make a second offer to Longmire at the original salary level, and after I secured agreement on that I called up Longmire and told him that we can offer him this salary and would he please come. Longmire said "Yes." He would come. However, he had accepted an invitation in the meantime at the Institute of Advanced Study and he now no longer could change his mind. Thereupon I said,

"Well, what about it if I try to get this chance? Come with us anyway for a year. After a year you can go back to the Institute. I will talk to Oppenheimer about this." Longmire said, "If Oppenheimer will agree to this, I will consider coming very seriously."

I thereupon called up Oppenheimer on the phone, and at least I believed I approached him directly, I am not sure, somebody approached him, but I think I did it directly, and I remember on that occasion Dr. Oppenheimer was exceedingly cooperative and did give whatever formal assurances he could give. It was not terribly formal. He gave assurances that after a year if Longmire wanted to come back to the Institute, he would be very welcome, and if he wants to go to Los Alamos, that is a very good idea, and so on, and after this was arranged, Longmire did come.

Q: This was when?

A: This was all, however, before anyone of us dreamed about the Russian explosion. That was in the early summer or late spring of 1949. I should also say that after Longmire got to Los Alamos, he not only worked effectively, but liked it so much that then on his own choice he really just stayed there, and is still there, although in the meantime he also taught for certain periods in Rochester, I believe, or in Cornell.

Q: Except for giving you this list of names that you have told us about of people all of whom refused to come, did Dr. Oppenheimer, after the President's decision in 1950, assist you in any way in recruiting people on the thermonuclear project?

A: To the best of my knowledge, not in the slightest.

Q: After the President's decision did Dr. Oppenheimer do anything so far as you know to assist you in the thermonuclear project?

A: The GAC did meet, did consider this matter, and its recommendations were in support of the program. Perhaps I am prejudiced in this matter, but I did not feel that we got from the GAC more than passive agreement on the program which we evolved. I should say passive agreement and I felt the kind of criticism which tended to be perhaps more in the nature of a headache than in the nature of enlightenment.

I would like to say that in a later phase there is at least one occurrence where I felt Dr. Oppenheimer's reaction to be different.

Q: Would you tell us about that?

A: I will be very glad to do that. In June of 1951, after our first experimental test, there was a meeting of the GAC and the AEC personnel and some consultants in Princeton at the Institute for Advanced Study. The meeting was chaired by Dr. Oppenheimer. Frankly I went to that meeting with very considerable misgivings, because I expected that the GAC and particularly Dr. Oppenheimer, would further oppose the development. By that time we had evolved something which amounted to a new approach, and after listening to the evidence of both the test and the theoretical investigations on that new approach, Dr. Oppenheimer warmly supported this new approach, and I understand that he made a statement to the effect that if anything of this kind had been suggested right away he never would have opposed it.

Q: With that exception, did you have any indication from Dr. O after January 1950 that he was supporting and approving the work that was being done on the thermonuclear?

A: My general impression was precisely in the opposite direction. However, I should like to say that my contacts with Oppenheimer were infrequent, and he might have supported the thermonuclear effort without my knowing it.

Q: When was the feasibility of the thermonuclear weapon demonstrated?

A: I believe that this can be stated accurately. On November 1, 1952. Although since it was on the other side of the date line, I am not quite sure whether it was November 1 our time or their time.

Q: What?

A: I don't know whether it was November 1 Eniwetok time or Berkeley time. I watched it in Berkeley.

Q: Did you have a conversation with Dr. Oppenheimer in the summer of 1950 about your work on the thermonuclear?

A: To the best of my recollection he visited Los Alamos in the summer of 1950 and then in early fall the GAC met in Los Alamos—I mean he visited in Los Alamos early in the summer, and then they met in Los Alamos sometime, I believe in September, and on both occasions we did talk.

Q: What did Dr. Oppenheimer have to say, if anything, about the thermonuclear?

A: To the best of my recollection he did not have any very definite or concrete advice. Whatever he had tended in the direction that we should proceed with the theoretical investigations, which at that time did not look terribly encouraging, before spending more money or effort on the experimental approach, which I think was at that time not the right advice, because only by pursuing the experimental approach as well as the theoretical one did we face the problem sufficiently concretely so as to find a more correct solution. But I also should like to say that the opinion of Dr. Oppenheimer given at that time to my hearing was not a very decisive or not a very strongly advocated opinion, and I considered it not helpful, but also not as anything that need worry us too much.

I must say this, that the influence of the GAC at that time was to the best of my understanding in the direction of go slow, explore all, completely all the designs before looking into new designs, do not spend too much on test programs, all of which advice I consider as somewhat in the nature of serving as a brake rather than encouragement.

Q: Doctor, I would like to ask for your expert opinion again.

In your opinion, if Dr. Oppenheimer should go fishing for the rest of his life, what would be the effect upon the atomic energy and the thermonuclear programs?

A: You mean from now on?

Q: Yes, sir.

A: May I say this depends entirely on the question of whether his work would be similar to the one during the war or similar to the one after the war.

Q: Assume that it was similar to the work after the war.

A: In that case I should like to say two things. One is that after the war Dr. Oppenheimer served on committees rather than actually participating in the work. I am afraid this might not be a correct evaluation of the work of committees in general, but within the AEC, I should say that committees could go fishing without affecting the work of these who are actively engaged in the work.

In particular, however, the general recommendations that I know have come from Oppenheimer were more frequently, and I mean not only and not even particularly the thermonuclear case, but other cases, more frequently a hindrance than a help, and therefore, if I look into the continuation of this and assume that it will come in the same way I think that further work of Dr. Oppenheimer on committees would not be helpful.

Q: What were some of the other recommendations to which you referred?

A: You want me to give a reasonably complete list? I would be glad to.

Q: Yes.

A: And not distinguish between things I know of my own knowledge and things I know from hearsay evidence?

Q: Yes.

Mr. Robb: May I go off the record just a moment?

(Discussion off the record.)

Mr. Gray: We will take a short recess.

(The last question and answer preceding the recess were read by the reporter.)

By Mr. Robb:

Q: Doctor, in giving your answer, I wish you would give the board both those items that you know of your own knowledge and the others, but I wish you would identify them as being either of your own knowledge or on hearsay.

(Added in *The New York Times*: [Dr. Teller was asked to specify some of Dr. Oppenheimer's recommendations, and list them as being either of his own direct knowledge or by hearsay. Dr. Teller, in so doing, listed some proposals that he had favored. Some of those he disapproved follow.])

A: Actually, most of them are on some sort of hearsay. I would like to include not only those things which have occurred in committee but also others.

I furthermore felt that I should like at least to make an attempt to give some impression of the cases in which Dr. Oppenheimer's advice was helpful. His first major action after the war was what I understand both from some part of personal experience and to some extent of hearsay, as I have described, his discussion which led at least to some discouragement in the continuation of Los Alamos. I think that it would have been much better if this had not happened.

Secondly, Oppenheimer published shortly after in connection with the Acheson-Lilienthal report a proposal or supported a proposal, I do not know which, which was based on his scientific authority to share denatured plutonium with others with whom we might agree on international control. I believed at that time and so did many others that denaturing plutonium is not an adequate safeguard.

One of the first actions of the General Advisory Committee—this is hearsay—

Q: Excuse me, doctor. Have you finished your discussion of the other matter?

A: I intended to have it finished but I will be glad to stop and answer questions.

Q: Let me ask a question in that connection as to whether or not Dr. Oppenheimer either at that time or subsequently recommended some inspection of the Russian atomic plants.

A: My understanding is that inspection was an integral part of the Acheson-Lilienthal report, and that, in turn, Dr. Oppenheimer had very actively participated in drafting this report.

I should like to say that in my personal opinion—perhaps I should have said that right away—the Acheson-Lilienthal proposal was a very good one, would have been wonderful had it been accepted, and the inspection to my mind was a very important portion of it. I did not follow these things very closely but I believe it was something with which Dr. Oppenheimer had also agreed or recommended. Which ever the case was, if I am not mistaken in this matter, I really should include that among the very valuable things he did after the war.

Q: Excuse me, and now go ahead.

A: Thanks for bringing up this matter.

One of the first actions of the General Advisory Committee was to advise that reactor work at Oak Ridge should be discontinued and the reactor work should be concentrated at the Argonne Laboratory in Chicago. That was recommended, as I understand, by a great majority.

I also understand that Fermi opposed this recommendation. All this is hearsay evidence but of the kind which I heard so often and so generally that I think it can be classed as general knowledge within AEC circles.

Now, I should like to say that it appeared to many of us at the time, and I think it has been proved by the sequel, that this recommendation was a most unfortunate one. It set our reactor work back by many years. Those exceedingly good workers who left—the great majority of those very good workers who left Oak Ridge—did not find their way into the Argonne Laboratory but discontinued to work on atomic-energy matters or else worked in a smaller group on the side very ineffectively. The very small and determined group which then stayed behind in Oak Ridge turned out in the long run as good work as the people at the Argonne Laboratory, and I feel that again being a little bit uncertain of what would have happened if this recommendation had not been and would not have been accepted, we would be now a couple of years ahead in reactor development. I would like to count this as one of the very great mistakes that have been made.

I understand, having finished with this one, that among the early actions of the General Advisory Committee was, after it was decided that Los Alamos should go on, to recommend strong support for Los Alamos and particularly for the theoretical group. I understand that Oppenheimer supported this and I again think that this was helpful. I have a little personal evidence of it, although it is perhaps somewhat presumptuous of me to say so, that Oppenheimer was active in this direction, for instance, by advising me unambiguously to go back at least for a limited period. I know similarly that in that period he helped us to get Longmire. I also have heard and have heard in a way that I have every reason to believe that in a number of minor but important details in the development of fission weapons, Oppenheimer gave his expert advice effectively, and this included the encouragement of further tests when these things came along.

Q: Tests on what?

A: Tests of atomic bombs, of fission bombs.

Now, the next item is very definitely in the hearsay category, and I might be quite wrong on it, but I have heard that Dr. Oppenheimer opposed earlier surveillance, the kind of procedures–

Mr. Silverman: I did not understand. Opposed what?

The Witness: Earlier surveillance, the sort of thing which was designed to find out whether or not the Russians have detonated an atomic bomb. If this should prove to be correct, I think it was thoroughly wrong advice. Then I think generally the actions of the General Advisory Committee were adverse to the thermonuclear development, but to what extent this is so and I believe that it is so, we have discussed and I do not need to repeat any of that.

Finally, when, about 3 years ago, the question arose whether this would be a good time to start a new group of people working in a separate laboratory, along similar lines as Los Alamos and competing with Los Alamos, the General Advisory Committee, or the majority of the General Advisory Committee and in particular Dr. Oppenheimer, was opposed to this idea, using again the argument which was used in the case of Oak Ridge, that enough scientific personnel is not available. In this matter, I am personally interested, of course, and I was on the opposite side of the argument and I believe that Dr. Oppenheimer's advice was wrong. Of course, it is quite possible that his advice was right and mine was wrong. In the meantime, however, we did succeed in recruiting quite a capable group of people in Livermore. I think this is essentially the extent of my knowledge, direct or indirect, in the matter. I think it would be proper to restrict my statements to things in close connection with the Atomic Energy Commission and to disregard advice that I heard that Oppenheimer has given to other agencies like the Armed Forces or the State Department. This would be hearsay evidence of a more shaky kind than the rest.

By Mr. Robb:

Q: Doctor, the second laboratory, is that the one in which you are now working at Livermore?

A: That is one at which I had been working for a year and at which I am now working part time. I am spending about half my time at the University of California in teaching and research and half my time in Livermore.

Q: Did you have any difficulty recruiting personnel for that laboratory?

A: Yes, but not terribly difficult.

Q: Did you get the personnel you needed?

A: This is a question I cannot really answer, because it is always possible to get better personnel. But I am very happy about the people whom we did get and we are still looking for very excellent people if we can get them, and I am going to spend the next 3 days in the Physical Society in trying to persuade additional young people to join us.

Q: Numerically at least, you have your staff; is that right?

A: I would say numerically we certainly have a staff but I do not think this answer to the question is relevant. It is always the question of whether we have the right sort of people and I do believe we have the right sort of people.

Q: Is that laboratory concerned primarily with thermonuclear weapons or is that classified?

A: To the extent that I can believe what I read in Time magazine, it is not classified, but I would like to say that my best authority on the subject is Time magazine.

Q: What does Time magazine say about it?

Mr. Silverman: Well—

Mr. Robb: I will skip that.

By Mr. Robb:

Q: I will ask you this, Doctor: Will you tell us whether or not the purpose of establishing a second laboratory was to further work on the thermonuclear?

A: That was a very important part of the purpose.

Mr. Robb: Mr. Chairman, that completes my direct examination, and it is now 5:30.

Mr. Gray: I think we had better ask the witness to return tomorrow morning at 9:30.

Mr. Garrison: Mr. Chairman, we only have one or two questions.

The Witness: I would be very glad to stay for a short time.

Mr. Gray: I have some questions, but I do not think it will take too long, and if you only have a few—

Mr. Silverman: We have so very few, I am almost tempted not to ask them.

Cross-Examination

By Mr. Silverman:

Q: You were just testifying about the Livermore Laboratory?

A: Right.

Q: Did Mr. Oppenheimer oppose the Livermore Laboratory as it was finally set up?

A: No. To the best of my knowledge, no.

Q: His opposition was to another Los Alamos?

A: It was to another Los Alamos, and when the Atomic Energy Commission, I think, on the advice from the military did proceed in the direction, the General Advisory Committee encouraged in particular setting up a laboratory at the site where it was set up. But prior to that, I understand that the General Advisory Committee advised against it.

Q: That is when there was a question of another Los Alamos?

A: Right.

Q: Dr. Teller, when was Livermore set up in its present form?

A: This is something which is more difficult—

Q: You think that is classified?

A: No. It is more difficult to answer than the question of when a baby is born because it is not born all at once. I think the contracts were signed with the Atomic Energy Commission sometime in July 1952. There was a letter of intent sent out earlier and the work had started a little before that. Actually, we moved to Livermore on the 2d of September 1952 and work before that was done in Berkeley.

Q: Do you now have on your staff at Livermore some people who had been or who are members of the Institute for Advanced Study? I am thinking particularly of Dr. Karplus.

A: The answer is no. Dr. Karplus has been consulting with us for a period. He had accepted an invitation to the University of California and he is maintaining his consultant status to the Radiation Laboratory in general, of which Livermore is a part. I believe, but this is again a prediction about the future and my expectation, that Dr. Karplus in the future will help us in Livermore by consulting, but I also believe that for the next couple of years, if I can predict his general plans at all and I talked a bit with him, this is likely not to be terribly much because he will have to adjust himself to the new surroundings first.

Q: Do you know whether Dr. Oppenheimer recommended that Dr. Karplus go to work at Livermore?

A: I have no knowledge whatsoever about it. It is quite possible that he did.

Mr. Silverman: I have no further questions.

Mr. Gray: Dr. Teller, I think earlier in your testimony you stated that in August 1945, Dr. Oppenheimer talked with you and indicated his feeling that Los Alamos would inevitably disintegrate. I believe those were your words, and that there was no point in your staying on there. Is my recollection correct?

The Witness: Yes. I am not sure that my statement was very fortunate, but I am pretty sure that this is how I said it.

Mr. Gray: Would you say that his attitude at that time was that it should disintegrate?

The Witness: I would like to elaborate on that for a moment. I think that I ought to say this: I do not like to say it. Oppenheimer and I did not always agree in Los Alamos, and I believe that it is quite possible, probably, that this was my fault. This particular discussion was connected with an impression I got that Oppenheimer wanted me particularly to leave, which at first I interpreted as his being dissatisfied with the attitude I was taking about certain questions as to how to proceed in detail. It became clear to me during the conversation—and, incidentally, it was something which was quite new to me because prior to that, while we did disagree quite frequently, Oppenheimer always urged no matter how much we disagreed in detail I should certainly stay and work. He urged me although on some occasions I was discouraged and I wanted to leave. On this occasion, he advised me to leave. I considered that at first as essentially personal matters. In the course of the conversation, it became clear to me that what he really meant at that time—I asked him—we disagreed on a similar thing and I forget the thing, but I do remember asking him in a similar discussion that, 3 months ago—"you told me by all means I should stay. Now you tell me I should leave." He said, "Yes," but in the meantime we had developed these bombs and the work looks different and I think all of us would have to go home—something to that effect. It was at that time that I had the first idea that Oppenheimer himself wanted to discontinue his work very rapidly and promptly at Los Alamos. I knew that changes were due but it did not occur to me prior to that conversation that they were due quite that rapidly and would affect our immediate plans just right then and there. I do not know whether I have made myself sufficiently clear or not.

I failed to mention this personal element before. I am sorry about that. I think it is perhaps relevant as a background.

Mr. Gray: Do you think that Dr. Bradbury has been an effective director of the Los Alamos Laboratory?

The Witness: I am quite sure of that.

Mr. Gray: It is my impression that he was selected by Dr. Oppenheimer. Do you know about that?

The Witness: I heard that statement. I also heard the statement that it was General Groves who recommended Bradbury. I have not the least information upon which to decide which of these statements or whether any of these statements are correct. Perhaps both of them are correct.

Mr. Gray: It could be. Were you aware of the presence of any scientists on the project following the January 1950 decision who were there for the purpose of proving that this development was not possible rather than proving that it was possible?

The Witness: I certainly would not put it that way. There have been a few who believed that it was not possible, who argued strongly and occasionally passionately for it. I do not know of any case where I have reason to suspect intellectual dishonestly.

Mr. Gray: Excuse me, Dr. Teller. I would like the record to show that it was not my intention to impute intellectual dishonesty to anybody, but you have no knowledge of this.

The Witness: I would like to say that on some visits when Bethe came there, he looked the program over some way critically and quite frankly he said he wished the thing would not work. But also he looked it over carefully and whatever he said we surely agreed. In fact, we always agreed.

Mr. Gray: Yes. I think that clears it up perhaps.

You talked with Dr. Fermi soon after the October 1949 meeting of the GAC, and whereas he was not at liberty to tell you what the GAC decided, you got the impression that they were not favorable to a crash program, as you put it.

The Witness: Actually, Dr. Fermi gave me his own opinion, and this was an essential agreement with the GAC. This discouraged me, of course. He also gave me the impression that the GAC really decided something else, something essentially different.

Mr. Gray: You subsequently saw the GAC report?

The Witness: I did.

Mr. Gray: Is my impression correct that the tenor of the report was not altogether only a question of not moving into a crash program but was opposed to the development of the weapon altogether.

The Witness: That was my understanding. In fact, that is definitely my recollection.

Mr. Gray: Now Dr. Teller, you stated that the GAC report stopped work at Los Alamos. I assume you meant work on thermonuclear devices.

The Witness: I said that and may I correct it, please. What I really should have said was prevented the start of work because work really did not get started.

Mr. Gray: I think that is important because I thought I heard you that you were instructed not to work. What you mean is that you were instructed not to start anything new.

The Witness: That is correct. I am sorry if I expressed erroneously.

Mr. Gray: Was a result of the GAC report that the 6 or 8 or 10 or whatever it was people who were then working, did they stop their work?

The Witness: No, certainly not. In fact, there was an increase of people working right then and there, which was in the relatively free community. Not all of the work was directed in this relatively free atmosphere. It was evident that some work would continue. It was quite clear that in the period November—December—January, we did do some work and more than we had done earlier. However, we did not make a jump from, let us say 6 people to 200, but we made a jump of from 6 people to 12 or 20. I could not tell you which.

Mr. Gray: Dr. Teller, General Nichols' letter to Dr. Oppenheimer, which I assume you have some familiarity with—

The Witness: I read it. That is, I read the New York Times. If that is assumed to be a correct version—

Mr. Gray: As far as I know, it is correct. There is one sentence which reads as follows:

"It was further reported that you departed from your proper role as advisor to the Commission by causing the distribution, separately and in private, to top personnel at Los Alamos of the majority and minority reports of the General Advisory Committee on development of the hydrogen bomb for the purpose of trying to turn such top personnel against the development of the hydrogen bomb."

If this conversation you had with Dr. Manley about which you have testified and in which he referred to our chairman or the chairman was the source of this report, am I right in assuming that your testimony is that you are not prepared to say that Dr. Oppenheimer did cause the distribution of this?

The Witness: My testimony says that I cannot ascertain that Dr. Oppenheimer caused distribution. I have presented in this matter all that I can remember.

Mr. Gray: Dr. Teller, your are familiar with the question which this board is called upon to answer, I assume.

The Witness: Yes, I believe so.

Mr. Gray: Let me tell you what it is and invite counsel to help me out if I misstate it. We are asked to make a finding in the alternative, that it will or will not endanger the common defense and security to grant security clearance to Dr. Oppenheimer.

I believe you testified earlier when Mr. Robb was putting questions to you that because of your knowledge of the whole situation and by reason of many factors about which you have testified in very considerable detail, you would feel safer if the security of the country were in other hands.

The Witness: Right.

Mr. Gray: That is substantially what you said?

The Witness: Yes.

Mr. Gray: I think you have explained why you feel that way. I would then like to ask you this question: Do you feel that it would endanger the common defense and security to grant clearance to Dr. Oppenheimer?

The Witness: I believe, and that is merely a question of belief and there is no expertness, no real information behind it, that Dr. Oppenheimer's character is such that he would not knowingly and willingly do anything that is designed to endanger the safety of this country. To the extent, therefore, that your question is directed toward intent, I would say I do not see any reason to deny clearance.

If it is a question of wisdom and judgment, as demonstrated by actions since 1945, then I would say one would be wiser not to grant clearance. I must say that I am myself a little bit confused on this issue, particularly as it refers to a person of Oppenheimer's prestige and influence. May I limit myself to these comments?

Mr. Gray: Yes.

The Witness: I will be glad to answer more questions about it to you or to counsel.

Mr. Gray: No, I think that you have answered my question. I have, I think, only one more.

I believe there has been testimony given to this board to the effect—and again I would like the assistance of counsel if I misstate anything—that the important and significant developments in the thermonuclear program since January of 1950 have indeed taken place at Los Alamos and not at Livermore. Am I wrong in stating that?

Mr. Robb: Somebody said that.

Mr. Gray: Do you recall?

Mr. Silverman: My recollection is that there was testimony that the important developments in the thermonuclear bomb which have thus far been tested out and which were the subject of the recent tests were developed at Los Alamos. I think that was the testimony.

Mr. Gray: Will you assume that we have heard something of that sort? Do you have a comment?

The Witness: Is there a ruling that I may answer this question in a way without affecting security? I would like to assume that. I think I should.

Mr. Rolander: If you have any worry on that point, perhaps the board may wish you to give a classified answer on that.

The Witness: I mean I would like to give an unclassified answer to it and if you think it is wrong, strike it later. I understand that has been done before. I would like to make the statement that this testimony is substantially correct. Livermore is a very new laboratory and I think it is doing a very nice job, but published reports about its importance have been grossly and embarrassingly exaggerated.

Dr. Evans: I have one question.

Dr. Teller, you understand—

The Witness: May I leave that in the record? I would like to.

Mr. Rolander: Yes.

Dr. Evans: You understand, of course, that we did not seek the job on this board, do you not?

The Witness: You understand, sir, that I did not want to be at this end of the table either.

Dr. Evans: I want to ask you one question. Do you think the action of a committee like this, no matter what it may be, will be the source of great discussion in the National Academy and among scientific men in general?

The Witness: It already is and it certainly will be.

Dr. Evans: That is all I wanted to say.

Mr. Robb: May I ask one further question?

Re-Direct-Examination

By Mr. Robb:

Q: Dr. Teller, you did a great deal of work on the thermonuclear at the old laboratory, too, at Los Alamos.

A: Certainly.

Mr. Silverman: I have one question.

Re-Cross-Examination

By Mr. Silverman:

Q: I would like you, Dr. Teller, to distinguish between the desirability of this country's or the Government's accepting Dr. Oppenheimer's advice and the danger, if there be any, in Dr. Oppenheimer's having access to restricted data. As to this latter, as to the danger in Dr. Oppenheimer's having access to restricted data without regard to the wisdom of his advice, do you think there is any danger to the national security in his having access to restricted data?

A: In other words, I now am supposed to assume that Dr. Oppenheimer will have access to security information?

Q: Yes.

A: But will refrain from all advice in these matters which is to my mind a very hypothetical question indeed. May I answer such a hypothetical question by saying that the very limited knowledge which I have on these matters and which are based on feelings, emotions, and prejudices, I believe there is no danger.

Mr. Gray: Thank you very much, Doctor.

(Witness excused.)

Mr. Gray: We will recess until 9:30 tomorrow.

(Whereupon, the hearing was recessed at 5:50 p.m., to reconvene at 9:30 a.m., Thursday, April 29, 1954.)

INDEX

Abbreviations used in this index:
AEC, Atomic Energy Commission; DAS, Department of Applied Science (Livermore Laboratory/UC, Davis); ET, Edward Teller; GAC, General Advisory Committee; JRO, J. Robert Oppenheimer; LASL, Los Alamos Scientific Laboratory, LLL, Lawrence Livermore Laboratory, RSC, Reactor Safeguard Committee; SDI, Strategic Defense Initiative; UC, University of California, WW I, World War I; WWII, World War II.

Index / 613

Hirohito vs. the War Cabinet, 215–16; surrender ends WWII, 215; takeover of Manchuria and, 83
Jastrow, Bob, 350
Jauch, J. M., 398
Javan, Ali, 409
Jensen, Carl, 482, 484
Jensen, Hans J., 242
Jesuits, the, 271
Jetty, Eric, 300
Jews, Gamow on, 124; Germany, post-WW I, 51; Hungary, post-WW I, 15, 16, 31–32; in Italy, 139; Jewish friends of ET, 119; "Jewish science," 231
John Paul II, Pope, 547
Johnson, Edwin C., 291
Johnson, Gerald (Jerry), 349, 479, 493
Johnson, Lyall, 392
Johnson, Lyndon, 489
Johnson, Montgomery, 349, 357, 400, 406, 430(n17)
Johnson, Ralph, 271
Joint Chiefs of Staff, 531. *See also* Pentagon, the
Joint Congressional Committee on Atomic Energy(JCCAE), 386, 412
Joliot, Frederick, 143, 146; vs. secrecy of fission research, 144
Joseph, Franz, 8, 9, 11
József, Pónya, 553
Judaism, 31, 32, 33
Juvancz, Ireneus, 12, 15

Kádár, János, 459(n8), 551(n1)
Kahn, Herman, 485
Kaiser Wilhelm Institute, 64, 229
Kalckar, Fritz, 103, 104
Kaldor, Nicholas, 119(n7)
Kansas City, 432
Kant, Immanuel, 99
Kantrowicz, Arthur, 156, 487(n12)
Kapitsa, Piotr, 107; at Erice, 546; Majorana Prize, 549; Nobel Prize, 546(n11)
Karlsruhe Technical Institute, 42–46
Kármán, Maurice von, 21
Kármán, Theodore von, 134, 335, 341, 415, 416, 458–59
Károlyi, Mihály, 11, 12
Kazakhstan, 557
Keck telescope, 354(n14)
Kekulé, Stradonitz von, 127–28
Kelemen, Geza and Elizabeth (ET's aunt and uncle) 20, 21(n4)
Kennedy, John Fitzgerald (Jack), 451, 463, 464–65, 466, 467; assassination of Ngo Diem and, 502; foreign policy and, 455; meets ET, 461–62; opposes ET speaking at the Southern Governor's Conference, 469

Kennedy, Joseph, 265
Kepler, Johann, 562
Kerr, Clark, 442, 478
Kerszthelyi, Nándor, 34, 35, 40–41, 551
Keyworth, Jay, 530, 533
Khariton, Yuli B., 558–59
Kikuchi, Seishi, 56
Kilpatrick, Pat, 354
Kinetic energy, 128; alpha particles and, 173(n9); fission and, 173(n10); missile defense and, 535
King, Perce, 191
Kirkpatrick, Jeane, 535
Kirz, András (ET's brother-in-law), 199–200
Kirz, Emmi (Teller – ET's sister), 4, 19, 20, 27, 29, 36; death, 460(n9); death of father, 307; deported from Budapest to Tálya, 326; permitted to return to Budapest, 366; during Nazi occupation of Hungary, 199–201; reunion with ET and emigration to the U.S., 460
Kirz, János (ET's nephew), 19; death of ET's father and, 307; deported from Budapest to Tálya, 326; permitted to return to Budapest, 366; escape to the U.S., 427; during Nazi occupation of Hungary, 199–201
Kissinger, Henry, 454, 476, 501, 503; supports ballistic missile defense, 509
Klug, Leopold, 22–23
Koestler, Arthur, 181, 182–83, 390
Koniye, Prince Fumamiro, 215
Konopinski, Emil (Kayski), 165, 402; publication with ET, 251; work on the hydrogen bomb, 158, 172, 191, 295, 296, 297
Konynenburg, Richard A., 488
Korean War, 307, 314, 352–53. *See also* South Korea
Körösy, Feri von, 44
KQED television, 432, 442
Khrushchev, Nikita, 433, 437; vs. Sakharov, 463–64
Kuckuck, Bob, 480(n7)
Kun, Béla, 12, 13
Kurchatov, I. V., 238, 431, 556
Kurchatov Institute, 556
Kuwait, 538

Lamp, the, 363(n8)
Landau, Lev, arrest of 107, 546(n11); characteristics of, 78, 95, 118, 181, 183; Nobel Prize for work in superfluidity, 107(n21); Gamow and, 117; Heisenberg on electrons and magnetism, 66; helps Tisza, 107; paper with, 107; student years, 56, 58, 59; Voronel on, 107–08
Landaur, Eric, 181